Contents

VOLUME IV
A Twentieth Century Overview

The Novels

CONTENTS

THOMAS HARDY

Critical Assessments

immense length of aisle & nave, the spire of St Thomas's, the pinnacled tower of the College, &, more to the right, the tower & gables of the ancient ~~palace~~ hospice, where to this day the pilgrim may receive his dole of bread & ale. Behind the city swept the rotund upland of St Catherine's Hill, further off, landscape beyond landscape, till the horizon was lost in the radiance of the sun hanging above it.

Against these far stretches of country rose, in front of the other city ~~erections~~ edifices, a large red brick building, with level gray roofs, & rows of short ~~barred~~ windows ~~bespeaking captivity~~, the whole contrasting greatly by its regularity with the ~~~~ quaint irregularities of the ~~~~ Gothic erections. It was somewhat disguised from the road in passing it by yews & evergreen oaks, but it was visible enough up here. From the middle of the building a flat-topped octagonal tower ascended against the east horizon, & viewed from this spot, on its shady side & against the light it seemed a blot on the city's beauty. ~~Yet it~~ yes with this blot & not with the beauty, that the two gazers were ~~~~ concerned.

Upon the cornice of the tower a tall staff was fixed, & on this ~~staff~~ their eyes were rivetted ~~on it~~. A few minutes after the hour had struck something ~~shot~~ moved slowly up the staff & extended itself upon the breeze. It was a black flag. & the President of the Immortals (in Æschylean phrase) had ended his sport with Tess And the D'Urberville knights & dames slept on in their tombs unknowing.

'Justice' was done ∤ the two speechless gazers bent themselves down to the earth, as if in prayer, & remained thus a long time, absolutely motionless: the flag continued to wave silently. As soon as they had strength they arose, joined hands again, & went on.

The End.

Final page of *Tess* ms. (British Library).

THOMAS HARDY

Critical Assessments

◆

Edited by

Graham Clarke

VOLUME IV
A Twentieth Century Overview

HELM INFORMATION

Selection and editorial matter
© 1993 Helm Information Ltd
Helm Information Ltd,
The Banks,
Mountfield,
near Robertsbridge,
East Sussex TN32 5JY

ISBN 1–873403–08–9

A CIP catalogue record for this book
is available from the British Library.

Frontispiece: Final page of *Tess of the d'Urbervilles* ms., British Library.

Typeset by Leaper & Gard Ltd, Bristol, England
Printed and bound by Hartnolls Ltd, Bodmin, Cornwall
on 'acid-free' paper.

A Postscript

The Novels

Under the Greenwood Tree: A Novel about the Imagination

◆

BARBARA HARDY

Although Thomas Hardy's novels show his interest in crafts and arts, religious, secular, and military music, verse, architecture, landscape painting, and story-telling on the public platform (in *The Hand of Ethelberta*), they do not directly reveal his interest in the art of fiction. He does not write artist-novels. Nevertheless, all his characters are active in the narrative forms of fantasy and memory, and in his most argumentative and ambitious novels, *The Mayor of Casterbridge*, *The Return of the Native*, *Tess of the d'Urbervilles* and *Jude the Obscure*, his interest in imagination is too wide to be confined to the nature and situation of the artist. Jude, Sue, Eustacia, and Tess, are examples of imaginative power. They all share a poor chance of survival, for their mental energy finds it impossible to conform to the restrictive and conventional demands of nature and society. To imagine is to imagine a better world, and in the Hardy world, to imagine a better world is to be subversive, and to be subversive is to be destroyed. Only one of his highly imaginative people, Elizabeth-Jane Farfrae in *The Mayor of Casterbridge*, comes to terms with life, and modestly but sensitively survives. However, she refuses to be 'demonstratively thankful', as Hardy says, for 'the doubtful honour of a brief transit through a sorry world'. She believes, and encourages others to believe, that life may be made endurable through 'those minute forms of satisfaction that offer themselves to everyone not in positive pain'. Even such mild anodynes are rare in Hardy.

Tess is more representative of his thinking characters. Her intelligence and imagination are articulated as finely as Elizabeth-Jane's, though she has less promising opportunity for intellectual self-improvement. Though at times inclined to speak with her author's voice, as when she compares our planet to a blighted apple, she speaks and meditates for the most part in a

SOURCE *The Novels of Thomas Hardy*, ed. Anne Smith, London, 1979, pp. 45–57.

personal style. Her individual eloquence shows a profound, passionate, and properly generalised sense of her situation, as in her retort to Angel Clare's typically Victorian offer to help her take up some 'course of study—history for example?':

> '... what's the use of learning that I am one of a long row only—finding out that there is set down in some old book somebody just like me, and to know that I shall only act her part; making me sad, that's all. The best is not to remember that your nature and your past doings have been just like thousands' and thousands', and that your coming life and doings'll be like thousands' and thousands'.'

(ch. xix)

I am less concerned with the content of what Elizabeth-Jane or Tess say, with their attitudes of pessimism or meliorism, than with their ability to ponder and perceive and their experience. They are endowed with an imaginative capacity sufficiently sophisticated and eloquent to act as a vehicle for Hardy to utter his ideas. But the vehicle is shaped, coloured, and fully characterised. He creates characters who meditate and formulate in terms that serve the dual purposes of the particularities of fiction and the larger lines of his own argument.

Like most writers, Hardy uses mouthpieces as well as examples. Of course, imaginative literature tends to be about imaginative people—Odysseus, Antigone, Lear, Hamlet, Henry Esmond, Dorothea Brooke, Marcel, Stephen Dedalus. But the imaginative artist's interest in imagination and creation of imaginative character may show itself less conspicuously and heroically. *Under the Greenwood Tree* takes its place with *The Woodlanders, Far from the Madding Crowd*, and *The Trumpet-Major*, all novels which speak of and through the superficially limited minds and styles of characters who are rarely permitted to generalise, but stay and speak from their allotted empirical experience. It seems inaccurate to call them naïve or even simple characters, because their apparent simplicity is not incompatible with intimations of imaginative grasp. The novels stand with other works of literature whose authors have decided to exclude their own close kin, those characters who can act as examples of expressive, bold, far-seeing, and inventive imagination. Among writings which take such a self-denying ordinance are Wordsworth's *Lyrical Ballads*, George Eliot's *Scenes of Clerical Life*, and Joyce's *Dubliners*. These poems and stories exclude characters directly and broadly representative of their authors' powers, and attempt instead to work through less expressive and refined intelligences of people for whom the world of general ideas barely exists, or seems not to exist at all. Their concerns are with their day-to-day existence, with their immediate environment, with the place and society in which they find themselves, with their families, work, pastimes, pleasures, births, loves, marriages, and deaths. The last-named major events in the human cycle immediately signal the occasion for analysis, speculation, and debate, and the works I am concerned with often avail themselves of the enlarged experiences of social and religious ritual. But even on such occasions, the cyclical or major events of human experience are usually presented and discussed empirically, and the human actors are not strongly sceptical, subversive, or solemn in their attitudes to their own mortality, and are never unconcerned with immediate and particular action.

Under the Greenwood Tree can scarcely be said to have themes in the usual sense understood by literary critics. Its double plot joins the love-story of Dick Dewy and Fancy Day with a vital and fatal chapter in the history of the Mellstock Quire. It can be pressed into thematic conformity with Hardy's other novels through its concern with time and history, but although it certainly suggests or proposes views on change, conformity, continuity, tradition, and modernity, such suggestions do not amount to an informing and conspicuous theme. To insist on such generalisation as dominant would, I believe, reduce or abstract much of the book's vitality and particularity. But I am not so much concerned to examine all the concerns of this novel, as to suggest the way in which one of them emerges. The emergence is subtle, natural, and unusually implicit.

The novel presents the novelist's interest in imagination entirely through its accretion of particulars. In *Under the Greenwood Tree* the characters, actions, and environment, show the human mind sensitively, benignly, and creatively at work. Such work, however humble, is characteristic of what we commonly call imagination. It synthesises and particularises, like Coleridge's favourite image of the shooting star which vividly condenses complex experience in Shakespeare's *Venus and Adonis*. The Imagination shows itself in *Under the Greenwood Tree* as founded on knowledge, sympathy, sensuous response and synthetic force.

Under the Greenwood Tree is a narrative unity which invites an orthodox analysis. It joins the obstacles and triumphs of the love-story with the dismissal of the Mellstock musicians, and its synthesis is made through parallels and contrasts. Fancy Day is the new organist who replaces the old choir, and her two unsuccessful lovers, the churchwarden and the parson, bring about the local change as a testimony to their feeling for her. The lovers are young and must hurry, the musicians middle-aged and old, and must give way. Attitudes to love, youth, ageing, and age are shown in fine blends and contrasts. The lovers are rapturous and blind, the middle-aged and elderly are calmly disenchanted. A sharply and fully realised natural environment creates Hardy's honest version of pastoral, neither wholly ideal nor wholly undesirable, in which the bitter-sweet human experiences are all chronicled.

The pastoral exerts its binding-power. Each part of the novel is what Coleridge would call an organ to the whole, beginning with the resonant title's quotation from that earlier pastoral, *As You Like It*. Sentences are resonant, suggesting the motion of nature's rituals, 'And winter, which modifies the note of such trees as shed their leaves, does not destroy its individuality' (in Chapter I), or perfect harmony, 'a couple ... so exactly in tune with one another as Dick and she' (in Chapter II) of the fruition and colour, in the description of grandfather William, 'an ardent vitality still preserved a warm and roughened bloom upon his face, which reminded gardeners of the sunny side of a ripe ribstone-pippin' (in Chapter III).

The image of William's face marks one of Hardy's favourite methods of describing his characters. He is closely attentive not only to appearances, but to the sensibility and sympathy which register them. He likes to show his characters through the variable responses of other people:

> William Dewy—otherwise grandfather William—was now about seventy; yet an ardent vitality still preserved a warm and roughened bloom upon his face, which reminded gardeners of the sunny side of a ripe ribstone-pippin; though a narrow strip of forehead, that was protected from the weather by lying above the line of his hat-brim, seemed to belong to some town man, so gentle-manly was its whiteness. His was a humorous and kindly nature, not unmixed with a frequent melancholy; and he had a firm religious faith. But to his neigh-bours he had no character in particular. If they saw him pass by their windows when they had been bottling off old mead, or when they had just been called long-headed men who might do anything in the world if they chose, they thought concerning him, 'Ah, there's that good-hearted man—open as a child!' If they saw him just after losing a shilling or half-a-crown, or accidentally letting fall a piece of crockery, they thought, 'There's that poor weak-minded man Dewy again! Ah, he's never done much in the world either!' If he passed when fortune neither smiled nor frowned on them, they merely thought him old William Dewy.
>
> (pt. 1, ch. iii)

This joint attention to a man and to the shifting external viewpoint which regards, interprets and judges him, is characteristic of Hardy's medium of presentation in this novel. He is not altogether giving up the descriptive authority of the author, but inclines to share it provisionally with his characters, while reserving his own total knowledge. He does not preserve this superior knowledge in order to create an ironical contrast between wisdom and ignorance, as George Eliot or Henry James occasionally do, but suggests and ultimately proves that good judgement and vision are native to Mellstock. Hardy speaks about his people, through them, and for them. To present a character is for him to present a variable, not a constent, so as to recognise a local truth, and to create a community of linked and separated people. He may be omniscient, but masks the omniscience out of regard for the minds and responses of his people, who have their own rights and powers. If he is attentive to nature, so are they; and his description of the natural world, like his description of people, uses his people's eyes and ears.

The novelist's familiar knowledge, and his appreciation of individual human and natural life, is drawn from his characters and is delegated to them. This is not a critical conceit. One might truly suggest that Hardy learnt to see, hear, and know by observing the originals of his characters, the creation of art being a circular process rather than an imitation of nature.

We learn then from Hardy's people how imagery and imagination function. The novel's first sentence reports that dwellers in a wood can tell trees apart by voice as well as feature; then Dick Dewey makes his entry, while his author observes that the plantation 'whispered thus distinctively to his intelligence'. The author's sensibility is interwoven with the character's. Hardy immediately proceeds to delineate Dick's nature, confining himself to Dick's confining darkness. Dick is first sensed and presented through the sounds he makes: 'All the evidences of his nature were those afforded by the spirit of his footsteps, which succeeded each other lightly and quickly, and by the liveliness of his voice as he sang in a rural cadence ...' These evidences of his nature, which are allowed to speak for themselves, carry great weight through being unendorsed yet unmistakable. Many of the novel's people meditate, observe, and respond to the world outside through their 'intelligence', a word Hardy uses rather broadly to include mind, feeling, senses. Reuben Dewy, the tranter, for instance, is first seen as his friends and neighbours arrive at his house, knowing 'by their footsteps that they were the expected old comrades' and so not bothering to look up from the hogshead he is about to broach. His son Charley is contemplating his own face in a small looking-glass, 'to learn how the human countenance appeared when engaged in crying, which survey led him to pause at various points in each wail that were more than ordinarily striking, for a thorough appreciation of the general effect'. His daughter Bessy is comparing the faded and unfaded pattern of her plaid dress, his wife testing the temperature of flitches of bacon which seem to be in possible danger from the festive fire's great heat. Hardy likes to show people engaged in fervent, absorbed, and curious attention to the things around them, including themselves. The child Charley is worth all the children in the novels of George Eliot put together, for that look in the glass, as he cries, and for his marvellous question about the inside of the cider cask, 'Idd it cold inthide te hole?' Hardy's grown men and women, as well as his children, are engaged in this barefaced and unmonitored response to life. Old William loves two things best, splitting apple-wood and playing the bass-viol. At one time Hardy intended to call the novel, *The Mellstock Quire*, and the whole choir is ruled by a musical passion, delighting in performance, discussing the merits and history of their instruments, and forcing music upon Farmer Shiner who can't stand their Christmas carols. This quality of fervour is a necessary aspect of imagination and sensibility, as Hardy conceives them. Fervour joins intellectual curiosity with physical and emotional response, to create the exhilarated and creative eating, drinking, singing, dancing and working of *Under the Greenwood Tree*.

The fullest instance of fervour is the music, a fervent labour and a fervent joy. But professional appreciation is also there in Fancy's expected 'sharp remark' which was expected of 'the village sharpener', in the villagers' disinterested praise of 'sellers' like old Sam Lawson, and in the tranter's history of his cider and its barrel. Reuben Dewy discourses on the subject of his cider, the apples of which it is made, their names (where known), and the places where they grew, the hoops and tap of the barrel, once used for port wine and dishonestly sold by Sam Lawson, in an articulate history. Professional fervour involves a way of organising and ordering experience, not exclusively or distortingly, like a humour, but affording an entry to experience and a means of organising it. It depends on knowledge of people, objects, and history. It is attentive to life, as Dick Dewey is when he attends to the swarm of bees even though it makes him slightly late for his wedding. It is presented through praise and delight. This knowledgeable fervour is more than a feeling for community and nature, for through its specialisation Hardy's people establish and order their lives and values. Mr Penny not only knows about shoes and feet, but tells his shoemaker's anecdotes to reveal an implicit feeling for family, neighbourhood, and individual people. Ruling passions can blind or blinker vision, but Hardy makes his people benevolent and sympathetic in the exercise and defence of their jobs:

> 'Well,' said the shoemaker, seeming to perceive that the interest the object had excited was greater than he had anticipated, and warranted the last's being taken up again and exhibited; 'now, whose foot do ye suppose this last was made for? It was made for Geoffrey Day's father, over at Yalbury Wood. Ah, many's the pair o' boots he've had off the last! Well, when 'a died, I used the last for Geoffrey, and have ever since, though a little doctoring was wanted to make it do. Yes, a very queer natured last it is now, 'a b'lieve', he continued, turning it over caressingly. 'Now, you notice that there' (pointing to a lump of leather bradded to the toe), 'that's a very bad bunion that he've had ever since 'a was a boy. Now, this remarkable large piece' (pointing to a patch nailed to the side), 'shows a' accident he received by the tread of a horse, that squashed his foot a'most to a pomace. The horse-shoe came full-butt on this point, you see. And so I've just been over to Geoffrey's, to know if he wanted his bunion altered or made bigger in the new pair I'm making.'
>
> (pt. 1, ch. iii)

and

> 'You used to know Johnson the dairyman, William?'
> 'Ay, sure: I did.'
> 'Well, 'twasn't opposite his house, but a little lower down—by his paddock, in front o' Parkmaze Pool. I was a-bearing across towards Bloom's End, and lo and behold, there was a man just brought out o' the Pool, dead; he had un'rayed for a dip, but not being able to pitch it just there had gone in flop over his head. Men looked at en; women looked at en; children looked at en; nobody knowed en. He was covered wi' a sheet; but I catched sight of his voot, just showing out as they carried en along. "I don't care what name that man went by," I said, in my way, "but he's John Woodward's brother; I can swear to the family voot." At that very moment up comes John Woodward, weeping and teaving, "I've lost my brother! I've lost my brother!"'
>
> (pt. 1, ch. iii)

In such professional humours experience is incised, remembered, and narrated. The anecdotes have their guiding theme or *motif*, whether it is shoes, music, drink, or Mrs Penny's harping on her marriage to her 'little small man'. As Penny talks to the group outside his shop window, he goes on stitching, and punctuates or emphasises remarks with the strong pulls of needle through leather. His special shoemaker's concern makes his responses sharply self-interested, and informed, and so keeps sympathy from spilling over into grandiose or sentimental effusions. Grandfather William's passion for strings allow him to remember warmly and acutely:

> 'Well, as to father in the corner there, the tranter said, pointing to old William, who was in the act of filling his mouth; 'he'd starve to death for music's sake now, as much as when he was a boy-chap of fifteen.'
> 'Truly, now,' said Michael Mail, clearing the corner of his throat in the manner of a man who meant to be convincing; 'there's a friendly tie of some sort between music and eating.' He lifted the cup to his mouth, and drank himself gradually backwards from a perpendicular position to a slanting one, during which time his looks performed a circuit from the wall opposite him to the ceiling overhead. Then clearing the other corner of his throat: 'Once I was a-setting in the little kitchen of the Dree Mariners at Casterbridge, having a bit of dinner, and a brass band struck up in the street. Such a beautiful band as that were! I was setting eating fried liver and lights, I well can mind—ah, I was! and to save my life, I couldn't help chawing to the tune. Band played six-eight time; six-eight chaws I, willynilly. Band plays common; common time went my teeth among the liver and lights as true as a hair. Beautiful 'twere! Ah, I shall never forget that there band!'
> 'That's as tuneful a thing as ever I heard of,' said grandfather James, with the absent gaze which accompanies profound criticism.
>
> (pt. 1, ch. viii)

These ruling passions are not despotic, and often divide their rule. Penny plays the fiddle as well as making shoes, grandfather William cleaves the apple-wood and knows how it will burn, Mr and Mrs Dewy and Mr and Mrs Penny tell a chequered but not cynical experience of married life. The passions chime in together. Grandfather William's thought of singing to Fancy Day follows Mr Penny's story of the drowned man's foot, but takes place with natural and easy enthusiasm, not jockeying for position. There is room for stories about strings, cider, shoes, and marriage, told by many story-tellers. Hardy's are not satirical humours. No one 'peculiar quality' diverts and distorts the 'effects and powers' of his people, making them 'in their confluction all to flow one way'. The bias gives shape to imagination. These people have a solid and special ground, from which to regard their own and each other's lives.

Despite the great praise of strings, the choir can put aside their special interest with tolerance and generosity. When their deputation marches off to see the parson, it is not to give it to him 'hot and strong' as local intelligence expects, but to accept the decision and ask modestly for a proper season for their going. William's mild detachment refuses to be insulting or unjust to their enemy the parson:

> 'Still, for my part,' said old William, 'though he's arrayed against us, I like the hearty borus-snorus ways of the new pa'son.'
>
> 'You, ready to die for the quire,' said Bowman reproachfully, 'to stick up for the quire's enemy, William!'
>
> 'Nobody will feel the loss of our church-work so much as I,' said the old man firmly: 'that you d'all know. I've a-been in the quire man and boy ever since I was a chiel of eleven. But for all that 'tisn't in me to call the man a bad man, because I truly and sincerely believe en to be a good young feller.'
>
> Some of the youthful sparkle that used to reside there animated William's eye as he uttered the words, and a certain nobility of aspect was also imparted to him by the setting sun, which gave him a Titanic shadow at least thirty feet in length, stretching away to the east in outlines of imposing magnitude, his head finally terminating upon the trunk of a grand old oak-tree.
>
> (pt. 2, ch. ii)

So Hardy evinces his approval of William's character and remarks. They are not sentimental, as their collective biography of the former parson makes clear:

> 'Ah, Mr Grinham was the man!' said Bowman. 'Why, he never troubled us wi' a visit from year's end to year's end. You might go anywhere, do anything: you'd be sure never to see him.'
>
> (pt. 2, ch. ii)

and

> 'And 'a was a very jinerous gentleman about choosing the psalms and hymns o' Sundays. "Confound ye," says he, "blare and scrape what ye will, but don't bother me!"'
>
> (pt. 2, ch. ii)

The quality of the Mellstock imagination is well-wishing but not soft, self-respecting but not egotistical, specialist but not warped. These moral and intellectual qualities are invariably conveyed in those narratives that are the prevailing genre within the novel. Music may be a collective enterprise, but so is story-telling, ritualised in village feasts and gatherings, part of the ordinary social flow of reminiscence, gossip, praise, criticism, entertainment, hopes, fears, jokes and ruminations, and seemingly extended naturally to form Hardy's art.

A remarkable feature of his story-tellers is their co-operation in narrative. The community is brought to life in its daily activities and its properties. Every object and every event tells many stories, and the stories are generous, but the actual harmony and community of the telling testifies and ministers to the benevolence. The tellers quote and build on other stories. Hardy's story-tellers are good men, and their sprightly and potent characters, with their ironic but tolerant acceptances, are expressed and implied in their stories. Perhaps the social psychology and morality of Hardy's narratives achieves its most complex response in the last sight we get of the community in *Under the Greenwood Tree*. In the last chapter, Hardy shows us the communal act of imagination, practised by the onlookers at the nuptial dance:

Here the gaffers and gammers whose dancing days were over told stories of great impressiveness, and at intervals surveyed the advancing and retiring couples from the same retreat, as people on shore might be supposed to survey a naval engagement in the bay beyond; returning again to their tales when the pause was over. Those of the whirling throng who, during the rests between each figure, turned their eyes in the direction of these seated ones, were only able to discover, on account of the music and bustle, that a very striking circumstance was in course of narration—denoted by an emphatic sweep of the hand, snapping of the fingers, close of the lips, and fixed look into the centre of the listener's eye for the space of a quarter of a minute, which raised in that listener such a reciprocating working of face as to sometimes make the distant dancers half wish to know what such an interesting tale could refer to.

(pt. 5, ch. ii)

Those whose dancing days were over remember festivities past, and loves and marriages are summoned up unromantically to testify to the binding-power of social ritual. The feeblest member of the Mellstock Quire is Thomas Leaf, who turns up, as so often, to take his place among his superiors. Like a good guest he makes his contribution to the ritual story-telling under the beech-tree. Thomas Leaf's story is scarcely an imaginative creation, but takes its place in the common ritual.

It is a feeble story, its rhetoric and form making it a model of how not to do it. His tale is one told by an idiot, flat, pointless, but generously offered for the occasion.[1]

'Once,' said the delighted Leaf, in an uncertain voice, 'there was a man who lived in a house! Well, this man went thinking and thinking night and day. At last, he said to himself, as I might, "If I had only ten pound, I'd make a fortune." At last by hook or by crook, he got the ten pounds!'

'Only think of that!' said Nat Callcome satirically.

'Silence!' said the tranter.

'Well, now comes the interesting part of the story! In a little time he had made that ten pounds twenty. Then a little time after that he doubled it, and made it forty. Well, he went on, and a good while after that he made it eighty, and on to a hundred. Well, by-and-by he made it two hundred! Well, you'd never believe it, but—he went on and made it four hundred! He went on, and what did he do? Why, he made it eight hundred! Yes, he did,' continued Leaf in the highest pitch of excitement, bringing down his fist upon his knee with such force that he quivered with the pain; 'yes, and he went on and made it A THOUSAND!'

'Hear, hear!' said the tranter. 'Better than the history of England, my sonnies!'

'Thank you for your story, Thomas Leaf,' said grandfather William; and then Leaf gradually sank into nothingness again.

(pt. 5, ch. ii)

The tranter and his father, two of the best tellers, in this novel full of telling, move their generous vote of thanks. In *Under the Greenwood Tree* the chorus often ceases to be choric, to take its prominent place in the centre of our attention. It holds such a place through its imaginative appreciation of the past, well-preserved and alive, but naturally conservative and conserving.

The middle-aged and the old men are constantly telling the comic story of courtship and marriage, wryly, drily, but not chillingly or cynically. The two lovers are naturally forward-looking. Hardy's appreciation of their amorous creations is beautifully balanced against the old stories. Dick's vision is a vision, delicately appreciated in its intensity and fervour, comedy insisting on its inventiveness and force. His exuberant ideality is contrasted with the acquired common-sense of the choir, whose unromantic and unvisionary look at love amazes the young lover. The choir's imagination dwells on the reliable pleasures of music, song, food, drink, and festivity, but they sigh over Dick tolerantly, their breath scarcely dimming the brilliant reflecting surface of creative love.

Dick Dewy sees visions. Fancy Day's imagination has been busy with a more complicated vision of future possibilities than Dick Dewy's. She follows Thomas Leaf's unimaginative simple tale with her carefully kept secret and her white lie. She had made up her plain tale of love and marriage with Dick, but into this realistic construction has strayed the less palpable vision of higher things, thoughts of marriage with Parson Maybold. This is a vision entertained but not followed through. She chooses the plain tale, though Hardy makes it truthfully apparent that her imaginative endeavours, in their selective and creative efforts, are painfully struggling, as Coleridge says of poets, to idealise and unify. The choir's creativity takes an understated form, right for its stoicism and sense of proportion. Fancy's imaginative infidelity is also understated, remaining a straying of the mind which reminds us, like the novel's title, that idylls are fictions. The personal autobiography we are all engaged in constructing as we look before and after depends on visions and revisions.

Note

1. I have discussed Thomas Leaf's story more fully in *Tellers and Listeners* (Athlone Press, 1975).

165

Hardy's Retroactive Self-censorship: The Case of *The Well-beloved*

◆

ANNE C. PILGRIM

From his earliest days as a novelist, Thomas Hardy presented his works to the public in two successive ways, first in serial installments in a periodical, and then in volume form. Beginning with his composition of *Far from the Madding Crowd* in 1874, he ran into the nervousness of editors who requested discreet alterations to his periodical stories; it was Leslie Stephen of the *Cornhill* who wanted him to 'omit the baby' from the scene in which Bathsheba Everdene opens Fanny Robin's coffin, and who also suggested that 'if the omission were made it might be restored on republication.'[1] By the closing stages of his novel-writing career in the 1890s, Hardy had become inured to the necessity of bowdlerizing the manuscripts of his novels for their first appearance and then restoring the materials which had been perceived as likely to give offense when the novels appeared in volume form. It is well known to students of Hardy that the versions of *Tess of the d'Urbervilles* which appeared in the *Graphic* and of *Jude the Obscure* which appeared in *Harper's New Monthly Magazine* were heavily censored by Hardy. What is much less well known is that on one occasion, in producing his last published novel *The Well-beloved*, Hardy worked in the opposite manner. In this instance, the serial text, dating from 1892, represented his original intention, and he substantially revised it later in such a way as to remove elements that might create difficulties when the novel came out in book form in 1897. The reasons for and the nature of this revision form the subject of this paper.

Although according to Hardy the story had been 'sketched many years before'[2] its serial publication, he did not write it until late in 1891, as a consequence then of having promised 'something light'[3] and considerably briefer to Tillotson and Son to replace the serial version of *Tess of the*

SOURCE *Victorian Authors and Their Works, Revision, Motivations and Modes*, ed. Judith Kennedy, Athens, Ohio, 1991, ch. 9, pp. 125–39.

d'Urbervilles, then known as *Too Late Beloved*, which Tillotson's had found entirely unsuitable for publication some two years before. The replacement tale, under the title *The Pursuit of the Well-beloved*, and a subtitle, 'A Sketch of a Temperament,' ran weekly from 1 October to 17 December 1892 in the *Illustrated London News*. Not only was the story 'light,' it was more than a little fantastic, a study of the artistic temperament rather than a dully realistic history, as the following necessarily condensed account of it will show.

The original plot, in thirty-three chapters, traces the romantic adventures of Jocelyn Pearston, a gifted young sculptor of twenty who returns from London to visit his Wessex home on the Isle of Slingers (i.e., Portland Bill). A lover of beauty for whom the abstract idea of the Well-beloved has already been embodied in many successive female forms, he now concludes that the Well-beloved has decided to remain in Avice Caro, a young island neighbour to whom he becomes engaged. But the Well-beloved abruptly migrates into the person of Marcia Bencomb, whom he takes back to London and impulsively marries. Quarrels, regrets and recriminations ensue; among the few things the pair agrees on are the defects of matrimony, their need for a permanent separation (Marcia departs to the Pacific coast of America), and their freedom to form new ties. The story moves forward to find Jocelyn at the age of forty returning to the island for the funeral of Avice Caro and discovering his Well-beloved in her daughter Ann Avice; his intention to marry her is checked only by his learning that she is secretly married already. In Part Third, after another twenty-year interval, he visits the now widowed Ann Avice, and meets her elegant, rather too-docile daughter Avice; this time he succeeds in marrying this final incarnation of the Well-beloved despite the great difference in their ages. His second marriage is also a disaster, for two reasons: Avice's physical aversion to Pearston and the surprise return of her true love Henri Leverre. She finds her husband truly magnanimous: he does not assert his right to sexual relations and in fact hatches a plan to leave the two young people free to marry. He places advertisements for his long lost wife so that he will be able to pretend to find her and leave Avice free. The serial has an ironic and painful surprise ending: Marcia does in fact answer his appeal, and the still-youthful Pearston finds that his lifelong pursuit of beauty is to end in his being yoked with a hideously aged wife who has returned for good.

There is no evidence that in 1892 Hardy regarded his story as suitable for publication in book form; in fact there is some firm evidence of his doubts in that regard. Early in 1892, when Harper and Brothers had already secured the rights to the American serial publication, they conveyed through their London agents Osgood and McIlvaine their readiness both to publish it in book form and to allow Hardy the opportunity to revise it. Hardy's reply displayed his usual canny prudence in managing his literary affairs: while agreeing that Harper and Brothers might publish the American edition of the volume form, and even discussing possible terms, he stipulated that

the story being short and slight and written entirely with a view to serial publication, it may be found upon consideration to be inadvisable in the interest of
future novels to issue this as a book at all; hence I reserve the right to withhold it
in that form either altogether, or until the story can be re-written.[4]

In fact four years went by before he picked the story up again, an
extremely busy and eventful period in his career. As well as writing verse
destined to appear in *Wessex Poems*, writing short stories, and collecting his
others into the 1893 volume *Life's Little Ironies*, Hardy wrote and published,
Jude the Obscure, a major novel into which he poured his energies; he was
involved in on-the-scene research and in a year and a half of writing, as well
as in the extra task of bowdlerizing the novel for its serial publication and
restoring it in the summer of 1895 for its appearance in book form in
November of that year. Overlapping with the final stages of work on *Jude*,
starting early in 1895, was Hardy's contribution in the form of textual work
(revision, corrections, and the writing of new prefaces) to the first uniform
edition of his Wessex novels, in sixteen volumes, being brought out by
Osgood, McIlvaine. The first edition of *Jude* appeared as Volume VIII in the
series, and as publication rights to such very early novels as *Desperate Remedies*
lapsed, Osgood, McIlvaine added them to the collected edition. The
sixteenth and last volume was *Under the Greenwood Tree*, in September 1896.
Much of this latter textual work by Hardy was carried on under the strain of
the sometimes violently adverse reaction to the frankness of *Jude*, and it is
little wonder that after writing his preface to *Under the Greenwood Tree* in
August he embarked on an eight-week holiday with his wife.

Hardy, now in his late fifties, was avowedly anxious—had been so for
some years—to return to his primary vocation as a poet after more than a
quarter century devoted to fiction. He did not do so immediately, however,
for in the last months of 1896 he agreed—whether at his own suggestion or
that of his publishers is not known—to revise *The Pursuit of the Well-beloved* for
publication as a belated seventeenth volume in the uniform edition. His
motives for doing so may have been gratified vanity, in finding that Osgood,
McIlvaine considered it worthy of inclusion, or a prudent concern with
keeping his name before the public in the interval before his first book of
poems could appear. Certainly to some extent they must have been financial,
for Osgood, McIlvaine was generous with royalties (in the case of their six-
shilling edition of *Jude* they returned one shilling six pence of the price of
each copy sold to the author),[5] and the 1891 passage of the American Copyright Act had meant that for each novel from *Tess* onward Hardy could
count on receiving royalties from any and all American publishers of his
work. As his biographer Michael Millgate points out, Hardy was looking
forward to becoming 'a retired novelist living on the proceeds of past work;'[6]
these proceeds could be—and in fact were—significantly enhanced by
royalties from *The Well-beloved*.

Although Hardy's doubts as expressed in 1892 about the advisability of issuing his story as a book were overcome, he stood by his right to revise it, not just because of his dissatisfaction with a work that had been 'written entirely with a view to serial publication' but also because of developments in the meantime. The revised version which appeared on 16 March 1897 suggests by the nature of the revisions—particularly the excision from the plot of Jocelyn's two unfortunate marriages—Hardy's response to three things: the 1895 publication of *Jude the Obscure*, the December 1896 publication of Richard Le Gallienne's novel *The Quest of the Golden Girl*, and Hardy's new and recent wish on the eve of his return to poetry to be conciliatory toward those whom he had lately offended—both his wife Emma and his reading public—by his tendentious attacks on marriage and his aggressive frankness about the role of sexuality in human relations.

Certain elements in each of the two novels which had appeared in the four years since his serial left Hardy open to the same imputation, that of a lack of originality: readers of a merely reprinted *Pursuit of the Well-beloved* might infer that he owed a debt either to his own novel or to Le Gallienne's. To modern scholars it is clear that *The Pursuit of the Well-beloved* was a preliminary treatment of issues which Hardy was to expand upon in *Jude*; however, to most of the readers of his novels, the serial was unknown (one observer said of it that 'it seems ... to have made little impression at the time'),[7] and a reader who had just recently finished *Jude*, or had even merely heard about it, might well conclude that Hardy was repeating himself if the serial version were not reworked. In his first marriage Jocelyn is all too like Jude: he contracts an early marriage unwisely and suffers for it; he finds himself involved with a strong-willed woman who is very articulate in her denunciation of marriage as an institution and who has 'advanced views.'[8] Marcia recalls both Arabella Donn, in her sensual appeal and her willingness to depart to the far side of the world, and Sue Bridehead. In his second marriage Pearston even more closely resembles Sue's husband Richard Phillotson, who declines to force himself on a fastidious young wife and sends her back to the arms of her youthful lover; in his letters he confides in his friend Alfred Somers as Phillotson does in his friend George Gillingham. As for the other novel, it seems merely an accident of literary history that Le Gallienne's *Quest of the Golden Girl* should come on the scene just as Hardy was about to reissue his *Pursuit of the Well-beloved*. Again, Hardy risked the imputation of debt where none was owed. Le Gallienne, an active journalist and reviewer, had of course had the opportunity to read Hardy's serial story, although his whimsical tale told by a poet of thirty who goes on a walking tour in search of the perfect woman—his Golden Girl—to make his wife owes much more to Sterne's *A Sentimental Journey* in the looseness of its structure and even in specific episodes, as well as in its sexual suggestiveness (its narrator is a lingerie fetishist and a libertine). Its ending managed to be both improper and mawkish, as the quester recognizes his true love in a Picadilly prostitute and marries her, only to have her die giving birth to a daughter and instructing him to 'let her be your little golden girl.'[9] The romance was an immediate success; a thousand copies were sold on publication day. One can only imagine Hardy's dismay at the thought that his novel might, especially if it retained its original title, invite comparison of the two.

After the fact, Hardy maintained that he had not been able to revise his serial as completely as he had intended,[10] but he did make many changes, both aesthetically and prudentially dictated, which went far beyond the shortening of his title to *The Well-beloved*. He made a number of incidental improvements such as changing the spelling of his hero's name to Pierston, thereby clarifying the pronunciation and adding an appropriate marine allusion. He added poetic epigraphs, from Crashaw, Wyatt, and Shakespeare, to each part; tinkered with chapter titles; and made Pierston 'A Young Man of 60' rather than of 59 at the outset of Part Third to enhance the symmetry of the tale. In other larger ways Hardy increased the geometric precision of the three-generation plot. He lopped off altogether an initial brief episode of Pierston in London burning love letters from smitten girls (eight names are specified) and thus started the action with Pierston's arrival on the island—a 'return of the native' motif which reviewers were quick to spot—and his discovery of Avice Caro, the first of the three Avices, *none* of whom he will, in the new version, marry. Major changes include having Pierston stop short of marrying Marcia in Part First, and a completely rewritten ending, in which the last seven chapters of the serial were removed and four new ones substituted. The effects of these latter changes must now be considered.

By having Pierston and Marcia quarrel and part before marrying, Hardy was able to excise from his novel passages that sound very much like ones in *Jude*—the sort of remarks about marriage that had made Mrs Oliphant in January 1896 describe that novel as 'intended as an assault on the stronghold of marriage, which is now beleaguered on every side.'[11] Barely is the couple home from the honeymoon, in the serial, before their regrets make them talk 'in complete accord of the curse of matrimony.' 'In their ill-matched junction on the strength of a two or three days' passion,' the narrator observes, 'they felt the full irksomeness of a formal tie,'[12] an insight identical to Jude's into his marriage with Arabella:

> Their lives were ruined, he thought; ruined by the fundamental error of their matrimonial union: that of having based a permanent contract on a temporary feeling which had no necessary connection with affinities that alone render a life-long comradeship tolerable.[13]

Not only their foolish haste but the nature of marriage itself is assailed by Marcia, who divines that she is 'her husband's property, like one of his statues that he could not sell.'[14] Marcia, like Sue, has reason to view the marriage tie with suspicion, and since the story is set back in the 1850s she has not even the possibility of divorce to rely on. Her 'advanced views' at the point of marital separation include an assertion that 'I fail to see why, in making each our own home, we should not make our own matrimonial laws if we choose.'[15] Following up on this radical notion, both she and Pearston contract bigamous second marriages, a fact which Hardy skims over lightly in the serial but which he was no doubt happy enough to eradicate from his more conventional book version.

In his reworking of the novel's ending, Hardy once again prevented a marriage founded on doubtful motives from taking place. Pierston wishes to marry the third Avice at least partly as a way of making amends for having abandoned the first, and she agrees to their engagement out of a wish to please and comfort her dying mother. The more timely reappearance of Henri Leverre, in the new version, and Avice's elopement with him on the eve of her wedding to Pierston places a counter-emphasis on mutuality and youthful passion and introduces as well the idea of poetic justice. Pierston refuses to blame his vanished bride, saying 'She didn't make the circumstances. I did ... It was how I served her grandmother.'[16] Pierston's generosity to Avice remains, but in the later version he is no longer called upon to be the generous-though-rebuffed elderly husband. By deleting their marriage, Hardy was able to omit from his text material that was troublesome both because it was indelicate in nature and because it so closely resembled that in *Jude*. The serial had dwelt, even in its chapter titles, on the idea of possession. Two of these titles which disappeared in revision were those for Chapter XXVII, 'He desperately clutches the form [of the Well-beloved],' and for Chapter XXVIII, in which is described the early married life of Pearston and Avice, 'He possesses it; he posseses it not.' Whether the idea is one of sequence or of simultaneity, it draws the reader's attention to the question of a husband's rights. Like Sue Bridehead, Avice in the serial displays nervousness, apprehension, and repugnance; when Pearston, listening at the door of her room, accidentally brushes against the handle, he hears her 'gasp and start.'[17] Like Phillotson, Pearston is noble, compassionate, and free-thinking; he repudiates legalities he sees as unjust, declaring that 'to me healthy natural instinct is true law, and not an Act of Parliament.'[18] Sincere such declarations no doubt were, on the part of both character and author, but by 1896 they must have come to seem needlessly provocative.

Pierston in the later version is much more of an artist—a lover of beauty in the abstract—and a dreamer than he is an amorist, for in the general reduction of the attention given to sexual matters in *The Well-beloved* Hardy drastically reduced his hero's sexual experience. The Pierston of the 1897 book version is not in his early youth so successful a lover that he has a large bundle of letters to dispose of; he does not marry a Junoesque island girl and live with her for four years; he does not marry and possess, however briefly, an eighteen-year-old when he is sixty; in fact he does not marry at all until Marcia returns to his side and he offers her 'such friendship as I am capable of ... till the end.'[19] His bride, when he finally has one, is so advanced in age and decrepitude (and presumably sexlessness) that she suffers an attack of rheumatism on their wedding day and 'after being well wrapped up' is 'wheeled into the church in a chair.'[20] Were it not for Pierston's few days of cohabitation with Marcia long before, one might believe him altogether virginal.

In both accounts Marcia, after her departure from London, has been married and widowed and on her return is discovered to be, rather improbably, stepmother to the youngest Avice's true love, Henri Leverre. The treatment of her return in each case is drastically different, however, and indicates a major shift in attitude on Hardy's part. In the serial her reappearance when least wanted seems the expression of a cosmic joke at Pearston's expense, and the closing chapter ends with his bitter laughter, 'so violent as to be an agony.'[21] In the new version Marcia returns out of concern for her stepson and transfers that concern to Pierston, especially when he falls ill; in the final chapter she shares with him in the experience of loss, renunciation, and resignation which gives the ending its muted tone. After his illness Pierston discovers that he has lost his artistic sense, his care for beauty, and in relief exclaims, 'Thank Heaven I am old at last.'[22] He leaves London forever, accompanied by Marcia who has also accepted her true age by presenting her face to Pierston's eyes denuded of all the 'beautifying artifices'[23] she is skilled in applying after a lifetime in society. Thus reduced, they return to the island for the last time and marry for convenience and companionship.

Virtually from the day of publication it was apparent that Hardy's scheme of purifying *The Pursuit of the Well-beloved* had been successful. Only four days later, on 20 March, the *Graphic* proclaimed in an editorial that Mrs Grundy would be happy with Hardy, since there was nothing in *The Well-beloved* to bring a blush 'to even the most inflammable cheek of maidenhood';[24] on the same day, an unsigned article in the *Saturday Review* welcomed Hardy back 'to his own province of the imagination,' contrasting *The Well-beloved*'s 'preoccupation with beauty' to the ugliness of *Tess* and *Jude*, which had been 'of set purpose squalid.'[25] As the weeks elapsed in the spring of 1897, reviewers on both sides of the Atlantic echoed this initial expression of pleasure and relief. The *Literary World* noted that *The Well-beloved* had 'few features in common with its two most recent predecessors' and was 'free from the grosser traits that sent staid matrons into hysterics of wrath';[26] the *Athenaeum* dourly referred to it as 'a more pleasing sample of Mr Hardy's later manner than some we could name' and expressed the hope that its appearance indicated 'a desire to renew those pleasant relations with his readers that should never have been interrupted.'[27] American journals also contrasted the new work to *Jude* in particular. William Lyon Phelps, writing in the *Book Buyer* in May, launched into a food metaphor, acclaiming *The Well-beloved* as a dish more 'palatable' which would 'take out the taste of *Jude the Obscure.*' The new work is 'innocuous' and makes him exclaim, 'For this relief much thanks.'[28] Not all critics were aware that the novel had appeared some years before as a serial, and those who mentioned the serial of 1892 were not always aware that it had been revised. One of these was William Morton Payne, who confessed in the *Dial* of Chicago his wish 'that *The Well-beloved* were a recently-written book, for it would represent a reaction from the mood of cynical bitterness that has been upon Mr Hardy of late, and all lovers of good literature would rejoice to learn that the 'blue devils' had been exorcised, and to find the novelist of *Far from the Madding Crowd* and *A Pair of Blue Eyes* restored to them. Such 'a return of the native' to his old-time scenes and themes would be welcome indeed.'[29]

The intensity of Hardy's desire to succeed in disarming the reviewers at this delicate moment in his career may perhaps be gauged by his over-reaction to one extremely negative anonymous review, 'Thomas Hardy, Humorist,' in the London *World*. It appeared barely a week after the release of *The Well-beloved*, on 24 March, and Hardy could certainly not foresee that it would be the only such attack on his work among more than two dozen reviews to come; still, he reacted with outrage and even a degree of panic, sending a flurry of letters from his Dorchester home to friends and literary associates. In two letters written on the same day, to Edmund Gosse and to Florence Henniker, he complained of the 'extraordinary stab in the back'[30] and the 'horrid stab'[31] delivered to his 'poor little innocent book,'[32] and expressed his amazement that it could give any offense. To Gosse he explained that 'one of the reasons why I consented to the reprinting of such a bygone, wildly romantic fancy was that it wd please Mrs Grundy & her young Person, & her respected husband, by its absolutely 'harmless' quality'; to Mrs Henniker he said that 'one of my reasons for letting the story be reprinted was that it cd not by any possibility offend Mr or Mrs Grundy, or their Young Persons.' The references to consenting and reprinting seem more than a little disingenuous; it is hard to believe that Hardy had forgotten his own activity and the extensive revisions he had so recently made.

Hardy's agitation is understandable, however, for the review in the *World*, which was both malicious and mendacious, posed a distinct threat to his plan to foster the public perception of *The Well-beloved* as 'harmless.' From the start, the unknown reviewer adopted a tone of sneering sarcasm, calling the new novel an example of 'the later Hardy at his best—so tasteful, reticent and amiable'[33] while singling out for attention any hint of the fleshly which could, with difficulty, be found in it. He (or she—there was some speculation later that a woman had written it) objected to a passage describing Pierston's progress through a crowded reception room with a close-up view of 'shoulder-blades, back hair, glittering headgear, necknapes, moles, hairpins, pearl-powder, pimples,' et cetera; remarked on his being diverted from Avice Caro 'by the more opulent attractions' of Marcia; found a deliberate reference to the flesh in the choice of surname for Avice ('*Caro, carnis* is the noun with the declension of which Mr Hardy is perpetually and everlastingly preoccupied in his new book'); and ended a long paragraph with a punning condemnation: 'Of all forms of sex-mania in fiction we have no hesitation in pronouncing the most unpleasant to be the Wessex-mania of Mr Thomas Hardy.' Two sentences, coming at the end of a flippant passage of plot summary, must have been particularly enraging. In them the reader was told 'Avice III elopes with the stepson of Marcia, and Marcia, now a faded and painted harridan, returns to appropriate the senile amorist. And thus ends Mr Thomas Le Gallienne Hardy's *Pursuit of the Golden Girl.*' Le Gallienne's hero had found his wife among the 'poor painted faces'[34] clustering at street corners in Piccadilly; the use of the adjective here unfairly blackened the character of Marcia, while the blending of the authors' names and the two titles impugned Hardy's originality.

His worst fears were thus realized; his revisions had gone for naught, or so it seemed for the moment. In fact Hardy received prompt reassurances and support of several kinds, including an invitation, which he declined, to reply directly to the *World* in the pages of the *Academy.* His friend Gosse, who had written the *Saturday Review* article, sprang into action and wrote another favorable review, this time signed, for the *St James's Gazette* of 31 March. Unexpected assistance came from Le Gallienne himself, whom Hardy knew only slightly; the younger man quickly produced a piece for the *London Star* of 29 March in which he deplored the outcry 'which already mounts to heaven from Philistia'[35] and observed that Hardy's novel invited comparison with *Liber Amoris* but was clearly superior to Hazlitt's work. He thus attempted to throw readers off the scent of his *Golden Girl* and—not incidentally—to promote his own 1893 edition of *Liber Amoris*, the only one then available. In the long run, Hardy had in fact nothing to worry about; favorable reviews continued to appear, and the sales of *The Well-beloved* were excellent (it was mentioned in the April *Bookman* as one of the month's bestsellers).[36] Still, he was not easily or soon mollified. When sorting the materials, over twenty years later, for the second part of his autobiography, *The Later Years of Thomas Hardy*, he saved and had reprinted in Chapter 4 extracts from three separate letters of his, defending *The Well-beloved* against this one 'ferocious review.'[37]

Other students of Hardy's work and his publishing career have commented, in various ways, on Hardy's revision of his serial into the novel *The Well-beloved.* Both versions of the story, but especially the later one, have been scrutinized for covert autobiography, whether crudely by Lois Deacon and Terry Coleman in their 1966 'exposé' of Hardy's relations with his cousin Tryphena Sparks, or more subtly and plausibly by others, such as Michael Millgate. Macmillan's New Wessex edition of the novel, published in 1975, includes an introduction by J. Hillis Miller, in which he provides a psychoanalytic reading of the plot and finds that 'a reading of the two versions reinforces the reader's sense that the novel is contrived, fantastic, openly fictional'; he sees in Hardy's 'late Victorian novel a text which anticipates twentieth-century experimentation,'[38] such as that carried on by John Fowles and J.L. Borges. A more precise parallel to Hardy's substitution of one ending for another, however, is one which Miller mentions only in passing, that is, Dickens's reworking of the ending of *Great Expectations* in 1861 at the instance of his friend Bulwer-Lytton, who argued successfully to have the first ending withdrawn and replaced by one which, Dickens agreed, would make 'the story ... more acceptable through the alteration.'[39] My account of the revision process with respect to *The Well-beloved* has emphasized for the first time similar motives of prudence and expediency, revealing the amount of energy, skill, and determination Hardy put into manipulating for his own ends the conditions of Victorian novel publication, and his success in doing so. One of the pleasant ironies of this often ironical history lies in the reassurance held out to Victorian readers by Gosse in his first review of *The Well-beloved*: 'Mr Hardy,' he said, 'is an artist of pure race, and no living writer is less moved by the laws of supply and demand. We must take what he chooses to give us; it is quite certain that he never allows himself to ask what we should like to receive.'[40]

Notes

1. Leslie Stephen, letter to Hardy, 13 April 1874, in *Thomas Hardy: A Bibliographical Study*, by Richard Little Purdy (London: Oxford University Press, 1954), app. II, p. 339.

2. Florence Emily Hardy, *The Later Years of Thomas Hardy* (London: Macmillan, 1930), p. 59.

3. Purdy, p. 94.

4. Harper and Brothers Contract Book VI, Columbia University Libraries, pp. 453–4.

5. Letter to Clarence McIlvaine, 24 February 1895, in *The Collected Letters of Thomas Hardy*, ed. Richard Little Purdy and Michael Millgate (Oxford: Clarendon Press, 1980), 2:69 (hereafter *Collected Letters*).

6. Michael Millgate, *Thomas Hardy: A Biography* (Oxford: Oxford University Press, 1982), p. 323.

7. William Morton Payne, 'Recent Fiction,' *Dial* (Chicago), 16 May 1897, p. 307.

8. Thomas Hardy, *The Pursuit of the Well-beloved, Illustrated London News*, 15 October 1892, p. 481 (hereafter abbreviated *ILN*).

9. Richard Le Gallienne, *The Quest of the Golden Girl* (London and New York: John Lane, 1896), p. 307.

10. *Collected Letters*, 2:152.

11. M.O.W. Oliphant, 'The Anti-Marriage League,' *Blackwood's Magazine*, January 1896, p. 141.

12. *ILN*, 15 October 1892, p. 481.

13. Thomas Hardy, *Jude the Obscure* (London: Macmillan, 1974), p. 90.

14. *ILN*, 15 October 1892, p. 481.

15. Ibid.

16. Thomas Hardy, *The Well-beloved* (London: Macmillan, 1975), p. 176.

17. *ILN*, 10 December 1892, p. 743.

18. *ILN*, 17 December 1892, p. 774.

19. Hardy, *The Well-beloved*, p. 192.

20. Ibid.

21. *ILN*, 17 December 1892, p. 775.

22. Hardy, *The Well-beloved*, p. 190.

23. Ibid., p. 188.

24. *Graphic*, 20 March 1897, p. 354.

25. *Saturday Review*, 20 March 1897, p. 296.

26. *Literary World*, 25 March 1897, p. 283.

27. *Athenaeum*, 10 April 1897, p. 471.

28. 'Incomparable Wessex, Again,' *Book Buyer* (New York), May 1897, p. 410.

29. *Dial*, 16 May 1897, p. 307.

30. Hardy to Edmund Gosse, 31 March 1897, *Collected Letters*, 2:156.

31. Hardy to Florence Henniker, 31 March 1897, *Collected Letters*, 2:157.

32. This phrase was directed to Mrs Henniker, 31 March 1897, *Collected Letters*, 2:157; to Gosse he described *The Well-beloved* as his 'poor innocent little tale,' 31 March 1897, *Collected Letters*, 2:156.

33. *World*, 24 March 1897, p. 13. All passages quoted appear on this page.

34. Le Gallienne, p. 294.

35. *Star*, 29 March 1897, p. 1.

36. *Bookman*, April 1897, p. 4.

37. Florence Emily Hardy, p. 61.

38. J. Hillis Miller, introduction to *The Well-beloved*, p. 17.

39. Dickens's letter to John Forster, 26 June 1861, quoted in *Charles Dickens: His Tragedy and Triumph*, by Edgar Johnson (New York: Simon and Schuster, 1952), 2:969.

40. *Saturday Review*, 20 March 1897, p. 297.

The Woodlanders as
Traditional Pastoral

◆

ROBERT Y. DRAKE, JR

The Woodlanders (1887), which is perhaps the least often read of Thomas Hardy's great Wessex novels, is often referred to by critics—and sometimes not without a tinge of condescension—as a pastoral, a charming idyl laid in a remote Arcadia which perhaps one pauses to read in the midst of grappling with the stern 'realities' of *The Mayor of Casterbridge* and *Tess of the D'Urbervilles*. Nevertheless, in relegating the novel to that green shade known as pastoral, they are perhaps according to it a dignity greater than they know.

If one regards the great flowering of pastoral in the Elizabethan era as substantially defining the tradition of English pastoral, he sees in subsequent periods of English literary history a steady decline in the vitality and per-suasiveness of pastoral as a genre—through the sentimentality ('God made the country, and man made the town') of eighteenth-century pastoral, which often seems a literature of escape, down to the often jejune optimism ('Nature never did betray the heart that loved her') which pervades much of the nature poetry of the Romantics. Finally, there is the scientifically de-mythologized nature, stripped of awful mysteries and unseen presences, of the later nineteenth and the twentieth centuries which substantially precludes the creation of any pastoral at all.

As I read it, traditional English pastoral (whether poetry or fiction) always assumes a Serpent in the Garden, a dualism in the natural world corre-sponding to the dualism in the human heart; and the struggle between these light and dark powers gives to it a pertinence it would not have if, as is often assumed, pastoral involved a 'retreat' from reality. Such pastoral always assumes a hierarchy of persons and loyalties; and the inevitable anti-pastoral force is often embodied in what Hallett Smith has called the 'aspiring mind,' which seeks to overthrow the accepted order and rise above its allotted station.[1] Also subversive of pastoral order and serenity are the pseudo-

SOURCE *Modern Fiction Studies*, VI, November 1960, no. 3, pp. 251–7.

pastoral 'escapist' desire to sport with Amaryllis in the shade and the invitation to 'come live with me and be my love,' which ignore the responsibilities of the Arcadian world, undermining its vitality and inviting its ultimate dissolution. Set in the midst of green pastures and still waters, traditional pastoral does perhaps embody a *simplification* of the human situation—and predicament; but this design signifies more the simplification of 'myth' than the distortion of 'romance.'

It is my thesis that *The Woodlanders*, though a product of the latter half of the nineteenth century, is a traditional pastoral. Unlike the Romantics (with perhaps the significant exception of Keats), Hardy viewed both nature and man as grounded in the same dualism, often grim and always inscrutable. Intellectually a rationalist, he accepted the contemporary scientific dogmas: nature was often red in tooth and claw and man's life was indeed lived on a darkling plain, and there was no 'myth' to explain or palliate these harsh realities. As Lord David Cecil has pointed out, however, Hardy's imagination always conceived of both dark and light powers in anthropomorphic or even supernatural terms: the 'President of the Immortals' in *Tess*, Egdon Heath in *The Return of the Native*, the Hintock woods themselves in *The Woodlanders*.[2] In short, Hardy, who Cecil argues was an Elizabethan in the imaginative conception of his work, was never able to de-mythologize the world around him; and, therefore, when he came to try his hand at the idyl of Little Hintock, the result was a not unworthy successor to the traditional pastoral of the great Elizabethans.

The remote Wessex village of Little Hintock, where most of the action of *The Woodlanders* takes place, is literally and spiritually a pastoral community. The timber cutters and farmers still adhere to their traditional agricultural employments and to their traditional beliefs—Christian and pagan. (Significantly, the village maidens actually *believe in* the rites of Midsummer's Eve, which are supposed to reveal their future husbands to them, though they also know that the 'visions' vouchsafed them are produced by the connivance of their swains.) But at the outset Hardy warns us against condescending to this pastoral milieu and, by implication, to the tale which is to follow; true pastoral signifies more than a picturesque chronicling of the short and simple annals of the poor.

> It was one of those sequestered spots outside the gates of the world where may usually be found more meditation than action, and more listlessness than meditation; where reasoning proceeds on narrow premises, and results in inferences wildly imaginative; yet where, from time to time, dramas of a grandeur and unity truly Sophoclean are enacted in the real, by virtue of the concentrated passions and closely-knit interdependence of the lives therein. (pp. 4–5)[3]

Although the Hintock woods are pervaded with a peaceful charm which seems of the essence of pastoral serenity, Hardy in the early pages of the novel calls to our attention the existence of subversive forces within the

natural world itself and thereby dramatically foreshadows the human
conflicts which will imperil the very existence of this Arcadia.

> They went noiselessly over mats of starry moss, rustled through interspersed
> tracts of leaves, skirted trunks with spreading roots whose mossed rinds made
> them like hands wearing green gloves; elbowed old elms and ashes with great
> forks, in which stood pools of water that overflowed on rainy days and ran down
> their stems in green cascades. On older trees still than these huge lobes of fungi
> grew like lungs. Here, as everywhere, the Unfulfilled Intention, which makes
> life what it is, was as obvious as it could be among the depraved crowds of a city
> slum. The leaf was deformed, the curve was crippled, the taper was interrupted;
> the lichen ate the vigour of the stalk, and the ivy slowly strangled to death the
> promising sapling. (pp. 58–9)

Like most of the Wessex novels (as Cecil has observed) and like most
pastoral, *The Woodlanders* is essentially a love story; it is perhaps to be
expected that, within its 'simplified' world, pastoral should center its various
conflicts in the tensions produced by that deepest and strongest of human
emotions. And the love conflicts in *The Woodlanders* are reminiscent of the
'cross-eyed Cupid' situation familiar in Elizabethan pastoral: A loves B who
loves C who loves D, and so on. As in traditional pastoral, however, there is
love which is faithful and content, accepting and supporting the pastoral
order, and love which 'aspires' and devours, undermining the *otium* which
characterizes the Arcadian world. Furthermore, in *The Woodlanders* the
conflicts between true pastoral love and its inverse (anti-pastoral) frequently
reflect the grand struggle which, often overtly, sometimes implicitly, is the
basis for the action in most of the Wessex novels: the conflict between
traditionalism and modernism. In a pastoral 'reading' of *The Woodlanders*,
the viewpoint of the traditionalist, who shapes and directs his life according
to the 'tested' and ordered conventions (whether social, political, or religious)
of the past, may be regarded as the pastoral attitude. On the other hand, the
view of the modernist that the *individual*, often ignorant or even contemptuous of past example, can impose on the community his own will (often
under the guise of a 'scientific' or 'rational' sanction), thereby disrupting its
traditional order, is of the essence of anti-pastoral. How, then, do the lovers
of *The Woodlanders* fit into a pastoral framework?

As true Arcadians we have Giles Winterborne and Marty South, both of
whom are in every way children of the soil, deriving from it both sustenance
and metaphysics. Indeed, Giles is nowhere more faithfully described than in
a passage which has been quite properly held to be reminiscent of the
pastoral tone of Keats' ode 'To Autumn'

> He looked and smelt like Autumn's very brother, his face being sunburnt to
> wheat-colour, his eyes blue as corn-flowers, his sleeves and leggings dyed with
> fruit-stains, his hands clammy with the sweet juice of apples, his hat sprinkled
> with pips, and everywhere about him that atmosphere of cider which at its first
> return each season has such an indescribable fascination for those who have
> been born and bred among the orchards. (pp. 246–7)

Giles and Marty, as true Arcadians, are alike in their 'intelligent intercourse with nature,' perceiving the natural world, with its ordered structure continually assailed by the 'Unfulfilled Intention,' as at once a reflection of and a parable for the lives of men. The modernist attitude is embodied in Edred Fitzpiers, the young doctor who comes to 'practice on' (in more ways than one) the natives of Little Hintock, and Felice Charmond, the handsome young widow who is the mistress of Hintock House. Between these diametrically opposed groups stands Grace Melbury, the daughter of a well-to-do timber merchant, who has been educated above her station by a doting but 'aspiring' father and in whom the various conflicts of the novel are most significantly focused; as a relatively 'uncommitted' character at first, she is, in some measure, an attractive prize for either side.

But Giles, who has loved Grace devotedly for years and to whom she has been promised by her father by way of redressing an old injury he had done Giles' father, has no proper strategy, as a traditionalist, for countering Melbury's growing determination to marry his daughter 'higher.' Giles, who appears ignorant and crude beside the handsome young doctor and whose final disqualification as a suitor (at least in Melbury's eyes) is accomplished when he loses most of his property, which he holds from Mrs Charmond's estate by a curious life-lease arrangement, can only magnanimously relinquish his 'claim' to Grace and retire for a time from the scene to love her from afar; he is indeed the 'faithful shepherd' of traditional pastoral. All the time, of course, he is loved just as faithfully himself by the self-effacing Marty South. Indeed, when two such Arcadians love, it is with the whole body and soul; their love is surely of the sort which bears and endures all things. But here once more is the 'Unfulfilled Intention,' the Serpent in the Garden: Giles loves someone else.

On the opposite side of the conflict, Dr Fitzpiers may easily be identified as an anti-pastoralist. Uncommitted to the life of Little Hintock and condescending toward the assumptions on which its inhabitants live, this scion of an impoverished 'great' family, who has chosen to practice medicine there mainly because it is equidistant from the 'practices' of all neighboring physicians, is interested only in his medical science and in the desultory pursuit of abstruse or even occult philosophical and scientific knowledge. Inevitably, he is regarded, not without some trepidation, by some of the woodlanders as a practitioner of the black as well as the healing arts. Mrs Charmond, whose very name (and Hardy was not above imparting to his characters' names a crude significance) suggests the alluring wiles of the Circean enchantress, is perhaps more of a pseudo-pastoralist. Characterized largely by 'inconsequence' and motivated chiefly by caprice, she lacks even the commitment which Dr Fitzpiers had made to science; her life is largely spent in gratifying the idle whims of a capricious fancy; and when she encounters Fitzpiers, whom she had known on the Continent some years before, shortly after his marriage to Grace, she at once sets to work to ensnare the all-too-willing doctor in her web.

However, it is the character of Grace Melbury that is most 'involved' in the conflicts between pastoral and anti-pastoral, traditionalism and modernism. And the course which these conflicts take and the resolution of them which is finally achieved within Grace more or less determine the outcome of the novel's action and the fate of the other characters. Therefore, I cannot agree with those critics who would see Marty South as the novel's heroine; lovable though she be, she is, for the most part, not crucially involved in the novel's conflicts (in many ways like Thomasin in *The Return of the Native*) and as such plays only a supporting role. Grace Melbury, despite the novelist's reported 'provocation' with her, is, in many ways, the most appealing of Hardy's heroines.[4] Unlike the tempestuous Eustacia Vye, who comes to grief through trying to impose her own will on the intractable Wessex world, or the docile Elizabeth-Jane, who survives catastrophe by following always the line of least resistance, Grace Melbury only once wavers in her traditional allegiance. Indeed, soon after her marriage with the fickle doctor she comes to apprehend fully her situation as an Arcadian unwillingly allied with the anti-pastoral world; and heartsick at her plight, she significantly upbraids the loving father who foolishly induced her to forsake her traditional loyalties.

> 'I wish you had never, never thought of educating me. I wish I worked in the woods like Marty South! I hate genteel life, and I want to be no better than she!'
> 'Why?' said her amazed father.
> 'Because cultivation has only brought me inconveniences and troubles. I say again, I wish you had never sent me to those fashionable schools you set your mind on. It all arose out of that, father. If I had stayed at home I should have married—'
> She closed up her mouth suddenly and was silent; and he saw that she was not far from crying.
> Melbury was much grieved. 'What, and would you like to have grown up as we be here in Hintock—knowing no more, and with no more chance of seeing good life than we have here?'
> 'Yes. I have never got any happiness outside Hintock that I know of, and I have suffered many a heartache at being sent away.' (pp. 266–7)

Later, after the elopement of Fitzpiers and Mrs Charmond to the Continent and the melodramatic death of the latter at the hands of a disgruntled American suitor—but not before the doctor had begun to tire of her, as Grace had predicted—the penitent Fitzpiers comes back to Little Hintock to attempt a reconciliation with his wife. But Grace, almost hysterical at the prospect of meeting the faithless husband she has come to abhor, flees from her father's house to the shelter of Giles' hut in the woods and indirectly hastens his death when Giles, already ill, chivalrously retires from the hut to sleep under an impoverished shelter where he is more or less at the mercy of the inclement weather. And in her anguish at perceiving what her lover's faithfulness (and perhaps her own original defection) has finally led to, she implores Giles, all 'aspiration' now cast aside, to come in out of the rain: 'Don't you want to come in? Are you not wet? *Come to me, dearest! I don't mind what they say or what they think of us any more*' (p. 374). Grace's reconciliation with the Arcadian world which she had momentarily betrayed in her marriage is now complete; nevertheless, Giles dies, attended by Grace and the faithful Marty and, in a professional capacity, by the repentant Fitzpiers, whom Grace, in her inconsolable grief, for a time allows to draw the 'extremist inference' about her presence in Giles' hut.

The remainder of the novel, which as other critics have noted is almost tediously prolonged, is devoted, then, to the anticipated reconciliation of Grace and Fitzpiers. In this reconciliation, however, there is no renunciation, on Grace's part, of Arcadian principles; there is, however, some apparent change in Fitzpiers' modernist principles in the direction of greater humility and devotion to duty. Therefore, they can resume their marital relationship with some prospect of quietly growing devotion, if not of passionate attachment; and at the novel's end they go forth from the Eden of Little Hintock to their new home in the Midlands like a chastened Adam and Eve.

But what of the Arcadian world itself? Has it been able to preserve anything from the onslaught of the enemy, and have its assumptions been vindicated despite the enemy's attempt to discredit them? Of all the lovers, only Marty is left in Little Hintock—Marty who has never questioned for one moment the assumptions of that Arcadian world. Quite properly the novel's final lines, which she speaks at Giles' grave, reaffirm, in a decidedly Biblical cadence, the essential if not historical permanence of the Arcadian world and the continued validity and significance of its assumptions in 'modern' times.

> As this solitary and silent girl stood there in the moonlight, a straight slim figure, clothed in a plaitless gown, the contours of womanhood so undeveloped as to be scarcely perceptible in her, the marks of poverty and toil effaced by the misty hour, she touched sublimity at points, and looked almost like a being who had rejected with indifference the attribute of sex for the loftier quality of abstract humanism. She stooped down and cleared away the withered flowers that Grace and herself had laid there the previous week, and put her fresh ones in their place.
>
> 'Now, my own, own love,' she whispered, 'you are mine, and only mine; for she has forgot 'ee at last, although for her you died! But I—whenever I get up I'll think of 'ee, and whenever I lie down I'll think of 'ee again. Whenever I plant the young larches I'll think that none can plant as you planted; and whenever I split a gad, and whenever I turn the cider wring, I'll say none could do it like you. If ever I forget your name let me forget home and heaven! ... But no, no, my love, I never forget 'ee; for you was a good man, and did good things!' (pp. 443–4)

Notes

1. See the chapter on Elizabethan pastoral in Hallet Smith, *Elizabethan Poetry* (Cambridge, Mass., 1952), pp. 1–63. My interpretation of pastoral is considerably indebted to Professor Smith's observations there.

2. See Lord David Cecil, *Hardy the Novelist* (London, 1943), pp. 149 ff.

3. All quotations from *The Woodlanders*, whose page numbers will be cited in the text, are taken from *The Writings of Thomas Hardy in Prose and Verse*, Anniversary Edition, VI (New York, 1921).

4. See Carl J. Weber, *Hardy and the Lady from Madison Square* (Waterville, Maine, 1952), p. 89. After a conversation with Hardy, his American Boswell-in-embryo, Rebekah Owen, recorded that 'he said that Grace never interested him much; he was provoked with her all along.'

167

Setting and Theme in *Far from the Madding Crowd*

◆

HOWARD BABB

Even casual readers of Thomas Hardy soon begin to sense that in his fiction the customary setting, the natural world, operates a good deal more force-fully than as sheer backdrop to the narrative. And the power of his settings is a commonplace among Hardy's critics, most of whom find the natural back-ground functioning symbolically at moments, though one of them speaks instead of a metaphoric dimension.[1] To anyone curious about Hardy's technique with his backgrounds, or generally inquisitive about the ways in which fiction may be structured and work for its effects, the relatively early *Far from the Madding Crowd* proves especially interesting. While not in the same class with Hardy's later achievements, this story shows—with some-thing approaching the obviousness of a textbook example—how setting can be used to reinforce and indeed at times to render theme. What I want chiefly to bring out in the following pages is both the number and variety of relationships that Hardy creates between setting and theme here: a host of interconnections that serves—along with the story's other structures, some of which I shall be glancing at—to saturate *Far from the Madding Crowd* with its theme. And I shall be suggesting incidentally that the novel's saturation with its theme helps to explain how we come to terms—if indeed we do—with several scenes of more or less questionable plausibility in which the natural setting plays a dominant part.

At bottom, Hardy's story juxtaposes two different worlds or modes of being, the natural against the civilized, and it insists on the superiority of the former by identifying the natural as strong, enduring, self-contained, slow to change, sympathetic, while associating the civilized with weakness, facility, modernity, self-centeredness. We are perhaps alerted for this theme by the title itself of the novel, which evokes the contrast in Gray's 'Elegy' between rural and urban values. But in any case, Hardy's juxtaposition of the natural and the civilized is reflected in even the barest outline of *Far from the Madding*

SOURCE *Journal of English Literary History*, 30, 1963, pp. 147–61.

Crowd's narrative. The first section of the story hinges on the unsuccessful marriage proposal made by Gabriel Oak—the simple, modest shepherd—to the self-assured and somewhat flightly Bathsheba Everdene; she turns him down mainly because she does not love him, to be sure, but also because she has her sights set on a way of life above, somehow more refined than, what he can offer her. By the end of the novel, however, she has learned through her sufferings on account of Boldwood and Troy how to value Gabriel, so Oak's patient love is rewarded at last. Between these opening and closing movements of the story, its foreground is largely given over to the entanglement of Bathsheba with Gabriel's two rivals for her heart. The first to present himself is the gentlemanly Boldwood, whose composure is so shattered by Bathsheba's valentine that he begins hounding her mercilessly to marry him. Then comes the fashionable Troy, who overwhelms Bathsheba with flattery, quickly marries her, tires of her almost as fast, and drifts away after quarreling with her over the dead Fanny Robin, a girl whom Troy seduced before meeting Bathsheba. Finally Boldwood steps forward again, now spurred by the assumption that Troy is dead to press Bathsheba more relentlessly than ever for a promise of marriage, only to have his fantasy exploded by the return of Troy, whom he shoots down in a burst of passion. Every so often during these romantic conflicts and maneuverings, Gabriel Oak will move to the front of the stage, perhaps to give Bathsheba some moral counsel, or to save her sheep, or to protect her grain during the storm. But for the most part he remains in the middle distance, allied with the processes of nature through performing the ordinary tasks of the farmer or shepherd, his feet firmly planted in the natural world. The most general impression created by the narrative, then, is of a running contrast between dignified naturalness and the feverish pursuit of selfish ends.

Whatever the local action that Hardy places in the foreground, he manages to keep us constantly aware of the natural world in the novel. Four characteristics of that world as it is revealed throughout Hardy's fiction have been admirably set forth by John Holloway: 'Nature is an organic living whole,' with all its parts having 'a life and personality of their own'; 'it is unified on a great scale through both time and space'; 'it is exceedingly complex,' with 'details that are sometimes even quaint or bizarre; these heterogeneous things are integrated, however obscurely, into a system of rigid and undeviating law.'[2] All of these qualities are apparent enough in *Far from the Madding Crowd*, as anyone may remind himself by rereading the famous Norcombe Hill scene at the beginning of chapter 2. But the natural world in this novel seems endowed with a fifth attribute as well, one that may surprise the reader of Hardy's other fiction. For in *Far from the Madding Crowd* nature is frequently represented as at least a sympathetic force, sometimes even as a moral agent—an assertion that I shall depend upon details cited later to bear out.

Even if the claim about a fifth attribute should prove tenuous, there can be no questioning the fact that again and again in this story Hardy uses his position as omniscient author to set the natural world and the civilized explicitly against each other in such a way that we have no doubt about which we are to prefer. Almost at the beginning of the novel, for instance, after he has developed so compelling a sense of nature's majesty in describing Norcombe Hill, the night sky, and the 'almost ... palpable movement' of the earth, Hardy remarks that this vivid experiencing of the universe is possible only when one has 'first expanded with a sense of difference from the mass of civilized mankind, who are dreamwrapt and disregardful of all such [natural] proceedings at this time' (2).[3] Further on in the story, when Hardy is leading up to the sheep-shearing by sketching the June landscape, he spells out the opposition once more, this time with obviously moral overtones: 'God was palpably present in the country, and the devil had gone with the world to town' (22). And the great shearing-barn itself provides the occasion for one of Hardy's most elaborate variations on this theme. First he treats the four-hundred-year-old building as an instance of that continuity between past and present which typifies the rural mode of life; then, in a separate paragraph, he contrasts the relative immutability of Weatherbury and its ways with the rapid change, the discontinuity between past and present, which characterizes London or Paris; and he comes out finally with the flat statement that 'the barn was naturall to the shearers, and the shearers were in harmony with the barn' (22). These examples will have suggested plainly enough not only that Hardy charges the natural background itself with value, but that he keeps taking advantage of his position as omniscient author to restate his theme openly in passages which focus mainly on the setting.

One of the basic methods by which any author dramatizes his theme, of course, is through ordering the similarities and differences between his characters in such a manner that these figures make up a pattern expressive of the novel's meaning. But instead of tracing the pattern in *Far from the Madding Crowd* as it emerges most directly, through the actions and motives of its persons, I want to emphasize two of the ways in which Hardy articulates it through relating his characters to the setting. The first of these— Hardy's naming of his men and women—is so evident that it needs little discussing.[4] Gabriel is as sturdy, as eminently natural, as an oak tree. Diametrically opposed to him is the Sergeant, whose name identifies that famous city which we perforce associate at least with weakness, given our many accounts of the fall of Troy, if not with decadence. The names Everdene and Boldwood do not formulate values quite so patly. But to my ear *Everdene* can hardly fail to echo *evergreen*; and according to the O.E.D., *dene* itself refers either to 'a low standhill' or, as a variant of *dean*, to 'a (wooded) vale.' This linking of Bathsheba with the natural is thoroughly appropriate, for the novel insists that her fundamental commitment—though she deviates from it for a time in her infatuation with Troy—is to the land

33

and to Gabriel. As for *Boldwood*, I think the name hints at a person somehow more than natural; in any case, the story shows us a man who, though he apparently *has* had his feet on the ground, is alienated from his farm and from himself through his obsessive pursuit of Bathsheba, and ends up as a murderer declared insane by the law. Even some of the minor figures bear names which mark out their allegiances in similar fashion, although Hardy is not absolutely consistent in this matter. Definitely members of the rustic group are Fanny Robin, Joseph Poorgrass, Matthew Moon; and doubtless Maryann Money belongs there as well in spite of her name. At this level of character the obvious outsider and villain is the bailiff whom Bathsheba discharges for stealing, the mercenary Pennyways, who finishes out the novel as the agent—predictably enough, given his name—of Troy. Clearly, then, Hardy does in effect evaluate many of his characters by the names he chooses for them.

The second way in which Hardy relates setting to character is less apparent, and one risks sounding impressionistic in talking about it. At or shortly after the introduction of each major figure, Hardy gives us a scene in which he uses the natural world to provide an oblique commentary on the person, the sense of which is verified through the rest of the novel. The first time that we see Gabriel Oak substantially located in a natural environment, for instance, is on Norcombe Hill. Of course in the opening chapter Hardy has already taken pains to distinguish him from the merely civilized world: by declaring Gabriel to be really at ease only 'on working days' and 'in his old clothes' (1); by laboring the joke about the watch which will not run and forces Oak to tell time by the stars; and by allowing Gabriel to announce the fault of Bathsheba, whom he has glimpsed looking in her mirror, as 'Vanity' (1). Then, after devoting two pages of the second chapter to the endurance, the spaciousness, the sublimity of Norcombe Hill and the night, Hardy places Gabriel in the scene by showing him attending to the lambing. After several more pages, indeed, Hardy relates the shepherd to the landscape even more directly by letting Gabriel read the time from the stars and by reporting that

> ... he stood still after looking at the sky as a useful instrument, and regarded it in an appreciative spirit, as a work of art superlatively beautiful. For a moment he seemed impressed with the speaking loneliness of the scene, or rather with the complete abstraction from all its compass of the sights and sounds of man. (2)

The general effect of this Norcombe Hill sequence is to associate the qualities of the landscape with Gabriel, and he lives up to them in the narrative that follows. Several chapters later on the author refers specifically to Gabriel's 'sublimity' (6). And towards the end of the novel, Hardy insists that Oak's moral status is almost more than human, as I understand the passage, by twice recording the shepherd's disagreement with an opinion which the law endorses, that Boldwood was insane when killing Troy. As for

34

Gabriel's endurance, it is manifest in his unwavering love for Bathsheba throughout the story.

The scene in which we are introduced to Troy is as different as can be from the one on Norcombe Hill. Instead of the sublime, Hardy emphasizes the 'dreariness' of a heavy snowfall (11); instead of a landscape vitalized by a multitude of minute natural details, we have a 'moor' whose 'irregularities were forms without features; suggestive of anything ... and without more character than that of being the limit of something else—the lowest layer of a firmament of snow'; and most strikingly, instead of the spacious, the suffocating:

> The vast arch of cloud above was strangely low, and formed as it were the roof of a large dark cavern, gradually sinking in upon its floor; for the instinctive thought was that the snow lining the heavens and that encrusting the earth would soon unite into one mass without any intervening stratum of air at all. (11)

While Troy is not placed literally in this setting (as Fanny Robin is), the somberness of the landscape and its deathlike quality condition our response to him at least to the extent of preparing us for a person contrasting sharply with Oak, even though the suggestions of the landscape are not mirrored directly in Troy's character. He stays inside the barracks during the scene, parrying Fanny's plaintive attempts to set a time for their marriage and thus apparently amusing his companions. But it is appropriate that we should first hear Troy when he is in a society of sorts, set apart from the natural world, for he remains fundamentally estranged from it. (To be sure he is a 'natural' child, but of a nobleman; and though more a native of Weatherbury than Oak or Bathsheba, he never seems thoroughly engaged in rural occupations, as they do—even in the passage about hiving the bees, Hardy stresses the flirtation interplay between Bathsheba and Troy rather than the deed itself.) The most dramatic proof of the Sergeant's estrangement from nature appears in two incidents that I shall deal with later on. For the present, the critical fact to recognize is the absolute difference between the central feature of Troy's personality and a dominant characteristic of the natural world. That world is marked by the continuity of past and present, by the gradualness of its change, whereas Troy—so Hardy reiterates when analyzing him for us—is the slave of impulse, irrevocably committed to a present discontinuous with the past or with the future: 'Simply feeling, considering, and caring for what was before his eyes, he was vulnerable only in the present ... That projection of consciousness into days gone by and to come ... was foreign to Troy. With him the past was yesterday; the future, to-morrow; never, the day after' (25). Trapped so completely in the present, Troy can have no sense of an act's consequences, is therefore incapable of a moral decision. And nowhere in the story does Hardy permit him to be governed by anything except impulse, making even Troy's self-condemnation following the death of Fanny Robin a mere fit of remorse (46). But to come back to Troy and the landscape itself. It may be worth noting that the image of a 'cavern' in the previous description of the snowfall finds vague echoes in the setting of Troy's first encounter with Bathsheba—the path roofed over and enclosed by trees which Hardy calls 'a vast, low, naturally formed hall' (24)—and in the setting for the sword-exercise, a 'hollow amid the ferns' (28).

The first scene in which we really became acquainted with Boldwood may remind us in several ways of the introduction of Troy. Once more the earth is covered with snow, and once more the tone is somber. But in this instance the landscape does mirror directly the condition of Boldwood. For he had just been knocked head over heels, as it were, by the anonymous valentine sealed with the message 'Marry Me,' never to right himself emotionally again. And of the natural world, Hardy writes at first:

> The moon shone to-night, and its light was not of a customary kind. His window admitted only a reflection of its rays, and the pale sheen had that reversed direction which snow gives, coming upward and lighting up his ceiling in an unnatural way, casting shadows in strange places, and putting lights where shadows had used to be. (14)

Then, as if to underline the 'unnaturalness' of nature here, Hardy describes the same effect at sunrise, when Boldwood leaves the house:

> ... the fields and sky were so much of one colour by the snow that it was difficult ... to tell whereabouts the horizon occurred; and in general there was here, too, that before-mentioned preternatural inversion of light and shade which attends the prospect when the garish brightness commonly in the sky is found on the earth, and the shades of earth are in the sky. (14)

However tempted we may be at times to sympathize with Boldwood, I take it that we do feel his behavior to be unnatural and perverse from here on, especially given the qualities attributed to nature and its norm—Gabriel Oak—in *Far from the Madding Crowd*. Catapulted immediately to an emotional extreme by the valentine, Boldwood keeps thrusting his attentions on Bathsheba, through not one suit but two, and the violence with which he declares to her his love, or anger, or envy is a world away from the restrained dignity that typifies Oak. The radical selfishness of Boldwood reveals itself in the fact that he goes on exacting promises from her though he quite realizes that she does not love him. Towards the end of the story, indeed, Hardy underlines the degree of the man's perverseness by allowing Boldwood to deny—though as a last desperate maneuver to win Bathsheba's hand—that he himself loves her, to deny his own nature: 'But do give your word! A mere business compact, you know, between two people who are beyond the influence of passion' (53). The novel does not, however, stop at defining Boldwood as different from Oak; it tellingly associates the gentleman farmer with Troy. For one thing, both of them turn their backs on the natural world (if for different reasons) in ignoring the storm that threatens their grain ricks. Besides, as Boldwood's quest after Bathsheba continues, he becomes more and more pointedly linked with a civilized world like Troy's. To image his career oversimply, but not untruthfully: shortly after Boldwood enters the story, we learn how he meditates in the barn, drawing comfort from the nearness of the horses (18); towards the end of the novel, we are shown him absorbed with his tailor in the fitting of a coat he will wear to his Christmas party for Bathsheba (52). In fact, Hardy spells out Boldwood's deviation from the natural and identifies the civilized strain as evil when describing the preparations for the party: 'Such a thing had never been attempted before by its owner, and it was now done as by a wrench ... A shadow seemed to move about the rooms, saying that the proceedings were unnatural to the place and the lone man who lived therein, and hence not good' (52).

Bathsheba does not have a scene in the natural world largely to herself near her introduction into the novel, as do Oak and Boldwood; nor are the landscapes against which we initially see her so powerfully suggestive as the snowstorm at the introduction of Troy. Still, two of our first three glimpses of her do supply a kind of commentary on Bathsheba. If our first sight is of a girl on a wagon full of furniture who glances at herself in a mirror, our third is of the same girl riding more than skilfully in the woods, 'quite at home,' as Hardy says, 'anywhere between a horse's head and its tail' (3). These vignettes hint, it seems to me, at the impulses which conflict in Bathsheba, swaying her now towards the socially refined and now towards the natural. At any rate, the course of the story shows her to be a rather artless woman whose vanity temporarily ensnares her in the civilized world, embodied primarily here by Troy, and who escapes from it at last to come to terms with Gabriel. Even during her captivity, however, Hardy represents her as loving Troy to the depths of her being and as possessing absolute integrity, that integrity she manifests by remaining loyal to her husband after he has deserted her—or by continuing to accept the consequences of having once sent the valentine to Boldwood. The fact that Bathsheba does belong essentially to the natural world is indicated over and over by Hardy in the figurative language he applies to her—another of the ways in which he relates character to theme and keeps reminding us of the novel's meaning. Thus he describes the 'rapidity' with which Bathsheba moves as 'that of a kingfisher' and the 'noiselessness that of a hawk' (3). Or he calls her 'excited, wild, and honest as the day' (26). Or, in commenting on her response to Troy, Hardy takes his figure of speech from the world of fashion and redefines it expressly to ally her with the world valued in the story:

> Though in one sense a woman of the world, it was, after all, that world of daylight coteries and green carpets wherein cattle form the passing crowd and winds the busy hum; where a quiet family of rabbits or hares lives on the other side of your party-wall, where your neighbor is everybody in the tything, and where calculation is confined to market-days. Of the fabricated tastes of good fashionable society she knew but little, and of the formulated self-indulgence of bad, nothing at all ... Her love was entire as a child's, and though warm as summer it was fresh as spring. (29)

Bathsheba's affiliation to the world of nature is also brought out by several incidents in the novel, notably the one in which she is spiritually regenerated by a night in a thicket after breaking with Troy at Fanny's coffin. But it will be more interesting to consider this passage after we have observed some of the effects which Hardy achieves through his use of the natural world in particular incidents.

In the introductory scenes just discussed, the settings remain primarily settings. But in the four incidents now at hand, the natural world functions as something more than a background for events, and by the last of them it has explicitly become a moral agent. In the first one, the journey of Fanny Robin's body through Yalbury Great Wood in an autumn fog, we may still tend to view the landscape mainly as a setting, if an appropriate one. Yet even in this scene, the underlying impression conveyed is of nature sympathizing with Fanny. The effect arises in part from several phrases by which Hardy suggests that the natural world itself undergoes a death of sorts here— 'There was no perceptible motion in the air, not a visible drop of water fell upon a leaf ... A startling quiet overhung all surroundings things ...' (42)— and in part from the climax of the description, the condensed fog dropping from the trees onto the coffin, which one can hardly keep from reading as nature's tears at the death of Fanny. A kindred sense of nature's almost personal affection for Fanny has been dramatized rather bluntly by Hardy in one of the story's earlier events, not that we are ever allowed any doubts about the world that she belongs to, given her name and the civilized Troy's ruthless exploitation of her. Nevertheless, Hardy drives the point home in plotting Fanny's desperate trip through the night to reach the Casterbridge Union-house before she collapses, a struggle that succeeds only because a dog miraculously appears to tow her in. As Hardy depicts him (40), this dog seems a good deal less mere dog than nature's minister to Fanny. Just when 'Hopelessness had come at last' to her, the dog materializes out of the natural surroundings: 'From the stripe of shadow on the opposite side of the bridge a portion of shade seemed to detach itself ...' The description of the dog is consciously generalized, separating him from any particular breed and elevating him to something approaching a force of nature: 'He seemed to be of too strange and mysterious a nature to belong to any variety ... He was the ideal embodiment of canine greatness—a generalization from what was common to all.' And in his next sentence, Hardy identifies the dog directly with a nature capable of kindness: 'Night, in its sad, solemn, and benevolent aspect, apart from its stealthy and cruel side, was personified in this form.' The significance of the dog is clinched for us at the end of the journey when civilization, in the person of the attendant at the Union-house, stones away the friend that nature has given Fanny. What the whole episode means is beyond argument, surely, but I am less certain about how a reader responds to it. Hardy's account of Fanny's anguished efforts to get on, even before the dog turns up, by making herself crutches, by hanging on a fence, and by

deceiving herself about the distance, seems on the face of it grossly sentimental. And the business of the dog arriving so opportunely, 'frantic in his
distress' to help her, appears in itself highly unlikely, if not incredible. Yet
the episode actually affects us, I would guess, as neither crassly sentimental
nor utterly implausible, precisely because it is so transparent an expression
of the theme with which the novel is drenched that, when we come to the
scene in context, we either accommodate it readily enough or never think to
question its authenticity as fiction.

If the incidents just mentioned show the sympathy of the natural world for
Fanny, the two that follow declare how hostile it is toward Troy. The first of
them, the wild storm that climaxes the Sergeant's drinking party with the
laborers in the barn and endangers the grain, serves also to contrast Troy
with Oak again. Whereas Troy asserts, absurdly enough, his mastery over
nature by denying that it will rain (36), Gabriel receives three separate
warnings 'direct ... from the Great Mother' (36). Perhaps the power of the
storm is supposed simply to mark nature's outrage as it answers Troy's
obtuse claim. But the violent unnaturalness of the event, which Hardy
recreates so memorably, strikes me rather as nature measuring in its own
fashion the ascendancy that the civilized Troy has gained on Bathsheba's
farm. He is, after all, recently married to her and 'ruling now in the room of
his wife', has just converted 'harvest home' into a celebration of his wedding,
and debauches the workmen by forcing them to drink brandy-and-water
rather than the 'cider and ale' natural to them (36)—thus incapacitating the
whole party, of course, to deal with the threat of the elements to the grain, a
task undertaken by Gabriel and an indignant Bathsheba. While in this storm
nature appears to be evaluating Troy for us, in a later scene Hardy compels
us to view the natural world as Troy's open antagonist and his moral judge.
For the pouring of the cloudburst through the gurgoyle to wash out the
flowers that Troy has planted on Fanny's grave is an act by which nature
rejects him absolutely from its community and rebukes him for his belated
effort to atone for his treatment of Fanny. The moral dimension of nature's
deed is insisted upon by Hardy when he refers to 'Providence' in describing
the Sergeant's reaction to what has happened: '... to find that Providence,
far from helping him into a new course ... actually jeered his first trembling
and critical attempt in that kind, was more than [Troy's] nature could bear'
(46). Certainly this whole episode, like the one about Fanny and the dog,
seems radically coincidental when viewed in the cold light of reason and
probability. But again I suspect that, by the time we encounter it in our
reading, Hardy has conditioned us so thoroughly to his theme that we come
to terms with the incident almost instinctively. If this claim sounds too
strong, it is at least clear that the incident articulates the theme of *Far from the
Madding Crowd* once more and is to that extent domesticated in the novel.[5]

It is worth emphasizing here, as a mark of how intensively Hardy
dramatizes his theme, that in the scene of Troy at Fanny's grave or of Fanny

on Casterbridge highway the natural world is not employed symbolically. (I am using that word in its loosest sense, simply to designate a unit that does not contain all its meaning within itself, that stands in part for something else.) The cloudburst and the dog are natural forces, literal presences, which as it were enact the story's theme rather than represent it with any obliqueness.[6] And even in the other two scenes I think we apprehend nature directly, as a sheer being, a thing in itself, rather than as a symbolic vehicle which signifies indirectly.

Perhaps I can make clear my sense of nature's non-symbolic functioning in these incidents by glancing at one other in which a bit of landscape, a swamp, does work symbolically for a while. As a result of her bitter quarrel with Troy at Fanny's coffin, during which Bathsheba has heard him declare that he values the dead girl more than his living wife, she is so shaken that even suicide suggests itself to her—'A vehement impulse to flee from him ... not stopping short of death itself, mastered Bathsheba now' (43)—and she rushes into the night. But a sleep under the trees cleanses her spirit, and against the 'cool air and colours' of the morning, 'her heated actions and resolves of the night stood out in lurid contrast' (44). Now she catches sight of a swamp nearby, one which Hardy makes into a symbol of her earlier despair (44). For he heaps up such noxious items as 'rotting leaves' and 'fungi' with 'clammy tops' or 'oozing gills,' imparting to them a moral dimension by writing that 'the general aspect of the swamp was malignant. From its moist and poisonous coat seemed to be exhaled the essences of evil things in the earth ...' And he concludes the description with 'The hollow seemed a nursery of pestilence small and great, in the immediate neighborhood of comfort and health, and Bathsheba arose with a tremor at the thought of having passed the night on the brink of so dismal a place,' words which in effect equate Bathsheba's physical with her moral situation. Another indication that this passage operates symbolically is the sense one has of a slight grinding in the gears when, on the next page, Hardy needs to use the swamp as a naturalistic fact at the appearance of Liddy Smallbury. Bathsheba tries to warn her against traversing it—still influenced, it would seem, by the symbolism of the swamp—but has lost her voice; and Liddy herself is forced by Hardy to acknowledge the swamp's dangers in remarking, 'It will bear me up, I think.' But as a matter of fact she crosses it safely enough: 'Iridescent bubbles of dank subterranean breath rose from the sweating sod beside the waiting-maid's feet as she trod, hissing as they burst ... Liddy did not sink, as Bathsheba had anticipated' (44). One feels a subdued clash here between the frightfully dark colors with which Hardy paints the swamp, colors determined largely by its earlier symbolism, and Liddy's ready success in negotiating it. Yet whatever the flaws in Hardy's performance at this moment, his major point in these pages about Bathsheba's awakening is that she has found refuge from Troy in nature and been morally regenerated by that world.

The setting of *Far from the Madding Crowd* impinges upon the consciousness of the reader in many ways, then: in some incidents as mere setting, or as symbol, or as a being in its own right; often through the relationship of various sorts established between it and the characters; sometimes as a complex whole more or less explicitly evaluated for us by Hardy. And whatever its local role may be, the setting keeps mediating the novel's theme. But we should guard against reading too much into these conclusions. Although *Far from the Madding Crowd* does in fact seem to me a thoroughly achieved and compelling novel, the variety and number of uses to which Hardy puts the setting do not of themselves guarantee the book's success as art, any more than they can insure that Hardy's theme itself will convince the reader. Indeed, one can find in *Lady Chatterley's Lover*, curiously enough, almost as various a use of setting as Hardy's, the novel also revealing quite comparable governing structures and substantially the same theme—yet Lawrence's story fails dismally as fiction. So, while the foregoing analysis does make clear *Far from the Madding Crowd*'s saturation with its theme, it remains ultimately as limited as any formal analysis: which is capable of showing *how* the piece of literature works, but incapable of showing *that* it works, of closing with the essential vitality that allows the piece of literature to possess us.

Notes

1. Carol R. Andersen, 'Time, Space, and Perspective in Thomas Hardy,' *Nineteenth-Century Fiction* 9 (1954), 192–208. The critic feels that in the case of Hardy 'we must take all the ordinary elements of the novel (landscape, characters, plot) and accept them as metaphorical equivalents of the theme' (p. 195), and later speaks of Hardy's 'backgrounds' as 'something more than a mere setting of scene. It appears to be the pathetic fallacy driven to such an extreme that it is no longer a fallacy but an artistic integer' (p. 203). These sentences convey an impression of Hardey's settings that seems to me much like my own, but the essay concentrates on metaphors of 'time' and 'space' in the novels.

2. *The Victorian Sage* (London, 1953), p. 252.

3. My Hardy quotations are from Harper's Anniversary Edition of *Far from the Madding Crowd* (New York and London, 1920).

4. Joseph Warren Beach has noted—in *The Technique of Thomas Hardy* (Chicago, 1922)—that the characters' 'names are chosen largely for their combination of biblical and rustic associations' (p. 52), but he goes on to mention some of the biblical echoes only. The topic of Beach's section on *Far from the Madding Crowd* is setting, which he seems to view mainly as a kind of inspired local color. Moreover, he makes its setting the major motive of the novel—which appears to him 'primarily a reconstruction of "realistic dream country"' (p. 51)—and thus in effect denies the story a theme, as in commenting that the early Hardy 'was treating a subject, but not a theme' and 'took up,' in the present novel, 'the subject of Wessex country life' (p. 90).

5. John Holloway finds the episode 'unconvincing' in that 'Hardy stresses a trivial incident of tedious length' (*The Victorian Sage*, p. 249). Overlong, perhaps, but I cannot agree with 'trivial,' for I think that in our reading we apprehend the incident as the climax in Troy's relationship with the natural world.

6. Here I am running counter to the argument of Richard C. Carpenter—in 'Hardy's "Gurgoyles,"' *Modern Fiction Studies* (Autumn, 1960), 227—that 'the gargoyle sets the tone' of the cloudburst scene and 'lets us know that this is a symbolic event, an instance of the disproportion that is art.' [See Chapter 195. Ed.]

Reading a Story: Sequence, Pace, and Recollection

◆

IAN GREGOR

I have been attempting to suggest ways in which the unfolding narrative of *Wuthering Heights* creates its own manner of attention, a manner involving the reader in a highly concentrated suspension of judgement. The novel may alter in narrative tempo in the second half, but it continues to require the kind of absorbed curiosity which prompted Lockweed to demand that Nelly begin her tale. *Wuthering Heights*, however it may appear in retrospect, demands a reading of the utmost intensity, the feeling present in the writing seems to seek a matching response in the reading. If we turn from the story that Emily Brontë tells to the kind of story that Hardy tells, we find a markedly different kind of reader being called into being, a reader who is to be drawn not so much into an intensity of response, but rather into a continual oscillation between intensity of involvement and contemplative detachment. We can see what this means in practice if we look at two novels which have been discussed elsewhere in this volume from a different point of view.

Chapter 40 of *Far From the Madding Crowd* can be thought of as the longest chapter in nineteenth-century fiction, not in terms of pages, which are few, but in terms of the experience it conveys. The chapter describes Fanny Robin's fateful journey on the Casterbridge highway to the lying-in hospital, and which, together with Troy's sword-play, the shearing supper and the great fire, make it one of the scenes that remains most vividly in the memory when the reading of the novel has been completed. It is not difficult to see why. It is deeply felt and intensely visual: the lonely girl '*in extremis*', half-walking, half-crawling, to the hospital, and then helped in the desperate, final stage by a friendly dog. With such elements the scene is almost cut free from its context to be offered as a suitable subject for a genre painting, with

SOURCE *Reading the Victorian Novel: Detail into Form*, London, 1980, pp. 98–104.

some title such as 'Deserted' or 'The Only Friend'.

But such an activity of detaching and framing is the scene viewed in retrospect; it is not how it strikes the reader coming to it fresh from the renewed quarrel between Bathsheba and Troy in the previous chapter. The breakup of the marriage is becoming evermore certain, the question is simply how it is to be brought about. It is now that Fanny, after a long absence from the novel (several weeks for the first readers of the serial) makes her dramatic reappearance. The reader's attention is quickened not simply by the recognition of the destructive agent, but by being made to remember again Troy's fickleness and Bathsheba's infatuation. Equally, the reader is being made to anticipate, through Oak's apprehensions, Bathsheba's reaction to Fanny's situation. In reading the story, as distinct from recollecting it, the reader travels through Chapter 40, vivid as it is, with memories freshened by the past and with renewed anticipation of what is to come.

Michael Irwin has discussed the melodramatic effect of the scene and pointed out that though an individual scene may be simple in the response it seeks, its effect in the emotional pattern of the unfolding drama can be complex. Certainly this is true of 'On the Casterbridge highway'. Hardy obtains through Fanny's plight a sharp injection of feeling into the novel through her isolation, through the way in which Fanny endures the sheer difficulty of her journey. The *deceleration* of pace allows the feeling to intensify and infiltrate the narrative. But Hardy in doing this is working not so much on behalf of Fanny as on behalf of Bathsheba. The reader has to be made to see the depth of her infatuation for Troy, never more present than when she has lost him. That, for Hardy, is to be the dramatic climax of the scene, not any revelation about Fanny or her child. When that revelation comes we sweep past it in a way that makes us almost surprised that we have done so, 'her tears fell fast beside the unconscious pair in the coffin'. The way is now clear for the real climax, not the effect on Bathsheba of 'the unconscious pair', but the effect on Bathsheba of Troy's reaction to that pair. This is what consumes her in the desperate cry, 'Don't don't kiss them. O Frank, I can't bear it— *You will, Frank, kiss me too?*' Rhythm, punctuation, underlining, all indicate and convey the intensity of emotional pressure behind a scene which modulates out of an explicitly melodramatic mode into a dramatic one. All the pathos of the desperate journey on the highway can now be drawn upon to generate the tragic feeling present in Bathsheba's recognition that her marriage to Troy is now truly at an end.

In the reading experience of the novel, Fanny acts as an emotional surrogate for Bathsheba, taking our thoughts away from individual caprice towards that universal woe attendant on the frustrations of love, no matter to whom it occurs. But if Fanny's destiny is to allow a deepening of feeling both by, and for Bathsheba, it is a destiny which has, in the dramatic economy of the novel, to be swiftly performed and not allowed to linger in the memory. It is crucial to Hardy's purpose that when the hospital door closes on Fanny, it should close also on the reader's memories of her. However sad Fanny's fate has been, it cannot be allowed to distract attention from Bathsheba; Hardy's management of this leads us to consider the function of Chapter 42, 'Joseph and his Burden—At the Buck's Head'.

At first sight that chapter seems something of a digression, not in Poorgrass's journey, but in the extended conversation at the inn. In fact, the whole scene has a precise dramatic role to perform. Poorgrass oppressed by the burden of bringing Fanny's body back from Casterbridge makes a grateful pause at 'The Buck's Head', where he finds Coggan and Mark Clark already installed:

> What's yer hurry, Joseph? The poor woman's dead, and you can't bring her back to life, and you may as well sit down comfortable, and finish another with us.

That is the tone that characterises the chapter. No longer are we to think unduly about the death of a particular individual, however distressing it may have been, but more of death as an inevitable, and daily, occurence in the life of any community. It is to be an occasion for Coggan to ponder the conditions for entry into heaven, to be unimpressed by the claims of the elect, and to favour the practical charity of Parson Thirdly, regardless of his ultimate destination. By the time Oak arrives, they all have 'the multiplying eye'. Just as Hardy uses the pathos of Fanny's journey to intensify and extend feelings present elsewhere, so now he uses comedy to allow that feeling to subside. Through the amiable generalities of the company in 'The Buck's Head', the poignant memory of Fanny's death is allowed to fade. Poorgrass's deserted wagon, at rest between 'The Buck's Head' and the churchyard, reminds us of that larger perspective which connects the living with the dead, and in that larger perspective Bathsheba's grief will be softened too. As the talk at 'The Buck's Head' goes on, the pathos and the melodrama began to disappear, and Hardy modulates his story in a way that will allow him, with ease and tact, to resume his main narrative journey in a novel which is to end, some ten chapters later, on a note of quiet resolve and harmony.

Taken together, 'On The Casterbridge Highway' and 'The Buck's Head', are instances of the way pace is used dramatically, to guide our response to the narrative. Both chapters exert a marked effect of deceleration, but where the first works to intensify the feeling, the second works to defuse it. This emerges clearly only when we see the effects made by the chapters in sequence; in isolation, their dramatic function is obscured and they emerge simply as 'scenes' classified as 'melodrama' and 'latterday pastoral'. The notion of sequence is, of course, inseparable from the activity of the reader who is continually filling in, and, in a sense akin to music, arranging the scenes in a way that makes him as mindful of the gaps between them as of the scenes themselves. Hardy's stories, unlike Emily Brontë's, ask to be read in a way which works through the interplay of sudden involvement followed by sudden detachment; we are made to *walk* with Fanny, we are made to look *at* Poorgrass, Coggan, and Clark, and simultaneously, we are made aware of the contemplative vision which holds both together.

If sequence can be thought of literally and locally, located in a continuous series of chapters it can also be thought of diffusely, creating effects which are spread throughout an entire novel. It is this effect I want to examine by looking at *The Mayor of Casterbridge*.

In a recent T.V. adaptation of the novel, faithful and felicitous as it often was in detail, the total impression created seemed alien to the novel. An outdoors novel had become an indoors one, there was a sense of unremitting gloom and claustrophobia, and the determining forces at work seemed to have more in common with Zola than with Hardy. The adaptation continually excised incidents and episodes which, in themselves, seemed to sit lightly to the main narrative but, taken cumulatively, enabled us to understand its significance. It is these details which safeguard the novel from being thought of as *The Life and Death of Michael Henchard*.

To see this kind of diffusing detail at work in the main narrative, we can turn to a point almost exactly halfway through the novel. It is Chapter 23 when Farfrae is calling at High Place Hall to renew his meetings with Elizabeth Jane. To his great embarrassment he meets, for the first time, Lucetta. The scene is short, but it is a crucial moment in the unfolding story, seeming to mark an end of Farfrae's relationship with Elizabeth Jane and initiating another relationship. In the middle of this chapter, however, the main narrative pauses, and the reader follows the gaze of Farfrae and Lucetta through the window into the market place:

> It was the chief hiring fair of the year, and different quite from the market of a few days earlier. In substance it was a whitey-brown flecked with white—this being the body of labourers waiting for places. The long bonnets of the women, like wagon-tilts, their cotton gowns and checked shawls, mixed with the carters, smock-frocks; for they, too, entered into the hiring. Among the rest, at the corner of the pavement, stood an old shepherd, who attracted the eyes of Lucetta and Frafrae by his stillness. He was evidently a chastened man. The battle of life had been a sharp one with him, for, to begin with he was a man of small frame. He was now so bowed by hard work and years that, approaching from behind, a person could hardly see his head. He had planted the stem of his crook in the gutter and was resting upon the bow, which was polished to silver brightness by the long friction of his hands. He had quite forgotten where he was, and what he had come for, his eyes being bent on the ground. A little way off negotiations were proceeding which had reference to him; but he did not hear them, and there seemed to be passing through his mind pleasant visions of the hiring successes of his prime, when his skill laid open to him any farm for the asking.

In *Far From the Madding Crowd* Hardy set up a narrative rhythm which was propulsive and overlapping, Bathsheba's anxiety and disillusion about Troy being present as a persistent undertone in both Fanny's journey and also at 'The Buck's Head'. In *The Mayor*, the narrative rhythm is such that it can accommodate a marked shift in pace without ever disturbing the strong sense of continuity. Hardy creates in that novel a contemplative mood, a habit of mind, which will allow, with the minimum of adjustment on the reader's part, a move forwards and backwards between characters and incidents of no importance at all. Major and minor, background and foreground, these distinctions are irrelevant to the manner of regard we bring to this novel. For the space of the page on which they appear, the shepherd, his son, and 'the crook polished to silver brightness by the long friction of his hands', have as much independence and life as Lucetta and Farfrae, and, were he to appear, Henchard himself.

The dramatic vignette has, of course, its function in the main narrative, enabling Hardy to quicken the feelings between Lucetta and Farfrae, as well as allowing the reader to be aware of their rather facile emotionalism. But the significance of the episode lies not inside High Place Hall, but outside. It is there to remind us—and in this it is representative of many such moments in the novel—of a world elsewhere, of characters indifferent to Farfrae and Lucetta and Elizabeth-Jane, and even to Henchard himself, of stories which remain untold. The hiring fair brings the market place into the novel—'the whitey-brown flecked with white'—and it brings too a sense of the passage of time both in the general passing of the seasons and in the juxtaposition of youth and age.

Reading *The Mayor of Casterbridge* has something in common with Henchard 'reading' the face of his sleeping daughter: 'He steadfastly regarded her features ... In sleep there came to the surface buried genealogical facts, ancestral curves, dead men's traits, which the mobility of daytime animation screens and overwhelms. ...' Such a 'regard' makes no distinction between 'surface' and 'depth'; it is akin to 'reading' a situation. Rod Edmond, in his essay on the novel, talks about the 'layering' of time in the novel, and although that is true, the layers have a transparency about them in our actual reading that makes us continually see the presence of the past in the present and the present terms of the past. It is this which gives resonance to the main narrative, so that stark as Henchard's story is in many of its aspects, it is always seen with a compassionate gaze which softens and transforms it.

I suggested earlier that the reading attention we give to a Hardy novel was a matter of oscillation between involvement and detachment, but as my remarks on *Far From the Madding Crowd* and *The Mayor of Casterbridge* suggest, it is an oscillation which can take different forms. With the earlier novel we are sharply aware of local intensities, local withdrawals, whereas in *The Mayor*, there is a persistent duality of effect which gives that novel an overall impersonality we associate with epic, but containing within it moments which glow with lyric intensity. Between the reader and the tale we feel the absorbed intentness of the narrative voice, which creates a mood hospitable to generalities and reflections, but which, at a shift in tone makes us aware of the immediacy of detail, its firm contingency. The final sentence of Chapter 23, blends, in cadence and substance, the duality of mood this novel so effortlessly solicits and satisfies, 'Her emotions rose, fell, undulated, filled her with wild surmise at their suddenness; and so passed Lucetta's experiences of that day'.

'What she offers is something that expands in the reader's mind'. Virginia Woolf's remark about Jane Austen has particular significance when we come to consider the ending of a story. Endings have received a good deal of attention in recent years, but the interest has been more metaphysical in character than aesthetic, and the impact an ending makes on the reader's attention has been neglected.

In looking at *Wuthering Heights* I tried to suggest ways in which Emily Brontë had, from the beginning of that novel, set up a narrative rhythm which encouraged not only immediacy of involvement in the story but an involvement so complete as to dispel any scepticism on the part of the reader about the credibility of its occasion. In *Far From the Madding Crowd* and *The Mayor of Casterbridge*, Hardy created a more contemplative mood for his tale, but a mood always open to the sudden access of feeling, always capable of responding to a switch in narrative intensity. In both Emily Brontë and Hardy, however, attention to the process of reading gives a heightened awareness of the way in which the narrative medium itself, with all its shifts and turns, can help to enact the story it relates ...

169

The 'Poetics' of
The Return of the Native

◆

JOHN PATERSON

If *The Return of the Native* suggests the most formal and even the most literary of Hardy's experiments in prose fiction, it is perhaps because his imagination was dominated at this juncture, as it had not been before and as it would not be again, by the legend and literature of Greece and Rome. This influence is first of all apparent in the dubious doctrine the novel was evidently designed to dramatize: 'The truth seems to be that a long line of disillusive centuries has permanently displaced the Hellenic idea of life.... What the Greeks only suspected we know well; what their Aeschylus imagined our nursery children feel.'[1] But it is also apparent in the frequency of the novel's references to Homer, Virgil, Aeschylus, and Sophocles as well as to more modern practitioners of epic and tragic form: e.g., Dante, Shakespeare, Milton, and (through Handel) Racine.[2]

That this influence entered the novel more especially as a dramatic influence Hardy was himself to acknowledge later. There is a virtue, he wrote of his late play, *The Famous Tragedy of the Queen of Cornwall*, in preserving the unities: 'the only other case I remember attempting it in was *The Return of the Native*.'[3] Hence the limitation of the action to the narrow space of Egdon Heath and of the time to a year and a day. Beyond this, Hardy employed, in Eustacia's moments of crisis, the convention of the set speech; dissociated the community of humble peasants from the gentility of the heath to create a rough equivalent of the Greek chorus; and, though compelled against his better judgment to add a sixth book,[4] originally conceived the novel in terms of five books in imitation, evidently, of the five acts identified with classical tragedy.

If a direct formal and structural correspondence was intended, however, it must in the process of composition have lapsed or become diffused. The claims of the main characters to aristocratic standing are, in the first place, seldom convincing: they qualify at best as a species of stuffy provincial

SOURCE *Modern Fiction Studies*, vol. VI, no 3, Autumn, 1960, pp. 214–22.

gentility. The stress of the novel falls, in the second place, not on one major figure but on several, the image of Eustacia Vye dominating, if at all, only after a debilitating struggle with the competing images of Thomasin, Clym, and Mrs Yeobright. Its center of gravity is in fact so unstable that its intensity as tragedy is ultimately dispersed, the complication of its plot suggesting more the loosely-fashioned pastoral romance of *Far From the Madding Crowd* and *The Woodlanders* than the rigorously-structured drama of Sophocles and Aeschylus. The novel displays, finally, infiltrations of romantic sympathy altogether foreign to the tragic vision of things. Unpersuaded of the existence of a just cosmic order, it fails to command, in the presence of human defeat, the detachment and equanimity of the classical imagination.[5] As features of form and structure, then, the preservation of the unities and the five-'act' division appear either as arbitrary or as ornamental.

In the end, however, the structure of the novel, its principle of organization, is less architectural than poetic or musical. For if Hardy failed to produce a formal and structural parallel with Greek tragedy, he managed to achieve, consciously or unconsciously, a reasonable artistic equivalent. By the sheer and almost systematic accumulation of allusions to the geography and history, the legend and literature, of classical antiquity, he evoked the large and heroic 'world' out of which Greek tragedy came and, by so doing, fixed the otherwise purely local action of the novel within a frame of reference that gave it dignity and meaning.[6] Thus the domestic landscape of Wessex is everywhere transfigured by the heroic landscape, real and imaginary, of an older and grander civilization. Egdon Heath recommends itself to the diminished modern consciousness as 'the new Vale of Tempe' (p. 5); the little hills on its lower levels look from Rainbarrow on a misty morning 'like an archipelago in a fog-formed Aegean' (p. 100); and Budmouth combines, in the unsophisticated imagination of the heath-folk, 'a Carthaginian bustle of building with Tarentine luxuriousness and Baian health and beauty' (p. 108). An ordinary chimney fire becomes, in the perspective of this novel, 'an Etna of peat' (p. 160).

More significantly, Egdon Heath itself is altogether transfigured in being juxtaposed with the grisly underworld of the ancients and, though less frequently, with its Christian equivalent. This identification is established immediately in the first chapter where, described as a 'Titanic form' ('Every night its Titanic form seemed to await something' [p. 4], the heath suggests Tartarus, the gloomy foster-home of rebel-gods. Soon afterward, Egdon is called upon to evoke the Limbo of Dante's (and Virgil's) imagination:

> The whole black phenomenon beneath represented Limbo as viewed from the brink by the sublime Florentine in his vision, and the muttered articulations of the wind in the hollows were as complaints and petitions from the 'souls of mighty worth' suspended therein (p. 17).

This image is elaborated in the setting of the novel's third chapter, where the fires that flare in the darkness suggest the inflammable landscape of the Christian Hell. Later still, the heath provokes a reference to 'Homer's Cimmerian land' (p. 60), the dark region at the outer rim of the world and the traditional location of the entrance to Hades.

If Egdon Heath suggests the grim underworld of the Greek and Christian imaginations, the main characters of the novel naturally suggest its ghostly and tormented inhabitants. Egdon is explicitly identified as Eustacia's 'Hades' (p. 77). The dignity that sits upon her brow is defined as 'Tartarean' (p. 77) and her removal from Budmouth to Edgon, like that of the Titans to Tartarus, as a banishment (p. 78). When Mrs Yeobright and Olly Dowden go down from Rainbarrow into the darker regions below, the vocabulary and imagery overwhelmingly suggest a descent into the underworld of the dead: 'Down, downward they went, and yet further down—their descent at each step seeming to outmeasure their advance. Their skirts were scratched nosily by the furze, their shoulders brushed by the ferns, which, though dead and dry, stood erect as when alive.' The situation of the two women at this point is designated, in fact, a 'Tartarean situation' (p. 38). Even the phlegmatic and apparently imperturbable Diggory Venn is seen in the same hyperbolic terms: as one who has suffered the pangs of unrequited love, he is said to have 'stood in the shoes of Tantalus' (p. 94).

Moreover, throughout the novel character and scene and incident are constantly evaluated, or more accurately, transvaluated, according to a scale provided by classical history and literature. Johnny Nunsuch's suspension between the vague menace of the reddleman and the certain wrath of Eustacia Vye is defined as 'a Scyllaeo-Charybdean position' (p. 84). His dying mother in his arms, Clym proceeds 'like Aeneas with his father' (p. 348) and, having learned the import of her last words, endures the anguish of Oedipus: 'his mouth had passed into the phase more or less imaginatively rendered in studies of Oedipus' (p. 384). Indeed, as the symbol of the diminished consciousness of modern times, Clym's is explicitly contrasted with the heroic consciousness of Hardy's prelapsarian Greeks: 'Should there be a classic period to art hereafter, its Pheidias may produce such faces' (p. 197).

While Clym suggests the deterioration of 'the Hellenic idea of life,' Eustacia suggests its anachronistic and hence foredoomed revival. When she is not being victimized by the gods and goddesses, she is visualized as one of them herself, her approximation to divinity providing the dominant note of the 'Queen of Night' Chapter. 'Eustacia Vye was,' the chapter begins, 'the raw material of a divinity. On Olympus she would have done well with a little preparation' (p. 75). 'The new moon behind her head,' the chapter records elsewhere, 'an old helmet upon it, a diadem of accidental dewdrops round her brow, would have been adjuncts sufficient to strike the note of Artemis, Athena, or Hera respectively.' (p. 77). Eustacia occasionally recalls the statuary of ancient Greece with its imagery of god-like heroes and heroic gods. 'One had fancied,' Hardy remarks, 'that such lip-curves were mostly lurking underground in the South as fragments of forgotten marbles' (p. 76). And the wound which she sustains at the hands of Susan Nunsuch is later said to look 'like a ruby on Parian marble' (p. 219). Elsewhere, informed that her association with Wildeve is likely to damage her character, Eustacia is 'as unconcerned at that contingency as a goddess at a lack of linen' (p. 109).

Also, throughout the novel the image of Eustacia Vye inevitably inspires allusions to the history and legend and literature of an exotic antiquity. Her profile justifies comparison with that of Sappho (p. 62); in moments of calm, she suggests the Sphinx (p. 75); she is said to have 'pagan eyes, full of nocturnal mysteries' and moods that recall the lotus-eaters (p. 76). When she does not choose to be direct, she can 'utter oracles of Delphian ambiguity' (p. 82); and her dream is described as having 'as many ramifications as the Cretan labyrinth' (p. 138). On the occasion of the Christmas party she plays the Venus to Clym's Aeneas: 'When the disguised Queen of Love appeared before Aeneas a preternatural perfume accompanied her presence and betrayed her quality' (p. 167). And prevented by her disguise from exercising her charms on Clym, she has 'a sense of the doom of Echo' (p. 169). In by far the most dazzling of her classical associations, Eustacia is established in virtually explicit terms, as a lineal descendant of Homeric kings: 'Where did her dignity come from? By a latent vein from Alcinous' line, her father hailing from Phaeacia's isle?' (p. 78). Identified by Mrs Yeobright as a band-master from the island of Corfu (p. 239)—Phaeacia's isle—Eustacia's father will be described more spectacularly by Thomasin as 'a romantic wanderer—a sort of Greek Ulysses' (p. 251).

Nothing contributes more, however, to the transfiguration of the novel's essentially domestic action than the Promethean theme and image. At the very least, the legend of the fallen god more narrowly delimits the field of the novel, exerts a stricter control over its form and meaning, than the rather widespread context provided by the system of classical allusions. It creates, indeed, a frame of reference that operates within, and cooperates with, the larger classical frame of reference.

The Promethean theme and metaphor are already active, if only in-directly, in the Tartarean analogy alluded to earlier. For the image of a 'Titanic form' that 'seemed to await something' suggests nothing so much as the figure of Prometheus awaiting the promised liberation from the torments of his imprisonment. Furthermore, the bonfires that have been lit ostensibly in observance of Guy Fawkes day are charged with a specifically Promethean significance:

> To light a fire is the instinctive and resistant act of man when, at the winter ingress, the curfew is sounded throughout Nature. It indicates a spontaneous, Promethean rebelliousness against the fiat that this recurrent season shall bring foul times, cold darkness, misery and death. Black chaos comes, and the fettered gods of the earth say, Let there be light (pp. 17–18).

51

Elsewhere Clym Yeobright himself is created in the image of the fallen god: 'As is usual with bright natures, the deity that lies ignominiously chained within an ephemeral human carcass shone out of him like a ray' (p. 162). In his role of the reformed Promethean, he is later called upon to sound that note only too baldly: 'Now, don't you suppose, my inexperienced girl,' he tells that unregenerate fire-worshipper, his wife, 'that I cannot rebel, in high Promethean fashion, against the gods and fate as well as you' (p 302).

As this reference may have indicated, however, the Promethean passion of the novel particularly concentrates itself in the image of Eustacia Vye. Her dialogue and, in general, the terms of her thinking and feeling have a rhetorical quality that unmistakably suggests the generic heroine of Greek tragedy, if not Prometheus himself. Thus she can confess to 'an agonizing pity for myself that I ever was born' (p. 232) and aspire 'to look with indifference upon the cruel satires that Fate loves to indulge in' (p. 243). Death seems to her the only relief 'if the satire of Heaven should go much further' (p. 305); and she is said to have good grounds for asking 'the Supreme Power by what right a being of such exquisite finish had been placed in circumstances calculated to make of her charms a curse rather than a blessing' (p. 305). 'How I have tried and tried to be a splendid woman,' she cries finally in her denunciation of the gods,

> and how destiny has been against me! … I was capable of much; but I have been injured and blighted and crushed by things beyond my control! O, how hard it is of Heaven to devise such tortures for me, who have done no harm to Heaven at all! (p. 422).

The Promethean motif affects the substance of the novel in an even more subtle and indirect way. In the fire-imagery, by inference Promethean, with which the text is virtually saturated, it becomes chemically active at the vital center of the novel. This is already apparent in the major imagery of scene and incident. The darkness of the heath is shattered in the third chapter by the grotesque bonfires that mark the anniversary of the Gunpowder Plot. In the almost parabolic episode of Chapter IV, Book Fourth, Wildeve makes his presence known to Eustacia by releasing at her window a moth that perishes in the flames of her candle. On the day of Mrs Yeobright's death, the universe of Egdon Heath is visualized as almost literally on fire:

> The sun had branded the whole heath with his mark, even the purple heath-flowers having put on a brownness under the dry blazes of the few preceding days. Every valley was filled with air like that of a kiln, and the clean quartz sand of the winter water-courses, which formed summer paths, had undergone a species of incineration since the drought had set in (pp. 326–7).

And Mrs Yeobright subsequently dies what amounts to a symbolic death-by-fire: 'The sun … stood directly in her face, like some merciless incendiary, brand in hand, waiting to consume her' (p. 342). Finally and most conclusively, Eustacia Vye herself perishes in the same fatal flames: she is burned in effigy by Susan Nunsuch (pp. 424–5), and acting out the parable of the moth-signal and making Susan's prophetic magic good, she hurls herself into what is called, inevitably, 'the boiling *caldron*' of the weir (p. 441).

The Promethean theme is expressed and supported not alone by the major imagery of action and setting, but also by the minor imagery, the local fire imagery, with which the language of the novel is from beginning to end surcharged. Egdon's 'crimson heather' is '*fired*' to scarlet by the July sun (p. 283). In the presence of Eustacia Vye, '*the revived embers* of an old passion *glowed* clearly in Wildeve' (p. 73) who sees himself as having upon him 'the curse of *inflammability*' (p. 71). And from the ravine which is the site of Diggory's encampment, Eustacia sees 'a sinister redness arising ... dull and lurid like a *flame in sunlight*' (p. 174). 'Why,' Mrs Yeobright cries, disappointed in her hopes for her son, 'should I go on *scalding* my face like this?' (p. 256). After her death Clym's eyes will be 'lit by a hot light, *as if the fire in their pupils were burning up their substance*' (p. 366).

The fire-imagery is never more emergent than when Eustacia Vye commands the attention of the novel. Thus the colour of her soul is fancied as '*flame-like.*' (p. 76). 'A *blaze* of love, and extinction' she prefers characteristically, to 'a lantern glimmer of the same' (p. 79). Antagonized by Wildeve's cool manner, indignation spreads through her 'like subterranean *heat*' (p. 72) and elsewhere angered by the reddleman, she lets him see '*how a slow fire could blaze on occasion*' (p. 107). She resembles the tiger-beetle 'which, when observed in dull situations, seems to be of the quietest neutral colour, but under a full illumination *blazes* with dazzling splendour' (p. 104). And when she laughs and opens her lips, the effect is at once more and less than human: 'the sun shone into her mouth as into a tulip, and *lent it a similar scarlet fire*' (p. 104).

After her first meeting with Clym, she is '*warmed with an inner fire,*' but is later alarmed at the thought of a rival like Thomasin 'living day after day in *inflammable* proximity to him' (p. 171). After their first kiss, Clym fears his mother will ask, 'What red spot is that *glowing* upon your mouth so vividly?' (p. 225). In her quarrel with Mrs Yeobright, Eustacia speaks out 'with *a smothered fire* of feeling' and '*scalding* tears' trickle from her eyes (pp. 288–9), events justifying Clym's allusion to their '*inflammable* natures' (pp. 293–4). In the period after Mrs Yeobright's death, Eustacia will be '*seared* inwardly' by the secret she dares not tell (p. 367).

The fire-imagery joins, then, with the specific allusions to, and evocations of, the Prometheus story to frame and transvaluate the otherwise purely domestic action of the novel. In their association with fire, Clym, Mrs Yeobright, Wildeve and, above all, Eustacia are identified as Promethean figures. Consumed in the flames of their own passion and in effect defeated by their own aggressive humanity, they stand in opposition to Thomasin, Diggory, and the modest members of the present community who are more reluctant to play with fire and to invite the retribution of jealous gods.[7]

The Promethean and classical analogy is not of course sustained throughout. The inspiration of the serial novelist is intermittent, tends to flag and falter.[8] Hardy sometimes shifts his focus from the classical to the Elizabethan: at the scene of Mrs Yeobright's death, for example, Egdon Heath suddenly suggests the landscape of *King Lear*; and when the indignant husband melodramatically confronts the erring wife, the scene suggests a domestic nineteenth-century notion of Jacobean grand drama. Even more crucially, the characters and incidents and scenes are not always equal to their heroic analogues; and when this is the case, the classical frame of reference merely serves to expose their insufficiency. The analogy with Oedipus, for example, far from celebrating the image of Clym Yeobright, merely indicates how appallingly far short of the tragic king he really falls.

For the most part, however, the major imagery of the novel is equal to its formidable frame of reference. Egdon Heath eventually connotes much more than the provincial landscape it denotes: it is a stage grand enough to bear the weight of gods and heroes; more specifically, it is Tartarus, the ancient underworld of the fallen Titans; and more specifically still, it is the prison-house of Prometheus, the fire-bearing benefactor of mankind. Similarly, Eustacia Vye is more than just another of Hardy's foreign and slightly spoiled aristocratic girls impatient of their dreary confinement in the provinces: she is the reincarnation not, perhaps, of any specific heroine of classical tragedy but, certainly, of the 'idea' of such a heroine; and her kinship is, in this sense, more with Clytemnestra and Antigone than with Felice Charmond and Lucetta La Sueur. Moreover, the action of *The Return of the Native*, which is perhaps intrinsically less an action of antique nobility and grandeur than a domestic action peculiar to ballad and pastoral romance, is placed in a medium of analogy, a frame of reference, that creates an illusion of antique nobility and graudeur. Whereas the larger classical frame of reference creates an heroic context in which the local elements of the narrative achieve by analogy a measure of status and dignity, the Promethean frame of reference defines in more specific terms the evaluating or transvaluating context.

In the last analysis, then, the artistic unity and coherence of the novel do not depend on those purely external features of form and structure represented by the preservation of the unities and the organization in five 'acts.' They depend, rather, on the application of a significant frame of reference and on the activity of a meaningful pattern of images. In this sense the novel obeys not so much the architectural concept of form favored by the Greek dramatists as the musical or poetic—i.e., less clearly rational—concept of form favored by modern experiments in prose fiction. Consciously or unconsciously, Hardy contrived in *The Return of the Native* that technique of spatialization which has been described as the twentieth century's particular contribution to the form of the novel.[9]

Notes

1. Thomas Hardy, *The Return of the Native*, Harper's Modern Classics (New York, 1922), p. 197. All page references, henceforward to be incorporated in the text, will be to this volume. The italics in the passages dealing with Hardy's fire imagery are, of course, mine.

2. Eustacia's moods are said to recall 'the march in "Athalie"' (p. 76).

3. Florence Hardy, *The Later Years of Thomas Hardy* (New York, 1930), p. 235.

4. See Hardy's footnote (p. 473) disclaiming responsibility for the sixth book.

5. Hardy managed only once, perhaps, and that was in the making of *The Mayor of Casterbridge*, to approximate the conditions of traditional tragedy. See John Paterson, '"The Mayor of Casterbridge" as Tragedy,' *Victorian Studies*, III (December 1959), 151–72.

6. In establishing his heroic context, Hardy evoked the antiquity of the Celts and Hebrews as well as that of the Greeks. The classical allusions, however, far outnumber the Celtic and Hebraic.

7. Hardy tended up to a certain point to see all men as Promethean martyrs. Certainly, Diggory's red color would suggest that only the middleclass apotheosis enforced by the extraneous Book Sixth kept him out of the company of the defeated romantics: Clym, Eustacia, Wildeve and Mrs Yeobright. And our first glimpse of the country-folk is of an almost demoniacal crew dancing about an impious bonfire. In the end, however, they are, like Thomasin, fully adjusted to the limitations of the human condition and hence untouched by the ecstasies and frustrations of the Promethean passion.

8. A study of the manuscript and variant editions does indicate, however, that Hardy was not wholly unaware of this sensitive inner movement of the novel. See John Paterson, *The Making of the Return of the Native*, University of California Publications, English Studies, No. 19 (Berkeley, 1960), Ch. V.

9. Joseph Frank, 'Spatial Form in Modern Literature,' in *Critiques and Essays in Criticism*, ed. Robert Wooster Stallman (New York, 1949), pp. 315–28.

170

Heroism and Pathos in
The Return of the Native

◆

LEONARD W. DEEN

Of all Hardy's novels, *The Return of the Native* is the one which most invites comparison with grand tragedy. It is full of elevating and sobering allusions to such tragic and heroic figures as Aeneas, Oedipus, Lear, and Cleopatra. Eustacia Vye, more than any other of Hardy's protagonists, seems intended to be grandly heroic, to exist on a higher level of significance than the other characters in the novel. She is alone, rebellious, even powerful—and so little explicable that she can be taken for a witch by the superstitious. Eustacia's state of heroic isolation is emphasized by a tragic chorus of country folk clearly set off from the actors in the drama. They provide a Shakespearean (grave diggers and porter) comic change-of-pace as well as a contrast of styles and levels of seriousness; and, functioning as Greek chorus, from a position of sanity and safety they comment on the illusion, ambition, or *hubris* of the antagonists. But for all these approaches to the heroic style, Hardy seems curiously uncertain whether his story constitutes high tragedy. *The Return of the Native* begins heroically, but slips more and more into the diminishing ironic and pathetic mode which characterizes Hardy's later tragedies.

Eustacia Vye is a young woman with romantic dreams of heroic love and social brilliance, who marries under the illusion that her husband, Clym Yeobright, will fulfill her dreams, and help her to escape her remote and isolated life on Egdon Heath. Disillusionment, conflict with her mother-in-law, and a violent quarrel with her husband lead her to attempt a desperate flight with a former lover, Damon Wildeve. On her way to meet him, she drowns, and Wildeve drowns in an attempt to rescue her. Hardy never tells us whether Eustacia's drowning is accident or suicide, but suicide is the inevitable explanation, since she considers herself trapped between the intolerable alternatives of staying on Egdon Heath or living with a lover she thinks vastly inferior to herself.

Given a bare synopsis of the plot, one is scarcely prepared for the Eustacia

SOURCE *Nineteenth Century Fiction*, vol. 15, 1960–1, pp. 207–19.

of the novel. At one time or another, Hardy suggests that she is a goddess (Aphrodite probably) in her power and capriciousness, a Titaness in her rebelliousness, a witch in her solitude and mystery, a *femme fatale* in her power to arouse passion in others, and a Cleopatra in her pride, her passion, and her scorn of consequences. Hardy is perhaps aiming at infinite variety, but his efforts in this kind are largely self-defeating. For one thing, his descriptions of Eustacia so complicate our impressions of her that it is almost impossible to form a consistent image of her, except that she is meant to be awe-inspiring. For another, he makes her more impressive than she has a right to be, considering her age and sex and the apparently frivolous nature of her desires. She does little to demonstrate or to justify the dazzling array of qualities Hardy ascribes to her.

Eustacia can remain mysterious and fatal only as long as our view of her is external and relatively long range, as it is at her first appearance. She is standing on an ancient grave on the summit of Rainbarrow, the highest hill in Egdon.

> There the form stood, motionless as the hill beneath. Above the plain rose the hill, above the hill rose the barrow, and above the barrow rose the figure. Above the figure was nothing that could be mapped elsewhere than on a celestial globe ... The scene was strangely homogeneous, in that the vale, the upland, the barrow, and the figure above it amounted only to unity. Looking at this or that member of the group was not observing a complete thing, but a fraction of the thing.[1]

At the approach of others Eustacia (whom Hardy has not yet identified) leaves.

> The imagination of the observer clung by preference to that vanished, solitary figure, as to something more interesting, more important, more likely to have a history worth knowing than these newcomers, and unconsciously regarded them as intruders. But they remained, and established themselves; and the lonely person who hitherto had been queen of the solitude did not at present seem likely to return (p. 14).

Silhouetted against the sky, Eustacia seems almost to have risen from the earth on which she stands. She is 'queen of the solitude', quite literally elevated, and she is 'discovered' standing on a grave, with which she is persistently associated throughout the novel. The scene is carefully composed for its heroic–tragic implications.

The heath on which Eustacia is first seen provides an index for all the other characters as well. As a symbol of man's unchangeable place in nature, and of his endurance, it measures each character's acceptance of his earthly fate. Clym, the native returned, as furze cutter symbolically submerges himself in the life of the heath; Thomasin Yeobright (his cousin) considers the heath her natural and appropriate environment. They have chosen the safer and more reasonable part, and thus, in the logic of the novel, they can be neither heroic nor tragic. Wildeve attempts to evade the heath; he loses his life, and Hardy intends his death to give him a certain dignity which he did not have alive. Mrs Yeobright, who has more force than Wildeve, and whose death is considerably more significant than his, is only less un-reconciled to her existence than Eustacia. Just before her death she has a vision of an intensely desired escape:

> She leant back to obtain more thorough rest, and the soft eastern portion of the sky was as great a relief to her eyes as the thyme was to her head. While she looked a heron arose on that side of the sky and flew on with his face towards the sun. He had come dripping wet from some pool in the valleys, and as he flew the edges and linings of his wings, his thighs, and his breast were so caught by the bright sunbeams that he appeared as if formed of burnished silver. Up in the zenith where he was seemed a free and happy place, away from all contact with the earthly ball to which she was pinioned; and she wished that she could arise uncrushed from its surface and fly as he flew then (p. 343).

Death is of course the only escape possible. The human involvement in the round of existence is inexorable, and all visions of freedom or of paradise are denied.

More proudly and intransigently than anyone else, Eustacia rebels against the heath. For Hardy this rebellion makes her not only tragic but heroic, though her situation as goddess misplaced in this sublunary world (she is repeatedly associated with the moon) is not without its irony:

> But celestial imperiousness, love, wrath, and fervour had proved to be some-what thrown away on netherward Egdon. Her power was limited, and the consciousness of this limitation had biassed her development. Egdon was her Hades, and since coming there she had imbibed much of what was dark in its tone, though inwardly and externally unreconciled thereto. Her appearance accorded well with this smouldering rebelliousness, and the shady splendour of her beauty was the real surface of the sad and stifled warmth within her. A true Tartarean dignity sat upon her brow, and not factitiously or with marks of constraint, for it had grown in her with years (p. 77).

The heath mirrors the minds of its inhabitants, and for Eustacia it is hell. She is not the initially triumphant hero, Oedipus or Agamemnon, but the bitterly enduring hero, Milton's Satan or Shelley's Prometheus. She is a romantic (she is a whole history of romanticism) seen romantically. She is emblematic of the feeling and infinite desire which rebel against inevitable limitation, and thus is the supremely tragic figure of the novel.

These early scenes have shown us Eustacia's outer character, built up by allusion and external description and the implications of setting. So far as her tragic heroism is evoked by these means, the tragic conception of *Return* is static; it consists mostly in the mysterious and superior isolation of the heroine, her singularity. It seems a tragedy of portentous mood and circum-stance; Eustacia looks tragic and acts tragic in a quite theatrical way. What James would presumably call tragic drama—action rendered by dialogue and dramatic confrontation—is often obscured by tragic scene or tableau, the trappings and the suits of woe.

What keeps external and scenic portent from swallowing the novel is the fact that it is excessive only in the opening scenes. It soon retires into the background (where it belongs of course), and the foreground is occupied by a tragic action which proceeds mainly on two levels—that of overt purpose, conflict, and misunderstanding, and that of symbolic and ritual revelation of Eustacia's inner life and character. The revelatory action presents a different Eustacia from the one we see first. She remains the central figure of a tragedy, but she is not so exaggeratedly heroic as she seems from outside.

The ritual or symbolic action begins with a dream which Eustacia has shortly after Clym's return, and before she has seen him (though she has heard his voice, and has fallen in love with him sight unseen). In her dream she finds herself ecstatically dancing with a helmeted knight. Suddenly they dive into a pool, and come out on the other side into a kind of 'iridescent' paradise. They kiss, and he crumbles like a pack of cards, without her having identified him. The dream, of course, is a prevision of Eustacia's drowning at the weir; what she interprets as a promise of ideally romantic love is instead a promise of death.

The symbolic action of the dream is bit by bit 'realized' in later scenes of the novel. In the first scene, Eustacia decides to join a party of mummers who are to present 'the well-known play of St George' at a Christmas party of the Yeobrights'. Disguised by hanging ribbons which represent the vizor of her helmet, Eustacia plays the part of the Turkish knight. In doing so, she seems both to take the role of the helmeted knight of the dream, and to undergo a ritual death at the hands of another helmeted knight, St George. Eustacia has two purposes in becoming a mummer—one recognized and the other buried. Driven by boredom and the hope that he might be the means of rescuing her from the heath, she is desperately anxious to meet Clym, who has just returned from Paris, the heart of the romantic and fashionable world. Although she does not dance with Clym, she hopes that he 'is' the knight of her dream. In the mumming scene Eustacia also reveals a second desire, a more destructive one, of which she is not conscious. As Hardy is careful to emphasize, in becoming a mummer Eustacia 'changes sex', and the whole episode is an adventure on the outer limits of female respectability. What is suggested elsewhere in the novel is clearly revealed here. Eustacia in the mumming assumes the heroic masculine role to which she is always aspiring. She wants to alter her essential human condition, to change her sex. A dissatisfaction so thoroughgoing amounts to a denial of life itself.

The second scene which carries out in reality the events of Eustacia's dream takes place after her marriage to Clym Yeobright. In it she dances, by moonlight, with Wildeve. She is again disguised, this time by a veil, and the dance is a 'pagan' throwing off of restraint, a celebration of the 'pride of life', and a ritual of passionate unreason which 'drives the emotions to rankness'. It is a 'riding upon the whirlwind' which deadens conscious control: 'her soul had passed away from and forgotten her features, which were left empty

and quiescent, as they always are when feeling goes beyond their register'
(p. 310). Wildeve's response is equally abandoned. He is repeatedly associated with the moth who immolates himself in the flame, and he is here seen
taking fire from Eustacia. Furthermore, the dance identifies Wildeve as the
partner with whom Eustacia dances in the dream, and who dives with her
into the pool—that is, the fellow-victim of her drowning. For both Eustacia
and Wildeve the dance is not only a sublimation of more specifically sexual
desires (the symbolic sexuality of the dances which occur in Hardy's novels
scarcely needs to be pointed out): it is also a ritual embracing of oblivion and
death. Wildeve had earlier ratified his own death, in the alien and overwhelming presence of the heath, by an unlucky cast of the dice—which are
'powerful rulers of us all, and yet at my command', as Christian Cantle
affirms.

The dream and the later scenes which are linked to it operate not only as
tragic portents, but as oblique revelations of weakness in the self. Eustacia
assumes in them two 'roles'—the conscious self which, desiring passionate
love above all things, nevertheless keeps this desire under reasonable control,
and the vizored knight, or its other manifestation, the veiled dancer. The
knight and the dancer reveal a tragic and sometimes Dionysian self-
destructiveness in Eustacia. The two dances, the dream dance and the dance
on the heath, have the significance Hardy ascribed to the mumming, itself a
kind of dance: they are all rites in which 'the agents seem moved by an inner
compulsion to say and do their allotted parts whether they will or no'
(p. 144). They are all rituals of which Eustacia's story is the mythical
development. Her buried self takes control of her and destroys her. Her
abandonment to it makes her death 'necessary', the fruit of her character as
much as of her circumstances and her luck. Beneath her external and superhuman mask as *femme fatale* or goddess of love, Eustacia is an all too human
victim of her own nature.

But the irony implicit in our double vision of Eustacia's role and personality is not firmly controlled. Hardy has implicated himself too deeply in her
appearance of being larger than life to be able to detach himself from it. It
has been clear throughout the novel that Eustacia acquiesces in illusion. Her
life is primarily nocturnal, a moonlight existence. While she recognizes what
she calls the 'mendacity of the imagination', she yields to its deception. 'Let
us only look at what seems', she says, and she has no patience with fact that
conflicts with desire. Her reason tells her that Wildeve is unworthy of her,
that Clym's aims are inconsistent with her own, and that his personality fails
to satisfy her dreams of the heroic; yet she succeeds, at different times, in
altering both Clym and Wildeve to something sufficiently like the image of
her desire. Hardy insists that this failing makes her more admirable. He
remarks of her falling in love with Clym before she has met him, 'The
fantastic nature of her passion, which lowered her as an intellect, raised her
as a soul' (p. 139). The fantastic nature of her passion does not exalt her,

though it is not incompatible with tragedy. In the overwhelming of her reason by her passions there is an imbalance, a simultaneous strength and weakness, to which admiration or condemnation is equally irrelevant. This self-destructive excess in Eustacia is tragic, but it is sometimes falsified by Hardy's explanatory comments and by a rhetoric which inflates Eustacia's 'real' character, the one revealed to us by the logic of actions and events.

The ritual scenes I have described establish the necessity of the catastrophe primarily by revealing Eustacia as a tragic type. In them she wordlessly acts out her character and fate. The more immediate causes of her death, of course, are in her conflicts with and misunderstandings of other characters. But the two levels of action illuminate each other by their interconnections. Running parallel to but ahead of the external drama, the submerged action gives the external events a deep resonance of dramatic irony.

The overt action turns largely on the forces which destroy Eustacia's and Clym's excessively romantic and illusory married happiness. (As the titles of Books III and V indicate, first comes the 'Fascination', then the 'Discovery'.) One of the essential destructive forces is, of course, their emotional and intellectual incompatibility. Hardy seems to have conceived Clym, at least in the beginning, as a kind of Hamlet—a superior mind and sensibility ravaged by that disease, thought, and misunderstood by the cruder world. Clym also has strong suggestions of the prophet who retires from a luxurious and self-indulgent society in order to criticize and to reform it; he intends to begin in the wilderness of the heath. His force as prophet is considerably weakened, however, by his becoming the inevitable victim of a world whose worldliness he does not comprehend. He is a prophet of the future who fails to see how intractably primitive the world of Egdon Heath is. And as overspiritualized modern man he is equally blind to Eustacia's primitiveness. She is all pagan self-assertion and passion; he has chosen the different way of self-denial and devotion to the good of others. The two almost become figures in an allegory of flesh and spirit, like the abstractly patterned interplay of flesh and spirit (or perverse spirit) in *Jude the Obscure*. Eustacia is not only less spiritually pure than Clym; she has many of the masculine qualities—energy, aggressiveness, ambition, and Promethean rebellion—which he lacks. If Eustacia is too fervid, Clym is too idealistic for life on earth, and suffers from blindness to the way of the world. He is, in fact, symbolically striken with blindness shortly after his marriage to Eustacia, and Hardy, perhaps too obviously, murmurs 'Oedipus'.

The primal flaw in Eustacia's and Clym's marriage is increased by the earlier conflicting but ineradicable emotional commitments each has made. Eustacia is unable to escape Wildeve's hold on her. Clym cannot free himself from his mother, and considers Eustacia his 'mother's supplanter'. The intentional conflict is between Eustacia and her mother-in-law, who end by destroying one another. Clym seems to exist primarily to define this conflict, as the rather passive and uncomprehending prize of the struggle between the two women. (Eustacia's and Mrs Yeobright's mutual distrust and dislike is well established in Book I, 'The Three Women', before Clym even appears.) The crisis of the struggle is the 'Closed Door' episode in which Eustacia, Wildeve, Clym, and Mrs Yeobright are involved. It is an implausible but expressionistically powerful scene which freezes all the actors in positions which expose their essential relations to one another. Clym is characteristically unaware of anything—in a more than natural sleep on the floor. Wildeve, innocently and yet not innocently, is talking to Eustacia, showing his regret at not having married her. As always, he plays the role of feckless catalyst of catastrophe: it is his presence which causes Eustacia, when she hears the knock at the door, to decide on the very measures which increase her apparent guilt. She looks out of the window, is seen by Mrs Yeobright, but does not open the door. She assumes that Clym will open it. The destructive moment for us is pure vision; for Mrs Yeobright it is fatefully ambiguous. To her Eustacia's action has the appearance of a deliberate and hateful denial, and Clym seems equally implicated in it. This shocking rejection, with unnecessary assistance from the heath, ends by killing Mrs Yeobright before she can reach home.

After his mother's death, the struggle between Eustacia and Mrs Yeobright continues within Clym, and the victory, such as it is, goes to Mrs Yeobright, who achieves it from beyond the grave. Playing out his role as Oedipus, Clym determinedly pursues his search into the mystery of his mother's death until he succeeds in destroying his own happiness, and Eustacia's as well. But not by learning the truth, as Oedipus does; he only exchanges ignorance for misinterpretation, for the deceptive outside view of Johnny Nunsuch and Mrs Yeobright. Deceived by the apparent meaning of Wildeve's presence and Eustacia's 'refusal' to open the door, he accuses Eustacia of infidelity and of causing his mother's death. Eustacia, who considers herself innocent (though guilty of having been afraid to tell Clym of the incident), is too proud to stoop to explanations, and after a violent quarrel with Clym she leaves the house. Her attempt at an escape with Wildeve, leading to the death of both, follows.

The last book, 'Aftercourses', is a descent from their stormy deaths to a spectacle of bitter suffering in which Clym takes the center of the stage, and the tragedy, or pathos, becomes his. After Eustacia's death the guilt with which he had responded to his mother's death is doubled: 'I spoke cruel words to her, and she left my house. I did not invite her back till it was too late. It is I who ought to have drowned myself. It would have been a charity to the living had the river overwhelmed me and borne her up. But I cannot die. Those who ought to have lived lie dead; and here am I alive!' (p. 449). To this Diggory Venn replies, 'You may as well say that the parents be the cause of a murder by the child, for without the parents the child would never have been begot'. Nevertheless, Clym's 'great regret' remains that 'for what I have done no man or law can punish me' (p. 449).

Hardy meant us to see Clym's sense of guilt as excessive. Clym had sent the letter of reconciliation to Eustacia in time to prevent her flight, but it never reached her. As usual in Hardy's novels, at the crisis the physical context of human action asserts itself abstractly and symbolically as the mischances of time and space—misplacing and mistiming. The effect is that of a hair-breadth rescue which at the last minute turns a happy ending into a catastrophe. But this effect does not bear analysis. The complicated series of thwarting mischances which causes Eustacia to miss the letter is clearly unnecessary to explain her death, nor would such a rescue have been very efficacious, given Eustacia's and Clym's deep incompatibility and Eustacia's reckless and despairing self-destructiveness. What Hardy intends, clearly, is an ironic parody of Providence. The pattern of events preceding Eustacia's death (including Susan Nunsuch's magical operations upon Eustacia's effigy) reveals a sinister and demonic 'providence' which, instead of saving, destroys. But the effective causes of the tragedy are of course deeper—in Clym's and Eustacia's inability to conceive one another, in the uncontrolled play of irrational forces in Eustacia, in past choices which prove to be irrevocable, and in the bitter enmity between Eustacia and Mrs Yeobright. Hardy's concatenation of last-minute unlucky events has the effect of doubly reinforcing a tragedy which is already necessary. This supererogation of tragic effects blurs the psychological and dramatic structure of the action in the interests of a 'philosophic' comment—an effort to indict the universe. The irony of the missed letter is excessively underlined, and as so often happens in Hardy's novels (and his poetry) the final effect of the irony is pathos. The episode tends to absolve both Eustacia and Clym of responsibility, and to make both appear to be the innocent victims of a malignant fate.

Irony and pathos dominate the last scenes of the novel. In the final scene, Clym becomes a lay preacher, or rather 'moral lecturer' who takes his texts from 'all kinds of books', delivers a discourse from the summit of Rainbarrow, on the following dutifully filial text (I Kings, 2:19):

> 'And the king rose up to meet her, and bowed himself unto her, and sat down on his throne, and caused a seat to be set for the king's mother; and she sat on his right hand. Then she said, I desire one small petition of thee; I pray thee say me not nay. And the king said unto her, Ask on, my mother: for I will not say thee nay' (pp. 484–5).

Towards Clym as 'lecturer on morally unimpeachable subjects' Hardy's attitude is ambiguous. Viewed sympathetically, Clym can be seen as cruelly misunderstood by an uncomprehending world. But from a more practical point of view, he is simply incapacitated for effective existence in the world.

> Some believed him, and some believed not; some said that his words were commonplace, others complained of his want of theological doctrine; while others again remarked that it was well enough for a man to take a preaching

who could not see to do anything else. But everywhere he was kindly received, for the story of his life had become generally known (p. 485).

At the end of the novel Clym remains emptied of his force, a diminished and pathetic victim.

Clym is much more typical of the tragic heroes of Hardy's later novels than Eustacia in her heroic aspects is. The two together, however, share the essential characteristics of Hardy's later protagonists. Eustacia has their self-destructiveness (disguised as rebellion against fate), and, finally, their pathos. Clym has both their pathos and their overgrown guilt and self-accusation. Michael Henchard, Tess Durbeyfield, Jude Fawley, and Sue Bridehead are all self-destructive, and self-accusation is an essential cause of their suffering. What accuses them, and Clym as well, is not so much conscience as the superego—which defines more exactly Hardy's belief that such tortures result in large part from taking internally and too seriously the external and rigid dictates of the moral codes of society. Partly, Hardy seems to want to exorcise the inflexibility and excess of the Victorian sense of guilt and duty. But his primary interest is in the victims of accusation. Towards them his feeling is excruciatingly sympathetic—so much so that they hover continually on the verge of being entirely pitiful figures. The dense and complex evocation of a culture which occupied the earlier Victorian novelists is missing from Hardy's novels. More accurately, when it exists, it does so peripherally, as a frame—as in the folk who act as chorus in *Return*. Hardy's attention is lyric and in-driving, towards the inmost emotional and suffering vulnerability of single figures isolated from one another and from the society which surrounds them. In his last novel, *Jude the Obscure*, society has become so internalized that the outer social world appears almost entirely as a reflected and distorted image; we see it only as it threatens or exiles his isolated heroes; and we see it less in its action than in their reaction. *Jude* is the logical development of a tendency towards the pathos of isolation and self-inflicted punishment clearly visible at least as early as *Return of the Native*.

The action of Hardy's tragedies is almost always the doomed struggle against isolation—the struggle towards a common world. Eustacia Vye is typical of all Hardy's tragic victims in finding it impossible to harmonize the outer world (both social and physical) with her inner world of feeling, and in dissipating her life in the struggle. The real struggle, or ironic discrepancy rather, is between hopes or dreams and the immovable and incalculable circumstances which frustrate them. The discovery is usually the characters' realization of the inevitability of frustration, and it is generalized as a recognition of their hopeless plight as sensitive and emotionally vulnerable beings in an unconscious and indifferent but seemingly malignant universe. Eustacia's last soliloquy has its parallel in almost all Hardy's tragic novels: 'O, the cruelty of putting me into this ill-conceived world! I was capable of much; but I have been injured and blighted and crushed by things beyond my control! O, how hard it is of Heaven to devise such tortures for me, who have done no harm to Heaven at all!' (p. 422).

The archetypal figures of Hardy's tragedies are Tantalus ('"Life offers—to deny!"')[2] and Job. His characters' response to the crushing of their hopes, to the withdrawal of life's offering, is most often Job's: '"Let the day perish."' Like Eustacia, they think themselves the victim of a demonic torturer, as Job is Satan's victim, and they are denied Job's final revelation. Hardy's tragedies end by revealing a gigantic flaw in the very conditions of life—in the discrepancy between personality and environment, sensibility and circumstance. There is no remedy for this flaw. One can only stoically adapt himself to it, as the animal who survives in the struggle for existence must adapt himself to his environment. In Hardy's tragedies impulse, energy, *élan* are almost always punished. Like Clym, those who survive learn (or try to learn) what to make of a diminished thing. The effect is pathos emphasized and underlined.

In spite of its elements of heroic tragedy *The Return of the Native* expresses essentially the same disillusioned-ironic tragic attitude that the later tragedies— *The Mayor of Casterbridge, Tess of the d'Urbervilles,* and *Jude the Obscure*—do. Because of their emphasis on pathos and irony, their reduction of the tragic figure to a pitiable one, some critics would deny that these novels (particularly *Tess* and *Jude*) are tragic at all. Perhaps Hardy's attempt to elevate Eustacia to the heroic level betrays the same doubt in his mind. Whether or not the novels are legitimate and perhaps peripheral modes of tragedy I am not prepared to argue. What is important to recognize, I think, is their disillusioned skepticism as to the possibility of romance and heroism, their concentrated drama and bold symbolism of the inner life, and their protagonists' acute sense of isolation in an alien society and in a universe abandoned or forgotten by a god who is after all only a fiction. In these elements they set the pattern for one of the dominant traditions of the modern novel.

Notes

1. *The Return of the Native*, p. 13. All quotations from *The Return of the Native* are from the Macmillan edition of *The Works of Thomas Hardy in Prose and Verse*, 23 vols (London, 1912–26) vol. IV.

2. 'Yell'ham-Wood's Story', *Collected Poems of Thomas Hardy* (New York, 1940), p. 280.

171

Introduction to
The Return of the Native

———————— ◆ ————————

JOHN PATERSON

The Return of the Native has been ranked by some indulgent readers with *The Mayor of Casterbridge* and *Tess of the d'Urbervilles* and *Jude the Obscure*; but, for all its superficial impressiveness, it doesn't really belong in their distinguished company. Too studied and self-conscious an imitation of classical tragedy, it doesn't have their immediate reality, their powerful authenticity. In the ceremonial chapters of Egdon Heath and Eustacia Vye, in the set speeches and soliloquies of the heroine, in the novel's conscientious observation of the unities of time and space, in its organization (as originally planned) in terms of the five parts or 'acts' of traditional tragedy, *The Return of the Native* was meant to recall the immensities of Sophocles and Shakespeare. But the facts of its fiction simply do not justify the application of so grand, so grandiose, a machinery. Its men and women are seldom equal after all to the sublime world they are asked to occupy. In the Vyes and the Yeobrights, Hardy evidently intended a little aristocracy fit to bear the solemn burdens of tragedy. But they remain a species of stuffy local gentility and as such incapable of heroic transformations. Eustacia may justify the formidable frame of reference in which she is set, but to associate Clym, the translated shopkeeper, with the likes of Oedipus and Aeneas is to emphasize how far short of them he really falls. Mrs Yeobright's identification with Lear—in her final agony she is equipped with a heath, a hovel and a fool—is perhaps more deserved, but it shows too visibly and seems only slightly less wilful than Clym's identification with heroes of classical fame. In the unfolding of her fate, money, her collection of precious guineas, surely plays a more crucial part than should consist with an action of Sophoclean or Shakespearean size. Even the death of the splendid Eustacia is in part determined by a shortage of funds.

The plot of the novel, then, lacks the terrific and terrifying logic of cause and effect that marks the plots of the greatest exercises in this line. That it

SOURCE New York, 1966.

operates the way it does is more accidental than necessary. If Diggory had known that half the guineas belonged to Clym, if Mrs Yeobright's arrival at her son's house had not coincided with Wildeve's, if Eustacia had not mistakenly thought her husband awake, if she had received his letter or had had a few more pence in her purse, then the tragic disaster would not have taken place at all. The presence of the fateful and the inevitable is felt as little in the 'action' of the characters as in the action of the plot. Their motives for doing what they do, for contriving their own undoing, are often only specious and arbitrary and seem determined by the needs of a tyrannical plot. Diggory's sentimental motive for haunting the heath speaks well for his heart but may impress the reader as odd and even gratuitous. Eustacia's reasons for not at once opening the door to Mrs Yeobright seem strained and dubious and even her reasons for doing herself in at the end are not wholly convincing. Hardy does manage on the whole to bring these things off, but not without arousing in the reader the uneasy sensation that he has had the narrowest of escapes, that all the time he has been skating on the thinnest of ice. The inexorability of its tragic development has seemed too often to express, in short, not the natural needs or necessities of the novel but the applied will or wilfulness of the author . . .

But *The Return of the Native* is better than its defects; it breathes a reality that its very manifest weaknesses are powerless to explain or explain away. The sources of this reality are not easily identifiable. That they don't exist in Hardy's conceptions that are usually trite or clumsy or obvious is clear enough. That they don't exist in the raw materials he worked with, in that traditional stockpile of ruined maids, mysterious strangers, dashing soldiers and sailors, lovers faithful or faithless, dark-dyed villains, etc., is equally clear. Few readers briefed in advance on the plots and characters of *Far From the Madding Crowd, The Woodlanders, Tess of the d'Urbervilles, The Return of the Native*, would think them worth the trouble of a further exploration. Their matter would seem too thin or too poor or too simple-minded for artistic conversion. It is just here, though, that the sources of Hardy's power to chasten and subdue disclose themselves. It was in the life and imagination he brought with so much simple faith and fervor to his large but crude conceptions, to his rude primitive images, that his power to persuade resides. In spite of the many excellent and obvious reasons for not believing in the experience of the novel, we do in the end believe in it because Hardy himself did. He wins our consent because what he records has been both closely observed and deeply felt . . .

In the end, however, the novel derives more from Hardy's imagination than from his observation and experience, so that the detail that provides its intensest and most vivid pages is better described as poetic than as realistic. Like Wordsworth, Hardy worked to transfigure the trivial and the commonplace, to make the ordinary extraordinary. The business of the artist was, he said, to make Nature's defects 'the basis of a hitherto unperceived beauty, by irradiating them with "the light that never was" ...' As the creatures of a tragic or symbolic or conceptual machinery, Hardy's people may sometimes fail at the purely realistic level, but because they are made to move as often as they are in an ambience of poetic beauty and wonder, these intermittent failures are not decisive. Images like Thomasin gathering holly boughs 'amid the glistening green and scarlet masses of the tree' or Eustacia unclosing her lips in a laugh 'so that the sun shone into her mouth as into a tulip and lent it a similar scarlet fire' exercise a chemical influence out of all proportion to their mass or quantity and have the effect of compensating for the novel's many flat and sandy moments. Even a character as tenuous and abstract as Clym can be quickened into vital life on occasion by the magic of Hardy's incandescent imagination as when 'the eclipsed moonlight shines upon [his] face with a strange foreign colour, and shows its shape as if it were cut out of gold'. The same transfiguring force enters the novel's individual scenes and episodes. Eustacia's voyage across the moonlit heath with the mummers, the weird nocturnal game of dice between Wildeve and the reddleman, the unearthly trancelike dance on the green at East Egdon—such radiant scenes as these have the power to cancel out the occasional lapses in the novel's plotting or causation. It was this power to change the ordinary stuff of reality into something rich and strange, this power to discover beneath the surface of ordinary life and being rare and mysterious states of life and being, that led D.H. Lawrence to discover in Hardy a brother under the skin.[1]

The same powerful imagination everywhere informs and transforms the novel. *The Return of the Native* can survive the defects of its plot because the plot as such all but disappears in the greater and more inclusive music of theme and imagery. Though its action scarcely qualifies as a tragic action, the novel does evoke, in its accumulating allusions to the geography, history and literature of classical antiquity, the heroic world out of which tragedy came and to this extent places the otherwise purely local or domestic action in a context that enlarges and enrichens. Variously described as the home of the Titans, as Dante's Limbo, as 'Homer's Cimmerian land', Egdon Heath can suggest the lightless underworld of the ancients. Representing the diminished consciousness of modern times, Clym's is explicitly contrasted with the heroic consciousness of Hardy's prelapsarian Greeks. Persistently identified with the legend and literature of antiquity, Eustacia, on the other hand, suggests the anachronistic and hence foredoomed revival of that consciousness. Her profile compares with Sappho's; she 'can utter oracles of Delphian ambiguity'; her dream has 'as many ramifications as the Cretan labyrinth'. In the most dazzling of her Mediterranean associations, she is established as the lineal descendant of Homeric kings, as the last of the house of Phaeacia's princely Alcinous.

What most energetically enters and irradiates the matter of *The Return of the Native*, however, is its Promethean theme and imagery. Clym and his Egdon Heath are specifically affiliated with the banished Titan, with the fallen benefactor of mankind; but it is the novel's fire imagery, by inference Promethean, that most fully asserts this primary motif. The darkness of the heath is thus disturbed, early in the novel, by fires that mark the anniversary of the Gunpowder Plot. Wildeve makes his presence known by releasing at Eustacia's window a moth that perishes in the flames of her candle. On the day Mrs Yeobright dies, the universe of Egdon is imagined as almost literally in flames and her death is a symbolic death-by-fire: 'The sun ... stood directly in her face, like some merciless incendiary, brand in hand, waiting to consume her.' Eustacia herself will perish in the same fatal flames: burned in effigy by Susan Nunsuch and acting out the parable of Wildeve's moth-signal, she will hurl herself into 'the boiling caldron' of the weir. This theme affects not only the major imagery of action and setting but also the minor imagery of word and phrase. In Eustacia's presence, 'the revived embers of an old passion glowed clearly in Wildeve', who fancies himself victimized by 'the curse of inflammability'. 'A blaze of love, and extinction' Eustacia herself prefers characteristically to 'a lantern glimmer of the same'. After first meeting Clym she is 'warmed with an inner fire' and she will later denounce Mrs Yeobright 'with a smothered fire of feeling' and with 'scalding tears' trickling from her eyes.

At the very last, however, the source of the novel's 'felt' life or power is much more elusive, less accessible, than the chemistry of its language and imagery. That ultimate source can only approximately be identified as what Francis Fergusson would call its 'action', the sensitive inner movement or motion of its feeling. It may be difficult to accept, to believe in, the novel's rickety and arbitrarily directed plot; but it is not at all difficult to accept and believe in its 'action', the curve of the emotion that animates it and is the true shape of its 'felt' life. What eventually overcomes us is the tragic rhythm of the action as it moves in the experience of the chief characters through the phases first of purpose or will or desire, then of passion or suffering as what the characters intend or desire is resisted and defeated, and finally of perception or knowledge as they recognize the limits of their world and of their power to change it. If *The Return of the Native* does not rank with the greatest novels, it is because it fails, in the imagery of character and plot, to enact with full and confident power this tragic rhythm of action. But if it remains a good or nearly great novel, it is because it does enact, however imperfectly, this powerful and profoundly felt rhythm ...

The novel as Hardy initially conceived it was a very different novel from the one we now have. Now Mrs Yeobright's niece and Clym's cousin, Thomasin was originally conceived as Mrs Yeobright's daughter and Clym's sister. Now a witch in only the metaphorical sense, Eustacia was at first imagined as a witch in the more literal sense and, as such, was more malevolently the persecutor of a helpless Thomasin Yeobright than she now is. In the novel's present form, Thomasin leaves one morning with Wildeve to be married but returns that evening alone, hysterical and unmarried because the license produced by her husband-to-be has proved invalid. According to the original or provisional terms of the novel, however, Thomasin was to have lived with Wildeve for a week before discovering that the marriage ceremony, perhaps by her paramour's wilful and malicious design, had been illegal. Hardy's decision to abandon the original program of the novel was doubtless determined by editorial pressure, 'a pressure emanating probably from the offices of the *Cornhill Magazine* to whose editor, Leslie Stephen, it was first shown. Responsible for the serial publication of *Far From the Madding Crowd* and *The Hand of Ethelberta*, Stephen had had already in the past to restrain Hardy's difficult and dangerous imagination. 'I may be over particular,' he wrote in connection with *The Hand of Ethelberta*, 'but I don't like the suggestion of the very close embrace in the London churchyard.' Now presented with *The Return of the Native* in an evidently embryonic form, the editor felt called upon again to correct and control his client. 'Though he liked the opening,' Hardy reported, 'he feared that the relations between Eustacia, Wildeve and Thomasin might develop into something "dangerous" for a family magazine, and he refused to have anything to do with it unless he could see the whole.' Although *The Return of the Native* was eventually serialized in *Belgravia*, not in the *Cornhill*, the anxious author was evidently inspired by Stephen's serious misgivings to subject the novel in its germinal form to the radical revision that resulted in the version we now have.

The history of the novel's distortion under editorial pressure was not to end with Hardy's separation from Stephen and the *Cornhill*. His employers on the board of *Belgravia* could have been no more liberal than his old employers had been. Though the opposition between Christian and pre-Christian values is vital to the novel's total effect, no specific denigration of the Christian religion was permitted to enter the text. In such outlandish spots as Egdon, Hardy planned to say, 'homage to nature, self-adoration, frantic gaieties, fragments of Teutonic rites to divinities whose names are forgotten, have in some way or other survived medieval Christianity'. Editorial tact prevailed, however, and the phrase 'medieval Christianity' was subsequently neutralized to 'medieval doctrine'. Even more damaging to the novel's free imaginative development was the suppression of all references to lips and legs and bodies. Though the force that brings Wildeve and Eustacia together is manifestly other than spiritual or sentimental, no explicit indication of its sexual character was permitted. These wicked lovers were not to be granted even the small freedom of a kiss. 'You are a pleasant lady to know,' Wildeve was at one time permitted to say, 'and I daresay as sweet [to kiss] as ever—almost.' The dangerous infinitive was rigorously removed, however, from the text of the manuscript. Just as tyrannical was the public passion for the happy ending. Hardy had intended, as he confessed in a foot-note on page 473 of the definitive edition of 1912, to conclude *The Return of the Native* with the fifth book: with the deaths of Wildeve and Eustacia, with the widowhood of Thomasin and the disappearance of the reddleman. He was forced by editorial policy, however, to add a sixth book: to arrange the marriage of a reconstructed reddleman and a rehabilitated widow and thus to dishonor his original intention....

[Paterson argues that it would be wrong to exaggerate the effect of Hardy's 'exposure to a prudential editorial policy'; he continues:]

There's even a question whether the energetic moral censorship of the time really affected more than the superficies of the novel. It did make it difficult for Hardy to represent his men and women as sexual as well as social creatures. But it didn't prevent him from forcibly expressing the novel's crucial criticism of Christianity. No explicit condemnation of the religious establishment was, of course, permitted to appear at the surface of the novel. But the condemnation is not the less a condemnation because it is not explicit. Indeed, much of its power may derive from the accident that it was driven underground, that Hardy was compelled by the nature of the circumstances to dramatize indirectly, at the level of artistic suggestion, what he couldn't plainly say. Identified with a world not yet touched by the spectral hand of Christianity, Eustacia Vye reincarnated on the withered parish of Egdon Heath the larger and braver vision of the ancient Greeks. In her suffering and death she dramatizes the tragic humiliation, in a diminished world, of the heroic pre-Christian understanding of things. It doesn't surprise us, therefore, that though no longer literally the witch, that immemorial antagonist of the Christian faith, she remains that black creature in the figurative sense at least. Nor does it surprise that of all the parts in the mummers' play, she should draw precisely that of the Antichrist, the Turkish Knight, who must, with ritual inexorability, suffer defeat and death at the hands of the Christian champion.

Eustacia stands in this in opposition to her husband, whose allegedly advanced views only thinly disguise the Christian champion. For if Clym consistently deceives himself and sometimes his creator, he doesn't deceive his mother, who correctly understands him as a missionary in disguise, or his wife, who associates him half-satirically with the Apostle Paul. Nor does he always deceive Hardy *either*, who sometimes exposes him to the most damaging ironies. Clym's theoretical and pious intelligence suffers, for example, when contrasted with the practical and instinctive intelligence of a still-unchristened peasant community very properly skeptical of his plans to improve it. ''Tis good-hearted of the young man', says one member of that community with a condescension that events will justify. 'But, for my part, I think he had better mind his own business.' The ironies at Clym's expense are especially trenchant at the novel's end where his denial of life in a spirit of Christian self-renunciation contrasts dramatically with the life-renewing rites both of Maypole-day and of Thomasin's marriage. Whether Hardy intended it or not—and it's hard to believe he didn't—Clym's theatrical conversion is reduced by the savage rites of spring and marriage to ludicrous terms.

As the unreconstructed reddleman, Diggory Venn was evidently meant to honor the stoic and realistic values of a pre-Christian way of life and, tacitly at least, to criticize the nicer, less permissive, values that come in with Christianity. Orignally meant 'to have retained his isolated and weird character to the last, and to have disappeared mysteriously from his heath', he was to have symbolized the displacement by the Christian dispensation of that elusive and nearly demoniacal spirit of fen and forest that had found its last resting place on Egdon. Identified with Cain, with Ishmael, with Mephistopheles, he was to have stood with Eustacia Vye, and to a certain extent still stands with her, outside the pale of Christian salvation. For the novel's anti-Christian character, however, the members of the peasant community with their hearty celebration of the natural life and their instinctive distrust of the church are mainly responsible. Their performances derive, that is, from levels of thinking and feeling older than and antagonistic to the innovations of Christianity. The bonfires they build in their first appearance have their antecedents in a barbaric Druidical and Anglo–Saxon past. As mummers they re-enact the old folk-play, the St George play, whose Christian veneer scarcely conceals the pre-Christian fertility rite. As participants in the ancient ritual of Maypole-day, they celebrate a vitality older and stronger than Christianity. 'In name they were parishioners,' Hardy notes with evident satisfaction, 'but virtually they belonged to no parish at all.' Hardy's denigration of Christianity is perhaps most explicit in the ludicrous figure of Christian Cantle, the caricature of the Christian man. Dissociated from the pagan community with its profane celebration of natural joy and virtue, the pious Christian alone refrains from joining the mad, demoniacal measure about the Promethean bonfire of November 5. His physical decrepitude and sexual impotence—he's the man no woman will marry—stand out beside the life-worshiping vitality of Grandfer and Timothy and the rest of that lusty crew. And where he lives in constant terror of the sights and sounds of the savage heath, they, complete pagans that they are, feel perfectly at home in this grimmest of all possible worlds. Though the subversive, anti-Christian argument of *The Return of the Native* could not openly be asserted, it was and remains everywhere active beneath the novel's unassuming surface. Hardy may have been hampered in the exercise of his artistic will by the virulent censorship of the time, but he couldn't, it's clear, be stopped by it. If his strong and stubborn imagination couldn't have its will one way, it would have it another ...

Note

1. D.H. Lawrence, 'Study of Thomas Hardy', in *Phoenix: The Posthumous Papers of D.H. Lawrence* (New York, 1936).

172

'The Past-marked Prospect': Reading: *The Mayor of Casterbridge*

———————◆———————

ROD EDMOND

1

Most of Hardy's writing is preoccupied in some way with the past, with history and memory. There is the deeply personal sense of the past, and the private memories that go with it, of the Poems of 1912–13, some of which finds its way into *A Pair of Blue Eyes*. There is the historical past which figures in novels as dissimilar as *The Trumpet Major* and *Return of the Native*. There is the recurring use in his fiction of the settings and remains of ancient civilisations and the remote past to explore continuities and ruptures between past and present. *A Laodicean* and *The Well-beloved*, among others, use details of the past in this expressive way.

But it is *The Mayor of Casterbridge* in which these issues of the past, of history and memory, have their most concentrated expression, and are brought into a complex relationship with the present which gives the novel an integration, thematic and structural, not found elsewhere in Hardy's fiction. As a result it offers a special kind of reading experience, and it is this which I want now to explore.

2

The morning after Susan and her daughter arrive in Casterbridge, Elizabeth-Jane is seen at the hotel window looking down on to the High Street (ch. 9). The story is poised, ready to move forward again after the detailed descriptions of the previous day which have run over six chapters. Elizabeth-Jane sees Henchard greet Farfrae, and watches the two men walk off together up the High Street, leaving her saddened at Farfrae's departure and failure to say goodbye. Inside the hotel room Susan is undecided whether or not to

SOURCE This is a specially revised version of an essay that originally appeared in *Reading the Victorian Novel: Detail into Form*, London, 1980, pp. 111–27.

approach Henchard, a dilemma solved for her by the sight of five large wagons laden with hay and bearing Henchard's name going past the window. She decides that for the sake of her daughter she must go through with her plan, and Elizabeth-Jane is sent off with a message which will imply that its bearer is Henchard's daughter. What is being set going here is the interplay of past, present, and future, which the novel explores on a much larger scale and indeed expresses through its very structure. The conversation between Henchard and Farfrae results in the latter staying on in Casterbridge as Henchard's manager. Elizabeth-Jane's interest in Farfrae looks forward to their eventual marriage; Susan's hesitations go back almost twenty years; the calculated misunderstanding her message and its bearer will produce looks back to the sale of Susan with which the novel begins, and forward to Henchard's rejection of Elizabeth-Jane and his own lonely death.

All this, of course, only becomes clear to the reader in retrospect. And yet even in the process of reading *The Mayor of Casterbridge* chapter 9 introduces a marked deceleration. The previous day, spread over six chapters, has been one of activity and discovery. Casterbridge has been entered, but at dusk, and the focus of our attention has narrowed to Henchard and Farfrae. Now, in the clear light of the following morning, Casterbridge is to be seen and contemplated in a more leisurely manner, setting and action are to assume a more equal significance, alerting the reader to the function of certain kinds of significant detail in the growth of the novel.

As Elizabeth-Jane walks slowly up the High Street towards her meeting with Henchard, she looks idly around her.

> The front doors of the private houses were mostly left open at this warm autumn time ... Hence, through the long, straight, entrance passages thus unclosed could be seen, as through tunnels, the mossy gardens at the back, glowing with nasturtiums, fuchsias, scarlet geraniums, 'bloody warriors', snap-dragons, and dahlias, this floral blaze being backed by crusted grey stone-work remaining from a yet remoter Casterbridge than the venerable one visible in the street. The old-fashioned fronts of these houses, which had older than old-fashioned backs, rose sheer from the pavement, into which the bow-windows protruded like bastions, necessitating a pleasing chassez–dechassez movement to the time-pressed pedestrian at every few yards. He was bound also to evolve other Terpsichorean figures in respect of door-steps, scrapers, cellar-hatches, church buttresses, and the overhanging angles of walls which, originally un-obtrusive, had become bow-legged and knock-kneed.
>
> (ch. 9)

This passage is characteristic of Hardy in the unusual angle from which things are seen, the finely observed detail and sense of solidity, its touch of quaintness, and its odd blend of objectivity and humour. It has a double movement, down the passages to the stonework of ancient Casterbridge and then back to the street and the more recent but still venerable house fronts, which in turn protrude into the daily activities of mid-nineteenth-century Casterbridge, acting picturesquely as a brake. ('Time-pressed' is doing a lot of work in this context.) The reader discovers that everything in Casterbridge has something older behind or beneath it; for example, the ancient door with its chipped, leering keystone is found at the back of High-Place Hall (ch. 21). The history of the town seems visibly layered, from remotest Casterbridge at the backs of the houses to the 'present' life of this busy early Victorian town in the streets and market place. There is nothing incidental about this passage, charming as it is. The whole of chapter 9, from its opening with Elizabeth-Jane at the window to her arrival at Henchard's yard, has been constructed with a view to the novel's overall design, and detail of this kind is integral to the way in which past, present, and future are being inter-woven.

'Casterbridge announced old Rome in every street, alley, and precinct' (ch. 11). This opening to the description of the Amphitheatre in which Henchard and Susan meet again is, like other settings of prehistoric earth forts, barrows, the Roman-British burial ground, the Franciscan Priory and mill, much more than 'background detail'. Throughout the novel significant action is held within some context of the past, gripped by it in a way which comes to alert the reader to the work that such detail is doing. The view from the cottage Henchard hires for Susan while they prepare to remarry is an example of this kind of placing.

> Beneath these sycamores on the town walls could be seen from the sitting room the tumuli and earth forts of the distant uplands; making it altogether a pleasant spot, with the usual touch of melancholy that a past-marked prospect lends.

(ch. 13)

This 'past-marked prospect' is both historical—the earth forts and the Roman wall on which the trees are growing—and personal, the melancholy coming not just from the historical perspective but also from Susan's own history which she contemplates now that Henchard prepares to set right his guilty act of twenty years earlier. It is the past-marked prospect in fact, which becomes for the reader an image of the novel as a whole.

Individual experience in the novel is rarely located simply in the present. Instead the reader normally views the events of the novel in the context of an ever lengthening past which moves back through the living memory of the community and the recent historical past of a relatively static pre-capitalist rural society, to the middle ages, Roman Britain, and prehistoric times. The movement, as in my opening example, is a double one, first backwards and then forwards, so that the recurring effect is one of shrinking and enlarging. In other words the reader is constantly having to refocus as character and action are first sited within an ever lengthening past, and then brought close again, as for instance when Henchard and Susan meet in the physically and historically dwarfing context of the Amphitheatre, confront their own past and plan their remarriage.

The reader experiences a similar kind of double movement *within* the lives of most of the main characters. Farfrae is the notable exception, Henchard the most fully developed example, and the opposition is significant. Henchard carries his history with him, most obviously in his memory of the sale of Susan and his consequent pledge of abstinence, but also in other, more detailed ways, which lead the reader to see him in this light. Waking the morning after the sale of his wife Henchard looks down on to the village of Weydon-Priors and across the surrounding countryside.

> The spot stretched downwards into valleys, and onwards to other uplands, dotted with barrows, and trenched with the remains of prehistoric forts. The whole scene lay under the rays of a newly risen sun ...
>
> (ch. 2)

New mornings bring their own promise, but cannot wipe out the past; an intimate connection is being established between Henchard's life and the past-littered landscape he inhabits. His past now clings to him like heavy mud to wet boots. The furmity woman reappears in the court Henchard is presiding over, and the sudden surfacing of his past, which has the effect of seeming to bring it close, completes his downfall. He returns to the places of his past, most notably Weydon-Priors. The associations of the past are too strong for him; he finds it impossible to refuse Lucetta's request for the return of her letters because the place she has chosen for the meeting, the Ring, is filled with the memory of his wronged wife and her return. And it is the Ring from which Henchard first spies on the meetings of Elizabeth-Jane and Farfrae on the Budmouth Road, the setting in this case working on the reader to heighten and dramatise the sense of Henchard ignoring the lessons of the past and once again acting in ways which will lead to his rejection and isolation.

This use of setting to induce the reader to recollect and make connections is developed in the scenes where Henchard spies on Elizabeth-Jane and Farfrae from the prehistoric fort of Mai Dun.

> Two miles out, a quarter of a mile from the highway, was the prehistoric fort called Mai Dun, of huge dimensions and many ramparts, within or upon whose enclosures a human being, as seen from the road, was but an insignificant speck. Hitherward Henchard often resorted, glass in hand, and scanned the hedgeless Via—for it was the original track laid out by the legions of the Empire—to a distance of two or three miles, his object being to read the progress of affairs between Farfrae and his charmer.
>
> (ch. 43)

Mai Dun functions like the Ring to shrink character and action by placing them in a setting redolent of the past. It is as if the reader looks back down the other end of the telescope at Henchard and sees his individual significance temporarily diminished in this lengthened setting. At the same time it works to remind the reader of Henchard's relationship to his own past. He is spying on Farfrae, his supplanter he cannot forgive, and Elizabeth-Jane, his substitute for the daughter he once lost whom he is now losing 'again'. Looking through the glass Henchard sees a male figure approaching.

> It was one clothed as a merchant captain; and as he turned in his scrutiny of the road he revealed his face. Henchard lived a lifetime the moment he saw it. The face was Newson's.
>
> (ch. 43)

'Lived a lifetime' is precise. The reader shares Henchard's shock of recognition, sees Henchard's past coming at him irresistibly, and with it the destruction of his relationship with Elizabeth-Jane. It is that evening Henchard leaves Casterbridge.

These general terms in which the reader is persuaded to see Henchard are constantly particularised through detail which itself expresses this larger meaning. Henchard's 'wardrobe' is a case in point, the clothes he wears being one of the specific ways in which the interplay of past and present in his life is expressed. The contrast between the fustian and corduroy of the hay trusser and the evening suit, jewelled studs, and heavy gold chain of the Mayor of Casterbridge which hits Susan when she sees him through the window of the King's Arms, underlines for us the extent of Henchard's transformation. This gentleman's garb persists, pathetically, after his ruin, and the shabby, thread-bare suit, silk hat, and satin stock of his mayoral days in which he works for Farfrae and attempts to give his own welcome to the Royal Personage dramatise for the reader that past which Henchard cannot relinquish and which holds him trapped. When that past finally drops away and Henchard prepares to leave Casterbridge it is an earlier past which surfaces as he reassumes the clothes of his original trade. Even 'the regularly interchanging fustian folds, now in the left leg, now in the right, as he paced along', of the opening page return as Elizabeth-Jane, watching him disappear across the moor, notices 'the creases behind his knees coming and going alternately till she could no longer see them' (ch. 43). This use of repetition is managed without strain, occurring quietly as a distant echo in the reader's memory rather than as something we consciously mark in the process of reading. It is, for example, very different from George Moore's self-conscious, almost ostentatious use of a similar device in *Esther Waters*, where the opening paragraph of the novel is artfully repeated four chapters from the end when Esther returns to Woodview. The cumulative effect of all this on the reader is to produce a sense of seeing character through a screen of detail which registers shifts in consciousness and circumstance. Henchard's last change of clothes, the 'rough yet respectable coat and hat ... new shirt and neck-cloth' (ch. 44) which he buys on his way back to Casterbridge for Elizabeth-Jane's wedding is painfully contrasted with the glimpse he gets of the white-waistcoated Newson through the half-open door at the wedding party. This contrast, deftly made, instantly compresses both the finality of Henchard's displacement and his renewed sense of dignity, both of which flow into the tragedy of his death in a crumbling eroded cottage on the edge of Egdon Heath.

Lucetta also carries her history with her, and is constantly seen by the reader in terms of her past. Her exclamation 'I won't be a slave to the past' (ch. 25) is deeply ironic. She has her own furmity woman figure in the person of Jopp, who knows of her past with Henchard. On one level Jopp isn't convincing. He is dragged in at various points to give impetus to the story, yet he is as important for Lucetta's future as the furmity woman is for Henchard's, and as his function in the novel's design becomes clear to the reader his staginess becomes less of a problem. The threads of Henchard and Lucetta's past are pulled together in Peter's Finger when Jopp and the furmity woman meet and she persuades him to read Lucetta's letters to the crowded pub, which results in the skimmity ride and Lucetta's death.

It is only Farfrae who is not bound by any past. The 'insight, briskness, and rapidity of his nature' (ch. 42) partly accounts for this, but it is also that, unlike the other characters in the novel, he enters it 'clean'. We know nothing of his past; he brings no memory with which to engage the reader's own. Solomon Longways is essentially correct when he describes the Scotsman as having 'travelled a'most from the North Pole' (ch. 8). Whereas Henchard is constantly seen in prehistoric, Roman, and medieval settings, Farfrae inhabits a world free of such associations; the Ring, Mai Dun, the Franciscan Priory and mill have no part in his history.

Yet by the end of the novel Farfrae has begun to acquire a past, one which is recorded by the collective memory of Casterbridge—Christopher Coney, Solomon Longways, Buzzford, Billy Wills, Mother Cuxsom, Nance Mockridge, and their friends. As Farfrae becomes a prosperous merchant, and then Mayor, he loses much of the charm he originally had for this group. Lucetta is disliked; sympathy is felt for Elizabeth-Jane; slowly Farfrae's history is assimilated to this collective memory, which functions throughout the novel as yet another kind of past within which character and action are sited. It is worth considering the ways in which the reader's response to the novel is affected by the presence of this collective memory; how it feeds our memory as we read; the view out into history which this group opens up for the reader.

This group is more than simply a 'touch of local colour', and even to describe its function as choric is distancing and flattening. It certainly carries a 'folkloric' knowledge of Casterbridge, as Buzzford's reflections suggest;

> Casterbridge is a old, hoary place o'wickedness, by all account. 'Tis recorded in history that we rebelled against the King one or two hundred years ago, in the time of the Romans, and that lots of us was hanged on Gallows Hill, and quartered, and our different jints sent about the country like butcher's meat;
>
> (ch. 8)

Buzzford makes this speech looking at the grain of the table, as if the memory of Monmouth's rebellion, and Judge Jeffrey's 'Bloody Assize', is held there in the wood. Yet this is not simply picturesque. Farfrae, Susan, Elizabeth-Jane, and Lucetta are all newcomers to Casterbridge, and Henchard was not born there. The Three Mariners' crowd expresses a local memory which goes back well beyond the arrival of any of the main characters in Casterbridge. The conversation as they gather outside the church on the morning of Henchard and Susan's wedding recalls Henchard's early days in Casterbridge, and then pushes back more than forty-five years to memories of Mrs Cuxsom's mother, and Mellstock parties at old Dame Ledlow's, farmer Shiner's aunt (ch. 13). This conversation, with its references to the world of *Under the Greenwood Tree*, surrounds the wedding with a body of local memory and judgement which has a strong resonance for both the reader of this novel, and the general Hardy reader.

Although this group carries most of the novel's humour, behind the stock comic roles is a whole social history, one which the novel itself invites us to read through to. The social rank of these characters is a 'middling' one, between the King's Arms on one hand, and Peter's Finger on the other. Within the Three Mariners they form 'an inferior set at the unlighted end', distinct from the master tradesmen who occupy the seats in the bow window (ch. 8). Billy Wills is a glazier, Buzzford a general dealer, Smart a shoe-maker. This social group, its collective memory, and the past it speaks for, is seen to be slowly disappearing. Some of these 'middling' sections of rural society—artisans, small life-holders and copyholders, that class of 'stationary cottagers' whose disappearance Hardy deplored in his introduction to *Far From the Madding Crowd*—have in *The Mayor of Casterbridge* been reduced to living in Mixen Lane (ch. 36). The signboard of the Three Mariners with its fading painting 'but a half-visible film upon the reality of the grain, and knots, and nails', can be seen as an image of their historical situation. The neglected state of this signboard is no fault of the landlord. It is because of 'the lack of a painter in Casterbridge who would undertake to reproduce the features of men so traditional' (ch. 6). In terms of the economy of Casterbridge and its surrounding villages this group is shown to be increasingly marginal as large scale trading edges out the small independent dealer, and rural society is more and more stratified into two main classes, the respectable farmers and dealers we see leaving the market place in Casterbridge late on Saturday afternoon, and those who replace them, the field labourers coming into town at the end of the day to do their weekly shopping (ch. 24).

Attempts at reading history into this novel have been taken to task. In his introduction to The New Wessex edition Ian Gregor reproves Douglas Brown for placing the significance of the repeal of the Corn Laws at the centre of the novel.[1] Brown's position here is not a strong one, but it seems important not to dismiss that kind of approach altogether. Ian Gregor's general conclusion that 'when concentration is made too directly on the historical implications of the novel, so that we see a precise agricultural crisis constituting its centre, the move is further and further away from its imaginative life', is in danger of confusing one specific example of this approach with the whole method itself.[2] This is no place to attempt to construct a methodology for moving between history and text. However I do want to argue that the reading experience itself directs our attention through *The Mayor of Casterbridge* out into history, not specifically to the Corn Laws or the movement of prices, but to something which goes on more quietly, page by page: that sense of an actively changing social structure which we register as we follow its effects on individuals and groups. This is felt most strongly in the Three Mariners' group, but it is found throughout the novel. Newly emerging class factors help define the relationships of all the main characters, from Henchard's embarrassment at Elizabeth-Jane's lack of refinement, to Farfrae's transfer of affection from Elizabeth-Jane to Lucetta, and Lucetta's calculated preference of Farfrae to Henchard.

This view is not obtained by 'deducing' things from Hardy's novel, nor by 'reading in' from history (although a priori there seems no reason why such approaches should be ruled out), but rather by reading *through* the fiction into that view of history which the novel itself opens up. The reader who fails to register the significance of detail of this kind is, directly or indirectly, a victim of certain limiting assumptions about the novel.

One of the scenes which does seem to open out into history in this way is that of the old shepherd at the hiring fair. Hardy had written about the reduced state of the agricultural labourer in an essay, 'The Dorsetshire Labourer'[3] published shortly before *The Mayor of Casterbridge*, and it was from here that he took the scene of the old shepherd and incorporated it, almost word for word, in the novel. This vignette of the old shepherd standing in the market place, eyes lowered, heedless of the negotiations going on between his son and a prospective employer, expresses, in the larger context of this novel which marks other, roughly parallel experiences, the kind of marginality which changes in the economic and social structure of Victorian rural society were producing. We don't view the scene simply as one views the passage of the seasons or as an emblematic confrontation of Youth with Age. Rather, the novel invites the reader to place it within a specific historical context.

Farfrae's hiring of the young man and his father is an act of calculation rather than sentiment, the real purchase being credit in the eyes of Lucetta, and in its ironic way is perfectly consonant with the new values which are entering Casterbridge life. It is Farfrae's excited account of recent buying and selling transactions which has just stirred Lucetta's interest in him. Indeed there is some irony in it being a hiring fair which forms the background to the early courtship of Farfrae and Lucetta. In a muted way it recalls the market place scene in *Madame Bovary*, where Rodolphe's love talk to Emma is punctuated with shouts from the Agricultural Show.[4]

There is nothing sudden or dramatic in this picture of a social structure in the process of transformation which the novel opens up to the reader, but the changes are there, within the society and encroaching on it. 'The railway had stretched out an arm towards Casterbridge at this time, but had not reached it by several miles as yet' (ch. 27); the clumsy construction gives an accurate rendering of the halting, uneven but unmistakable map of change.

As the map becomes more detailed and comprehensive Coney and his friends will be threatened. But this is in the future. Like the old shepherd they are significantly and vividly present for the reader, even as history is moving away from them. It is here that the novel is poised between two worlds, exploring and enacting continuity and dislocation through that familiar double movement between present and past.

3

My main interest in the previous section was with how history and the past, as themes within the novel, are conveyed to the reader. I want now to examine in less objective, more directly affective terms, the way in which time is experienced by the reader as he or she turns the pages.

The Mayor of Casterbridge is a novel written in the 1880s, about the 1840s, which begins in the 1820s. It looks further back to Casterbridge as it was before Henchard's arrival, and it ends with Elizabeth-Jane looking into the future, as Henchard already begins to recede into a vanishing past. The reader begins viewing the narrative—'One evening of late summer, before the nineteenth century had reached one-third of its span ...'—from his or her own present, but becomes drawn into the careful construction of all its other time layers. This offers a distinctive kind of reading experience, and one which is peculiarly well suited to the novel's thematic preoccupation with time.

As we read the novel we are reminded that Hardy is looking back to Dorchester as he knew it in his childhood. The description of the evening chimes of the local church is footnoted: 'These chimes, like those of other country churches, have been silenced for many years.' A description of the old timber houses in the High Street is similarly footnoted: 'Most of these old houses have now been pulled down'. This footnote is then dated (1912), having been inserted at the time of the 1912 Wessex edition of Hardy's novels, adding yet another layer of time to the novel's structure. Both these footnotes occur in Chapter 4, which marks the novel's entry into Casterbridge, and they help establish that complex relationship between fictional Casterbridge and historical Dorchester of which the novel is constantly reminding us. A later footnote to another detailed description of Casterbridge emphasises this: 'The reader will scarcely need to be reminded that time and progress have obliterated from the town that suggested these descriptions many or most of the old-fashioned features here enumerated' (ch. 9).

This sense of historical retrospection the reader experiences is not, of course, confined to Hardy's curious use of footnotes or his more formal set-piece descriptions of Casterbridge. It is a distinguishing feature of the narrative throughout. Consider, for example, the episode in which Henchard is shamed and angered by Elizabeth-Jane's inability to write 'ladies-hand' (ch. 20). This is how Hardy describes Elizabeth-Jane's writing.

> She started the pen in an elephantine march across the sheet. It was a splendid round, bold hand of her own conception, a style that would have stamped a woman as Minerva's own in more recent days. But other ideas reigned then:

As the contrast between past and present is inserted the perspective lengthens for the reader. Yet the effect is not so much one of distancing the scene or reducing its immediacy, as of lending depth and resonance to the narrative and suggesting that Elizabeth-Jane's time is still to come. Another example of this kind of effect is the description of the end of the fight between Henchard and Farfrae.

> He instantly delivered the younger man an annihilating turn by the left fore-hip, as it used to be expressed, and following up his advantage thrust him towards the door, never loosening his hold till Farfrae's fair head was hanging over the window-sill, and his arm dangling down outside the wall.
>
> (ch. 38)

What is particularly significant here is the parenthetical comment, 'as it used to be expressed', inserted into the culmination of one of the novel's most dramatic and vividly rendered scenes. At precisely the moment Farfrae is beaten and apparently about to be killed, we are reminded that Hardy is describing an old mode of conduct, almost of a gladiatorial kind, which like so much else in the novel has now vanished. As if to reinforce this, Henchard relents and flings himself down in a corner of the loft, while Farfrae picks himself up and goes off to Weatherbury on business. Again the lengthening of the perspective doesn't detract from the power of the scene, but gives it that sense of depth which, in this case almost subliminally, is a central part of the reading experience of the novel ...

The narrative itself therefore, which constantly reminds us we are looking back in time, is one of several 'presents' within the novel. The 1820s, the 1840s, the 1880s, 1912 (1979), all constitute separate layers of time which structure both the novel and the reader's experience of it. As readers, our involvement in this layering is not simply through an awareness of the author's intention, but also through memory. Within the novel it is memory which connects past and present, carrying one into the other, holding and retaining experience in a way which is analogous to the novel's overall design. In a sense the whole novel is structured around the reappearance of characters from the past and the memory they bring with them. This is true of Susan and Elizabeth-Jane, Lucetta, Jopp, Newson, and the furmity woman, all of whom are entangled in Henchard's past and carry memories which affect him. But the reader is also involved rather differently, through the way in which his or her own memory is exercised in the act of reading the novel. Indeed *The Mayor of Casterbridge* makes peculiar demands on our memory as readers.

On the most obvious level, our memory gives us privileged access to Henchard's past. We revisit Weydon-Priors fair eighteen years after Henchard's sale of Susan, and we are able to see that it is dying, so that when

Mrs Goodenough, the furmity woman, complains to Susan, 'the world's no memory' (ch. 3), we as readers are exempt from the charge. It is because we do remember, that we are able to understand the significance of the decline of Weydon-Priors fair, both for Henchard and for Wessex. There are other, more detailed ways, in which the reader is involved, through memory, in the text. Like Henchard, we are given signs and clues to the past which memory can discover. At the beginning of the novel we are told that Elizabeth-Jane has black eyes (ch. 1). When she 'reappears' with Susan eighteen years later there is an uncharacteristic lack of detail in the several descriptions we are given of her, and this persists until her visit to Henchard the morning after her arrival in Casterbridge. As Elizabeth-Jane and Henchard face each other, the 'dark pupils' of Henchard's eyes are noted, and quickly followed by a description of tears rising to Elizabeth-Jane's 'aerial-grey eyes' (ch. 10). Immediately after Henchard and Susan have remarried we get another description of Elizabeth-Jane's 'grey, thoughtful eyes', and this is followed by Henchard's musing on the colour of Elizabeth-Jane's hair 'brown—rather light than dark', and his question to Susan '... didn't you tell me that Elizabeth-Jane's hair promised to be black when she was a baby?' (ch. 14). All this is preparing us for Susan's posthumous disclosure of Elizabeth-Jane's true parentage, and Henchard's candlelight examination of Elizabeth-Jane's face, in search of a past which is confirmed as illusory. Eye colour is a peculiarly haunting yet palpable clue to the past. The signs of Susan's disclosure are there to read; our memory as readers is exercised in a manner which shadows Henchard's own.

Much of the later part of Henchard's tragedy rests on his inability to reconcile the memory of his original Elizabeth-Jane with the fact of Susan's second daughter. Yet although Henchard's tragedy dominates the novel, it does not override it. *The Mayor of Casterbridge* finishes with Elizabeth-Jane and the long view into her future, so that although our memory remains engaged with Henchard and the past, our attention is directed, through Elizabeth-Jane, to the future. And more generally, the use of different time perspectives and the depth these give to the novel creates for the reader a sense of space within the novel which Henchard cannot entirely fill, nor is intended to.

My use of the word 'space' should not be confused with the term 'bulk'. By Victorian standards *The Mayor of Casterbridge* is not a long novel. It has one or two loose ends perhaps, but it is not a 'baggy monster'. What I mean by 'space' is something opened up within the novel as we read it, and hardly dependent on length at all. It is the cumulative product of factors I have considered in the course of this essay: Hardy's selective use of expressive detail concerned with history and the past; the function of memory both within the novel and in terms of our reading experience; the construction of its different layers and perspectives, and the reader's involvement in this whole process.

From the moment we read the title of the novel, which emphasises the town and the office of mayor, our attention is directed towards the historical space which that town and that office occupy. There are three Mayors of Casterbridge in the novel—Henchard, Dr Chalkfield, and Farfrae—and we are encouraged to place them within a much longer line of succession. Throughout the novel time is continually stretched, and the effect of this is to help open up those large spaces within which we view the events of the novel, and which give us our full sense of its meaning. The clocks in Casterbridge don't strike 8 p.m. at precisely the same minute. The church clock is followed by the gaol clock, that of the alms-house, and then by those inside the clock-maker's shop, so that some 'were appreciably on their way to the next hour before the whole business of the old one was satisfactorily wound up' (ch. 4). The stuttering effect this creates is a small example of the way in which Hardy opens out time within the novel, giving it that sense of depth and space which makes it so much more than its subtitle, 'A Story of a Man of Character', and helps account for the special satisfactions it offers. This space allows the reader an imaginative freedom, a sense of incompleteness which exists in contrast to the completeness of Henchard's tragedy and surrounds it. It is within this space that our total impression of the novel and our memory of it lives.

Notes

1. Ian Gregor, *The Mayor of Casterbridge*, intro. The New Wessex Edition, pp. 26–8.
2. A much cruder example of this tendency occurs in Laurence Lerner's *Thomas Hardy's The Mayor of Casterbridge: Tragedy or Social History* (1975). Lerner's approach is evident from the tired opposition of the title—tragedy or social history? and is laid bare in this passage:

> To read through a book like *The Agricultural Revolution 1750–1880* by Chambers and Mingay with Hardy in mind is to notice how little it has to tell us about the concerns of his novel. The upward and downward movement of prices; the relative prosperity of the labourer in corn-growing areas and in pasture; the increase in the size of farms—these are not the issues that appear in Hardy, and underlying economic forces of this kind could never be deduced from his fiction. (p. 83)

The methodology used here—take a piece of history, apply it to a literary text, does it fit? no—is so crude that the rejection of this kind of significance for the novel follows inevitably from the attempt.
3. 'The Dorsetshire Labourer', *Thomas Hardy; Personal Writings*, ed. Harold Orel, (London, 1967).
4. Flaubert, *Madame Bovary*, Part 2, Ch. 8.

173

The Mayor of Casterbridge: A New Fiction Defined

◆

FREDERICK R. KARL

From George Eliot to Thomas Hardy, and particularly from *Adam Bede* (1859), with its artisan protagonist, to *The Mayor of Casterbridge* (1886), with its field-worker 'hero,' is a distance far greater than the passage of twenty-seven years would indicate. Although Hardy's roots, like George Eliot's, were solidly within a nineteenth-century intellectual framework—a pre-Freudian world of Darwin, Spencer, and Huxley—nevertheless, his characters and plots move in a sphere unknown to his contemporaries, an area that no other Victorian, excepting Dickens in some of his minor characters, had attempted to define.

The century that began with Jane Austen's well-balanced heroines of strong will, who literally 'will' themselves into normal behavior, rushes toward its end with the wilful self-destructiveness of Hardy's heroines and heroes, who 'will' themselves not into normality but into an obsession with guilt and penance. From the suave, unquestioned inner-direction of Darcy and Mr Knightley, who live within an intensely realistic world of everyday fact, we pass to a completely different kind of inner-direction in Henchard, whose compulsive life is played out in a fabulous puppet show rather than in a real world. In *The Mayor of Casterbridge*, as in several of his other major novels, Hardy evidently aimed at a different kind of realism from that exhibited in George Eliot, Dickens, Jane Austen, and Thackeray. When he wrote in 1886 that his 'art is to intensify the expression of things ... so that the heart and inner meaning is made vividly visible,'[1] he foreshadowed Conrad's oft-repeated and justly famous definition of realism, that 'by the power of the written word to make you hear, to make you feel—it is, before all, to make you *see*.' This kind of realism entails, among other things, a new type of protagonist and a new way of developing scenes: one finds, for example, characters and scenes that relate to the narrative on both a non-realistic and realistic basis, in the same way that some of the seemingly non-

SOURCE *Modern Fiction Studies*, vol. VI, no. 3, Autumn, 1960, pp. 195–213.

functional passages work in Conrad's major novels and in Lawrence's *The Rainbow* and *Women in Love*. To define Hardy's realism, particularly that of *The Mayor of Casterbridge*, is to reveal a major turning point in the development of the English novel: the novel is no longer solely an important social document but has become as well as significant psychological history.

Hardy once wrote that 'Coleridge says, aim at *illusion* in audience or readers—*i.e.*, the mental state when dreaming, intermediate between complete *delusion* (which the French mistakenly aim at) and a clear perception of falsity.'[2] In this 'suspension of disbelief,' Hardy found a way of both raising the implausible to a philosophic system and demonstrating that art is a 'disproportioning' of reality. As aware as George Eliot that the realism of the naturalist is not art, Hardy used chance as a way of infusing 'imaginative realism' into his narratives, for chance not only suggested something supernatural, but it also fitted the terms of his own beliefs.

In *The Mayor of Casterbridge*, as well as in *The Return of the Native*, *Jude the Obscure*, and *Tess of the d'Urbervilles*, chance becomes a universal symbol of Hardy's personal philosophy; what he calls chance is everything over which man has no control. Although man's will is not nullified by chance, neither can will itself overcome chance; the latter is, in its functioning, the will of the universe, what Hardy, in his long narrative poem, *The Dynasts*, later called the Immanent Will. This force operates in the world without conscious design; even though it is not a controlling force, in that it does not direct man, it frequently seems to evoke more malignity than benevolence. Hardy claimed, notwithstanding, that chance is not a sinister intelligence, that it can work either for good or evil. With Michael Henchard, it seems more apparently sinister because he lacks proportion and balance, is himself sinister in the original sense of the word. That Henchard—also, Jude, Clym Yeobright, Tess, and Eustacia Vye—happens to be constituted *this* way is, however, of no consequence to the principle of chance. Each may have been completely different, Hardy suggests but, except for Tess, each would still have become a victim because he is obsessed by some inexplicable force that wastes his energies. As D.H. Lawrence, with some disappointment, noted, Hardy 'used' chance as a way of punishing his social deviates, while at the same time claiming that chance itself is an indifferent force.

Nevertheless, this philosophy of chance, while certainly neither original nor consistent, did allow Hardy to move from the realistic–romantic nineteenth-century mold into his unique expression of changing values. In *The Mayor of Casterbridge*, the unreality of a chance-filled world is at once indicated in the fable-like beginning, with its simple evocation of distance and timelessness. Hardy writes:

> One evening of late summer, before the present century had reached its thirtieth year, a young man and woman, the latter carrying a child, were approaching the large village of Weydon-Priors, in Upper Wessex, on foot. They were plainly but not ill clad, though the thick hoar of dust which had

accumulated on their shoes and garments from an obviously long journey lent a disadvantageous shabbiness to their appearance just now.[3]

The straightforward style, almost matter-of-fact in its artlessness, conveys both the immediate setting and the potential doom awaiting the couple. They walk along the road together, yet alone, and their isolation here foreshadows their inability to connect personally, even though later they do remarry. The fact is, Henchard must always be alone and isolated ('his taciturnity was unbroken, and the woman [Susan] enjoyed no society whatever from his presence' [p. 2]). She and he walk to the fair grounds unknown and unknowing, only to be separated even further by his perverse act of selling her and the child. Later, the still isolated Henchard enters Casterbridge, painfully builds up a business alone, tries unsuccessfully to win a friend in Farfrae, unsuccessfully woos Lucetta, then remarries Susan, who is dutiful but unloving, tries unsuccessfully to win Elizabeth-Jane as his daughter, and gradually loses each in turn, leaving Casterbridge as alone, stripped, and alienated as when he entered.

Henchard's rashness of temperament and lack of moderation, leading to bursts of anti-social behavior while he is drunk, do not by themselves adequately explain his character. In his bull-like force (Hardy emphasizes his physical strength in the fight with Farfrae), in his inability to love (he offers marriage, but never love), in his need to humiliate himself (among other things, his marriage with Susan lowers him in public opinion), in his anti-heroic tendencies (he rises in stature paradoxically as he demeans himself)—in all of these Henchard is more an inexplicable force than a frail human. Like Conrad's Jim, he seems personally to make the terms of his own victimizing, and yet he is unable to help himself—the kind of forces that are to destroy him are, as Freud indicated, too deep in the unconscious to manifest themselves in easily recognizable form. Henchard's quest in life is to pursue a course of action that will satisfy both his destructive drives and the overt desires of his social life. He is, Hardy suggests, a man obsessed by a singular passion, and, therefore, a man doomed in a world that rewards flexibility.

By moving at the extremes of behavior which he himself cannot understand, Henchard recalls in part, among Hardy's contemporaries, Dickens' Steerforth (*David Copperfield*) and Bradley Headstone (*Our Mutual Friend*) and foreruns Conrad's Lord Jim, Gide's Lafcadio, and Camus' Meursault, each of whom is obsessed by demons that remain unrecognizable, although all perceive that there is something within they must control. When control, nevertheless, becomes impossible, they commit actions which directly or indirectly injure others while also laying the groundwork for their own destruction. Only Dickens among other major nineteenth-century English novelists was aware of the self-destructive demons nourished within an otherwise respectable and controlled individual, although he, like Hardy after him, was unable to account for them.

Hardy's other immediate predecessors and contemporaries, Thackeray,

George Eliot, and Meredith, were so far committed to a 'normal' world that they avoided all extremes of social behavior; but Hardy, like Dickens in his later novels, attempted to create a society in which the extremist, what Dostoevsky considered the criminal and later French novelists the rebel, clashed with the social norm. Hardy differed from Dickens, however, by concerning himself *primarily* with what happened to the radical who is the potential criminal and rebel: Henchard, Jude, Clym, Eustacia, and all those who are destroyed by their intransigence and/or their obsession with a single mode of behavior. Moreover, since they are unable to help themselves, Hardy's world seems excessively cruel, even antagonistic to individual needs, a world in which chance becomes a malevolent rather than an indifferent force. Yet the savagery of Hardy's world—in which continued cruelty, pain, and suffering become the norm for his heroes and heroines—is merely a reflection of man's insignificance when he attempts to exert more force than he has or tries to function without self-understanding. Hardy's protagonist usually means well and is, as Henchard, basically decent. But his obsessions are clearly uncontrollable—like Gide's Lafcadio and Conrad's Jim, he must defy the restrictions placed upon him, and in his defiance there lies the stuff of his self-destruction.

Henchard's fixed behavior further strengthens the fable or fairy tale atmosphere that surrounds the narrative, with its seeming simplification of character development, and also becomes the substance of Hardy's anti-realism. The Fair scene itself, with its readers of Fate, its games of chance, its auctions of animals, its waxworks and peep shows and conning medical men, with its hag-like furmity woman, who, like a Fate from *Macbeth*, stirs her large pot, is a timeless symbol of man's irrational quest for pleasure in a grim world of expedience. Moreover, at a Fair, anything goes; normal behavior is no longer adhered to, and eccentricity can itself become the norm. In Freudian terms, the id can here triumph over (or force out) the censorship of the superego, and man's ego, his ultimate behavior, is deflected into cruel acts both to his loved ones and to himself. Thus, the relatively simple act of auctioning horses at the Fair becomes an unambiguous fore-shadowing of Henchard's sale of Susan, and the swallow circling through the tent trying to escape is an obvious reference to Henchard's desire to escape a marriage that he claims has bound him in penury. The Fair, then, assumes its traditional significance: a place where people are liberated from personal cares and freed from their daily burdens. Like the quickly curving swallow, Henchard is to fly from the tent alone.

Escape itself becomes, ironically, a form of isolation that Henchard can never avoid; and the sordid business at the Fair becomes the terms both of his freedom and his thralldom. When he sells Susan, that act is the only one in which *he* throws off another human being; the rest of the novel finds him 'being sold' and thrown off. Hardy remarks: 'Henchard's wife was dissevered from him by death; his friend and helper Farfrae by estrangement;

Elizabeth-Jane by ignorance' (p. 146). Moreover, Lucetta leaves him for marriage with Farfrae; the sailor Newsom returns to claim Elizabeth-Jane; the town itself casts him out as Mayor. Further, one part of Henchard is dissociated from the other, so that his personality is split, manifest on the surface as the sober part and the drunken part, but of course the division goes far deeper. Hardy evidently lacked the psychological equipment to analyze the double role that grips Henchard, although his artistic suggestion of the type is psychologically true. Conrad, in *Lord Jim*, likewise lacked the analytical knowledge, but he was able to create a 'true' type: in Jim, the split occurs between his romantic ideals and his realistic situations, and his tragedy is his inability to reconcile the two. Henchard's tragedy, similarly, is his inability to reconcile drunkenness (romance) and soberness (realism). The self-destructive Henchard cannot perceive that the latter preserves while the former destroys.

Henchard's isolation from himself is given nearly exact definition in Hardy's use of several overlapping scenes that both indicate his alienation and emphasize the element of fable. Man is split and isolated, first, by his juxtaposition to surroundings that dwarf his stature and diminish his spirit. In Chapter 19, for example, Henchard gazes at the cliffs outside Casterbridge and his eyes alight on a square mass of buildings cut into the sky. Hardy describes the bulky monument as a pedestal missing its statue, the missing element significantly being a corpse; for the buildings were once the county jail, their base forming the gallows where crowds would gather to watch executions. This passage occurs soon after Henchard was read Susan's letter telling him that Elizabeth-Jane is not his daughter, Henchard having recently tried to convince the girl that she is his. Then, after Henchard learns the facts, Newsom's daughter comes to him and says that she does accept him as her father. We recognize that the missing corpse is the doomed Henchard, caught between uncontrollable forces, one part trying to gain love and life, the other, unable to effect an attachment, caught by death.

This powerful scene in which the split Henchard foresees his own doom recurs in a different context when, after the cruel mummery, the despondent and suicidal outcast thinks of drowning in the river as a solution to his misery. The sight, however, of his straw effigy floating in the water—the same effigy that had horrified Lucetta and caused her fit—suggests his own death, acts out, as it were, a substitute death, and dissuades him. 'Not a man somewhat resembling him, but one in all respects his counterpart, his actual double, was floating as if dead in Ten Hatches Hole' (p. 360). The supernatural aspect of the sight impresses Henchard, and, ironically, the effigy, which in another way has helped destroy him, here saves his life. 'That performance of theirs killed her [Lucetta], but kept me alive' (p. 361).

'Supernatural' aspects of the fable further appear when man is enclosed in a historical setting that indicates his fate. The Roman amphitheatre at Casterbridge serves the purpose of a meeting-ground and at the same time frames the puny dimensions of puppet-like man against a mighty historical past. Henchard, who has been heroic amidst the townspeople, is now diminished by the immensity of the ampitheatre where he meets Susan; and their immediate problems, when viewed against the melancholy background, seem petty indeed.

This kind of scene recurs in various forms: it appears, as we saw, when Henchard gazes at the Franciscan priory with its gallows and missing corpse; it re-appears with intended irony near the end of the novel in the form of the pre-historic fort, Mai-Dun, where Henchard hides, telescope in hand, to spy on Farfrae and Elizabeth-Jane. The fort is described as 'of huge dimensions and many ramparts, within or upon whose enclosures a human being, as seen from the road, was but an insignificant speck' (p. 375). Here, Henchard, already in decline because of his personal losses, squanders even his physical dimensions, dwarfed as he is by the fort and made to seem still smaller by the meanness of his objective—to scan the Roman *Via* for the two lovers. Then the ampitheatre itself recurs as a meeting-place for Henchard and Lucetta, the successor to Susan; within the huge enclosure, her pathetic figure revives in his soul 'the memory of another ill-used woman who had stood there ... [so that] he was unmanned' (p. 301). As they meet, the sun rests on the hill 'like a drop of blood on an eyelid,' a half-closed eyelid which sees reality only absently, masked as the latter is by personal ambition and willful revenge. His strength drained, the once heroic Henchard finds his feeling for the woman turning from revenge to pity and disdain amidst the hugeness of their overwhelming enclosure.

Not only is man insignificant in relation to natural surroundings, Hardy suggests, but also in his contacts with uncontrollable human forces. The reappearance of the furmity woman, that Fate who reveals the iniquity of Henchard's past, indicates how limited his career can be once he has offended the order of the universe. Further, his reliance on the weather-prophet, a person deep within superstition, exemplifies Henchard's growing insecurity and also puts him at the mercies of a human interpretation of the uncertain elements. That Henchard should rely on a fabulous prophet, who, mysteriously, seems to be expecting him, demonstrates his recurring fears now that Farfrae opposes him. The 'hero' can no longer rely on his own devices and by taking counsel from a false prophet wills a destiny that will destroy him. The furmity woman and the weather-prophet 'destroy' Henchard on the fable level as much as Farfrae, Lucetta, Elizabeth-Jane, Susan, and the town itself nullify him on the realistic level. Split by the two forces, Henchard is indeed trapped.

II

Hardy had the poetic ability, as Lawrence did after him, to suggest the whole in every part, to bring into each scene a miniature of the entire work. This is particularly evident in *The Mayor of Casterbridge* where the structure is tight, the plot limited to essentials, and the main characters few. One recognizes the novel's stylization in the anti-realism of implausible events, in the somewhat evident symbolic patterns, and in the poetic evocation of characters and events. As Albert Guerard has pointed out, at the poetic and imaginative level, Hardy is capable of tragedy, although when he thinks philosophically he seems commonplace and his limitations become obvious. His finest scenes, consequently, are those in which 'pure thought' does not dominate, scenes which remain close to a fable tradition and can be suggested poetically rather than realistically.

Unlike George Eliot and Thackeray, whose obvious forte was realism, Hardy, like Conrad and Lawrence, was more at home when he could avoid a head-on realistic scene and, instead, evoke the conflict obliquely. He could, so to speak, be true to human feeling but not to human truth. Lacking the philosophical orderliness of George Eliot and Thackeray's uniformity of viewpoint, as well as the sheer vivacity of Dickens and Meredith, Hardy retreated to the oddities of life which determine man's frail existence. Thus, as we suggested above, his reliance on cosmic irony and the chance occurrences of implausible events bolstered his way of working; for a dependence on chance enabled him to touch his subject, as it were, from the side and gave substance to his oblique attacks upon complacency, deviation, and immoderation. Chance, in effect, was his weapon to strike through surface reality to areas where the poetry of man offers resistance to the drab starkness of a malevolent universe.

We can see, then, that certain short but powerful scenes fulfill Hardy's genius, although they may well seem peripheral or incidental to the unsympathetic reader. In Chapter 29, for example, Lucetta and Elizabeth-Jane encounter a rambling bull, whose uncertainty seems to be theirs as well as Henchard's. The bull proves to be dangerous, an old cranky one, and uncontrollable except by an experienced hand. It begins to pursue the two women, the air from its nostrils blowing fear over them, until Henchard runs up, seizes the stick attached to the nose-ring, and subdues the frustrated animal. How ironical the scene becomes! for Henchard is recognizably the bull, or at least suggestive of the bull first in its brazen fierceness and then in its flinching half-paralysis once a stronger force masters it. Henchard himself is literally imprisoned in a nose-ring of events, and the two women whom he saves are, ironically, the Furies who will not give him rest.

This kind of intense scene, otherwise ordinary, joins with several others of the same type to comment indirectly upon the main characters and to create an atmosphere of lost opportunities and muddled human relationships. Earlier, upon recognizing that Lucetta and Farfrae are lovers, Henchard is offered an apple by the nervous Lucetta, which he rejects just as she has rejected his proposal: both offers are based on deceit and both are to bring unhappiness. Then, late in the novel, the dead body of the goldfinch in Henchard's gift to the Farfraes is a sentimentalized but effective symbol of the isolated Henchard, his life snuffed-out, forgotten, and alone in the darkness. The selling-scene itself, which runs like a leitmotif through the novel—for it becomes the basis both of Henchard's potential salvation and his real destruction—contains the grotesqueness and expediency that are essential to a world that pays only lip service to the amenities of life. Similarly, the grotesqueness recurs in Henchard's fight with Farfrae; the declining mayor realizes that he cannot kill his rival, for at the moment of triumph he is struck by the sadness of his inhuman act in the past, and to think of killing Farfrae is to relive his former shame at the Fair.

This scene itself is duplicated by one shortly after. As Farfrae is defeated by Henchard at the height of his good fortune (as, conversely, the Scotsman had triumphed over the Mayor), so too Lucetta, at her peak of assurance, is trapped by the satirical mummery, which causes her death. Everyone closely associated with Henchard's past is tainted by his misfortune. Only Farfrae and Elizabeth-Jane can escape because they are outside Henchard's range and remain flexible: they can move *with* chance and defy the Fates, although Farfrae escapes death or serious injury only because Henchard is guilt-ridden. The tragedy of Lucetta, on the other hand, is the tragedy of any Hardy woman who seeks a clear path to happiness without the perceptive awareness of potential evil, and who tries to defy the precepts of a malevolent universe that demands obedience to its strict terms of behavior.

Henchard himself, confused by the pressures of the outside world, declines rapidly once he foregoes his twenty-year penance and returns to drink, his position in the town having been exploded by the return of the furmity woman. He honors the breaking of his oath, appropriately, with the recitation of verses from the 109th Psalm, to the effect that a wicked man shall lose his family, his riches, even all semblance of dignity; and, his name despised, he will be swiftly destroyed. Hardy evidently conceived of Henchard as an enduring Job, an inarticulate sufferer of destiny's wager, but one without the possibility of salvation through faith. Henchard, like Job, is caught amidst forces he cannot understand, caught among forces, however, created by the terms of his own character rather than those strictly imposed upon him. Therefore, Henchard's tragedy is potentially greater than Job's (he is closer to the Greeks than he is to the Hebrews), for his only salvation would be to transcend himself, an impossibility for one who is condemned to be destroyed.

All of Henchard's acts reveal a fatalism, as if he must drive himself until he falls. Thus, his seeming impetuousness in ignoring all advice is more than mere rashness or ill temper. It is the chief constituent of an innate need to debase himself, to act out a role that will ultimately diminish him. Nowhere more than in the scene when the obsessed ex-Mayor kneels to welcome the Royal Personage passing through Casterbridge is his growing insignificance stressed. Fortified by drink and carrying a small Union Jack, Henchard, wearing a brilliant rosette over his weatherbeaten journeyman garments, tries to regain some of his former glory without disguising his present misery. Advancing to the Personage, Henchard waves the flag and attempts to shake his hand, until, seized by Farfrae, he is removed forcibly. From the large-sized individual who struggled against powers he could not understand, Henchard here dwindles into the court fool, whose pathetic figure, however, causes not comedy but vexation and annoyance. Reduced from his former self and diminished by the blows of chance, Henchard allows his former employee to sweep him aside as a foolish meddler.

Nevertheless, Hardy's Henchard, although dwarfed by his natural surroundings, isolated by his townsmen, and made absurd by his grotesque acts, is still of heroic stature, evidently a nineteenth-century counterpart of an Aeschylean or Euripidean protagonist. Hardy had early recognized that Aristotle's definition of classical tragedy needed to be transformed or amended to suit present-day realities and wrote his own definition shortly after completing *The Mayor of Casterbridge*: 'Tragedy. It may be put there in brief: a tragedy exhibits a state of things in the life of an individual which unavoidably causes some natural aim or desire of his to end in catastrophe when carried out.'[4] Within these terms, Henchard, as well as Clym, Jude, and several others of low birth, is a tragic hero, frustrated and hindered by the very things he hopes to attain and blinded by the obsessive nature of his quest. Clearly, Henchard's flaw is, as we suggested, more than a rash temper; his whole character, Hardy is careful to indicate in his definition, is his fate.

His character, like Lear's, is of heroic proportions, although so molded that the vast energies are dissipated in foolish acts of pride and vanity. As an outcast, Henchard gains identification with a whole host of alienated figures, Oedipus, the Ancient Mariner, Lear himself, but, most of all, the Cain of the Bible, whom Hardy made the prototype of all outcasts. Once fallen from his eminence, Henchard, now no different from the 'naked' man who had entered Casterbridge nearly a quarter of a century before, leaves the town: '"I—Cain—go alone as I deserve—an outcast and a vagabond. But my punishment is *not* greater than I can bear"' (p. 379). Henchard's ordeal—all part of the universe's unconscious design—is a peculiarly nineteenth-century one even though Hardy carefully drew attention to its Greek and Biblical counterparts. True, Henchard is caught within the workings of a destiny he cannot understand, but he has committed a crime against the universe, the unnatural act of ridding himself of a family burden, and this while frenzied (drunk). Further, while his free will can work successfully within a certain sphere—only by sheer energy and drive has he become mayor, for Henchard is a man of small ability—it nevertheless is restricted to a line of action in which the whole person is not engaged. Still further, while the novel is sub-titled 'A Story of a Man of Character,' indicating that the emphasis is to be on man and on character, the definitive acts in the novel clearly derive from an area outside Henchard's control. A split individual, a mysterious universe, a misdirected will—all these elements help define a new type of nineteenth-century man.

If, once again, we compare Henchard with Adam Bede, we can distinguish sharply between two kinds of lower class protagonists and show further how Hardy was moving from the traditional matter of the novel. Adam is in the line of somewhat prosaic young men whose aims are restricted to what they can possibly attain. Imperfect in certain ways, these characters do not set goals that are outside their reach, and they display relative equanimity and moderation in their quests. Adam himself is by no means perfect, but his imperfections are of a kind that will provide only disappointment, not nullification. Moreover, the terms of his desires are themselves small and always bounded by the explicable. There is little in the world that Adam could not understand, George Eliot leads us to believe, provided he was mature and intelligent enough to extend himself. What is true of Adam is also true of Dickens' protagonists, Thackeray's middle-class gentlemen, Jane Austen's genteel provincials, and Meredith's romantic heroes: the world holds few secrets from those who would banish ego and vanity in favor of comon sense. Henchard's world is obviously quite different. While a simple frettish woman disappoints Adam, a whole series of re-appearing women seem to doom Henchard, and each time he fails it is almost always over a woman or related to one. Moreover, while imperfections of character are merely a sign of immaturity in Adam, they *constitute* the character of Henchard. While Adam has to go through an emotional ordeal in order to purge himself of his temper and to gain an insight into real love, the ordeal of Henchard is not a matter of development but of life and death, the ordeal of the tragic hero set back by phenomena outside his control. In addition, while Adam has to understand only visible things, Henchard must master invisible forces and obviously he cannot succeed, for he himself engenders several of the forces which help destroy him. Furthermore, Adam is the lower-class 'hero' who is *like* everyone else despite low birth, while Henchard is *unlike* anyone else—he is marked, like Cain, almost from the beginning, and marked he goes through the novel, a grotesque figure of wasted energies and misdirected will. Adam was not intended to be, and cannot be, a tragic hero, while Henchard could not be the center of a conventional love story or the protagonist in a dramatic narrative lacking tragedy.

George Eliot was interested in presenting the detailed grandeur of passions that Wordsworth considered 'incorporated with the beautiful and permanent forms of nature.' Hardy, also, was interested in the 'permanent forms of nature,' though not as something necessarily ennobling; rather, as a background for human tragedy and as a silent force supposedly indifferent both to man and to its own powers. Nature, like society, gives Henchard something to be isolated from, helping to define the terms of his alienation, while in George Eliot it brings about attachment and purification. This distinction is important, for Hardy turned the Victorian lower-class 'hero' into an unreasonable, guilt-stricken, and alienated figure who is denied even the saving powers of nature.

The seeming simplicity of Henchard's actions should not obscure Hardy's not so simple conception of his character. The grotesqueness and obsessiveness of Henchard's position—in several ways he is not unlike a muscular version of Kafka's K.—become more meaningful when we see that his tragedy, like K.'s, is played out against a relatively calm and imperturbable background. The townspeople themselves are under no pall of tragedy; even Farfrae is untouched by the deeper aspects of Henchard's position, as is Elizabeth-Jane, whose insubstantiality precludes her suffering too much. Susan, likewise, is too simple and flexible to suffer little more than shame at her position, and her early removal from Henchard would seem more a source of happiness than misery. Perhaps Lucetta suffers for a short time on a scale comparable to that of Henchard, but she, like Elizabeth-Jane and Susan, is not solid enough to transform suffering into tragic feeling. Only Henchard is tragic, only Henchard really suffers, and this emphasis helps convey his monumental anguish. His profile denominates Casterbridge, and even in decline he has size and scope.

Although Henchard is diminished by juxtaposition with the amphitheatre, as well as with the Roman road and the Chapel on the Cliff, he nevertheless gains identity from their massive impressiveness at the same time he is dwarfed by their grandeur. One is reminded here of that great scene in *Tess of the D'Urbervilles* (1891) in which Tess lies immolated on the stone slab of Stonehenge, the pretty dairy girl identified with a vast history of martyrs and victims. So too, Henchard gains in massiveness and substance through identification with his surroundings. Like many other Hardy heroes, together with several from Wordsworth through Lawrence, Henchard cannot be separated from the earth, which denotes both defeat and life to him. The spirit of place remains close to him: he works in the earth before coming to Casterbridge and dies close to the earth after leaving. He places his trust in the earth, and when it, like everything else, fails him, he willingly forsakes life.

III

The outline of *The Mayor of Casterbridge*, as befitting a tragedy, is quite simple, despite the several new incidents occurring in each chapter. Hardy himself was afraid that the demands of weekly publication, with the need to force an incident into each installment, would strain the credulity of the reader of the novel as a whole; but while the play of intercrossing incidents—especially those concerning the returned sailor Newsom—does seem overworked at times, the main profile is clear. Perhaps the very simplicity of the novel caused Henry James to call the author, 'the good little T —— H ——,' a remark that caused Hardy considerable discomfort.

The important elements, however, do stand out boldly, so boldly that

Joseph Warren Beach thought the spareness was closer to a motion picture scenario than to a novel. Yet fullness of development could not have been Hardy's intention, certainly not the fullness of *Tess of the d'Urbervilles* or *The Return of the Native*, both of which are longer novels with fewer single incidents. What Hardy evidently intended was a Greek tragedy appropriate for his own time. Certainly the formal patterns of the novel (although these elements are not necessarily its virtues) attempt the simple line of Greek tragedy, with the evident rise and fall of incident leading to the hero's recognition of his situation. Even the moral alienation of Henchard, which places him close to a twentieth-century 'hero,' finds its source in the isolation of Aeschylus' and Euripides' protagonists. Consider, also, the leitmotif of the furmity woman, together with the recurrence of themes of isolation, the reappearance of key people, the use of the weather prophet, the prevalence of classical architecture, the starkness of the landscape, the morbidity of Henchard's 'sickness,' the victimizing of the hero by women, the use of folk customs like the skimmity ride, the presence of the townspeople as a chorus, the aura of fatalism cast over the main character because of events lying outside his control, the inability of the main character to find happiness as long as there is a taint on his conscience—all these are a throwback to the chief elements of Greek tragedy now reproduced and brought to bear upon the novel, elements, moreover, that have become the common staple of the novel after Hardy.

Henchard is an Oedipus who instead of marrying his mother after twenty years remarries Susan after a similar lapse of time; in another way, he is an Orestes whose revenge is against himself, not his mother, for having killed a part of his own being. Henchard can never be free from himself, just as he can never be free from society. Often, the conflict in a Hardy protagonist is between social convention, which restricts, and the individual need to be free, which can never be fulfilled in the terms the individual expects. This conflict can take several forms, although rarely does Hardy shape it solely along the simple line of duty versus passion. Frequently, he complicates the terms of the inner conflict by showing that duty itself can be and often is degrading, while passion can as frequently lead to fear and insecurity as it does to personal happiness. Doubtless, Hardy changed the terms of the traditional conflict (especially strong in the Victorian novel) because they would, under certain conditions, lead to qualified happiness and heroization, both of which he felt falsified a tragic sense of life. As several critics have remarked, the criticism of Hardy during his novel-writing days was directed more toward his pessimism than toward his so-called sexual themes. Perhaps Hardy's readers would have more readily accepted Lucetta's happiness (after sufficient penance) than the cruel death that she must suffer. D.H. Lawrence, for instance, was outraged that Hardy killed off his 'living' characters and let the prosaic ones escape, and Lawrence, here, was not far from the general public's dismay at Hardy's lack of optimism. Hardy himself wrote in 1886:

'These venerable philosophers seem to start wrong; they cannot get away from a prepossession that the world must somehow have been made to be a comfortable place for man.'[5] Hardy suggests his own prepossession in the last line of *The Mayor*: 'that happiness was but the occasional episode in a general drama of pain.'

The frequent criticism is that Hardy as a counter to mid-Victorian optimism (or what passed for it) would not allow anyone to be happy who could feel deeply or think widely. There is some truth to this stricture, for Hardy had been strongly influenced by Darwin's work during his maturing years prior to his first published novel in 1871. The battle between man and nature, manifest in the mysterious and even malevolent power that determines the process of natural selection, becomes translated into a cosmic pessimism in which man is countered at every turn by antagonistic forces. Because man can never be sure of himself—like the Greek hero, he can be struck down at the peak of his success—Hardy's novels seem cruel. Henchard undergoes rebuffs that appear in excess of what his original crime demands, and his punishment appears more than what a basically decent man deserves. That Hardy will not give him the chance to recover after penance, a kind of resurrection traditional in the nineteenth-century novel, is evident in his relationship with Elizabeth-Jane. During his decline, Henchard has hopes of living closer to the girl: 'In truth, a great change had come over him with regard to her, and he was developing the dream of a future lit by her filial presence, as though that way alone could happiness lie' (p. 352). This passage is measured against a later one in which the girl, now married, rebuffs his attempt at reconciliation: '"Oh how can I love, or do anything more for, a man who has served us like this [deceived her about her real father]"' (p. 396). Thus, one of Henchard's few real acts of demonstrable affection is rejected out of hand, and rejected, moreover, by a girl now secure with a husband and a father. The cruelty here is unbearable for the reason that Henchard has been discarded by one who is solidly part of society, while, previously, his rejections had at least been at the hands of people equally insecure. Now, Elizabeth-Jane, respectable, cared-for, loved, confident, and youthful, strikes at Henchard's last vestige of dignity: he indeed becomes the dead goldfinch forgotten in the dark cage.

The cruelty of the main lines of the novel does help prevent a potentially sentimental tale from getting mawkish. Hardy, like Conrad, Lawrence, Joyce, and Virginia Woolf after him, was clearly reacting to Victorian sentimentality, although he did not evade it on several occasions when he was sure his audience desired tears. However, by imposing the starkness of Greek classical tragedy on an 1820's rural English setting, and intermixing that with a Darwinian cosmos, Hardy tried to avoid an excess of direct feeling. Nevertheless, he failed to recognize that Greek tragedy is not necessarily bleak and pessimistic but merely the working out of man's conflicts with himself or with his state and gods. He did recognize, though, that to approximate such tragedy he would have to manipulate much artificially in order to make his philosophy—one necessarily alien to the surrounding culture—work out consistently. The Greek tragedian could write with his entire culture behind him, while Hardy was generally isolated from the practices of his literary contemporaries and certainly from the beliefs of a dominant part of his audience. Therefore, we sense the strain, the need to impose consistency even at the expense of art.

The cruelty of Hardy's pursuit of Henchard is mitigated, if only partially, by the latter's stubborn resistance to forces that would soon have defeated a man of lesser stature. The mere array of circumstances aligned against Henchard—in this sense comparable to Job's ordeal—makes his struggle seem epical. Henchard's standing up to the onslaughts of chance incidents, each of which might demolish him, exemplifies his power of defiant endurance. When he declares scornfully, ' "But my punishment is *not* greater than I can bear," ' he seems, in his Promethean strength, to become as large as the forces which are attempting to nullify him. The fact that Henchard *is* tragic—that despite several excessive circumstances, Hardy is still able to convey a tragic sense—gives him a power beyond that of a mere mortal, who would appear pathetic, not Promethean. When Henchard has been defeated, one has witnessed the conflict of a powerful will with an implacable force, and his dying wishes give him the unearthly power of a maddened Lear, whose defiant cry of ' "Ere they shall make us weep! We'll see 'em starved first." ' should be the epitaph for Casterbridge's former mayor. Hardy wrote significantly in his diary just two days after finishing *The Mayor* his own epitaph on Henchard's struggle: 'The business of the poet and novelist is to show the sorriness underlying the grandest things, and the grandeur underlying the sorriest things.'

Henchard, we should remember, is a decent man whose early sins are not indicative of a cruel or ill-intentioned character, rather the mistakes of a man carried away by a frenzy he finds impossible to control. In his dealings in Casterbridge, he is particularly fair and honest. He willingly destroys himself by admitting the furmity woman's accusation in court, and his action in remarrying Susan is an attempt to do what is right even though no love is involved. Although Henchard is a primitive in his inarticulateness, he recognizes the need for a softer side at the same time he is unable to summon these feelings. He agrees, out of duty, to take care of Susan, Elizabeth-Jane, Farfrae, and Lucetta, feeling intimately only about Farfrae, who returns mere decency for the Mayor's compulsive need for companionship. Henchard, however, so dominates all relationships that he disallows any opposition; lacking love, which itself forces flexibility, he loses all hold upon humanity, including his own. His inability to love is equated to his self-destructive tendencies, and it is difficult to distinguish where each begins or ends. Consequently, Henchard often seems harsher than his character warrants simply because he smashes certain moral bonds by acting from duty rather than love. Moreover, Hardy appears to nullify him exactly as he, in turn, nullifies others by refusing them the deeper feelings that he himself is unable to summon. The disparity between Henchard's abortive attempts to be decent and the ill results of his efforts is the extent to which Hardy's philosophy precluded uncontested happiness.

The quality of one's happiness is determined by his flexibility and aims; if he can, like Farfrae and Elizabeth-Jane, remain outside any dominating obsession and live more by common sense than force of will, he will not be destroyed or even seriously injured. Hardy indicates that if one is an idealist—that is, one who tries to impose his will upon an antagonistic or indifferent world—then his exertions create a Promethean conflict leading to his destruction; if, however, one is a realist and does not attempt to change himself or the world, his chances of destruction are minimized. This pattern is not of course always true for Hardy's characters—Tess is an evident exception—but it does define the major figures of *The Mayor*.

Nevertheless, even to suggest that the other characters in the novel have individual lives is to see how far Henchard overshadows them and how much of *The Mayor* is his novel alone. To a much larger extent than either George Eliot, Thackeray, Meredith, or the later Dickens, Hardy used a single character to dominate his narratives. Even Becky Sharp fails to predominate in *Vanity Fair* to the degree that Henchard controls Hardy's novel, and we must return to *Wuthering Heights* to find a comparable figure, that of the all-powerful Heathcliff. We recognize that for Hardy the domination of the central character, even though he be an anti-hero, was another carryover from Greek tragedy, the nature of whose protagonist determined the nature of the drama. If the novel is, as Hardy believed, an outgrowth of events from a particular character who shapes them (except those things which chance controls), then the novel must be directed in its details by this single force. Thus, the events that help nullify Henchard are those that develop from his own character: he literally makes the world that first envelops and then squeezes him to death. The title, we note again, is 'A Story of a Man of Character.'

Hardy's use of the town, similar to George Eliot's presentation of Middlemarch as a comment upon the main characters, creates a chorus that is as malevolent in its gossip as it is a form of social commentary. Hardy took the Greek chorus as both a representation of public opinion and a force for warning the protagonist of excesses, and remolded it into an interfering group of townspeople who directly influence the protagonist's fortunes. Accordingly, the town is both public opinion and participant in the drama: its opinion is more than mere warning, it can force its way. George Eliot and Hardy realized that the town's opinion in a democratic age would entail more than mere commentary; with class mobility less restricted, the individual's business was no longer his sole concern: the individual now belonged to everyone. In *Middlemarch*, town gossip cuts through Bulstrode's hypocrisy and ruins his reputation, while in *The Mayor* the skimmity ride destroys Lucetta's hopes for happiness. In each, the town becomes a force for reliving the past, whose unwelcome recurrence is the basis for gossip and hearsay.

Both George Eliot and Hardy showed a sharp awareness of social structure, recognizing that the mighty (Bulstrode) and the outsider (Lucetta and Henchard) can each be destroyed by a demonstration of majority opinion, whether it be justified or not. Further, both use country customs, implicit in the chorus, as a way of trapping the urbanized characters, and by so doing remove the country from mere picturesqueness and take the romance from the pastoral. This is not to claim that George Eliot and Hardy forsake the picturesque quality of rural life—one need think only of the Poysons in *Adam Bede* or of the dairy workers in *Tess*—but it is to suggest that in their later work they discount the pictorial quality in favor of a more individualized comment. The farmer and his wife are no longer merely decorative; they now have sentiments that must be heeded and values that can upset those whom they oppose. Thus, the chorus of townspeople and farmers has come full turn; in a democratic age, it loses its aloofness and sense of cosmic justice. Now, it too is involved, and no one can escape its approval, condemnation, or interference in his personal life. The chorus, as Kafka's K. was to learn, can impose its will regardless of the individual's rights, more often than not sending the alienated protagonist into exile. Hardy's Henchard, then, is in some ways the English prototype of the twentieth-century's isolated hero, the dominating figure in a world suddenly inexplicable by human reason.

Hardy is important, therefore, not only intrinsically but also historically. If we compare him again with Jane Austen, Thackeray, Dickens, Meredith, and George Eliot and then with the nearest pivotal English novelist after him, Joseph Conrad, we can see how he has changed the nineteenth-century novel, although change in itself is of course no criterion of quality. Granted, obviously, that his major predecessors and contemporaries had each brought individual genius to the novel, it is nevertheless in Hardy that we find the first sustained attempt to examine new aspects of late Victorian reality and to probe into areas barely suggested before. In Hardy, almost for the first time, we have an author who is counter to the central tendencies of his age, what we can claim for Dickens and Meredith only marginally. Hardy recognized that idealism is a component of egoism, and that the true idealistic hero is not one who conquers or triumphs as Christ did, but one who can destroy himself in muddle and non-comprehension. Hardy was primarily interested in the stranger whose attempts to get inside society are self-destructive. Already, we recognize a world that is somewhat subversive and anti-social; Greek tragedy now serves modern sensibilities, and its external determinism is now internalized and seen as of man's own making. The stranger is indeed Promethean in his quest for a particular kind of truth, but the mere fact that he is a stranger is sufficient to doom him. In his perception of the great grotesque depths lying beneath conventional morality, Hardy, in *The Mayor of Casterbridge* and his other major novels, wrote a parable for our times. The lesson is that life itself destroys even when man is basically good.

Notes

1. Florence Hardy, *The Early Life of Thomas Hardy, 1840–1891* (New York, 1928), pp. 231–2.
2. Florence Hardy, p. 197.
3. *The Mayor of Casterbridge* (New York, 1922), p. 1. All further references will be to this Harper's Modern Classics Edition and will appear in the text of my paper.
4. Florence Hardy, p. 230.
5. Florence Hardy, p. 234.

174

Character and Fate in
The Mayor of Casterbridge

◆

ROBERT C. SCHWEIK

Perhaps the most compelling evidence of really fundamental inconsistencies in *The Mayor of Casterbridge* is to be found, not in those analyses intended to show that the novel is seriously flawed,[1] but in the startlingly divergent interpretations proposed by critics who have attempted to discover some underlying consistency in Hardy's treatment of the relationship of Henchard's character to his fate. Two recent discussions of *The Mayor of Casterbridge* exemplify the almost polar extremes to which this divergence can tend: as John Paterson has interpreted the novel, Henchard is a man guilty of having violated a moral order in the world and thus brings upon himself a retribution for his crime; but, on the other hand, as *The Mayor of Casterbridge* has been explicated by Frederick Karl, Henchard is an essentially good man who is destroyed by the chance forces of a morally indifferent world upon which he has obsessively attempted to impose his will.[2] The fact is that *The Mayor of Casterbridge* is capable of supporting a variety of such conflicting assessments both of Henchard's character and of the world he inhabits, and further discussion of the novel must proceed, I think, by giving this fact more serious attention. Hardy strenuously insisted that both as novelist and as poet he dealt with 'impressions' and made no attempt at complete consistency;[3] what is worth considering is whether or not Hardy put his inconsistency to any use and what, if any, advantage he may have gained by doing so.

The sacrifice of simple consistency in fiction can yield some important compensations, particularly in the freedom it allows a novelist to manipulate detail and aspect as a means of controlling and shifting reader attitude as the work progresses. It is possible to make a rhetorical use of elements whose implications will not add up to a logically consistent whole. Clearly such a rhetoric can serve the imaginative purpose of the novel if it is arranged to generate an initial image of life which is then altered by subsequent changes

SOURCE *Nineteenth Century Fiction*, vol. 21, 1966–7, pp. 249–62.

in the handling of character and event, and when the progress of the whole is such as to move the reader from one way of looking at things to another less immediately acceptable view of them. A novelist may meet his readers by providing a view of life which is socially orthodox, familiar, and comforting, then more or less deliberately shift his ground and, in effect, undertake to persuade his audience to adjust or abandon that view in order to accommodate some other less familiar or less comforting one. In such cases, it is not in the sum of its particulars but in the organization of their presentation that the novel will have its unity, and this, I believe, is true of the organization of *The Mayor of Casterbridge*.

The largest elements in *The Mayor of Casterbridge* are four relatively self-contained and structurally similar 'movements' of progressively diminishing lengths, roughly comprising chapters I–XXXI, XXXI–XL, XLI–XLIII, and XLIV–XLV. Each provides a variation on a common pattern: an initial situation which seems to offer some hope for Henchard is followed by events which create doubt, fear, and anxious anticipation for an outcome that comes, finally, as a catastrophe. Furthermore, in each of these succeeding movements there is a reduction in the scope of Henchard's expectations and a corresponding increase in the emphasis which Hardy puts both upon Henchard's anxiety for success and upon the acuteness of his subsequent feeling of failure. Much of our response to Hardy's account of Henchard's final withdrawal and lonely death depends, certainly, upon the cumulative impact of these successively foreshortened and intensified movements from hope to catastrophe; but the particular tragic response which *The Mayor of Casterbridge* seems calculated to evoke is also the product of other adjustments in detail and emphasis from movement to movement which have the effect of repeatedly shifting our perception of Henchard's character, of the kind of world he inhabits, and of the meaning of the catastrophes which he suffers.

The first and by far the longest of these movements (slightly more than half of the novel) falls into two almost equal parts. The opening fourteen chapters of *The Mayor of Casterbridge* establish a situation which seems to offer hope for Henchard's success. Following the brief prefatory account of Henchard's economic and moral nadir at Weydon Priors and his resolution to make a 'start in a new direction',[4] Hardy abruptly bridges an intervening eighteen years to reveal the outcome of Henchard's vow; and not only does Henchard reappear transformed into a figure of affluence and social standing, but events now seem to augur his further financial and social success: he gains the commercial support and personal companionship of Farfrae, effects a reconciliation with his lost wife and child, and seems about to find a solution to the awkward aftermath of his affair with Lucetta. Hardy implies, certainly, that Henchard has undergone no equivalent moral transformation; we learn that he is conscientiously abstemious, but is otherwise simply 'matured in shape, stiffened in line, exaggerated in traits; disciplined,

103

thought-marked—in a word, older', and what details contribute to our first impression of the new Henchard—his aloofness, his harsh laugh, the hint of moral callousness in his stiff reply to complaints about his bad wheat—tend to support, as Hardy remarks, 'conjectures of a temperament which would have no pity for weakness, but would be ready to yield ungrudging admiration to greatness and strength. Its producer's personal goodness, if he had any, would be of a very fitful cast—an occasional almost oppressive generosity rather than a mild and constant kindness (V).' Yet, an examination of the following nine chapters will reveal that it is precisely Henchard's fitful personal goodness that Hardy does emphasize. Henchard's consistent if 'rough benignity', his gruff friendliness and frankness with Farfrae, his concern for Lucetta, his efforts to make amends to Susan and Elizabeth-Jane, his determination to 'castigate himself with the thorns which these restitutory acts brought in their train', and his humanizing acknowledgements of his own loneliness and need for companionship—these are the most prominent signs of Henchard's character in chapters VI–XIV; they tend to minimize his earlier harshness, so that by chapter XIV, at the high-water mark of Henchard's apparent success. Hardy's bland comment that he was as kind to Susan as 'man, mayor, and churchwarden could possibly be' squares so well with the repeated evidences of Henchard's gruff personal goodness in action that it carries little more than a muted suggestion of stiffness and social pride.

The remaining chapters of the first movement (XV–XXXI) then reverse the course of Henchard's fortunes, and as Hardy gradually increases the sharpness of Henchard's disappointments and anxieties, he also arranges the action so that Henchard's frustrated wrath is vented with increasing vehemence and with more obvious moral culpability on persons who appear to deserve it less and who suffer from it more intensely. In short, the 'temperament which would have no pity for weakness' gradually re-emerges, and by the conclusion of the first movement it is again the dominant feature of Henchard's character. The first sign of this progressive deterioration in Henchard – his grotesque attempt to punish Abel Whittle (XV)—is almost immediately countered by a revelation of Henchard's previous charities to Whittle's mother and by the frankness he displays in his reconciliation with Farfrae. But as the action continues Hardy develops situations which manifest more and more clearly the vehemence and injustice of Henchard's conduct. A first petty annoyance at his loss of popularity turns gradually into the more clearly misplaced and unjustly envious anger which prompts Henchard to dismiss Farfrae and to regard him as an 'enemy'. It is in this context that Hardy supplies an often quoted authorial comment which broadly implies a connection between Henchard's moral stature and his fortune: 'character is fate', Hardy reminds his readers, and he pointedly observes that Farfrae prospers like Jacob in Padan-Aram as he blamelessly pursues his 'praiseworthy course', while the gloomy and Faust-like

Henchard has 'quitted the ways of vulgar men without light to guide him on a better way' (XVII).

The chapters which follow seem designed to illustrate this point, for as Henchard's harshness and pitilessness become more apparent, his fortunes decline. What begins in Henchard's impulsive desire for a 'tussle ... at fair buying and selling' (XVII) develops into his more desperately planned and culpably savage effort to destroy Farfrae's career, 'grind him into the ground', and 'starve him out' (XXVI). Henchard's turning on Farfrae is followed by his more cruelly felt coldness to the unsuspecting Elizabeth-Jane, who is the innocent victim of Henchard's anger over the ironic turn of events by which he has discovered the secret of her parentage. And, finally, in his last exasperated effort to best Farfrae, Henchard takes the still more obviously vicious course of wringing an unwilling promise of marriage from Lucetta by mercilessly threatening to reveal their former relations (XXVII). At this point in the action, Hardy reintroduces the furmity woman, whose public exposure of Henchard's past wrong to his wife not only helps to bring about Henchard's fall but also serves to reinforce momentarily the sinister aspect of his character which the previous chapters have made increasingly evident.

Thus, throughout the long first movement of *The Mayor of Casterbridge* Hardy uses both action and authorial comment to shift our impression of Henchard's moral stature in a curve which parallels his economic rise and fall. Nature and chance are repeatedly made to serve what seems to be a larger moral order in the world; Henchard himself comes to feel that some intelligent power is 'bent on punishing him' (XIX) and is 'working against him' (XXVII); and the course of Henchard's career might stand as testimony for the familiar and comforting belief that the wise and good shall prosper and the wicked and rash shall fail. Certainly there is almost a fable-like congruity in the sequence by which Hardy gradually brings Henchard back to something like his moral nadir at Weydon Priors just before public disgrace and bankruptcy come like a retribution and precipitate him to social and economic ruin. Hence, in spite of its really complex and ambiguous cause and effect relationships,[5] the first movement of *The Mayor of Casterbridge* does seem to exemplify the dictum that 'character is fate'; it does so largely because Hardy maintains a general correspondence between the changes in Henchard's apparent moral stature and the changes in his fortunes.

Henchard's fall marks, however, the beginning of another tragic cycle in the novel—a second movement which again opens on a note of rising hope that is followed by a reversal and a falling action which terminates in catastrophe. Hardy clearly intends to leave no doubt about Henchard's fate after the furmity woman has revealed his past: 'On that day—almost at that minute—he passed the ridge of prosperity and honour, and began to descend rapidly on the other side' (XXXI). But having predicted the imminent collapse of Henchard's fortunes, Hardy once more shifts the aspect in which he presents Henchard's character and career; and out of his account of Henchard's failure he contrives to establish a situation which seems to offer renewed hope. Thus he makes the court incident an occasion for a comment which puts Henchard's career in a more favorable light:

> The amends he had made in after life were lost sight of in the dramatic glare of the original act. Had the incident been well-known of old and always, it might by this time have grown to be lightly regarded as the rather tall wild oat, but well-nigh the single one, of a young man with whom the steady and mature (if somewhat headstrong) burgher of today had scarcely a point in common (XXXI).

Thereafter, Hardy stresses Henchard's generosity and integrity. We learn that it was the failure of a debtor whom Henchard had 'trusted generously' which brought about the final collapse of his fortunes, and the bankruptcy proceedings themselves serve to dramatize Henchard's scrupulous integrity as well as the finer instinct for justice which prompts him to sell his watch in order to repay a needy cottager. In short, Henchard now begins to appear in a character which seems worthy of the general approval of his creditors and the renewed sympathies of his townsmen, who, we are told, come to regret his fall when they have perceived how 'admirably' he had used his energy (XXXI). These signs of a hopeful change in Henchard's public reputation are followed in the next chapter by indications of a corresponding change in his private attitudes. Hardy suggests, first, the possibility of Henchard's reconciliation with Farfrae by a scene in which the kindness of Farfrae prompts Henchard to admit, 'I—sometimes think I've wronged 'ee!' and to depart, after shaking hands, 'as if unwilling to betray himself further'. This is followed by Henchard's reconciliation with Elizabeth-Jane, who tends him through a brief illness; and the result, Hardy remarks, is a distinct alteration in Henchard's outlook:

> The effect, either of her ministrations or of her mere presence, was a rapid recovery ... and now things seemed to wear a new colour in his eyes. He no longer thought of emigration, and thought more of Elizabeth. The having nothing to do made him more dreary than any other circumstance; and one day, with better views of Farfrae than he had held for some time, and a sense that honest work was not a thing to be ashamed of, he stoically went down to Farfrae's yard and asked to be taken on as a journeyman hay-trusser. He was engaged at once (XXXII).

Through the space of two chapters, then, Hardy repeatedly presents Henchard in ways which not only emphasize his maturity, integrity, and good sense but also suggest the possibility that he may now successfully accommodate himself to his new situation.

But in the following chapters there is an abrupt reversal, a second descending action, and what at first appears to be a second corresponding degeneration of Henchard's character. In rapid succession we are told that

Henchard has undergone a 'moral change' and has returned to his 'old view' of Farfrae as the 'triumphant rival who rode rough-shod over him' (XXXII); that Henchard's drinking has brought on a new 'era of recklessness' (XXXIII); and that 'his sinister qualities, formerly latent' have been 'quickened into life by his buffetings' (XXXIV). Certainly, the series of progressively heightened crises which follow depend upon and repeatedly dramatize Henchard's sinister potential for hatred and violence. But they do so with an important difference: previously Henchard's antagonisms have been checked by external forces; now Hardy emphasizes the internal compulsions toward decency and fairness which at critical moments in the action decisively frustrate Henchard's destructive intent. Thus the crisis which Henchard precipitates by reading Lucetta's letters to Farfrae comes to an unexpected conclusion:

> The truth was that, as may be divined, he had quite intended to effect a grand catastrophe at the end of this drama by reading out the name: he had come to the house with no other thought. But sitting here in cold blood he could not do it. Such a wrecking of hearts appalled even him (XXXIV).

Twice more Henchard brings matters to the brink of violence, and in each case the crisis is resolved when he is prompted by some inner compulsion to desist. In his determination to defy Farfrae and personally greet the Royal Visitor, Henchard presses the issue to a point just short of violence, only to be moved by an 'unaccountable impulse' to respect Farfrae's command and give way (XXXVII). This incident precipitates Henchard's attack on Farfrae in the hayloft; and once again, at the moment when Farfrae's life is in his hands, Henchard is so touched by Farfrae's reproachful accusation that he feels compelled to relent. Instead, he flings himself down on some sacks 'in the abandonment of remorse' and takes 'his full measure of shame and self reproach' (XXXVIII). What seems central to Hardy's characterization of Henchard throughout these crises, then, is that incapacity for callous destructiveness which repeatedly frustrates his reckless antagonism. Then, as the action continues through the events which culminate in the death of Lucetta, it is the frustration of Henchard's attempt to redeem himself which brings about his personal catastrophe. For Henchard is 'possessed by an overpowering wish ... to attempt the well-nigh impossible task of winning pardon for his late mad attack' (XXXVIII): he vainly attempts to save Lucetta's life, and finding himself unable to persuade Farfrae to return to his wife, he is brought, finally, to the point of despair:

> The gig and its driver lessened against the sky in Henchard's eyes; his exertions for Farfrae's good had been in vain. Over this repentant sinner, at least, there was to be no joy in heaven. He cursed himself like a less scrupulous Job, as a vehement man will do when he loses self-respect, the last prop under mental poverty (XL).

When we attend closely to what Hardy has been doing with Henchard's character in chapters XXXIII–XL, it is apparent, then, that although he exploits situations which depend for their effects upon our awareness of Henchard's potential for reckless cruelty, he in fact uses those situations to gradually strip Henchard of the features which earlier in the novel gave rise to 'conjectures of a temperament which would have no pity on weakness'. But more is involved here than a change of the aspect in which Henchard's character appears; there is really a marked change in tragic mode as well—a shift from that fable-like correspondence of fate and character which earlier in the novel seemed to dramatize a connection between Henchard's moral offense and a just retribution which followed upon it. Now something less than an ideal justice seems to govern the grim irony of events, unknown to Henchard, through which his decent attempt to return Lucetta's letters is turned to her destruction by the viciousness of Jopp and his degenerate companions from Mixen Lane; and what Hardy repeatedly dramatizes is Henchard's frustrated incapacity to find either the will to destroy or the means to win pardon. It is, finally, the failure of his well-intentioned acts which brings about Henchard's second catastrophe—that loss of self-respect which verges on despair—and in his second fall he appears no longer as a Faust figure but rather, in Hardy's new image, as a 'less scrupulous Job' and a self-tormented 'repentant sinner' who curses himself for the failure of his own redemptive efforts.

The death of Lucetta marks another major turning point in the novel and the opening of a third cycle from hope to catastrophe for Henchard. Shorn of other interests, he now begins to feel his life centering on his stepdaughter and dreams of a 'future lit by her filial presence' (XLI). By one desperate and unthinking lie he turns away Newson and manages for a while to persevere in the hope that he can fulfill his dream. But just as the furmity woman returned to ruin Henchard by her exposure of his past, so Newson now returns to expose Henchard's lie and dash his hope. But the parallel serves mainly to emphasize a difference, for Henchard appears in a greatly altered character, and Hardy's account of his loss of Elizabeth-Jane and his withdrawal from Casterbridge as a self-banished outcast is clearly intended to evoke quite another kind of tragic effect. Hardy now presents Henchard in a character so soberly chastened as to seem 'denaturalized' (XLII). He is reduced to suicidal despair at the thought of losing Elizabeth-Jane and to anxiously calculating what he says and does in an effort to avoid her displeasure—so much so, Hardy remarks, that 'the sympathy of the girl seemed necessary to his very existence; and on her account pride itself wore the garments of humility' (XLII). Hence, while he looks forward with dread to living like a 'fangless lion' in the back rooms of his stepdaughter's house, Henchard comes to acknowledge that 'for the girl's sake he might put up with anything; even from Farfrae; even snubbings and masterful tongue scourgings. The privilege of being in the house she occupied would almost outweigh the personal humiliation' (XLIII).

But it is not only Henchard's pathetic subjection to Elizabeth-Jane which Hardy stresses; he now directs attention to Henchard's conscious moral struggles (as opposed to those 'unaccountable' impulses which previously checked his drunken recklessness), and he makes increasingly clear that Henchard now thinks and acts with heightened conscientiousness. Thus, when Henchard is again prompted by his perverse instinct to oppose Farfrae, Hardy pointedly reminds his readers that in the past 'such instinctive opposition would have taken shape in action' but that 'he was not now the Henchard of former days'. Instead, Hardy portrays Henchard's struggle against his instinct: Henchard vows not to interfere with Farfrae's courtship of Elizabeth-Jane even though he is convinced that by their marriage he will be 'doomed to be bereft of her', and when the impulse returns, he rejects it as a temptation, wondering, 'Why should I still be subject to these visitations of the devil, when I try so hard to keep him away?' (XLII). At the same time, Henchard now suffers through moments of self-doubt and agonized casuistry in which, after the lie to Newson, his 'jealous soul speciously argued to excuse the separation of father and child' (XLI). The problem, Hardy suggests, continues to trouble him:

> To satisfy his conscience somewhat, Henchard repeated to himself that the lie which had retained for him the coveted treasure had not been deliberately told to that end, but had come from him as the last defiant word of an irony which took no thought of consequences. Furthermore, he pleaded with himself that no Newson could love her as he loved her, nor would tend her to his life's extremity as he was prepared to do cheerfully (XLII).

And, finally, when Henchard leaves Casterbridge, Hardy makes clear that he goes as a self-condemned man, hoping that Elizabeth-Jane will not forget him after she knows all his 'sins' yet assenting both to the fact of his guilt and the appropriateness of his fate: 'I—Cain—go alone as I deserve—an outcast and a vagabond. But my punishment is *not* greater than I can bear!' (LXII).

In view of the crushed submissiveness, remorse, earnest casuistry and conscious moral effort which have come to figure so prominently in Henchard's character, this self-accusation and self-imposed exile is certainly designed to impress us as excessively harsh. But by having Henchard accept an excessive burden of guilt and determine to bear it, Hardy does enable him to achieve a kind of expiation; and although excessiveness is certainly a constant in Henchard, in his third catastrophe we are brought to see in him a kind of excess which makes claims upon our sympathy in a way that his earlier excesses of moral callousness, antagonism, drunkenness, and frustrated violence have not. In short, Henchard now appears to suffer disproportionately, and he has taken on qualities of character which serve to justify on the moral level the pity and sympathy for him which Hardy evokes in other ways by emphasizing his declining health, his morbid sensitivity, his fears of 'friendless solitude', his character as an 'old hand at bearing anguish in silence', and his lack of friends who will speak in his defense.

The final two chapters of *The Mayor of Casterbridge* form a short coda which, on a still lower level, again involves a movement from hope to catastrophe—from that slightest of hopes which prompts Henchard to consider that he need not be separated from Elizabeth-Jane to the rebuke which leads to his second departure from Casterbridge and his lonely death. Despite its brevity, this fourth movement has the important function both of further shifting our perception of Henchard's character and situation and of establishing more explicitly the final meaning of his tragedy. Hardy describes Henchard's journey from Casterbridge to Weydon Priors as a kind of pilgrimage carried out 'as an act of penance'. There Henchard mentally relives his past and retraces the foiled course of his career; and from both Henchard's reflections and Hardy's authorial comment upon his situation there emerges a central point—that Henchard's present situation is a consequence of 'Nature's jaunty readiness to support unorthodox social principles'. For as Henchard grimly reflects on the 'contrarious inconsistencies' of Nature which have nullified his recantation of ambition and foiled his attempts to replace ambition with love, Hardy comments on another of those contrarious inconsistencies—that Henchard, as a result of his suffering, has acquired 'new lights', has become capable of 'achieving higher things', and has found a 'wisdom' to do them precisely when an almost malicious machination in things has caused him to lose his zest for doing (XLIV). Henchard does make a final effort to return to Casterbridge and ask forgiveness of Elizabeth-Jane, but now, in being condemned and rebuffed by her, it is he who is made to appear more sinned against than sinning. Even Farfrae, toward whom Hardy has been otherwise sympathetic or at least relatively neutral, is momentarily brought forward to contrast with Henchard's sincere repentance by being put in a hypocritical posture, 'giving strong expression to a song of his dear native country, that he loved so well as never to have revisited it' (XLIV), and, most significantly, Elizabeth-Jane comes to regret her own harshness and attempts too late to make amends.

It is in the last chapters of the novel, then, that Hardy emphasizes most strongly the disjunction between Henchard's moral stature and the circumstance which has blindly nullified his repentance, his recantation of ambition, and his new capacity for a higher kind of achievement; and in doing so Hardy seems intent on reversing the fable-like correspondence between character and fate which figures so conspicuously in the first half of the novel. If throughout the opening portion of *The Mayor of Casterbridge* both nature and the course of events seem joined in support of the reassuring belief that the good shall prosper and the wicked fail, the remainder of the novel seems designed to reveal with progressively greater clarity that the fable is false. At its conclusion we are told that Elizabeth-Jane has learned the 'secret ... of making limited opportunities endurable' by 'the cunning enlargement ... of those minute forms of satisfaction that offer themselves to everybody not in positive pain'. Henchard obviously has not learned that

110

secret, and, by contrast, he remains characteristically excessive and tragically mistaken even in his last acts—in 'living on as one of his own worst accusers' and in executing a will which bears testimony to his final acceptance of a terribly disproportionate burden of guilt. But at the same time, by having Henchard persist in these acts, Hardy continues to dramatize his acceptance of a moral responsibility which now tends to set him quite apart from—and above—the indifferent circumstances which has frustrated his effort and contributed to his defeat. It is appropriate, then, that *The Mayor of Casterbridge* should end with the reflections of Elizabeth-Jane, who has found the cunning to make the most of limited opportunities, as she gravely ponders the mysterious 'persistence of the unforeseen' in men's destinies and concludes that 'neither she nor any human being deserved less than was given' while 'there were others receiving less who had deserved much more'. Certainly that pointed distinction with which the novel closes—the distinction between what men deserve (which is a question of worth) and what men receive (which may be enlarged and made endurable by self-control, good sense, and cunning stratagems) is central to the final meaning which Hardy puts upon Henchard's tragedy; for although Hardy makes clear that Henchard fails ultimately because he lacks those qualities of character by which he might make the most of his opportunities, he clearly expects, at the same time, to have brought his readers to see that Henchard must finally be classed among those 'others receiving less who had deserved much more'.

There is, then, a marked contrast between that image of a morally ordered world projected by the long opening movement of *The Mayor of Casterbridge* and the more sombre, disenchanted vision of man's predicament with which the novel closes; and what is suggested about the relationship of Henchard's character to his fate by the first part of the novel is clearly inconsistent with the implications of its conclusion. Yet, considered rhetorically, such an arrangement probably worked to Hardy's advantage, for it enabled him to avoid abruptly confronting many of his readers with a view of life which would have sharply conflicted with their own assumptions and attitudes. Instead, Hardy first met his audience on the more readily acceptable ground of the moral fable; only after he had worked out Henchard's rise and fall on this level did he undertake to bring his readers to face the much more grim image of the human condition with which the novel closes, and even then the change was effected gradually, almost imperceptibly, by those various adjustments in detail and emphasis from movement to movement which I have attempted to trace in the preceding pages.

But, however rhetorically advantageous such an arrangement might have been, it need not be assumed to have been the outcome of a deliberate and preconceived plan. I think it more likely, rather, that the progressive changes which I have noted in *The Mayor of Casterbridge* came about in the process of its composition and were the result of Hardy's effort to develop his subject and to work out its implications. There is nothing really surprising in the fact that Hardy began *The Mayor of Casterbridge* with an action which strongly implied a connection between Henchard's moral stature and his fate; for, although Hardy had intellectually rejected the traditional belief in an ethically ordered universe, that belief retained a strong and pervasive hold upon his mind at the level of imagination and feeling, and certainly it shaped some of his most deeply rooted and habitual attitudes towards life.[6] But these attitudes remained at variance with his intellectual commitments, and the gradual shift in aspect and emphasis which takes place throughout the second half of *The Mayor of Casterbridge* suggests that, as composition of the novel progressed, Hardy began to exhaust the line of development which stemmed from his more immediate imaginative grasp of his subject and that thereafter he tended to reflect more deliberately upon the implications of Henchard's fall and did so within the framework of his consciously considered views on man's place in a Darwinian world. Yet it is important to note that even then Hardy's treatment of Henchard's character implies his continued respect for an older, pre-scientific conception of man's dignity and worth as a moral agent, and the conclusion of the novel seems to be as much an affirmation of faith in the transcendent worth of the human person as it is an acknowledgment of man's precarious situation in a blind and uncertain universe.

Notes

1. See, for example, James R. Baker, 'Thematic Ambiguity in *The Mayor of Casterbridge*', *Twentieth Century Literature*, I (April 1955) 13–16; Robert B. Heilman, 'Hardy's "Mayor" and the Problem of Intention', *Criticism*, V (Summer 1963) 199–213.

2. John Paterson, '*The Mayor of Casterbridge* as Tragedy', *Victorian Studies*, III (December 1959) 151–72; and Frederick R. Karl, '*The Mayor of Casterbridge*: A New Fiction Defined', *Modern Fiction Studies*, VI (Autumn 1960) 195–213.

3. *The Works of Thomas Hardy*, Wessex Edition (London, 1912) I, xii and xviii.

4. *Works*, Wessex Edition, V, ch. ii. All further citations are to this edition and are indicated by chapter numbers inserted parenthetically in the text.

5. Both Hardy's authorial comments and his handling of the action suggest that Henchard's first downfall is the product of a variety of interconnected causes, some related to Henchard's character (as he is variously prompted by instinctive antagonism, superstitiousness, Southern doggedness, disappointment, unconscious cravings, rashness, rivalry in love) and some more clearly matters of chance (coincidental discoveries, inopportune revelations, the vagaries of the weather): there seems, moreover, no way of establishing any clear causal priority among these.

6. I think that what Delmore Schwartz has had to say about the way belief is involved in Hardy's poetry applies, *mutatis mutandis*, to Hardy's prose fiction as well. See 'Poetry and Belief in Thomas Hardy', *The Southern Review*, VI (Summer 1940) 64–77.

175

On *Tess of the d'Urbervilles*

———— ◆ ————

DOROTHY VAN GHENT

It was Hardy who said of Meredith that 'he would not, or could not—at any rate did not—when aiming to represent the "Comic Spirit," let himself discover the tragedy that always underlies comedy if you only scratch deeply enough.' Hardy's statement does not really suggest that comedy is somehow tragedy *manqué*, that writers of comedy would write tragedies if they only 'scratched deeply enough.' What he says is what Socrates said to Aristophanes and Agathon at the end of the *Symposium*—that the genius of tragedy is the same as that of comedy. It is what Cervantes knew, whose great comic hero, Quixote, walks in the same shades with Orestes and Oedipus, Hamlet and Lear. It is what Molière knew. Even Jane Austen knew it. The precariousness of moral consciousness in its brute instinctual and physical circumstances, its fragility as an instrument for the regeneration of the will: this generic disproportion in the human condition comedy develops by grotesque enlargement of one or another aberrated faculty; tragedy, by grotesque enlargement of the imbalance between human motive and the effect of action. The special point to our purpose is, however, another: neither tragic figure nor comic figure is merely phenomenal and spectacular if it truly serves the function common to both genres—the catharsis; acting as scapegoats for the absurdity of the human dilemma, they are humanity's thoughtful or intuitive comment on itself. We return, thus, deviously by way of the kinship of tragedy and comedy, to the matter of 'internal relations.' The human condition, whether in the 'drawing-room of civilized men and women' or on a wild heath in ancient Britain, shows, if scratched deeply enough, the binding ironies that bind the spectacular destiny of the hero with the unspectacular common destiny; and it is in the internal relations of the art form, the aesthetic structure, that these bonds have symbolic representation. The aesthetic failure of the *The Egoist* is thus a diagnostic mark of a crucial failure of vision, a weakness and withdrawal of vision before the common dilemma and the common destiny.

SOURCE *The English Novel: Form and Function*, New York, 1953, pp. 193–209.

To turn to one of Hardy's great tragic novels is to put 'internal relations' in the novel to peculiar test, for there is perhaps no other novelist, of a stature equal to Hardy's, who so stubbornly and flagrantly foisted upon the novel elements resistant to aesthetic cohesion. We shall want to speak of these elements first, simply to clear away and free ourselves from the temptation to appraise Hardy by his 'philosophy'—that is, the temptation to mistake bits of philosophic adhesive tape, rather dampened and rumpled by time, for the deeply animated vision of experience which our novel, *Tess*, holds. We can quickly summon examples, for they crop out obviously enough. Before one has got beyond twenty pages one finds this paragraph on the ignominy and helplessness of the human estate:

> All these young souls were passengers in the Durbeyfield ship—entirely dependent on the judgment of the two Durbeyfield adults for their pleasures, their necessities, their health, even their existence. If the heads of the Durbeyfield household chose to sail into difficulty, disaster, starvation, disease, degradation, death, thither were these half-dozen little captives under hatches compelled to sail with them—six helpless creatures, who had never been asked if they wished for life on any terms, much less if they wished for it on such hard conditions as were involved in being of the shiftless house of Durbeyfield. Some people would like to know whence the poet whose philosophy is in these days deemed as profound and trustworthy as his song is sweet and pure, gets his authority for speaking of 'Nature's holy plan.'

Whenever, in this book, Hardy finds either a butt or a sanction in a poet, one can expect the inevitable intrusion of a form of discourse that infers proofs and opinions and competition in 'truth' that belongs to an intellectual battle-field alien from the novel's imaginative concretions. On the eve of the Durbeyfield family's forced deracination and migration, we are told that

> to Tess, as to some few millions of others, there was ghastly satire in the poet's lines:
>
> *Not in utter nakedness*
> *But trailing clouds of glory do we come.*
>
> To her and her like, birth itself was an ordeal of degrading personal compulsion, whose gratuitousness nothing in the result seemed to justify, and at best could only palliate.

Aside from the fact that no circumstances have been suggested in which Tess could have had time or opportunity or the requisite development of critical aptitudes to brood so formidably on Wordsworth's lines, who are those 'few millions' who are the 'like' of Tess? as, who are the 'some people' in the previous quotation? and in what way do these statistical generalizations add to the already sufficient meaning of Tess's situation? At the end of the book, with the 'Aeschylean phrase' on the sport of the gods, we feel again that intrusion of a commentary which belongs to another order of discourse. The gibbet is enough. The vision is deep and clear and can only be marred by any exploitation of it as a datum in support of abstraction. We could even do without the note of 'ameliorism' in the joined hands of Clare and Tess's younger sister at the end: the philosophy of an evolutionary hope has nothing essential to do with Tess's fate and her common meaning; she is too humanly adequate for evolutionary ethics to comment upon, and furthermore we do not believe that young girls make ameliorated lives out of witness of a sister's hanging.

What philosophical vision honestly inheres in a novel inheres as the signifying form of a certain concrete body of experience; it is what the experience 'means' because it is what, structurally, the experience *is*. When it can be loosened away from the novel to compete in the general field of abstract truth—as frequently in Hardy—it has the weakness of any abstraction that statistics and history and science may be allowed to criticize; whether true or false for one generation or another, or for one reader or another, or even for one personal mood or another, its status as truth is relative to conditions of evidence and belief existing outside the novel and existing there quite irrelevant to whatever body of particularized life the novel itself might contain. But as a structural principle active within the particulars of the novel, local and inherent there through a maximum of organic dependencies, the philosophical vision has the unassailable truth of living form.

We wish to press this difference a bit further by considering—deliberately in a few minor instances, for in the minor notation is the furthest reach of form—the internality and essentiality of Hardy's vision, just as we have previously considered instances of its externalization and devitalization. Significantly, his 'ideas' remain the same in either case. They are abruptly articulated in incident, early in the book, with the death of Prince, appearing here with almost ideographical simplicity.

> The morning mail-cart, with its two noiseless wheels, speeding along these lanes like an arrow, as it always did, had driven into [Tess's] slow and unlighted equipage. The pointed shaft of the cart had entered the breast of the unhappy Prince like a sword, and from the wound his life's blood was spouting in a stream, and falling with a hiss into the road.
> In her despair Tess sprang forward and put her hand upon the hole, with the only result that she became splashed from face to skirt with the crimson drops ...

The mail cart leaves, and she remains alone on the road with the ruin.

> The atmosphere turned pale; the birds shook themselves in the hedges, arose, and twittered; the lane showed all its white features, and Tess showed hers, still whiter. The huge pool of blood in front of her was already assuming the iridescence of coagulation; and when the sun rose, a million prismatic hues were reflected in it. Prince lay alongside still and stark, his eyes half open, the hole in his chest looking scarcely large enough to have let out all that had animated him.

With this accident are concatenated in fatal union Tess's going to 'claim kin' of the d'Urbervilles and all the other links in her tragedy down to the murder of Alec. The symbolism of the detail is naïve and forthright to the point of temerity: the accident occurs in darkness and Tess has fallen asleep—just as the whole system of mischances and cross-purposes in the novel is a function of psychic and cosmic blindness; she 'put her hand upon the hole'—and the gesture is as absurdly ineffectual as all her effort will be; the only result is that she becomes splashed with blood—as she will be at the end; the shaft pierces Prince's breast 'like a sword'—Alec is stabbed in the heart with a knife; with the arousal and twittering of the birds we are aware of the oblivious manifold of nature stretching infinite and detached beyond the isolated human figure; the iridescence of the coagulating blood is, in its incongruity with the dark human trouble, a note of the same indifferent cosmic chemistry that has brought about the accident; and the smallness of the hole in Prince's chest, that looked 'scarcely large enough to have let out all that had animated him,' is the minor remark of that irony by which Tess's great cruel trial appears as a vanishing incidental in the blind waste of time and space and biological repetition. Nevertheless, there is nothing in this event that has not the natural 'grain' of concrete fact; and what it signifies—of the complicity of doom with the most random occurrence, of the cross-purposing of purpose in a multiple world, of cosmic indifference and of moral desolation—is a local truth of a particular experience and irrefutable as the experience itself.

In the second chapter of *Tess* the gathering for the May-day 'club-walking' is described, a debased 'local Cerealia' that has lost its ancient motive as fertility rite and that subsists as a social habit among the village young people. Here Clare sees Tess for the first time, in white dress, with peeled willow wand and bunch of white flowers. But it is too late for him to stop, the clock has struck, he must be on his way to join his companions. Later, when he wants to marry Tess, he will tell his parents of the 'pure and virtuous' bride he has chosen, when her robe is no longer the white robe of the May-walking but the chameleon robe of Queen Guinevere,

> *That never would become that wife*
> *That had once done amiss.*

In the scene of the May-walking, the lovers are 'star-crossed' not by obscure celestial intent but by ordinary multiplicity of purposes and suitabilities; but in the submerged and debased fertility ritual—ironically doubled here with the symbolism of the white dress (a symbolism which Clare himself will later debase by his prudish pervisity)—is shadowed a more savage doom brought about by a more violent potency, that of sexual instinct, by which Tess will be victimized. Owing its form entirely to the vision that shapes the whole of Tess's tragedy, the minor incident of the May-walking has the assurance of particularized reality and the truth of the naturally given.

Nothing could be more brutally factual than the description of the swede field at Flintcomb-Ash, nor convey more economically and transparently Hardy's vision of human abandonment in the dissevering earth.

The upper half of each turnip had been eaten off by the live-stock, and it was the business of the two women to grub out the lower or earthy half of the root with a hooked fork called a hacker, that this might be eaten also. Every leaf of the vegetable having previously been consumed, the whole field was in color a desolate drab; it was a complexion without features, as if a face, from chin to brow, should be only an expanse of skin. The sky wore, in another color, the same likeness; a white vacuity of expression with the lineaments gone.

The visitation of the winter birds has the same grain of local reality, and yet all the signifying and representative disaster of Tess's situation—its loneliness, its bleak triviality, its irrelevance in the dumb digestion of earth—is focused in the mirroring eyes of the birds.

> ... strange birds from behind the North Pole began to arrive silently ... gaunt spectral creatures with tragical eyes—eyes which had witnessed scenes of cataclysmal horror in inaccessible polar regions, of a magnitude such as no human being had ever conceived, in curdling temperatures that no man could endure; which had beheld the crash of icebergs and the slide of snow-hills by the shooting light of the Aurora; been half blinded by the whirl of colossal storms and terraqueous distortions; and retained the expression of feature that such scenes had engendered. These nameless birds came quite near to Tess and Marian, but of all they had seen which humanity would never see they brought no account. The traveller's ambition to tell was not theirs, and, with dumb impassivity, they dismissed experiences which they did not value for the immediate incidents of this upland—the trivial movements of the two girls in disturbing the clods with their fragile hackers so as to uncover something or other that these visitants relished as food.

There is the same sentitive honesty to the detail and expression of fact, the same inherence of vision in the particulars of experience, in the description of the weeds where Tess hears Clare thrumming his harp. The weeds, circumstantial as they are, have an astonishingly cunning and bold metaphorical function. They grow at Talbothays, in that healing procreative idyl of milk and mist and passive biology, and they too are bountiful with life, but they stain and slime and blight; and it is in this part of Paradise (an 'outskirt of the garden'—there are even apple trees here) that the minister's son is hidden, who, in his conceited impotence, will violate Tess more nastily than her sensual seducer: who but Hardy would have dared to give him the name Angel, and a harp too? It is Hardy's incorruptible feeling for the actual that allows his symbolism its amazingly blunt privileges and that at the same time subdues it to and absorbs it into the concrete circumstance of experience, real as touch.

The dilemma of Tess is the dilemma of morally individualizing consciousness in its earthy mixture. The subject is mythological, for it places the human protagonist in dramatic relationship with the non-human and orients his destiny among preternatural powers. The most primitive antagonist of consciousness is, on the simplest premise, the earth itself. It acts so in *Tess*, clogging action and defying conscious motive; or, in the long dream of Talbothays, conspiring with its ancient sensuality to provoke instinct; or, on the farm at Flintcomb-Ash, demoralizing consciousness by its mere geological flintiness. But the earth is 'natural,' while, dramatically visualized as antagonist, it transcends the natural. The integrity of the myth thus depends, paradoxically, upon naturalism; and it is because of that intimate dependence between the natural and the mythological, a dependence that is organic to the subject, that Hardy's vision is able to impregnate so deeply and shape so unobtrusively the naturalistic particulars of the story.

In *Tess*, of all his novels, the earth is most actual as a dramatic factor—that is, as a factor of causation; and by this we refer simply to the long stretches of earth that have to be trudged in order that a person may get from one place to another, the slowness of the business, the irreducible reality of it (for one has only one's feet), its grimness of soul-wearing fatigue and shelterlessness and doubtful issue at the other end of the journey where nobody may be at home. In *Tess* the earth is *primarily not a metaphor but a real thing* that one has to moive on in order to get anywhere or do anything, and it constantly acts in its own motivating, causational substantiality by being there in the way of human purposes to encounter, to harass them, detour them, seduce them, defeat them.

In the accident of Prince's death, the road itself is, in a manner of speaking, responsible, merely by being the same road that the mail cart travels. The seduction of Tess is as closely related, causally, to the distance between Trantridge and Chaseborough as it is to Tess's naïveté and to Alec's egoism; the physical distance itself causes Tess's fatigue and provides Alec's opportunity. The insidiously demoralizing effect of Tess's desolate journeys on foot as she seeks dairy work and field work here and there after the collapse of her marriage, brutal months that are foreshortened to the plodding trip over the chalk uplands to Flintcomb-Ash, is again, as directly as anything, an effect of the irreducible *thereness* of the territory she has to cover. There are other fatal elements in her ineffectual trip from the farm to Emminster to see Clare's parents, but fatal above all is the distance she must walk to see people who can have no foreknowledge of her coming and who are not at home when she gets there. Finally, with the uprooting and migration of the Durbeyfield family on Old Lady Day, the simple fatality of the earth as earth, in its measurelessness and anonymousness, with people having to move over it with no place to go, is decisive in the final event of Tess's tragedy—her return to Alec, for Alec provides at least a place to go.

The dramatic motivation provided by natural earth is central to every aspect of the book. It controls the style: page by page *Tess* has a wrought density of texure that is fairly unique in Hardy; symbolic depth is communicated by the physical surface of things with unhampered transparency while the homeliest conviction of fact is preserved ('The upper half of each turnip had been eaten off by the live-stock'); and one is aware of style not as a specifically verbal quality but as a quality of observation and intuition that are here—very often—wonderfully identical with each other, a quality of lucidity. Again, it is because of the *actual* motivational impact of the earth that Hardy is able to use setting and atmosphere for a symbolism that, considered in itself, is so astonishingly blunt and rudimentary. The green vale of Blackmoor, fertile, small, enclosed by hills, lying under a blue haze—the vale of birth, the cradle of innocence. The wide misty setting of Talbothays dairy, 'oozing fatness and warm ferments,' where the 'rush of juices could almost be heard below the hiss of fertilization'—the sensual dream, the lost Paradise. The starved uplands of Flintcomb-Ash, with their ironic mimicry of the organs of generation, 'myriads of loose white flints in bulbous, cusped, and phallic shapes,' and the dun consuming ruin of the swede field—the mockery of impotence, the exile. Finally, that immensely courageous use of setting, Stonehenge and the stone of sacrifice. Obvious as these symbolisms are, their deep stress is maintained by Hardy's naturalistic premise. The earth exists here as Final Cause, and its omnipresence affords constantly to Hardy the textures that excited his eye and care, but affords them wholly charged with dramatic, causational necessity; and the symbolic values of setting are constituted, in large part, by the responses required of the characters themselves in their relationship with the earth.

Generally, the narrative system of the book—that is, the system of episodes—is a series of accidents and coincidences (although it is important to note that the really great crises are psychologically motivated: Alec's seduction of Tess, Clare's rejection of her, and the murder). It is [an] accident that Clare does not meet Tess at the May-walking, when she was 'pure' and when he might have begun to court her; coincidence that the mail cart rams Tess's wagon and kills Prince; coincidence that Tess and Clare meet at Talbothays, *after* her 'trouble' rather than before; accident that the letter slips under the rug; coincidence that Clare's parents are not at home when she comes to the vicarage; and so on. Superficially it would seem that this type of event, the accidental and coincidental, is the very least credible of fictional devices, particularly when there is an accumulation of them; and we have all read or heard criticism of Hardy for his excessive reliance upon coincidence in the management of his narratives; if his invention of probabilities and inevitabilities of action does not seem simply poverty-stricken, he appears to be too much the puppeteer working wires or strings to make events conform to his 'pessimistic' and 'fatalistic' ideas. It is not enough to say that there is a certain justification for his large use of the accidental in the fact that 'life is like that'—chance, mishap, accident, events that affect our lives while they remain far beyond our control, are a very large part of experience; but art differs from life precisely by making order out of this disorder, by finding causation in it. In the accidentalism of Hardy's universe we can recognize the profound truth of the darkness in which life is cast, darkness both within the soul and without, only insofar as his accidentalism *is not itself accidental* not yet an ideology-obsessed puppeteer's manipulation of character and event; which is to say, only insofar as the universe he creates has aesthetic integrity, the flesh and bones and organic development of a concrete world. This is not true always of even the best of Hardy's novels; but it is so generally true of the construction of *Tess*—a novel in which the accidental is perhaps more preponderant than in any other Hardy—that we do not care to finick about incidental lapses. The naturalistic premise of the book—the condition of earth in which life is placed—is the most obvious, fundamental, and inexorable of facts; but because it is the physically 'given,' into which and beyond which there can be no penetration, it exists as mystery; it is thus, even as the basis of all natural manifestation, itself of the quality of the supernatural. On the earth, so conceived, coincidence and accident constitute order, the prime terrestrial order, for they too are 'the given,' impenetrable by human *ratio*, accountable only as mystery. By constructing the *Tess*-universe on the solid ground (one might say even literally on the 'ground') of the earth as Final Cause, mysterious cause of causes, Hardy does not allow us to forget that what is most concrete in experience is also what is most inscrutable, that an overturned clod in a field or the posture of herons standing in a water mead or the shadows of cows thrown against a wall by evening sunlight are as essentially fathomless as the procreative yearning, and this in turn as fathomless as the sheerest accident in event. The accidentalism and coincidentalism in the narrative pattern of the book stand, thus, in perfectly orderly correlation with the grounding mystery of the physically concrete and the natural.

But Hardy has, with very great cunning, reinforced the *necessity* of this particular kind of narrative pattern by giving to it the background of the folk instinctivism, folk fatalism, and folk magic. If the narrative is conducted largely by coincidence, the broad folk background rationalizes coincidence by constant recognition of the mysteriously 'given' as what 'was to be'—the folk's humble presumption of order in a rule of mishap. The folk are the earth's pseudopodia, another fauna; and because they are so deeply rooted in the elemental life of the earth—like a sensitive animal extension of the earth itself—they share the authority of the natural. (Whether Hardy's 'folk,' in all the attributes he gives them, ever existed historically or not is scarcely pertinent; they exist here.) Their philosophy and their skills in living, even their gestures of tragic violence, are instinctive adaptations to 'the given'; and because they are indestructible, their attitudes toward events authoritatively urge a similar fatalism upon the reader, impelling him to an imaginative acceptance of the doom-wrought series of accidents in the foreground of the action.

We have said that the dilemma of Tess is the dilemma of moral consciousness in its intractable earthy mixture; schematically simpified, the signifying form of the *Tess*-universe is the tragic heroism and tragic ineffectuality of such consciousness in an antagonistic earth where events shape themselves by accident rather than by moral design; and the *mythological* dimension of this form lies precisely in the earth's antagonism—for what is persistently antagonistic appears to have its own intentions, in this case mysterious, supernatural, for it is only thus that the earth can seem to have 'intentions.' The folk are the bridge between mere earth and moral individuality; of the earth as they are, separable conscious ego does not arise among them to weaken animal instinct and confuse response—it is the sports, the deracinated ones, like Tess and Clare and Alec, who are morally individualized and who are therefore able to suffer isolation, alienation, and abandonment, or to make others so suffer; the folk, while they remain folk, cannot be individually isolated, alienated, or lost, for they are amoral and their existence is colonial rather than personal. (There is no finer note of this matter— fine in factual and symbolic precision, and in its very inconspicuousness—than the paragraph describing the loaded wagons of the migrating families:

> The day being the sixth of April, the Durbeyfield wagon met many other wagons with families on the summit of the load, which was built on a well-nigh unvarying principle, as peculiar, probably, to the rural laborer as the hexagon to the bee. The groundwork of the arrangement was the position of the family dresser, which, with its shining handles, and finger marks, and domestic evidences thick upon it, stood importantly in front, over the tails of the shaft-horses, in its erect and natural position, like some Ark of the Covenant which must not be carried slightingly.

Even in the event of mass uprooting, the folk character that is preserved is that of the tenacious, the colonial, the instinctive, for which Hardy finds the simile of the hexagon of the bee, converting it then, with Miltonic boldness, to its humanly tribal significance with the simile of the Ark of the Covenant.) Their fatalism is communal and ritual, an instinctive adaptation as accommodating to bad as to good weather, to misfortune as to luck, to birth as to death, a subjective economy by which emotion is subdued to the falling out of event and the destructiveness of resistance is avoided. In their fatalism lies their survival wisdom, as against the death direction of all moral deliberation. There is this wisdom in the cheerful compassion of the fieldwomen for Tess in her time of trouble: the trouble 'was to be.' It is in Joan Durbeyfield's Elizabethan dities of lullaby:

> *I saw her lie do-own in yon-der green gro—ve;*
> *Come, love, and I'll tell you where.*

—the kind of ditty by which women of the folk induce maturity in the child by lulling him to sleep with visions of seduction, adultery, and despair. It is in the folk code of secrecy—as in Dairyman Crick's story of the widow who married Jack Dollop, or in Joan's letter of advice to her daughter, summoning the witness of ladies the highest in the land who had had their 'trouble' too but who had not told. Tess's tragedy turns on a secret revealed, that is, on the substitution in Tess of an individualizing morality for the folk instinct of concealment and anonymity.

While their fatalism is a passive adaptation to the earthy doom, the folk magic is an active luxury: the human being, having a mind, however incongruous with his animal condition, has to do something with it—and if the butter will not come and someone is in love in the house, the coexistence of the two facts offers a mental exercise in causation (though this is not really the 'rights o't,' about the butter, as Dairyman Crick himself observes; magical lore is not so dainty); yet the magic is no less a survival wisdom than the fatalism, inasmuch as it does offer mental exercise in causation, for man cannot live without a sense of cause. The magic is a knowledgeable mode of dealing with the unknowledgeable, and it is adaptive to the dooms of exist-ence where moral reason is not adaptive to the dooms of existence where moral reason is not adaptive, for moral reason seeks congruence between human intention and effect and is therefore always inapropos (in Hardy's universe, tragically inapropos), whereas magic seeks only likenesses, corre-spondences, analogies, and these are everywhere. Moral reason is in complete incommunication with the 'given,' for it cannot accept the 'given' as such, cannot accept accident, cannot accept the obscure activities of instinct, cannot accept doom; but magic can not only accept but rationalize all these, for the correspondences that determine its strategies are themselves 'given'—like is like, and that is the end of the matter. As the folk fatalism imbues the foreground accidents with the suggestion of the supernaturally motivated; and motivation of whatever kind makes an event seem 'neces-sary,' suitable, fitting. The intricate interknitting of all these motifs gives to Hardy's actually magical view of the universe and of human destiny a backing of concrete life, as his evocation of the earth as Cause gives to his vision the grounding of the naturalistic.

The folk magic is, after all, in its strategy of analogy, only a specialization and formalization of the novelist's use of the symbolism of natural detail, a symbolism of which we are constantly aware from beginning to end. Magical interpretation and prediction of events consist in seeing one event or thing as a 'mimicry' of another—a present happening, for instance, as a mimicry of some future happening; that is, magic makes a system out of analogies, the correlative forms of things. Poets and novelists do likewise with their symbols. Burns's lines: 'And my fause luver staw my rose, / But ah! he left the thorn wi' me,' use this kind of mimicry, common to poetry and magic. When a thorn of Alec's roses pricks Tess's chin, the occurrence is read as an omen—and omens properly belong to the field of magic; but the difference between this symbol which is an omen, and the very similar symbol in Burns's lines, which acts only reminiscently, is a difference merely of timing—the one 'mimics' a seduction which occurs later, the other 'mimics' a seduction and its consequences which have already occurred. And there is very little difference, functionally, between Hardy's use of this popular symbol as an *omen* and his symbolic use of natural particulars—the chatter-ing of the birds at dawn after the death of Prince and the iridescence of the coagulated blood, the swollen udders of the cows at Talbothays and the heavy fertilizing mists of the late summer mornings and evenings, the ravaged turnip field on Flintcomb-Ash and the visitation of the polar birds. All of these natural details are either predictive or interpretive or both, and prediction and interpretation of events through analogies are the professions of magic. When a piece of blood-stained butcher paper flies up in the road as Tess enters the gate of the vicarage at Emminster, the occurrence is natural while it is ominous; it is realistically observed, as part of the 'given,' while it inculcates the magical point of view. Novelistic symbolism is magical strategy. In *Tess*, which is through and through symbolic, magic is not only an adaptive specialization of the 'folk,' but it also determines the reader's response to the most naturalistic detail. Thus, though the story is grounded deeply in a naturalistic premise, Hardy's use of one of the commonest tools of novelists—symbolism—enforces a magical view of life.

Logically accommodated by this view of life is the presentation of supernatural characters. Alec d'Urberville does not appear in his full otherworldly character until late in the book, in the episode of the planting fires, where we see him with pitchfork among flames—and even then the local realism of the planting fires is such as almost to absorb the ghostliness of the apparition. The usual form of his appearance is as a stage villain, complete with curled mustache, checked suit, and cane; and actually it seems a bit easier for the reader to accept him as the Evil Spirit itself, even with a pitchfork, then in his secular accoutrements of the villain of melodrama. But Hardy's logic faces its conclusions with superb boldness, as it does in giving Angel Clare his name and his harp and making him a minister's son; if Alec is the Evil One, there will be something queer about his ordinary tastes, and the queerness is shown in his stagy clothes (actually, this melodramatic stereotype is just as valid for a certain period of manners and dress as our own stereotype of the gunman leaning against a lamppost and striking a match against his thumbnail). Alec is the smart aleck of the Book of Job, the one who goes to and fro in the earth and walks up and down in it, the perfectly deracinated one, with his flash and new money and faked name and aggressive ego. If he becomes a religious convert even temporarily it is because he is not really so very much different from Angel (the smart aleck of the Book of Job was also an angel), for extreme implies extreme, and both Angel and Alec are foundered in egoism, the one in idealistic egoism, the other in sensual egoism, and Angel himself is diabolic enough in his prudery. When Alec plays his last frivolous trick on Tess, lying down on one of the slabs in the d'Urberville vaults and springing up at her like an animated corpse, his neuroticism finally wears, not the stagy traditional externals of the Evil Spirit, but the deeply convincing character of insanity—of that human evil which is identifiable with madness. Both Angel and Alec are metaphors of extremes of human behavior, when the human has been cut off from community and has been individualized by intellectual education or by material wealth and traditionless independence.

Between the stridencies of Angel's egoism and Alec's egoism is Tess—

with her Sixth Standard training and some anachronistic d'Urberville current in her blood that makes for spiritual exacerbation just as it makes her cheeks paler, 'the teeth more regular, the red lips thinner than is usual in a country-bred girl'; incapacitated for life by her moral idealism, capacious of life through her sensualism. When, after Alec's evilly absurd trick, she bends down to whisper at the opening of the vaults, 'Why am I on the wrong side of this door?' her words construct all the hopelessness of her cultural impasse. But her stabbing of Alec is her heroic return through the 'door' into the folk fold, the fold of nature and instinct, the anonymous community. If both Alec and Angel are spiritually impotent in their separate ways, Tess is finally creative by the only measure of creativeness that this particular novelistic universe holds, the measure of the instinctive and the natural. Her gesture is the traditional gesture of the revenge of insinct, by which she joins an innumerable company of folk heroines who stabbed and were hanged—the spectacular but still anonymous and common gesture of common circumstances and common responses, which we, as habitual readers of newspaper crime headlines, find, unthinkingly, so shocking to our delicate notions of what is 'natural.' That she goes, in her wandering at the end, to Stonehenge, is an inevitable symbolic going—as all going and doing are symbolic—for it is here that the earthiness of her state is best recognized, by the monoliths of Stonehenge, and that the human dignity of her last gesture has the most austere recognition, by the ritual sacrifices that have been made on these stones.

176

Colour and Movement in
Tess of the d'Urbervilles

◆

TONY TANNER

the discontinuance of immobility in any quarter suggested confusion (*The Return of the Native*)

the least irregularity of motion startled her (*Tess of the d'Urbervilles*)

I

Every great writer has his own kind of legibility, his own way of turning life into a language of particular saliences, and in Hardy this legibility is of a singularly stark order. If we can think of a novelist as creating, among other things, a particular linguistic world by a series of selective intensifications of our shared vocabulary, then we can say that Hardy's world is unusually easy to read. The key words in his dialect, to continue the image, stand out like braille. It is as though some impersonal process of erosion had worn away much of the dense circumstantial texture of his tales, revealing the basic resistant contours of a sequence of events which Hardy only has to point to to make us see—like ancient marks on a barren landscape. And Hardy above all does make us see. Just as he himself could not bear to be touched, so he does not 'touch' the people and things in his tales, does not interfere with them or absorb them into his own sensibility. When he says in his introduction to *Tess of the d'Urbervilles* that 'a novel is an impression, not an argument', or in his introduction to *Jude the Obscure* that 'like former productions of this pen, *Jude the Obscure* is simply an endeavour to give shape and coherence to a series of seemings, or personal impressions', we should give full stress to the idea of something seen but not tampered with, some thing scrupulously watched in its otherness, something perceived but not made over. Hardy's famous, or notorious, philosophic broodings and asides are part of his reactions as a watcher, but they never give the impression of violating the people and objects of which his tale is composed. Reflection and

SOURCE *Critical Quarterly*, 10, Autumn 1968.

perception are kept separate (in Lawrence they often tend to merge), and those who complain about the turgidity of his thoughts may be overlooking the incomparable clarity of his eyes.

II

This illusion that the tale exists independently of Hardy's rendering of it *is* of course only an illusion, but it testifies to art of a rather special kind. For all Henry James's scrupulous indirectness, Hardy's art is more truly impersonal. He goes in for graphic crudities of effect which James would have scorned, yet, as other critics have testified, the result is an anonymity which we more commonly associate with folk-tale, or the ballads. By graphic crudity of effect I am referring, for instance, to such moments as when Tess, shortly after being seduced, encounters a man who is writing in large letters 'THY, DAMNATION, SLUMBERETH, NOT.' There are commas between every word 'as if to give pause while that word was driven well home to the reader's heart'. This is not unlike Hardy's own art which is full of prominent notations, and emphatic pauses which temporarily isolate, and thus vivify, key incidents and objects. On the level of everyday plausibility and probability it is too freakish a chance which brings Tess and the painted words together at this point. In the vast empty landscapes of Hardy's world, peoples' paths cross according to some more mysterious logic—that same imponderable structuring of things in time which brought the *Titanic* and the iceberg together at one point in the trackless night sea. (See the poem 'The Convergence of the Twain'.) A comparable 'crudity' is discernible in the characterisation which is extremely schematic, lacking in all the minute mysteries of individual uniqueness which a writer like James pursued. *Angel* Clare is indeed utterly ethereal; his love is 'more spiritual than animal'. He even plays the harp! On the other hand Alec d'Urberville is almost a stage villain with his 'swarthy complexion ... full lips ... well-groomed black moustache with curled points', his cigars and his rakish way with his fast spring-cart. If we turn from character to plot sequence we see at once that the overall architecture of the novel is blocked out with massive simplicity in a series of balancing phases— The Maiden, Maiden No More: The Rally, The Consequence; and so on. Let it be conceded at once that Hardy's art is not subtle in the way that James and many subsequent writers are subtle. Nevertheless I think it is clear that Hardy derives his great power from that very 'crudity' which, in its impersonal indifference to plausibility and rational cause and effect, enhances the visibility of the most basic lineaments of the tale.

III

I want first to concentrate on one series of examples which show how this manifest visibility works. For an artist as visually sensitive as Hardy, colour is of the first importance and significance, and there is one colour which literally catches the eye, and is meant to catch it, throughout the book. This colour is red, the colour of blood, which is associated with Tess from first to last. It dogs her, disturbs her, destroys her. She is full of it, she spills it, she loses it. Watching Tess's life we begin to see that her destiny is nothing more or less than the colour red. The first time we (and Angel) see Tess, in the May dance with the other girls, she stands out. How? They are all in white except that Tess 'wore a red ribbon in her hair, and was the only one of the white company who would boast of such a pronounced adornment'. Tess is marked, even from the happy valley of her birth and childhood. The others are a semi-anonymous mass; Tess already had that heightened legibility, that eye-taking prominence which suggests that she has in some mysterious way been singled out. And the red stands out because it is on a pure white background. In that simple scene and colour contrast is the embryo of the whole book and all that happens in it.

This patterning of red and white is often visible in the background of the book. For instance 'The ripe hue of the red and dun kine absorbed the evening sunlight, which the white-coated animals returned to the eye in rays almost dazzling, even at the distant elevation on which she stood.' This dark red and dazzling white is something seen, it is something there; it is an effect on the retina, it is a configuration of matter. In looking at this landscape Tess in fact is seeing the elemental mixture which conditions her own existence. In the second chapter Tess is described as 'a mere vessel of emotion un-tinctured by experience'. The use of the word 'untinctured' may at first seem surprising; we perhaps tend to think of people being shaped by experience rather than coloured by it—yet the use of a word connected with dye and paint is clearly intentional. In her youth Tess is often referred to as a 'white shape'—almost more as a colour value in a landscape than a human being. And on the night of her rape she is seen as a 'white muslin figure' sleeping on a pile of dead leaves; her 'beautiful feminine tissue' is described as 'practically blank as snow'. The historic precedent for what is to happen to this vulnerable white shape is given at the start when we read that 'the Vale was known in former times as the Forest of White Hart, from a curious legend of King Henry III's reign, in which the killing by a certain Thomas de la Lynd of a beautiful white hart which the king had run down and spared, was made the occasion of a heavy fine'. Against all social injunctions, white harts are brought down. And in Tess's case the 'tincturing'—already prefigured in the red ribbon—starts very early.

The next omen—for even that harmless ribbon is an omen in this world—occurs when Tess drives the hives to market when her father is too drunk to do the job. When she sets out the road is still in darkness. Tess drifts, sleeps, dreams. Then there is the sudden collision and she wakes to find that Prince, their horse, has been killed by another cart.

> The pointed shaft of the cart had entered the breast of the unhappy Prince like a sword, and from the wound his life's blood was spouting in a stream and falling with a hiss on the road. In her despair Tess sprang forward and put her hand upon the hole, with the only result that she became splashed from face to

skirt with the crimson drops. Then she stood helplessly looking on. Prince also stood firm and motionless as long as he could, till he suddenly sank down in a heap.

It is possible to say different things about this passage. On one level the death of the horse means that the family is destitute, which means in turn that Tess will have to go begging to the d'Urbervilles. Thus, it is part of a rough cause and effect economic sequence. But far more graphic, more disturbing and memorable, is the image of the sleeping girl on the darkened road, brutally awakened and desperately trying to staunch a fatal puncture, trying to stop the blood which cannot be stopped and only getting drenched in its powerful spurts. It adumbrates the loss of her virginity, for she, too, will be brutally pierced on a darkened road far from home; and once the blood of her innocence has been released, she too, like the stoical Prince, will stay upright as long as she can until, all blood being out, she will sink down suddenly in a heap. Compressed in that one imponderable scene we can see her whole life.

After this Tess is constantly encountering the colour red—if not literal blood, manifold reminders of it. When she approaches the d'Urberville house we read: 'It was of recent erection—indeed almost new—and of the same rich red colour that formed such a contrast with the evergreens of the lodge.' And the corner of the house 'rose like a geranium bloom against the subdued colours around'. Tess, with her red ribbon, also stood out against 'the subdued colours around'. Mysteriously, inevitably, this house will play a part in her destiny. And if this red house contains her future rapist, so it is another red house which contains her final executioner, for the prison where she is hanged is 'a large red-brick building'. Red marks the house of sex and death. When first she has to approach the leering, smoking Alec d'Urberville, he forces roses and strawberries on her, pushing a strawberry into her mouth, pressing the roses into her bosom. Hardy, deliberately adding to the legibility I am describing, comments that d'Urberville is one 'who stood fair to be the blood-red ray in the spectrum of her young life'. On the evening of the rape, Tess is first aware of d'Urberville's presence at the dance when she sees 'the red coal of a cigar'. This is too clearly phallic to need comment, but it is worth pointing out that, from the first, d'Urberville seems to have the power of reducing Tess to a sort of trance-like state, he envelops her in a 'blue narcotic haze' of which his cigar smoke is the most visible emblem. On the night of the rape, at the dance, everything is in a 'mist', like 'illuminated smoke'; there is a 'floating, fusty *débris* of peat and hay' stirred up as 'the panting shapes spun onwards'. Everything together seems to form 'a sort of vegeto-human pollen'. In other words it becomes part of a basic natural process in which Tess is caught up simply by being alive. fecund and female. D'Uberville is that figure, that force, at the heart of the haze, the mist, the smoke, waiting to claim her when the dance catches her up (we first saw her at a dance and she can scarcely avoid being drawn in). It is in a brilliant continuation of this blurred narcotic atmosphere that Hardy has the rape take place in a dense fog, while Tess is in a deep sleep. Consciousness and perception are alike engulfed and obliterated. When Tess first leaves d'Urberville's house she suddenly wakes up to find that she is covered in roses; while removing them a thorn from a remaining rose pricks her chin. 'Like all the cottagers in Blackmoor Vale, Tess was steeped in fancies and prefigurative superstitions; she thought this an ill omen.' The world of the book is indeed a world of omens (*not* symbols) in which things and events echo and connect in patterns deeper than lines of rational cause and effect. Tess takes it as an omen when she starts to bleed from the last rose pressed on her by Alec. She is right; for later on she will again wake up to find that he has drawn blood—in a way which determines her subsequent existence.

After the rape we are still constantly seeing the colour red. The man who writes up the words promising damnation is carrying 'a tin pot of red paint in his hand'. As a result 'these vermilion words shone forth'. Shortly after, when Tess is back at home, Hardy describes a sunrise in which the sun 'broke through chinks of cottage shutters, throwing stripes like red-hot pokers upon cupboards, chests of drawers, and other furniture within'. (The conjunction of sun-light and redness is a phenomenon I will return to.) And Hardy goes on: 'But of all ruddy things that morning the brightest were two broad arms of painted wood ... forming the revolving Maltese cross of the reaping-machine.' We will later see Tess virtually trapped and tortured on a piece of red machinery, and her way will take her past several crosses until she finds her own particular sacrificial place. When Tess is working in the fields her flesh again reveals its vulnerability. 'A bit of her naked arm is visible between the buff leather of the gauntlet and the sleeve of her gown; and as the day wears on its feminine smoothness becomes scarified by the stubble, and bleeds.' Notice the shift to the present tense: Hardy makes us look at the actual surfaces—the leather, the sleeve, the flesh, the blood. One of the great strengths of Hardy is that he knew, and makes us realise, just how very much the surfaces of things mean.

Of course it is part of the whole meaning of the book that there is as much red inside Tess as outside her. Both the men who seek to possess her see it. When Tess defies d'Urberville early on, she speaks up at him, 'revealing the red and ivory of her mouth'; while when Angel watches her unawares, 'she was yawning, and he saw the red interior of her mouth as if it had been a snakes's'. When Angel does just kiss her arm, and he kisses the inside vein, we read that she was such a 'sheaf of susceptibilities' that 'her blood (was) driven to her finger ends'. Tess does not so much act as re-act. She would be content to be passive, but something is always disturbing her blood, and all but helplessly she submits to the momentums of nature in which, by her very constitution, she is necessarily involved. As for example when she is drawn by Angel's music 'like a fascinated bird' and she makes her way through, once again, a misty atmosphere ('mists of pollen') of uncontrollable swarming fertility and widespread insemination. It is a place of growth, though not wholly a place of beauty. There are 'tall blooming weeds' giving off 'offensive smells' and some of the weeds are a bright 'red'.

> She went stealthily as a cat through this profusion of growth, gathering cuckoo-spittle on her skirts, cracking snails that were underfoot, staining her hands with thistle-milk and slugslime, and rubbing off upon her naked arms sticky blights which though snow-white on the apple-tree trunks, made *madder* stains on her skin … (my italics).

In some of the earlier editions (certainly up to the 1895 edition) that final phrase was 'blood-red stains on her skin'; only later did Hardy change 'blood-red' to 'madder', a crimson dye made from a climbing plant. This change clearly reveals that he intended us once again to see Tess's arm marked with red, though he opted for a word which better suggested something in nature staining, 'tincturing', Tess as she pushes on through 'this profusion of growth'. And once again Hardy presents us with redness and snow-whiteness in the same scene—indeed, in the same plant.

After Tess has been abandoned by Angel and she has to renew her endless journeying the red omens grow more vivid, more violent. She seeks shelter one night under some bushes and when she wakes up:

> Under the trees several pheasants lay about, their rich plumage dabbled with blood; some were dead, some feebly twitching a wing, some staring up at the sky, some pulsating quickly, some contorted, some stretched out—all of them writhing in agony, except for the fortunate ones whose torture had ended during the night by the inability of nature to bear more.

There is much that is horribly apposite for Tess in these bloody writhings. (It is worth noting that Hardy uses the same word to describe the torments of the onset of sexual impulse; thus he describes the sleeping girls at Talbothays who are all suffering from 'hopeless passion'. 'They writhed feverishly under the oppressiveness of an emotion thrust on them by cruel Nature's law—an emotion which they had neither expected nor desired.' The writhings of life are strangely similar to the writhings of death.) Looking at the dying birds Tess reprimands herself for feeling self-pity, saying 'I be not mangled, and I be not bleeding'. But she will be both, and she too, will have to endure until she reaches 'the inability of nature to bear more'. Like the white hart and the pheasants she is a hunted animal; hunted not really by a distinct human individual, but by ominous loitering presences like the cruel gun-men she used to glimpse stalking through the woods and bushes—a male blood-letting force which is abroad. Later when she makes her fruitless trek to Angel's parents she sees 'a piece of blood-stained paper, caught up from some meat-buyer's dustheap, beat up and down the road without the gate; too flimsy to rest, too heavy to fly away, and a few straws to keep it company'. It is another deliberate omen. Tess, too, is blood-stained, she, too, is beat up and down the road without the gate; too flimsy to rest, too heavy no door opens to her; and she, too, very exactly, is too flimsy to rest, too heavy to fly away. (cf. Eustacia Vye's envy of the heron. 'Up in the zenith where he was seemed a free and happy place, away from all contact with the earthly ball to which she was pinioned; and she wished that she could arise uncrushed from its surface and fly as he flew then.') The blood-stained piece of paper is not a clumsy symbol; it is one of a number of cumulative omens. When Alec d'Urberville renews his pressure on Tess, at one point she turns and slashes him across the face with her heavy leather gauntlet. 'A scarlet oozing appeared where her blow had alighted and in a moment the blood began dropping from his mouth upon the straw.' (Notice again the conjunction of blood and straw.) The man who first made her bleed now stands bleeding from the lips. Blood has blood, and it will have more blood. We need only to see the scene—there, unanalysed, un-explained; a matter of violent movement, sudden compulsions. Hardy spends more time describing the glove than attempting to unravel the hidden thoughts of these starkly confronted human beings. Few other writers can so make us feel that the world is its own meaning—and mystery, requiring no interpretative gloss. Seeing the heavy glove, the sudden blow, the dripping blood, we see all we need to see.

At one point shortly before her marriage, Tess comes into proximity with a railway engine. 'No object could have looked more foreign to the gleaming cranks and wheels than this unsophisticated girl, with the round bare arms....' This feeling that her vulnerable flesh is somehow menaced by machinery is realised when she is later set to work on that 'insatiable swallower', the relentless threshing machine. It is a bright red machine, and the 'immense stack of straw' which it is turning out is seen as 'the *faeces* of the same buzzing red glutton'. Tess is 'the only woman whose place was upon the machine so as to be shaken bodily by its spinning'. She is beaten into a 'stupefied reverie in which her arm worked on independently of her consciousness' (this separation, indeed severance, of consciousness and body is a crucial part of Tess's experience). Whenever she looks up 'she beheld always the great upgrown straw-stack, with the men in shirt-sleeves upon it, against the grey north sky; in front of it the long red elevator like a Jacob's ladder, on which a perpetual stream of threshed straw ascended ...' There it is. We see Tess, trapped and stupefied in the cruel red man-made machine. Whenever she looks up in her trance of pain and weariness she sees—the long red elevator, the growing heap of straw, the men at work against the grey sky. It is a scene which is, somehow, her life: the men, the movement, the redness, the straw (blood and straw seem almost to be the basic materials of existence in the book—the vital pulsating fluid, and the dry, dead stalks). At the end of the day she is as a 'bled calf'. We do not need any enveloping and aiding words; only the legibility of vibrant, perceived detail.

The end of the book is sufficiently well known, but it is worth pointing out how Hardy continues to bring the colour red in front of our eyes. The land-lady who peeps through the keyhole during Tess's anguish when Angel has returned reports that, 'her lips were bleeding from the clench of her teeth

131

upon them'. It is the landlady who sees 'the oblong white ceiling, with this scarlet blot in the midst', which is at once the evidence of the murder and the completion of a life which also started with a red patch on a white back-ground, only then it was simply a ribbon on a dress. The blood stain on the ceiling has 'the appearance of a gigantic ace of hearts'. In that shape of the heart, sex and death are merged in utmost legibility. After this we hardly need to see the hanging. It is enough that we see Tess climb into a vast bed with 'crimson damask hangings', not indeed in a home, for she has no home, but in an empty house to be 'Let Furnished'. And in that great crimson closed-in bed she finds what she has wanted for so long—rest and peace. Apart from the last scene at Stonehenge, we can say that at this point the crimson curtains do indeed fall on Tess; for if she was all white at birth, she is to be all red at death. The massed and linking red omens have finally closed in on Tess and her wanderings are over.

Tess is a 'pure woman' as the subtitle, which caused such outrage, specifi-cally says. The purest woman contains tides of blood (Tess is always blushing), and if the rising of blood is sexual passion and the spilling of blood is death, then we can see that the purest woman is sexual and mortal. Remember Tess watching Prince bleed to death—'the hole in his chest looking scarcely large enough to have let out all that animated him'. It is not a large hole that Alec makes in Tess when he rapes her, but from then on the blood is bound to go on flowing until that initial violation will finally 'let out all that animated her'. Hardy is dealing here with the simplest and deepest of matters. Life starts in sex and ends in death, and Hardy constantly shows how closely allied the two forms of blood-letting are in one basic, unalterable rhythm of existence.

IV

I have suggested that the destiny of Tess comes to us as a cumulation of visible omens. It is also a convergence of omens and to explain what I mean I want to add a few comments on the part played in her life by the sun, altars and tombs, and finally walking and travelling. When we first see Tess with the other dancing girls we read that they are all bathed in sunshine. Hardy, ever conscious of effects of light, describes how their hair reflects various colours in the sunlight. More, 'as each and all of them were warmed without by the sun, so each of them had a private little sun for her soul to bask in'. They are creatures of the sun, warmed and nourished by the sources of all heat and life. Tess starts sun-blessed. At the dairy, the sun is at its most active as a cause of the fertile surgings which animate all nature. 'Rays from the sunrise drew forth the buds and stretched them into stalks, lifted up sap in noiseless streams, opened petals, and sucked out scents in invisible jets and breathings.' This is the profoundly sensuous atmosphere in which Tess, despite mental hesitations, blooms into full female ripeness. Hardy does something very suggestive here in his treatment of the times of day. Tess and

Angel rise very early, before the sun. They seem to themselves 'the first persons up of all the world'. The light is still 'half-compounded, aqueous', as though the business of creating animated forms has not yet begun. They are compared to Adam and Eve. As so often when Tess is getting involved with the superior power of a man, the atmosphere is misty, but this time it is cold mist, the sunless fogs which precede the dawn. In this particular light of a cool watery whiteness, Tess appears to Angel as 'a visionary essence of woman', something ghostly, 'merely a soul at large'. He calls her, among other things, Artemis (who lived, of course, in perpetual celibacy). In this sunless light Tess appears to Angel as unsexed, sexless, the sort of non-physical spiritualised essence he, in his impotent spirituality, wants. (At the end he marries 'a spiritualized image of Tess'). But Tess is inescapably flesh and blood. And when the sun does come up, she reverts from divine essence to physical milkmaid: 'her teeth, lips and eyes scintillated in the sunbeams, and she was again the dazzlingly fair dairymaid only ...' (That placing of 'only' is typical of the strength of Hardy's prose.) Soon after this, the dairy-man tells his story of the seduction of a young girl; 'none of them but herself seemed to see the sorrow of it'. And immediately we read, 'the evening sun was now ugly to her, like a great inflamed wound in the sky'. Sex is a natural instinct which however can lead to lives of utter misery. The same sun that blesses, can curse.

Tess drifts into marriage with Angel (her most characteristic way of moving in a landscape is a 'quiescent glide'), because 'every wave of her blood ... was a voice that joined with nature in revolt against her scrupulous-ness', but meanwhile 'at half-past six the sun settled down upon the levels, with the aspect of a great forge in the heavens'. This suggests not a drawing-up into growth, but a slow inexorable downward crushing force, through an image linked to that machinery which will later pummel her body. It is as though the universe turns metallic against Tess, just as we read when Angel rejects her that there is in him a hard negating force 'like a vein of metal in a soft loam'. This is the metal which her soft flesh runs up against. Other omens follow on her journey towards her wedding. Her feeling that she has seen the d'Urberville coach before; the postillion who takes them to church and who has 'a permanent running wound on the outside of his right leg'; the ominous 'afternoon crow' and so on. I want to point to another omen, when the sun seems to single out Tess in a sinister way. It is worth reminding ourselves that when Angel finally does propose to Tess she is quite sun-drenched. They are standing on the 'red-brick' floor and the sun slants in 'upon her inclining face, upon the blue veins of her temple, upon her naked arm, and her neck, and into the depths of her hair'. Now, on what should be the first night of her honeymoon we read: 'The sun was so low on that short, last afternoon of the year that it shone in through a small opening and formed a golden staff which stretched across to her skirt, where it made a spot like a paint-mark set upon her'. She has been marked before—first, with the blood of a dying beast, now with a mark from the setting sun. We find other descriptions of how the sun shines on Tess subsequently, but let us return to that crimson bed which, I suggested, effectively marked the end of Tess's journey. 'A shaft of dazzling sunlight glanced into the room, revealing heavy, old-fashioned furniture, crimson damask hangings, and an enormous four-poster bedstead ...' The sun and the redness which have marked Tess's life, now converge at the moment of her approaching death. Finally Tess takes her last rest on the altar of Stonehenge. She speaks to Angel—again, it is before dawn, that sunless part of the day when he can communicate with her.

> 'Did they sacrifice to God here?' asked she.
> 'No', said he.
> 'Who to?'
> 'I believe to the sun. That lofty stone set away by itself is in the direction of the sun, which will presently rise behind it.'

When the sun does rise it also reveals the policemen closing in, for it is society which demands a specific revenge upon Tess. But in the configuration of omens which, I think, is the major part of the book, Tess is indeed a victim, sacrificed to the sun. The heathen temple 'is fitting, since of course Tess is descended from Pagan d'Urberville, and Hardy makes no scruple about asserting that women 'retain in their souls far more of the Pagan fantasy of their remote forefathers than of the systematized religion taught their race at a later date'. This raises an important point. Is Tess a victim of society, or of nature? Who wants her blood, who is after her, the policemen, or the sun? Or are they in some sadistic conspiracy so that we see nature and society converging on Tess to destroy her? I will return to this question.

To the convergence of redness and the sun we must add the great final fact of the altar, an altar which Tess approaches almost gratefully, and on which she takes up her sacrificial position with exhausted relief. She says (I have run some of her words to Angel together): 'I don't want to go any further, Angel ... Can't we bide here? ... you used to say at Talbothays that I was a heathen. So now I am at home ... I like very much to be here.' Fully to be human is partly to be heathen, as the figure of Tess on the altar makes clear. (And after all what did heathen originally mean?—someone who lived on the heath; and what was a pagan?—someone who lived in a remote village. The terms only acquire their opprobrium after the advent of Christianity. Similarly Hardy points out that Sunday was originally the sun's day—a spiritual superstructure has been imposed on a physical source.) Tess's willingness to take her place on the stone of death has been manifested before. After she returns from the rape we read 'her depression was then terrible, and she could have hidden herself in a tomb'. On her marriage night, Angel sleepwalks into her room, saying 'Dead! Dead! Dead! ... My wife—dead, dead, dead!' He picks her up, kisses her (which he can now only manage when he is unconscious), and carries her over a racing river. Tess almost wants to jog him so that they can fall to their deaths: but Angel can negotiate the dangers of turbulent water just as he can suppress all passion. His steps are not directed towards the movement of the waters but to the stillness of stone. He takes Tess and lays her in an 'empty stone coffin' in the 'ruined choir'. In Angel's life of suppressed spontaneity and the negation of passional feeling, this is the most significant thing that he does. He encoffins the sexual instinct, then lies down beside Tess. The deepest inclinations of his psyche, his very being, have been revealed.

Later on, when things are utterly desperate for Tess's family and they literally have no roof over their heads, they take refuge by the church in which the family vaults are kept (where 'the bones of her ancestors—her useless ancestors—lay entombed'). In their exhaustion they erect an old 'four-post bedstead' over the vaults. We see again the intimate proximity of the bed and the grave. This sombre contiguity also adumbrates the ambiguous relief which Tess later finds in her crimson four-post bed which is also very close to death. On this occasion Tess enters the church and pauses by the 'tombs of the family' and 'the door of her ancestral sepulchre'. It is at this point that one of the tomb effigies moves, and Alex plays his insane jest on her by appearing to leap from a tomb. Again, we are invited to make the starkest sort of comparison without any exegesis from Hardy. Angel, asleep, took Tess in his arms and laid her in a coffin. Alec, however, seems to wake up from the tomb, a crude but animated threat to Tess in her quest for peace. Angel's instinct towards stillness is countered by Alec's instinct for sexual motion. Together they add up to a continuous process in which Tess is simply caught up. For it is both men who drive Tess to her death: Angel by his spiritualised rejection, Alec by his sexual attacks. It is notable that both these men are also cut off from any fixed community; they have both broken away from traditional attitudes and dwellings. Angel roams in his thought; Alec roams in his lust. They are both drifters of the sort who have an unsettling, often destructive impact in the Hardy world. Tess is a pure product of nature; but she is nature subject to complex and contradictory pressures. Angel wants her spiritual image without her body (when he finds out about her sexual past he simply denies her identity, 'the woman I have been loving is not you'); Alec wants only her body and is indifferent to anything we might call her soul, her distinctly human inwardness. The effect of this opposed wrenching on her wholeness is to induce a sort of inner rift which develops into something we would now call a schizophrenia. While still at Talbothays she says one day: 'I do know that our souls can be made to go outside our bodies when we are alive.' Her method is to fix the mind on a remote star and 'you will soon find that you are hundreds and hundreds o' miles away from your body, which you don't seem to want at all'. The deep mystery by which consciousness can seek to be delivered from the body which sustains it, is one which Hardy had clearly before him. That an organism can be generated which then wishes to repudiate the very grounds of its existence obviously struck Hardy as providing a very awesome comment on the nature of nature. Tess is robbed of her integrated single-ness, divided by two men, two forces. (This gives extra point to the various crosses she passes on her travels; the cross not only indicating torture, but that opposition between the vertical and the horizontal which, as I shall try to show, is ultimately the source of Tess's—and man's—sufferings in Hardy.) It is no wonder that when Alec worries and pursues her at the very door of her ancestors' vault, she should bend down and whisper that line of terrible simplicity—'Why am I on the wrong side of this door?' (A relevant poem of great power is 'A Wasted Illness' of which I quote three stanzas which are very apt for Tess:

> *'Where lies the end*
> *To this foul way?' I asked with weakening breath.*
> *Thereon ahead I saw a door extend—*
> *The door to Death.*
>
> *It loomed more clear:*
> *'At last!' I cried. 'The all-delivering door!'*
> *And then, I know not how, it grew less near*
> *Than theretofore.*
>
> *And back slid I*
> *Along the galleries by which I came,*
> *And tediously the day returned, and sky,*
> *And life—the same.*

Tess at this moment is utterly unplaced, with no refuge and no comfort. She can only stumble along more and rougher roads; increasingly vulnerable, weary and helpless, increasingly remote from her body. Her only solution is to break through that 'all-delivering door', the door from life to death which opens on the only home left to her. This she does, by stabbing Alec and then taking her place on the ritual altar. She has finally spilled all the blood that tormented her; she can then abandon the torments of animateness and seek out the lasting repose she has earned.

V

This brings me to what is perhaps the most searching of all Hardy's pre-occupations—walking, travelling, movement of all kinds. Somewhere at the heart of his vision is a profound sense of what we may call the mystery of motion. *Tess of the d'Urbervilles* opens with a man staggering on rickety legs down a road, and it is his daughter we shall see walking throughout the book. Phase the Second opens, once again, simply with an unexplained scene of laboured walking.

> The basket was heavy and the bundle was large, but she lugged them along like a person who did not find her especial burden in material things. Occasionally

she stopped to rest in a mechanical way by some gate or post; and then, giving the baggage another hitch upon her full round arm, went steadily on again.'

Such visualised passages carry the meaning of the novel, even down to the material burdens which weigh down that plump, vulnerable flesh: the meaning is both mute and unmistakable. At the start of Phase the Third, again Tess moves: 'she left her home for the second time'. At first the journey seems easy and comfortable in 'a hired trap'; but soon she gets out and walks, and her journey again leads her into portents of the life ahead of her. 'The journey over the intervening uplands and lowlands of Egdon, when she reached them, was a more troublesome walk than she had anticipated, the distance being actually but a few miles. It was two hours, owing to sundry turnings, 'ere she found herself on a summit commanding the long-sought-for vale ...' The road to the peaceful vale of death is longer and harder than she thinks. Always Tess has to move, usually to harsher and more punishing territories, and always Hardy makes sure we *see* her. After Angel has banished her: 'instead of a bride with boxes and trunks which others bore, we see her a lonely woman with a basket and a bundle in her own porterage ...' Later she walks to Emminster Vicarage on her abortive journey to see Angel's parents. She starts off briskly but by the end she is weary, and there are omens by the way. For instance, from one eminence she looks down at endless little fields, 'so numerous that they look from this height like the meshes of a net'. And again she passes a stone cross, Cross-in-Hand, which stands 'desolate and silent, to mark the site of a miracle, or murder, or both'. (Note the hint of the profound ambivalence and ambiguity of deeds and events.) At the end of this journey there is nobody at home and there follows the incident of Tess losing her walking boots, another physical reminder that the walking gets harder and harder for her. 'Her journey back was rather a meander than a march. It had no sprightliness, no purpose; only a tendency.' Her movements do get more leaden throughout, and by the end Hardy confronts us with one of the strangest phenomena of existence—motion without volition. (Interestingly enough, Conrad approaches the same phenomenon in *The Secret Agent* where walking is also the most insistent motif.) The only relief in her walking is that as it gets harder it also approaches nearer to darkness. Thus when she is summoned back to her family: 'She plunged into the chilly equinoctial darkness ... for her fifteen miles' walk under the steely stars'; and later during this walk from another eminence she 'looked from that height into the abyss of chaotic shade which was all that revealed itself of the vale on whose further side she was born'. She is indeed returning home, just as Oedipus was returning home on all his journeyings. Perhaps the ultimate reduction of Tess, the distillation of her fate, is to be seen when she runs after Angel having murdered Alec. Angel turns around. 'The tape-like surface of the road diminished in his rear as far as he could see, and as he gazed a moving spot intruded on the white vacuity of its perspective.' This scene has been anticipated when Tess was working at Flintcomb-Ash:

> The whole field was in colour a desolate drab; it was a complexion without features, as if a face, from chin to brow, should be only an expanse of skin. The sky wore, in another colour, the same likeness; a white vacuity of countenance with the lineaments gone. So these two upper and nether visages confronted each other all day long . . . without anything standing between them but the two girls crawling over the surface of the former like flies.

In both cases we see Tess as a moving spot on a white vacuity. And this extreme pictorial reduction seems to me to be right at the heart of Hardy's vision.

VI

To explain what I mean I want to interpose a few comments on some remarkable passages from the earlier novel, *The Return of the Native*. Chapter I describes the vast inert heath. Chapter II opens 'Along the road walked an old man'. He in turn sees a tiny speck of movement—'the single atom of life that the scene contained'. And this spot is a 'lurid red'. It is, of course, the reddleman, but I want to emphasise the composition of the scene—the great stillness and the tiny spot of red movement which is the human presence on the heath. Shortly after, the reddleman is scanning the heath (Hardy's world is full of watching eyes) and it is then that he first sees Eustacia Vye. But how he first sees her is described in a passage which seems to me so central to Hardy that I want to quote at length.

> There the form stood, motionless as the hill beneath. Above the plain rose the hill, above the hill rose the barrow, and above the barrow rose the figure. Above the figure there was nothing that could be mapped elsewhere than on a celestial globe.
>
> Such a perfect, delicate, and necessary finish did the figure give to the dark pile of hills that it seemed to be the only obvious justification of their outline. Without it, there was the dome without the lantern; with it the architectural demands of the mass were satisfied. The scene was strangely homogeneous. The vale, the upland, the barrow, and the figure above it amounted to unity. Looking at this or that member of the group was not observing a complete thing, but a fraction of a thing.
>
> The form was so much like an organic part of the entire motionless structure that to see it move would have impressed the mind as a strange phenomenon. Immobility being the chief characteristic of that whole which the person formed portion of, the discontinuance of immobility in any quarter suggested confusion.
>
> Yet that is what happened. The figure perceptibly gave up its fixity, shifted a step or two, and turned round.

Here in powerful visual terms is a complete statement about existence. Without the human presence, sheer land and sky seem to have no formal, architectural significance. The human form brings significant outline to the brown mass of earth, the white vacuity of sky. But this moment of satisfying formal harmony depends on stillness, and to be human is to be animated, is to move. Hardy's novels are about 'the discontinuance of immobility'; all the confusions that make up his plots are the result of people who perceptibly give up their fixity. To say that this is the very condition of life itself is only to point to the elemental nature of Hardy's art. All plants and all animals move, but much more within rhythms ordained by their native terrain than humans—who build things like the *Titanic* and go plunging off into the night sea, or who set out in a horse and cart in the middle of the night to reach a distant market, in both cases meeting with disastrous accidents. Only what moves can crash. Eustacia moves on the still heath, breaking up the unity: there is confusion ahead for her. Not indeed that the heath is in a state of absolute fixity; that would imply a dead planet: 'the quality of repose appertaining to the scene ... was not the repose of actual stagnation, but the apparent repose of incredible slowness'. Hardy often reminds us of the mindless insect life going on near the feet of his bewildered human protagonists; but to the human eye, which after all determines the felt meaning of the perceptible world, there is a movement which is like stillness just as there is a motion which seems to be unmitigated violence. The 'incredible slowness' of the heath, only serves to make more graphic the 'catastrophic dash' which ends the lives of Eustacia and Wildeve. And after the 'catastrophic dash'— 'eternal rigidity'.

The tragic tension between human and heath, between motion and repose, between the organic drive away from the inorganic and, what turns out to be the same thing, the drive to return to the inorganic, provides Hardy with the radical structure of his finest work. The human struggle against— and temporary departure from—the level stillness of the heath, is part of that struggle between the vertical and the horizontal which is a crucial part of Hardy's vision. We read of the 'oppressive horizontality' of the heath, and when Eustacia comes to the time of her death Hardy describes her position in such a way that it echoes the first time we saw her, and completes the pattern of her life. She returns to one of those ancient earthen grave mounds, called barrows. 'Eustacia at length reached Rainbarrow, and stood still there to think ... she sighed bitterly and ceased to stand erect, gradually crouching down under the umbrella as if she were drawn into the Barrow by a hand from underneath.' Her period of motion is over; her erect status above the flatness of the heath terminates at the same moment; she is, as it were, drawn back into the undifferentiated levelness of the earth from which she emerged. At the same time, you will remember, Susan is tormenting and burning a wax effigy of Eustacia, so that while she seems to be sinking back into the earth Hardy can also write 'the effigy of Eustacia was melting to nothing'. She is losing her distinguishing outline and features. Hardy describes elsewhere how a woman starts to 'lose her own margin' when working the fields. Human life is featured and contoured life: yet the erosion of feature and contour seems to be a primal activity of that 'featureless convexity' of the heath, of the earth itself.

VII

This feeling of the constant attrition, and final obliteration, of the human shape and all human structures, permeates Hardy's work. Interviewed about Stonehenge he commented that 'it is a matter of wonder that the erection has stood so long', adding however that 'time nibbles year after year' at the structure. Just so he will write of a wind 'which seemed to gnaw at the corners of the house'; of 'wooden posts rubbed to a glossy smoothness by the flanks of infinite cows and calves of bygone years'. His work is full of decaying architecture, and in *The Woodlanders* there is a memorable picture of the calves roaming in the ruins of Sherton Castle, 'cooling their thirsty tongues by licking the quaint Norman carving, which glistened with the moisture'. It is as though time, and all the rest of the natural order, conspired to eat away and erase all the structures and features associated with the human presence on, or intrusion into, the planet. Of one part of the heath Hardy says, in a sentence of extraordinarily succinct power, 'There had been no obliteration, because there had been no tending'. Tess working at Flintcomb-Ash in a landscape which is 'a complexion without features', and Tess running after Angel, 'a moving spot intruding on the white vacuity', is a visible paradigm of the terms of human life—a spot of featured animation moving painfully across a vast featureless repose. Like Eustacia, and like her wounded horse Prince, having remained upright as long as possible, she, too, simply 'ceases to stand erect' and lies down on the flat sacrificial stone, as though offering herself not only up to the sun which tended her, but to the obliterating earth, the horizontal inertia of which she had disturbed.

Life is movement, and movement leads to confusion. Tess's instinct is for placidity, she recoils from rapid movements. Yet at crucial times she finds herself in men's carriages or men's machines. She has to drive her father's cart to market and Prince is killed. Alec forces her into his dog-cart which he drives recklessly at great speed. Of Tess we read 'the least irregularity of motion startled her' and Alec at this point is disturbing and shaking up blood which will only be stilled in death. Angel, by contrast, takes Tess to the wedding in a carriage which manages to suggest something brutal, punitive, and funereal all at once—'It had stout wheel-spokes, and heavy felloes, a great curved bed, immense straps and springs, and a pole like a battering-ram.' All these man-made conveyances, together with the ominous train, and that 'tyrant' the threshing machine, seem to threaten Tess. And yet she is bound to be involved in travelling, and dangerous motion, because she has no home. At the beginning the parson telling Tess's father about his noble lineage says an ominous thing. To Jack's question, 'Where do we d'Urbervilles live?' he answers: 'You don't live anywhere. You are extinct—as a county family.' Tess does not live anywhere. The one home she finds, Angel turns her out of. That is why she is bound to succumb to Alec. He provides a place but not a home. Alec takes her to Sandbourne,, a place of 'detached mansions', the very reverse of a community. It is a 'pleasure city', 'a glittering novelty', a place of meretricious fashion and amusement. '"Tis all lodging-houses here ...' This is the perfect place for the modern, de-racinated Alec. It is no place at all for Tess, 'a cottage girl'. But we have seen her uprooted, forced to the roads, ejected from houses, knocking on doors which remain closed to her; we have seen the process by which she has become an exhausted helpless prey who is finally bundled off to a boarding house. Her spell in this place is a drugged interlude; she seems finally to have come to that state of catatonic trance which has been anticipated in previous episodes.

Angel realises that 'Tess had spiritually ceased to recognize the body before him as hers—allowing it to drift, like a corpse upon the current, in a direction dissociated from its living will'. Tess has been so 'disturbed' by irregularities of motion, so pulled in different directions, that she really is sick, split, half dead. Hardy was very interested in this sort of split person— for instance, people with primitive instincts and modern nerves, as he says in another book—and we can see that Tess is subjected to too many different pressures, not to say torments, ever to achieve a felicitous wholeness of being.

VIII

This brings me to a problem I mentioned earlier. We see Tess suffering, apparently doomed to suffer; destroyed by two men, by society, by the sun outside her and the blood inside her. And we are tempted to ask, what is Hardy's vision of the *cause* of this tale of suffering. Throughout the book Hardy stresses that Tess is damned, and damns herself, according to man-made laws which are as arbitrary as they are cruel. He goes out of his way to show how Nature seems to disdain, ignore or make mockery of the laws which social beings impose on themselves. The fetish of chastity is a ludi-crous aberration in a world which teems and spills with such promiscuous and far-flung fertility every year (not to say a brutal caricature of human justice in that what was damned in the woman was condoned in the man). So, if the book was an attempt to show an innocent girl who is destroyed by society though justified by Nature, Hardy could certainly have left the opposition as direct and as simple as that. Social laws hang Tess; and Nature admits no such laws. But it is an important part of the book that we feel Nature itself turning against Tess, so that we register something approaching a sadism of *both* the man-made *and* the natural directed against her. If she is tortured by the man-made threshing machine, she is also crushed by the forge of the sun; the cold negating metal in Angel is also to be found in the 'steely stars'; the pangs of guilt which lacerate her are matched by the 'glass splinters' of rain which penetrate her at Flintcomb-Ash. Perhaps to under-stand this feeling of almost universal opposition which grows throughout the book, we should turn to some of Hardy's own words, when he talks of 'the universal harshness ... the harshness of the position towards the temperament, of the means towards the aims, of today towards yesterday, of hereafter towards today'. When he meditates on the imminent disappearance of the d'Urberville family he says, 'so does Time ruthlessly destroy his own romances'. This suggests a universe of radical opposition, working to destroy what it works to create, crushing to death what it coaxes into life. From this point of view society only appears as a functioning part of a larger process whereby the vertical returns to the horizontal, motion lapses into stillness and structure cedes to the unstructured. The policemen appear as the sun rises: Tess is a sacrifice to both, to all of them. Hardy's vision is tragic and penetrates far deeper than specific social anomalies. One is more inclined to think of Sophocles than, say, Zola, when reading Hardy. The vision is tragic because he shows an ordering of existence in which nature turns against itself, in which the sun blasts what it blesses, in which all the hopeful explorations of life turn out to have been a circuitous peregrination towards death. 'All things are born to be diminished' said Pericles at the time of Sophocles; and Hardy's comparable feeling that all things are tended to be obliterated, reveals a Sophoclean grasp of the bed-rock ironies of existence.

Tess is the living demonstration of these tragic ironies. That is why she who is raped lives to be hanged; why she who is so physically beautiful feels guilt at 'inhabiting the fleshly tabernacle with which Nature had endowed her'; why she who is a fertile source of life comes to feel that 'birth itself was an ordeal of degrading personal compulsion, whose gratuitousness nothing in the result seemed to justify'. It is why she attracts the incompatible forces represented by Alec and Angel. It is why she who is a lover is also a killer. Tess is gradually crucified on the oppugnant ironies of circumstance and existence itself, ironies which centre, I have suggested, on the fact of blood, that basic stuff which starts the human spot moving across the white vacuity. Blood, and the spilling of blood; which in one set of circumstances can mean sexual passion and the creation of life, and in another can mean murderous passion and death—two forms of 'red' energy intimately related—this is the substance of Tess's story. Any why should it all happen to her? You can say, as some people in the book say fatalistically, 'It was to be'. Or you could go through the book and try to work out how Hardy apportions the blame—a bit on Tess, a bit on society, a bit on religion, a bit on heredity, a bit on the Industrial Revolution, a bit on the men who abuse her, a bit on the sun and the stars, and so on. But Hardy does not work in this way. More than make us judge, Hardy makes us see; and in looking for some explanation of why all this should happen to Tess, our eyes finally settle on that red ribbon marking out the little girl in the white dress, which already foreshadows the red blood stain on the white ceiling. In her beginning is her end. It is the oldest of truths, but it takes a great writer to make us experience it again in all its awesome mystery.

IX

Hardy specifically rejected the idea of offering any theory of the universe. In his General Preface to his works, he said

> Nor is it likely, indeed, that imaginative writings extending over more than forty years would exhibit a coherent scientific theory of the universe even if it had been attempted—of that universe concerning which Spencer owns to the 'paralyzing thought' that possibly there exists no comprehension of it anywhere. But such objectless consistency never has been attempted ...

Hardy 'theorizes' far less than Lawrence, but certain images recur which serve to convey his sense of life—its poignancy and its incomprehensibility—more memorably than any overt statement. Death, the sudden end of brilliance and movement, occupied a constant place in his thoughts. 'The most prosaic man becomes a poem which you stand by his grave and think of him' he once wrote; and the strange brightness of ephemeral creatures is something one often meets in his fiction—pictorially, not philosophically. 'Gnats, knowing nothing of their brief glorification, wandered across the shimmer of this pathway, irradiated as if they bore fire within them, then passed out of its line, and were quite extinct.' Compare with that the description of the girls returning from the dance: 'and as they went there moved onward with them ... a circle of opalized light, formed by the moon's rays upon the glistening sheet of dew. Each pedestrian could see no halo but his or her own ...' Hardy is often to be found stressing the ephemeral nature of life—'independent worlds of ephemerons were passing their time in mad carousal', 'ephemeral creatures, took up their positions where only a year ago other[s] had stood in their place when these were nothing more than germs and inorganic particles'—and it often seems that the ephemeral fragments of moving life are also like bubbles of light, temporary illuminations of an encroaching darkness. One of the great scenes in all of Hardy is in *The Return of the Native* when Wildeve and Venn, the reddleman, gamble at night on the heath. Their lantern makes a little circle of light which draws things out of the darkness towards it. 'The light of the candle had by this time attracted heath-flies, moths and other winged creatures of night, which floated round the lantern, flew into the flame, or beat about the faces of the two players.' Much more suggestively as they continue to throw dice: 'they were surrounded by dusky forms about four feet high, standing a few paces beyond the rays of the lantern. A moment's inspection revealed that the encircling figures were heath-croppers, their heads being all towards the players, at whom they gazed intently.' When a moth extinguishes the candle, Wildeve gathers glow worms and puts them on the stone on which they are playing.

> The incongruity between the men's deeds and their environment was great. Amid the soft juicy vegetation of the hollow in which they sat, the motionless and the uninhabited solitude, intruded the chink of guineas, the rattle of dice, the exclamations of the reckless players.

143

Again, it is one of those scenes which seems to condense a whole vision of human existence—a strange activity in a small circle of light, and all round them the horses of the night noiselessly gathering at the very perimeter. And in *Tess of the d'Urbervilles* Hardy develops this scene into a metaphor of great power. He is describing how Tess's love for Angel sustains her:

> it enveloped her as a photosphere, irradiated her into forgetfulness of her past sorrows, keeping back the gloomy spectres that would persist in their attempts to touch her—doubt, fear, moodiness, care, shame. She knew that they were waiting like wolves just outside the circumscribing light, but she had long spells of power to keep them in hungry subjection there ... She walked in brightness, but she knew that in the background those shapes of darkness were always spread.

I have singled out this image not only because I think there is something quintessentially Hardyan in it, but also because I think it is an image which profoundly influenced D.H. Lawrence. Here is a final quotation, taken from the culmination of perhaps his greatest novel, *The Rainbow*. Ursula is trying to clarify her sense of her own presence in the world.

> This world in which she lived was like a circle lighted by a lamp. This lighted area, lit up by man's completest consciousness, she thought was all the world: that here all was disclosed for ever. Yet all the time, within the darkness she had been aware of points of light, like the eyes of wild beasts, gleaming, penetrating, vanishing. And her soul had acknowledged in a great heave of terror only the outer darkness. This inner circle of light in which she lived and moved, wherein the trains rushed and the factories ground out their machine-produce and the plants and the animals worked by the light of science and knowledge, suddenly it seemed like the area under an arc lamp, wherein the moths and children played in the security of blinding light, not even knowing there was any darkness, because they stayed in the light.
> But she could see the glimmer of dark movement just out of range, she saw the eyes of the wild beast gleaming from the darkness, watching the vanity of the camp fire and the sleepers; she felt the strange, foolish vanity of the camp, which said 'Beyond our light and our order there is nothing', turning their faces always inwards toward the sinking fire of illuminating consciousness, which comprised sun and stars, and the Creator, and the System of Righteousness, ignoring always the vast shapes that wheeled round about, with half-revealed shapes lurking on the edge ...
> Nevertheless the darkness wheeled round about, with grey shadow-shapes of wild beasts, and also with dark shadow-shapes of the angels, whom the light fenced out, as it fenced out the more familiar beasts of darkness. . . .

Lawrence, more insistent as to the torments and sterilities of consciousness, confidently ascribes positive values to the shapes prowling around the perimeter of the circle of light. But Lawrence's *interpretation*—itself an act of consciousness—of the population of the dark, is only something overlayed on the *situation*, that irreducible configuration which is to be found, I suggest, at the heart of Hardy's work. 'She walked in brightness, but she knew that in the background those shapes of darkness were always spread.'

Tess, Nature, and the Voices of Hardy

◆

DAVID LODGE

Thomas Hardy might be described as an 'in-spite-of' novelist. That is, he figures in literary criticism and literary history as a great novelist 'in spite of' gross defects, the most commonly alleged of which are his manipulation of events in defiance of probability to produce a tragic–ironic pattern, his intrusiveness as authorial commentator, his reliance on stock characters, and his capacity for writing badly. In my view, the last of these alleged faults involves all the others, which, considered in the abstract as narrative strategies, are not necessarily faults. If we have reservations about them in Hardy's work, it must be because of the way they are articulated—or inadequately articulated.

Does Hardy write badly? One method of trying to answer such a question is that of Practical Criticism: the critical analysis of a passage extracted from its context. I therefore begin by citing an example of Practical Criticism *avant la lettre* performed by Vernon Lee upon five hundred words taken at random from *Tess of the d'Urbervilles*.[1] The unsatisfactoriness of her conclusions, I suggest, can only be made good by returning the passage to its context—the whole novel, and by trying to define the linguistic character of the novel in terms of its literary purpose. Using the perspective thus established, I turn to the consideration of another passage from the novel, one which has attracted a good deal of conflicting commentary. My intention is primarily to try and define as clearly as possible the sense in which the author of *Tess* may be said to 'write badly'; and to show that the consideration of this question, even when based on the close examination of short extracts, must inevitably involve us in the consideration of the meaning and artistic success of the novel as a whole.

The passage discussed by Vernon Lee is from Chapter XVI, the first chapter of the third 'Phase' of the novel, entitled 'The Rally'. It follows immediately after Tess, on her journey from her home at Marlott in the Vale

SOURCE *Language of Fiction*, 1966, from ch. IV.

of Blackmoor to the dairy of Talbothays, where she hopes to make a new start after her seduction by Alec d'Urberville, breaks into the 148th Psalm; and it describes her descent into the valley of the Var:

> However, Tess found at least approximate expression for her feelings in the old *Benedicite* that she had lisped from infancy; and it was enough. Such high contentment with such a slight initial performance as that of having started towards a means of independent living was a part of the Durbeyfield temperament. Tess really wished to walk uprightly, while her father did nothing of the kind; but she resembled him in being content with immediate and small achievements, and in having no mind for laborious effort towards such petty social advancement as could alone be effected by a family so heavily handicapped as the once powerful d'Urbervilles were now.
>
> There was, it might be said, the energy of her mother's unexpended family, as well as the natural energy of Tess's years, rekindled after the experience which had so overwhelmed her for the time. Let the truth be told—women do as a rule live through such humiliations, and regain their spirits, and again look about them with an interested eye. While there's life there's hope is a conviction not so entirely unknown to the 'betrayed' as some amiable theorists would have us believe.
>
> Tess Durbeyfield, then, in good heart, and full of zest for life, descended the Egdon slopes lower and lower towards the dairy of her pilgrimage.
>
> The marked difference, in the final particular, between the rival vales now showed itself. The secret of Blackmoor was best discovered from the heights around; to read aright the valley before her it was necessary to descend into its midst. When Tess had accomplished this feat she found herself to be standing on a carpeted level, which stretched to the east and west as far as the eye could reach.
>
> The river had stolen from the higher tracts and brought in particles to the vale all this horizontal land; and now, exhausted, aged, and attenuated, lay serpentining along through the midst of its former spoils.
>
> Not quite sure of her direction Tess stood still upon the hemmed expanse of verdant flatness, like a fly on a billiard table of indefinite length, and of no more consequence to the surroundings than that fly. The sole effect of her presence upon the placid valley so far had been to excite the mind of a solitary heron, which, after descending to the ground not far from her path, stood with neck erect, looking at her.
>
> Suddenly there arose from all parts of the lowland a prolonged and repeated call —
>
> 'Waow! waow! waow!'
>
> From the furthest east to the furthest west the cries spread by contagion, accompanied in some cases by the barking of a dog. It was not the expression of the valley's consciousness that beautiful Tess had arrived, but the ordinary announcement of milking-time—half-past four o'clock, when the dairy men set about getting in the cows.

The interested reader will find it rewarding to read Vernon Lee's commentary in its entirety, but I must confine myself to extracts from it. Her basic objection to this passage is 'that we are *being told about* the locality, not what is necessary for the intelligence of the situation'[2]—the 'then', she argues, poses falsely as a connective between the description of the valley and the meditative commentary that precedes it[3]—and that even as a straight-forward description it is awkwardly and untidily written:

> Notice how he tells us the very simple fact of how Tess stops to look round: 'Tess ... stood still upon the hemmed expanse of verdant flatness, like a fly on a billiard-table of indefinite length.' '*Hemmed* expanse,' that implies that the expanse had limits; it is however, compared to a billiard-table 'of indefinite length'. Hardy's attention has slackened, and really he is talking a little at random. If he visualized that valley, particularly from above, he would not think of it, which is bounded by something on his own higher level (*hemmed*, by which he means *hemmed in*), in connection with a billiard table which is bounded by the tiny wall of its cushion. I venture to add that if, at the instant of writing, he were feeling the variety, the freshness of a valley, he would not be comparing it to a piece of cloth, with which it has only two things in common, being flat and being green; the utterly dissimilar flatness and greenness of a landscape and that of a billiard-table.
>
> We are surely in the presence of slackened interest, when the Writer casts about for and accepts any illustration, without realizing it sufficiently to reject it. Such slackening of attention is confirmed by the poor structure of the sentence, 'a fly on a billiard-table of indefinite length *and* of no more consequence to the surroundings than that fly'. The *and* refers the 'of no more consequence' in the first instance to the billiard-table. Moreover, I venture to think the whole remark was not worth making: why divert our attention from Tess and her big, flat valley, surely easy enough to realize, by a vision of a billiard-table with a fly on it? Can the two images ever grow into one another? is the first made clearer, richer, by the second? How useless all this business has been is shown by the next sentence: 'The sole effect of her presence upon the placid valley so far had been to excite the mind of a solitary heron, which, after descending to the ground not far from her path, stood, with neck erect, looking at her.' Leave out all about the billiard-table, and the sentences coalesce perfectly and give us all we care to know.[4]

Vernon Lee's discussion of the rest of the passage is equally severe, finding everywhere a 'general slackening of attention, the vagueness showing itself in the casual distribution of the subject matter; showing itself, as we ... see in lack of masterful treatment of the Reader's attention, in utter deficiency of logical arrangement. These are the co-related deficiencies due to the same inactivity and confusion of thought.'[5] In her closing remarks, however, Vernon Lee glaringly declines to accept the critical conclusions which follow from her analysis:

> The woolly outlines, even the uncertain drawing, merely add to the impression of primeval passiveness and blind, unreasoning emotion; of inscru-table doom and blind, unfeeling Fate which belong to his whole outlook on life. And the very faults of Hardy are probably an expression of his solitary and matchless grandeur of attitude. He belongs to a universe transcending such trifles as Writers and Readers and their little logical ways.[6]

This disingenuous conclusion conceals either a failure of nerve before the Great Reputation, or an admission that the total effect of *Tess* is rather more impressive than the analysis of the extract suggests. I suspect that the latter is the case, and that if we consider the peculiarities of the passage in the context of the whole novel we shall arrive at a view of Hardy somewhere between the semi-illiterate blunderer exposed by Vernon Lee's commentary and the majestic figure transcending ordinary critical standards postulated in her conclusion. Such a consideration must start with an attempt to describe the function of the 'author's voice' in *Tess*, and proceed to discuss the attitudes of that author to Nature.

Underlying all Vernon Lee's criticism we can detect a prejudice against omniscient narration and in favour of Jamesian 'presentation'; against 'telling' and in favour of 'showing'. Just how dangerously narrowing and exclusive such prescriptive interpretation of Jamesian precept and practice can be, has been fully and persuasively argued by Wayne Booth in *The Rhetoric of Fiction*. But to note the existence of this element in Vernon Lee's approach to Hardy by no means disposes of her objections for a candid appraisal of *Tess* will reveal a fundamental uncertainty about the author's relation to his readers and to his characters, an uncertainty which is betrayed again and again in the language of the novel.

Tess, we are told, 'spoke two languages: the dialect at home, more or less; ordinary English abroad and to persons of quality' (III). To some extent the same is true of Hardy as narrator. There is the Hardy who can recreate dialect speech with flawless authenticity, who shows how closely he is in touch with the life of an agrarian community through being in touch with its idiom; and there is the Hardy speaking to 'the quality' in orotund sentences of laboured syntax and learned vocabulary, the Hardy who studied *The Times*, Addison, and Scott to improve his style.[7] It is probably the second Hardy who is responsible for the most spectacular stylistic lapses. But to regard the second Hardy as a regrettable excrescence superimposed upon the first 'true', Hardy would be mistaken. For while one aspect of the novelist's undertaking in *Tess* demands a quality of immediacy, of 'felt life', achieved through his empathetic identification with his characters, particularly his heroine—in other words, the voice of the first Hardy—other aspects demand a quality of distance, both of time and space, through which the characters can be seen in their cosmic, historical and social settings—in other words, the voice of the second Hardy. And some of the most effective passages in the book—the description of the mechanical thresher, for instance (XLVII)—are articulated by this second Hardy.

Several accents are mingled in this voice. The author here is a combination of sceptical philosopher, and local historian topographer, antiquarian, mediating between his 'folk'—the agricultural community of Wessex—and his readers—the metropolitan 'quality'. About the sceptical philosopher critics have had much to say, and most of them have regretted his presence. But if we reject such intrusions *qua* intrusions, we must reject other kinds of intrusion in the novel, in which case we shall not be left with very much in our hand. On the whole I think it will be found that these intrusions offend when they are crudely expressed. The sentence in Vernon Lee's passage, 'While there's life there's hope is a conviction not so entirely unknown to the "betrayed" as some amiable theorists would have us believe', for example, alienates rather than persuades the reader because it attempts to overthrow a social–moral cliché (that sexual betrayal is irredeemable) by nothing more potent than a proverbial cliché ('while there's life there's hope') and an ironic cliché ('amiable'). Compare the bitingly effective comment on the burial of Tess's child:

> So the baby was carried in a small deal box, under an ancient woman's shawl, to the churchyard that night, and buried by lantern-light, at the cost of a shilling, and a pint of beer to the sexton, in that shabby corner of God's allot-ment where He lets the nettles grow, and where all unbaptized infants, notorious drunkards, suicides and others of the conjecturally damned are laid. (XIV)

There is much to admire in this sentence. It begins with a subdued literal description of the pathetic particulars of the child's burial. A hint of irony appears in the shilling and the pint of beer. This becomes overt in the axis of the sentence which marks the transition from impersonal narration to comment—'That shabby corner of God's allotment where He lets the nettles grow'—where, through the conventional idea that the churchyard is ground dedicated to God, He is held responsible for the behaviour of His earthly representatives—is presented, in fact, as a cynically careless smallholder, a stroke which has particular appropriateness in the agrarian environment of the story. The irony is sustained and intensified in the conclusion of the sentence, in the grouping of unbaptized infants with drunkards and suicides, and in the juxtaposition of the cool 'conjecturally' with the uncompromising 'damned', which effectively shocks us into awareness of the arrogance and inhumanity of presuming to forecast the eternal destiny of souls.

The author of *Tess* as local historian has received less attention than the author as sceptical philosopher, but his presence in unmistakable. The title-page tells us that the story of Tess is 'Faithfully Presented by Thomas Hardy'; and the explanatory note to the first edition of 1891 describes the novel, rather equivocally, 'as an attempt to give artistic form to a true sequence of things'. Although no dates are specified in the novel, we are often made to feel that Tess's story is not taking place in a continuum in which author and reader keep pace with the action and, so to speak, discover its outcome with the protagonists; but that it is already finished, that it took place in living memory, and is being reported to us by someone who lived in the locality, who knew her, though only slightly, who has received much of his information at second-hand, and whose account is one of imaginative reconstruction:

> The name of the eclipsing girl, whatever it was, has not been handed down. (II)

> ... the stopt-diapason note which her voice acquired when her heart was in her speech, and which will never be forgotten by those who knew her. (XIV)

> It was said afterwards that a cottager of Wellbridge, who went out late that night for a doctor, met two lovers in the pastures, walking very slowly, without converse, one behind the other, as in a funeral procession, and the glimpse he obtained of their faces seemed to denote that they were anxious and sad. (XXXV)

This voice of the author as local historian, dependent upon secondary sources, is in a state of uneasy co-existence with the voice of the author as creator and maker, as one acquainted with the deepest interior processes of his characters' minds. The uneasiness manifests itself notably in Hardy's hesitation about how far to attempt an imitation of the verbal quality of Tess's consciousness. Often he does not attempt it at all: the morning after Angel's sleep-walking, for instance, we are told that, 'It just crossed her mind, too, that he might have a faint recollection of his tender vagary, and was disinclined to allude to it from a conviction that she would take amatory advantage of the opportunity it gave her of appealing to him anew not to go' (XXXVII). That Hardy was not entirely happy about using vocabulary and syntax so far removed from Tess's natural idiom is suggested by this quotation: 'She thought, *without actually wording the thought*, how strange and godlike was a composer's power, who from the grave could lead through sequences of emotion, which he alone had felt at first, a girl like her who had never heard of his name ...' (XIII—*my italics*). Of course, in the strict sense, there is no 'real' Tess, and everything we know about her proceeds from the same source. But in terms of literary illusion, the distinction between Tess's consciousness and the author's articulation of it is a real one. Consider for example the account of her disappointment at the appearance of Alec d'Urberville:

> She had dreamed of an aged and dignified face, the sublimation of all the d'Urberville lineaments, furrowed with incarnate memories representing in hieroglyphic the centuries of her family's and England's history. But she screwed herself up to the work in hand, since she could not get out of it, and answered —
> 'I came to see your mother, sir.' (V)

The first sentence is a consciously literary paraphrase of Tess's vague, romantic expectations; whereas the second sentence is tough, simple and idiomatic, precisely rendering the verbal quality of Tess's consciousness. Each sentence is written in a mode which is legitimate and effective. But the transition between the two is too abrupt: a slight disturbance and confusion is created in the movement of the language, of a kind which we experience persistently in Hardy. It is particularly noticeable when he employs free indirect speech, for it would appear that the novelist who uses this device is obliged to be particularly faithful to the linguistic quality of his character's consciousness—the omission of the introductory verb 'he thought', 'he said', etc., seems to break down the literary convention by which we accept that the writer and his characters operate on quite different levels of discourse. Here is an example: 'Was once lost always lost really true of chastity? she would ask herself. She might prove it false if she could veil bygones. The recuperative power which pervaded organic nature was surely not denied to maidenhood alone' (XV). The structure of the last sentence indicates that it is a rendering, in free indirect speech, of Tess's thought; but its vocabulary belongs to the voice of the authorial commentator.

This duality in the presentation of Tess's consciousness is paralleled in the treatment of Nature (understanding Nature in its general cosmic sense and more specific sense of landscape, the earth, flora and fauna). Ian Gregor has commented acutely on the contradiction that exists in *Tess* between a 'Rousseauistic view of Nature' as essentially life-giving, healthy, opposed to the inhibiting, destructive forces of society and convention which alone generate human misery, and the 'deterministic [view] which Hardy runs alongside it', in which the world appears as a 'blighted star' and the three dairymaids in love with Angel 'writhed feverishly under the oppressiveness of an emotion which they neither expected nor desired'.[8] This contradiction applies not only to generalizations about Nature, but also to the treatment of landscape, and Gregor's own assertion that 'at every stage of the tale interior states are visualized in terms of landscape'[9] must be qualified. It would be difficult to refute Vernon Lee's point that in the passage she quotes the description of the landscape does *not* reflect Tess's interior state of mind. On the other hand, we must not assume that such a relationship between character and setting is a necessary feature of imaginative prose, or that Hardy failed to establish it through incompetence. The truth of the matter is rather more complex.

No attentive reader can fail to note how persistently Tess is associated and identified with Nature, on several different levels. On the social level, in terms of the rural/urban or agrarian/industrial antithesis on which the values of the novel are largely based, she is a 'daughter of the soil' (XIX), almost timeless and anonymous—'Thus Tess walks on; a figure which is part of the landscape, a fieldswoman pure and simple, in winter guise' (XLII) (the present tense here having an effect of timelessness rather than of immediacy)—a quasi-symbolic 'object . . . foreign to the gleaming cranks and wheels' of the railway engine (XXX). In religious or spiritual terms, Tess is a Nature-worshipping pagan. Her beliefs are 'Tractarian as to phraseology' 'but Pantheistic as to essence' (XXVII). 'You used to say at Talbothays that I was a heathen', says Tess to Angel, as she lies on a stone 'altar' at Stonehenge, 'So now I am at home' (LVII). 'Did they sacrifice to God here?' she asks later. 'No . . . I believe to the sun', he replies (LVIII). And we may recall here, that at their second embrace at Talbothays the sun had shone through the window 'upon her inclining face, upon the blue veins of her temple, upon her naked arm, and her neck, and into the depths of her hair' (XXVII).

This schematic association of Tess with Nature is enforced by insistent allusion, literal and figurative, to flora and fauna. Early in the novel she appears with 'roses at her breast; roses in her hat; roses and strawberries in her basket to the brim' (VI). Her hair is 'earth-coloured' (V), her mouth 'flower-like' (XIV), and her breath tastes 'of the butter and eggs and honey on which she mainly lived' (XXXVI). She is compared to a 'plant' (XXVII) and a 'sapling' (XX); the dew falls on her as naturally as on the grass (XX). To Angel, 'her arm, from her dabbling in the curds, was cold and damp to his mouth as new-gathered mushrooms' (XXVIII). While her physical appearance finds its metaphorical equivalents in the vegetable world, her behaviour is often compared to that of animals, particularly cats and birds. She 'wears the look of a wary animal' (XXXI). 'There was something of the habitude of the wild animal in the unreflecting instinct with which she rambled on' (XLI). She is as unresponsive to sarcasm as a 'dog or cat' (XXXV). She listens to Angel's harp like a 'fascinated bird', and moves through an overgrown garden 'as stealthily as a cat' (XIX). After sleep, 'she was as warm as a sunned cat' (XXVII). When she is happy her tread is like 'the skim of a bird which has not quite alighted' (XXXI). She faces d'Urberville with 'the hopeless defiance of the sparrow's gaze before its captor twists its neck' (XLVII).

This network of imagery and reference encourages us to think of Tess as essentially 'in touch' with Nature. Her character is defined and justified by metaphors of flora and fauna, and the changing face of the earth both directs and reflects her emotional life. At such moments we are least conscious of the literary *persona* of the author, and of his distance from the story. But it is equally true that Nature is quite indifferent to Tess and her fate. It is simply 'there', the physical setting against which the story takes place, described by the local historian with a wealth of geological and topographical detail, its moral neutrality emphasized by the sceptical philosopher.

This is surely the case in the passage quoted by Vernon Lee, particularly the two paragraphs beginning, 'The marked difference, in the final particular, between the rival vales now showed itself'. These paragraphs have the very tone of the guide-book, the tone of the parallel description of the Vale of Blackmoor:

> It is a vale whose acquaintance is best made by viewing it from the summits of the hills that surround it—except perhaps during the droughts of summer. An unguided ramble into its recesses in bad weather is apt to engender dissatisfaction with its narrow, tortuous, and miry ways (II).

But this earlier description is deliberately and clearly detached from the narrative, most obviously by its use of the present tense. Whereas in the passage quoted by Vernon Lee there is a fumbling attempt to relate the guide-book view to Tess. It is true that the two valleys might present themselves to Tess as in some sense 'rivals', but not in such impersonal, topographical terms.

A similar problem is raised by the simile of the fly, of which Vernon Lee asks, 'Why divert our attention from Tess and her big, flat valley, surely easy enough to realise, by a vision of a billiard table with a fly on it?' The answer surely is that Hardy, having got Tess into the valley, wants to give us, not a horizontal picture of the situation from her point of view, but a vertical, bird's eye picture; and he wants to do so in order to bring out her defence-lessness, her isolation, her insignificance, in the eye of impersonal nature. (One is reminded of the later description of Flintcomb, in which the earth and the sky are compared to two vacant faces, 'the white face looking down on the brown face, and the brown face looking up at the white face, without anything standing between them but the two girls crawling over the surface of the former like flies' (XLIII), and even of the lines from *Lear* quoted in the Preface to the Fifth and later editions:

> *As flies to wanton boys are we to the gods;*
> *They kill us for their sport.*

The trouble, once again, is that the structure of the sentence is confused and misleading. 'Not quite sure of her direction Tess stood still ...' arouses expectations that any subsequent image will define her sense of uncertainty, whereas it does nothing of the sort. This confusion in the handling of the point of view, with its consequent disturbance of tone and meaning, is the essential basis of Vernon Lee's criticism; and I do not see how it can be dismissed, here or elsewhere in the novel.

On the other hand her critique can be challenged on two grounds. Firstly, she does not seem to have given her text the careful attention which close criticism demands. Her transcription of the passage (from an unspecified 'cheap edition') runs together the three paragraphs beginning 'Tess Durbeyfield, then', 'The marked difference', and 'The river had stolen', and adds on the following sentence to make one paragraph ending with 'fly'. This considerably increases the confusion in the point of view. For in my text the first of these three paragraphs stands as a self-contained statement of Tess's mood and action, which seems to have a sufficient logical connection with the preceding commentary to justify the use of the connective 'then'; and the third stands as a self-contained statement of the geological history of the valley. The attempt to provide some transition between the two in the second paragraph remains, however, a muddle.[10]

A more significant limitation of Vernon Lee's critique is her assumption that landscape in fiction must be vividly realized in sensuous terms, and reflect characters' states of consciousness. The fly and billiard table image does neither of these things, and is dismissed as the mechanical gesture of a nodding writer. She does not consider the possibility that it is a deliberately homely and bathetic image, designed to dissociate us from Tess at this point, to check any tendency to find reassurance in the identification of Tess's renewed hope with the fertile promise of the valley.

Ruskin called such identification the 'pathetic fallacy', and Hardy's ambiguous treatment of Nature throughout *Tess* might be formulated as his inability to decide whether the pathetic fallacy was fallacious or not. For of course it is Hardy himself who has encouraged us to make this kind of identification between Tess and her environment. A page or two before the passage quoted by Vernon Lee, we have the following description of Tess on a summit overlooking the valley into which she later descends:

> The bird's eye perspective before her was not so luxuriantly beautiful, perhaps, as that other one which she knew so well; yet it was more cheering. It lacked the intensely blue atmosphere of the rival vale, and its heavy soils and scents; the new air was clear, bracing, ethereal. The river itself, which nourished the grass and cows of these renowned dairies, flowed not like the streams in Blackmoor. Those were slow, silent, often turbid; flowing over beds of mud into which the incautious wader might sink and vanish unawares. The Froom waters were clear as the pure River of Life shown to the Evangelist, rapid as the shadow of a cloud, with pebbly shallows that prattled to the sky all day long. There the water-flower was the lily; the crowfoot here.
>
> Either the change in the quality of the air from heavy to light, or the sense of being amid new scenes where there were no invidious eyes upon her, sent up her spirits wonderfully. Her hopes mingled with the sunshine in an ideal photosphere which surrounded her as she bounded along against the soft south wind. She heard a pleasant voice in every breeze, and in every bird's note seemed to lurk a joy. (XVI)

Here we have the 'rivalry' of the two valleys defined in a quite different way, a way that is verbally related to Tess's sensuous and emotional experience (the pedantic 'photosphere' striking the only incongruous note). The suggestions of hope and recovery are unmistakable, and appropriate to the first chapter of a 'Phase' of the novel entitled 'The Rally'. And yet, as Tess descends this same valley, the 'Froom waters ... clear as the pure river of life shown to the Evangelist', become a river exhausted by aeons of geological activity, and we are sharply reminded that Tess was of not the slightest consequence to her natural surroundings, that the sudden burst of sound 'was not the expression of the valley's consciousness that lovely Tess had arrived'. 'Who in his senses would have thought that it was? asks Vernon Lee. The answer is surely, a Romantic poet—Wordsworth, perhaps, to whom Hardy twice alludes in sarcastic asides elsewhere in the novel (III and LI). Hardy's undertaking to defend Tess as a pure woman by emphasizing her kinship with Nature[11] perpetually drew him towards the Romantic view of Nature as a reservoir of benevolent impulses, a view which one side of his mind rejected as falsely sentimental. Many Victorian writers, struggling to reconcile the view of Nature inherited from the Romantics with the discoveries of Darwinian biology, exhibit the same conflict, but it is particularly noticeable in Hardy.

A passage which seems especially revealing in this respect is that which describes Tess's gloomy nocturnal rambling in the weeks following her seduction, where she is explicitly shown entertaining the pathetic fallacy, and her mistake explicitly pointed out by the author:

> On these lonely hills and dales her quiescent glide was of a piece with the element she moved in. Her flexuous and stealthy figure became an integral part of the scene. At times her whimsical fancy would intensify natural processes around her till they seemed a part of her own story. Rather they became a part of it; for the world is only a psychological phenomenon, and what they seemed they were. The midnight airs and gusts, moaning amongst the tightly-wrapped buds and bark of the winter twigs, were formulae of bitter reproach. A wet day was the expression of irremediable grief at her weakness in the mind of some vague ethical being whom she could not class definitely as the God of her childhood, and could not comprehend as any other.
>
> But this encompassment of her own characterization, based on shreds of convention, peopled by phantoms and voices antipathetic to her, was a sorry and mistaken creation of Tess's fancy—a cloud of moral hobglobins by which she was terrified without reason. It was they that were out of harmony with the actual world, not she. Walking among the sleeping birds in the hedges, watching the skipping rabbits on a moonlit warren, or standing under a pheasant-laden bough, she looked upon herself as a figure of Guilt intruding into the haunts of Innocence. But all the while she was making a distinction where there was no difference. Feeling herself in antagonism she was quite in accord. She had been made to break an accepted social law, but no law known to the environment in which she fancied herself such an anomaly. (XIII)

Here we have two paragraphs, one describing Tess's subjective state of mind, and the second describing the objective 'reality'. We are meant to feel that the second cancels out the first, that 'guilt' is a fabrication of social convention, something unknown to the natural order which Tess distorts by projecting her own feelings into it. It seems to me, however, that there is an unresolved conflict in Hardy's rhetoric here. Not only are the 'midnight airs and gusts, moaning amongst the tightly wrapped buds and bark of the winter twigs' images of sorrow and remorse too moving and impressive to be easily overthrown by the rational arguments of the second paragraph; we are explicitly told that 'the world is only a psychological [i.e. subjective] phenomenon', in which case the view expressed in the second paragraph is as 'subjective' as that expressed in the first, and has no greater validity. If Tess felt herself in antagonism she *was* in antagonism. But in fact 'antagonism' is a clumsy formulation of the experience so delicately expressed in the first paragraph. That Nature should present its most sombre aspect to Tess when she is most desolate is, in a way, evidence of how deeply she is 'in accord' with Nature. There are many other places in the book where Hardy 'intensifies natural processes around Tess till they seem part of her story', without suggesting that she is deceiving herself, e.g.

> She was wretched—O so wretched ... The evening sun was now ugly to her, like a great inflamed wound in the sky. Only a solitary cracked-voiced reed-sparrow greeted her from the bushes by the river, in a sad, machine-made tone, resembling that of a past friend whose friendship she had outworn (XXI)

There is further ambiguity about the 'actual world' of nature with which, according to the author, Tess is in accord without realizing it. Is she mistaken in thinking herself guilty, or Nature innocent, or both? Elsewhere in the novel it is true to say that when Nature is not presented through Tess's consciousness, it is neither innocent nor guilty, but neutral; neither sympathetic nor hostile, but indifferent. When Tess and her young brother are driving their father's cart through the night, 'the cold pulses' of the stars 'were beating in serene dissociation from these two wisps of human life' (IV). The birds and rabbits skip happily and heedlessly round the defenceless Tess at her seduction (XI); and the Valley of the Var has no interest in her arrival. Is not Tess more human in preferring a sad but sympathetic Nature to a gay but indifferent one?

Hardy, then, here undermines our trust in the reliability of Tess's response to Nature, which is his own chief rhetorical device for defending her character and interesting our sympathies on her behalf. Without this winterpiece, which the author dismisses as a delusion of Tess's mind, we would lose the significance of Tess's renewal of energy in the spring which urges her towards the Valley of the Var and her 'rally':

> A particularly fine spring came round, and the stir of germination was almost audible in the buds; it moved her, as it moved the wild animals, and made her passionate to go ... some spirit within her rose automatically as the sap in the twigs. It was unexpended youth, surging up anew after its temporary check, and bringing with it hope, and the invincible instinct towards self-delight. (XV)

But of course the instinct is, in the event, vincible ... and so we return to the basic contradiction pointed out by Ian Gregor, of which he says: 'the small measure in which this confusion, which is central to the theme of the novel, really decreases its artistic compulsion, suggests how effectively the latter is protected against the raids of philosophic speculation'.[12] I find myself in some disagreement with this verdict for, as I have tried to show, the confusion is not merely in the abstractable philosophical content of the novel, but inextricably woven into its verbal texture ...

Notes

1. Vernon Lee, *The Handling of Words and Other Studies in Literary Psychology* (London, 1923) pp. 222–41. Vernon Lee's method does not of course anticipate I.A. Richards' procedure in *Practical Criticism* (London, 1929) exactly. His is primarily pedagogic in purpose; hers, critical. He deals with complete short poems, the context from which they are extracted being historical knowledge of the poem's origins; she deals with extracts from novels which are identified, though they are not discussed as wholes. The similarity resides mainly in their mutual reliance on the close analysis of limited pieces by reference to certain constant assumptions about good literary language.
2. Lee, *The Handling of Words*, p. 224
3. *Ibid.* p. 233.

4. *Ibid.* pp. 227–8.

5. *Ibid.* p. 234.

6. *Ibid.* pp. 240–1.

7. Douglas Brown, *Thomas Hardy* (London, 1954; reprinted 1961) p. 103.

8. Ian Gregor and Brian Nicholas, *The Moral and the Story* (London, 1962) pp. 143–4.

9. *Ibid.*, p. 137

10. Vernon Lee also omits from her transcription the line 'Waow! waow! waow!'; and when quoting the sentence with the fly simile a second time, she omits the comma after *length*, which removes the grammatical ambiguity of which she complains.

11. In the Preface to the 5th edition (1895), Hardy says of readers who had objected to the description of Tess as a 'pure' woman: 'they ignore the meaning of the word in Nature.'

12. Gregor and Nicholas, *The Moral and the Story*, p. 144

178

Psychic Evolution: Darwinism and Initiation in *Tess of the D'Urbervilles*

◆

ELLIOTT B. GOSE, JR

The novels of Thomas Hardy have often been praised for their concern with the issues which the Victorian era was forced to face by developments in philosophy and science, and by social change. Although all of these concerns can be found in *Tess of the d'Urbervilles*, the most central to the book are Hardy's interpretation of two specialized developments in mid-Victorian thought, Darwinism and anthropology. The impact of the Darwinian controversy on Hardy is well known, but his interest in the new science of anthropology has not been much remarked. Commentators have, of course, frequently noted his interest in folklore and superstition, but usually as an indication of the cultural and intellectual conflict which was so important in making Hardy the kind of Victorian writer he was. Victorian England was characterized not only by conflicts but by attempts at synthesis; the concept of evolution, for instance, was not confined to the study of biology but spread to the humanities as well. Its most obvious application was in charting the history and culture of man; thus, most of Hardy's novels deal in some form with the problems of social evolution. He usually goes behind contemporary problems, however, to what is always a key relation to him, that of man to nature. Specifically, in *Tess* he brings together the evolutionary view of man as a product of nature with the anthropological findings about early man's attempt to control nature through primitive rituals.

On December 18, 1890, shortly after he finished writing *Tess*, Hardy made the following entry in his notebook:

> Mr E. Clodd this morning gives an excellently neat answer to my question why the superstitions of a remote Asiatic and a Dorset labourer are the same: 'The attitude of man,' he says, 'at corresponding levels of culture, before like phenomena, is pretty much the same, your Dorset peasants representing the

SOURCE *Nineteenth Century Fiction*, vol. 18, no. 3, December 1963, pp. 261–72.

persistence of the barbaric idea which confuses persons and things, and founds wide generalizations on the slenderest analogies.'

(This 'barbaric idea which confuses persons and things' is, by the way, also common to the highest imaginative genius—that of the poet.)[1]

Mr E Clodd of the quotation was Edward Clodd, an anthropologist friend, and from references in *Tess* there can be no doubt that Hardy had been doing a fair amount of reading in anthropology. To begin demonstrating Hardy's use of it, we might look at a passage in the novel which indicates his interest in primitive rites.

> The house ... was of recent erection—indeed almost new—and of the same rich colour that formed such a contrast with the evergreens of the lodge. Far behind the corner of the house—which rose like a geranium bloom against the subdued colours around—stretched the soft azure landscape of The Chase—a truly venerable tract of forest land, one of the few remaining woodlands in England of undoubted primæval date, wherein Druidical mistletoe was still found on aged oaks, and where enormous yew-trees, not planted by the hand of man, grew as they had grown when they were pollarded for bows. All this sylvan antiquity, however, though visible from The Slopes, was outside the immediate boundaries of the estate.[2]

Hardy's contrast between the newness, neatness, and tameness of The Slopes, and the antiquity and wildness of The Chase is intensified by the mention of the 'Druidical mistletoe ... still found on aged oaks.' He is referring to Pliny's famous description of the central rite of the Druids, who

> esteem nothing more sacred than the mistletoe and the tree on which it grows, provided only that the tree is an oak. But apart from this they choose oak-woods for their sacred groves ... After due preparations have been made for a sacrifice and a feast under the tree, they hail it as the universal healer and bring to the spot two white bulls, whose horns have never been bound before. A priest clad in white robe climbs the tree and with a golden sickle cuts the mistletoe, which is caught in a white cloth. Then they sacrifice the victims, praying that God may make his own gift to prosper with those upon whom he has bestowed it. They believe that a potion prepared from mistletoe will make barren animals to bring forth.[3]

It is to The Chase that Alec takes Tess the night he seduces her. And Hardy reminds us of its character in that scene too. 'Darkness and silence ruled everywhere around. Above them rose the primeval yews and oaks of The Chase.' Slight though this allusion is, it serves as a clue linking the scene with the pattern of sacrificial images which are present in the most vivid scenes in the novel. Before going on to analyze them, however, we must look briefly at the images which forbode Tess' rape. One of these, Hardy specifically has Tess interpret as prefigurative, the pricking of her chin by a thorn on the red roses given her by Alec (chap. vi). Earlier, he has Alec smoke a red-tipped cigar in front of Tess, and then offer her a strawberry:

> He stood up and held it by the stem to her mouth.
> 'No—no!' she said quickly, putting her fingers between his hand and her

lips. 'I would rather take it in my own hand.'

'Nonsense!' he insisted; and in a slight distress she parted her lips and took it in (chap. v)

Tess' passivity is emphasized heavily in the first two sections of the book and, as this incident indicates, is an important ingredient in her becoming Alec's victim. Although the victim of a ritual sacrifice and the aspirant in a ritual initiation can be easily distinguished by intellectual analysis, in this novel we shall find Hardy tying the two together in an emotionally convincing manner.

In 1887, three years before beginning *The Golden Bough*, James Frazer had published *Totemism*, an authoritative statement on a subject which Western man was just beginning grasp. Although we have no proof that Hardy read the book, we may assume that by 1889 he would have known some of the rituals documented by Frazer, including a common form of totemic initiation, being 'smeared with blood.' The meaning of this ceremony, according to Frazer, is indicated

> by the following custom. Among the Gonds, a non-Aryan race of Central India, the rajas, by intermarriage with Hindus, have lost much of their pure blood and are half Hindus; hence one of the ceremonies at their installation is 'the touching of their foreheads with a drop of blood drawn from the body of a pure aborigine of the tribe they belong to' (pp. 42–3).

This custom of symbolic initiation among primitive tribes is imaginatively adapted by Hardy to form an important figurative pattern in the plot of *Tess*. It makes its appearance in the death of Prince, the incident earlier in the book which caused Tess to go to The Slopes. She had fallen asleep on a wagon she was driving to market with the result that her horse was run down by the mail cart.

> The pointed shaft of the cart had entered the breast of the unhappy Prince like a sword, and from the wound his life's blood was spouting in a stream, and falling with a hiss into the road.
>
> In her despair Tess sprang forward and put her hand upon the hole, with the only result that she became splashed from face to skirt with the crimson drops.[4]

The consequence of Tess' falling asleep is to deprive her father of his means of livelihood. Her guilt causes her to go to The Slopes where Alec, after telling her he has sent a new horse to her father, seduces her. Cause and effect on a symbolic level are also evident. Like the d'Urbervilles, Prince's name shows him to be of noble blood, though like them he is decrepit. The rendered image of his death by the 'pointed shaft' is parallel with the covert image of Tess' rape by Alec.

As indicated by these two incidents and the description of the slaughter of rodents at harvest (chap. xiv), Hardy saw that man's relation to nature was based on certain harsh realities and inexorable cycles which would necessarily be reflected in primitive rituals. Yet looked at more closely, Hardy's characterization of Tess indicates that rape may be too strong a word for what happens in The Chase. In chapter xii we find out that, 'temporarily blinded' by Alec's 'ardent manners,' Tess 'had been stirred to confused surrender awhile.' In other words Tess is not merely a victim of Alec's lust, nor of Hardy's view of nature's ironic and fateful law of cause and effect; despite her mother's bad advice and her own physical weariness, she is finally responsible for her own nature and development. Hardy emphasizes her no longer having a peasant mentality like her mother's, and her having lost contact with the real meaning of natural processes. In fact at the end of chap. xiii he rebukes her for the Victorian moral conscience with which her modern education has provided her.

Then in 'Phase the Third' of the novel, Hardy puts her in a situation where her consciousness of being outside the social pale is in conflict with the unconscious 'appetite for joy which pervades all creation, that tremendous force which sways humanity to its purpose' (chap. xxx). In making this and similar statements, Hardy is affirming a certain attitude toward nature, an attitude that puts a somewhat different emphasis on the relations among natural creatures than did Darwin's notion of the survival of the fittest. The two views are not, of course, incompatible as Hardy's term 'appetite' indicates, and I shall show presently how Darwin's concept is connected with the initiation ritual we have noted in *Tess*. But first I would like to distinguish between Darwin's theory of natural selection and the older theory of evolution. Where Darwin's theory emphasizes competition for survival, the other asserts the connection of all life and leaves room for the concept of co-operation. Hardy was aware of both, but he saw man's progress as being tied to evolution. Of several notebook entries on this subject, I pick the most relevant. 'The discovery of the law of evolution, which revealed that all organic creatures are of one family, shifted the center of altruism from humanity to the whole conscious world collectively.'[5] In the light of such a belief we can appreciate Tess' reaction to the burial of Prince. 'The children cried anew. All except Tess. Her face was dry and pale, as though she regarded herself in the light of a murderess' (chap. iv). We might also notice how the idea of initiation becomes associated with the idea of evolution at this point. Both beliefs connect the individual who accepts them with the past and determine his future actions. Noting Tess' emotional adherence to both, we may draw some interesting conclusions about her nature. Her reaction to suffering can be seen as a weakness because it leaves her vulnerable, but it can also be seen as a strength because it makes her aware as she had not been before. As we noted, Hardy felt that ' "the barbaric idea which confuses persons and things" is ... also common to the highest imaginative genius—that of the poet.' Tess' retrogression to anthropomorphism may thus be seen as a step forward in Hardy's conception of what I would like to call psychic evolution.

The conception of psychic evolution is evident from many hints in Hardy's writing, but especially from a comment he wrote the year before he finished *Tess*.

> A 'sensation-novel' is possible in which the sensationalism is not casualty, but evolution; not physical but psychical ... [In the latter] the casualty or adventure is held to be of no intrinsic interest, but the effect upon the faculties is the important matter to be depicted (*Early Life*, p. 268).

Tess is obviously such a 'sensation-novel.' Reading it, we must forget the sensationalism and melodrama (Hardy felt that 'it is not improbabilities of incident but improbabilities of character that matter,' *Early Life*, p. 231). But once we have seen what Hardy intends us to focus on, we can sympathize with Tess' struggle to advance on the scale of psychic evolution and we can appreciate the insight Hardy showed in connecting the psychical and the physical, in rendering the struggles of mind through evolutionary and ritualistic images. Although he tends to make a dichotomy between mind and body, he always ties them together, always makes us aware that Tess cannot separate her spiritual rapture from her position in the environment. Perhaps the scene where this is brought home most strikingly is the one in which she moves through the garden listening to Angel's flute. Despite the exaltation she feels from the music, her body is being stained by 'sticky blights which, though snow-white on the apple-tree trunks, made madder stains on her skin' (chap. xix).

The scene in the garden may be taken as one of many omens that Tess' effort to achieve psychic evolution will finally be unsuccessful. Although Hardy favored evolution with its sympathy and co-operation, he did not forget natural selection with its competitive lack of compassion. Man's aggressive nature must be reckoned with, as we have seen in Alec's seduction of Tess. A variation on this active–submissive relation is given much later in the novel when Alec makes another bid for Tess on the platform of the threshing machine at Flintcomb Ash. In response to his suggestion.

> She passionately swung the glove by the gauntlet directly in his face. It was heavy and thick as a warrior's, and it struck him flat on the mouth. Fancy might have regarded the act as the recrudesence of a trick in which her armed progenitors were not unpractised. Alec fiercely started up from his reclining position. A scarlet oozing appeared where her blow had alighted, and in a moment the blood began dropping from his mouth upon the straw ...
>
> 'Now, punish me!' she said, turning up her eyes to him with the hopeless defiance of the sparrow's gaze before its captor twists its neck. 'Whip me, crush me; you need not mind those people under the rick! I shall not cry out. Once victim, always victim—that's the law!'
>
> ... He stepped across to her side and held her by the shoulders, so that she shook under his grasp. 'Remember, my lady, I was your master once! I will be your master again. If you are any man's wife you are mine!'[6]

Although Tess says that once victim, always victim is the law (of nature), she has actually taken the first step toward denying the dominance Alec gained when he sealed their relation with her blood. When she finally kills him, she draws all his blood, and Hardy has her say afterwards, 'I feared long ago, when I struck him on the mouth with my glove, that I might do it some day for the trap he set for me in my simple youth.' The image depicts man's aggressive nature, for the trap was to catch a bird, as is clear both from an earlier comment of Hardy's that she 'had been caught during her days of immaturity like a bird in a springe,' and from one of her accusations against Alec: 'O, you have torn my life all to pieces ... made me a victim, a caged wretch.'[7] It is evident, therefore, that despite Hardy's hatred of cruelty and his hope that in man co-operation based on evolutionary kinship would overcome competition based on natural selection, he recognized the strong hold of the more brutal means of maintaining relations.

In *Tess* Darwinian self-assertion manifests itself in an aggressive–submissive pattern which has its locus in the relations of Alec and Tess but is generalized to include society past and contemporary. In his commentary on the seduction scene earlier, Hardy includes a hint that retribution for past misconduct by Tess' ancestors might be involved. He immediately repudiates such visiting of 'the sins of the fathers upon the children' (chap. xi) on philosophic grounds, but the connection of the aristocracy with aggression is based symbolically throughout the novel, as in her striking Alec with the warrior's glove. Another important use of it is in the legend of the d'Urberville coach, which is mentioned twice, but never fully explained. The first time, Angel tells her about it. 'A certain d'Urberville of the sixteenth or seventeenth century committed a dreadful crime in his family coach and since that time members of the family see or hear the old coach whenever— But I'll tell you another day—it is rather gloomy' (chap. xxxiii). Later, Alec adds a little more: 'One of the family is said to have abducted some beautiful woman, who tried to escape from the coach in which he was carrying her off and in the struggle he killed her—or she killed him—I forget which' (chap. li). Taking the relation between Alec and Tess as a modern repetition of this legend, we can see that the moral of it will be that the victim can turn on her aggressor. That is certainly the outcome in Tess' life. The connection of the coach with the problem is evident: the legend is mentioned in the first place because Tess was bothered by the sight of the coach she and Angel were to use on their wedding night.

> A close carriage was ordered from a roadside inn, a vehicle which had been kept there ever since the old days of post-chaise travelling. It had stout wheel-spokes, and a heavy felloes, a great curved bed, immense straps and springs, and a pole like a battering-ram. The postilion was a venerable 'boy' of sixty—a martyr to rheumatic gout, the result of excessive exposure in youth, counteracted by strong liquors—who had stood at the inn-doors doing nothing for the whole five-and-twenty years that elapsed since he had no longer been required to ride professionally, as if expecting the old times to come back again. He had a permanent running wound on the outside of his right leg, originated by the

constant bruising of aristocratic carriage-poles during the many years that he had been in regular employ at the King's Arms, Casterbridge (chap. xxxiii).

Just as Prince is the victim of the battering ram of the mail coach, and Tess is of Alec, so the postilion is of the 'aristocratic carriage-poles.' The development of this 'boy' has been arrested at that point in the past when he was forced to submit to aristocratic dominance to be used as an object instead of a person. We might almost say that the postilion has undergone a ceremony of blood initiation which commits him for life, whether or not conditions change afterward and his position becomes anomalous. In a similar way, Tess in her youth has also been initiated by her blood bath from the victim Prince. Both she and the 'boy' have become victims bound always to submit in the presence of an aggressor. As victims they belong to an almost sub-human order, one closely tied to brute nature. But Tess has the possibility of changing her state by marrying Angel. He himself realizes the symbolic import of their wedding, that after it Tess will no longer be a peasant, forced to submit to the toils of manual labour. He even decorates the bridal chamber appropriately: Tess looks at

> the tester of white dimity; something was hanging beneath it, and she lifted the candle to see what it was. A bough of mistletoe. Angel had put it there; she knew that in an instant. This was the explanation of that mysterious parcel ... whose contents he would not explain to her, saying that time would soon show her the purpose thereof (chap. xxxv)

But the marriage is never consummated, and the blood seal of Alec, given under the mistletoe in the darkness of The Chase, is consequently never revoked.

After leaving Angel, Tess undergoes a reversal of psychic evolution. Having lost her chance of breaking free of Alec's seal, of becoming a fuller individual guided by Angel's high spiritual nature, she reverts first to the peasant with her family, and then below that to the animal level after she leaves them. 'There was something of the habitude of the wild animal in the unreflecting instinct with which she rambled on—disconnecting herself by littles from her eventful past at every step, obliterating her identity.' This reversion to instinct is imaged also in her re-enactment of the circumstances leading up to her earlier despoilment.[8] In The Chase Alec had 'made a sort of couch or nest for her in the deep moss of dead leaves.' This time 'her haunted soul' causes Tess to enter an upland plantation where 'she scraped together the dead leaves till she had formed them into a large heap, making a sort of nest in the middle. Into this Tess crept.' She moves herself back up to the human level after one of the most striking incidents in the book. She hears strange sounds and when daylight comes

> Under the trees several pheasants lay about, their rich plumage dabbled with blood; some were dead, some feebly twitching a wing, some staring up at the sky, some pulsating quickly, some contorted, some stretched out—all of them writhing in agony, except the fortunate ones whose tortures had ended

during the night by the inability of nature to bear more ...

'Poor darlings—to suppose myself the most miserable being on earth in the sight o' such misery as yours!' she exclaimed, her tears running down as she killed the birds tenderly. 'And not a twinge of bodily pain about me! I be not mangled, and I be not bleeding, and I have two hands to feed and clothe me' (chap. xli)

As her dialect indicates, Tess reacts as a peasant here, but this again leaves her a potential victim. Despite her rejection of Alec on the machine, she has to give in to him finally when her father dies, and her family is left homeless. As we might expect, her life with him, while materially good, is sensual, soulless. When Angel meets her again at the 'pleasure city' of Sandbourne, he has 'a vague consciousness of one thing, though it was not clear to him till later; that his original Tess had spiritually ceased to recognize the body before him as hers—allowing it to drift, like a corpse upon the current, in a direction dissociated from its living will' (chap. lv). He should be completely conscious of what has happened, however. For the climax of his belated conversion had been his realization that 'the beauty or ugliness of a character lay not only in its achievements, but in its aims and impulses; its true history lay, not among things done, but among things willed' (chap. xlix). Alec has subdued her pride and will, immersed them in luxury, but upon her meeting Angel again, that will comes to life. She stabs Alec to sever finally the blood bond between them. The image describing his fate is very similar to that used in the scene with Prince, whose death was almost directly responsible for putting her under Alec's domination. 'The wound was small, but the point of the blade had touched the heart of the victim.' Murdering him is the only way left to her, and to do it she has to regress as far down the human scale as Alec had in The Chase, back that is to the pagan Druids. Angel feels 'amazement at the strength of her affection for himself, and at the strangeness of its quality, which had apparently extinguished her moral sense altogether' (chap. lvii). And the last important scene in the novel is given a background appropriate to Tess' state: 'At an indefinite height overhead something made the black sky blacker, which had the semblance of a vast architrave beneath and between; the surfaces echoed their soft rustle; but they seemed to be still out of doors. The place was roofless.' They have reached the Druid's Stonehenge, and when Tess asks if it is a 'heathen temple,' Angel replies, 'Yes. Older than the centuries; older than the d'Urbervilles.' By chance or instinct she falls asleep on the Stone of Sacrifice. 'Her breathing now was quick and small, like that of a lesser creature than a woman ... Soon the light was strong, and a ray shone upon her unconscious form, peering under her eyelids and waking her' (chap. lviii). She is taken away by the representatives of society, who have surrounded her while she slept.

A combination of social pressure, mischance, and willfulness have put Tess in a position where she can gain temporary happiness only by discarding civilized self-restraint. As a result of her blood sacrifice of Alec, her own death has become inevitable. Although Tess was obeying the kinship-through-evolution code when she put the pheasants out of their misery, in brutally freeing herself from a brute relationship, she moved down the scale of psychic evolution to the primitive level. Seen, therefore, in the perspective of the patterns Hardy has constructed, her death is called for by the dark law of man's earliest relation to nature as much as by any unlightened social law. And set in the elemental grandeur of Stonehenge, it would have been a fitting primitive sacrifice.

Early in the novel Hardy had speculated whether 'at the acme and summit of the human progress [human relations] will be corrected by a finer intuition, a closer interaction of the social machinery than that which now jolts us around and along; but such completeness is not to be prophesied, or even conceived as possible' (chap. v). This analysis, adequate enough as a statement of the central problems in *Jude the Obscure*, refers to only a part of what actually goes on in *Tess of the d'Urbervilles*. Through his feeling for man's place in the evolutionary scale of progress and regress, and his insight into the ritual necessities of man's relation to nature, Hardy makes Tess appealing not as a victim of society but as a human being caught in the ebb and flow of history, environment, and self.

Notes

1. Florence Hardy, *The Early Life of Thomas Hardy* (London, 1928), pp. 301–2. Clodd's contention was a truism by 1891, being in fact the necessary premise for comparative anthropology. Hardy's observation had precedent too. In *Primitive Culture* (first ed. 1871), Edward Tylor, the father of English anthropology, frequently made the point. See for instance the end of chap. viii: 'A poet of our own day has still much in common with the minds of uncultured tribes in the mythologic stage of thought.'

2. Since there are so many editions of *Tess* available, I will make my citations by chapter. This passage is from chapter v.

3. Quoted by Frazer in chapter lxv of his one volume abridgement of *The Golden Bough*. Also quoted by Bullfinch in *The Age of Fable* (1855).

4. Chapter v. This scene is analyzed both by Dorothy Van Ghent in *The English Novel: Form and Function* (New York, 1953), and by Arnold Kettle, *An Introduction to the English Novel*, Vol. II (London, 1953).

5. Florence Hardy, *The Later Years of Thomas Hardy* (London, 1930), p. 138. Although Hardy wrote this particular version of his belief in 1909, he had written a similar one the year before he began *Tess* (*Early Life*, p. 294). And he is completely straightforward in *Tess* itself, referring to the cruelty of the pheasant hunters, 'at once so unmannerly and so unchivalrous towards their weaker fellows in Nature's teeming family' (chap. xli).

6. Chap. xlvii. After she descends from the machine, Alec says to her, in an image reminiscent of primitive sacrifice, 'How the little limbs tremble! You are weak as a bled calf, you know you are.'

7. Chap. lvi. Ellipsis Hardy's. This is an early version of the passage, available in the Modern Library hardcover edition of *Tess*. The revised version is much less illuminating: 'O, you have torn my life all to pieces ... made me be what I prayed you in pity not to make me be again!'

8. This parallel is noted by John Holloway in his article 'Hardy's Major Fiction' in *From Jane Austin to Joseph Conrad*, ed. Rathburn and Steinmann (Minneapolis, 1958). Holloway also comments on the Darwinian motifs in *Tess*.

Jude the Obscure as a Tragedy

———————— ◆ ————————

ARTHUR MIZENER

> *. . . who cannot see*
> *What Earth's ingrained conditions are.*
> *— 'Seventy-four and Twenty.'*

I suppose no one will question Hardy's right to the title of 'the first great tragedian in novel form,' taking *tragedy* in its looser sense. Yet there seems to be a general feeling that somehow his novels are not successful, are not, for all their deep sense of the horror of ordinary life, really tragic. 'There is,' as Mr E.M. Forster says, 'some vital problem that has not been answered, or even posed, in the misfortunes of Jude the Obscure.' The cause of that feeling is, I think, an attitude which is probably more the product of his age than of Hardy's own understanding. In a sense the courage of Hardy's profoundest conviction failed him, precisely as Tennyson's did, under the pressure of the reasoning of his age.

Hardy, to be sure, refused to identify what he called 'the ideal life' with the conventional views of his times, and this refusal saved him from the superior fatuousness of people like Tennyson and Browning at their worst. He could, indeed, be devastating about these conventional views: 'How could smug Christian optimism worthy of a dissenting grocer find a place inside a man [Browning] who was so vast a seer and feeler when on neutral ground?'[1] Yet at bottom Hardy's attitude suffered from the same kind of fault as Browning's. Browning tried to convince himself that because God was in his heaven all must be right with the world. Hardy's objection to this view of things was that it believed in heaven at all; for Hardy, using Browning's logic in reverse, tried to convince himself that because all was obviously not right with the world, there could be no heaven. The only source of hope left him, therefore, was the belief that the world would, by a process of moral evolution, become a kind of heaven in time.[2] This kind of hope was the only kind Hardy could discover, once he had denied any

SOURCE *The Southern Review*, 1940–1, vol. 6, pp. 193–213

independent reality to the dream of perfection, and without some hope not only tragedy but life itself is impossible.

The trouble with this view, for tragedy, is that its possessor is incapable of facing squarely the paradox of evil. Browning felt that, having accepted the proposition that God is the all-great and the all-loving too, he had committed himself to a denial of evil; life was therefore an exhilarating battle in which one proved his worth for heaven —

> *Only they see not God, I know,*
> *Nor all that chivalry of his,*
> *The soldier-saints who, row on row,*
>
> *Burn upward each to his point of bliss —*
> *Since, the end of life being manifest,*
> *He had burned his way thro' the world to this.*[3]

Hardy, feeling profoundly the ingrained evil of human and animal life, thought that feeling committed him to a denial of heaven. Thus both Browning and Hardy found it impossible not to deny, for the sake of a smaller consistency, one of the realities which must be recognized and accepted for the larger consistency of tragedy. Both found it impossible to believe in 'the goodness of God' and 'the horrors of human and animal life'; neither, in Keats's phrase, was 'capable of being in uncertainties, mysteries, doubts, without any irritable reaching after fact and reason.' They felt called upon either to explain the real life as a logical corollary of the ideal life, or to explain the ideal life as a logical corollary of the real. They were thus incapable of representing in the same fiction the meaning and splendor of both lives and of using each to illuminate the limitations of the other.

But this inability to escape the smaller consistency was the central weakness of late nineteenth-century literature as a whole:

> there is the assumption that Truth is indifferent or hostile to the desires of men; that these desires were formerly nurtured on legend, myth, all kinds of insufficient experiment; that, Truth being known at last in the form of experimental science, it is intellectually impossible to maintain illusion any longer, at the same time that it is morally impossible to assimilate Truth.[4]

It is in this sense that Hardy's attitude is more the product of his age than of his own understanding. It is probably more remarkable, under the circumstances, that he came as close as he did to escaping from the trap his age unconsciously set for itself than that he was, in the end, caught.

The code Hardy evolved as a description of the ideal life is a secularized version of the Sermon on the Mount, a thoroughly fumigated New Testament morality. The real subject of *Jude* is the evolution of this code in Jude's mind ('a species of Dick Whittington, whose spirit was touched to finer issues than a mere material gain' [89]). In so far as this code is a statement of the potentialities of humanity, it is the possibility of their realization somewhere, somehow, which gives Jude's death meaning. In so far as it is not a statement of the potentialities of humanity Jude is mad and his death meaningless: this alternative was obviously no part of Hardy's intention. But Hardy had no place outside of the actual world of time where he could visualize these potentialities as being realized; he saw no possibility that the noting of death itself, when the long sickness of health and living begins to mend, would bring all things. So he ended by implying the realization of these human potentialities in this world; ended, that is, by denying his most profound conviction, that earth's conditions are ingrained. And if it is difficult to believe that life is evil and God good, it is even more difficult to believe that the evil of life is ingrained and that it will nevertheless presently come unstuck.

That Hardy produced such powerful novels, in spite of his inability to conceive an ideal life with an existence either very strong or outside of time and in spite of the formal limitations which this attitude inevitably imposed on him, is a tribute to his profound rectitude. The power of Hardy's novels is the power of Hardy's character; the consistency and purity of the feeling throughout both the novels and the poems proves that his vision of evil is, quite simply, what he saw. Such feeling cannot be faked. This power makes itself felt in spite of Hardy's fumbling inability to think his way through to an understanding of his personal impressions or to a form which would organize them in terms of their meaning.

2

About his idea in *Jude* Hardy was quite explicit: *Jude* was 'to show the contrast between the ideal life a man wished to lead, and the squalid real life he was fated to lead.... [This] idea was meant to run all through the novel.' It was to be a tragedy 'of the WORTHY encompassed by the INEVITABLE.'[5] Such an idea requires for its successful representation a form which is consciously an artifice, a verisimilar and plausible narrative which the novelist values, not for its own sake, but as the perfect vehicle for his idea. He must keep his narrative alive at every turn with his idea, for he cannot, once committed to it, afford the luxury of a meaningless appeal to his reader's delight in recognition and suspense. The characters of such a novel, as Aristotle said of the characters in the tragedy of his day, are there for the sake of the action, and the action or fable is there, ultimately, for the sake of the idea—*is* the idea.

Yet Hardy, with such an essentially tragic idea never freed himself wholly from the naturalistic assumption that narrative must be significant histori-cally rather than fabulously.[6] In the case of *Jude* this assumption forced him to identify himself as author with his hero instead of with the action as a whole. Jude is not a character in a larger composition, the dramatization of one of several presented points of view which go together to make up the author's attitude, because Hardy's attitude was not complex and inclusive but simple and exclusive. He therefore sought to contrast the ideal life with the real life, not of man but of *a* man. That is to say, he wrote a naturalistic

169

novel, a history of his hero, in which the hero is the author, for Jude is obviously autobiographical in the general sense.[7] The essential meaning of his fiction for Hardy is its narrative or 'historical' meaning, and Jude's understanding of that history is Hardy's. All that the narrative which is a perfect artifice ever proves according to Hardy is the historical existence of a 'consummate artist'; all that it even tempts us to believe in is the historical reality of the events it presents. Hardy never really faced the possibility that a great work of art aims at a kind of truth superior (but not necessarily contradictory) to a scientific and historical verisimilitude.[8] For Hardy, therefore, the true narrative was one which conformed to a historical conception of the truth from which the fabulous was very carefully excluded; and the truest of these was, in the general sense, autobiographical, since only the man who had lived through experiences generally like those described in the narrative could represent with historical accuracy not only the external events but the thoughts and opinions of a participant in these events.

Yet because Hardy had an idea he was not content simply to tell a story. If that idea was not finely enough conceived to drive him to discard the naturalistic form, it was strong enough to make him stretch that form to the breaking point by the use of devices which have no place in his kind of novel. There is, for example, nothing to be said against the use of a certain amount of coincidence in the novel which is consistently an artifice, but it only weakens a novel which depends for its acceptance on the reader's conviction of the distinguishably historical truth of its hero's career. In the same way Hardy's carefully devised contrasts fail of their full purpose because he is writing a novel at whose center there is no final contrast.[9] These contrasts are not, therefore, means for enriching a central contrast between a vision of the ideal life and a vision of the real life; they are but means for contrasting a single view of things, which is true, with all other views of things, which are false. And this is the contrast of melodrama rather than of tragedy. In the same way, too, Hardy's use of symbolic incident, for all its immense immediate effectiveness, remains a kind of desperate contrivance in a novel which is not itself a symbol but 'a true historie.' These incidents do not, that is, have in them implications of contrasted views of experience; they are merely poetic projections of the hero's view of things. The result of all this is a novel which is formally neither fish, flesh, nor good red herring, a novel whose tremendous verisimilar life is constantly being sapped by a series of irrelevant devices and yet remains, as a systematic artifice, 'a paradise of loose ends.'

3

The nearest Hardy came to escaping from the strangling limitations of his attitude and the naturalistic form to which it committed him was in his pastoral idealization of the life of his Wessex peasants. He might, by completing this idealization, have produced profound romantic comedy; for he could see so clearly that

> it is the on-going—*i.e.*, the 'becoming'—of the world that produces its sadness.
> If the world stood still at a felicitous moment there would be no sadness in it.
> The sun and the moon standing still on Ajalon was not a catastrophe for Israel,
> but a type of Paradise (*The Early Life*, p. 265).

It is his feeling that the world had come perceptibly closer to standing still at
a felicitous moment for his Wessex peasants in the old days which tempted
him to see their life as a type of Paradise.

Yet he did not know how to subdue the rational fact of the matter. The
on-going of the world worked among the Wessex people too, if more slowly;
and even if it did not, only the illusion of nostalgia could make one who
knew that earth's conditions are ingrained suppose there had even been a
felicitous moment in the past. The life of these peasants can be, for Hardy,
only a charming anachronism; and their comments, though Hardy uses
them chorically in his novels, are really irrelevant to any meaning which is
possible for him. When Mrs Edlin comments on Sue's marriage—'In my
time we took it more careless, and I don't know that we was any the worse
for it!' (438)—or when she is to be heard 'honestly saying the Lord's Prayer
in a loud voice, as the Rubric directed' (333), she is only an example of how
much simpler and easier life was before man had progressed in the hands of
inescapable time to his present high state of nervous and emotional organization. She cannot be, as Hardy's use of her sometimes seems to imply she is,
an image from a timeless and ideal pastoral world, an Arden to which his
hero will escape from the squalid real world of Duke Frederick's court. For
much as Hardy longed, however unconsciously, to make out of the world of
his Wessex peasants an ideal pastoral world, the weary weight of its unintel-
ligible actuality so burdened him that he was never able to see it as a type of
Paradise, to make it a part of his means for 'holding in a single thought
reality and justice.' It was indeed Hardy's tragedy as a writer that he never
found any such means. Mrs Edlin and the rest of his peasants remain
meaningful only at the level of history; they are samples of the simpler and
easier way of life in the past, preserved for Hardy's day by an eddy in time.

The moments of happiness which come in most of Hardy's novels just
before the catastrophes are particular instances of his inability to make the
country life a type of Paradise. Grace and Giles in Sherton Abbey while they
still believe the divorce possible, Tess and Angel between the murder of Alec
and the arrest at Stonehenge, Jude and Sue at the Wessex Agricultural
Show, these felicitous moments are always moments when the protagonists
believe they have won their way back to the Garden of Eden, to purity of
heart and to a kindly country world which will be a satisfactory home for the
pure in heart. Only a rather staggering amount of coincidence in the
narrative or naïveté in the characters can provide moments of such delusion
in the real world as Hardy knew it; and because Hardy was committed to a
naturalistic form he not only had to produce these moments by coincidence
and naïveté, but to demonstrate that, except as faint foreshadowings of a

reformed humanity, they were fool's paradises. Thus Hardy's time-bound universe and the naturalistic form which it forced on him as a novelist prevented his imagining or presenting an artificial world which contained both reality and justice.

Committed as he was to the truth of abstract reason rather than the truth of imagination, Hardy therefore had no choice but to conceive his ideal life as a felicitous moment some place in the future of the real life, since this ideal life was the only kind which could be reached by strict reason from his premise. Hardy's faith in this kindly country world to which humanity would win in the course of history is seldom explicit in the novels, since to make it explicit is to make explicit also the contradiction between his faith and Hardy's overwhelming conviction that Earth's conditions are ingrained. That faith is, however, of necessity everywhere implicit in his presentation of the events of human and natural life; it is his only source for the light which reveals the horror of these events.[10]

In that Hardy's novels rest, in this indirect fashion, on a belief in the world's progress toward a felicitous future, their meaning is the meaning of sentimental pastoral. They are what *As You Like It* would be without Jaques to remind us and the senior Duke that 'the penalty of Adam' was not merely 'the season's difference' but the knowledge of good and evil, without Touchstone to show us that weariness of the legs is as significant in its way as weariness of the spirit in its, and his love of Jane Smile as real as Silvius's love of Phoebe or Orlando's of Rosalind. For however much Hardy failed to recognize it, his whole view of things was based on the assumption that the world of *The Woodlanders* without Fitzpiers and Mrs Charmond and an educated Grace would be an ideal world, a world of

> *Men surfeited of laying heavy hands*
> *Upon the innocent,*
> *The mild, the fragile, the obscure content*
> *Among the myriads of thy family.*
> *Those, too, who love the true, the excellent,*
> *And make their daily moves a melody.*
> *[The Dynasts]*

The success of such poems as 'In Time of "The Breaking of Nations"' depends on the implication that the life of the man harrowing clods and the maid and her wight is not only eternal—a world that stands still; but felicitous—a world which knows only the sweet adversity of 'the season's difference' and not the adversity of evil. Such a pastoral vision of a still point of the turning world was the source of Hardy's sense of the squalid evil of real life. But because he refused to use the life of his Wessex peasants, or any other life, to body forth his forms of things unknown, he was unable to turn those forms to shapes at all.

But if Hardy's combination of half-despairing, scientific humanitarianism, and the naturalistic form which he thought it committed him to, was incapable of pastoral, it was even more incapable of tragedy. Hardy's feeling that the evil of this world was incurable is tragic. But because he was unable to place the source of the idealism by which he measured the world and found it wanting outside of time and therefore, *faute de mieux*, came to believe 'in the gradual ennoblement of man,' his attitude is such as to preclude a formal structure which pits the idealist against the practical man in equal combat. There is no basic, unresolvable tragic tension between the real and the ideal in his attitude, and there is as a consequence no tragic tension in the formal structure it invokes as its representation. The objection to Hardy's form for tragedy is, therefore, not a matter of his occasional awkwardness or carelessness; it is radical.[11]

The assumption which justifies the naturalistic novel is that there can be only one kind of reality, and this is Hardy's assumption. But if there is only one kind of reality there can be also only one kind of truth, and that truth, in *Jude*, is the melioristic view of the world which is the only belief Hardy can find.[12] As author Hardy is therefore unable to represent justly in *Jude* those kinds of men according to whose ideas the world must be run if earth's conditions are ingrained. In his fictional world such people can be shown only in the light of the single true view of things which Hardy and Jude share. It is as if Shakespeare had first made Hamlet altogether incapable of believing the evil of the world incurable and had then shown us Claudius only as Hamlet saw him. Hardy's Claudiuses are not mighty opposites; they are inexplicable villains. At best he can give them credit for being better adjusted to the world as it is at the moment. And for the same reason the only irony he can direct against his hero is the irony to be derived from a demonstration of his temporary maladjustment in a world which, if it is not meaningless, will presently realize that hero's ideal. There is thus neither permanent justification in Hardy for the Arabellas nor permanent irony for the Judes. *Jude* cannot display the very real if limited truth of Claudius's

> *For what we know must be, and is as common*
> *As any the most vulgar thing to sense,*
> *Why should we in our peevish opposition*
> *Take it to heart? Fie! 'tis a fault to heaven,*
> *A fault against the dead, a fault to nature,*
> *To reason most absurd . . .*

nor the very real if terrible absurdity of Hamlet's 'Go to, I'll no more on't; it hath made me mad. I say, we will have no more marriage: . . .'

But if the actions of the Arabellas are seen only as Jude saw them, they must remain for the reader what they were for Jude, the consequences of an inexplicable and brutal stupidity rather than of a different kind of wisdom to Jude's. Thus Hardy's attitude and the form it invoked excluded from his representation, despite the fact that no one knew them better than he did, the point of view of those men and women for whom 'the defence and salvation of the body by daily bread is still a study, a religion, and a desire.' It excluded, too, an understanding of how a woman like Sue might, not in weakness but in strength, deny the validity of Jude's humanitarian idealism. It is one thing, that is, for Jude to preach to Sue the horror of her final surrender to Phillotson and conventional conduct or for Hamlet to preach to his mother the horror of surrender to Claudius and a 'normal' life. It is quite another for Hardy, who does, or Shakespeare, who does not, to commit himself completely as author to this sermon.

At the same time, however, that Hardy presents the almost universal opposition to Jude as inexplicably cruel, he is forced to present people and animals—of which there are a great many in Hardy—in such a way as to support Jude's view of them. In other words, Hardy presents the same kinds of objects at once unjustly and sentimentally. And this is the manifestation in the 'verbal correlative' of Hardy's attitude of the contradiction inherent in that attitude. Because he can see only a single reality, that of the time-bound actual world, the life of that reality has to be at once incurably evil and potentially good.

4

Jude the Obscure is, then, the history of a worthy man's education. Part one, for example, is primarily an account of Jude's youth up to the moment he departs for Christminster in search of learning. From the very beginning, however, Jude and the world through which he moves are presented as they appear to the eyes of one who has accepted the view of things which will be the end-product of Jude's education. In so far as Jude understands this view of things, he is not dramatized; he is the author. In so far as, in his innocence, he ignores the necessities and their implications which this view sees, he is dramatized, objectified by Hardy's irony. Hardy's narrative is, then, secondarily, a demonstration of the consequences of Jude's innocent ignorance of 'Nature's logic'—in Part One in the matter of sex. Nature takes its revenge by entangling Jude irretrievably with Arabella. Hardy gives this demonstration a complex poetic elaboration, and it is easy to suppose as a consequence that his narrative is fundamentally symbolic, the pitting of two different views of experience—Jude's and Arabella's—against each other in a neutral arena. That it is not is evident from that fact that Hardy as the narrator takes advantage of every opportunity to support Jude's attitude. Furthermore, this part cannot, as symbolic narrative, be fitted into any pattern which runs through the book as a whole, for the only pattern *Jude* has is the pattern of history.

Nevertheless the poetic elaboration of this episode is interesting as an example, characteristic of the procedure of the book as a whole, of how Hardy's idea, striving to establish a form which will make sense of it, is constantly breaking through the limits of the naturalistic form. The meeting of Arabella and Jude, for example, is brought about by Arabella's hitting

Jude with a pig's pizzle. No better image for what drew Arabella and Jude together could be found, and, a symbol of their meeting, the pig's pizzle hangs on the bridge rail between them throughout their first meeting. Thereafter, Arabella scarcely appears in this part unaccompanied by pigs. In the same way Jude's dream of an education which will take him through Christminster to a career as a philanthropic bishop is associated with a vision of Christminster as seen from the roof of the old Brown House against the blaze of the setting sun, like the heavenly Jerusalem, as the child Jude says solemnly to the tiler. It is also associated with the New Testament. The New Testament, in its strictly moral aspect, is the textbook of Hardy's humanitarian morality, and in so far as Jude values its morality he is demonstrating his instinctively humanitarian feelings. But Jude's Testament represents for him also religion and, in that it is a Greek text, learning; and in valuing it on these counts he is demonstrating his illusions.

During the wooing of Arabella by Jude there are sporadic recrudescences of these symbols. For example, Hardy is constantly bringing the two lovers back to the rise on which the old Brown House stands, from which Jude had once seen his vision of the heavenly Jerusalem and where, under the influence of an impulse rather awkwardly explained on the narrative level, he had also once knelt and prayed to Apollo and Diana, the god and goddess of learning and chastity (33). Under the influence of Arabella, Jude 'passed the spot where he had knelt to Diana and Phoebus without remembering that there were any such people in the mythology, or that the sun was anything else than a useful lamp for illuminating Arabella's face' (46). Hardy carefully notes, too, that a picture of Samson and Delilah hangs on the wall of the tavern where the two lovers stop for tea but instead, partly at Arabella's suggestion, drink beer (48, 79, 451). The linkage of Arabella and liquor (she had been a barmaid) is valuable to Hardy not only as a piece of naturalism but because it makes Arabella an incarnation of what Jude later calls 'my two Arch Enemies ... my weakness for women and my impulse to strong liquor' (420).

Yet these symbols, effective as they are, are sporadic and unsystematized. Hardy never deserts his naturalistic narrative and commits his meaning to them completely, and so the reader never feels to the full in him what Henry James once so beautifully called the renewal 'in the modern alchemist [of] something like the old dream of the secret of life.' Hardy never thought of himself as a modern alchemist but only as a historian. This fact is plain enough in the climactic scene of this part, the pig-killing scene, for here the pig is not primarily a symbol but an object at the naturalistic level. Arabella takes toward it, as such, an attitude perfectly consistent with the attitude she has maintained throughout. Her concern is for the salableness of the meat, and even her urging that Jude kill the pig quickly when it cries out is determined by her conventional fear lest the cry reveal to the neighbors that the Fawley's have sunk to killing their own pig. 'Poor folks must live,' she says when Jude protests against the inhumanity of slowly bleeding the pig to death (72). And though Hardy's description of the incident precludes any sympathy for Arabella, this statement is profoundly true within the limits of the world Arabella is aware of.

In direct contrast to Arabella's practical view of this killing, Hardy sets Jude's idealistic view of it: 'The white snow, stained with the blood of his fellow-mortal, wore an illogical look to him as a lover of justice, not to say a Christian; ...' (73). There is irony here, of course, but it is directed solely to the point that Hardy 'could not see how the matter was to be mended' (73), not at all to the point that in one very real sense—the sense that Arabella understood—it could and ought never to be mended.[13] This is so because Hardy is in fact and, as a consequence, by the form he has chosen committed to Jude's view of this incident. That commitment is clear in every word Hardy himself writes about the pig; for example: 'The dying animal's cry assumed its third and final tone, the shriek of agony; his glazing eyes rivetting themselves on Arabella with the eloquently keen reproach of a creature recognizing at last the treachery of those who had seemed his only friends' (71).

The consequence of the author's putting the full weight of his authority in this way behind one of the conflicting views of the events is to take the ground out from under the other. The events are presented only as Jude saw them, so that Arabella's view of them seems to the reader simply inexplicably hard-hearted, however commonplace. Hardy can see that Arabella's attitude, in its complete ignorance of Jude's, is grimly funny: ' "'Od damn it all!" she cried, "that ever I should say it! You've over-stuck un! And I telling you all the time—" ' (71). But he cannot see that it is in any sense justified. The result of this commitment of the author is that the scene as a whole becomes sentimental; and it is difficult to resist the temptation to read it as 'a burlesque of the murder of Duncan' with the pig substituted for the king ('Well—you must do the sticking—there's no help for it. I'll show you how. Or I'll do it myself—I think I could.' [70]).

This pig-killing scene is of course meant to connect in the reader's mind with the earlier episode where Farmer Troutham whips Jude for allowing the rooks to eat his corn. For Jude the rooks 'took upon them more and more the aspect of gentle friends and pensioners. ... A magic thread of fellow-feeling united his own life with theirs. Puny and sorry as those lives were, they much resembled his own' (10).[14] Here again Hardy presents these birds and Jude only as Jude sees them. For all his knowledge of 'the defence and salvation of the body' he signally fails to do justice to Farmer Troutham's view of them, just as he fails to do justice to Arabella's view of Jude and the pig, because he cannot present two kinds of truth in a naturalistic novel. Hamlet, to say nothing of Shakespeare, could understand and yet defy augury both for himself and the sparrow, since he knew well in the end from experience what was well enough known to him from his reading from the start, that there is a 'special providence' in these matters, so that 'the readiness is all.' Hardy, like Jude and Jaques, could only weep, knowing no providence at all. Shakespeare could therefore write 'The Phoenix and the Turtle,' Hardy only 'Compassion: An Ode in Celebration of the Centenary of the Royal Society for the Prevention of Cruelty to Animals.'

Part Two (at Christminster) brings Hardy's spiritual Whittington to his London where he is taught that his desire for learning had been only 'a social unrest which had no foundation in the nobler instincts; which was purely an artificial product of civilization' (151). At the very beginning he catches a glimpse of the truth: 'For a moment there fell on Jude a true illumination; that here in the stone-yard was a centre of effort as worthy as that dignified by the name of scholarly study within the noblest of the colleges' (96).[15] Apart from his narrative function Phillotson is used in this part to fore-shadow Jude's discovery of this truth and to reveal what happens to a weaker person at such a disappointment (116–17). Arabella's temporary conversion after Cartlett's death has the same kind of formal relation to Sue's con-version, with the additional irony that Sue's conversion involves a return to active sexual life which she hates, Arabella's a loss of it which she cannot endure (373). Jude's discovery of the fraudulence of learning leaves him only his Christianity; that he will discover this too is 'as dead as a fern-leaf in a lump of coal' Hardy tell us directly (96–7). That it has been replaced by a German-Gothic fake he suggests by his references to the tearing down of the 'hump-backed, wood-turreted, and quaintly hipped' Marygreen church and to the 'tall new building of German–Gothic design' erected in its place (6, 146).

Meanwhile Jude meets his cousin Sue, whom Hardy always keeps before the reader as Jude first saw her in the picture at Marygreen, 'in a broad hat, with radiating folds under the brim like the rays of a halo' (88), not only because she remains always for Jude a saint but because, by a terrible irony, she literally becomes one at the end of the book. Sue has twice Jude's quick-ness of wit and half his strength of character.[16] She therefore saw from the beginning that there was nothing in the universe except 'Nature's law'; but because of her lack of real profundity, she thought also that it was 'Natures ... *raison d'être*, that we should be joyful in what instincts she afforded us ...' (403). When she discovered that nature had no *raison d'être* and that paganism was as false as Christianity had seemed to her, she did not have the strength to face it and went back to conventional wifehood and conventional Christianity. All this, even the impermanence of Sue's paganism (the figures of Venus and Apollo are plaster and come off on her gloves and jacket), is implicit in the episode of the images in Chapter II and in the recollections of Sue's childhood in Chapter VI. By a fine piece of irony—since Sue is, while her strength lasts, a saint of Hardy's humanitarian faith—Hardy has Jude focus not only his physical but his religious feelings on Sue. Gradually he learns from her and experience the omnipotence of Nature's law. But mean-while Jude sees this imperfect saint of humanitarianism as an Anglican saint.

Of the irony of this illusion Hardy makes much (e.g., 123), and in incident after incident, until Jude unlearns his Christianity, he reëmphasizes the irony of this love between the pagan and delicately sexed Sue and the Christian and passionate Jude.

In Part Three Jude, having realized that learning is vain and that only his 'altruistic feeling' had any 'foundation in the nobler instincts,' goes to Melchester, partly because it is 'a spot where worldly learning and intellectual smartness had no establishment' (152), partly because Sue is there. There follows a series of episodes which represent the conflict between Sue's daring humanitarian faith and her weak conventional conduct, on the one hand, and Jude's 'Tractarian' faith and courageously honest conduct, on the other. In the end, of course, Hardy arranges events so as to demonstrate the omnipotence of 'the artificial system of things, under which the normal sex-impulses are turned into devilish domestic gins and springes to noose and hold back those who want to progress' (257), and Sue marries Phillotson. In Part Four Jude's education is almost lost sight of in the welter of narrative detail. Occasionally its progress is marked for the reader, as when Jude replies to Sue's question whether she ought to continue to live with Phillotson: 'Speaking as an order-loving man—which I hope I am, though I fear I am not—I should say yes. Speaking from experience and unbiassed nature, I should say no' (248). Though Sue and Jude determine to sacrifice their love to right conduct, their coming together on the occasion of their aunt's death at Marygreen finally forces Jude to recognize the evil of the church's marriage system and Sue to realize that she must leave Phillotson for Jude. Sue tries at first to avoid marriage and an active sexual life, but Arabella's return, ironically, forces her to yield to Jude in order to hold him.[17]

There follows in Part Five a period when 'the twain were happy—between their times of sadness ...' (341). Hardy shows them as devoted lovers at the Great Wessex Agricultural Show, where they are carefully contrasted with the conventional married couple Arabella and Cartlett (Chapter V). But the pressure of the conventional world on them as unmarried lovers forces them down and down until Jude, 'still haunted by his dream' (395), brings Sue and the children to a 'depressing purlieu' of Christminster. Here Jude makes a speech, from the cross, as it were, to the Roman soldiers of Christminster in which he states the result of his education: 'I perceive there is something wrong somewhere in our social formulas: what it is can only be discovered by men or women with greater insight than mine—if, indeed, they ever discover it—at least, in our time' (388).

It is here at Christminster that Hardy makes the most extreme use of his one completely symbolic character, Father Time.[18] All through Part Five he has been used to strike the ominous note which reminds us that Sue and Jude's moderate happiness is a snare and a delusion. Now, under the influence of his perfectly arbitrary melancholy and the misinterpretation of something Sue says, he kills all the children, including himself. Father Time

178

is Jude and Arabella's son brought up by Jude and Sue, in order that Hardy may say (400):

> On that little shape had converged all the inauspiciousness and shadow which had darkened the first union of Jude, and all the accidents, mistakes, fears, errors of the last. He was their nodal point, their focus, their expression in a single term. For the rashness of those parents he had groaned, for their ill-assortment he had quaked, and for the misfortunes of these he had died.

The effect of this incident on Jude and Sue is to place each of them in the position from which the other had started at the beginning of the book (409):

> One thing troubled him more than any other, that Sue and himself had mentally travelled in opposite directions since the tragedy: events which had enlarged his own views of life, laws, customs, and dogmas had not operated in the same manner on Sue's. She was no longer the same as in the independent days, when her intellect played like lambent lightning over conventions and formalities which he had at that time respected, though he did not now.

Sue returns to Christianity and Phillotson as a consequence of this change; and Jude, partly because of a kind of stunned indifference (he takes to drink), and partly because of Arabella's predatory sexuality, returns to his first wife. It is perfectly apparent that in Hardy's opinion Sue has done an unforgivably inhuman thing to save a perfectly imaginary soul.[19]

But Hardy is at least willing to suggest a conflict in Sue between her affection for Jude and her religious belief, even if he is capable of seeing only one right in that conflict. Thus, when Jude departs from their last meeting, to which he had gone knowing that he was committing suicide, 'in a last instinct of human affection, even now unsubdued by her fetters, she sprang up as if to go and succor him. But she knelt down again, and stopped her ears with her hands till all possible sound of him had passed away' (466). On his way home Jude feels 'the chilly fog from the meadows of Cardinal as if death-claws were grabbing me through and through' (469); Hardy catches the whole complex of 'stern reality' in this symbolic statement by Jude. College, church, social convention, the very things which Jude had at the beginning believed in as the representatives of his ideal, have killed him, either by betraying him directly or by teaching Sue to betray him.

When Hardy comes to Jude's actual death, he also presents Arabella with a choice, the choice of staying with the dying Jude or going to the Remembrance games. The representation of her here is perhaps the best brief illustration in the book of the melodramatic effect which resulted from Hardy's exclusive attitude toward his material. There is not the slightest sign of conflict in Arabella over her choice; she goes without question to the games, flirts with the quack physician Vilbert, and is upset only by the thought that 'if Jude were discovered to have died alone an inquest might be deemed necessary' (485). As in the pig-killing scene, Arabella is shown as feeling only brute passion and fear of convention; she is the parody villainess of melodrama, not the mighty opposite of tragedy. Thus the immediate pathos of Jude's death in part derives from Arabella's villainous neglect of him; like the cheers of the Remembrance day crowd which are counterpointed against Jude's dying quotation from *Job*, however, this neglect illustrates only the complete indifference of society to Jude's dream of an ideal life. The rest of the pathos derives from Jude's uncertainty as to why he had been born at all. But the meaning of his death, in so far as it has one, derives from such conviction as Hardy can muster that Jude's life has not been in vain, but the unfortunate life of a man who had tried to live the ideal life several generations before the world was reformed enough to allow him to. Jude's death is not, therefore, in our ordinary understanding of the word, tragic; since it is the result of a conflict between the ideal life a man wished to lead and the only temporarily squalid real life which he was forced to lead.

Jude the Obscure is then, not a tragedy, not a carefully devised representation of life the purpose of which is to contrast, at every turn, the permanently squalid real life of man, with the ideal life (or, if you will, man's dream of an ideal life). It is the history of how an obscure but worthy man, living a life which Hardy conceived to be representative, learned gradually 'that the social moulds civilization fits us into have no more relation to our actual shapes than the conventional shapes of the constellations have to the real star-patterns' (242), learned what the true morality of 'unbiased nature' is. In the process of learning this optimistic morality he discovered also that neither nature nor society even recognized it, to say nothing of living by it. In so far as Hardy gave him hope at the end that in time they would, he denied what he otherwise saw so clearly, that earth's conditions are ingrained; in so far as he did not give Jude this hope he denied the possibility of the only ideal life he could conceive and made his hero's life and death essentially meaningless.

The instructive comparison to *Jude* is of course *Hamlet*. For Shakespeare too saw most profoundly the horror of life's ingrained conditions. But because he could also understand and represent the attitude of those who sought to adjust themselves to life's conditions, he saw that the only hope he could give his hero was for that consummation he so devoutly wished, and death is the only felicity Hamlet ever deems possible. Hamlet's death is not death in a universe in which there is no place without bad dreams; neither is it a death justified by a hope that some day the world's ingrained conditions will come unstuck. Jude's death is a little bit of both.

Hardy says in the preface to *Jude* that it 'is simply an endeavor to give shape and coherence to a series of seemings, or personal impressions, the question of their consistency or their discordance ... being regarded as not of the first moment.' In that the feeling of the presented life in *Jude* has a powerful coherence this is a justified defense of it. But it is precisely because Hardy never really posed for himself the question of how the meaning of his impressions could be coherent without being consistent that *Jude*, for all the power of its presented life, is not a tragedy.

Notes

1. Hardy to Sir Edmund Gosse, 3 March 1899. This letter is reproduced in T.J. Wise, *A Browning Library*, opposite p. 118. Cp., *Jude*, p. 410. For convenience's sake I have made all page references to the Modern Library edition of *Jude*.

2. When Dr A.B. Grosart, having found 'abundant evidence that the facts and mysteries of nature and human nature have come urgently before Mr Hardy's penetrative brain,' wrote in that wonderful Victorian way to ask Hardy for his views on the problem of reconciling the absolute goodness of God with 'the horrors of human and animal life, particularly parasitic,' Hardy characteristically replied: 'Perhaps Dr Grosart might be helped to a provisional view of the universe by the recently published Life of Darwin, and the works of Herbert Spencer and other agnostics.' F.E. Hardy, *The Early Life of Thomas Hardy*, p. 269.

3. 'The Statue and the Bust.' This was Hardy's favourite Browning poem, presumably because its doctrine that 'he who endureth to the end shall be saved' was Hardy's, though he could not, I think, have said, as Browning—perhaps too surely—can, what he meant by *saved*. (*The Early Life*, pp. 252, 261; *Jude*, p. 281.) It should be said for Browning that he was capable, in such poems as 'A Toccata of Galuppi's,' of doing full justice to the splendor of human life as an autonomous existence.

4. Allen Tate, *Reactionary Essays on Poetry and Ideas*, p. 96

5. F.E. Hardy, *The Later Years of Thomas Hardy*, pp. 41 and 14.

6. Let me repeat that I think this is not simply a case of Hardy's making an unfortunate choice. In any age when history and fable seem mutually exclusive there is no fortunate choice.

7. Hardy frequently and quite rightly denied that *Jude* was autobiographical in the specific sense (see *The Later Years*, pp. 44, 196), for the events of Jude's life are not in any specific sense the events of Hardy's. But Hardy certainly thought of Jude's experiences as representative of the same kind of experiences he had had and therefore believed it would be scientifically accurate to make the history of his own mind the history of Jude's. 'April 28 [1888]. A short story of a young man—"who could not go to Oxford"—His struggles and ultimate failure. Suicide. There is something [in this] the world ought to be shown, and I am the man to show it to them—though I was not altogether hindered going, at least to Cambridge, and could have gone up easily at five-and-twenty.' (Hardy's journal, quoted in *The Early Life*, pp. 272–3). What is crucial here is the evidence that Hardy identified himself with Jude so far as thoughts and feelings go, that Jude's attitude toward the events of the narrative is, with minor qualifications to be noted presently, Hardy's.

8. 'But in these Bible lives and adventures there is the spherical completeness of perfect art. And our first, and second, feeling that they must be true because they are so impressive, becomes, as a third feeling, modified to, "Are they so very true, after all?" Is not the fact of their being so convincing an argument, not for their actuality, but for the actuality of a consummate artist who was no more content with what Nature offered than Sophocles and Pheidias were content?' *The Early Life*, p. 223.

9. 'Of course the book is all contrasts—or was meant to be in its original conception ... e.g., Sue and her heathen gods set against Jude's reading the Greek testament; Christminster academical, Christminster in the slums; Jude the saint, Jude the sinner; Sue the Pagan, Sue the saint; marriage, no marriage; &c., &c.' *The Later Years*, p. 42

10. It may be added here that the war destroyed all Hardy's belief in the gradual ennoblement of man, a belief he had held for many years ... He said he would probably not have ended *The Dynasts* as he did end it if he could have foreseen what was going to happen within a few years.' (*The Later Years*, p. 165.) See also Hardy's remarks on the Golden Rule, *Early Life*, p. 294.

11. Hardy, like so many naturalistic novelists, seems to have had considerable faith in the efficacy of carelessness: 'The whole secret of a living style and the difference between it and a dead style, lies in not having too much style—being—in fact, a little careless, or rather seeming to, here and there.' (*The Early Life*, p. 138). '"Why!" he said, "I have never in my life taken more than three, or perhaps four, drafts for a poem. I am afraid of it losing its freshness."' (Robert Graves, *Good-bye to All That*, p. 362.) The result is, as Maughan once wrote, that 'he gave you the impression of writing with the stub of a blunt pencil.' (*Cakes and Ale*, p. 134.)

12. '... the time was not ripe for us! Our ideas were fifty years too soon to be any good to us' (478). 'Christminster is ... any old-fashioned University about the date of the story, 1860–70, before there were such chances for poor men as there are now.' (*The Later Years*, p. 249).

13. It is interesting here to compare the way Shakespeare handles Jaques's moralizing of the wounded stag. To begin with, Shakespeare makes precise and explicit what is only vaguely implicit in Hardy's fiction because Hardy is too much concerned with the actual level, that is the fact that this grief for an animal is really the image of a grief for the neglect of the exceptional man in an indifferent world—'Sweep on you fat and greasy citizens.' In the second place, Shakespeare does not present Jaques 'weeping and commenting/Upon the sobbing deer'; we hear of it from another lord who, though not without sympathy for the deer ('and indeed, my lord/The wretched animal heaved forth such groans ...'), conveys quite clearly the absurdity of Jaques's grief in the practical world. Shakespeare is as sure of the justice of this anonymous lord's view of the matter as he is of the different justice of Jacques's view of it. It is as if Hardy had given Arabella as eloquent a statement of her view of the pig-killing as he gives Jude of his.

14. Birds also occasionally achieve the status of symbols in Hardy—'All are caged birds the only difference lies in the size of the cage.' (*The Early Life*, p. 224.) Thus the pair of pigeons which Jude and Sue are forced to sell to the poulterer and which Sue later surreptitiously releases (363) are an image of Jude and Sue caged and sold by society for reasons quite independent of their own feelings and worth. For other uses of this bird symbol, see *Jude*, pp. 316, 318, 398, 436; *The Mayor of Casterbridge*, Chap. XLIV–XLV *The Dynasts*, Pt. 2, p. 214. Hardy would not, of course, have used these birds at all if he had not thought their dilemma terrible in its own right. In other words, their primary meaning is still their naturalistic meaning. The same thing is true of the trapped rabbit (252).

15. This passage is an example of what Henry James called 'the platitude of statement.' Hardy indulged in it constantly, both in the prose and the poems, without, apparently any sense that it was destructive of the life of his representation. Like his description of the objects of his narrative from Jude's point of view, it is an outgrowth of his inability to see how necessary it was for him not to commit himself as author to one view of things.

16. Hardy seems to have felt that this kind of spiritual weakness was an inherent characteristic of the more delicate sex (165, 263). It was a common enough Victorian idea—

> *Woman is the lesser man, and all thy passions, match'd with mine,*
> *Are as moonlight unto sunlight, and as water unto wine—*

but it is a little difficult to see how Hardy reconciled this conviction with *Tess*. The resemblance between 'Locksley Hall' and *Jude*, however, even down to the parallel uses of Arabella and Tennyson's 'savage woman,' is astonishing. The only difference between them is that Tennyson, like Browning, found it a little easier to view conventional life optimistically—at least officially he did, for there is much to be said for the argument that Tennyson was at bottom pure mystic and that 'The Mystic' rather than 'Locksley Hall' represents his deepest feelings about the secular and material faith of his day.

17. On the marriage question, from Sue's point of view: '... she fears it would be breaking faith with Jude to withhold herself at pleasure, or altogether, after it; though while uncontracted she feels at liberty to yield herself as seldom as she chooses. This has tended to keep his passions as hot at the end as at the beginning, and helps to break his heart. He has never really possessed her as freely as he desired.' (*The Later Years*, p. 42.) Hardy confessed that the delicacy of public sentiment in the period prevented his dwelling on this point as he wished to, made it impossible for him to show clearly, for example, that Jude's spending the night with Arabella when they met unexpectedly in Melchester (216) was a demonstration of how powerfully sheer physical desire was fighting against suppression in him.

18. Father Time as an excellent illustration of the kind of sensational sentimentality which results from trying to represent the essence of life's squalor in a naturalistic narrative: 'The doctor says [says Jude] there are such boys springing up amongst us—boys of a sort unknown in the last generation—the outcome of new views of life ... He says it is the beginning of the coming universal wish not to live' (400).

19. 'Do not do an immoral thing for moral reasons! You have been my social salvation. Stay with me for humanity's sake! You know what a weak fellow I am. My two Arch Enemies you know—my weakness for women and my impulse to strong liquor. Don't abandon me to them, Sue, to save your own soul ...' (420).

180

On *Jude the Obscure*

———————— ◆ ————————

BARBARA HARDY

It may be thought that I am merely betraying impatience with the simplicities of Christian dogma rather than describing some of their consequences, so I hasten at least to extend my impatience to Hardy's pessimistic
vision, which has the very opposite metaphysical implications, but similar
formal results. In *Jude the Obscure* Hardy, like Charlotte Brontë, succeeds in
combining animated and realistic psychology with ideological pattern. His
story also depends on an arrangement of action which reflects his general
conclusions about the universe. This is the world without a Providence,
where there is no malignant President of the Immortals, but conditions in
nature and society which, in the absence of Providence, work together to
frustrate energy and intelligence.[1] Those who best serve the life-force, like
Arabella, prosper best, but those who have imagination and aspiration meet
with the frustrations of nature's blind biological purpose and society's
conventional restrictions. So 'nobody comes, because nobody does come',
and Providence can be on occasion invoked with awful irony, because all is
working towards frustration, not prosperity. At every point in his career Jude
is checked: by his sexuality, by his poverty and class, by his love for and
affinity with Sue. Her career ironically combines with his to make frustration
definite: there is not only the fatal irony of their marriages, which overlap,
but the irony of their ideological cross-purposes. Father Time is the symbolic
short-cut which corresponds to Charlotte Brontë's Providential telepathy.
This novel would surely be no different if Hardy had literally believed in a
malignant supernatural improvidence. His 'crass casualty' imposes an
energetic and external pattern as well as merely revealing itself in social and
biological conditions. There is the same short-circuiting of internal and
social determinism, though this shows itself unconvincingly only at one
point, in the children's deaths, and on the whole does not lay an impossible
implausibility on his materials.

There is another feature of ideological form, common both to the
Providence novel and to Hardy's late novels, which is important. In the

SOURCE *The Appropriate Form: An Essay on The Novel*, London, 1964, from ch. III.

novels of Dickens, George Eliot, Meredith, and Tolstoy, free from this kind of metaphysical pattern, there is the constant play of opposites. If Romola progresses, Tito deteriorates, if Dorothea has a muted success, Lydgate has a failure, if Fred Vincy is redeemed, Bulstrode is all but lost. A similar play of variations is present in Dickens and, most impressively and movingly, in Tolstoy. Life has a clear and schematic pattern, but it is like a game of snakes and ladders, at least in the presence of possibilities of success and failure, redemption and damnation, though not, like the game, in the pure environment of chance. Defoe and Charlotte Brontë choose a pattern where there are very few snakes. There are some characters in *Jane Eyre* who do not illustrate conscience and passion like Jane, Rochester, and St John Rivers, but there are no contrary examples illustrating the flouting of Providence unless we count John Reed and his mother who are too grossly foreshortened to act as proper counter-examples. Ideologically there is no reason why there shouldn't be. We are not asking for the kind of novel where the existence of Providence is both suggested and doubted, but merely for a novel where there are failures as well as successes, delineated in detail and substance within the author's ideological terms. We see what happens to those who flout Heaven in Robinson Crusoe's early career and in the case of Rochester, but the material is subdued to the optimistic selection, and here no doubt there are the pressures of wish-fulfilment as well as the pressures of strong belief. Defoe's interest in writing best-selling success stories and Charlotte Brontë's wishfulfilment fantasy need not have conflicted with the Providential scheme. Commercial needs, private gratification, and ideology could co-operate to the one end, and are in any case perhaps not very easily separable as different causes, when we look at the actual novels.

It is even simpler in Hardy's late novels, for he has less possibility of acknowledging variation and exception. He is here writing from the belief that all worked for the worst. Although we can see him loading the dice, as when he chooses the ghastly examples of other marriages to warn and frighten Jude and Sue, this is scarcely even a distortion, according to his own terms. This game has all snakes and no ladders, and there are indeed moments when we feel that the strong statement of his vision leads to exaggeration or distortion, as in the multiplication of fatal coincidences in defiance of probability, or in the symbolic short-circuit. We can describe his moral pattern as one which excludes the possibility of another answer, or contrary evidence, but pessimism is by definition selective.

I do not think that this kind of dogmatically organized novel with its special features of single-track action and symbolic short-cuts is confined to the 'religious novel' written to a consistent belief, like the belief in Providence or the belief in the implications of an absent Providence. I should like therefore to end this chapter with the suggestion that the same kind of ideological form is to be found in a modern novelist, whose beliefs are not as easily codified as Defoe's or Charlotte Brontë's or Hardy's.

Note

1. Those of us who share Hardy's metaphysical beliefs must still observe that Jude suffered from being born before the rise of the meritocracy.

The Symbolical Use of Image and Contrast in *Jude the Obscure*

———— ◆ ————

FREDERICK P.W. McDOWELL

I

Sixty years after publication, Thomas Hardy's *Jude the Obscure* still elicits controversial judgments. The majority of recent critics, such as William R. Rutland, Lord David Cecil, R.A. Scott-James, Douglas Brown, and Evelyn Hardy, have judged the book a relative failure because of its violations of probability, its morbidity, or its philosophical pretentiousness.[1] Other critics, such as Lascelles Abercrombie, H.C. Duffin, Joseph Warren Beach, Arthur McDowall, and Albert Guerard, have acclaimed the book as possibly Hardy's best.[2] I agree with the most recent critic in this group, Albert Guerard, who finds *Jude the Obscure*, despite the 'naturalistic paraphernalia,' a haunting symbolic rendition of the modern age as it appeared to a compassionate pessimist.[3] In order to arrive at a sound approach to the novel, I have had recourse less to book-length studies of Thomas Hardy—except for Abercrombie and Guerard these are disappointing—than to articles and incidental treatments of Hardy in more general books.

Though I disagree with them in part, two of the most perceptive of these accounts—Arthur Mizener's and Walter Allen's—can serve as basis for further discussion.[4] These critics maintain that Hardy's naturalistic technique in *Jude* sets it off from his earlier fiction. More than in his preceding books, Hardy does stress the effects both of heredity and environment upon his characters, the conviction that social laws operate like natural laws, the presence of a strong if still incomplete determinism in human affairs, the need to present the unsavory and animalistic aspects of experience, the sense that primitive and eruptive forces are part of human nature, the insistence that Darwinian postulates underlie any modern world view, the belief that

SOURCE *Modern Fiction Studies*, vol. VI, no. 3, Autumn, 1960, pp. 233–50 individualistic force is needed to break from an inherited morality, and the view that ethics are inductively derived from experience. Granted that these premises obtrude with greater force in *Jude the Obscure* than in the other novels, still Thomas Hardy primarily remained faithful in *Jude the Obscure* to his earlier defined, more fluid theory of the art of fiction.

Thomas Hardy departed from naturalistic convention in *Jude the Obscure* in being unable to efface his temperament from his work. *Jude the Obscure* thus illustrates Hardy's view that a writer should be free to select his materials, to give shape and form to them, to explore their poetical and metaphysical implications, and to declare his belief, however tentative or qualified, in values which he deems to have some permanent validity in experience.[5] Hardy felt that 'scientific' novelists were to be commended for their desire to present the full truth and for their hatred of the false and hypocritical; but he also felt that artistic effectiveness derived more from a 'sympathetic appreciativeness of life in all its manifestations' than from a sensitive eye and ear alone.[6] He alleged, therefore, that 'art' in poetry and novel writing results in an illumination of subject material, going beyond mere reportage.[7] The mission of poetry, he said, is to record impressions and not convictions;[8] in the preface to *Jude the Obscure* he expressed himself similarly upon the art of the novel. This book, he maintained, was like former productions of his in being 'simply an endeavor to give shape and coherence to a series of seemings, or personal impressions, the question of their consistency or their discordance, of their permanence or their transitoriness, being regarded as not of the first moment.'[9]

Disregard or misconstruction of this statement has led Mizener and Allen to emphasize too completely the realism of *Jude the Obscure*. Mr Mizener contends that its symbolic embellishments, which represent Hardy's attempt to give order to his impressions, are ineffective, and represent 'a kind of desperate contrivance' in a basically naturalistic novel.[10] The symbolism in *Jude the Obscure*, I feel, is not adventitious but organic; it prevades the whole and provides those shades of ineffable and expanded significance which Mizener finds absent.

Allen's view that the power and impressiveness of the novel derive from 'Hardy's very refusal to employ his great poetic talents in it' is, I think, similarly debatable.[11] It is just his exercise of these gifts in concentrated form which gives the book its full life. Allen apparently views the symbolism of *Jude the Obscure* as almost wholly ironic, existing primarily to provide implicit rational commentary upon incident, character, and value. Such is indeed the case, but most of the images in the novel haunt the imagination as well as gratify the mind. In an ineffable and poetic dimension, they give nuance, resonance, and intensity to action, psychology, and idea, and carry the fabric—of which they form part—away from an objectively rendered and obviously typical reality. In *Jude the Obscure* we have a naturalistic novel, but a naturalistic novel with a difference. Thus when *Jude the Obscure* is compared with *A Mummer's Wife* or *The Nether World*, its imagined universe stands out in far sharper relief.

Norman Holland, in his important '*Jude the Obscure*: Hardy's Symbolic Indictment of Christianity,'[12] has developed Guerard's insight that *Jude* is primarily a symbolic depiction of the chaotic modern age. Holland also admirably illustrates Morton D. Zabel's related insight that Hardy is a realist 'developing toward allegory' and, in the process, getting away increasingly from 'slavery to fact.'[13] If anything, Holland errs in an opposite direction from Mizener and Allen, and concludes that *Jude the Obscure* is more allegorical than realistic. In the images of the novel Holland finds a pattern through which Hardy denies the relevance of Christianity to the modern world. The hanging by Father Time—a modern Jesus Christ—of himself and the two Fawley children is, in Holland's view, an atonement which is not efficacious in a spiritually barren society. Holland's interpretation is perhaps extreme: Hardy not only indicts Christianity, but by inference throughout the novel also condemns modern society for its failure to exemplify Christian ethical values. Furthermore, Father Time is 'an enslaved and dwarfed Divinity' (p. 336) and in his narrow wilfulness becomes a parody upon, as well as counterpart to, the Christian Saviour. My purpose is to approach the novel with a method similar to Holland's but to give my discussion a less allegorical focus. Thus I shall endeavor to relate, more closely than Holland has done, the images and clusters of images in the novel to the actual lives of Sue Bridehead and Jude Fawley in society.

I wish also to develop the importance of one aspect of Hardy's technique, which Guerard has dismissed with slighting comment: his purposeful use of contrast.[14] All the contrasts in *Jude* are not so purely factitious and geometrical as Guerard indicates. Many of the parallel incidents provide a symbolic and metaphysical commentary upon the characters and their problems, just as the characters in parallel situations throw light upon one another and the action as a whole. In short, the ramifications and contortions of plot are in themselves provocative, and open up unexpected ranges of meaning. My examination of Hardy's marshalling of images and symbols in the novel, in conjunction with his skilled use of significant contrasts, will, I think, amplify Guerard's view that the lasting impression produced by *Jude* is its spiritual 'trueness' for a time of moral, intellectual, and spiritual dislocation.[15]

II

The first function of the images, symbols, and symbolic or parallel incidents in *Jude the Obscure* is to deepen and reinforce the realistic and psychological aspects of the narrative, our impressions of the characters who figure in it, and the various developments arising from it. A number of images, first encountered in the early part of the novel, operate in this way. There is, for example, the well at Marygreen into whose depths Jude peered as a boy. Its 'long circular perspective' indicates the path of Jude's own existence which many times converges circularly upon Marygreen. In somewhat the same manner, the schoolmaster Phillotson returns recurrently to Marygreen, where he had first been a teacher. The well also suggests infinity, and conveys an impression of the continuity of nature and of life itself. It hints at psychic and spiritual renewal and acts, therefore, as a counterweight to many of the death-connoting images in the novel. The well is in part a natural phenomenon and as such will survive man-made objects: thus it has outlasted the old church which has been supplanted by a newer, less aesthetically pleasing structure. Along with the suggestion of infinity, the well has given to the young Jude intimations of sadness and of the inscrutability of life; these impressions are, of course, heightened in him and us by his destiny.

The well has possible sexual connotations, too, and suggests the darkness, the mystery, the security, and the fertile energies of the womb. It thus reinforces the animal imagery which betokens physical sexuality and which is especially prominent in the early part of the novel.[16] There are the copulating earthworms which Jude as a boy tries to avoid crushing in a wet pasture. They are responding to the same natural force motivating the peasant youths and maidens who make love in upland privacy and populate thereby the neighboring villages. Somewhat later, Jude and Arabella become such lovers themselves. Arabella is, of course, associated with pigs throughout the novel; she is twice referred to as a 'tiger,' and at the Aldbrickham hotel when Sue visits her, she springs from bed like a beast from its lair. The most celebrated of the animal images is the pig's pizzle which Arabella throws at Jude to attract his attention when, at the brookside, she is washing a slaughtered pig for her father. One of the most arresting scenes is the subsequent flirtation on the bridge, after Arabella hangs on the rail the pizzle which Jude surrenders to her in a ritualistic yielding of his own virginity to her. The coarse and sensual nature of their soon developing affair is explicit, then, from its outset.

The first of a group of images and incidents relating to music appears early in the book. In the opening section Phillotson has difficulty getting a piano moved which he has never learned to play. His failure to master it is linked with his inability to play, subtly and potently, upon the keyboard of a woman's sensibility; with the defeat of his other aspirations, social, intellectual, and spiritual; and with the absence of emotional depths in his nature. While Sue is Phillotson's wife at Shaston, she and Jude are brought together when he plays upon this piano a newly written hymn which appeals with power to both of them. Almost from the first, then, Sue and Jude share, to Phillotson's detriment, experiences from which he is excluded. In addition to his sexual magnetism, Jude has greater spiritual reserves, in general, than Phillotson. Thus Jude achieves considerable distinction in church music at Melchester, singing with deep feeling the church chants while he accompanies himself with ease on a harmonium.

Events at Christminster are often subtly developed by references to music. Jude is greatly moved by the Gregorian chant which he hears at the cathedral church of Cardinal College: 'Wherewithal shall a young man cleanse his way?' (p. 106). At this point he has begun struggling against his feeling for Sue, and the chant seems to have a special significance for him as sinner. His feeling of guilt disappears when he sees Sue in the cathedral and becomes conscious that they are both steeped in the same exalted harmonies. As Jude leaves Christminster in despair at the defeat of his intellectual ambitions, he cannot respond to the gay promenade concert. Some years later upon his return to Christminster he is much more susceptible to the spirited music which, on Remembrance Day, peals from the theater organ. The spell exerted by Christminster upon Jude is greater, therefore, than the bitterness engendered in him by his failure to become part of the university. In ironic counterpoint to the tragedy at Christminster when little Father Time hangs himself and the Fawley children is the joyous tumult of the organ sounding from a nearby chapel ('Truly God is loving unto Israel,' [p. 412]) after the bodies have been discovered. The same incongruity obtrudes on the second Remembrance Day when the lilting strains of a waltz from Cardinal College penetrate the chamber where Jude has just died. Sue's early view of ultimate reality, in part Hardy's own, is expressed by a musical metaphor. She had thought that 'the world resembled a stanza or melody composed in a dream' (p. 418), full of ineffable suggestion to the half-perceiving mind but 'absurd' to the completely awakened intelligence. Sue's later distress, of course, involves a retreat from this position to a less aesthetically satisfying concept of God as an anthropomorphic being who does not hesitate to punish those who flout convention.

Images in the novel drawn from the Bible also serve to intensify its realism and the psychic impulses of its characters. The relationship between Jude and Arabella is given by the picture of Samson and Delilah at the inn where the lovers decide to get tea during their courtship and are forced to get beer instead. As Holland observes, Arabella thereby combines the two forces which undermine Jude, his passion for women and his developing taste for strong drink.[17] When he is duped a second time into marrying Arabella, she appropriately thinks of him as 'her shorn Samson' (p. 464). Biblical and ecclesiastical images are also associated with Sue Bridehead, who looks like a saint with a halo of light in her portrait at Marygreen and who is engaged in an apparently saintly occupation at Christminster. She is an artist for an ecclesiastical warehouse and is designing, when Jude first sees her through the shop window, the word *Alleluia* in zinc. Without knowing her 'Voltairean' propensities, he feels that she would be a sweet companion for him in the Anglican worship, opening for him new social and spiritual possibilities and soothing him 'like the dew of Hermon' (p. 107). In her marital difficulties she identifies herself with the Christian drama in Eden. Writing to Phillotson from her school room, she wishes that Eve had not fallen, so that a more delicate mode of reproduction than sex might have peopled Paradise. In her developing asceticism after the death of her children, she regards the flesh as 'the curse of Adam' (p. 421). If, as she had said previously, she was 'the Ishmaelite' as a result of her disregard of convention, she feels still more of an outcast after she tries to expiate her tragedy by mortification of the flesh.

In view of his devotion to Christianity in the first half of the novel, Jude is linked even more firmly with Biblical incident than is Sue. At Shaston Sue describes Jude as 'Joseph, the dreamer of dreams' (p. 247) and as 'St Stephen who, while they were stoning him, could see heaven opened' (pp. 247–8). Here Sue refers, at least by implication, to Jude's scarcely practicable dreams, first of entering Christminster and then of becoming an altruistic licentiate, to his early vision of Christminster as a 'heavenly Jerusalem,' and to the scorn merged with indifference which his unusual ambition arouses among his Marygreen and Christminster acquaintances. When Jude gets to Christminster, he is fascinated by a model of ancient Jerusalem while Sue as a skeptic is indifferent to it. This model of Jerusalem anticipates that made by Jude and Sue some years later of his 'new Jerusalem,' Cardinal College, for the Great Wessex Agricultural Show at Stoke-Barehills.

The completeness of Jude's defeat at Christminster is implied when he climbs into the octagonal lantern of the theater and sees the city spread out before his eyes as if it were a Pisgah view of the Promised Land which he is never to reach. He then leaves the town, broken in spirit, and returns to Marygreen, 'a poor Christ' (p. 147). When he comes back to Christminster in the last part of the novel, he lingers nostalgically outside the theater where he had first realized that study at Christminster was impossible for a man of his resources. Like Jude, the New Testament scribe who sought to reclaim his lapsed contemporaries to the love of Christ by citing the punishments meted to those in the Old Testament who defied God, Jude Fawley is a prophetic figure, seeing further than most of his contemporaries and deploring the placid indifference of most of them to the demands of Christian charity. As a stranger, too, to people in his own class, he is likened the last time at Christminster to Paul among the Lycaonians. Jude at this point is translating a Latin inscription and describing a carving to assembled strangers from the town side of Christminster. Jude, 'the Tutor of St Slums,' had been thrust out of Christminster as Paul had been from Lystra; and like Paul, who returns to the city after persecution to preach again his gospel, Jude later comes back to Christminster to voice his radical social ideas to the crowd. On this return to his old haunts, he observes that leaving Kennet-bridge for Christminster was like going from Caiaphas to Pilate. There is, by implication, no place anywhere for a man of his talents from his humble class.

Images drawn from pagan and classical sources also heighten character and incident. Pagan allusions gather around Sue early in the novel: the atmosphere surrounding her 'blew as distinctly from Cyprus as from Galilee' (p. 107). A vivid scene occurs when she is walking on a hill outside Christminster and sees some statuary of classical deities, carved by an itinerant foreigner, spread out before her and half obliterating the distant towers of the city. Sue's pagan skepticism gets between her and the Christian traditions of the city which from the first secure Jude's allegiance. Her Pisgah view of the city shows her that the secular is fast encroaching upon the religious and indeed must continue to do so if the University is ever to recover intellectual leadership.

A pagan in her sympathies, Sue purchases statues of Venus and Apollo which upon nearer view seem to her embarrassingly large and naked. In theory, then, she embraces a pagan abandon which, in the actuality discomposes her. She wraps the statues in leaves and brings her 'heathen load' into the Christian city, much to the later horror of Miss Fontover, Sue's pious employer, who grinds one of the images with her heel and breaks its arm. Like ecclesiastical Christianity, then, pagan humanism is an incomplete philosophy for the modern age and its survival even more precarious, since its enlarged perspectives so often go counter to convention. Sue's own paganism is imperfect, possibly transient: the clay of the statues rubs off easily. At night she places candles before them as before Christian icons and communes with them raptly. At one such time she reads Swinburne, who expresses her own regret that 'the pale Galilean' has conquered. While she peruses Swinburne and Gibbon, Jude in his lodging is studying the Greek New Testament. In the diffused light the statues stand out commandingly against the wall ornaments: Christian texts, pictures of martyrs, and a gothic framed Latin cross, the figure on which is shrouded by shadows. This obscurely seen cross, which signifies the present abeyance of Christian sentiment in Sue, is in complete contrast to the brightly jeweled Latin cross in the church of St Silas under which Jude finds Sue towards the end of the novel when, as a result of personal tragedy, Christian conventions become prominent in her life.

After Sue escapes from the training school at Melchester, where she had previously appeared 'nunlike' to Jude, she seems to him 'clammy as a marine deity' (p. 171) from having forded the river behind the school. Like a latter-day Venus Anadyomene, she seems to have materialized spontaneously out of the waters. If in this sequence she brings to mind the pagan goddess of love, Sue is no sensual Pandemos-like deity but the Venus Urania of heavenly love with whom she somewhat later identifies herself. Her garments also cling to her 'like the robes upon the figures in the Parthenon frieze' (p. 171). In her most expansive moods, she seems to Jude, after they live together at Aldbrickham, to be a serene Roman matron or an enlightened woman from Greece who may have just been watching Praxiteles carving his latest Venus. Later, of course, Sue renounces Greek joyousness for Christian asceticism, and 'the pale Galilean' in actuality does conquer.

Although Jude is most often seen in a Christian ambience, he is some-times described in terms of the pagan past. As a devout young aspirant to intellectual culture who momentarily forgets his Christianity before his first sojourn at Christminster, he repeats the 'Carmen Saeculare' and invokes on his knees the gods of moon and sun in parallel sequence to Sue's later worship of her statues at night. When Jude returns defeated from Christ-minster, he is described as a Laocöon contorted by grief; the pagan image implies that the bonds of Christian orthodoxy are loosening even now, primarily as a result of his unpermitted passion for Sue. He is also sensitive to the pessimistic, as well as to the harmonious aspects, of classical antiquity. After the Widow Edlin in Aldbrickham has told the lovers of their ill-fated ancestor who had been hanged as the ultimate result of a marital quarrel, Sue feels that the curse of the house of Atreus hangs over the family, and Jude then compares its doom to that haunting the house of Jeroboam. Later in the novel, however, it is Jude who resorts to the *Agamemnon* to demonstrate that Sue's premonition concerning the ancestral curse hanging over the Fawleys had been correct: 'Things are as they are, and will be brought to their destined issue' (p. 415) … When the seriously ill Jude perceives the ghosts of the Christminster worthies a second time (after his final trip to Marygreen), he poignantly quotes *Antigone* to signify his own anomalous and wretched situation: 'I am neither a dweller among men nor ghosts' (p. 483). Despite his discouragement and enervation, Jude's persisting moral force resembles that of a stolid, stoic man of antiquity. This is suggested when he is described on his final trip to Marygreen as being 'pale as a monumental figure in alabaster' (p. 476), or when he is seen by Arabella to be 'pale' and 'statuesque' in death with his features like 'marble.'

Another group of symbolic incidents is concerned with action taking place at windows or casements. At Melchester, Sue jumps from a window at the training college in order to escape the hateful discipline imposed there; at Shaston she jumps from a window to escape from Phillotson and the regimentation imposed by marriage. When Sue springs from the window at the Melchester school and wades neck-deep through the river to escape, she is making a sharp break with her past and is being borne into another life with Jude at its center. Her break for freedom takes her to the lodgings of the man she loves, but destiny prevents her then from seeing where her affections are centered. Hearing from Jude that he had been married previously, she is precipitated into her union with Phillotson, an impulsive action toward Phillotson in contrast with her later bold jump through the window away from him at Shaston. When Jude comes to visit her at Shaston, she talks to him from a casement, strokes his forehead, and calls him a dreamer; a similar episode takes place at Marygreen a few weeks later after Jude mercifully kills a maimed rabbit caught in a gin. She then leans far out of the window at Mrs Edlin's and lays her tear-stained face on his hair. Seen so often from a relatively inaccessible casement, Sue is in part the immured enchanted maiden, also a kind of inverted Juliet talking to her ardent lover from the safety of a balcony, to which she does not invite him. Somewhat later Jude, living at Aldbrickham with Sue, talks to Arabella from an upper window of the house when she comes to tell him of the existence of the child, Father Time. Whereas Sue had to this time kept the passionate Jude at a distance, the walls of this house—primly erected upon Sue's inconsistent adherence to the conventions she affects to despise—are hardly proof against Arabella's frankly competitive, more direct animal energies. Afraid of losing Jude to Arabella, Sue yields at last to his ardor to possess her.

Other images or symbolic episodes give the novel a richer texture than that usually found in a realistic narrative. Thus the agonies of jealousy experienced by Sue's lovers at various points in the novel gain strength by being counterpointed with each other. Jude is tortured after the marriage at Melchester by the thought that any children born to Sue would be half Phillotson's. After Sue's visit to him in an illness following her departure from him, Phillotson himself is in jealous agony at the thought of Jude as Sue's physical lover (at this point he is not, so Phillotson's jealousy is wasted). Sue also experiences momentary discomfiture when she first sees Father Time, the child of Jude and Arabella, and thinks that he is as much Arabella's as Jude's. In his distressing final interview with Sue at Marygreen, what sustains Jude is her declaration that she is a wife to Phillotson only in name, whereas what later breaks him down is the Widow Edlin's report to him that Sue has physically become Phillotson's wife as a punishment for having returned Jude's kisses with passion. Sue's statement that she was the only mourner to attend the funeral of her early Christminster lover gathers poignancy when one remembers her absence from the deathbed of the man whom she has loved even more. When she excludes Jude from their bedroom at Christminster, the scene is made intense by his ritualistic gesture of farewell: he flings his pillow to the floor, an act which signifies, he says, the rending of the veil of the temple of their marriage.

Sue, in effect, says farewell to the passions of the flesh in a similarly poignant scene toward the end of the novel. By mistake she had brought with her to Marygreen a beautifully embroidered nightgown. She impulsively tears it and throws the tatters into the fire, thus figuratively eliminating from her nature all stain of unpermitted earthly passion. In its place she will wear a plain nightdress, which impresses the Widow Edlin as similar to the sackcloth which Sue, in her passion for self-centered suffering, would now like to wear. The destruction of the nightgown also recalls another strong incident, Jude's burning his divinity books on a kind of funeral pyre to his religious aspirations when he realizes at Marygreen that he can no longer be licentiate in the church and continue to love Sue. In burning the nightgown Sue aspires, almost successfully, to invalidate the flesh; in burning the books, Jude relinquishes, to the stronger call of the flesh, his aspirations. He decides that he will give up all for love, but he later finds with a kind of hopeless irony that Sue has not fully reciprocated. Jude's destruction of his books also anticipates Arabella's thrusting her religious pamphlets into the hedge when as Cartlett's widow she decides she is still in love with Jude; in both cases, formal religion is unable to restrain a powerful passion. Arabella, moreover, seems to act as a kind of catalyst in the varying relationships between Sue and Jude. The effect of her first visit to the married couple at Aldbrickham is to thrust Sue into Jude's arms and to bring about the consummation of their union. Her second visit to the couple, after the tragedy to the children, confirms Sue in her opinion that she is no longer Jude's and must return to Phillotson, since she has come to the orthodox view that her early marriage is indissoluble.

III

The images and symbolic patterns in the novel not only deepen its signifi-cance, but give it scope and amplitude. The full and extended represen-tations of locale help give the novel its broadened perspectives and take it again beyond the unadorned content of most naturalistic novels. In Hardy's evocation the physical Christminster is replete with Gothic grace and charming if irregular architectural harmonies. Shaston 'the ancient British Palladour,' is described as 'the city of a dream' (p. 239) and its past glories are suggested as they would now appeal to the sensitive beholder of the picturesque town. Melchester with its towering cathedral is presented with similar immediacy, though no set description of town or cathedral is given.

Although Marygreen is a desolate and remote spot, Hardy savored its uniqueness and quaintness. In particular, the features of the spacious countryside nearby are assimilated effectively into the action of the novel. The highway ascending the downs from Alfredston to Marygreen is one of the most consistently used topographical images in the novel. This is the road that Jude walks with Arabella in the early days of their relationship, it is along this road that the newly married pair settle, and it is by this road that Jude returns several times to his native village. Along this road occurs the fateful kiss between Jude and Sue; here Arabella, as the 'volupshious widow' of Cartlett, relives the early days with Jude and determines to get him back. Phillotson's history is also intimately connected with the highway. The surrounding landscape is full of associations for Jude: the field where he chased the crows for Farmer Troutham, the Brown House from which he first had his view of Christminster in the distance, the milestone upon which he carved the word *thither* and an arrow pointing toward Christminster, and the gibbet upon which one of his ancestors was reputed to have been hanged. The sequence at Melchester when Jude and Sue climb the downs about Wardour Castle inevitably recalls the courtship walks with Arabella across the heights near Marygreen. One instance of Hardy's skilled use of these topographical images occurs at the novel's close. Jude's inscription on the milestone at Marygreen has now been almost effaced by moss: the implication is that Jude's aspirations have been slowly undermined with the years and are soon to be extinguished in his approaching death.

Other types of nature imagery similarly enlarge the realistic framework of the novel by suggesting that the life of nature underlies the social life of man even when that life is led in urban rather than in rural surroundings. Thus weather becomes as important as the terrain in establishing the emotional impress of *Jude the Obscure*. The Christminster fog, for example, hangs over the last sequences of the novel and adds to their chill and depressing effect. In one of these scenes, Jude in effect commits suicide by going back to Marygreen in a driving rain after he has begun to show symptoms of consumption. He also lies down to rest by the milestone near the Brown House where wind and rain are fiercest and coldest. Wind and storm continue when Sue that evening forces herself to yield to her husband. In ironic counterpoint to the brilliance of the sun and to the happy Remembrance Day games going on outside, Jude comes to his solitary shadowed end at Christminster. The classical and Biblical allusions, previously analyzed, also give the novel wider reference than a chronicle of contemporary events would normally possess, by suggesting that situations in the present somehow reach back through time and are comparable to conditions at remote dates in the history of humanity.

Both Sue and Jude live in a world of personal fantasy and illusion. The descriptions of their mental reactions and the images used to define them go counter to a strict realism by suggesting that an individualistic life in the mind is often fully as intense as life in society. Jude's inspiriting view of Christminster which his later experience cannot dispel, the lovers' enthusiasm for each other's company as a kind of paradisal union before tragedy strikes, and Jude's imaginative summoning of the spirits of the departed worthies that still haunt the university are all instances in Sue and Jude of concentrated mental vision, related only tangentially to the verisimilar life recorded in the book. Jude at times feels that he is as much a disembodied spirit as a struggling young man, upon occasion a 'self-spectre' (p. 91) who is 'spectre-seeing always' (p. 180); at the same time he regards Sue, despite her physical beauty, as ethereal and bodiless. Sue and Jude at various times see one another as naive and ethusiastic children; other spectators like Phillotson and Arabella comment upon their childlike quality. Emma Clifford has shown convincingly that part of the imaginative universe of *Jude the Obscure* consists of a childlike realm of fantasy.[18] She has demonstrated, moreover, that this realm of fantasy sometimes becomes malignant and approaches nightmare. The malevolence of life is epitomized, for example, by the obtrusive policeman who always acts as a kind of censor whenever the characters are at their most spontaneous. The aged and ageless child, Father Time, with his warped view of life, contributes, too, to the grim fantasy in the novel. Existence seen through the eyes of this precocious and humorless boy becomes a sinister and sick horror, at its most unrelieved, of course, in the hanging of his half-brother, his half-sister, and himself.

IV

The metaphors and metaphorical incidents in the novel often illustrate Hardy's philosophical ideas and values. The indifference of God, or the powers that control the universe, to man and his destiny are indicated figuratively at many points. The hard life of the crows which Jude must scare from Farmer Troutham's field leads him to think that 'mercy towards one set of creatures was cruelty towards another' (p. 15); and the selling of her pet pigeons to the poulterer at the removal from Aldbrickham prompts Sue like-wise to ask, 'Oh, why should Nature's law be mutual butchery!' (p. 376). The imagery deriving from sickness reveals the futility of the characters' lives, their basic neuroticism, and the indifference of the cosmic powers to them. At the close of the novel when Sue as the source of his life's meaning is with-drawn from him, Jude gradually loses the desire to live. In despair he goes to a part of Christminster 'where boughs dripped, and coughs and consump-tion lurked' (p. 444). His life becomes increasingly fevered and reaches a climax of desperation after the sordid saturnalia behind Donn's Christ-minster sausage shop which leads to his remarriage to Arabella. Sub-sequently, he is in physical pain from his loss of health and in mental pain from his loss of Sue and from his sense of degradation in having abandoned himself again to Arabella. After his farewell journey to Marygreen, 'a deadly chill' penetrates his bones; back in Christminster he totters 'with cold and lassitude,' and becomes more fevered still. The inescapable conclusion is that only in a malignant universe could there be so much undeserved suffering.

The theme of modern restlessness, which Hardy had hitherto explored in *The Return of the Native,* is also dominating in his last major novel. This theme is not only explicitly stated several times but illustrated through the imagery. Early in the action Jude is described as 'a tragic Don Quixote' (p. 247) and as a 'Dick Whittington, whose spirit was touched to finer issues than a mere material gain' (p. 89)—the man, in other words, who will give over the ordinary securities and rewards to seek the all but unattainable. In serene Christminster the very buildings seem engaged in an insensate struggle for survival and comment implicitly upon the restlessness and the lack of ideal harmonies in modern society. At Christminster the angularity and precision of the stones cut by modern masons are deceptive. Modern thought is chaotic, less orderly and ordered by far than medieval, even if the relics of medievalism do not have the surface sharpness of modern stones. Jude's social unrest has its counterpart in the vagrancy of the itinerant show people who hibernate at Shaston. Sue, moreover, describes herself as a woman 'tossed about, all alone, with aberrant passions and unaccountable anti-pathies' (p. 248). When Sue and Jude leave a settled life at Aldbrickham for a nomadic existence despite Sue's giving birth thereafter to two children, we may conclude that the social and domestic roots of the couple have dissolved. They spend two and a half years wandering from place to place and finally get back to Christminster. At this juncture Jude describes himself to by-standers as lost in 'a chaos of principles—groping in the dark—acting by instinct and not after example' (p. 399). Thus, like Sue, he is symbolic of spiritual malaise and lacks a firm substratum of moral and intellectual values.

The opposition of the forces of life and death, fundamental to the complete meaning of the novel, is conveyed through appropriate images. Thus the past is seen both as a positive and a negative influence. Jude feels the vital energy emanating from Christminster infused into him when he strokes the stones of the buildings during his first night there. Though the university at night is a haunt of the dead, their spirits whisper a message of light and hope to him in these days. Jude remains loyal to the spiritual effluence of the university even when intellectual assent to its values is no longer complete. Jude's continued idealization of the Christian city would, in fact, imply that Christianity can still exert an authentic appeal to the imagination and the moral sensibilities even in a skeptical age. In his early vision of Christminster as a heavenly Jerusalem, he sees its topaz lights go out like 'extinguished candles' as he looks toward the city. This image prefigures Jude's own later relation to Christminster, as its Christian influence dwindles over him and as his own hopes for matriculating disappear. His first vision of the lighted city through the momentarily lifted fog also emphasizes his own difficulties in his attempt to reach it and to become identified with its life-giving spirit. The later associations of Christminster with fog indicate that it is not quite the clear intellectual center that Jude felt it to be in his early days. Jude becomes aware, moreover, that he is further away from Christminster when he is living in the town than he had been previously. The division between what he is and what he wants to be is the greater now that only a 'wall' lies between him and the colleges. On Jude's final return to Christminster, this image of a separating wall is used again when only a wall quite literally divides his family's temporary lodgings from the college at the back of the house.

The precious spiritual heritage from the past is all present in Christminster but it has been greatly dissipated by inertia and decay. This is the belief of Sue who is oppressed by Sarcophagus College with its 'four centuries of gloom, bigotry, and decay' (p. 406). As if to confirm her insight, 'the quaint and frost-eaten stone busts' (p. 400) encircling the theater look down with disdain upon intruders like Jude and his family as an affront to their rock-bound conservatism. As an 'outsider' to the end of his days (see Sue's earlier description of herself as an Ishmaelite), Jude daily repairs the colleges he will never enter and the windows he will never look from.

The images connected with Sue reveal her as an ambiguous moral force, and illustrate Hardy's conviction that positive and negative energies can be exerted, almost simultaneously and often unconsciously, by a gifted and unusual person. At first she seems to Jude to be a part of the atmosphere of light characterizing Christminster, and the fact that she is in the city helps determine him to come there. At this time she is a figure of mystery and suggestion; when Jude finally sees her he is impressed by her vibrancy and by her graciousness. She possesses 'a kindling glance'; and later Jude refers to her intellect in these years as 'a shining star' or as 'lambent lightning.' Phillotson, too, refers to her intellect as sparkling 'like diamonds.'

In the Melchester sequences before her marriage to Phillotson, her influence becomes more ambivalent. Generally a focus of light and life, she wishes 'to ennoble some men to high aims' (p. 182) by infusing into them some of her intellectual energy. Like some women who wish to exert undue control over the destinies of men, she ends by destroying or depressing three men instead of exalting any of them. In the exercise of her vitality she is also curiously irresponsible. Thus she revels in new sensations, irrespective of their influence upon others. An 'epicure in emotions' (p. 207), she visits in Jude's company the chapel in which she is to be married at Melchester little thinking of the torture that this experience entails for the cousin who loves her but who is unable to marry her himself.

Jude's desire to live survives the death of his children; and, despite the horror of the occurrence, he feels that tragedy has enlarged his views while it has narrowed Sue's. Sue's latent revulsion from life, indicated in her Schopenhauerian conviction expressed at Aldbrickham that people in the future may will the extinction of the race, is intensified by the family tragedy. More given to depression than Jude, Sue had felt from the first greater spontaneous sympathy with little Father Time. As a result of his disruption of their family life, Sue embraces the negations that had previously warped the child's nature. Her children's deaths, in part the result of her indiscreet and evasive confidences to Father Time, symbolize her failure to emancipate herself from tradition and, incidentally, her death-bringing influence. The Widow Edlin recalls Sue's uncanny ability as a child to actualize the presence of the raven of death when she recited Poe's poem. Thus Sue, a vessel of the life-force, was also from her early years a potential force for death. Her secret wishes also carry her, she confides to Jude, backward to the security of infancy—ostensibly to the peace of the womb—rather than forward into life: 'I like reading and all that, but I crave to get back to the life of my infancy and its freedom' (p. 164).

Jude's comment after the death of the children reveals how delicately balanced the conflicting energies of life and death are in Sue. She is mistaken in feeling that she is an ascetic, he says; rather she is healthy in her emotional responses, delicate but not inhumanly sexless. He does accuse her of never having loved him as he has loved her: her 'heart does not burn in a flame' (p. 432), whereas he had been earlier seen with 'his ardent affection for her burning in his eyes' (p. 288). In essence, he perceives that she has drained him of his life energies, at the same time that she is their all too volatile source. Now that the cosmic powers seem bent on vengeance, she is deaf to

Jude's entreaty for her to stay with him and offers herself in a sacrificial rite to Christian convention by going back to Phillotson. At this point one recalls Sue's own pitying attitude toward the bride at Aldbrickham: Sue had then felt that the woman, bedecked with flowers, was a lamentable sacrifice on the altar of custom, answering a purpose similar to the sacrifice of bedecked heifers on Grecian altars to gods and principles now seen to be superstitions.

Possibly the characters in *Jude the Obscure* are relatively static, and possibly incident is for the most part contrived, since both men and society alike are controlled by deterministic natural law. Yet this is only one impression produced by the novel, I feel, and not the most important one. If *Jude the Obscure* possesses some of the stationary quality which often characterizes realism in the graphic arts, still as in the masterworks of realistic painting and sculpture the details of the composition and the relationships among them are not immediately available to the critic. Similarly the full ramifications of pattern emerge in *Jude the Obscure* only after these details have been studied, that is, only after an exhaustive analysis has been made of the images and parallel situations in it. New chains of connection among these subsidiary and component elements of the book are continually being suggested to the contemplative, inquiring intelligence. In spite, then, of its somewhat rigid structural lines and philosophical framework, *Jude the Obscure*, as a pulsating organism within such limits, is continually alive with ever-expanding significance. This novel is, as it were, a kind of kaleidoscope: the pattern formed by image, event, character, and idea continually changes with the angle from which it is viewed. The fluid contours of the novel reform and reshape to furnish changing vistas of meaning; new impressions of the whole which are yet related to our previous impressions continually emerge.

Notes

1. *Thomas Hardy: A Study of His Writings and Their Backgrounds* (New York, 1938), pp. 256–7; *Hardy the Novelist* (New York, 1943), pp. 172–3, 189–92; *Thomas Hardy* (New York, 1951: *Writers and Their Work*, No. 21), p. 26; *Thomas Hardy* (New York, 1954), pp. 98–100; *Thomas Hardy: A Critical Biography* (London, 1954), pp. 246, 253.

2. *Thomas Hardy: A Critical Study* (London, 1912), p. 161; *Thomas Hardy: A Study of the Wessex Novels* (New York, 1916), p. 173; *The Technique of Thomas Hardy* (Chicago, 1922), pp. 242–43; *Thomas Hardy: A Critical Study* (London, 1931), p. 88; *Thomas Hardy: The Novels and the Stories* (Cambridge, Mass., 1949), p. 159.

3. *Thomas Hardy: The Novels and the Stories*, p. 82.

4. '*Jude the Obscure* as a Tragedy,' *Southern Review*, VI (Summer 1940), 193–213; and *The English Novel* (New York, 1954), pp. 285–304.

5. See the essays 'The Profitable Reading of Fiction' and 'The Science of Fiction,' reprinted in *Life and Art*, ed. Ernest Brennecke, Jr. (New York, 1925).

6. '*The Science of Fiction*,' p. 89.

7. Florence E. Hardy, *The Early Life of Thomas Hardy, 1840–1891* (New York, 1928), p. 150.

8. Florence E. Hardy, *The Later Years of Thomas Hardy, 1892–1928* (New York, 1930), p. 178).

9. *Jude the Obscure*, 1895 text as reprinted in The Modern Library Edition, p. vi. Page references in my article are to this edition.

10. *Southern Review*, VI (Summer 1940), 197.

11. *The English Novel*, p. 302.

12. *Nineteenth Century Fiction*, IX (June 1954), 50–61.

13. 'Hardy in Defense of His Art,' *Craft and Character: Texts, Method, and Vocation in Modern Fiction* (New York, 1957), p. 94.

14. *Thomas Hardy: The Novels and the Stories*, p. 82.

15. *Ibid.*, p. 33.

16. The patterns of animal imagery in the novel are more fully analyzed in Holland's article, note 12 above.

17. *Nineteenth Century Fiction*, IX (June 1954), 51.

18. 'The Child: The Circus: and *Jude the Obscure*,' *Cambridge Journal*, VIII (June 1954), 531–46.

182

Jude the Obscure: Afterword

———————— ◆ ————————

A. ALVAREZ

Jude the Obscure is Hardy's last and finest novel. Yet its publication in 1895 provoked an outcry as noisy as that which recently greeted *Lady Chatterley's Lover.* The press attacked in a pack, lady reviewers became hysterical, abusive letters poured in, and a bishop solemnly burnt the book. The fuss may seem to us, at this point in time, incredible and even faintly ridiculous, but its effect was serious enough: '... the experience,' Hardy wrote later, 'completely cur[ed] me of further interest in novel-writing.' After *Jude* he devoted himself exclusively to his poetry, never returning to fiction.

What caused the uproar? It was not Hardy's fatalism; after *Tess* his public had learned to live with that and even love it. Nor was his attack on social and religious hypocrisy particularly virulent, though there was certainly a good deal of entrenched resentment of his criticism of those two almost equally venerable institutions: marriage and Oxford. Zola's name was invoked by one or two reviewers, but not seriously. The real blow to the eminently shockable Victorian public was the fact that Hardy treated the sexual undertheme of his book more or less frankly: less frankly, he complained, than he had wished, but more frankly than was normal or acceptable.

Despite the social criticism it involves, the tragedy of *Jude* is not one of missed chances but of missed fulfillment, of frustration. It is a kind of *Anna Karenina* from the male point of view, with the basic action turned upside down. Where Anna moves from Karenin to Vronsky, from dessication to partial satisfaction, Jude, swinging from Arabella to Sue, does the opposite. For all his—and Hardy's—superficial disgust, Jude and Arabella are, physically, very much married: their night at Aldbrickham after years apart is made to seem the most natural thing in the world; Jude's subsequent shame is prompted less by the act itself than by his anger at missing Sue and fear that she will somehow find out. On the other hand, his great love for Sue remains at its high pitch of romance and fatality largely because she never

SOURCE *Jude the Obscure*, New York, 1961.

202

really satisfies him. Hardy himself was quite explicit about this in a letter he wrote after the novel was published:

> One point ... I could not dwell upon: that, though she has children, her intimacies with Jude have never been more than occasional, even when they were living together (I mention that they occupy separate rooms, except towards the end, and one of her reasons for fearing the marriage ceremony is that she fears it would be breaking faith with Jude to withhold herself at pleasure, or altogether, after it; though while uncontracted she feels at liberty to yield herself as seldom as she chooses). This has tended to keep his passion as hot at the end as at the beginning, and helps to break his heart. He has never really possessed her as freely as he desired.[1]

So Jude's tragedy, like every true tragedy, comes from inner tensions which shape the action, not from any haphazard or indifferent force of circumstance. Jude is as frustrated by Sue, his ideal, intellectual woman, as he is by Oxford, his equally shining ideal of the intellectual life. Frustration is the permanent condition of his life.

I am not, of course, suggesting that the book has no theme beyond the sexual relations of Jude, Sue, Arabella, and Phillotson. That was D.H. Lawrence's interpretation in his wonderfully perceptive, startlingly uneven *Study of Thomas Hardy*. But then, Lawrence was writing not as a critic but as an imaginative artist who owed a great personal debt to Hardy. His critical method was simply to retell Hardy's plots as though he himself had written them, isolating only what interested him. The result was considerable insight and an equally considerable shift of emphasis away from the novel Hardy actually wrote.

Obviously, *Jude the Obscure* does have its declared social purpose: to criticize a system which could, for mainly snobbish reasons, keep out of the universities 'one of the very men,' as Sue says, 'Christminster was intended for when the colleges were founded; a man with a passion for learning, but no money, or opportunities, or friends ... You were elbowed off the pavement by the millionaires' sons.' A figure who for Thomas Gray, a Cambridge don elegizing in his country churchyard, was an object of mildly nostaligic curiosity, became in Hardy's work a living, tragic hero. And by this shift of focus Hardy helped make the issue itself live. In his postscript of 1912 he wrote 'that some readers thought ... that when Ruskin College[2] was subsequently founded it should have been called the College of Jude the Obscure.' Hardy may not have had as direct an influence on social reforms as Dickens; but he helped.

Yet *Jude the Obscure* is clearly more than a criticism of the exclusiveness of the major English universities. Surprisingly early in the book Jude realizes that his Christminster ambitions are futile. After that, though the university remains an obsession with him, it plays very little part in the novel itself. Instead, it is a kind of subplot echoing the main theme in slightly different terms, just as Gloucester and his sons repeat on a smaller scale the tragedy of

King Lear and his daughters. But with this difference: that Jude is the hero of both the main plot and the subplot. Christminster may drop out of the major action, but his continuing obsession with it repeats, in another tone of voice, his obsession with Sue. In the beginning, both Sue and the university seem objects of infinitely mysterious romance; both, in the end, land Jude in disillusion. Both seem to promise intellectual freedom and strength; both are shown to be at bottom utterly conventional. Both promise fulfillment; both frustrate him. All Jude's intellectual passion earns him nothing more than the title 'Tutor of St Slums,' while all his patience and devotion to Sue loses him his job, his children, and finally even his title of husband.

Hardy himself knew perfectly well that the Christminster, social-purpose side of the novel was relatively exterior to its main theme. Years later, when there was talk of turning *Jude* into a play, he wrote: 'Christminster is of course the tragic influence of Jude's drama in one sense, but innocently so, and merely as cross obstruction.'[3] There is, however, nothing exterior in the part Sue plays in Jude's tragedy. At times, in fact, she seems less a person in her own right than a projection of one side of Jude's character. Even Phillotson remarks on this; 'I have been struck,' he said, 'with ... the extraordinary sympathy, or similarity, between the pair. He is her cousin, which perhaps accounts for some of it. They seem to be one person split in two!' And, in harmony with the principle by which all the major intuitions in the novel are given to the men, Jude himself perceives the same thing: when he lends Sue his clothes after she has escaped from the training college and arrived, soaking wet, at his lodgings,

> He palpitated at the thought that she had fled to him in her trouble as he had fled to her in his. What counterparts they were! ... Sitting in his only arm-chair he saw a slim and fragile being masquerading as himself on a Sunday, so pathetic in her defencelessness that his heart felt big with the sense of it.

The situation, in which the hero dresses in his own clothes his wet, lost, desperate double, is exactly the same as that of the masterpiece of double identity, Conrad's *The Secret Sharer.*

Considering the ultimate differences between Sue and Jude, Hardy perhaps thought that their similarities merely emphasized the contrasts of which, he wrote, the book was full: 'Sue and her heathen gods set against Jude's reading the Greek testament; Christminster academical, Christminster in the slums; Jude the saint, Jude the sinner; Sue the Pagan, Sue the saint; marriage, no marriage; &c., &c.'[4] But the geometrical neatness of Hardy's plan does not make his psychological insight any less profound or compelling. All through the book Sue is Jude 'masquerading as himself on a Sunday.' As even her name implies (Sue, Hardy says himself, is a lily, and Bridehead sounds very like maidenhead), she is the untouched part of him, all intellect, nerves, and sensitivity, essentially bodiless. That is why her most dramatic and typical appearances have always something ghostly about them. When, for example, Jude suddenly and guiltily comes across her after his night with Arabella at Aldbrickham, 'Sue stood like a vision before him— her look bodeful and anxious as in a dream.' Or, when she unexpectedly returns to Phillotson in his illness, and does her odd, characteristic conjuring trick with the mirror: 'she was in light spring clothing, and her advent seemed ghostly—like the flitting in of a moth.' It is this combination of nonphysical purity with exaggeratedly sharp intellect and sensitivity which preserves her for Jude as an object of ideal yearning, hopeless and debilitating. It is a yearning for his own lost innocence, before his Christminster ambitions were diverted by Arabella. Even when he finally rounds on her, after all their years and tragedies together, he can still only call her 'a sort of fey, or sprite—not a woman!' Despite everything he can do, she remains a bodiless idea, an idea of something in himself.

Sue and Arabella are, in fact, like the white and black horses, the noble and base instincts, which drew Plato's chariot of the soul. But because Hardy too has a passion for Sue's kind of frigid purity ('She is,' he wrote, 'a type of woman which has always had an attraction for me'), he exaggerated the case against Arabella almost to the point of parody. Lawrence wrote:

> He insists that she is a pig-killer's daughter; he insists that she drag Jude into pig-killing; he lays stress on her false tail of hair. That is not the point at all. This is only Hardy's bad art. He himself, as an artist, manages in the whole picture of Arabella almost to make insignificant in her these pig-sticking, false-hair crudities. But he must have his personal revenge on her for her coarseness, which offends him, because he is something of an Angel Clare.

Where Hardy thought Arabella 'the villain of the piece,' Lawrence tried to make her out the heroine. Both views are wrong—not because Sue is any more or less of the heroine than Arabella, but because *Jude the Obscure* is fundamentally a work without any heroines at all. It has only a hero. I will return to this. Lawrence was, however, right when he said that Arabella survives Hardy's deliberate coarsening of her. The artist does her justice against the grain of his tastes. So it is she, not Sue, who shows flashes of real intelligence:

> 'I don't know what you mean,' said Sue stiffly. 'He is mine if you come to that!'
> 'He wasn't yesterday.'
> Sue coloured roseate, and said 'How do you know?'
> 'From your manner when you talked to me at the door. Well, my dear, you've been quick about it, and I expect my visit last night helped it on . . .'

And it is also she, not Sue, who really wants Jude:

> In a few moments Arabella replied in a curiously low, hungry tone of latent sensuousness: 'I've got him to care for me: yes! But I want him to more than care for me; I want him to have me—to marry me! I must have him. I can't do without him. He's the sort of man I long for. I shall go mad if I can't give myself to him altogether! I felt I should when I first saw him!'

With fewer exclamation marks and without the moralizing qualification 'of latent sensuousness'—as though that were so reprehensible!—Arabella's words would sound more frank and serious than any protestation Sue manages in the whole book. Similarly, despite everything, it is Arabella whom Jude really wants physically. There is no doubt about this from the moment when, without a flicker of distaste, he picks up the pig's pizzle she has thrown at him:

> ... somehow or other, the eyes of the brown girl rested in his own when he had said the words, and there was a momentary flash of intelligence, a dumb announcement of affinity *in posse*, between herself and him, which, so far as Jude Fawley was concerned, had no sort of premeditation in it. She saw that he had singled her out from the three, as a woman is singled out in such cases ... The unvoiced call of woman to man, which was uttered very distinctly by Arabella's personality, held Jude to the spot against his intention—almost against his will, and in a way new to his experience.

This may have in it none of the refinement of Jude's passion for Sue, but it is considerably more human and spontaneous. Jude, after all fell in love with Sue's photograph before he fell in love with Sue herself; and the first time she saw him 'she no more observed his presence than that of the dust-motes which his manipulations raised into the sunbeams.' So they are never really married because the connection between them is of the sensibility, not of the senses. The only real moment of ecstasy Jude shares with Sue is bodiless, precipitated by the scent and brilliance of the roses at the agricultural show. 'The real marriage of Jude and Sue was,' as Lawrence said, 'in the roses.' So it is Arabella who gets the last word; however much Hardy may have disliked her in principle, artistically he acknowledged the sureness of her physical common sense, to the extent at least of allowing her to make the final, unqualified judgment of the tragedy:

> 'She may swear that on her knees to the holy cross upon her necklace till she's hoarse, but it won't be true!' said Arabella. 'She's never found peace since she left his arms, and never will again till she's as he is now!'

Yet although his final attitude to Sue may have been ambiguous, in creating her Hardy did something extraordinarily original: he created one of the few totally narcissistic women in literature; but he did so at the same time as he made her something rather wonderful. Her complexity lies in the way in which Hardy managed to present the full, bitter sterility of her narcissism and yet tried to exonerate her.

Bit by bit even Jude is made to build up the case against her: she is cold, incapable of real love,' 'an epicure of the emotions,' and a flirt; she wants to be loved more than she wants to love; she is vain, marrying Phillotson out of pique when she learns that Jude is married, and going to bed with Jude only when Arabella reappears on the scene; she is even cruel, in a refined way, her deliberate, 'epicene' frigidity having killed one man before the novel even starts. Yet despite all this, Jude loves her. Part of his love, of course, is rooted in frustration: he wants her endlessly because he can never properly have her. And he loves her, too, because he loves himself; he has in himself a narcissism which responds to hers, a vanity of the intellectual life, of his ideals and ambitions, of the refinement of intellect and sensibility which he had first projected onto Christminster.

But the truth and power of the novel lie in the way in which Jude, in the end, is able to understand his love for Sue *without lessening it.* Until the closing scenes, he manages to make her conform to his ideal by a kind of emotional sleight of mind: he dismisses his glimpses of the unchanging conventionality below the bright surface of her nonconformity by invoking both his own worthlessness and that vague marriage-curse which has been the lot of his family. The turning point is the death of the children:

> One thing troubled him more than any other; that Sue and himself had mentally travelled in opposite directions since the tragedy: events which had enlarged his own views of life, laws, customs, and dogmas, had not operated in the same manner on Sue's. She was no longer the same as in the independent days, when her intellect played like lambent lightning over conventions and formalities which he at that time respected, though he did not now.

Where Jude matures as a man, reconciling himself to the endless tragedies and disappointments until he can accept them more or less without self-pity, Sue remains fixed in her narcissism. She does not change, she simple shapes her outer actions to the commonplaces which at heart had always ruled her. Convention—which she calls High Church Sacramentalism—is simply a way of preserving her vanity intact. To break her self-enclosed mould would mean laying herself open to the real tragedy of her relationship with Jude— of which she, not Fate, is the main instrument—and thus giving herself to him completely. Because she is unable to do this, she denies the true marriage between them and perverts it to fit a conventional idea of matrimony. Arabella may occasionally have turned whore for practical ends— that, presumably, is how she raised the money to make Jude drunk before remarrying him—but it is Sue whom he accuses, when she returns to Phillotson, of 'a fanatic prostitution.' What began as intellectual freedom ends as prostitution to an idea. So when Jude finally turns on her with the cry 'Sue, Sue, you are not worth a man's love!' he is passing judgment not only on her but also, because he never once denies that he loves her, on something in himself. That cry and Arabella's closing words represent a standard of maturity which Jude only slowly and painfully attains.

There is something puzzling about *Jude the Obscure* as a work of art: in impact it is intensely moving; in much of its detail it is equally intensely false. The dialogue, for example, is, with very little exception, forced and awkward. Even granted the conventional formalities of the time, no character ever properly seems to connect with another in talk. Despite all the troubles they have seen together, Jude and Sue speak to each other as though they had just been introduced at a vicarage teaparty; as a result, their grand passion becomes, on their own lips, something generalized, like the weather or religion or politics. They are, in Sue's own words, 'too sermony.' Conversely, Arabella, apart from her few moments of truth and an occasional, ponderous slyness, is reduced to a kind of music-hall vulgarity of speech. Widow Edlin is archly folksy and Father Time is almost a caricature of Hardy at his most Hardyesque. The only people who seem able to talk more or less naturally to others are the solitaries, Phillotson and, in a slighter way, Vilbert.

It may be that Hardy had very little ear for dialogue; it is something he rarely does well. But his clumsiness in *Jude* is more than a fault, it is part of the nature of the work. For the essential subject of the novel is not Oxford, or marriage, or even frustration. It is loneliness. This is the one condition without which the book would show none of its power. When they are together the characters often seem amateurishly conceived, and sometimes downright false. But once they are left to themselves they begin to think, feel, act, and even talk with that strange poignancy which is uniquely Hardy's. The brief, almost cursory paragraph in which Jude tries to drown himself after the failure of his first marriage is a far more effective and affecting scene than, for example, the elaborately constructed pig-killing—and largely, I think, because nothing is said. None of the emotional impact is lost in heavy moralizing or awkwardness. When Jude is on his own, as he is for a great deal of the novel, walking from one village to the next, one Christminster college to another, then he emerges as a creation of real genius.

The novel's power, in fact, resides in that sustained, deep plangency of note which is the moving bass behind every major incident. This note is produced not by any single action but by a general sense of tragedy and sympathetic hopelessness which the figure of Jude provokes in Hardy. And the essence of this tragedy is Jude's loneliness. He is isolated from society because his ambitions, abilities, and sensibility separate him from his own class while winning him no place in any other. He is isolated in his marriage to Arabella because she has no idea of what he is about, and doesn't care. He is isolated in his marriage to Sue because she is frigid. Moreover, the sense of loneliness is intensified by the way in which both women are presented less as characters complete in themselves than as projections of Jude, sides of his character, existing only in relation to him. In the same way, the wonderfully sympathetic and moving treatment of Phillotson in the scenes at Shaston— his surprising delicacy and generosity and desolating loneliness—is essentially the same as the treatment of Jude. The two men, indeed, are extraordinarily alike: they are both in love with the same woman, both fail in much the same way at Christminster, both inhabit the same countryside and suffer the same loneliness. Their difference is in age and ability and passion. Phillotson, in short, is as much a projection of Jude as the two women. He is a kind of Jude Senior: older, milder, with less talent and urgency, and so without the potentiality for tragedy. In one sense, the entire novel is simply the image of Jude magnified and subtly lit from different angles until he and his shadows occupy the whole Wessex landscape. And Jude in turn is a embodiment of the loneliness, deprivation, and regret which are both the strength and constant theme of Hardy's best poetry. Hardy may have been perfectly justified in denying that the book was at all autobiographical, but it is a supremely vivid dramatization of the state of mind out of which Hardy's poetry emerged.

This is why Father Time fails as a symbol. He is introduced in one of the most beautiful passages of the novel:

> He was Age masquerading as Juvenility, and doing it so badly that his real self showed through crevices. A ground-swell from ancient years of night seemed now and then to lift the child in this his morning-life, when his face took a back view over some great Atlantic of Time, and appeared not to care about what it saw.

And he is finally left in a paragraph of equal force:

> The boy's face expressed the whole tale of their situation. On that little shape had converged all the inauspiciousness and shadow which had darkened the first union of Jude, and all the accidents, mistakes, fears, errors of the last. He was their nodal point, their focus, their expression in a single term. For the rashness of those parents he had groaned, for their ill assortment he had quaked, and for the misfortunes of these he had died.

But in between these two points, his ominous remarks, desolation, and self-consciously incurable melancholy are so overdone as to seem almost as though Hardy had decided to parody himself. Even the death of the children, and Father Time's appalling note—'*Done because we are too menny*'—is dangerously close to being laughable: a situation so extreme, insisted on so strongly, seems more appropriate to *grand guignol* than to tragedy. But Hardy, I think, was forced to overdraw Father Time because the child is redundant in the scheme of the novel. What he represents was already embodied in fully tragic form in the figure of Jude. There was no way of repeating it without melodrama.

The power of *Jude the Obscure* is, then, less fictional than poetic. It arises less from the action or the fidelity of the setting than from the wholeness of the author's feelings. It is a tragedy whose unity is not Aristotelian but emotional. And the feelings are those which were later given perfect form in Hardy's best poetry. The work is the finest of Hardy's novels because it is the one in which the complex of emotions is, despite Father Time, least weakened by melodrama, bad plotting, and that odd incidental amateurishness of detail by which, perhaps, Hardy, all through his novel-writing period, showed his dissatisfaction with the form. It is also the finest because it is the novel in which the true Hardy hero is most fully vindicated, and the apparently fascinating myth of immaculate frigidity is finally exploded. But I wonder if Hardy was not being slightly disingenuous when he claimed that the treatment of the book by the popular reviewers had turned him, for good, from the novel to poetry. After *Jude the Obscure* there was no other direction in which he could go.

Notes

1. *The Later Years of Thomas Hardy* by F.E. Hardy, 1930, p. 42.
2. Ruskin, Oxford, was the first college designed to provide opportunities at the university for working-class men who, for one reason or another, had not had a chance to go to a university after leaving school; it has since been supplemented by a wide system of government and local grants.
3. F.E. Hardy, *op. cit.*, p. 249.
4. F.E. Hardy, *op. cit.*, p. 42.

183
Hardy's Sue Bridehead

———— ◆ ————

ROBERT B. HEILMAN

In *Jude the Obscure*, a novel in which skillful characterization eventually wins the day over laborious editorializing, Thomas Hardy comes close to genius in the portrayal of Sue Bridehead. Sue takes the book away from the title character, because she is stronger, more complex, and more significant, and because her contradictory impulses, creating a spontaneous air of the inexplicable and even the mysterious, are dramatized with extraordinary fullness and concreteness, and with hardly a word of interpretation or admonishment by the author. To say this is to say that as a character she has taken off on her own, sped far away from a conceptual role, and developed as a being whose brilliant and puzzling surface provides only partial clues to the depths in which we can sense the presence of profound and representative problems.

Sue's original role, of course, is that of counterpoint to Arabella: spirit against flesh, or Houyhnhnm against Yahoo. Sue and Arabella are meant to represent different sides of Jude, who consistently thinks about them together, contrasts them, regards them as mutually exclusive opposites (e.g. III, 9, 10; IV, 5). Early in their acquaintance he sees in Sue 'almost an ideality' (II, 4), 'almost a divinity' (III, 3); the better he gets to know her, the more he uses, in speech or thought, such terms as 'ethereal' (III, 9; IV, 3; VI, 3), 'uncarnate' (III, 9), 'aerial' (IV, 3), 'spirit, ... disembodied creature ... hardly flesh' (IV, 5), 'phantasmal, bodiless creature' (V, 1), 'least sensual', 'a sort of fay, or sprite' (VI, 3). She herself asks Jude to kiss her 'incorporeally' (V, 4), and she puts Mrs Edlin 'in mind of a sperrit' (VI, 9).

The allegorical content in Hardy's delineation of Sue has also a historical base: she is made a figure of Shelleyan idealism. When Phillotson describes the rather spiritualized affinity that he perceives between Jude and Sue, Gillingham exclaims 'Platonic!' and Phillotson qualifies, 'Well, no. Shelleyan would be nearer to it. They remind me of Laon and Cythna' (IV, 4), the idealized liberators and martyrs in *The Revolt of Islam* (which is quoted later in another context—V, 4). Sue asks Jude to apply to her certain lines from

SOURCE *Nineteenth Century Fiction*, 20, 1965–6.

Shelley's 'Epipsychidion'— '... a Being whom my spirit oft/Met on its visioned wanderings far aloft ... A seraph of Heaven, too gentle to be human' (IV, 5)—and Jude later calls Sue a 'sensitive plant' (VI, 3).

Deliberately or instinctively Hardy is using certain Romantic values as a critical instrument against those of his own day, a free spirit against an oppressive society, the ethereal against commonplace and material. But a very odd thing happens: in conceiving of Sue as 'spirit', and then letting her develop logically in such terms, he finds her coming up with a powerful aversion to sex—in other words, with a strong infusion of the very Victorianism that many of her feelings and intellectual attitudes run counter to. On the one hand, her objection to allegorizing the Song of Solomon (III, 4) is anti-Victorian; but when, in refusing to have intercourse with Jude, she says, 'I resolved to trust you to set my wishes above your gratification', her view of herself as a supra-sexual holder of prerogative and of him as a mere seeker of 'gratification' is quite Victorian. She calls him 'gross', apparently both for his night with Arabella and for desiring her physically, and under her pressure he begs, 'Forgive me for being gross, as you call it!' (IV, 5). Again, he uses the apologetic phrase, 'we poor unfortunate wretches of grosser substance' (V, 1). All of Sue's terms for Arabella come out of middle-class propriety: 'fleshy, coarse woman', 'low-passioned woman', 'too low, too coarse for you', as does her argument that Jude should not go to help her because 'she's not your wife ...' Jude is not entirely pliant here; in fact, there is some defiance in his saying that perhaps he is 'coarse, too, worse luck!' But even while arguing against her refusal of sex he can say that 'your freedom from everything that's gross has elevated me', accepting the current view of the male as a lower being who needs to be lifted up to a higher life (V, 2). Even when, near the end, he is vehemently urging Sue not to break their union, he can entertain the possibility that in overturning her proscription of sex he may have 'spoiled one of the highest and purest loves that ever existed between man and woman' (VI, 3); the 'average sensual man' all but gives up his case to a conventional opinion of his own time. Other aspects of Sue's vocabulary betray the Victorian tinge: when she first calls marriage a 'sordid contract' (IV, 2) it seems fresh and independent, but the continuing chorus of 'horrible and sordid' (V, 1), 'vulgar' and 'low' (V, 3), 'vulgar' and 'sordid' (V, 4) suggests finally an over-nice and complacent personality. The style is a spontaneous accompaniment of the moral elevation which she assumes in herself and which in part she uses—Hardy is very shrewd in getting at the power-sense in self-conscious 'virtue'—to keep Jude in subjection.

There is a very striking irony here: perhaps unwittingly Hardy has forged or come upon a link between a romantic idea of spirit (loftiness, freedom) and a Victorian self-congratulatory 'spirituality'—a possibly remarkable feat of the historical imagination. He has also come fairly close to putting the novel on the side of the Houyhnhnms, a difficulty that he never gets around quite satisfactorily. But above all he has given a sharp image of inconsistency in Sue, for whatever the paradoxical link between her manifestations of spirit, she nevertheless appears as the special outsider on the one hand and as quite conventional on the other. In this he continues a line of characterization that he has followed very skillfully from the beginning. Repeatedly he uses such words as 'perverseness', 'riddle' (III, 1), 'conundrum' (III, 2), 'unreasonable ... capricious' (III, 5), 'perverse', 'colossal inconsistency' (III, 7), 'elusiveness of her curious double nature', 'ridiculously inconsistent' (IV, 2), 'logic ... extraordinarily compounded', 'puzzling and unpredictable' (IV, 3), 'riddle' (IV, 4), 'that mystery, her heart' (IV, 5), 'ever evasive' (V, 5). With an inferior novelist, such an array of terms might be an effort to do by words what the action failed to do; here, they only show that Hardy knew what he was doing in the action, for all the difficulties, puzzles, and unpredictability have been dramatized with utmost variety and thoroughness. From the beginning, in major actions and lesser ones, Sue is consistently one thing and then another: reckless, then diffident; independent, then needing support; severe, and then kindly; inviting, and then offish. The portrayal of her is the major achievement of the novel. It is an imaginative feat, devoid of analytical props; for all of the descriptive words that he uses, Hardy never explains her or places her, as he is likely to do with lesser characters. She simply is, and it is up to the reader to sense the inner truth that creates multiple, lively, totally conflicting impressions. With her still more than with the other characters Hardy has escaped from the allegorical formula in which his addiction to such words as 'spirit' might have trapped him.

From the beginning her inconsistency has a pattern which teases us with obscure hints of an elusive meaningfulness. Her first action characterizes her economically; she buys nude statues of classical divinities, but 'trembled', almost repented, concealed them, misrepresented them to her landlady, and kept waking up anxiously at night (II, 3). She reads Gibbon but is superstitious about the scene of her first meeting with Jude (II, 4). She criticizes unrestrainedly the beliefs of Jude and Phillotson, but is wounded by any kind of retort (II, 5); repeatedly she can challenge, censure, and deride others but be hypersensitive to even mild replies, as if expecting immunity from the normal reciprocities of argument and emotion (III, 4; IV, 5; VI, 3, 4, 8). She reacts excessively to the unexpected visit of the school inspector, snaps at Phillotson 'petulantly', and then 'regretted that she had upbraided him' (II, 5). Aunt Drusilla reports that as a girl Sue was 'pert ... too often, with her tight-strained nerves', and an inclination to scoff at the by-laws of modesty; she was a tomboy who would suddenly run away from the boys (II, 6).

These initial glimpses of Sue prepare for the remarkable central drama of the novel: her unceasing reversals, apparent changes of mind and heart, acceptances and rejections, alternations of warmth and offishness, of evasiveness and candor, of impulsive acts and later regrets, of commitment and withdrawal, of freedom and constraint, unconventionality and propriety. She is cool about seeing Jude, then very eager, then offish (III, 1). She escapes from confinement at school but appears increasingly less up to the exploit already concluded (III, 3–5). She tells Jude, 'You mustn't love me', then writes 'you may', quarrels with him, and writes, 'Forgive ... my petulance ...' (III, 5). Before and after marriage she resists talking about Phillotson ('But I am not going to be cross-examined ...') and then talks about him almost without reserve (III, 6, 9; IV, 2). Again she forbids Jude to come to see her (III, 9), then 'with sweet humility' revokes the prohibition (III, 10), is changeable when he comes, invites him for the next week (IV, 1), and then cancels the invitation (IV, 2). She 'tearfully' refuses to kiss Jude, and then suddenly kisses him (IV, 3). Hardy identifies, as a natural accompaniment of her shifting of attitude and mood, a tendency to shift ground under pressure. Since she dislikes firm reply, argument, or questioning from others, she may simply declare herself 'hurt'. Another ploy is to make a hyperbolic statement of desolation or self-condemnation. 'I *wish* I had a friend here to support me; but nobody is ever on my side!' (III, 5), 'I am in the wrong. I always am!' (IV, 3), 'I know I am a poor, miserable creature' (IV, 5). Another self-protective situation-controlling move is to fall back directly on her emotional responsiveness to a difficult moment. She will not sleep with Jude but is jealous of Arabella; so she simply tells Jude, '... I don't like you as well as I did!' (IV, 5). When she will not acknowledge loving him and he remarks on the danger of the game of elusiveness, her reply, 'in a tragic voice', is 'I don't think I like you today so well as I did ...' (V, 1). For all of her intellectual freedom, she seems to accept the ancient dogma of 'women's whims' (IV, 5) and calls Jude 'good' because 'you give way to all my whims!' (V, 4).

Through all the sensitiveness, fragility, and caprice there appears an impulse for power, for retaining control of a situation, very delicately or even overtly, in one's own terms. The Victorian acceptance of woman's pedestal implies a superiority to be acknowledged. Early in the story, just after Jude sees 'in her almost a divinity' (III, 3), Sue states candidly that she 'did want and long to ennoble some man to high aim's (III, 4)—which might be pure generosity or an idealism infected with egoism.[1] She trusts Jude not to pursue her with a desire for 'gratification' (IV, 5). She would rather go on 'always' without sex because 'It is so much sweeter—for the woman at least, and when she is sure of the man' (V, 1). The reappearance of Arabella so disturbs Sue's confidence in ownership that she tries to get rid of Arabella without Jude's seeing her, and when that fails, accepts the sexual bond only as a necessary means of binding Jude to her (V, 2). This gives her new confidence—'So I am not a bit frightened about losing you, now ...'—and hence she resists marriage (V, 3). Behind this near-compulsion to prescribe terms is a need which Sue states three different times: 'Some women's love of being loved is insatiable' (IV, 1); 'But sometimes a woman's *love of being loved* gets the better of her conscience ...' (IV, 5); 'the craving to attract and captivate, regardless of the injury it may do the man' (VI, 3). Here again,

Hardy avoids both allegory and that idealizing of a character whom her own associates find it easy to idealize.

At the center of hypersensitivity he perceives a self-concern which can mean a high insensitivity to others and hence a habit of hurting them which may actually embody an unconscious intention (another version of the power-sense). Despite her formal words of regret and self-censure, Sue seems almost to relish the complaint of the student that she 'was breaking his heart by holding out against him so long at such close quarters; (III, 4). Though she resents criticism of or even disagreement with her, all that Jude believes in and holds dear she attacks with an unrestraint that ranges from inconsiderateness to condescension to an outright desire to wound—the church, the university, and their traditions (III, 1, 2, and 4). Always careless of Phillotson's feelings, she does not even let him know about her expulsion from school (III, 6). Hardy presents her desire to leave Phillotson as understandable and defensible, but at the same time he portrays her style with Phillotson as fantastically inconsiderate. For instance, as he 'writhed', she upbraided him in a doctrinaire style for not having a free mind as J.S. Mill advised (IV, 3); later, he lies 'writhing like a man in hell' (IV, 6) as she lets him think that her relation with Jude is adulterous. She is indifferent to Jude's feelings when she refuses to have sexual intercourse with him. She insists that Jude must 'love me dearly' (V, 3), but when he gives her an opening for speaking affectionately to him, she says only, 'You are always trying to make me confess to all sorts of absurdities' (V, 5). She moves variously toward self-protection, self-assertion, and self-indulgence. One of the most remarkable cases of giving way to her own feelings in complete disregard of their impact on others is her telling Father Time, 'vehemently', that 'Nature's law [is] mutual butchery!' (V, 6)—a view that with any imagination at all she would know him utterly unfitted to cope with. It prepares for her thoughtless reply of 'almost' to his statement that it 'would be better to be out o' the world than in it' and her total ineptitude in dealing with his surmise that all their trouble is due to the children and with his desperation in finding that there is to be another child. Sue actually provides the psychological occasion, if not the cause, of the double murder and suicide (VI, 2)—the disasters that, with massive irony, begin her downward course to death-in-life.

The final touch in Sue as Victorian is her 'I can't explain' when Father Time is driven frantic by the news that there will be another child. This is a lesser echo of Sue's embarrassment in all matters of sex—a disability the more marked in one who enters into otherwise intimate relations with a series of men. In her feeling free to deny the very center of the relationship what looks like naiveté or innocence masks a paradoxical double design of self-interest: she wants to be sexually attractive and powerful but to remain sexually unavailable. Sue has something of 'La Belle Dame Sans Merci', leaving men not 'palely loitering' but worse off than that: of the three men who have desired her, one finally has her but only as a shuddering sacrificial victim, and the other two die of 'consumption', which modern medical practice regards as predominantly of psychosomatic origin. She does give in to Jude, indeed, but immediately begins campaigning against marriage, and in terms so inapplicable—she repeatedly argues from the example of their earlier marriages, which are simply not relevant (e.g. V, 4)—that they exist not for their own sake but as a symbolic continuation of the resistance to sex. They secretly help to prepare us for her eventual flight from Jude, and to keep us from crediting her later statement that she and Jude found a pagan joy in sensual life (Hardy's belated effort to do something for sex, which he has hardly moved an inch from the most conventional position). True, she declares, just before resuming sexual relations with Phillotson, 'I find I still love [Jude]—oh, grossly!' (VI, 9), but at this time the words seem less an intuition of truth than a reaction from the horror of her penitential life; and it is noteworthy that, in whatever sense they may be true, they are spoken by her only when the action they imply is now finally beyond possibility.

La Belle Dame Sans Merci cannot practice mercilessness without being belle—beautiful, or charming, or fascinating. Though Sue may be, as Arabella puts it, 'not a particular warm-hearted creature' and 'a slim, fidgety little thing' who 'don't know what love is' (V, 5), even Gillingham feels what the three men in her life respond to, her 'indefinable charm' (VI, 5). She is always spontaneous, often vivacious, occasionally kindly and tender. More important, Hardy has caught a paradoxical and yet powerful kind of charm: the physical attractiveness of the person who seems hardly to have physical existence and hence evokes such terms as 'aerial' and 'ethereal'. The possibility that she unconsciously holds out to men in the enrichment of the ordinary sensual experience by its very opposite: all modes—or rather, the two extremes—of relationship are present at once in an extraordinary fusion. But this special charm is tenuously interwoven with the much more evident charm, the sheer power to fascinate, of an unpredictable personality. Though Sue may, as she herself theorizes, get into 'these scrapes' through 'curiosity to hunt up a new sensation', she does not have in her very much of the cold experimenter. Jude senses sadistic and masochistic elements in her (elements much noted by more recent critics). He theorizes that she 'wilfully gave herself and him pain' for the pleasure of feeling pity for both, and he suspects that she will 'go on inflicting such pains again and again, and grieving for the sufferer again and again' (III, 7). Her selfishness is never consistent; she can be virtually ruthless in seeking ends, and then try to make reparation. She can be contemptuous and cutting, and then penitent and tearful. She can be daring and then scared ('scared' and 'frightened' are used of her repeatedly); inconsiderate, and then generous; self-indulgent, and then self-punishing; callous, and then all but heartbroken—always with a kind of rushing spontaneity. Such endless shifts as these, which Hardy presents with unflagging resourcefulness, make Jude call Sue a 'flirt' (IV, 1). Jude merely names what the reader feels on page after page: the unconscious coquetry that Sue practices. The novel is, in one light, a remarkable treatment of coquetry, for it implicitly defines the underlying bases of the style. The ordinary coquette may tease and chill by plan, invite and hold off deliberately, heighten desire by displaying readiness and simulating retreat: the piquant puzzle. This is what Arabella offers with great crudity in the beginning: Hardy's preparation, by contrast, for the brilliant unconscious tactics of Sue.

The true, ultimate coquette, the coquette in nature, has no plans, no deliberations, no contrived puzzles. Her inconsistency of act is the inconsistency of being. She goes this way, and then that way, for no other reason than that she cannot help it. She acts in terms of one impulse that seems clear and commanding, and is then pulled away by another that comes up and, though undefined, is not subject to her control. On the one hand, she freely puts conventional limitations behind her; on the other, she hardly comes up to conventional expectations. She has freedom of thought but not freedom of action and being. She is desirable but does not desire. She wishes to be desirable, which means making the moves that signify accessibility to desire; the cost of love is then a commitment from which she must frantically or stubbornly withdraw. She is thoughtless and even punitive, but she has pangs of conscience; yet to be certain that she has conscience, she must create situations that evoke pity for others and blame of self. Hardy catches very successfully the spontaneity of each of her acts and gestures; they are authentic, unprogrammed expressions of diverse elements in her personality. Coquetry is, in the end, the external drama of inner divisions, of divergent impulses each of which is strong enough to determine action at any time, but not at all times or even with any regularity. The failure of unity is greater than that of the ordinary personality, and the possibilities of trouble correspondingly greater. If the coquette is not fortunate in finding men with great tolerance for her diversity—and ordinarily she has an instinct for the type she needs—and situations that do not subject her to too great pressure, she will hardly avoid disaster.

The split that creates the coquette is not unlike the tragic split; the latter, of course, implies deeper emotional commitments and more momentous situations. Yet one might entitle an essay on Sue 'The Coquette as Tragic Heroine'. Because she has a stronger personality than Jude, has more initiative, and endeavors more to impose her will, she is closer to tragic stature than he. Like traditional tragic heroes, she believes that she can dictate terms and clothe herself in special immunities; like them, she has finally to reckon with neglected elements in herself and in the order of life. If the catastrophe which she helps precipitate is not in the first instance her own, nevertheless it becomes a turning point for her, a shock that opens up a new illumination, a new sense of self and of the moral order. After the death of the children Sue comes into some remarkable self-knowledge. She identifies precisely her errors in dealing with Father Time (VI, 2). Her phrase 'proud in my own conceit' describes her style as a free-swinging critic of others and of the world. She recognizes that her relations with Jude became sexual only when 'envy stimulated me to oust Arabella'. She acknowledges to Jude, '... I merely wanted you to love me ... it began in the selfish and cruel wish to make your heart ache for me without letting mine ache for you.' Such passages, with their burden of tragic self-understanding, predominate over others in which Sue looks for objects of blame, falls into self-pity, or frantically repeats her ancient self-protective plea, 'Don't criticize me, Jude—I can't bear it!' (VI, 3).

But the passages that indicate growth by understanding are predominated over, in turn, by others in which Sue violently and excessively blames herself and pronounces on herself a life sentence of the severest mortification that she can imagine. Under great stress the precarious structure of her divided personality has broken down, and it has been replaced by a narrow, rigid unity under the tyrannical control of a single element in the personality—the self-blaming, self-flagellating impulse which Sue now formulates in Christian terms but which has been part of her all along. In place of the tragic understanding there is only black misery. Hence she ignores all Jude's arguments; Hardy may sympathize with these, but he knows what development is in character for Sue. A basic lack of wholeness has been converted, by heavy strains, into illness. Not that an imposition of a penalty is in itself pathological; we see no illness in the self-execution of Othello, or, more comparably, in the self-blinding of Oedipus. Facts become clear to them, and they accept responsibility by prompt and final action. Sue not only judges her ignoble deeds but undiscriminatingly condemns a whole life; she converts all her deeds into vice, and crawls into an everlasting hell on earth. Remorse has become morbid, and punishment seems less a symbolic acknowledgement of error than the craving of a sick nature.

The problem is, then, whether the story of Sue merely touches on tragedy, with its characteristic reordering of a chaotic moral world, or becomes mainly a case history of clinical disorder, a sardonic prediction of an endless night. As always, the problem of illness is its representativeness: have we a special case, interesting for its own sake, pitiable, shocking, but limited in its relevance, or is the illness symbolic, containing a human truth that transcends its immediate terms? There is a real danger of reading Sue's story as if its confines were quite narrow. If she is simply taken as an undersexed woman, the human range will not seem a large one. If she is simply defined as 'sado-masochistic', we have only an abnormality. If she appears only as the victim of conventions which the world should get rid of, the romantic rebel unjustly punished, the intellectual range will seem too narrow, wholly without the comprehensiveness of George Eliot, who could see at once the pain inflicted by, and the inevitability of, conventions. If she seems simply a person of insufficient maturity—and Hardy uses the words *child* and *children* repeatedly of Jude and Sue, and makes Sue say, '... I crave to get back to the life of my infancy and its freedom' (III, 2)—we will seem to have only the obvious truth that it is risky for a child to be abroad in a man's world. If she seems simply an innocent or idealist done in by a harsh world, the story will seem banal, if not actually sentimental. A Christian apologist might argue that her history shows the inescapability of Christian thought; an anti-Christian, that she is the victim of wrong ideas without which she would have been saved. The answer to the former is that such a Christian triumph would be a melancholy and hardly persuasive one, and to the latter that Sue's nature would find in whatever system of values might be available, religious or secular, the doctrinal grounds for acting out her own disorder.

She does not strike us, in the end, as of narrow significance. She is the rather familiar being whose resources are not up to the demands made upon them. This is not so much a matter of weakness and bad luck as it is of an impulsiveness and wilfulness that carry her beyond her depth; even as a child she shows signs of strain and tension. She has many of the makings of the nun, but she wants the world too; she is peculiarly in need of protection, but she wants always to assert and attack. She works partly from an un-recognized egotism, sometimes from an open desire to wound and conquer; her aggressiveness leads her into injurious actions not unlike those of tragic protagonists. Aside from inflicting unfulfilled relationships upon three men, she does a subtler but deeper injury to Jude: with a mixture of the deliberate and the wanton she helps undermine the beliefs that are apparently essential to his well-being; she cannot stand that he should have any gods but her own. She has the style of the blue-stocking who has found a new key to truth and is intolerant of all who have not opened the same door. Though she is sympathetic with Jude in many ways, she lacks the imagination to under-stand the real needs of his nature; instead of understanding either him or her substantial indifferences to his well-being, she volubly pities him because the university and the world are indifferent to him. Having lost his faith and hope, he leans heavily on her; then she takes that support away when her own needs set her on another course. Symbolically, she comes fairly close to husband-murder.

In them Hardy activates two important, and naturally hostile, strains of nineteenth-century thought and feeling. Jude is under the influence of the Tractarian Movement, which, appealing to some of the best minds in university and church, displayed great vitality in pursuing its traditionalist and anti-liberal aims. Yet his allegiance does not hold up under the blows of Sue's modernist criticism; she looks at Jude as a sort of archaelogical specimen, 'a man puzzling out his way along a labyrinth from which one had one's self escaped' (III, 2) and refers sarcastically to his 'Tractarian stage' as if he had not grown up (III, 4). So he falls into a secular liberalism which simply fails to sustain him. Sue, on the other hand, has felt the influence of utili-tarianism (she quotes Mill to Phillotson very dogmatically); but her skepticism wilts under catastrophe, and she falls into an ascetic self-torment which utterly distorts the value of renunciation (the reduction of hubris to measure). Sue often talks about charity, but, despite her moments of sweetness and kindliness, it is hardly among her virtues; as a surrogate for charity to others she adopts a violent uncharitableness to herself.

Hardy may be intentionally commenting on the inadequacy of two important movements, perhaps because neither corresponds enough to human complexity. But as novelist he is rather exhibiting two characters who in different ways fail, despite unusual conscious attention to the problem, to find philosophical bases of life that are emotionally satisfactory. They like to think of themselves as ahead of their times, but this is rather a device of self-reassurance in people who are less ahead of their times than not up to them. One suspects that in the twentieth century, which has done away with the obstacles that loomed large before their eyes, they would be no better off—either because they lack some essential strength for survival or because they elect roles too onerous for them. Hardy, indeed, has imagined characters who could hardly survive in any order less than idyllic.

In Sue the inadequacy of resources is a representative one that gives her character great resonance. The clue is provided by a crucial experience of her intellectual hero, John Stuart Mill: under the strain of a severe logical discipline he broke down and discovered the therapeutic value of poetry. Sue, so to speak, never finds a therapy. In all ways she is allied with a tradition of intellect; she is specifically made a child of the eighteenth century. She dislikes everything medieval, admires classical writers and architecture, looks at the work of neo-classical secular painters, conspicuously reads eighteenth-century fiction and the satirists of all ages. Jude calls her 'Voltairean', and she is a devotee of Gibbon. She is influenced, among later figures, by Shelley as intellectual rebel, by Mill's liberalism, and by the new historical criticism of Christianity. Rational skepticism, critical intelligence are her aims; in his last interview with her, Jude attacks her for losing her 'reason', 'faculties', 'brains', 'intellect' (VI, 8). Much as she is an individual who cannot finally be identified by categories, she is a child of the Enlightenment, with all its virtues and with the liabilities inseparable from it. Hardy was very early in intuiting, though he did not expressly define it, what in the twentieth century has become a familiar doctrine: the danger of trying to live by rationality alone.

In Sue, Hardy detects the specific form of the danger: the tendency of the skeptical intelligence to rule out the nonrational foundations of life and security. Sue cuts herself off from the two principal such foundations—from the community as it is expressed in traditional beliefs and institutions and from the physical reality of sex. The former she tends to regard as fraudulent and coercive, the latter as 'gross'; in resisting marriage she resists both, and so she has not much left. Her deficiency in sex, whatever its precise psychological nature (we need not fall into the diagnositis of looking for a childhood trauma), is a logical correlative of her enthroning of critical intellect; thus a private peculiarity takes on a symbolic meaning of very wide relevance. The rationalist drawing away from nonrational sources of relationship creates the solitary; Sue is that, as she implies when, considering marriage because of the arrival of Father Time, she remarks, sadly, '... I feel myself getting intertwined with my kind' (V, 3). Precisely. But she is unwilling to be quite the solitary, and for such a person, the anchorite in search of an appropriate society, the natural dream is a private utopia—an endless unconsummated idyll with a single infinitely devoted lover.

At the heart of the drama of Sue is the always simmering revolt of the modes of life which she rejects, the devious self-assertion of the rejected values. Hence much of her inconsistency, of the maddening reversals that constitute a natural coquetry, the wonderfully dramatized mystery that simply stands on its own until the clues appear in the final section. Sue cannot really either reject or accept men, and in attempting to do both at once she leaves men irritated or troubled or desperate, and herself not much better off. She revolts against conventions, but never without strain; and here Hardy introduces an inner drama of conventions far more significant than the criticisms leveled by Jude and Sue. He detects in conventions, not merely inflexible and irrational pressures from without, but a power over human nature because of the way in which human nature is constituted. Sue is one of the first characters in fiction to make the honest mistake of regarding a convention as only a needless constraint and forgetting that it is a needed support, and hence of failing to recognize that the problem admits of no easy pros or cons. As a social critic Hardy may deplore the rigidity of conventions or the severity of their impact, but as an artist he knows of their ubiquity in human experience and of their inextricability from consciousness. They are always complexly present in the drama. At first Jude thinks that there is 'nothing unconventional' in Sue (III, 2); then he decides that 'you are as innocent as you are unconventional' (III, 4); still later he accuses her of being 'as enslaved to the social code as any woman I know' (IV, 5). The Sue who is devastatingly witty about institutions finds herself constantly acting in terms of traditional patterns. On one occasion she assures Jude that 'she despised herself for having been so conventional' (III, 10); on another she has to acknowledge, 'I perceive I have said that in mere convention' (IV, 1); and above all she says to Phillotson, '... I, of all people, ought not to have cared what was said, for it was just what I fancied I never did care for. But ... my theoretic unconventionality broke down' (IV, 3). Then Jude, shocked when she joins him but will not sleep with him, finds relief in the thought that she has 'become conventional' rather than unloving, 'Much as, under your teaching, I hate convention ...' (IV, 5). Here she is not clear herself, and she falls back mainly upon a concept whose conventionality she appears not to recognize, 'woman's natural timidity'. It is then that Jude accuses her of being 'enslaved to the social code' and that she replies, 'Not mentally. But I haven't the courage of my views ...' Her words betray the split between reason and feeling, between the rational critique of the forms and the emotional reliance upon them. This steady trail of comments, clashes, and partial acknowledgements leads up to the key event: in Christminster, she catches sight of Phillotson on the street, and she tells Jude, '... I felt a curious dread of him; an awe, or terror, of conventions I don't believe in' (VI, 1). It is the turning point; her suppressed emotions, her needs, so long harried by her 'reason', are seriously rebelling at last. 'Reason' can still phrase her assessment of the event: 'I am getting as superstitious as a savage!' Jude can lament the days 'when her intellect played like lambent lightning over conventions and formalities' (VI, 3) and somewhat complacently attack her for losing her 'scorn of convention' (VI, 8). But the defensiveness behind these criticisms soon emerges: as the defender of reason, Jude has also failed to find emotional anchorage, and his new independence of mind has provided him with no sustaining affirmations; and so he must blame Sue for deserting him.

Hardy has faithfully followed the character of Sue and has not let himself be deflated by his own sermonizing impulses. From the beginning he senses the split in her make-up—between rejections made by the mind, and emotional urgencies that she cannot deny or replace. If she is an 'epicure in emotions', it may partly be, as she says apologetically, because of a 'curiosity to hunt up a new sensation' (III, 7), but mostly it is that a turmoil of emotions will not let the mind, intent on its total freedom, have its own way. Much more than he realizes Jude speaks for both of them when he says, 'And [our feelings] rule thoughts' (IV, 1). Sue's sensitivity, her liability to be 'hurt', is real, but she uses it strategically to cut off Jude's and Phillotson's thoughts when they run counter to those that she freely flings about; understandably Jude exclaims, 'You make such a personal matter of everything!' (III, 4). Exactly; what appears to be thought is often personal feeling that must not be denied. Answerability, in ordinary as well as special situations, shakes her. On buying the Venus and Apollo she 'trembled' and at night 'kept waking up' (II, 3). When the school inspector visits, she almost faints, and Phillotson's arm around her in public makes her uncomfortable (II, 5). Repeatedly her feelings are very conventional: her embarrassment when Jude comes into the room where her wet clothes are hanging (III, 3), her discomfort after rebelling at school (III, 5), her jealousy of Arabella (III, 6: V, 2, 3). She is 'evidently touched' by the hymn that moves Jude, she finds it 'odd ... that I should care about' it, and she continues to play it (IV, 1). She is 'rather frightened' at leaving Phillotson (IV, 5). When she refuses to sleep with Jude, it is less that she is 'epicene' and 'boyish as a Ganymede' (III, 4) or that her 'nature is not so passionate as [his]' (IV, 5) than that joining Jude is an act of mind, of principled freedom, that does not have emotional support. Hence her singular scruple that 'my freedom has been obtained under false pretences!' (V, 1)—a rationalizing of feelings that, for all of her liking of Jude, run counter to their mode of life. Hardy rightly saw that only some very powerful emotional urgency could get her over the barrier between Jude and herself, and he supplies that in her jealousy of Arabella. It is a common emotion that her mind would want to reject; and it is notable that after giving in to Jude she gives voice to another conventional feeling—assuring him, and herself, that she is 'not a cold-natured, sexless creature' (V, 2).

In a series of penetrating episodes whose cumulative effect is massive, Hardy shows that her emotions cannot transcend the community which her mind endeavors to reject. With a deficiency of the feeling needed to sustain the courses laid out by the detached critical intellect, she would predictably return under pressure, to whatever form of support were available, to those indeed to which, while professing other codes, she has regularly been drawn. Though it would not take too much pressure, Hardy serves several ends at once by introducing the violent trauma of the death of the children. From here on he has only to trace, as he does with devastating thoroughness and fidelity, the revenge of the feelings that, albeit with admirable intellectual aspirations, Sue has persistently endeavored to thwart. They now counter-attack with such force that they make her a sick woman. Although her self-judgements take the superficial form of tragic recognition, what we see is less the recovery that accompanies the tragic anagnorisis than the disaster of a personality distorted by the efforts to bear excessive burdens and now blindly seeking, in its misery, excessive punishments. Illness is something other than tragic.

Whatever Hardy may have felt about the course ultimately taken by Sue, he was utterly faithful to the personality as he imagined and slowly constructed it. That is his triumph. His triumph, however, is not only his fidelity to the nature of Sue, but the perception of human reality that permitted him to constitute her as he did. We could say that he envisaged her, a bright but ordinary person, attempting the career that would be possible only to the solitary creative intellect, the artist, the saint, whose emotional safety does lie in a vision somewhere beyond that of the ordinary community. Sue does not have that vision; she is everyman. She is everyman entirely familiar to us: her sense of the imperfections around her leads her into habitual rational analysis that tends to destroy the forms of feeling developed by the historical community and to be unable to find a replacement for them. The insistence on the life of reason has become increasingly emphatic in each century of modern life, and Sue as the relentless critic of institutions incarnates the ideal usually held up to us in abstract terms. On the other hand, as if in defiance of rationalist aspirations, the twentieth century has seen destructive outbreaks of irrational force that would have been supposed incredible in the nineteenth. But a still more impressive modern phenomenon, since it entirely lacks the air of aberration, is a growing concern with the threat of intellect to the life of feelings and emotions. From some of the most respected guides of modern thought come warnings against arid rationality, and visions of a reconstructed emotional life essential to human safety and well-being. The present relevance of such cultural history is that it contributes to our understanding of Hardy: in *Jude the Obscure*, and primarily in the portrayal of Sue, he went to the heart of a modern problem long before it was understood as a problem. Yet the 'modern' is not topical, for the problem is rooted in the permanent reality of human nature. Neurotic Sue gives us, in dramatic terms, an essential revelation about human well-being.

Note

1. Just a little before *Jude* Ibsen was investigating this operation of the power-sense beneath the appearance of exerting a noble influence on a man—in *Rosmersholm* (1886) and *Hedda Gabler* (1890). In Rebecca West, the chief woman character in *Rosmersholm*, Ibsen was also noting the presence of irrational impulses in a woman strongly committed to modernist and rationalist views.

Hardy:
The General Context

184

The Early Life of Thomas Hardy

◆

JOHN FREEMAN

I

The Early Life of Thomas Hardy faithfully prepared by his widow from notes left by him and other matter, has an interest beyond that which is proper to mere incident and mere fact. The book covers the first fifty years of his life, which were scarcely more uneventful than the rest. It records neither exultations nor agonies, at the worst a vexation at the touch of a reviewer's fang when the *Spectator* dealt with *Desperate Remedies* far more harshly than unjustly. Failure did not overwhelm him, misgivings did not torture him, death did not divide him from affection, hopeless love did not madden him, and that sharpest of serpents, ambition, did not poison his nights. Yet in this copious story of early achievements and great designs there is a singular stimulation. Reading it, we must revise our easy notion of genius as being always scorned, art always betrayed and the world always oppressive; for in the life of Thomas Hardy we find a man meeting the world on its own terms, living by his wits without privation and certainly without compliant, pursuing prose when he could not live by verse, and then, after steadily plodding on to eminence as a novelist and finding himself at length able to live without writing at all, returning to verse and making a higher claim to immortality.

II

It is an odd practical commentary upon a philosophy of disillusion. Hardy started life, I suppose, with the same illusions as most of us have prized, but he never permitted himself to be illuded through perversity; he bowed to what he found inevitable. Rebuffed here, he would try there, and there, until Fate, so often capable of amusement and inclined to indulgence, gave way and let him alone. That philosophy which has been termed sombre, that spirit, as we have thought it, of nescience, was not the sum of circumstance

SOURCE *The London Mercury*, 1928, Vol. XIX, pp. 400–7.

but the expression of character. He was a happy man with a sad philosophy—sad for others, he was happy in himself. He had to think about the Universe in order to be sad, and it was only when he saw something physically dreadful—disease, poverty, agony—that his emotion surged with unhappiness.

Seldom, in fact, has the life of an imaginative writer showed more tranquillity. As an artist he claims no indulgence for his own passions, perhaps because he hardly ever regards himself as an artist and perhaps because he hardly ever shows passion. When he went to a ballet at the Alhambra in the early 'nineties, at the time when Mr Arthur Symons was persuading us that the ballet was a mystical and exalting ceremonial, he saw it as merely mechanical, but at the same time dangerous to the performers:—their morality could not be judged by the same standard as that of people leading slower lives, and so they should be forgiven as irresponsibles. He felt himself to be in no such danger; he was affectionate, his emotions were quickly touched, but he was self-possessed.

In another man than a poet we should say simply that common sense saved him from emotional extravagance, and that his mind was clear of cant; but a poet, I suppose, must not be credited with common sense if a philosophy can be attributed to him instead. And yet is it not the very honesty underlying common sense that makes the portrait of Thomas Hardy so attractive? I do not mean merely his portrait as drawn in this admirable volume, though chiefly this, but also his portrait as we discover it for ourselves in years of growing familiarity with the whole map of his being. He does not falsify, he does not lie, and gradually you become more and more interested in the man who is writing, as well as in what he has written, for the man himself, the whole man, is expressed in his work, in the whole work.

Thus to read Mrs Hardy's pages is to read something familiar. The dates may be new to us, the places identified, incidents fixed in their proper sequence—yes, but nothing is capable of surprizing us because Hardy has already unfolded himself to our eyes in a modest candour throughout more than twenty volumes. Her book confirms what we knew, amplifies it, justifies speculations and so gives us an undeserved sense of being part-author with her.

When he was born he was thrown aside as dead until the nurse saw that what seemed death was really that calm inanimation which characterizes so much of his work and keeps his image steady as we seek to understand it. With this, there was a precocity in the small child which showed itself mainly in music, and this eager, precocious skill in music is plain as a pikestaff in his poetry. No poetry of modern times has advanced farther towards the eventual harmony of the form of verse with the power of music. Mrs Hardy records that he hated being touched, and without asking a psycho-analyst which particular suppression this points to, it is consonant with his extreme physical susceptibility and the emotion or pain which, in his life and his work alike, as I have already suggested, was so readily quickened. He was in love with thoughts of death:—does any reader need proof? This *Early Life* teems with it. What Mrs Hardy tells here of his engagement to superintend the removal of coffins and bones from the old St Pancras churchyard is precisely what Hardy himself related in the last year of his life and is the memory responsible for many a poem and passage in prose:

> Throughout the late autumn and early winter (of probably the year 1865 or thereabouts) Hardy attended at the churchyard—each evening between five and six, as well as sometimes at other hours. There after nightfall, within a high hoarding that could not be overlooked, and by the light of flare-lamps, the exhumation went on continuously of the coffins that had been uncovered during the day, new coffins being provided for those that came apart in lifting, and for loose skeletons; those that held together being carried to new ground on a board merely; Hardy supervising these mournful processions when present, with what thoughts may be imagined, and Blomfield sometimes meeting him there. In one coffin that fell apart was a skeleton and two skulls. He used to tell that when, after some fifteen years of separation, he met Arthur Blomfield again and their friendship was fully renewed, among the latter's first words were: 'Do you remember how we found the man with two heads at St Pancras?'

Perhaps it may be surprising that when he found he could not live by poetry he should have inclined to the Church, and contemplated taking orders, with a view to a country curacy. Theological reasons dispelled this notion, but it is not very strange that he should have held it for a time, for doctrinal points, as part of the full spiritual apprehension of the world, retained his interest through most years of his life. Whatever the Church might have gained in the Rev. Thomas Hardy, poetry would have lost; and although the Rev. Laurence Sterne was able to write *Tristram Shandy*, the generation that was shocked by *Tess* would not have been appeased had it been discovered to be the work of a clergyman. He would hardly have published:

> *I asked the Lord: 'Sire, is this true*
> *Which hosts of theologians hold,*
> *That when we creatures censure you*
> *For shaping griefs and ails untold*
> *(Deeming them punishments undue)*
> *You rage, as Moses wrote of old? . . . '*
>
> *He: 'Save me from my friends, who seem*
> *That I care what my creatures say!*
> *Mouth as you list: swear, rail, blaspheme,*
> *O manikin, the livelong day,*
> *Not one grief-groan or pleasure-gleam*
> *Will you increase or take away. '*

—No bolder, doubtless, than Matthew Arnold, but less discreet.

And passing to his more ardent inclination for his first wife (whose orthodoxy in faith was emphatic enough), the biography hardly makes more lucid the abundantly clear allusions of Hardy's verse. He was thirty, but she thought him much older: 'he had a beard, and a rather shabby great-coat, and had quite a business appearance.' You may see him in this, and in this other note: 'I found him a perfectly new subject of study and delight ... He was quite unlike any other person who came to see us, for they were slow of speech and ideas.' They drove to places which Swinburne was to celebrate in one of his hundred elegies:

> *Tintagel and the long Trebarwith strand,*
> *Lone Camelford and Boscastle divine—*

places which, in their mere ringing, remembered names, were to yield recurrent delight to Hardy in later poems. And beyond all this, the *Early Life* bears witness to a fact which it is easy to overlook when we dwell too much upon Hardy's preoccupation with rural scenes, namely, his comfortable sociability. He did not invite the sneer of *Snob!* which snobs have flung at Henry James because he loved to dine with the well-to-do; but he was no awkward recluse. Partly because he liked it, partly because it gave the novelist the chance of noting manners and society, he was ready to meet people who wanted him. True that his friends were, at first, fellow-writers, men as different as Leslie Stephen and Pater, Henry James and Stevenson, but the group extended until it touched if it did not include many eminent 'society' people; and we may be sure that he was not the man to go un-welcomed, and that his welcome was due simply to his growing popularity as an author. It is the chief instance of what I have called his readiness to meet the world on its own terms.

The opportunity of observing people was a valuable one. He went into society as Mrs Hardy tells us he went to the police courts, 'to get novel padding.' He had resigned himself to novel-writing 'as a trade, which he had never wanted to carry on as such. He now went about the business mechanically.'

III

At one time he looked to architecture as a means of getting a living, and for a while combined architecture and novel-writing, *Under the Greenwood Tree* being written while he was preparing designs for the London Board Schools, some of which, unfortunately, still survive to afflict the sight. It was the gradual recognition of his powers as a novelist, in particular his skill and punctuality in writing serial stories, that led him to drop designing schools and depend upon novels for a livelihood. It was no urgent demand of art, there was no pretence of inspiration, but a frank desire to earn an honest living in the readiest way. None of the arrogance of genius was his, but all the persistence of a man loyal to his own powers. Since verse would not pay and novels would, he would become as good a novelist as might be; hence his haunting of police-courts, clubs and drawing-rooms, his visits to country houses, his travels here and there for brief periods; and hence the secure indifference with which he could accept the dictation which must often be galling to imaginative minds:

> The truth is that I am willing, and indeed anxious, to give up any points which may be desirable in a story when read as a whole, for the sake of others which shall please those who read it in numbers. Perhaps I may have higher aims some day, and be a great stickler for the proper artistic balance of the completed work, but for the present circumstances lead me to wish merely to be considered a good hand at a serial.

His indifference, his steadfastness, match Trollope's, whose *Autobiography* reveals something of the honesty of view that gives a constant direction to Hardy's work and tempts one to say that if Hardys and Trollopes were a little more common we should have to revise our notion that genius is divinely capricious and wholly irresponsible. Hardy lacked that riotous fecundity which enabled Dickens to pour forth his prodigious improvisations as a whale spouts water, but nevertheless he bent his mind to tasks which were, in his own regard, never other than tasks; and he found himself attracting a fame which had never been within his conception. *Desperate Remedies, Under the Greenwood Tree, A Pair of Blue Eyes, Far From the Madding Crowd* and *The Hand of Ethelberta* were produced so rapidly that you might think he had not another care in the world; yet the cares of architecture, courtship and marriage were borne no less lightly at the same time. Perhaps the oddest of results was that, some years later, his recognition as a novelist became so wide that he was pressed to join the Rabelais Club, as being the most virile of imaginative writers, while Henry James, who had never watched professionally the opening of old graves nor designed schools nor set up housekeeping with a door-scraper and a bookcase, as Hardy had done, was ignominiously rejected.

IV

Mrs Hardy has recited these events and prompted these reflections with a happy economy, and so left room for what is the most useful and delightful addition to our knowledge of Thomas Hardy. She has given few letters but innumerable notes from diaries and casual memoranda, never intended by their author for the public eye, but most valuable in their offer of intimacy with his thoughts. Here Hardy, turning from his trade of serial novelist, is permitting his mind to think aloud in prose, a random picking of his notes yielding these:

> In architecture, men who are clever in details are bunglers in generalities. So it is in everything whatsoever.
> More conducive to success in life than the desire for much knowledge is the being satisfied with ignorance on irrelevant subjects.

231

The world does not despise us: it only neglects us.

End of December, 1865. To insects the twelvemonth has been an epoch, to leaves a life, to tweeting birds a generation, to man a year.

April 19. The business of a poet and novelist is to show the sorriness underlying the grandest things, and the grandeur underlying the sorriest things.

His power of grim description was not the result of deep pondering, for he jots down:

> *March* 9. British Museum Reading Room. Souls are gliding about here in a sort of dream—screened somewhat by their bodies, but imaginable behind them. Dissolution is gnawing at them all, slightly hampered by renovations. In the great circle of the library Time is looking into Space. Coughs are floating in the same great vault, mixing with the rustle of book-leaves risen from the dead, and the touches of footsteps on the floor.

His physical sensibility is shewn here again:

> *July* 13. After being in the street: what was it on the faces of those horses?— Resignation. Their eyes looked at me, haunted me. The absoluteness of their resignation was terrible. When afterwards I heard their tramp as I lay in bed, the ghosts of their eyes came in to me saying, 'Where is your justice, O man and ruler?'

This comes from his own sick bed, a characteristic observation:

> *January* 31. Incidents of lying in bed for months. Skins gets fair: corns take their leave: feet and toes grow shapely as those of a Greek statue. Keys get rusty: watch dim, boots mildewed: hat and clothes old-fashioned: umbrella eaten out with rust; children seen through the window are grown taller.

Here and there are briefer notes which are not less acute and sardonic. Thus of Leslie Stephen as critic he writes:—'His approval is disapproval minimized'; and of Pater that 'his manner is that of one carrying weighty ideas without spilling them.'

But scarce a word of himself which another might not have written, and not a single word of complaint against the Fate that damned him to prose when it was poetry he longed for! When Coventry Patmore read *A Pair of Blue Eyes* he told Hardy that he regretted at almost every page that such unequalled beauty and power had not assured themselves the immortality which the form of verse would have given them. Considering this, Hardy notes the secret difference between a living style and a dead style—it is in not having too much style, and in being and seeming to be a little careless here and there:

> Otherwise your style is like worn half-pence—all the fresh images rounded off by rubbing, and no crispness or movement at all.
>
> It is, of course, simply a carrying into prose of the knowledge I have acquired in poetry—that inexact rhymes and rhythms now and then are far more pleasing than correct ones.

When he wrote this he had been driven from poetry as a thirsty dog may be driven from water, but the thirst for poetry remained. The period covered by the present volume is not concerned with his poetry but with the traffic of prose, and it was not until *Wessex Poems* appeared in 1898, when he was fifty-eight, that he could permit himself to tempt Fame with verse once more. Was it an extraordinary assurance or an extraordinary modesty that enabled him to keep silent so long, when lesser spirits itch with agony if they are silent for twelve months? I think it was simply modesty. He would quite freely admit in conversation that when his early verses were rejected he contented himself with putting them aside and writing others, never presuming to question the judgment of editors. Poets were born, they faded and died, or faded without dying, but for more than thirty years Hardy kept patient and only began to publish selections from his vast accumulation of verse when he had finished his labour at prose. Almost the only sign that verse was constantly in his mind is the allusiveness to *The Dynasts* in one form or another, the earliest reference being thirty-three years before the first volume was issued in 1908. The heart knows its own bitterness, but whatever Hardy felt he kept characteristically to himself.

There was, perhaps, one other cause for bitter disappointment, of which a single hint is given in the *Early Life* and none, I believe, elsewhere. When Hardy was thirty-seven, and married, a servant was detected in flight with her lover. A few weeks later he notes: 'We hear that Jane, our late servant, is soon to have a baby. Yet never a sign of one is there for us.'

V

The frontispiece to this volume is a portrait of Hardy aged sixteen, a remarkable, an astonishing portrait. The face has a touch of foreignness—the family derived from Jersey—and a beauty which, as we look at it now, is prophetic. The brow is unusually broad in one so young, the nose, lips and chin shapely, and the separate features under rather heavy hair compose a countenance of masculine firmness and sweetness, almost prematurely tranquil. And in the last months of his great age the moving face showed not a jot more heaviness, and a sweetness and serenity almost unmarred. The loss of flesh and the growth of bone had imparted nothing of the harshness of time, but had given the features a Roman look, so that you might think they had grown into the likeness of the Roman knights whose bones slept in the soil of his garden at Dorchester. Mrs Hardy quotes an anonymous description of his appearance halfway through life:

> A somewhat fair-complexioned man, a trifle below the middle-height [he was actually five ft. six and a half ins.] of slight build, with a pleasant thoughtful face, exceptionally broad at the temples, and fringed by a beard trimmed after the Elizabethan manner [this beard was shaved off about 1890, and he never grew another, but had always a moustache]; a man readily sociable and genial, but one whose mien conveys the impression that the world in his eyes has rather more of the tragedy than the comedy about it.

VI

It is a notable coincidence that Hardy's *Early Life* should be published at the same moment as *The Life of Charles M. Doughty*. They were born and died within a few years of each other; each of them wrote prodigiously in prose and verse, each turned eagerly to verse in maturity, each pursued it till death with indefatigable ardour. They never met, and Doughty, in 1909, said that he had never heard of *The Dynasts* or its author. Hardy's story suggests few difficulties in the author's way, apart from that harsh suppression of his poetry, but Doughty's presents an almost life-long discouragement of his prose and the most absolute disregard of his many volumes of verse. Hardy's *Early Life* discloses an abundance of friendly human encounters, but Doughty's were very few. In one superb characteristic they were precisely equal—the religious fidelity with which they preserved their creative powers and refused the corruption of the time.

Doughty's life was illuminated by his great travels in the East, begetting *Arabia Deserta*, but apart from what he tells us there, little seems left to tell. When the imaginative hour has passed he is inarticulate. With Hardy it is different, for apart from his own words there was very much to tell and we are the richer for this volume. But while the creative hour lasts, for Doughty or for Hardy, how wonderful seems their gift! Words thrill us and speech is divinity. In a page, almost in a phrase, Doughty brings before us the dizzy, sunstruck desert, the nomads of centuries, the ancient world indifferently swaying past the modern, each incomprehensible to the other; or in verse he calls up the freshness of an earlier England, and in a line restores us to consciousness of an ancient heritage. And not less does Hardy, when with his massive exactitude and brilliant felicity he conjures up heath and woodland, and the inhabitants of a cruder world, or sings in his curiously reverberating verse a song which it is sometimes a pain, often a delight, and always a stimulation to remember.

The Early Novels
of Thomas Hardy

◆

SIR ARTHUR QUILLER-COUCH

I

Among the many studies devoted to Thomas Hardy, and after the spate of journalistic *réclame* that so surprisingly burst upon us after his death and vulgarised his obsequies; I still hope, Gentlemen, that it may interest you to listen for fifty minutes or so, to what one can recall of the impressions made by his earlier writings as they appeared—the expectations they raised, disappointed, revived—the enthusiasms he had a knack of teasing—in the breasts of many who made him a hero but found him also a grave cause of anxiety.

To be so interested you must suppose yourself at your present age, but back almost fifty years ago. You must conceive yourselves to be just as fiery and avid then for letters and the future of letters as you are to-day (surely you have imagination for that?), and moreover perhaps that you have a dream of being yourself a writer one of these days—either a very successful one or at least one whose collected works the initiate will take down from their shelf and dust more or less affectionately, saying 'this fellow could write, after all?'

The period to which you throw yourselves back, is, say, 1882–6, a four years' span of undergraduate life. Your acquaintance with Hardy began with *Far from the Madding Crowd*. You found it at school, in the Sixth Form Library; and, young as you were, it produced the like impression on you as James Greenwood, editor of the *Gazette*, took when—attracted by his own name in its title—he cut the opening pages of *Under the Greenwood Tree*, and felt like a man who has overed a stile upon an undiscovered country, and that yet this country was the England he had always known. You saw it now, this background of our race and its daily doings, as Greenwood saw it—with washed eyes.

Now to none of you, I hope, need I recall, to enlarge upon it, my frequent caution against handbook divisions of our literature into periods parcelled by

SOURCE *The Poet as Citizen*, Cambridge, 1934, pp. 197–213.

dates or by names. Such divisions may be useful enough for examiners and lecturers, in setting out syllabuses with 'specified books' and 'books recommended'. Luckier than the courtiers of King Canute, *The Student's Guide* can command the tide 'Thus far and no farther'. But actually, of course in our literature, though a line of dry weed may mark the last impulse of a tide from which it receded, there is no searchable line in the deeps where the waters rallied and gathered. To change the simile, a man may dig a trench at the end of his garden as deep as was ever dug through England by the Conquest, or in Reformation time, or in 1642, or 1660, or (if you will) by the War of 1914–18: but the seeds carry over and germinate—as (to mention only our present author) the seed of Hardy has come across that last ditch. In fact, Gentlemen, changes in literature are always, if you search, in the air long before any book, afterwards called epoch-making, condenses them: perhaps as unconsciously as Virgil's *Pollio* Eclogue condensed the world's unconscious expectation of a Messiah.

II

Still—to compare small things with great—this man Thomas Hardy did catch and plant and acclimatise in our fiction that sensitive and 'subjective' intimacy with the country-side—its fauna, flora, contours, significant differences of scenery—which to-day is cultivated in so many literary gardens. If one quote Tennyson's

> *Most can grow the flower now*
> *For all have got the seed*

—it is with no intent at all to disparage such exquisite later cultivators as W.H. Hudson and Edward Thomas—as certainly not such genial, jovial interpreters of merry England as Messrs Belloc and Chesterton and the genius which invented or recaptured *Puck of Pook's Hill.* But the seed, as I trace back the gardening, was afloat in the early 'seventies of the last century—possibly stirred up and sent adrift unawares by Ruskin and Morris—and captured (as I see it) by Richard Jefferies and Hardy. (If you are interested in tracing the movement I recommend the pioneer books of James Owen who called himself 'A Son of the Marshes'.) I will not disparage for a moment the literary charm of these introspective observers of nature, with their reactions and fine writing: but only say that, as the grandson of an old-school naturalist who, intent on his observations, was satisfied with recording them accurately, communicating them to the notice of his fellow-scientists simply as facts illustrating the infinite and curious work of God, I prefer the way of the old school of naturalists. And who can help admiring the quiet classical close its masterpiece, White's *Natural History of Selborne?*

> When I first took the present work in hand I proposed to have added an *Annus Historico-naturalis* or the Natural History of the Twelve Months of the Year: which would have comprised many incidents and occurrences that have not fallen in my way to be mentioned in my series of letters—but as Mr Aiken

of Warrington has lately published somewhat of this sort, and as the length of my correspondence has sufficiently put your patience to the test, I shall here take a respectful leave of you and natural history together, and am, with all due deference and regard, your most obliged and most humble servant.

GIL. WHITE.

Selbourne
    June 25, 1787.

Or compare White's sober admiration of the Sussex Downs:

> As you pass along, you command a noble view of the wild, or weald, on one hand and sea on the other. Mr Rae used to visit a family just at the foot of these hills, and was so ravished with the prospect from *Plumpton Plain*, near *Lewes*, that he mentions these scapes in his 'Wisdom of God in the Works of the Creation' with the utmost satisfaction ...

Compare (I say) Mr Rae's satisfaction in his time with the personal impressions made by the Sussex Downs on Mr Hudson and Mr Thomas, or any of their many imitators, and you will at once detect the difference—difference maybe of an introspective age. For my part I enjoy this observation of natural scenery (when sincere) in relation to the writer's mood. It throws me back to certain momentary scenes of my own boyhood—to one in particular, when the sight of a green glade shelving down to a stream through Bradley Woods in Devon brought tears out of nothing but its sheer beauty, and a child's ache to run and 'tell about it'.

III

But my point here is that, in those days, while our poets had long been actively denouncing the ruin of our lovely valleys and streams, from Blake with his dark Satanic mills, to Elizabeth Barrett Browning with her *Cry of the Children*, and with Ruskin cursing the leprosy of factories, and the Pre-Raphaelites harking back to a medieval England of tapestries, ingle-nooks, sackbuts, fish-ponds, and leathern bottles, these new men of the 'seventies did bring us back, in prose, to a new outlook on the rural inheritance. And I believe true what I wrote a few years ago, of some study, in prefacing a collection of English Prose, that 'It is curious to observe in contrast with our poets, who sing of green country all the time, what a disproportionate mass of our prose is *urban*, and how rarely it contrives, at the best, to get off the pavement'.

And especially is this true, if you will observe, of our novelists up to that date. They had dealt with social themes, or with romantic adventure (throwing in the ruggedness of nature, rocks and cataracts, for a background); with politics and dinner-table talk. Save for George Eliot in occasional scenes—treated with shrewdness and some feeling yet with a certain 'literary' condescension—the great ones had neglected the countryside with the human joys and woes of those who tilled it. Nor indeed was this neglect of rural life confined to the novelists. It is, up to the period of which I speak, a very curious 'missment'—to use a rural phase—through the whole of our prose literature. Those of you who have skill in languages to follow it up, will, I hazard, find other of the prose literatures of Europe almost correspondently at fault. Even as a child in a household, whose first instinct it was of a morning, to run to the window and guess 'what the weather was going to be, where the wind sat, what the fish were likely to be doing', I seem to remember a certain dissatisfaction with so much prose literature as reached the nursery—a dissatisfaction scarcely suppressed by *The Swiss Family Robinson*, only relieved when the boy was let loose, later, upon Scott and Marryat.

The true reason may be found in this: The compelling impulse of our earlier poets was to *popularise* their themes, to *vulgarise* them (in the old and better meaning of the word, i.e. to translate them into the vulgate or English of daily converse, then rapidly ousting Norman–French or Anglo–French even among the ruling classes). Theirs was a great artistic achievement, enormously helped at its crisis by the genius of Chaucer: and as you study its artistry your admiration will increase. But the *motive* of it, apart from the adventurous joy of attempting a new thing, lay in the desire (as with Langland) to awaken Englishmen to a sense of their own worth; to interest them (as with the ballad makers) in legends of their race and its past: to translate for their enlivenment (as with Chaucer) romantic and amusing stories already current over the Continent. The England of those times being predominantly rural, an atmosphere of the country pervaded their writings: and to this the second or Elizabethan flush of our poetry of purpose occurred. Historically, for instance, we make a serious mistake if we regard Spenser first and foremost as a 'poets' poet' or a courtly one. It was part of his theory and earnest practice to revive local phrases, rustic idioms.

On the other hand our prose-writers were from the start essentially aristocratic; their audience the courtly, cultivated few. If you hunt down the list, I think you will be astonished to find, before the nineteenth century, how seldom, unless artificially or with patronage, they take the air in the green fields of England.

IV

But especially was it true of the novel when Hardy started to write—that is in or about 1870, the year of Dickens' death. Now the blaze of Dickens' genius not only shrivelled and ate up (for the general good) a growth of low-class Cockney fiction—Samuel Warren's *Ten Thousand a Year*, Albert Smith's *Christopher Tadpole* and that sort of thing: it killed for years the very seed of it. Called in his life 'the inimitable', he left no school, though he influenced many here and over Europe; and I think you will agree that his individuality could have been bequeathed to no school. Thackeray, on the other hand, came of a long tradition which he left improved. In 1870, for example, George Eliot was writing *Middlemarch*, George Meredith *The Adventures of Harry Richmond*, and Trollope filling an industrious interval between the Barchester novels and *The Eustace Diamonds*. So, even after the success of *Far from the Madding Crowd* backed [by] the possibly less popular but recognised artistic success of *Under the Greenwood Tree*, we find Hardy all a-twitter over the supposed and distasteful obligation to take—as one may put it—a course in society manners to qualify as a novelist. To confirm this, let me quote one passage from *The Early Life of Thomas Hardy* so carefully compiled, so delicately yet penetratingly written, by his second wife.

> He was now committed by circumstances to novel-writing as a regular trade, as much as he had previously been to architecture; and that hence he would, he deemed, have to look for material in *manners*—in ordinary social and fashionable life as other novelists did. Yet he took no interest in manners, but in the substance of life only. So far what he had written had not been novels at all—as usually understood—that is pictures of modern customs and observances—and might not long sustain the interest of the circulating library subscriber who cared mainly for those things. On the other hand, to go about to dinners and clubs and crowds as a business was not to his mind. Yet that was necessary meat and drink to the popular author. Not that he was unsociable, but events and long habit had accustomed him to solitary living ... He mentioned this doubt of himself one day to Miss Thackeray, who confirmed his gloomy misgivings by saying with surprise: 'Certainly: a novelist must necessarily like society!'

V

Well, Gentlemen, you surely see how stupid all that is: how excusable, if commercial, in a young man throwing the dice with fortune: how unworthy, however coupled with a mind already nursing the germ of *The Dynasts*. One of these days science, exploring history, may render some account to us of what the world's sum of poetry—its most priceless possession—has lost through its poets' eternal lack of pence—though I hope it never can, our world being sad enough, just now, without that information. But you probably divine how this 'inferiority complex' debilitated many of Hardy's earlier novels. Let me record how his early worshippers felt it. 'Here is a man', we felt, 'capable of lifting the English novel out of a social rut. Passage after passage proves that he can write pure, melodious prose: but, more than this, passage after passage suggests that here is a universal man, with a sense of the stars in their immensity, with a sense of his own and his neighbour's pulse and its harmony with them'. 'He could not go on for ever writing about shepherds?' No, for his mind was stretching out all the while to grasp and interpret Napoleon as a puppet of fate: instead of which he must bother himself about the troubles of a woman in society whose father, as butler, is sedately pouring champagne across her shoulder. Well, that is a situation which Meredith could have managed—as no reader of *Evan Harrington* will doubt. Meredith would have made the guests talk fantastically, as no company ever did talk or, it is to be hoped, ever could. His are conversational exercises in fancy dress: but the point is, the interlocutors *do* wear their fancy dress as if it fitted them and they had no awkwardness in it. Nor is it insincere, inasmuch as it comes straight from the author's disposition and demands your willing suspension of disbelief, almost a *credo quia impossibile* such as you carry away from the Mad Hatter's Tea-party. The converse of Hardy's society people does not fit in this way; and—which is worse—you feel that they do not fit Hardy; that he has bought a suit of clothes to come to the party. To be sure, when you think of it, Agamemnon never talked in hexameters, nor Virgil in *terza rima*, nor Coriolanus in blank verse, nor Phaedra in Alexandrines: but you are made to forget they did not. The conversation of 'ladies' and 'gentlemen' in these earlier novels (to which I confine myself) too often goes on stilts with occasional and distressing tumbles, as when, in *Two on a Tower*—a story that just misses the idyllic best by stilted talk between amorous lips—Louis Glanville lets us and his sister Lady Constantine down together by adjuring her not to be such a 'flat' as to refuse her hand in marriage when the Bishop has 'popped'.

VI

I am anticipating, however. Let us revert to the position for which I invited your curiosity—that of a young admirer who, arrested by *Far from the Madding Crowd* and fascinated as by something new and strange, sought back for all its author had previously written, and, possessed of this, became, as further books appeared, his constant reader; often delighted, almost as often perplexed, sometimes faint, but always pursuing. Take it, if you will, as cautionary: a study in unwisdom before the event. You all know now, as we did not know then, that Hardy, a struggling architect and writer of unsaleable poetry—an accepted and devoted lover, but with small prospect of earning enough by his profession to support a wife—turned to fiction as a sort of 'desperate remedy' with little sense of it as yet as a fine and difficult art, and—one may assert—with small aptitude for it as he understood it.

We know the story of his first attempt—of the novel which did not survive. He entitled it *The Poor Man and the Lady—by the Poor Man*, and he sent the MS. first to Mr Alexander Macmillan who consulted with John Morley upon it. They agreed that the performance was 'very curious and original', that the writer had stuff and purpose in him, that certain of the scenes were wildly extravagant 'so that they read like some clever lad's dream' and that the book in short was unsaleable. Hardy then visited Messrs Chapman and Hall with the MS. under his arm. That firm turned it over to their 'reader', George Meredith; who by-and-by gave the author an interview and advised him in substance that the book was raw and violent—in fact a sweeping dramatic satire of the squirearchy and nobility, London society, the vulgarity of the middle class, modern Christianity, church restoration, and political and domestic morals in general. It sounds fairly comprehensive.

No one knows what afterwards became of the MS. But I think we may gather— if only from the title itself—that Hardy was already possessed with a self-conscious indignation which distressed and haunted him almost throughout his life, breaks out again and again in his novels, takes charge of

some, and finally explodes in *Jude the Obscure*; at a time of life when he might
have known by unprejudiced observation that if

> *Slow rises worth by poverty depressed,*

the last place to search for illustration of this mournful truth would be one or
other of our ancient Universities, which, if any seminaries on earth do in my
observation—now continued over many years—present at least the best-
known realisation of a democracy, and reduce (whether by encouragement
or by kicks) a young man to the level of his worth.

But we deal here with Hardy's earlier novels. The figure of a young man
of genius, conscious of his power but awkward and diffident in company—in
dreams a king, but, waking, no such matter—is familiar enough in literary
annals; as is the tragedy of some who have mistaken the patronage of 'noble
dames' for a warmer personal interest. From this misfortune we may allow
that Hardy was saved by an early and passionate attachment. That yet he
was born and bred liable to it—that the shadow of it dogged him—may, I
think, be read into tale after tale of his, that contrive tragedy on the complication of a luxurious woman's fancy for a man below her in rank or wealth. I
choose today, not for convenience' sake but for a reason we shall consider, to
draw a dividing line at *Two on a Tower*. But this *imbroglio* persists beyond that
book and breeds the disease of *The Woodlanders* (to my thinking his loveliest if
not his strongest book), as of many a later short story.

VII

Balanced with this you have his uncanny, suspicious sense of the *other
woman*'s motives in loving. It has been said that 'every woman sees a home
through her engagement ring'. Possibly. *Mutatis mutandis*, the same may be
said of birds. But that women in love bring quite such a calculating eye to it
as (for one example of many) does Fancy Day in *Under the Greenwood Tree*;
that they have quite such second thoughts as she shares with the heroines of
A Pair of Blue Eyes and *A Laodicean*, with Ethelberta or even with *Eustacia Vye*
in the intervals of her passion, few men before Hardy had been apt to guess,
no women willing to allow. Certainly I can think of no writer, before or since,
who rings the changes as Hardy does on the *arrière-pensées* of the well-
beloved: and there my nescience must leave you with the fact that while he
wrote anonymously he was generally accused, by female readers, of being a
woman or, alternatively, of knowing too much.

So let us leave it at that—with one addition which I should be loth to
make, had he not patently and admittedly taken the world into confidence of
his own courtship—time, place, person, circumstance—in the story *A Pair of
Blue Eyes*, and also in many a dated lyric. It will probably never be disclosed
by the hand which has so delicately written the story of his early life—and yet
there seems no harm in telling an innocent thing of which all who had
privilege of converse with him in his last years were reverently aware—that

241

his widowhood had constructed a pure fairy-tale of that youthful time, bathed in romantic colour: that the mere presence of one familiar with those scenes, the houses he had visited on his honeymoon, the families and the tale of their descendants; where this love-lane led or that farm had decayed— with such an auditor to assure or prompt a memory he would sit happy, retracing, always reclothing, dressing up, the dream. Actually his first wife, to those who met her, was a woman of remarkably strong character, difficult, straightly loyal, for years distrustful that novel-writing was not quite the occupation to which this queer wonderful husband of hers should demean himself; she herself being connected with the clergy—niece, indeed, to an Archdeacon.

VIII

Now set this against Hardy's authenticated taking to fiction at first as a means of livelihood. Set against it or beside it the fact (now known to all) that secretly from the first he was a poet, though an unaccepted and a baffled one: and we face the paradox which, explicable now, in those early years perplexed and, time and again, disheartened the devotee. *Desperate Remedies* to start with (though few of us had read it); then *Under the Greenwood Tree* (so nearly perfect); then *A Pair of Blue Eyes* with its emotional uncertainty and stage tricks in dialogue and structure; then *Far from the Madding Crowd* and the feeling that genius had all but found itself; then a disconcerting let-down with *The Hand of Ethelberta*; a tremendous recovery with *The Return of the Native* and the triumph apparently assured; a happy pause on the level with *The Trumpet-Major*; and then—the plumb pitfall of *A Laodicean*. We knew not then of this mysterious writer (how could we?) as we learned at long later, that the major part of *A Laodicean* had been dictated from a sick bed in intervals of pain and haemorrhage, heroically, to fulfil a signed contract: but to anyone then unknowing—

> *The moving finger writes: and, having writ,*
> *Moves on . . .*

with what a zig-zag left on the chart!

Let us go back and observe how Meredith has sent Hardy away, advising him to attempt something with a more 'complicated' plot. You, who know your *Poetics*, will guess (as one who has heard Meredith's talk may pretty well assure you) that he airily used that Aristotelian term 'complicated plot' assuming that Hardy understood. Hardy goes away supposing that by 'complicated' is meant 'sensational *plus* intricate', after the fashion of Wilkie Collins, Mrs Henry Wood, Miss Braddon ... authors just then in vogue— yes, and in their way, let me assure you, as artists by no means to be despised. If any young aspirant in fiction nowadays care to study the *anatomy* of the business, let him spend study on Wilkie Collins' *Moonstone*; or let him take a forgotten tale by Miss Braddon, *Henry Dunbar*, strip it to the bone, and he will discover an anatomy quite Sophoclean in the story of a daughter sworn to hunt down her father's murderer, tracking him to bay to discover that the murderer is her father himself! All the material of Sophoclean irony is there under the muslin flounces.

Hardy then, mistaking Meredith, attempts a 'sensational' novel, which complicates it, with the result of *Desperate Remedies*. It is obvious that, whatever the talent of this young man as an architect, he started with little for constructing a plot. This and succeeding novels are full (to keep the architectural simile) of stays, struts and buttresses, hasty props, balances to keep the building solid, even plasterings to cover mistakes—or, in plain words, of coincidences, intercepted letters, interferences by convulsion of nature, audible soliloquies, stage asides and eaves-droppings. The eaves-droppings, for example—overhearings of secret conversations for furtherance of the plot—in these earlier novels have only to be counted to suggest some strange youthful ailment after being separately dismissed as incredible. Twice at least the whole intrigue of *A Laodicean* violates probability, but, as we know, *A Laodicean* was dictated in sickness, so let us take an earlier specimen. A brother and sister are exchanging confidences: on the other side of a hedge a malignant woman is tracking them—

> Their conversation [says the story], of which every word was clear and distinct, in the still air of the dawn, to the distance of a quarter of a mile, reached her ears.

[Lecturers, please copy!]

Again—

> 'Do you believe in such odd coincidences?' said Cytherea.
> 'How do you mean? [sic] They occur sometimes.'

They occur, indeed, so often that, opening a chapter headed precisely, 'From Ten to Half-past Eleven p.m.', we read without any amazement—

> 'A strange concurrence of phenomena now confronts us.'

IX

Yes, but wait a moment! Meredith, while rejecting *The Poor Man and the Lady*, had noted in it a certain knack with circumstantial detail, used to convey a sense of events actually happening, in the way of Defoe, curiously reminiscent of Defoe. Therefore, after wasting this moment, do not waste another over that silly sentence and confession of inept design—'A strange concurrence of phenomena now confronts us'—but read straight on into the description of the fire at the Tranter's, how it grew step by step from smouldering to a fierce blaze (four pages of it), and I am mistaken if, in the long range of English fiction between Defoe and Hardy, you will find anything *just like that*. Then compare this fire, if you will, with that in *Far from the Madding Crowd*, and note how man's strength and will is brought into the epic. Consider next (I but offer this as one clue for your curiosity) the famous lay-out of Egdon Heath in *The Return of the Native*. Read it by the light of an entry in his note-book under date September 28, 1877—

> An object or mark raised or made by man on a scene is worth ten times any such formed by unconscious Nature. Hence clouds, mists and mountains are unimportant beside the wear on a threshold, or the print of a hand.

Set this beside an earlier declaration—

> The poetry of a scene varies with the minds of the perceivers. Indeed it does not lie in the scene at all.

and you have some bearing (I think) on the development of the epic passages in the Novel—as played with by Fielding, occasionally gripped by the Brontés, elaborated by Reade, by the Kingsleys—to name none later—but born in Scott and Dickens, well grasped by Hardy and, when you come to size them, letting loose upon conventional technique force that gives *magnitude*: as it did with Cervantes and later with Tolstoy.

X

Yet as I read Hardy's earlier novels over again the secret of his later ones seems in some measure to explain itself. Suddenly, by a page or two in *Two on a Tower*—a page or two at which story I have chosen to draw a line between his earlier and later work; a shadowy line, I must admit: as shadowy perhaps as any line traceable between literary 'periods'. To me some pages of *Two on a Tower* provide almost a touch-stone of that kind of genius (Shakespeare's for a palmary instance) which explodes in any number of different directions before disclosing the central fire. Anyhow, the crucial pages for me in Hardy's development are those in which he opens, through the lips of an immature astronomer, the illimitable depths and despair of the heavens. Listen to a few words only of his—

> And to add a new weirdness to what the sky possesses in its size and formlessness there is involved the quality of decay. For all the wonder of these everlasting spheres, eternal stars and what not, they are not eternal: they burn out like candles. You see that dying one in the body of the Greater Bear. Two centuries ago it was as bright as the others. The senses may become terrified by plunging among them and they are, but there is a pitifulness even in their glory. Imagine them all extinguished, and a mind feeling its way through a heaven of total darkness, occasionally striking against the black invisible cinders of those stars. If you are cheerful, and wish to remain so, leave the study of astronomy alone. Of all sciences, it alone deserves the character of the terrible.

Now you know, Gentlemen, that the old educational course of the Middle Ages, as we call them, divided itself into the elementary, or *Trivium*, consisting of Grammar, Rhetoric and Dialectic; and the more advanced *Quadrivium*, embracing Music, Arithmetic, Geometry and Astronomy.

Well, now not speaking as an Educational Reformer (Heaven forbid!) I have sometimes wondered if some acquaintance with astronomy ought not to be a compulsory part of any gentleman's education. It would, I think, most profitably correct any sense of his own importance in the scheme of things and, by consequence, soften his manners through such a phase as he inherits on this little planet. The test is, knowing yourself a man, to face these immensities and not to be frightened: to recognise that there are still friends about you, counsellors—Plato for instance—and that, if you stand steady, the swing of the Universe goes round 'on time', the angels are in the sentry boxes, and your own little pulse without any of your own stupid interference ticking away in tune.

This regulating purpose is just what Hardy cannot recognise. He has looked into those inter-stellar depths, realised them, with a shudder, and so far as he has done this his novels are 'universal', but only so far: for in the dazzle he sees but anomalies, odds and ends, misfits, blind alleys, cast off pluckings (damnably painful to the victims) from the web that, to no evident pattern or purpose, a drowsy immanent Will goes on shuttling weaving.

XI

But just here comes in the paradox and the smiling irony of the Gods upon their rebel and declared ironeïst. This man, taking up the trade of fiction with no great zest, certainly under the urgency of no clear call, learns to achieve success; and promptly, to the dismay of his publishers, turns away from it to attempt new things—and this not once, but sundry times. He deems himself to be choosing, while actually he is being driven by the un-satisfied poet implanted within him. Accusing what he calls the Immanent Will, or President of the Immortals, of weaving life without a purpose, or even of fashioning it as in mockery as *hocus-pocus*, he lays down his pen on that final taunt in *Tess*, and takes up another, still unaware that he himself has been working to pattern all the while, and by working the pattern out has won the poet's emancipation, leisure, and with leisure power, to write *The Dynasts*. All the while of course the poet within him was struggling: and it seems to me characteristic that, although he sometimes dated his lyrics, sometimes jotted down the place of composition so that the date can be sought out by us, his own memory concerning their time and order as often as not found itself a fault, so that, even with aid of these insufficient *data*, the casual reader might easily mistake him for a pessimist born and to the end untaught by enterprise, enquiry or event. Let me give just one personal anecdote to illustrate this. The last letter he wrote me, not long before his death, put the staggering question 'Why had I [in a certain anthology called the *Oxford Book of English Verse*] preferred certain poems—call them *A, B* and *C*—to *X, Y* and *Z* which, on reflection, I must surely acknowledge to be better'. To which, of course, the simple answer had to be that in 1900—the date of my selection—these better lyrics did not happen to have been given to the world, and—though you put a murrain on his business—the poor anthologist cannot ply his trade upon things non-existent, or, at any rate, non-apparent. And I conclude upon this little story as on a parable.

186
Hardy

———— ◆ ————

JOSEPH WARREN BEACH

Hardy

Thomas Hardy heralds the disappearance from English poetry of nature with a capital N. Even more vigorously than Tennyson he denies the benevolence of nature conceived as the unity of things personified or as the sum of natural laws. And since he has no religious power, like Tennyson's God, to set up in contrast to nature, as a guarantee of happiness for spiritual beings, nothing is left in him of the optimistic *Weltansicht* characteristic of the palmy days of nature-poetry. He has neither the naturalism of Wordsworth nor his religion-inspired optimism.

First and last, in his poems and novels, he has many references to what, as he says in *The Dynasts,*

> *Men love to dub Dame Nature—that lay-shape*
> *They use to hang phenomena upon—*
> *Whose deftest mothering in fairest spheres*
> *Is girt about by terms inexorable!*[1]

But Hardy seems to be clear enough through all his writing that nature is nothing more than a lay-shape, or convenient personification, and that she is strictly conditioned by 'terms inexorable' which have no reference to our human notions of goodness and benevolence.

It is true that, especially in his earliest work, he sometimes refers to nature in a conventional way as the course of things which, if it could be left unopposed by artificial human arrangements, would naturally work for good ends. Thus in the earliest dated of his poems in which he uses the term nature, the sonnet 'Discouragement':

> *To see the Mother, naturing Nature, stand*
> *All racked and wrung by her unfaithful lord,*

SOURCE *The Concept of Nature in Nineteenth Century English Poetry*, New York, 1936, ch. XIX, pp. 503–21, 608–10

246

Her hopes dismayed by his defiling hand,
Her passioned plans for bloom and beauty marred:

Where she would mint a perfect mould, an ill;
Where she would don divinest hues, a stain,
Over her purposed genial hour a chill,
Upon her charm of flawless flesh a blain:

Her loves dependent on a feature's trim,
A whole life's circumstance on hap of birth,
A soul's direction on a body's whim,
Eternal Heaven upon a day of Earth,
Is frost to flower of heroism and worth,
And fosterer of visions ghast and grim.[2]

Nature and the 'Universal Harshness'

It is interesting to find Hardy thus referring to the scholastic *natura naturans* ('Naturing Nature'), whose passioned plans are for bloom and beauty, and echoing Wordsworth's complaint of 'what man has made of man.' But even here there are suggestions of flaws inherent in the natural design itself, such that man could hardly be expected to be happy in following his impulse— 'Her loves dependent on a feature's trim'—'A soul's direction on a body's whim.' In a poem of the same period, Hardy describes a meeting of two lovers in a church. The man is going to die; the woman to comfort him protests that she loves him; but struck by the tragic irony of the case, she could not prize—

A world conditioned thus, or care for breath
Where Nature such dilemmas could devise.[3]

Another poem records the passing of Hardy's illusions in regard to nature. The glory has departed, and the poet looks back sadly on the time when he—

Wrought thee (nature) for my pleasure,
Planned thee as a measure
For expounding
And resounding
Glad things that men treasure.[4]

'In a Wood' (1887–96) records his discovery that the vegetable world is, like the world of men, a scene of fighting and mutual destruction.[5] In 'Nature's Questioning' Hardy quite reverses Wordsworth's procedure. Instead of going to 'field, flock and tree' for an answer to his own questions about the universe, he represents these natural creatures as coming to him for light on questions that leave them entirely bewildered.[6] In 'The Bullfinches,' the poet informs the birds that while "all we creatures" are, according to the faeries of Blackmoor Vale, under the care of 'the Mother,' yet she never tries to protect us from danger, but works on dreaming and heedless.[7] The indifferences of 'the Matron,' or 'the Great Dame,' to her children's fate is expressed in 'At a Bridal'[8] and 'To an Orphan Child';[9] her blindness and unconsciousness in 'The Lacking Sense,'[10] 'Doom and She,'[11] 'The Sleep-Walker.'[12]

The altered feeling towards Dame Nature is strikingly exhibited in Hardy by the type of landscape, season, weather, which dominates his poetry and prose. The gentle, the sublime, the luxuriant, the cheerful aspects of nature have largely given place to the severe, the sombre, the meagre. An unusually large number of pieces is devoted to aspects of weather hostile to man and beast—'Winter in Durnover Field,'[13] 'A Backward Spring,'[14] 'A Wet August,'[15] 'If it's Ever Spring Again,'[16] 'An Unkindly May,'[17] 'Snow in the Suburbs,' and a whole series of snow pieces.[18] The romantic and picturesque landscapes of 'Alastor' and 'Endymion' have given place to 'Winter's dregs' and 'the land's sharp features.' The soaring ecstasy of Shelley's skylark and the 'shadows and sunny glimmerings' of Wordsworth's green linnet have given place to—

> An aged thrush, frail, gaunt and small,
> In blast-beruffled plume.[19]

The sombre philosophy of Hardy harmonizes with the prevailing sombreness of nature, whether in his poems or novels. And in the reciprocal action of his philosophy and his temperament, gravely musing and saturnine, it is impossible to say which has more affected the other. At any rate, he appears to have a natural preference in taste for aspects of nature which reflect the modified gloom of his intellectual outlook. His own rationale of this is given in a classic passage in his famous description of Egdon Heath.

> Indeed, it is a question if the exclusive reign of this orthodox beauty is not approaching its last quarter. The new Vale of Tempe may be a gaunt waste in Thule: human souls may find themselves in closer and closer harmony with external things wearing a sombreness distasteful to our race when it was young. The time seems near, if it has not actually arrived, when the chastened sublimity of a moor, a sea, or a mountain will be all of nature that is absolutely in keeping with the moods of the more thinking among mankind. And ultimately, to the commonest tourist, spots like Iceland may become what the vineyards and myrtle-gardens of South Europe are to him now; and Heidelberg and Baden be passed unheeded as he hastens from the Alps to the sand-dunes of Scheveningen.[20]

In his novels Hardy's references to personified nature exhibit the same general attitude as in his poems. There is this one apparent exception to be noted, that, where there is opposition between natural impulse and the restrictions of law and convention, natural impulse is assumed to be right. This opposition is strongest in *Tess of the d'Urbervilles* (1891) and *Jude the*

Obscure (1894–5). Tess, about to bear her illegitimate child in the rural seclusion of Blackmoor, reproached herself for her guilt, as if she were out of harmony with the world. She was terrified without reason by 'a cloud of moral hobgoblins.'

> Walking among the sleeping birds in the hedges, watching the skipping rabbits on a moonlit warren, or standing under a pheasant-laden bough, she looked upon herself as a figure of Guilt intruding into the haunts of Innocence. But all the while she was making a distinction where there was no difference. Feeling herself in antagonism, she was quite in accord. She had been made to break an accepted social law, but no law known to the environment in which she fancied herself such an anomaly.[21]

So in ironic vein the author refers to her short-lived infant as 'that bastard gift of shameless nature who respects not the civil law.' When Angel Clare made love to her later at the dairy farm, she felt in honor bound to reject his suit, but this was against nature. 'Every see-saw of her breath, every wave of her blood, every pulse singing in her ears, was a voice that joined with Nature in revolt against her scrupulousness.'[22] Her very instinct not to tell him of her 'past' was 'her instinct of self-preservation.'[23] After their marriage, when she had at length told him, Clare could not bear to go on living with her 'while that [other] man lives, he being your husband in the sight of Nature, if not really.'[24] But this appeal to nature seems to the author perverse; he suggests on the contrary: 'Some might risk the odd paradox that with more animalism he would have been the nobler man.'

In *Jude* there is a considerable number of references to nature as running counter to the religious restrictions upon the sex-impulse. Gibbon is quoted on 'insulted nature' in reference to the excessive chastity of the early saints.[25] Sue's sticking to her husband, whom she loathes, is by Jude ruled to be wrong, 'speaking from experience and unbiassed nature.'[26] of her marriage to himself, Jude declares, 'Nature's own marriage it is, unquestionably!' But though they were legally married, Sue, taking the high ecclesiastical point of view, protests that this is not 'Heaven's marriage.' In the eyes of God she considers herself still married to her first husband.[27] And in this whole debate there is no doubt that Hardy's sympathy is on the side of nature as against the notions of conventional religion. Jude reflects as follows on his frustrated career:

> Strange that his first aspiration—towards academical proficiency—had been checked by a woman, and that his second aspiration—towards apostleship—had also been checked by a woman. 'Is it,' he said, 'that the women are to blame; or is it the artificial system of things, under which the normal sex-impulses are turned into devilish domestic gins and springes to noose and hold back those who want to progress?'[28]

And Sue, before she turns religious, reflects thus upon her own dilemma: 'It is none of the tragedies of love that's love's usual tragedy in civilized life, but a tragedy artificially manufactured for people who in a natural state would find relief in parting!'[29]

But while Hardy recognizes, like every one else, the distress caused when natural impulse is balked by artificial codes of conduct, none realizes more acutely than he that nature herself is full of cruelty. Social codes are themselves a part of nature; and, beyond all that can be controlled by social codes, are the infinitely complicated lines of circumstance which tend to make impossible the attainment of happiness by any created being.

> In the ill-judged execution of the well-judged plan of things, the call seldom produces the comer, the man to love rarely coincides with the hour for loving. Nature does not often say 'See!' to a poor creature at a time when seeing can lead to happy doing; or reply 'Here!' to a body's cry of 'Where?' till the hide-and-seek has become an irksome, outworn game.[30]

Men's harshnesses towards women are but an outgrowth of 'the universal harshness ... the harshness of the position towards the temperament, of the means towards the aims, of to-day towards yesterday, of hereafter towards today.'[31] Thus in the interplay of human desire and aspiration with the circumstances under which they are to be gratified, there is an inherent want of adjustment which, in many different ways, determines their frustration and disappointment.

The very natural impulses which Hardy champions against the conventions of society bring misery with them. Referring to the half-dozen Durbeyfield children condemned by nature to sail along in one ship with their heedless parents, Hardy remarks:

> Some people would like to know whence the poet whose philosophy is in these days deemed as profound and trustworthy as his song is sweet and pure, gets his authority for speaking of 'Nature's holy plan.'[32]

Referring to the hopeless passion of the dairy maids for Clare, he speaks of 'cruel Nature's law.'[33] Tess, after making her confession to Clare, still looked absolutely pure, 'Nature, in her fantastic trickery, had set such a seal of girlishness upon [her] countenance.'[34]

In *Jude* the principal characters are unanimous in finding nature indifferent or hostile to man. Jude often felt 'the scorn of Nature for man's finer emotions, and her lack of interest in his aspirations.'[35] Phillotson, reflecting on the misery of Sue, declares: 'Cruelty is the law pervading all nature and society; and we can't get out of it if we would!'[36] Sue finds that 'Nature's law [is] mutual butchery.'[37] And the author in his own person, referring to the weakness of women as a sex, declares that they 'by no possible exertion of their willing hearts and abilities could be made strong while the inexorable laws of nature remain what they are.'[38] Above all, the young Jude is revolted by his realization that, in nature's plan, the lower animals must be the victims of man, through that 'flaw in the terrestrial scheme, by which what was good for God's birds was bad for God's gardener.'[39]

This idea of a flaw in the terrestrial scheme is everywhere present in Hardy's writing. Thus in *The Return of the Native* (1878), he speaks of the 'long

250

line of disillusive centuries' which have permanently displaced the cheerful Hellenic idea of life. 'That old-fashioned revelling in the general situation grows less and less possible as we uncover the defects of natural laws, and see the quandary that man is in by their operation.'[40]

Other Formulations: God, Chance, Fate

Nature is but one of many alternative terms used by Hardy for designating the unity of process and the directing power in the world. Fate and destiny are words found more often in the mouths of the characters, who reflect the superstitious philosophy of untrained country-people. God and providence are terms they take up from their religious culture. Chance, hap, circumstance are words suggestive of the seeming capriciousness of events, their irrelevance to human aims and direction. None of these terms is to be regarded as indicating that Hardy seriously adhered to the philosophy implied in its use. At no period of his writing did Hardy share the religious views of his characters, and God or the gods, providence, chance, fate, must all be taken in a figurative and dramatic sense, as reflecting the point of view of human beings caught in a web too large and complicated for mortal understanding.

That Hardy was a scientific determinist in his interpretation of how things come about is evident from many passages in the novels. Thus, in *The Mayor of Casterbridge* (1886), he comments as follows on the seeming element of chance in a certain act of Lucetta, involving a striking coincidence.

> That she had chosen for her afternoon walk the road along which she had returned to Casterbridge three hours earlier in a carriage was curious—if anything should be called curious in concatenations of phenomena wherein each is known to have its accounting cause.[41]

Again, he comments on Henchard's superstitious notion of the intervention of a sinister intelligence.

> Henchard, like all his kind, was superstitious, and he could not help thinking that the concatenation of events this evening had produced was the scheme of some sinister intelligence bent on punishing him. Yet they had developed naturally.[42]

His explanation of how these events came about is immediately followed by reference to the 'mockery' of the case and 'this ironical sequence of things'; and so we know that the mockery and the irony are not in nature, but simply in the relation of certain natural events to man's intentions, as seen from the point of view of the man himself. So in *The Woodlanders* (1887) a certain fateful letter of Marty South is called 'the tiny instrument of a cause deep in nature.'[43] Of men's attitude towards a causality which they cannot trace Hardy speaks in the same book.

> The petulance that relatives show towards each other is in truth directed against that intangible Causality which has shaped the situation no less for the offenders than the offended, but is too elusive to be discerned and cornered by poor humanity in irritated mood.[44]

In *Tess*, again, Hardy speaks of Tess and Clare balanced on the edge of passion. 'All the while they were none the less converging, under the force of irresistible law, as surely as two streams in one vale.'[45]

That the doings of individuals form a part of the entire pattern of cause and effect which makes up the universe is a point often emphasized.

> Hardly anything could be more isolated or more self-contained than the lives of these two walking here in the lonely antelucan hour, when gray shades, material and mental, are so very gray. And yet, looked at in a certain way, their lonely courses formed no detached design at all, but were part of the pattern in the great web of human doings then weaving in both hemispheres from the White Sea to Cape Horn.[46]

In this web, since all happens naturally and according to law, nothing comes about capriciously. But in the relation between outward circumstances and the needs and desires of men, there is infinite possibility for what men call accident, chance, fate, destiny, and the irony of circumstances that throw jeering reflections on one another.

> That Knight should have been thus constituted: that Elfride's second lover should not have been one of the great mass of bustling mankind ... was the chance of things. That her throbbing, self-confounding, indiscreet heart should have to defend itself unaided against the keen scrutiny and logical power which Knight ... would sooner or later be sure to exercise against her, was her misfortune. A miserable incongruity was apparent in the circumstance of a strong mind practising its unerring archery upon a heart which the owner of that mind loved better than his own.[47] ... Circumstance has, as usual, overpowered her purposes—fragile and delicate as she—liable to be overthrown in a moment by the coarse elements of accident.[48] ... That waggery of fate which started Clive as a writing clerk, Gay as a linen-draper, Keats as a surgeon, and a thousand others in a thousand other odd ways, banished the wild and ascetic heath lad to a trade whose sole concern was with the especial symbols of self-indulgence and vainglory.[49] ... The next slight touch in the shaping of Clym's destiny occurred a few days after.[50] ... And then, as a hoop by gentle knocks on this side and on that is made to travel in specific directions, the little touches of circumstance in the life of this young girl shaped the curves of her career.[51] ... Thus these people with converging destinies went along the road together.[52] ... Out of which maladroit delay sprang anxieties, disappointments, shocks, catastrophes—and what was called a strange destiny.[53]

By fate or destiny Hardy means the course of a man's life as determined by all the antecedent circumstances in the chain of causality. There is nothing here of the Greek religious conception of fate, or of a destiny or nemesis having us individually in mind. Fate is not arbitrary, being only another name for natural causality. The seeming arbitrariness of fate is an illusion of men; it overrules our will because, in its large and impersonal working, it has no reference to our will. An accident is a mere crossing of two sets of circumstances, an intersection of two orbits, which registers as an interference. Circumstances are the separate moments in the chain of causation. Circumstance is another name for the conditions under which we carry on our lives—most noted when unfavorable.

Throughout Hardy's work the emphasis is thrown, both by the author and by the characters of his fiction, on those elements in circumstance which are unfavorable to men's hopes.

> 'There's a back'ard current in the world, and we must do our utmost to advance in order just to bide where we be.'[54] ... 'Having found man's life to be a wretchedly conceived scheme, I renounce it.'[55] ... A fancy some people hold, when in a bitter mood, is that inexorable circumstance only tries to prevent what intelligence attempts.[56] ... So the two forces were at work here as everywhere, the inherent will to enjoy, and the circumstantial will against enjoyment.[57] ... 'There is something external to us which says, "You shan't!" First it said, "You shan't learn!" Then it said, "You shan't labor!" Now it says, "You shan't love!"'[58]

Too numerous to mention are the instances in the poems of this hostility of circumstance to men's desires and aspirations. Whole volumes are devoted to its exemplification, as indicated by the titles, *Satires of Circumstance, Time's Laughingstocks*. The upshot of volumes of poems is stated in general terms in 'Yell'ham-Wood's Story.' Yell'ham-Wood is one of Hardy's many impersonations of nature, and the general lesson of nature as stated by the voice of this forest is as follows:

> *It says that Life would signify*
> *A thwarted purposing:*
> *That we come to live, and are called to die.*
> *Yes, that's the thing*
> *In fall, in spring,*
> *That Yell'ham says:—*
> *'Life offers—to deny!'*[59]

Hardy does not believe in any God, or gods, or providence having regard for men or other creatures. But he recognizes the anthropomorphic disposition to invent gods and blame them for the ills of life. He expressly declares that his characters are mistaken in doing so; and when he himself uses these terms, it is clear that it is ironically and satirically.

> 'Providence, whom I had just thanked, seemed a mocking tormentor laughing at me.'[60] ... Even then Boldwood did not recognize that the impersonator of Heaven's persistent irony towards him, who had once before broken in upon his bliss, scourged him, and snatched his delight away, had come to do these things a second time.[61] ... But Providence is nothing if not coquettish; and no sooner had Eustacia formed this resolve than the opportunity came which, while sought, had been entirely withholden.[62] ... Yet, instead of blaming herself for the issue she had laid the fault upon the shoulders of some

indistinct, colossal Prince of the World, who had framed her situation and ruled her lot.[63] ... But the ingenious machinery contrived by the Gods for reducing human possibilities of amelioration to a minimum—which arranges that wisdom to do shall come *pari passu* with the departure of zest for doing—stood in the way of all that.[64] ... This consciousness upon which he had intruded was the single opportunity of existence ever vouchsafed to Tess by an unsympathetic First Cause[65] ... 'Justice' was done, and the President of the Immortals (in Æschylean phrase) had ended his sport with Tess.[66]

The Immanent Will

The final term chosen by Hardy for designating the unity and the directing power of the universe is one taken, in all probability, from Schopenhauer,— the Immanent Will. Mr Ernest Brennecke, in *Thomas Hardy's Universe*, has drawn many parallels between Hardy's philosophy in *The Dynasts* and that of Schopenhauer in *Die Welt als Wille und Vorstellung*; and he and Mr Stevenson have traced through the poems the gradual replacement of Chance, Circumstance, God, Providence, Nature, and other unsatisfactory terms, by the more satisfactory—but still admittedly tentative and groping term—the Immanent Will. Hardy's characterization of the Immanent Will in *The Dynasts*—in many ways identical with his earlier characterization of God in the poems—will make clear why it was that the sometimes alternative term nature had ceased to have for him the cheerful and mystical significance it had for poets like Wordsworth and Shelley and later for poets like Emerson, Whitman, Swinburne and Meredith—had altogether ceased indeed to be a term to conjure with.

Mr Brennecke is at some pains to make us understand that Schopenhauer's Will—and more dubiously, Hardy's—implies an idealistic metaphysic. The term will, taken from man's conscious and purposive action, is extended to cover all operations of the organic and inorganic world. But it amounts to no more than an urge in things which gives them the direction and the form which they have. The idealism is found altogether in the formative, the organizing character of this urge, which follows certain patterns vaguely suggestive of the world-patterns of Aristotle and Plato. Whatever may be the case with Hardy, Schopenhauer had a growing aversion to materialistic systems as incapable of explaining the organizing and formative character of this power. The behavior of the universe as a whole and in all its parts is the expression of an inherent, and as we might say, protoplasmic nature, an inner urge, and not merely the result of impulsion from without. In this sense the system of Schopenhauer, and of Hardy after him, is idealistic.

But the idealism of Schopenhauer and Hardy, as I understand it, is distinguished from most idealistic systems by the fact that it does not imply rationality. Hardy, at any rate, does not attribute intelligence to the universal

Will, or assume the existence of any intelligent supreme back lying [at the] back of or explaining the Will. Intelligence is a late and secondary development, to a large extent a delusion, and at any rate following upon the urge and action of the Will. Consequently the teleology of these men is sharply distinguished from that of most idealists, and in particular from that of writers like Cudworth and the eighteenth-century natural theologians. The Will follows unconsciously a plan inherent in itself, and the universe is purposive in that in every detail it carries out the original plan. But that this original plan implies the special adjustment of each part, of each organ and each organism, to the rôle it is to play in the universe, is certainly not remotely suggested in Hardy's writing; there is no suggestion that living creatures, including man, were destined to happiness under this plan; that it is benevolent in its particular dispositions; or that—as in the favorite eighteenth-century systems, in Shaftesbury, Pope, Wordsworth—the particular dispositions, however unsatisfactory by themselves, may be conceived of as building up in a whole which is harmonious and good taken altogether.

The word Will in Hardy and Schopenhauer carries for the most part implications quite the contrary of what it carries for religious thinkers like Coleridge. It is not the expression of intelligent thought, of 'spirit,' but of an unconscious impulse, better described in terms of animal instinct, vegetable irritability, and the insensitive—though formal—operations of inorganic matter, in the formation of crystals, the phenomena of electricity, etc. The impersonal and automatic working of this Will leaves no place for freedom in the action of men, so that the system is thoroughly unmoral and deterministic or necessarian.

Thus the Spirit of the Years describes the working of the will in human history.

> So the will heaves through Space, and moulds the times,
> With mortals for Its fingers! We shall see
> Again men's passions, virtues, visions, crimes,
>   Obey resistlessly
> The purposive, unmotived, dominant Thing
> Which sways in brooding dark their wayfaring![67]

The unconsciousness of the Will is again stated thus:

> In that immense unweeting Mind is shown
> One far above forethinking; purposive,
> Yet superconscious; a Clairvoyancy
> That knows not what It knows, yet works therewith.[68]

Again, of the Immanent Will:

> It works unconsciously, as heretofore,
> Eternal artistries in Circumstance,

255

Whose patterns, wrought by rapt æsthetic rote,
Seem in themselves Its single listless aim,
And not their consequence.[69]

There is something to remind us of Cudworth's Plastic Nature in this Immanent Will, which works purposively and aesthetically but without consciousness of what it does, proceeds like a thinking being but without thought—

Which thinking on, yet weighing not Its thought,
Unchecks Its clock-like laws.[70]

But in Cudworth the Plastic Nature is purposive and organizing in character by virtue of the Supreme Intelligence whose agent it is, whereas in Hardy the unconscious and unintelligent Will is the supreme principle of the universe, and—as the Spirit of the Years declares:

In the Foretime, even to the germ of Being,
Nothing appears of shape to indicate
That cognizance has marshalled things terrene,
Or will (such is my thinking) in my span.
Better they show that, like a knitter drowsed,
Whose fingers play in skilled unmindfulness,
The Will has woven with an absent heed
Since life first was; and ever will so weave.[71]

The mechanism of this Will and of the human beings and other forms of vitalized matter which form a part of it is figured, poetically, in terms derived from anatomy, as a gigantic brain, more suggestive of materialistic science, it seems to me, than of the vague metaphysical idealism which Mr Brennecke ascribes to Hardy. It is 'a seeming transparency ... exhibiting as one organism the anatomy of life and movement in all humanity and vitalized matter included in the display.' Strange waves pass back and forth along gossamer-like threads.

These are the Prime Volitions,—fibrils, veins,
Will-tissues, nerves, and pulses of the Cause,
That heave throughout the Earth's compositure.
Their sum is like the lobule of a Brain
Evolving always that it wots not of;

A Brain whose whole connotes the Everywhere,
And whose procedure may not be discerned
By phantom eyes like ours; the while unguessed
Of those it stirs, who (even as ye do) dream
Their motions free, their orderings supreme ...[72]

Throughout *The Dynasts* terms are used for designating this Will which emphasize the deterministic character of its action, making mere puppets of men, and its want of consciousness and intelligence. 'It is,' Mr Brennecke notes, 'the Great Necessitator, the Eternal Urger, the High Influence that sways the English realm with all its homuncules, the Master-Hand that plays the game alone, the Back of Things that hauls the halyards of the world.'[73] In the After Scene, with which the drama closes, it is called the Great Foresightless, the Inadvertent Mind, and—

> ... *the dreaming, dark, dumb thing*
> *That turns the handle of this idle show.*

It is expressly stated here, and elsewhere, that this Will, being foresightless and inadvertent, has no concern with the sufferings of mortals—though obviously it is responsible for them—and that the entire universe, like the small part of it exhibited in this epic of the Napoleonic wars, is, so far as one can make out by reason, 'inutile all.' The only hope for souls who would like to think well of the universe is that, as man in the course of the ages has evolved consciousness, so conceivably might the supreme will, with happy results for the creation—

Consciousness the Will informing, till It fashion all things fair!

This mitigating concession, made virtually without preparation at the end of a uniformly hopeless chronicle, is not to be regarded seriously as an element in Hardy's philosophy. It is radically inconsistent with the general concept of the Immanent Will, which expressly rules out the notion of a spirit external to the universe, being conceived as the mere principle of action inherent in the behavior of things. Altogether the Immanent Will is not a concept to arouse the enthusiasm of mortals like the Christian God or the nature of eighteenth-century poetry. It is nothing more than a metaphysical convenience,—a term for expressing the unity and pattern of existing things.

Evolution

The Darwinian theory of evolution was from the beginning assumed by Hardy, and it underlies all his general speculation. As he wrote in 1876, 'the evolution of species seems but a minute and obvious process' in the general world-movement, in which 'all things merge into one another—good into evil, generosity into justice, religion into politics, the years into the ages, the world into the universe.'[74] But the concept of evolution gave him none of the comfort that it did Meredith—quite the contrary. Mr Stevenson remarks that certain of Hardy's poems have the air of direct rebuttals to Meredith's hopeful evolutionary teaching. Hardy is, for the most part, doubtful of the possibility of any man's contributing to the progress of the race.[75] Heredity, he finds, works 'according to mechanical principles, beyond the control of human will.'[76] Nature shows no intention of improving the race by the process of reproduction.[77] Hardy fails to find any general tendency to good in the world.[78] In 'Nature's Questioning,'[79] field, pool, and tree interrogate the poet on the ruling power of the world, reviewing the various alternatives. Is it some 'vast Imbecility,' good at building but 'impotent to tend'; or an 'Automaton unconscious of our pains'; or is there some 'high Plan as yet not understood,' which involves so much suffering as incident to its operation?

The evolution of thought and sensibility, on which Meredith relies for his hopeful view of man's destiny, and for his entire ethical system, is with Hardy the main evidence of the blundering ineptitude of nature or God. It has occasioned untold suffering in both man and the lower animals. This view is more than once expressed by Hardy in his notebooks at different periods.

> Law has produced in man a child who cannot but constantly reproach its parent for doing much and yet not all, and constantly say to such parent that it would have been better never to have begun doing than to have *over*done so indecisively; that is, than to have created so far beyond all apparent first intention (on the emotional side) without mending matters by a second intention and execution, to eliminate the evils of the blunder of overdoing. The emotions have no place in a world of defect, and it is a cruel injustice that they should have developed in it.[80] ... A woeful fact—that the human race is too extremely developed for its corporeal conditions, the nerves being evolved to an activity abnormal in such an environment. Even the higher animals are in excess in this respect. It may be questioned if Nature, or what we call Nature, so far back as when she crossed the line from invertebrates to vertebrates, did not exceed her mission. This planet does not supply the material for happiness to higher existences. Other planets may, though one can hardly see how.[81]

Hardy's most impressive statement of this view in poetry is in 'The Mother Mourns,'[82] Here for the nonce the poet assumes, what he for the most part denies, that Mother Nature is aware of the sufferings of her creatures, and he represents her as regretting her evolutionary experiment, which has given man intelligence capable of judging and condemning her plan.

> *'I had not proposed me a Creature*
> *(She soughed) so excelling*
> *All else of my kingdom in compass*
> *And brightness of brain*
>
> *As to read my defects with a god-glance,*
> *Uncover each vestige*
> *Of old inadvertence, annunciate*
> *Each flaw and each stain*
>
> . . . .

Why loosened I olden control here
To mechanize skywards,
Undeeming great scope could outshape in
A globe of such grain?

Man's mountings of mind-sight I checked not,
Till range of his vision
Has topped my intent, and found blemish
Throughout my domain.

He holds as inept his own soul-shell—
My deftest achievement—
Contemns me for fitful inventions
Ill-timed and inane:

No more sees my sun as a Sanct-shape,
My moon as the Night-queen,
My stars as august and sublime ones
That influences rain:

Reckons gross and ignoble my teaching,
Immoral my story,
My love-lights a lure, that my species
May gather and gain.'

This poem, in which the evolution of the mind is represented as a sheer blunder, is, as Mr Stevenson suggests, a blasting reply to Meredith's 'Earth and Man.' In this one poem, for dramatic purposes, nature is figured as a conscious and planning goddess. But, in the group of poems printed with it in *Poems of the Past and Present* ('The Lacking Sense,' 'Doom and She,' 'The Sleep-Worker,' 'The Bullfinches,' 'God-Forgotten,' The Bedridden Peasant to an Unknowing God'), Mother Nature, or the alternative God, is shown as blind and dumb, a mere somnambulist. This is the price which Hardy pays—like Mill before him—for his supposition that the ruling power is not the deliberate planner of mortal miseries. The ruler of the universe, as they both hold, cannot be benevolent and omniscient at the same time.

Strictly speaking, in Hardy, the ruling power is neither omniscient nor benevolent. It is blind and indifferent. The Immanent Will, or Fundamental Energy, is no more than the sum total of all the activity in the universe. In the development of man's intelligence it works by natural selection, which is carried out by mere 'random sequence' of events.

The cognizance ye mourn, Life's doom to feel,
If I report it meetly, came unmeant,
Emerging with blind gropes from impercipience
By random sequence—luckless, tragic Chance,
If ye will call it so. 'Twas needed not

In the economy of Vitality,
Which might have ever kept a sealed cognition
As doth the Will Itself.[83]

It will be observed what an extremely attenuated version of teleology it is that will consist with this Epicurean–Lucretian notion of luckless Chance as the conductor of evolution. Nothing remains of purposiveness but the vague aesthetic recognition of unity and pattern in things. Conscious design, providence, harmony, benevolence have all evaporated from the concept of nature. As a subject for poetic exaltation it no longer has any value; and inevitably it goes into the discard, together with concepts more strictly theological. Thomas Hardy sounds the death-knell of the old nature-poetry.

Notes

1. *The Dynasts*, Part First (1904), Act. I, Scene vi, p. 54. All excerpts from Hardy's poems reprinted with kind permission of the Macmillan Co.
2. 'Discouragement' (1863–7), in *Human Shows and Far Fantasies* (1925), p. 275.
3. 'Her Dilemma' (1866), in *Wessex Poems and Other Verses* (1898), p. 22.
4. 'To Outer Nature,' *ibid.*, 150.
5. *Ibid.*, 158.
6. *Ibid.*, 165.
7. *Poems of the Past and Present* (1901), p. 97.
8. 'At a Bridal' (1866), in *Wessex Poems*, etc., p. 11.
9. *Ibid.*, 163.
10. *Poems of the Past and Present*, p. 82.
11. *Ibid.*, 88.
12. *Ibid.*, 95.
13. *Ibid.*, 165.
14. *Moments of Vision* (1st ed. 1917), p. 143.
15. *Late Lyrics and Earlier* (1922), p. 35.
16. *Ibid.*, 67.
17. *Winter Words* (1928), p. 15.
18. *Human Shows Far Fantasies*.
19. 'The Darkling Thrush,' in *Poems of the Past and Present*, p. 170.
20. *The Return of the Native*, Chap. 1.
21. *Tess of the d'Urbervilles*, Chap. XIII.
22. *Ibid.*, XXVIII.
23. *Ibid.*, XXX.
24. *Ibid.*, XXXVI.
25. *Jude the Obscure*, Part III, Chap. X.
26. *Ibid.*, IV, ii.
27. *Ibid.*, VI, iii.
28. *Ibid.*, IV, iii.
29. *Ibid.*, IV, ii.
30. *Tess of the d'Urbervilles*, Chap. V.
31. *Ibid.*, XLIX.
32. *Ibid.*, III.
33. *Ibid.*, XXIII.
34. *Ibid.*, XXXVI.
35. *Jude the Obscure*, III, viii.
36. *Ibid.*, V, viii.

37. *Ibid.*, V, vi.
38. *Ibid.*, III, iii.
39. *Ibid.*, I, ii.
40. *The Return of the Native*, Book III, Chap. i.
41. *The Mayor of Casterbridge*, Chap. XXIX.
42. *Ibid.*, XIX.
43. *The Woodlanders*, Chap. XLV.
44. *Ibid.*, XI.
45. *Tess of the D'Urbervilles*, XX.
46. *The Woodlanders*, III.
47. *A Pair of Blue Eyes*, XXX.
48. *Ibid.*, XL.
49. *The Return of the Native*, III, i.
50. *Ibid.*, III, iii.
51. *The Woodlanders*, XI.
52. *Ibid.*, VI.
53. *Tess*, V.
54. *Desperate Remedies*, Chap. XXI, Section i.
55. *Ibid.*
56. *A Pair of Blue Eyes*, XXII.
57. *Tess*, XLIII.
58. *Jude the Obscure*, VI, ii.
59. 'Yell'ham-Wood's Story,' in *Time's Laughingstocks* (first ed. 1909), p. 207.
60. *Desperate Remedies*, XXI, i.
61. *Far from the Madding Crowd*, LIII.
62. *The Return of the Native*, II, iii.
63. *Ibid.*, IV, viii.
64. *The Mayor of Casterbridge*, XLIV.
65. *Tess*, XXV.
66. *Ibid.*, LIX.
67. *The Dynasts*, Part Second, Act II, Scene iii.
68. *Ibid.*, First, V, iv.
69. *Ibid.*, Fore Scene.
70. *Ibid.*
71. *Ibid.*
72. *Ibid.*
73. Ernest Brennecke, Jr., *Thomas Hardy's Universe*, Boston 1924, p. 97. The references are to Part First, VI, iii; I, iii; Second II, iv; Third, VIII, vii.
74. Lionel Stevenson, *op. cit.*, pp. 240–1.
75. *Ibid.*, 255–7.
76. *Ibid.*, 258.
77. 'At a Bridal.'
78. Stevenson, pp. 261–3, refers to 'The Farm Woman's Winter,' 'In a Wood,' 'A Meeting with Despair,' 'To Life,' 'On a Fine Morning.'
79. *Wessex Poems*, etc., p. 165.
80. Florence Emily Hardy, *The Early Life of Thomas Hardy*, New York 1928, p. 192 (May, 1881). Reprinted by kind permission of the Macmillan Co.
81. *Ibid.*, pp. 285–6 (April 1889). Reprinted by kind permission of the Macmillan Co.
82. *Poems of the Past and Present*, p. 69.
83. *The Dynasts*, Part First, V, iv.

Thomas Hardy:
A Study of his Writings
and Their Background

◆

WILLIAM R. RUTLAND

Chapter III
The Background to Hardy's Thought

It has been the fashion to write books about Hardy's philosophy. Patrick Braybrooke's *Thomas Hardy and his Philosophy* is little more than a discursive essay lacking either philosophical or literary background, in which *The Dynasts* is disposed of in one astounding sentence.[1] There are two American theses, of widely divergent character. Helen Garwood's well-written Essay was the earliest attempt at a systematic comparison of Hardy with Schopenhauer,[2] of which more hereafter. George Swann's dissertation[3] is devoted to the drawing of real or imagined parallels between Defoe and Aristotle, Richardson and Kant, Fielding and Hume, Dickens and J.S. Mill, Meredith and Hegel, and Hardy and von Hartmann. It calls in the aid of mathematical formulæ, and states that 'the starting point of Hardy's thought was Schopenhauer,' ignoring the fact that Hardy did not read Schopenhauer until he was over forty. Ernest Brennecke's *Thomas Hardy's Universe: A Study of a Poet's Mind* is a very thorough exposition of *Die Welt als Wille und Vorstellung* and an anthology of quotations from *The Dynasts*, in alternate chapters. The correlation of the two is not always happy; as for example when Mr Brennecke writes 'Particularly in his treatment of the theme of love does Mr Hardy follow the disillusioned Schopenhaurian view of the dominant will,' the illustration chosen is the ditty sung by the Ironic Spirits on the betrothal of Napoleon to Marie Louise:

(Part 2, Act v, Sc. vii)
First 'twas a finished coquette,

SOURCE Oxford, 1938, chs III and IV.

And now 'tis a raw ingenue—
Blonde instead of brunette,
An old wife doffed for a new.
She'll bring him a baby
As swiftly as maybe
And that's what he wants her to do,
    Hoo, hoo!
And that's what he wants her to do.

Hardy himself repeatedly disclaimed the title of philosopher.[4] If the word is to be taken in its strictly technical sense, he was justified in so doing. For he was before all things an artist: if his work endures, it will endure as art. But that his art owes something of its greatness to his thought can hardly be denied. That he was a thinker in the sense that all great artists are thinkers, he tacitly admitted in the Apology prefixed to *Late Lyrics and Earlier*; when he rounded upon the critics, who accused him of pessimism, with this question: 'Should a shaper of such stuff as dreams are made on disregard considerations of what is customary and expected, and apply himself to the real function of poetry, the application of ideas to life (in Matthew Arnold's familiar phrase)?' That Hardy applied ideas to life needs no demonstration. So far did he go in the process that, to one reader of it at least, his last novel seems to be constructed wholly for the sake of ideas, round which is draped the insufficient and transparent fabric of a thin romance. The point must be amplified in another chapter. It has been generally agreed that even *Tess*, his most powerful although not his best, novel, is partly marred by the protrusion of arguments into the artistic illusion, like girders through ill-fitting scenery. It is significant that neither in *Tess* nor in *Jude*, nor the *The Dynasts*, in which Hardy carried the application of ideas to life so far that he created a new form of literature in the process, are the 'ideas' wholly of the intellect. With the artist, especially the poet, arguments continued by the mind are apt to be initiated by the heart. And with Hardy himself, if the mind argued when the question was once raised, it was often the heart which first questioned. The Ancient Spirit of the Years is the mind in *The Dynasts*. But there would be no *Dynasts*, and no Wessex novels, for that matter, without the Pities.

It would seem a truism that every man is the product of his age. Hardy was most certainly the product of the age in which he lived. And yet scarcely any of those who have attempted to examine his thought, have even glanced at the thought of that age in which Hardy came to maturity. An almost perfect example of the manner in which *not* to approach an investigation of Hardy's intellectual formation is provided in the latest American thesis upon him; in which the writer quotes very unfavourable comments by him upon Nietzsche and Bergson, and says of them: 'They completely refute the usual concept that the trend of Hardy's ideas was shaped by the authors he read.'[5]

Leaving out of account that there is no such 'usual concept' except with regard to Schopenhauer, it needs small proof that Hardy can have read not one word of either Nietzsche or Bergson until he was well on in middle life. Hardy did not read German easily: Nietzsche was not available in English until the 'nineties; that Hardy read him later is proved by a letter which appeared in the *Manchester Guardian* on October 12th, 1914, in which he said of Nietzsche:

> He used to seem to me (I have not looked into him for years) an incoherent rhapsodist who jumps from Macchiavelli to Isaiah as the mood seizes him, whom it is impossible to take seriously as a mentor.

Bergson was nineteen years younger than Hardy, and only began to assume importance when the bulk of Hardy's work was written. Neither of these philosophers can provide the smallest shred of evidence as to the shaping of Hardy's ideas by the authors he read. For that we must look to the authors whom he read, not after he was sixty, but before he was thirty-five. The point is worth making only because this apparently obvious course has not been taken by any of Hardy's critics. The only approach to it is made in the last chapter of Dr de Ridder Barzin's excellent analysis of Hardy's ideas; and even this chapter, entitled 'Hardy et le Courant des Idées en Angleterre au XIX Siècle' is only intended as a sketch, and is based upon textbooks of English literature, not upon original knowledge.[6]

To give long quotations of passages, detached from their contexts, out of Hardy's works, as specimens of his thought, is unscientific. If it be not clear from the works themselves what Hardy thought about, there is an admirable and fully documented summary entitled *Le Pessimisme de Thomas Hardy* in which his ideas are set forth with Latin clarity and precision. Assuming these to be known, it remains to give an account of the most important influences which may have helped to mould his intellect. When all is said, an artist of the calibre of Hardy remains himself, trace influences as we may. Some things which were absorbed into his consciousness may be pointed out; they do not explain the happily inexplicable mystery of creative genius.

It is fashionable at the present time to regard the 'mid-Victorian' years as a period of barren complacency and intellectual stagnation. In point of fact, the 'sixties witnessed a crisis in English intellectual life to which our times offer no parallel. The twentieth year of Hardy's life produced two events which are landmarks; he entered upon the threshold of manhood at the moment when there began what has probably been the most rapid change in our cultural history. This period can conveniently be dated from the publication of two books. The first edition of Charles Darwin's *Origin of Species* appeared on November 24th, 1859, and was sold out on the day of publication; the second edition became available in January 1860. In 1860 there also appeared a volume entitled *Essay and Reviews*. It is hardly too much to say that these books shook England to its centre.

Writing long afterwards of the appearance of *Essays and Reviews*, Leslie Stephen said, 'Nobody who remembers the time can doubt that it marked the appearance of a very important development of religious and philosophical thought.'[7] We have Mrs Hardy's testimony that Hardy read this book shortly after its publication, and that it impressed him much.[8] Small wonder that it impressed him. It should be remembered that he was at this time seriously considering ordination,[9] and that he was deeply interested both in the Bible (in which he remained interested always), and in the Church; and the special significance of *Essays and Reviews* has been thus described:

> The importance of this book in the history of religious thought in England lies in the proclamation of a view of Scripture which, at the time of its publication, seemed, as put forward by ordained ministers of the national church, nothing less than revolutionary. This view would not have excited surprise if found in the writings of opponents of orthodoxy or even of scholars unpledged to any particular position; it was in the enunciation of it by clergymen that the startling novelty lay.[10]

The effect which the thorough study of this book produced upon young Hardy, who, while he had been devoutly brought up in strict orthodoxy, was at this very time in what may be called a state of intellectual renaissance effected by study of the classics, can best be suggested by passages from the book itself. One of the most powerful articles in it was that 'On the Interpretation of Scripture' from the pen of Benjamin Jowett, who had then for some years been Regius Professor of Greek at Oxford. In the course of this article, which was in the main a piece of textual criticism, Jowett made a potent attack upon the stupidity of conventional orthodoxy.

> Consider, for example, the extraordinary and unreasonable importance attached to single words, sometimes of doubtful meaning, in reference to any of the following subjects: Divorce; Marriage with a Wife's Sister; Inspiration; the Personality of the Holy Spirit; Infant Baptism; Episcopacy; Divine Right of Kings; Original Sin.

Jowett examined the orthodox bases of each of these dogmas with devasting effect, and continued:

> There is indeed a kind of mystery in the way in which the chance words of a simple narrative, the occurrence of some accidental event, the use even of a figure of speech or a mistranslation of a word in Latin or English, have affected the thoughts of future ages and distant countries. Nothing so slight that it has not been caught at, nothing so plain that it may not be explained away.

This insistence upon doctrines often scarcely supported by Biblical authority was contrasted with the entire neglect of other precepts repeatedly and clearly given by our Lord; e.g., the blessedness of poverty. The close of this section ran thus:

> The conduct of our Lord to the woman taken in adultery affords a painful

contrast to the excessive severity with which even a Christian society punishes the errors of women.

The conclusion of the article contained a paragraph to which it is not hard to imagine young Hardy's vibrant response; it is at the same time eloquent concerning the atmosphere in which he was growing to maturity:

> It is a mischief that critical observations which any intelligent man can make for himself should be ascribed to atheism or unbelief. It would be a strange and almost incredible thing that the Gospel which at first made war only on the vices of mankind should now be opposed to one of the highest and rarest of human virtues—the love of truth. And that in the present day the great object of Christianity should be, not to change the lives of men, but to prevent them from changing their opinions; that would be a singular inversion of the purposes for which Christ came into the world.

It has sometimes been asked why Hardy chose Oxford as the type of intellectual obscurantism and obstructionism, and said, in the most bitter of all his works, that if Christminster could not move with the times, Christminster must go.[11] It might be remembered that most of the collaborators to *Essays and Reviews* were Oxford scholars; their position may be illustrated by the case of the most conspicuous of them. On February 20th, 1863, Benjamin Jowett was prosecuted for heresy in the Vice-Chancellor's Court. The prosecution was ultimately dropped on the advice of counsel against application to the Court of Queen's Bench. Foiled in their attempt to eject him from the University, Jowett's enemies next tried to ruin him. Of the four Regius Professorships, his was the only one whose salary had not been adjusted to modern conditions, but had remained the forty pounds granted under the mediæval foundation. A measure was introduced to endow the chair, and upon February 4th, 1864, there was a debate in Congregation upon it. The proposal ultimately went through; despite a memorial drawn up by Jowett's enemies, in the course of which they said:

> The Regius Professor of Greek in this University is charged—and that not hastily, or by a few persons, or a single party, but by the general voice of Christian people in Oxford and throughout the land—with holding and affirming doctrines subversive of the Church's faith. The fact of that faith having lost its hold upon the minds of the generality of those who have been brought within the sphere of his influence is but too evident.[12]

Hardy, who was still in Dorchester, had an opportunity of witnessing the working of obscurantism nearer home. Early in 1861, Rowland Williams, who, in the review of Bunsen's Biblical Researches in *Essays and Reviews*, had written that the command to Abraham to sacrifice his son Isaac had been given 'by the fierce ritual of Syria with the awe of a divine voice,' was indicted for heresy before the Court of Arches by William Kerr Hamilton, Bishop of Salisbury. He was condemned in that court, and suspended. But the decision was reversed by the Judicial Committee of the Privy Council. This case, being of great local interest—for Dorchester is in the Diocese of

Salisbury—almost filled the *Dorset County Chronicle* during several weeks with polemical correspondence and controversy. It produced at least one leading article, in which the Editor gave as an example of the blasphemy of the new heretics the view that the whole of the book of Daniel was not written by Daniel, which, he said, amounted to a charge of forgery against the Almighty.[13] Hardy was then reading the *Dorset County Chronicle* every day.

What must have impressed Hardy even more than the conclusions in *Essays and Reviews* was the method, which was imported from science, and was at that date new to theology. An excellent example is to be found in the article on the Mosaic Cosmogony, by C.W. Goodwin. The author there refers to the attempt made to reconcile the recent findings of science with the traditional interpretations of the Bible:

> In a text book of theological instruction widely used (Horne's Introduction to the Holy Scriptures, 10th ed., 1856) we find it stated in broad terms: 'Geological investigations, it is now known, all prove the perfect harmony between Scripture and Geology in reference to the history of creation.' In truth, however, if we refer to the plans of conciliation proposed, we find them at variance with each other and mutually destructive. The conciliators are not agreed among themselves, and each holds the view of the other to be untenable and unsafe. The ground is perpetually shifted, as the advance of geological science may require. The plain meaning of the Hebrew record is unscrupulously tampered with, and in general the pith of the whole process lies in divesting the text of all meaning whatever.

The writer of that was not a geologist but a Doctor of Divinity.

To pursue the history of the controversy further would here be out of place. Another *cause célèbre* resulted in 1862 from the publication, by John William Colenso, first Bishop of Natal, of a book entitled *Introduction to the Pentateuch*; for which, in the following year, his metropolitan, Robert Gray, Bishop of Capetown, deposed him from his see as an heretic. Although the deposition had no legal force and was disregarded by Colenso, it caused a storm at the time. And the young Hardy was not the only writer who was interested. Browning's *Dramatis Personæ*, when it appeared in 1864, contained a poem called 'Gold Hair: A Story of Pornic in Brittany,' the penultimate stanza of which runs:

> *The candid incline to surmise of late*
> *That the Christian faith proves false, I find;*
> *For our Essays-and-Reviews debate*
> *Begins to tell on the public mind,*
> *And Colenso's words have weight.*

Of even greater influence upon the whole of English thought in the later nineteenth century was the theory of evolution propounded in Darwin's epoch-making book, *The Origin of Species*, and in its sequel, *The Descent of Man* (1871). When Darwin died in 1882, Hardy attended his funeral in Westminster Abbey on April 26th. 'As a young man,' says Mrs Hardy, 'he had been among the earliest acclaimers of *The Origin of Species*.'[14] Writing the Preface to *Late Lyrics* in February 1922, Hardy, in his eighty-third year, lamented that he had fallen upon a period 'when belief in witches of Endor is displacing the Darwinian theory, and "the truth shall make you free."' The famous book, which became the gospel of so many in Hardy's youth, does not itself contain any philosophical speculation. It is a strict work of science, the contents of which may be concisely described in one sentence from the famous third chapter, 'The Struggle for Existence': 'I should infer from analogy,' wrote Darwin, 'that probably all the organic beings which have ever lived on this Earth have descended from some one primordial form, into which life was first breathed.' That this conclusion, if true, destroyed at one stroke the cosmogony of the Pentateuch and with it the doctrine of the infallibility of Holy Writ, was much; but still more were the further implications, which are described by Professor C.C.J. Webb:

> The importance to religious thought of the introduction of the idea of evolution was of course far greater than it would have been, had it merely, in its application in a particular form to a particular case, led to a questioning of the claim of Scripture to be considered as possessing infallible authority in respect of its statements regarding matters which fall within the domain of natural science. Regarded as the enunciation of a principle valid throughout the Universe, it seemed, at any rate to some minds, to explain by processes going on *within* the universe what it had previously been commonly maintained that an intelligent Power *beyond* and *above* the Universe was required to account for. If this use of the idea of evolution was to be reconciled with religion at all, it must plainly be by some doctrine of divine *immanence*, which should replace an instantaneous operation of *transcendent* divine power, calling the world into existence out of nothing in a form substantially the same from the first as it wears to-day, such as was then commonly supposed to be implied by the term 'creation,' by a gradual operation of God whereby some simple germ or seed might be developed into an ever progressively richer variety of forms. Moreover, if the world process were thus to be conceived after the analysis of the known facts of organic life, it would almost inevitably follow that individual members of any species, and therefore individual human beings among the rest, would come to be envisaged rather as transitory embodiments of relatively abiding types than as themselves the supremely important realities for the sake of which the whole process exists.[15]

This, then, was the intellectual atmosphere into which Hardy entered as he entered manhood; the two dominant ideas were, firstly that the Primal Cause was Immanent in the Universe, not transcendent to it; and, secondly, that the individual human being was of very small significance in the scheme of things. All the critics are agreed that these two conceptions are those which dominate all Hardy's work. Such of them as have sought the sources of this thought at all have gone to Schopenhauer and von Hartmann. It will be shown later in this chapter that Hardy studied both these philosophers in the 'eighties, and did in fact owe something to them in his last novels and in *The Dynasts*; but Hardy grew to manhood in the 'sixties. It was in the spring of 1862 that he came to make his fortune in London; and it was in those early, lonely, years in London that his personality was formed.

The speculative writer whose name is especially associated with the doctrine of the *immanence* of the Primal Cause as a means of reconciling religion and science, is Herbert Spencer (1820–1903). Spencer, who was a friend of Darwin and Huxley, and who coined the phrase 'survival of the fittest,' had already published four works by 1860. It was in 1862 that there appeared the first instalment of the great system of philosophy which is Spencer's monument in the history of thought. *First Principles* is almost certainly the earliest work of Spencer with which Hardy became acquainted. The metaphysical part of this work is that which has found least favour with either science or religion, and is generally regarded as the least important part of Spencer's philosophy. But to the student of Hardy, who, it is certain, was deeply impressed by this book in his early twenties, it is intensely interesting. The first part of the book is called 'The Unknowable'; and at the conclusion of the second chapter Spencer writes:

> If Religion and Science are to be reconciled, the basis of reconciliation must be this deepest, widest and most certain of all facts—that the Power which the Universe manifests to us is utterly inscrutable.

The third chapter on Ultimate Scientific Ideas consists of a 'reductio ad absurdum.' 'What,' asks Spencer, 'are Space and Time?', and proceeds to show that Space, Time, Matter, and, indeed, any ultimate scientific idea, are all representative of realities that cannot be comprehended. At which a reader of *The Dynasts* cannot but recall the ditty of the Spirits:

What are space and time? A Fancy—(Pt. 3, Act i, Sc. iii)

or the chorus of the Intelligences (at the close of the fore-scene) considering

> ... *the Prime that willed ere wareness was,*
> *Whose brain, perchance, is Space, whose thought its laws,*
> *Which we as threads and streams discern,*
> *We may but muse on, never learn.*

Or the sarcasm of the Spirit of the Years at the end of Sc. viii, Act vii, Part 3:

> *Your knowings of the Unknowable declared,*
> *Let the last Picture of the Play be bared.*

The conclusion of the fifth chapter of *First Principles* contains a passage, not hitherto mentioned by a single critic of Hardy, which Hardy must have known by heart when he was two-and-twenty; and which, if he had chosen, he might have written in 1903 upon the title-page of his greatest contribution to our literature:

> Thus the consciousness of an inscrutable Power, manifested to us through all phenomena, has been growing ever clearer; and must eventually be freed

from its imperfections. The certainty that on the one hand such a power exists, while on the other hand its nature transcends intuition and is beyond imagination, is the certainty towards which intelligence has from the first been progressing.

Hardy's biography provides a piece of external evidence that he knew Herbert Spencer, which, taken with the above, is most significant. In 1888 a certain Rev. Dr Grosart wrote to Hardy asking him if he could suggest any explanation of certain terrible facts of life which could reconcile them to the hypothesis of the absolute goodness and non-limitation of God. To which Hardy replied that he could suggest no such explanation, but that 'Perhaps Dr Grosart might be helped to a provisional view of the Universe by the recently published Life of Darwin, and the works of Herbert Spencer.'[16]

The man who, more than any other, was the active champion of the theory of evolution was Thomas Henry Huxley (1825–95). While Darwin remained in comparative seclusion, Huxley, one of the most agile intellects of the century and one of the most fearless men who ever lived, resolutely set out to secure fair public hearing for the new theories. At the beginning he fought the battle almost single-handed against formidable odds. For ten years, at least, he was popularly considered as the personification of the new doctrines; and it is hardly too much to say that no inconsiderable portion of the orthodox public regarded him as Antichrist.

There is about Huxley something which captures the imagination, even at this distance. To the men who were then young, and who, like Hardy, had acclaimed the new dawn of truth, he must have seemed a very Ajax striding into the ranks of obscurantism and scattering them before him. It was not until the 'seventies that Hardy met this champion face to face. Then, says Mrs Hardy, 'For Huxley he had a liking which grew with the knowledge of him—though that was never great—speaking of him as a man who united a fearless mind with the warmest of hearts and the most modest of manners.'[17] But from the written word he knew him long before.

The review in *The Times* of *The Origin of Species*, although nominally by *The Times* critic, was in fact by Huxley; the critic having applied to him for help in a matter beyond his own competence, and having complied with the letter of the law by prefixing a paragraph of his own to Huxley's article.[18] Entirely from Huxley's pen was the review in the *Westminster Review* for April 1860. This was in the main a carefully reasoned and dispassionate scientific review. But it contained two paragraphs which have a ring as of trumpet calls, and which are even more eloquent of the conditions in which it was possible to write them than they are in themselves:

> The myths of paganism are as dead as Osiris and Zeus, and the man who should revive them, in opposition to the knowledge of our time, would be justly laughed to scorn; but the coëval imaginations current among the rude inhabitants of Palestine, recorded by writers whose very name and age are admitted by every scholar to be unknown, have unfortunately not yet shared their fate, but,

even at this day, are regarded by nine-tenths of the civilised world as the authoritative standard of fact and the criterion of the justice of scientific conclusions, in all that relates to the origin of things, and among them, of species. In this nineteenth century, as at the dawn of modern physical science, the cosmogony of the semi-barbarous Hebrew is the incubus of the philosopher and the opprobrium of the orthodox. Who shall number the patient and earnest seekers after truth, from the days of Galileo until now, whose lives have been embittered and their good name blasted by the mistaken zeal of bibliolaters? Who shall count the host of weaker men whose sense of truth has been destroyed in the effort to harmonize the impossibilities—whose life has been wasted in the attempt to force the generous new wine of science into the old bottles of judaism, compelled by the outcry of the same strong party?

It is true that if philosophers have suffered, their cause has been amply avenged. Extinguished theologians lie about the cradle of every science as the strangled snakes beside that of Hercules; and history recalls that whenever science and orthodoxy have been fairly opposed, the latter has been forced to retire from the lists, bleeding and crushed, if not annihilated; scotched, if not slain. But orthodoxy is the Bourbon of the world of thought. It learns not, neither can it forget; and though at present bewildered and afraid to move, it is as willing as ever to insist that the first of Genesis contains the beginning and end of sound science, and to visit with such petty thunderbolts as its half-paralyzed hands can hurl those who refuse to degrade nature to the level of primitive Judaism.

Orthodoxy picked up the glove thrown into the lists with such superb audacity. In June 1860 there was held in Oxford the annual meeting of the British Association for the Advancement of Science. To this meeting there came, besides the men of science from all countries, Samuel Wilberforce, Bishop of Oxford; whose First Class in Mathematics in his youth gave him, in some orthodox eyes, standing in matters of science as well as in those of doctrine. Whatever he may have been in his youth, Wilberforce was an experienced and formidable controversialist; and he came to Oxford fully primed by the palaeontologist, Richard Owen, whom Huxley had demolished some little time before. On Saturday, June 30th, Dr Draper, of New York, read a paper: 'On the intellectual development of Europe considered with reference to the views of Mr Darwin and others that the progression of organisms is determined by law.' At the conclusion of this paper, there followed a general discussion, which soon became tempestuous. One speaker, who went to the blackboard and began 'Let the point A be Man, and let the point B be the mawnkey ...' was howled down with cries of 'mawnkey!' The President demanded that the discussion be confined to scientific matters only. After a short speech by another scientist, the Bishop rose and began to ridicule Darwin, savagely attacking Huxley:

> The Bishop spoke thus for full half an hour with inimitable spirit, emptiness and unfairness. In a light, scoffing tone, florid and fluent, he assured us there was nothing in the idea of evolution; rock pigeons were what rock pigeons had always been. Then, turning to the antagonist with a smiling insolence, he begged to know, was it through his grandfather or through his grandmother that he claimed his descent from a monkey.[19]

Huxley, who was at this point heard to remark 'The Lord hath delivered him into my hand,' sat patiently till the Bishop had said his say; and even refused to rise until repeatedly called for. He then made a speech in which he showed that the Right Reverend Father did not know what he was talking about when it came to physiology.

> But if this question is treated, not as a matter for the calm investigation of science, but as a matter of sentiment, and if I ask whether I would choose to be descended from the poor animal of low intelligence and stooping gait, who grins and chatters as we pass, or from a man, endowed with great ability and a splendid position, who should use these gifts to discredit and crush humble seekers after truth, I hesitate what to answer.

The conclusion of the sentence was drowned in cheers.

It was in such an atmosphere as this that Hardy came of age. It was, not improbably, with a memory of the events of the 'sixties that, when he was finishing *Jude the Obscure*, he wrote in his notebook: 'Never retract. Never explain. Get it done, and let them howl.'[20] By a curious coincidence, the most sensational episode in the storm over *Jude* was provided by a Bishop, who wrote to the *Yorkshire Post* that he had thrown the novel into the fire: 'probably,' said Hardy, 'in his despair at not being able to burn me.' In the rather bitterly ironical second Preface to *Jude* he added:

> To do Bludyer and the conflagratory bishop justice, what they meant seems to have been only this: 'We Britons hate ideas, and we are going to live up to that privilege of our native country. Your picture may not show the untrue or the uncommon, or even be contrary to the canons of art; but it is not the view of life that we who thrive on conventions can permit to be painted.'

There is in *Wessex Poems* a sonnet addressed 'To a Lady, offended by a book of the Writer's,' which is of a higher seriousness:

Now that my page is exiled—doomed, maybe,
Never to press thy cosy cushions more,
Or wake thy ready yeas as heretofore,
Or stir thy gentle vows of faith in me:

Knowing thy natural receptivity,
I figure that, as flambeaux banish eve,
My sombre image, warped by insidious heave
Of those less forthright, must lose place in thee.

So be it, I have borne such. Let thy dreams
Of me and mine diminish day by day,
And yield their space to shine of smugger things;
Till I shape to thee but in fitful gleams,
And then in far and feeble visitings,
And then surcease. Truth will be truth alway.

It is possible wholly to understand Hardy, both as a man and as a writer, only if we understand in what school he was brought up. Of the masters whose example inspired him in early manhood and whose principles he never forgot, Huxley was not the least. By the time he was thirty-five, Hardy had lost all religious faith. No one has regretted that loss more bitterly than he (as can be seen by such a moving poem as 'The Impercipient' in *Wessex Poems*). It was the inevitable result of an evolution of character conditioned by the age. In the volume of Essays called *Lay Sermons* which Huxley published in 1870, there is one upon Descartes. After describing Descartes's condition for the assent to any proposition, Huxley wrote:

> The enunciation of this first great commandment of science consecrated doubt. It removed doubt from the seat of penance among the grievous sins to which it had long been condemned, and enthroned it in that high place among the primary duties which is assigned to it by the scientific conscience of these later days.

What Hardy and those whom he followed lost, irreparable as it was, was at least lost in no ignoble quest. Huxley himself thus described the principles that had guided him:

> To promote the increase of natural knowledge and to further the application of scientific methods of investigation to all the problems of life to the best of my ability, in the conviction, which has grown with my growth and strengthened with my strength, that there is no alleviation for the sufferings of mankind except veracity of thought and action, and the resolute facing of the world as it is, when the garment of make-believe, by which pious hands have hidden its ugly features, is stripped off.[21]

That lesson Hardy learnt well and truly. All his novels and all his poetry are permeated with it. He was over eighty when he wrote, looking back upon his life:

> If I may be forgiven for quoting my own old words, let me repeat what I printed in this relation more than twenty years ago, and wrote much earlier, in a poem entitled 'In Tenebris.'
>
> *If a way to the Better there be, it exacts a full look at the Worst:*
>
> that is to say, by the exploration of reality, and its frank recognition stage by stage, along the survey, with an eye to the best consummation possible.[22]

The nature of Huxley's influence upon Hardy's thought is shown most clearly in a letter written by the latter on February 27th, 1902, to Edward Clodd, thanking him for his book on Huxley. This letter is in Mr T.J. Wise's Ashley Library,[23] and has not been published. In it Hardy wrote:

> What is forced upon one again after reading such a life as Huxley's, is the sad fact of the extent to which Theological lumber is still allowed to discredit religion, in spite of such devoted attempts as his to shake it off. If the doctrines of the supernatural were quickly abandoned to-morrow by the church, and 'reverence and love for an ethical ideal' alone retained, not one in ten thousand would object to the readjustment, while the enormous bulk of thinkers

excluded by the old teaching would be brought into the fold, and our venerable old churches and cathedrals would become the centres of emotional life that they once were.

Well: what we gain by science is, after all, sadness, as the Preacher saith. The more we know of the laws and nature of the Universe, the more ghastly a business one perceives it all to be—and the non-necessity of it. As some philosopher says, if nothing at all existed, it would be a completely natural thing; but that the world exists is a fact absolutely logicless and senseless.

In that letter we have the concise history of Hardy's mental and emotional development, and an illustration of the results to which it led.

Huxley, although the outstanding figure in the battle over evolution, was not alone as a fearless thinker in his day. In 1864 there was published a small volume which has become one of the major classics of English philosophy. The third chapter of it treats of Individuality as one of the elements of well-being; and in this we may read, as all the young men of that day, Hardy among the rest, read:

> There is now scarcely any outlet for energy in this country except business. The energy expended in this may still be regarded as considerable. What little is left from that employment, is expended on some hobby, which may be a useful, even a philanthropic, hobby, but is always some one thing, and generally a thing of small dimensions. The greatness of England is now all collective; individually small, we only appear capable of anything great by our habit of combining; and with this our moral and religious philanthropists are perfectly contented. But it was men of another stamp than this that made England what it has been; and men of another stamp will be needed to prevent its decline.

The writer of those words was John Stuart Mill (1806–73), and the book is the famous treatise *On Liberty*, the appearance of which raised Mill to the zenith of his fame. This was two years after Hardy had come to London; in the following year, Mill was elected to Parliament as Member for Westminster. Among the tributes called forth forty years later by the centenary of Mill's birth, there was a letter in *The Times* of May 21st, 1906, in which Hardy described a personal experience of that election:

> This being the hundredth anniversary of J. Stuart Mill's birth, and as writers like Carlyle, Leslie Stephen and others have held that anything, however imperfect, which affords an idea of a human personage in his actual form and flesh, is of value in respect of him, the few following words on how one of the profoundest thinkers of the last century appeared forty years ago to the man in the street may be worth recording as a footnote to Mr Morley's admirable estimate of Mill's life and philosophy in your impression of Friday.
>
> It was a day in 1865, about three in the afternoon, during Mill's candidature for Westminster. The hustings had been erected in Covent Garden, near the front of St Paul's Church; and when I—a young man living in London—drew near to the spot, Mill was speaking. The appearance of the author of the treatise *On Liberty* (which we students of that date knew almost by heart) was so different from the look of persons who usually address crowds in the open air that it held the attention of people for whom such a gathering in itself had little

interest. Yet it was, primarily, that of a man out of place. The religious sincerity of his speech was jarred on by his environment—a group on the hustings who, with few exceptions, did not care to understand him fully, and a crowd below who could not. He stood bareheaded, and his vast pale brow, so thin-skinned as to show the blue veins, sloped back like a stretching upland, and conveyed to the observer a curious sense of perilous exposure. The picture of him as personified earnestness surrounded for the most part by careless curiosity derived an added piquancy—if it can be called such—from the fact that the cameo clearness of his face chanced to be in relief against the blue shadow of a church, which on its transcendental side, his doctrines antagonized. But it would not be right to say that the throng was absolutely unimpressed by his words; it felt that they were weighty, though it did not quite know why.

The peculiar value of this most suggestive letter—and who but an artist could convey what is given by that touch of the cameo clear face against the blue shadow of a church?—is the direct testimony it affords of Mill's influence upon Hardy when the younger writer was just becoming a man. He knew the treatise *On Liberty* almost by heart. To get that treatise by heart is an experience which could leave no intellectual man quite as he was before it. In the second chapter on the Liberty of Thought and Discussion, the young Hardy read:

> No one can be a great thinker who does not recognise that as a thinker it is his first duty to follow his intellect to whatever conclusions it may lead. Truth gains even more by the errors of one, who, with due study and preparation, thinks for himself, than by the true opinion of those who only hold them because they do not suffer themselves to think.

It is not too much to say that the whole of Hardy's life, and all his writings, were profoundly influenced by thoughts that had come out of that vast pale brow, which he glimpsed on an afternoon in 1865. Thirty years later, in the third chapter of the fourth part of *Jude the Obscure*, he made Sue Bridehead quote to Phillotson a passage out of the third paragraph of the third chapter of the treatise *On Liberty*: 'She or he who lets the world, or his own portion of it, choose his plan of life for him, has no need of any other faculty than the ape-like one of imitation.' As must be shown in another chapter, *Jude the Obscure* occupies a place by itself among Hardy's writings in that it was primarily written for the sake of propagating certain ideas. The whole attitude of mind in which the book was written bears traces of Hardy's early studies in John Stuart Mill; although it may be conjectured that the result would have considerably startled Mill himself. When the storm broke upon Hardy after the publication of *Jude*, a far more effective reply than that which he actually made, would have been supplied by Mill's words:

> If any opinion is compelled to silence, that opinion may, for aught we can certainly know, be true. To deny this is to assume our own infallibility. Though the silenced opinion be an error, it may, and very commonly does, contain a portion of truth; and since the general and prevailing opinion on any subject is rarely or never the whole truth, it is only by the collision of adverse opinions that the remainder of the truth has any chance of being supplied.[24]

Hardy's first study in Mill was doubtless the treatise *On Liberty* in the 'sixties. But it would not be hard to show that his reading extended further also. As a brief example, we may take the *Three Essays on Religion* which first appeared in 1874 after Mill's death. The first of these, the Essay on Nature, written between 1850 and 1858, contains the following paragraph:

> That much applauded class of authors, the writers on natural theology, have, I venture to think, entirely lost their way and missed the sole line of argument which could have made their speculations acceptable to any who can perceive when two propositions contradict one another. They have exhausted the resources of sophistry to make it appear that all the suffering in the world exists to prevent greater—that misery exists, for fear lest there should be misery; a thesis which, if ever so well maintained, could only avail to explain and justify the works of limited beings, compelled to labour under conditions independent of their own will; but can have no application to a Creator assumed to be omnipotent, who, if he bends to a supposed necessity, himself makes the necessity which he bends to. If the maker of the world *can* all that he will, he wills misery, and there is no escape from the conclusion.

No reader of *Tess* or of *The Dynasts* will require further comment. There are a few passages in the novel, and several in the drama, so exactly corresponding to this that, given the knowledge that Hardy was a devoted admirer of Mill, the possibility of pure coincidence in the resemblance is practically ruled out. Simply because it is less generally known than his creative work, a passage may also be quoted from a letter which Hardy wrote concerning an essay in Maeterlinck's *Le Temple Enseveli*, that appeared in *The Academy* of May 17th, 1902 (at the time when he was putting the finishing touches to *The Dynasts*):

> Far be it from my wish to disturb any comforting phantasy, it if be barely tenable. But alas, no profound reflection can be needed to detect the sophistry in M. Maeterlinck's argument, and to see that the original difficulty recognised by thinkers like Schopenhauer, Hartmann, Haeckel, etc., and by most of the persons called pessimists, remains unsurmounted.
>
> Pain has been, and pain is: no new sort of morals in Nature can remove pain from the past and make it pleasure for those who are its infallible estimators, the bearers thereof. And no injustice, however slight, can be atoned for by her future generosity, however ample, so long as we consider Nature to be, or to stand for, unlimited power. The exoneration of an omnipotent Mother by her retrospective justice becomes an absurdity when we ask, What made the foregone injustice necessary to her omnipotence?

No comment upon this is needed, except that Hardy was perfectly familiar with the idea expressed in the last paragraph quoted, at least ten years before he had read a word of Schopenhauer or of von Hartmann (who were not translated into English until the 'eighties). It is true that three books by Haeckel were translated during the 'seventies, of which more hereafter. But it seems superfluous to invoke Haeckel when we know how Hardy studied Mill.

Before leaving Mill, there is one exceedingly suggestive point to be made, which has never, as far as I am aware, been made hitherto. It is commonly supposed and stated that the Doctrine of the unconscious Immanent Will, which forms the great theme of Hardy's greatest work, owes a debt to the writings of Schopenhauer and von Hartmann. This must later be discussed. But in the second of the *Essays on Religion*, that on Theism, written between 1868 and 1870, which is Mill's last important work, there is in the third chapter dealing with the Evidences of Theism a discussion of the theory of Will as the Prime Cause. Mill, who is of course combating the argument of those who use Will as synonymous with Personality, rejects this; but he makes a comment upon it which, in conjunction with the known facts of Hardy's attitude, is highly suggestive; Mill himself is dissenting from the proposition which he describes:

> The assertion is that physical nature must have been produced by a will because nothing but will is known to us as having the power of originating the production of phenomena ... That nothing can *consciously* produce Mind but Mind is self-evident, being involved in the meaning of the words; but that there cannot be *unconscious* production must not be assumed.

It need hardly be said that the theory of the production of conscious mind by unconscious process is the very kernel and heart of *The Dynasts*. Says the Ancient Spirit of the Years:

> *The cognisance ye mourn, Life's doom to feel,*
> *If I report it meetly, came unmeant,*
> *Emerging with blind gropes from impercipience*
> *By listless sequence—luckless, tragic chance,*
> *In your more human tongue.*

To which the Pities reply:

> *And hence unneeded*
> *In the economy of Vitality,*
> *Which might have ever kept a sealed cognition*
> *As doth the Will itself.*

(Pt. I, Act v, Sc. iv.)

Until further evidence is forthcoming, the first place in which Hardy can have found the germ of that idea would seem to be the writings of John Stuart Mill, which he studied long and lovingly.

Among the writers whom Hardy studied in his twenties, and whose work left upon him a deep and lasting impression, there remains to be mentioned a poet whose name rings strangely in the porch of the philosophers. And yet a dispassionate consideration of the evidence suggests that no writer whom he read in the 'sixties impressed young Hardy more than Algernon Charles Swinburne. The nature of the impression was obviously very different from that made by the philosophers and rationalists mentioned hitherto. If J.S. Mill influenced Hardy by an appeal to his intellect, Swinburne influenced him by an appeal to his emotions. Now Hardy, for all his claims to be scientific and rational, was primarily a being of emotion, as are most great creative artists. His stature as an artist is, indeed, the measure of the depth and intensity of his emotional nature; for intellectually he is smaller than many great writers have been; smaller, to make an obvious comparison, than Browning. Even his response to philosophical stimulus was largely emotional; as may be seen in *The Dynasts*; where his broodings upon the suggestions of thinkers, from Mill to Schopenhauer and von Hartmann, issue in the cry of the Pities:

> *O, the intolerable antilogy*
> *Of making figments feel!*

> (Pt. I, Act iv, Sc. v.)

To the young architect—poet adrift in London, and still more perilously adrift upon the strange seas of thought into which the loss of religious convictions had launched him, the appearance of *Atalanta in Calydon* in 1865, of *Poems and Ballads* in 1866, of *Songs Before Sunrise* in 1871 must have been events that stirred him to his depths. There is in the Ashley Library a letter which he wrote thirty years later, in reply to a letter from Swinburne praising *The Well-beloved*, which gives a glimpse of what those experiences must have been:

> Max Gate, Dorchester. April 1st, 1897.
>
> DEAR MR SWINBURNE,
>
> I must thank you for your kind note about my fantastic little tale, which, if it can make, in its better parts, any faint claims to imaginative feeling, will owe something of such feeling to you, for I often thought of lines of yours during the writing; and indeed was not able to resist the quotation of your words now and then.
>
> And this reminds me that one day, when examining several English imitations of a well-known fragment of Sappho, I interested myself in trying to strike out a better equivalent for it than the commonplace. 'Thou, too, shalt die,' which all the translators had used during the last hundred years. I then stumbled upon your 'Thee, too, the years shall cover,' and all my spirit for poetic pains died out of me. Those few words present, I think, the finest *drama* of Death and Oblivion, so to speak, on our tongue. Having rediscovered this phrase, it carried me back to the buoyant time of thirty years ago, when I used to read your early works walking along the crowded London streets to my imminent risk of being knocked down.
>
> > Believe me to be,
> > Yours very sincerely,
> > THOMAS HARDY.[25]

Beside this letter must be placed one written when he heard of Swinburne's death in 1912, which is printed by Mrs Hardy on pp. 135–6 of *Later Years*:

For several reasons I could not bring myself to write on Swinburne immediately I heard that, to use his own words, 'Fate had undone the bondage of the gods' for him.

No doubt the press will say some good words about him now he is dead and does not care whether it says them or no. Well, I remember what it said in 1866, when he did care, and how it made the blood of some of us young men boil.[26]

Was there ever such a country—looking back at the life, work and death of Swinburne—is there any other country in Europe whose attitude towards a deceased poet of his rank would have been so ignoring and almost contemptuous? I except *The Times*, which has the fairest estimate I have yet seen. But read the *Academy* and the *Nation*.

The kindly cowardice of many papers is overwhelming him with such toleration, such theological judgments, hypocritical sympathy and misdirected eulogy that, to use his own words again, it makes one sick in a corner—or, as we say down here in Wessex, it is enough to make every little dog run to mixen.

However, we are getting on in our appreciativeness of poets. One thinks of those other two lyricists, Burns and Shelley, at this time for obvious reasons, and of how much harder it was with them. We know how Burns was treated at Dumfries, but by the time that Swinburne was a young man Burns had advanced so far as to be regarded as no worse than 'the glory and the shame of literature' (in the words of a critic of that date). As for Shelley, he was not tolerated at all in his lifetime. But Swinburne has been tolerated—at any rate since he has not written anything to speak of. And a few months ago, when old and enfeebled, he was honoured by a rumour that he had been offered a complimentary degree at Oxford. And Shelley, too, in these latter days of our memory, has been favoured so far as to be considered no lower than an ineffectual angel beating his luminous wings in vain.

I was so late in getting my poetical barge under way, and he was so early with his flotilla—besides my being between three and four years younger, and being nominally an architect (an awful imposter at that, really)—that though I read him as he came out I did not personally know him till many years after the *Poems and Ballads* year.

Three days later, Hardy wrote in his diary that it was the day of Swinburne's funeral, to which he could not go because of his rheumatism; and he thought of some of Swinburne's lines: that on Shelley: 'O sole thing sweeter than thine own songs were'; two out of *Songs Before Sunrise* (one of which, on Man, 'Save his own soul he hath no star' was used as a chapter heading in *Jude*); and one from the sonnet on Newman and Carlyle. The latter is perhaps the most significant to the present purpose. This sonnet first appeared in the *Athenaeum* of January 8th, 1876, under the title of 'Two Leaders,' who were Newman and Carlyle. In it, Swinburne bade farewell, in the words of the Athenians' Farewell to the Eumenides, to two men who represented that older order of thought which he and Hardy were the most conspicuous English writers to discard. It is significant of the influence which his older contemporary had exercised upon him that on the day of Swinburne's funeral, Hardy should have thought of this sonnet:

With all our hearts we praise you whom ye hate,
High souls that hate us; for our hopes are higher,

And higher than yours the goal of our desire,
Though high your ends be as your hearts are great.
Your world of gods and kings, of shrine and state,
Was of the night when hope and fear stood nigher,
Wherein men walked by light of stars and fire
Till man by day stood equal with his fate.
Honour, not hate, we give you, love, not fear,
Last prophets of past kind, who fill the dome
Of great dead gods with wrath and wail, nor hear
Time's word and Man's: 'Go honoured hence, go home,
Night's childless children; here your hour is done;
Pass with the stars and leave us with the sun.'[27]

It is highly significant that in both the letters reproduced here, Hardy should have quoted from the same famous poem in the notorious volume of 1866. 'Anactoria' was, indeed, after 'Dolores,' the most famous of the 'pièces damnées.' And 'Anactoria,' besides what Hardy considered the finest drama of death and oblivion in our language, contained one of the most frenzied denunciations of Providence which English poetry had produced:

Were I made as he
Who hath made all things, to break them one by one,
If my feet trod upon the stars and sun
And souls of men as his have alway trod,
God knows I might be crueller than God.

. . . . . .

Is not his incense bitterness? His meat
Murder? His hidden face and iron feet
Hath not man known, and felt them on their way
Threaten and trample all things and every day?
Hath he not sent us hunger? Who hath cursed
Spirit and flesh with longing? Filled with thirst
Their lips who cried unto him? Who bade exceed
The fervid will, fall short the feeble deed,
Bade sink the spirit and the flesh aspire,
Pain animate the dust of dead desire,
And life yield up her flower to violent fate?

Although Hardy could not go to Swinburne's funeral, he went the year after to see the grave at Bonchurch; and in memory of the 'Singer Asleep' he wrote what is by common consent one of the most beautiful of all his poems (published in *Satires of Circumstance*). To quote this poem partially is to spoil it. The allusion to Sappho is perhaps the most exquisite touch in Hardy's poetry. One stanza alone must be quoted from the poem for our present purpose:

O that far morning of a summer day
When, down a terraced street whose pavements lay
Glassing the sunshine into my bent eyes,
I walked and read with a quick glad surprise
    New words, in classic guise—

What were those words that went so near to the heart of the young poet masquerading as an architect as he walked down Adelphi Terrace? 'Anactoria,' with its drama of death and oblivion, and its astonishing blasphemy; and the 'Hymn to Proserpine,' In the third chapter of the second part of *Jude* Sue Bridehead comes home with statuettes of Apollo and Venus (whom she describes to Miss Fontover as St Peter and St Mary Magdalen); she places them in her bedroom, and enacts a strange and significant scene:

> Placing the pair of figures on the chest of drawers, a candle on each side of them, she withdrew to the bed, flung herself down thereon, and began reading a book she had taken from her box, which Miss Fontover knew nothing of. It was a volume of Gibbon, and she read the chapter dealing with the reign of Julian the Apostate. Occasionally she looked up at the statuettes, which appeared strange and out of place, there happening to be a Calvary print hanging between them, and, as if the scene suggested the action, she at length jumped up and withdrew another book from her box—a volume of verse—and turned to the familiar poem—

> *Thou hast conquered, O pale Galilean:*
> *The world has grown grey from thy breath. . .*[28]

It is certain that Hardy's memory of the 'words in classic guise' which moved him so in his youth included another volume, published the year before *Poems and Ballads*, which he perhaps came to know through them. The copy of *Atalanta in Calydon*, which is still in the Library at Max Gate, dates from the 'eighties, for in the 'sixties Hardy could not afford to buy books that he could get from Mudie. But that he knew *Atalanta* in the 'sixties is certain. In the copy still to be seen in his library, there is a pencil line drawn against the fourth Stasimon:

For now we know not of them; but one saith
The Gods are gracious, praising God; and one,
When hast thou seen? or hast thou felt his breath
Touch, nor consume thine eyelids as the sun,
Nor fill thee to the lips with fiery death?
    None hath beheld him, none;
Seen above other gods and shapes of things,
Swift without feet and flying without wings,
Intolerable, not clad with death or life,
Insatiable, not known of night or day,
The lord of love and loathing and of strife
Who gives a star and takes a sun away:

> *Who shapes the soul and makes her a barren wife*
> *To the earthly body and grievous growth of clay;*
> *Who turns the large limbs to a little flame*
> *And binds the great sea with a little sand;*
> *Who makes desire, and slays desire with shame;*
> *Who shakes the heaven as ashes in his hand;*
> *Who, seeing the light and shadow for the same,*
> *Bids day waste night as fire devours a brand,*
> *Smites without sword and scourges without rod;*
>   *The supreme evil, God.*

Hardy was twenty-five or twenty-six when first he read that. Simultaneously, he was steeping himself in the writings of agnostics—to use the phrase coined by Huxley—who proved to his satisfaction that the omnipotence of a First Cause was incompatible with its goodness. In the light of these facts, it is easy to understand *Tess of the d'Urbervilles*, with its famous ending:

> Upon the cornice of the tower a tall staff was fixed. Their eyes were riveted on it. A few minutes after the hour had struck something moved slowly up the staff, and extended itself upon the breeze. It was a black flag.
>
> 'Justice' was done, and the President of the Immortals, in Aeschylean phrase, had ended his sport with Tess.[29]

By the time that Hardy entered his thirties, the rationalism which had made so determined an onslaught in his twentieth year, had practically gained the day. Some conception of the prodigious change which had taken place in opinion inside the church itself within twenty years may be gathered by a comparison. It was in 1853 that Frederick Denison Maurice, one of the most influential figures of the religious world in his generation, was expelled from his Professorship at King's College, London, for pointing out the inconsistency between the assertion that God is love, and the assertion that the majority of the human race must, for failure to repent during the earthly life, be doomed to everlasting damnation. It was to this expulsion that Tennyson alluded in the poem addressed to Maurice. The views upon this question expressed twenty-five years later by Canon Farrar, afterwards Dean of St Paul's, in a volume of sermons called *Our Eternal Hope* published in 1878, were thus described by Leslie Stephen: Canon Farrar does not deny the existence of hell; he only thinks that fewer people will go there and perhaps find it much less disagreeable than is generally supposed.[30] But it was not only the severer doctrines of the Church which had lost their hold upon the intellect and conscience of Christian people. The Church itself, and the religion for which it stood, had lost their hold upon a large section of the English public. The position is described by Matthew Arnold in the Preface to *Literature and Dogma*. How much Arnold's own beliefs had been shaken is evident in such a poem as 'Dover Beach.' But he never became a complete agnostic; his plea, in *Literature and Dogma*, is that the assertion concerning a

282

Great Primal Cause, which is unverifiable, must be replaced by that of 'an enduring Power, not ourselves, that makes for righteousness.' Thus far, Arnold himself remained in agreement with the church. But he wrote in 1873:

> And yet, with all this agreement, both in words and in things, when we behold the clergy and ministers of religion lament the neglect of religion and aspire to restore it, how much one must feel that to restore religion as they understand it, to re-enthrone the Bible as explained by our current theology, whether learned or popular, is absolutely and forever impossible!—as impossible as to restore the predominance of the feudal system, or the belief in witches. Let us admit that the Bible cannot possibly die; but then the churches cannot even conceive the Bible without the gloss they at present put upon it; and this gloss, as certainly, cannot possibly live. And it is not a gloss which one church or sect puts upon the Bible and another does not; it is the gloss they all put upon it, and call the substratum of belief common to all Christian churches, and largely shared by them even with natural religion. It is this so-called axiomatic basis which must go, and it supports all the rest; and if the Bible were really inseparable from this, and depended upon it, then Mr Bradlaugh[31] would have his way, and the Bible would go too; for this basis is inevitably doomed. For whatever is to stand must rest upon something that is verifiable, and not unverifiable. Now the assumption with which all the churches and sects set out, that there is a great Personal First Cause, the moral and intelligent Governor of the Universe, and that from Him the Bible derives its authority, can never be verified.[32]

While, upon one hand, a large proportion of the intellectual world of England was taking the direction which Matthew Arnold, the apostle of culture, took; on the other some misguided champions of orthodoxy took steps ill-judged to conciliate thinking minds. One such step, which had very wide publicity at the time, may be described in the words used by Leslie Stephen, in an article entitled 'An Agnostic's Apology,' which first appeared in the *Fortnightly Review* in June 1876:

> Not long ago there appeared in the papers a string of propositions framed— so we were assured—by some of the most candid and most learned of living theologians. These propositions defined by the help of various languages the precise relations which exist between the persons of the Trinity. It is an odd, though far from an unprecedented, circumstance that the unbeliever cannot quote them for fear of profanity. If they were translated into the pages of the *Fortnightly Review* it would be impossible to convince anyone that the intention was not to mock the simple-minded persons who, we must suppose, were not themselves intentionally irreverent. It is enough to say that they defined the nature of God Almighty with an accuracy from which modest naturalists would shrink in describing the genesis of a black beetle.

There is a reference to this same manifesto in *Literature and Dogma*, where Arnold characterized it as 'the faiery tale of the three Lord Shaftesburys'; and the gentle Arnold was devout if compared to Leslie Stephen. It was because Stephen exercised no small influence over the mind of Hardy in the 'seventies that he is of importance to this inquiry.

283

It is the literary side of Leslie Stephen's activities which has proved the most enduring. We think of him to-day primarily as the moving spirit of the *Dictionary of National Biography*, or as the author of *Hours in a Library*, rather than as a philosopher. If we connect him with philosophy at all, it is with the philosophy of an age not his own, as the author of the *History of English Thought in the Eighteenth Century*. But during the third quarter of the nineteenth century he was a militant rationalist, and proved himself one of the most acrimonious controversialists of that age of bitter controversy. His articles on questions of religion are mostly collected into two volumes: *Essays on Freethinking and Plain Speaking* and *An Agnostic's Apology*, published in 1873 and 1893 respectively. Nearly all of them first appeared during the 'seventies and early 'eighties in the pages of the *Fortnightly Review* or in those of *Frazer's Magazine*. Hardy first became acquainted with Stephen in 1871, when the latter was Editor of the *Cornhill Magazine*. The literary side of this relationship belongs to the history of *Far from the Madding Crowd*. It was really to Stephen that Hardy owed the secure establishment of his reputation as a novelist. The two men remained close friends for some years. *The Hand of Ethelberta* came out under Stephen's command, following *Far from the Madding Crowd* in the *Cornhill*. Stephen refused *The Return of the Native* in 1877. They continued in correspondence until the early 'eighties, after which they lost sight of each other for many years. *The Life and Letters of Leslie Stephen*, by F.W. Maitland, contains half a chapter by Hardy (p. 270 *et seq.*), as well as the poem on the Schreckhorn 'With Thoughts of Leslie Stephen,' afterwards reprinted in *Satires of Circumstance*.

It is a curious thing that the writers on Hardy's philosophy should have overlooked Leslie Stephen. The probability is very strong that, given the known facts of their close friendship during Hardy's early thirties and Hardy's state of mind at that time, the older man would try to persuade the younger into his own rationalistic attitude. There is also unmistakable evidence of this influence in Hardy's writings. But Mrs Hardy puts the matter beyond possible doubt. She makes two definite statements:

> On a visit to London in the winter (of 1873) Hardy had made the personal acquaintance of Leslie Stephen, the man whose philosophy was to influence his own for many years, indeed, more than that of any other contemporary. (*Early Life*, p. 132.)
>
> Since coming into contact with Leslie Stephen about 1873, Hardy had been much influenced by his philosophy and also by his criticism. (*Early Life*, p. 167.)

The general tone of Stephen's rationalist essays can best be shown by quotations. The *Fortnightly Review* for March 1873, when Hardy was becoming personally intimate with him, contained an article by Stephen called 'Are we Christians?' In this he examined evidence of Christian attitude and conduct in England:

> Are we to look to those popular platitudes which bring down the applause of crowded audiences and sell cheap newspapers by the hundred thousand? From them we may learn, for example, that the British workman will not have the Bible excluded from his schools, and will not have the Sunday desecrated. Certainly these are two of the most definite points in the popular creed. Our reverence for the Bible is, as Dr Newman tells us, the strong point of Protestantism; and our observance of the Sunday is the one fact which tells a foreigner that we have a religious faith. No one, whatever his opinions, should undervalue those beliefs, or, if they must so be called, superstitions. An English Sunday, with all its gloom and with all its drunkenness, is a proof that we do in fact worship something besides our stomachs.

The word 'agnostic' came into general use in the early 'seventies. It is said that it was suggested by Huxley at a party held previous to the formation of the Metaphysical Society at Mr James Knowle's house on Clapham Common one evening in 1869. Huxley took it from St Paul's mention of the altar to the Unknown God.[33] In the *Fortnightly Review* for June 1876, Leslie Stephen published an article entitled 'An Agnostic's Apology,' already quoted in which he contended that the position of Agnostic was the only one compatible with intellectual honesty, and in which he gave very short shrift to his opponents:

> Let us then ask once more, does Christianity exhibit the ruler of the universe as benevolent or as just? If I were to assert that of every ten beings born into this world, nine would be damned, that all who refused to believe what they did not hold to be proved, and all who sinned from overwhelming temptation, and all who had not the good fortune to be the subjects of a miraculous conversion or the recipients of a grace conveyed by a magical charm, would be tortured to all eternity, what would an orthodox theologian reply? He could not say 'That is false'; I might appeal to the highest authorities for my justification; nor, in fact, could he on his own showing deny the possibility. Hell, he says, exists; he does not know who will be damned; though he does know that all men are by nature corrupt and liable to be damned if not saved by supernatural grace. He might, and probably would, now say: 'That is rash. You have no authority for saying how many will be lost and how many saved; you cannot even say what is meant by hell or heaven; you cannot tell how far God may be better than His word, though you may be sure that He won't be worse than His word.' And what is all this, but to say We know nothing about it? In other words, to fall back on Agnosticism. The difficulty, as theologians truly say, is not so much that evil is eternal as that evil exists. That is in substance a frank admission that, as nobody can explain evil, nobody can explain anything. Your revelation, which was to prove the benevolence of God, has proved only that God's benevolence may be consistent with the eternal and infinite misery of most of His creatures; you escape only by saying that it is also consistent with their not being eternally and infinitely miserable. That is, the revelation reveals nothing.

Of an attitude of mind savouring distinctly of Leslie Stephen there are many traces in *Tess*. Perhaps the clearest are to be found in the fourteenth and the eighteenth chapters, both in connection with ecclesiastics. The first is the parson to whom Tess comes to ask if her baptism of her baby Sorrow is as effective as his would have been: 'Having the natural feelings of a tradesman at finding that a job he should have been called in for had been unskilfully botched by his customers among themselves, he was disposed to say no.' And again, when he replies that it will be just the same whether the poor little body is buried in Christian burial or not: 'How the Vicar reconciled his answer with the strict notions he supposed himself to hold on these subjects it is beyond a layman's power to tell, though not to excuse.' Had Leslie Stephen written *Tess*, he would have made both answers 'no.' He might, however, have written the phrase describing Angel Clare's father: 'A firm believer—not as the phrase is now elusively construed by theological thimble-riggers in the church and out of it, but in the old and ardent sense of the Evangelical School.' The 'theological thimble-riggers' is an echo of Stephen's article on the Broad Church.[34] The whole matter of Angel's beliefs, however, is a particularly interesting one, as there seems reason to believe that Hardy is here giving a piece of his own spiritual autobiography. It must be remembered that Hardy had neither the asperity nor the pugnacity of Stephen.[35] Hardy, moreover, retained all his life a sort of affection for the English Church, of which he had once wished to become a priest, even though he no longer believed her creeds; and he used occasionally to go to a service almost until he died. It is significant that Stephen, who had started life as a tutor at Cambridge entitled 'The Reverend Leslie Stephen,' chose Hardy as witness to his deed renunciatory of Holy Orders.[36] But Hardy came in later years to feel that 'rationalists err as far in one direction as Revelationists or Mystics in the other.' The same notes from which this is taken contain other entries, which are most revealing, and pathetic:

> We enter church, and we have to say 'We have erred and strayed from thy ways like lost sheep,' when what we want to say is 'Why are we made to err and stray like lost sheep?' Then we have to sing 'My soul doth magnify the Lord,' when what we want to sing is 'O that my soul could find some Lord that it could magnify!' Till it can, let us magnify good works, and develop all means of easing mortals' progress through a world not worthy of them.[37]

A word must be said of a philosopher with whose writings Hardy certainly became acquainted during the 'seventies. Mrs Hardy says that it was about 1873 that he read Comte.[38] She also reproduces an extract from his diary for 1880:

> If Comte had introduced Christ among the worthies in his calendar, it would have made Positivism tolerable to thousands who, from position, family connection or early education, now decry what in their heart of hearts they hold to contain the germs of a true system.[39]

There is also a reference to Comte in the Preface to *Late Lyrics*; and another in the article 'Candour in English Fiction,' written in 1889. It would have been strange had Hardy not read Comte; for, from the time when the writings of the French philosopher became available in English about the middle of the century,[40] 'Positivism' became a very popular word; although whether all those who so lightly bandied it about had ever looked into Comte's work may be doubted. To such an extent did this word enter into the popular vocabulary, that it caused great annoyance to other philosophers to whom it was applied indiscriminately. The Essays of Herbert Spencer contain a vigorous protest against this affiliation; and Huxley made an attack on Positivism in an essay 'The Scientific Aspects of Positivism' in *Lay Sermons* (1870), in which he wrote:

> It has been a source of periodical irritation to me to find M. Comte put forward as a representative of scientific thought; and to observe that writers whose philosophy had its legitimate parent in Hume or in themselves were labelled 'Comtists' or 'Positivists' by public writers, even in spite of vehement protests to the contrary. It has cost Mr Mill hard rubbings to get that label off; and I watch Mr Spencer as one regards a good man struggling with adversity, still engaged in eluding its adhesiveness, and ready to tear away skin and all rather than let it stick. My own turn might come next.

That the philosophy of Auguste Comte had no small influence in England in the latter half of the last century is undeniable. George Eliot was a student of Comte; and even many of those who were not were yet affected by ideas in the air which derived from him. For example, Swinburne, whom no one has yet accused of being a Comtist, was voicing the essential doctrine of the 'Philosophie positive' when he wrote in *Songs Before Sunrise*: 'Not each man of all men is God, but God is the fruit of the whole.' Comte did, in fact, attempt to devise an immanentist religion in which a transcendent God was displaced by Humanity, conceived as a single entity and advancing towards perfection:

> A deeper study of the great universal order reveals to us at length the ruling power within it of the true Great Being, whose destiny it is to bring that order continually to perfection by constantly conforming to its laws.

The lengths to which Comte developed his Religion of Humanity caused Huxley to describe it as 'ultramontane Christianity without Christ.' This doctrine can never have been very congenial to Hardy who never had any such bent towards sociological idealism as had Shelley or Swinburne. He naturally read Comte; but it is doubtful whether he took anything from him. The hope of the gradual perfection of the world order which is faintly suggested in *The Dynasts* bears very little, if any, resemblance to anything in Comte. As far as it was not Hardy's own, it was the fruit of hints from J.S. Mill, and von Hartmann. Moreover, cognate ideas were common enough in the later nineteenth century; they are to be found, for instance in Renan.[41] In many important respects, the ideas which Comte entertained for the emergence of a better order of things were diametrically opposed to those of Hardy.[42]

It was towards the close of the eighteen-seventies that there crept over Hardy a deep and incurable nostalgia, very clearly to be traced in his writing. He had never been gay. The author of *A Pair of Blue Eyes* was a potential—

perhaps more than a potential—tragedian. There is tragedy of a kind in *Far from the Madding Crowd*. But the tragedy darkens in *The Return of the Native*; and, above all, it takes a philosophical tinge of universality for which we should seek vainly in the early writings. It can best be illustrated by example. In the very first, famous, chapter of *The Return* we may read:

> The new Vale of Tempe may be a gaunt waste in Thule; human souls may find themselves in closer and closer harmony with external things wearing a sombreness distasteful to our race when it was young. The time seems near, if it has not actually arrived, when the chastened sublimity of a moor, a sea, or a mountain will be all of nature that is absolutely in keeping with the moods of the more thinking among mankind.

In the fifth chapter of the second book, Yeobright's face is described:

> He already showed that thought is a disease of the flesh, and indirectly bore evidence that ideal physical beauty is incompatible with emotional development and a full recognition of the coil of things.

The beginning of the third book contains a still more significant passage:

> The truth seems to be that a long line of disillusive centuries has permanently displaced the Hellenic idea of life, or whatever it may be called. What the Greeks only suspected, we know well; what their Aeschylus imagined, our nursery children feel.[43] That old-fashioned revelling in the general situation grows less and less possible as we uncover the defects of natural laws, and see the quandary that man is in by their operation.

The Return of the Native was written in 1877. By that time, the first wave of enthusiasm over the theory of evolution had spent its force, and it was giving place to a profound disillusion. For such men as Hardy, science had utterly destroyed the basis of religion. And, at least in Hardy's case, it had not left him the permanent consolation of a perpetual 'progress' in its stead. It was inevitable that he should now be writing about 'the defects of natural laws and the quandary that man is in by their operation.'

Hardy was not the only writer who had come to despair over the plight of humanity. The 'seventies saw the appearance of one of the most profoundly sorrowful writings in the English language. On March 22nd, 1874, James Thomson's *City of Dreadful Night* began to appear in the pages of the *National Reformer*, a periodical which had been founded by a group of free-thinkers in 1860, and which was conducted for some thirty years by Charles Bradlaugh. This poem is a most eloquent illustration of the pessimism produced by the free-thinking crusaders of the mid-century, who had destroyed religion for many minds, and had given nothing in return but a deterministic nihilism. Without suggesting that Hardy was especially influenced by Thomson, it is interesting to show how Thomson expressed ideas which were later made more famous by Hardy. The substance of much of the philosophical argument in *The Dynasts* is given by the Preacher in the Church in the *City of Dreadful Night*:

We bow down to the universal laws,
Which never had for man a special clause
Of cruelty or kindness, love or hate.
If toads and vultures are obscene to sight,
If tigers burn with beauty and with might,
Is it by favour or by wrath of fate?

All substance lives and struggles evermore
Through countless shapes continually at war,
By countless interactions interknit:
If one is born a certain day on earth,
All times and forces tended to that birth,
Nor all the world could change or hinder it.

I find no hint throughout the Universe
Of good or ill, of blessing or of curse;
I find alone Necessity supreme;
With infinite Mystery, abysmal, dark,
Unlighted ever by the faintest spark
For us the flitting shadows of a dream.

There is a famous passage in the fourth chapter of *Tess*, in which Tess's little brother asks her if the stars are worlds; and in which the girl is made to reply that they are worlds, like apples on the stubbard tree, and that we live on a blighted one. And in the fourth chapter of *Two on a Tower*, St Cleeve is expounding some of the mysteries of astronomy to Lady Constantine. He says that twenty million stars are visible in a powerful telescope; 'So that, whatever the stars were made for, they were not made to please our eyes. It is just the same in everything. Nothing was made for man.'

He then goes on to expound to her the size of the stellar universe, which is of that order which reaches ghastliness:

> And to add a new weirdness to what the sky possesses in its size and formlessness, there is involved the quality of decay. For all the wonder of these everlasting stars, eternal spheres, and what not, they are not everlasting, they are not eternal; they burn out like candles. You see that dying one in the body of the great Bear? Two centuries ago it was as bright as the others. The senses may become terrified by plunging among them as they are, but there is a pitifulness even in their glory. Imagine them all extinguished, and your mind feeling its way through a heaven of total darkness, occasionally striking against the black invisible cinders of those stars. . .

That could only have been written in the later nineteenth century. The theory of the universe upon which it is based is described by Sir James Jeans in the first chapter of *The Mysterious Universe*. But what were only theories concerning supposed physical facts to the scientists, became terrible to the artists who invested them with philosophical significance:

With such a living light these dead eyes shine,
These eyes of sightless heaven, that as we gaze
We read a pity, tremulous, divine
Or cold majestic scorn in their pure rays.
Fond man! They are not haughty, are not tender;
There is no heart or mind in all their splendour,
They thread mere puppets all their marvellous maze.

If we could near them with the flight unflown,
We should but find them worlds as sad as this,
Or suns all self-consuming like our own
Enringed by planet worlds as much amiss:
They wax and wane through fusion and confusion;
The spheres eternal are a grand illusion,
The empyrean is a void abyss.

When Edward Fitzgerald, in the 'fifties, was producing the remarkable poem, which is called a translation from Omar Khayyám, but which contains much that is so typical of the pessimism of the later nineteenth century in England, he was anticipating Thomson by twenty years. The first edition of his Rubáiyát in 1859 was stillborn. But by the 'eighties it had reached four editions; for then many had come to believe, with Hardy, that 'nothing is made for man.' And Fitzgerald bears the same burden as Thomson:

And that inverted bowl we call the sky,
Whereunder cooped we crawling live and die,
Lift not thy hands to it for help—for it
Rolls impotently on, as thou or I.

When the century had grown beyond its threescore years and ten, the strength of its thought indeed turned to labour and sorrow.

It is, then, against the whole background that has been outlined, that Hardy's later work must be regarded if we are to understand the deepening and darkening of his inspiration. If, in 1877, he wrote of the quandary in which man finds himself through the operation of defective natural laws, it was because the canker of thought had been at work. If, in 1880, he shuddered at the horrible abyss of heaven and grieved that nothing had been made for man, it was because he had eaten of the fruit of the Tree of Knowledge. Therefore, writing of the Dorsetshire labourer in *Longman's Magazine*, in July 1883, he wrote: 'It is among such communities as these that happiness will find her last refuge upon earth, since it is among them that a perfect insight into the conditions of existence will be longest postponed.' Therefore, the conclusion of *The Mayor of Casterbridge*, written in 1885, is that happiness is but an occasional episode in the general drama of pain.

290

Whether or no the physicists of the seventeenth century were right when they said that nature abhors a vacuum, it is certainly true that human natures does. Having reached a stage of spiritual vacuum by about 1880, Hardy seems to have set about trying to fill it by reading philosophy. As has already been shown, this was not the favourite of his younger years; and apart from such occasional allusions as might be found in the writing of any well-educated man, there is hardly a trace of philosophy, in the technical sense of the word, in his early works. Philosophy became the study of his middle life. On the last day of 1901 he wrote in his diary:

> After reading various philosophic systems, and being struck with their contradictions and futilities, I have come to this: Let every man make a philosophy for himself out of his own experience. He will not be able to escape using terms and phraseology from earlier philosophers, but let him avoid adopting their theories if he values his own mental life. Let him remember the fate of Coleridge, and save years of labour by working out his own views as given him by his surroundings.[44]

When he was eighty, he composed a ditty which appears in *Winter Words*:

'Our Old Friend Dualism'

All hail to him, the Protean! A tough old chap is he;
Spinoza and the monists cannot make him cease to be.
We pound him with out 'Truth, Sir, please!' and quite appear to still him:
He laughs, holds Bergson up, and James; and swears we cannot kill him.
We argue them pragmatic cheats. 'Aye,' says he. 'They're deceiving:
But I must live; for flamens plead I am all that's worth believing!'

To this had the study of philosophy brought him in his old age ... It is, however, very interesting to trace the beginning of his philosophical studies in his writing in the mid-'eighties. They are very clearly visible in *The Woodlanders*, which was begun in 1885, and finished during 1886; where they are exemplified in the person of Fitzpiers, and his studies in philosophy. To avoid falling into the error of some of the earnest American thesis writers, it must be admitted that Hardy sometimes had his tongue in his cheek, even on the subject of philosophy. He makes Grammar Oliver describe Fitzpiers thus:

> And yet he's a projick, and says the oddest of rozums. 'Ah Grammer, he said at another time, 'Let me tell you that Everything is Nothing. There's only Me and Not Me in the whole world.' And he told me that no man's hands could help what they did, any more than the hands of a clock.

But Hardy was now too much sicklied o'er with the pale cast of thought to jest as he had jested in *Far from the Madding Crowd*. Two pages later we are made to follow Melbury and his daughter into a wood which at once confronts us again with the problem of the Universe:

291

> Here, as everywhere, the Unfulfilled Intention, which makes life what it is, was as obvious as it could be among the depraved crowds of a city slum. The leaf was deformed, the curve was crippled, the taper was interrupted; the lichen ate the vigour of the stalk, and the ivy slowly strangled to death the promising sapling.

This could be compared to many of Hardy's poems. It was in an attempt to solve the riddle of the Unfulfilled Intention that he turned to the philosophers, with their enigmas of 'Me and Not Me.' That Fitzpiers quotes Spinoza (in Chap. XVI), and Schleiermacher (in Chap. XIX), is in itself little. What is significant is that Hardy should now be studying the problem of the 'ipsa hominis essentia,' and the riddle of Reality. How this study progressed could easily be illustrated out of *Tess* and *Jude*. But so many catalogues have already been made of the passages in which Tess is described as a 'psychological phenomenon', and what not, that time need not be wasted in repeating them. Moreover, they are largely misleading. The character of Marty South, the pity and the beauty of the life and death of Tess, which are great possessions in our literature, owe nothing to Hardy's wrestlings with the theories of the 'Thing-in-Itself.' The work which does owe something of its essential character to Hardy's speculations upon the nature of reality and the Universe, and to his philosophical studies during the last fifteen years of the century, is *The Dynasts*.

The subject of the philosophy of *The Dynasts* has by now been discussed almost *ad nauseam*. It was naturally pounced upon by the reviewers when the work first appeared, with its provocative preface about 'the wide prevalence of the Monistic theory of the Universe ... and the abandonment of the masculine pronoun in allusions to the First or Fundamental Energy.' The author of the article on *The Dynasts* in the *Edinburgh Review* in 1908 took Hardy severely to task[45]; and all the critics since that date have had their say about the philosophy of *The Dynasts*. It would probably be difficult to improve upon the original verdict pronounced upon the First Part by Max Beerbohm:

> The book closes, and (so surely has it cast its spell upon us) seems quite a fugitive and negligible piece of work. We wonder why Mr Hardy wrote it; or rather, one regrets that the Immanent Will put him to the trouble of writing it. 'Wot's the good of anythink? Wy, Nothink!' was the refrain of a popular coster song some years ago, and Mr Hardy has set it ringing in our ears again. But presently the mood passes. And, even as in the stage directions of *The Dynasts* we see specks becoming mountain tops, so do we begin to realise that we have been reading a really great book.
> Cries Mr Hardy's Spirit of the Pities:
>
> > *This tale of Will,*
> > *And Life's impulsion by Incognisance*
> > *I cannot take.*
>
> Nor can I. But I can take, and treasure with all gratitude, the book in which that tale is told so finely.[46]

The same thing was said more seriously by Dr Lascelles Abercrombie when he wrote of the supernatural part of *The Dynasts*: 'It would be easy to say that as a philosophy of existence, this will not do. But as a tragedy of existence it is surely magnificent.'[47]

So much has been written about Hardy's real or supposed debt to Schopenhauer that there would appear little left to be said. While Gosse maintained that Hardy's philosophy was complete by 1874, that he had never then heard of Schopenhauer, and that he owed nothing to Schopenhauer whatever,[48] Brennecke in *Thomas Hardy's Universe*, derives the entire scheme of *The Dynasts* from *Die Welt als Wille und Vorstellung*, and wholly ignores everything that Hardy read in the first forty-five years of his life. Both these positions are obviously untenable. In a well-written but rather slight essay published at Philadelphia in 1911, Helen Garwood discussed the resemblances between Hardy and Schopenhauer, and came to the conclusion that:

> The two men are not entirely alike in the details of their problem, not at all alike in their solution; they are alike in starting from the same basis, the basis of utter purposelessness. It might be possible to parallel many a passage in Schopenhauer with a like one in Hardy. Such a process is neither entertaining nor entirely trustworthy. It savours too much of seeing what we want to see. But without unduly stretching the material to fit the theory, it is possible to say that they are alike in the spirit which drives them to utterance.[49]

Without being dogmatic, it is possible by a few quotations to suggest what Hardy may have owed to Schopenhauer, as it has been suggested what he owed to Herbert Spencer and J. S. Mill. It is essential to remember, as critics in their haste for affiliations have not always done, that Hardy did not read German with ease; and that it can therefore only be a question of English translations when the subject of his debt to German philosophy is raised. There had been some talk of Schopenhauer in England during the 'seventies.[50] But the first English version of *Die Welt als Wille und Vorstellung* was that by Haldane and Kemp, which was published in three volumes in 1883. Hardy bought this book, and it is still in his library.

In the second book of *The World as Will and Idea*, which treats of the objectification of the Will, Schopenhauer defines Will, and explains his preference for the concept of Will to that of Force as the underlying Principle of the Universe. He then, in Section 23, continues:

> The *Will* as a thing in itself is quite different from its phenomenal appearance, and entirely free from all the forms of the phenomenal, into which it first passes when it manifests itself, and which therefore only concern its objectivity … The uncaused nature of will has been actually recognised, where it manifests itself most distinctly, as the will of man, and this has been called free, independent. But on account of the uncaused nature of the will itself, the necessity to which its manifestation is everywhere subjected has been overlooked, and actions are treated as free, which they are not … The fact is overlooked that the individual, the person, is not will as a thing-in-itself, but is a

phenomenon of will, is already determined as such, and has come under the form of the phenomenal, the principle of sufficient reason. Hence arises the strange fact that everyone believes himself *a priori* to be perfectly free, even in his individual actions and thinks that at every moment he can commence another manner of life. But *a posteriori*, through experience, he finds to his astonishment that he is not free, but subjected to necessity.

This is the doctrine which the Pities find so hard to accept in the Forescene of *The Dynasts*, even when shown the 'anatomy of the Immanent Will,' which, says the Spirit of Years, is:

> *the while unguessed*
> *Of those it stirs, who (even as ye do) dream*
> *Their motions free, their orderings supreme;*
> *Each life apart from each, with power to mete*
> *Its own day's measures; balanced, self-complete;*
> *Though they subsist but atoms of the One*
> *Labouring through all, divisible from none;*
> *But this no further now. Deem yet man's deeds self-done.*

In Section 25, Schopenhauer deals with the unity of the will:

The thing-in-itself is, as such, free from all forms of knowledge, even the most universal, that of being an object for the subject. In other words, the thing-in-itself, is something altogether different from the idea.[51] If, now, this thing is the *will*, as I believe I have fully and convincingly proved it to be, then, regarded as such and apart from its manifestation, it lies outside time and space and therefore knows no multiplicity and is consequently *one*.[52] Yet, as I have said, it is not one in the sense in which an individual or a concept is one, but as something to which the condition of the possibility of multiplicity, the *principium individuationis*, is foreign. The multiplicity of things in space and time, which collectively constitutes the objectification of the will, does not affect the will itself, which remains individual notwithstanding it.

In Section 28 there is a further remark upon the unity of the will:

As the magic-lantern shows many different pictures which are all made visible by one and the same light, so in all the multifarious phenomena which fill the world together or throng after each other as events, only *one will* manifests itself, of which everything is the visibility, the objectivity, and which remains unmoved in the midst of this change; it alone is thing-in-itself; all objects are manifestations, or, to speak the language of Kant, phenomena.

In Section 29, Schopenhauer deals with the question:

Every will is a will towards something, has an object, an end of its willing; what then is the final end, or towards what is that will striving that is exhibited to us as the being-in-itself of the world? This question rests, like so many others, upon the confusion of the thing-in-itself with its manifestations. The principle of sufficient reason, of which the law of motivation is also a form, extends only to the latter, not to the former. It is only of phenomena, of individual things, that a ground can be given, never of the will itself.

Schopenhauer's conclusion on the subject of the will is this:

> In fact, freedom from all aim, from all limits, belongs to the nature of the will, which is an endless striving ... Eternal becoming, an endless flux, characterizes the revelation of the inner nature of the will.

This is the constant burden of the Spirits in *The Dynasts*. As good an example as any is to be found in the antiphonal chant of the semichoruses of the Ironic Spirits during Waterloo (Pt. 3, Act vii, Sc. viii):

> *Of Its doings if It knew*
> *What It does It would not do!*
> *Since It knows not, what far sense*
> *Speeds its spinnings in the Immense?*
> *None; a fixed foresightless dream*
> *Is Its whole philosopheme.*
> *Just so; an unconscious planning,*
> *Like a potter raptly panning!*
> *Are then Love and Light its aim—*
> *Good its glory, Bad its blame?*
> *Nay; to alter evermore*
> *Things from what they were before.*

Although, as has been shown, he may have taken a hint from Herbert Spencer twenty years before, there cannot be any doubt that it was Hardy's reading in Schopenhauer after 1884 which determined the final form of the poem on the Napoleonic wars which he had long been meditating.[53] The correspondence between the presentation of the Immanent Will in *The Dynasts*, and Schopenhauer's discussion of the objectification of the Will in the second book of *The World as Will and Idea*, cannot be merely fortuitous. Brennecke rightly claims that the evidence of the language alone would refute such a theory. An interesting point of detail is the conception of Napoleon. In Section 26 of his second book, Schopenhauer, considering man as an objectification of the Will, writes:

> Motives do not determine the character of a man, but only the phenomena of his character, that is his actions; the outward fashion of his life, not its inner meaning and content. These proceed from the character which is the immediate manifestation of the will, and is therefore groundless ... Whether a man shows his badness in petty acts of injustice, cowardly tricks and low knavery which he practises in the narrow sphere of his circumstances, or whether as a conqueror he oppresses nations, throws a world into lamentation and sheds the blood of millions; this is the outward form of his manifestation, that which is unessential to it, and depends upon the circumstances in which fate has placed him, upon his surroundings, upon external influences, upon motives, but his decision upon these motives can never be explained from them; it proceeds from the will, of which man is a manifestation.

It has often been brought as a criticism against *The Dynasts* that Napoleon is a mere puppet. Says the Spirit of the Years at Ulm:

> *So let him speak, the while we clearly sight him*
> *Moved like a figure on a lantern slide.*
> *Which, much amazing uninitiate eyes,*
> *The all-compelling crystal pane but drags*
> *Whither the showman wills—*

(Pt. 2, Act iv, Sc. vi.)

Hardy, possibly partly under the influence of Haeckel (whose *Riddle of the Universe*, translated into English in 1900, he must have read just before writing *The Dynasts*), was a much more thorough determinist than Schopenhauer, who was born in the eighteenth century. In the chorus of the Spirits before Austerlitz, the Ironic Spirits ask:

> *O Innocents, can ye forget*
> *That things to be were shaped and set*
> *Ere mortals and this planet met?*

And Hardy would have said that the surroundings, external influences and motives which are the phenomena of a man's character, proceed as much from the 'All urging Will, raptly magnipotent,' as does the inner nature of the man himself—the *ipsa hominis essentia*, as Spinoza called it.

The fourth book of *The World as Will and Idea* deals with the assertion and denial of the will, and contains an elaborate exposition of the necessity of universal suffering. There is a close similarity between the tone of this and that of Hardy's last works on a large scale, especially *Jude*:

> It is really incredible how meaningless and void of significance when looked on from without, how dull and unenlightened by intellect when felt from within, is the course of the life of the great majority of men. It is a weary longing and complaining, a dreamlike staggering through the four ages of life to death, accompanied by a series of trivial thoughts. Such men are like clockwork, which is wound up, and goes it knows not why; and every time a man is begotten and born, the clock of human life is wound up anew to repeat the same old piece it has played innumerable times before, passage after passage, measure after measure, with insignificant variations. Every individual, every human being and his course of life, is but another short dream of the endless spirit of nature, of the persistent will to live; is only another fleeting form, which it carelessly sketches on its infinite page, space and time, allows to remain for a time so short that it vanishes into nothing in comparison with these, and then obliterates to make new room. And yet, and here lies the serious side of life, every one of these fleeting forms, these empty fancies, must be paid for by the whole will to live, in all its activity, with many and deep sufferings and finally with a bitter death.

In the nineteenth chapter of *Tess of the d'Urbervilles*, Tess says to Angel Clare:

> What's the use of learning that I am one of a long row only—finding out that there is set down in some old book somebody just like me and to know that I shall only act her part; making me sad, that's all. The best is not to remember that your nature and your past doings have been just like thousands' and thousands', and that your coming life and doings'll be like thousands' and thousands'.

Such sentiment is depressing stuff. And there is a large quantity of it in Schopenhauer. The realization that Hardy steeped himself in such reading helps to an understanding of *Jude the Obscure*. The paragraph quoted might, indeed, be the text upon which *Jude* is a sermon; and it explains why, to many critics and readers, *Jude* is so much inferior to Hardy's great novels; for out of futility it is not possible to make anything great. That *Jude* was largely the result of Hardy's reading in Schopenhauer is, of course, only conjecture. The conjecture is, however, supported by one very significant piece of internal evidence. The last part of the fourth book of *The World as Will and Idea* is devoted to the denial of the will to live. Schopenhauer preaches that the overcoming of suffering and the attainment of peace can be achieved through the denial of the will to live by asceticism and self-denial. It is, he says, only by denying the will to live, of which his own body is the objectification, that man can pierce the veil of Maya and escape from the *principium individuationis*. In the horrible second chapter of the sixth part of *Jude the Obscure*, when Arabella's son Time has hanged Sue's children and himself, Jude says:

> It was in his nature to do it. The Doctor says there are such boys springing up amongst us—boys of a sort unknown in the last generation—the outcome of new views of life. They seem to see all its terrors before they are old enough to have staying power to resist them. *He says it is the beginning of the coming universal wish not to live.*

Now, although Schopenhauer devotes an entire section (69) to suicide, which he demonstrates to be actually the strongest possible assertion of the will to live, and which he calls 'the masterpiece of Maya,' it can hardly be denied that the man who wrote the words just quoted from *Jude* had been reading the chapter on the denial of the will to live. His speech betrays him.

In connection with the metaphysics of *The Dynasts*, there is another philosopher to be mentioned to whom Hardy once acknowledged that he owed something. The nature of the debt is not difficult to show, although the only attempt hitherto made to draw a 'parallelism' between Hardy and Eduard von Hartmann is most unsatisfactory.[54] In a volume entitled *Real Conversations* which William Archer published in 1904, there is one with Hardy. In the course of it he reports Hardy as saying:

> A ghost story that should convince me would make me a happier man. And if you come to that, I don't know that the grotesqueness, the incompleteness of the manifestations (of spiritualism) is at all conclusive against their genuineness. Is not this incompleteness a characteristic of all phenomena, of the universe at large? It often seems to me like a half-expressed, an ill-expressed, idea. Do you

know Hartmann's philosophy of the Unconscious? It suggested to me what seems almost like a workable theory of the great problem of the origin of evil—though this, of course, is not Hartmann's own theory—namely, that there may be a consciousness, infinitely far off, at the other end of the chain of phenomena ...?

It is much to be regretted that Archer did not simply confess his ignorance of von Hartmann, and bring Hardy out a little further, instead of trying to cover it up, and drawing a red herring across the trail by talking about the Manichaean heresy. His further report of Hardy's words shows that he did not understand what Hardy was referring to. But there is enough to show that Hardy did speak of *The Philosophy of the Unconscious*.

Von Hartmann began to be discussed in England in the later 'seventies.[55] *Die Philosophie des Unbewusstes* was translated into English by W.C. Coupland, and published in three volumes in 1884. Even if Hardy had not said so, there would be no doubt that he had read this work; especially that part of it which deals with the metaphysics of the Unconscious. It is curious that he should have told Archer at the beginning of the century what is obviously true, namely, that Hartmann had suggested to him a working theory of the origin of evil, which he embodied in *The Dynasts* as the theory of the unconscious nature of the First Cause; and then that he should later have claimed entire originality for the theory of the gradual emergence of consciousness, which is an integral part of von Hartmann's philosophy. This theory peeps out in places elsewhere, but is adumbrated in set terms in the After Scene. The Spirit of the Pities says to the Spirit of the Years:

> *Thou arguest still the Inadvertent Mind.*
> *But even so, shall blankness be for aye?*
> *Men gained cognition from the flux of time,*
> *And wherefore not the Force informing them,*
> *When far-ranged aions past all fathoming*
> *Shall have swung by, and stand as backward years?*

And *The Dynasts* ends upon the hope of

> '*Consciousness the Will informing, till It fashion all things fair—*'

In a letter on *The Dynasts* which Hardy wrote in 1914,[56] he said:

> The assumption of unconsciousness in the driving force is, of course, not new. But I think the view of the unconscious force as gradually *becoming* conscious; i.e., that consciousness is creeping further and further back towards the origin of force, had never (as far as I know) been advanced before *The Dynasts* appeared.

The third chapter of von Hartmann's *Metaphysics of the Unconscious* is on the origin of consciousness; and in it he says:

> We have seen (in the first chapter) how Will and Idea are united in the

Unconscious as an inseparable unity, and we shall see further in the final chapters how the salvation of the world depends on the emancipation of the intellect from the Will, the possibility of which is given in consciousness, and how the whole world process is tending slowly towards this goal.

In order to appreciate what the metaphysics of *The Dynasts* may have owed—almost certainly did owe—to von Hartmann, it is necessary to glance at the seventh chapter of the *Metaphysics of the Unconscious*, which is entitled 'The Unconscious and the God of Theism.' Here von Hartmann writes:

If hitherto theism has eagerly insisted on assigning to God a consciousness of his own in the sphere of his divinity, this has happened for two reasons, both of which had their justification, but from which an illegitimate conclusion was drawn, because the possibility of an unconscious intelligence had never been conceived. These two grounds are: firstly, as regards man, repugnance to the thought, in default of a conscious God, of being a blind product of natural forces, an unintended, unwatched, purposeless and transient result of fortuitous necessity. Secondly, as regards God, the fear of thinking this supreme existence ... to be destitute of that excellence which passes with the human mind for the highest, namely clear consciousness and distinct self-consciousness. Both scruples, however, disappear before a correct estimation of the principles of the Unconscious, which hold the golden mean between a theism constructed of the floating human ideal made absolute, and a naturalism in which the highest flowers of the mind and the eternal necessity of natural law from which they have sprung, are mere results of a casual actuality, imposing to us on account of our importance—the right mean between conscious teleology, which is conceived after the human prototype, and entire renunciation of final causes. This right mean just consists in the recognition of a final causality which, however, is not represented according to the pattern of conscious human purposive activity by discursive reflection, *but as immanent unconscious teleology of an intuitive unconscious intelligence is revealed in natural objects and individuals by means of the same activity, which, in the last chapter, we described as continual creation or conservation, or as real phenomenon of the All-One Existence.*

If there is such a thing as close resemblance between one abstract conception and another, surely we have an instance here. The sentences here italicised may be regarded as the immediate origin of Hardy's metaphysic of the Immanent Will.

What almost amounts to proof on internal evidence is provided by the next paragraph in the same chapter:

In our inability positively to apprehend the mode of perception of this intelligence, we are only able to indicate it through the contrast to our own form of perception (consciousness); thus, only to characterise it by the negative predicate of Unconsciousness. But we know from the previous enquiries that the function of this unconscious intelligence is anything but blind, rather far seeing, nay, even *clairvoyant*, although this seeing can never be aware of its own vision, but only of the world, and without the mirrors of the individual consciousness can also not see the seeing eye. Of this unconscious clairvoyant intelligence we have come to perceive that in its infallible purposive activity, embracing out of time all ends and means in one, and always including all necessary data within its ken, it infinitely transcends the halting, stilted gait of the discursive reflection of consciousness, ever limited to a single point, dependent on sense-perception, memory and inspirations of the Unconscious. *We shall then be compelled to designate this intelligence, which is superior to all consciousness, at once unconscious and super-conscious.*

In Scene iv, Act v of the First Part of *The Dynasts*, following the death of Nelson, there occurs one of the high-water marks of the supernatural debate. After the Spirit of the Pities has quoted Sophocles, and a chorus of Pities has reviled the morality of the Immanent Will, the Spirit of the Years replies:

> *Nay, blame not! For what judgment can ye blame?*
> *In that immense unweeting Mind is shown*
> *One far above forethinking; processive,*
> *Yet super-conscious; a Clairvoyancy*
> *That knows not what It knows, yet works therewith.*

As to Hardy's claim—which, it should in justice be said, was made when he was seventy-four and cannot have had perfect memory—that the idea of the becoming-conscious of the Will was his own, it hardly seems to stand; for in the same chapter of the Metaphysics of the Unconscious there occurs this passage:

> Unquestionably, besides its value for the individual as such, consciousness has also in addition a universal significance for the redemption of the world, i.e., for the conversion of the World Will ... For this final purpose the All-One does in fact need consciousness, and accordingly it possesses the same—namely in the sum of individual consciousnesses, whose common subject it is.

In the letter to the *Academy* in 1902, which has already been quoted, Hardy mentioned Haeckel; from which it is to be inferred that he had at least looked into that writer. Ernst Haeckel (1834–1919) was primarily a scientist, and was, indeed, the most distinguished German zoologist of his generation. In the introduction to *The Descent of Man* in 1871, Darwin wrote of his *Natürliche Schöpfungsgeschichte*: 'If this work had appeared before my essay had been written, I should probably never have completed it.' One or two of Haeckel's works were translated into English fairly early. *Freedom in Science and Teaching*, which was largely concerned with a controversy over Evolution in the German scientific world, appeared in 1879 with a prefatory note by Huxley. It was followed by *The Pedigree of Man and Other Essays* in 1883. Both these books, however, were so largely scientific as to be unlikely to appeal to a layman like Hardy. That one of Haeckel's works which had the widest circulation among the ordinary public was *Die Welträtsel* (1899). This was translated into English and appeared in 1900 as *The Riddle of the Universe*. It was much discussed at the time, and provoked a reply from Sir Oliver Lodge; and Hardy would certainly have looked into it. *The Riddle of the Universe* is a popular exposition, in rather provocative language, of an extreme form of materialism. Haeckel claims that science has conclusively established that there is no such thing as soul; that all deductions from the hypothesis of soul, including, of course, all religion, are mere delusions; and that the religion of the twentieth century will be 'scientific monism.' Reading *The Riddle of the Universe* with its cocksure assumptions, one can understand why Sir James Jeans in 1930 wrote at the end of *The Mysterious Universe*: 'Our main contention can hardly be that the science of to-day has a pronouncement to make. Perhaps it ought rather to be that science should leave off making pronouncements.' If Hardy had shared that view of science, he would have been a happier man; but he took the scientists of the nineteenth century at their own estimation. It is unlikely that he took much from Haeckel, who in any case has no standing in philosophy; but it may be that a recent reading of *The Riddle of the Universe* was responsible for the phrase in the Preface to *The Dynasts*: 'The wide prevalence of the Monistic theory of the Universe in this twentieth century ...' The assumption is not necessary, for such a student of philosophy as Hardy had become must long since have been familiar with the term 'monism' and all that it implied, although it was chiefly popularized by Haeckel.[57]

Other writers might be added, who influenced Hardy's thought from 1860 onwards. Gibbon, for example, was certainly one. Like many other agnostics, Hardy had made a study of the famous fifteenth and sixteenth chapters of the *Decline and Fall*; and their author is one of the 'Christminster Ghosts' in *Jude*. The significant reference to the chapter on Julian the Apostate in *Jude* has already been quoted. There is an equally significant reference to Gibbon in the Preface to *The Woodlanders*.[58] The caustic poem in *Poems of the Past and Present*, inspired by Gibbon's garden at Lausanne, was written while Hardy was still smarting from the lash of the critics of *Jude*— episcopal and other; so that it is not surprising that he made the shade of the historian say to him:

> *How fares the Truth now? Ill?*
> *Do pens but slyly further her advance?*
> *May one not speed her but in phrase askance?*
> *Do scribes aver the Comic to be Reverend still?*
>
> *Still rule those minds on earth*
> *At whom sage Milton's wormwood words were hurled:*
> *'Truth like a bastard comes into the world*
> *Never without ill fame to him who gives her birth'?*

The quotation is from Milton's *Doctrine and Discipline of Divorce*, which is also quoted for the chapter heading to the fourth part of *Jude*; so that we may add some of Milton's more daring prose works to Hardy's philosophical studies.

Another book which Hardy read was Strauss's *Life of Jesus* as translated by George Eliot. The edition of this book which is still in his library is that of 1892; and he must have studied it extensively if he went to the expense of buying it. It was certainly from here that he started upon the track which caused him to produce what is perhaps the only one of his productions that dishonours him, the offensive poem called 'Panthera,' in *Time's Laughing-stocks*. Even David Strauss describes the subject of this poem as 'the ancient Jewish blasphemy, which we find in Celsus and the Talmud.[59] From the note at the head of this poem (of which the references are taken out of Strauss), we have incidental proof that Hardy had read *The Riddle of the Universe*; for it is there that Haeckel describes the legend, one most congenial to him.

A work which it is interesting to find in Hardy's not very large library is the French translation of Leopardi in three volumes, by F.A. Aulard, which was published in Paris in 1880. It is not surprising that the greatest pessimistic poet of the nineteenth century should, even if only in translation, appear on Hardy's shelves; their names have been coupled more than once,[60] and there is a reference to Leopardi in *Tess* (Chap. XXV). Hardy, whose faith in God, in life and in happiness had been destroyed by 'rationalism,' might well have echoed the words of Leopardi:

> *E figurato è il mondo in breve carta;*
> *Ecco tutto è simile, e discoprendo*
> *Solo il nulla s'accresce.*[61]

For the one as for the other, nothing remained after that study except sorrow:

> *Il certo e solo*
> *Veder che tutto è vano altro che il duolo.*[62]

It seems unlikely that Hardy can have been materially affected by reading Leopardi in French after he was forty. And yet, if he wished to feel that others before him had walked through the Slough of Despond, he could hardly have found in the literature of Europe a poet more suitable to his purpose:

> *Or poserai per sempre*
> *Stanco mio cor. Peri l'inganno estremo*
> *Ch'eterno io mi credei. Peri. Ben sento,*
> *In noi di cari inganni,*
> *Non che la speme, il desiderio è spento.*
> *Posa per sempre. Assai*
> *Palpitasti. Non val cosa nessuna*
> *I moti tuoi, nè di sospiri è degna*
> *La terra. Amaro e noia*
> *La vita, altro mai nulla; e fango è il mondo.*
> *T'acqueta omai. Dispera*
> *L'ultima volta. Al gener nostro il fato*

Non donò che il morire. Omai disprezza
Te, la natura, il brutto
Poter che, ascoso, a commun danno impera,
E l'infinita vanita del tutto.[63]

For three-quarters of a century, Hardy had studied such writings as these, from the days when, as a child in Stinsford church, he had heard read out the lamentation of the Preacher—'Vanity of Vanities, all is vanity.' For him, too, at last, the day drew night in which all the daughters of music should be brought low. Some hours before he died, after long silence and as dusk was falling, he asked his wife to read to him a certain verse from Fitzgerald's Omar; and she read:

O Thou who man of baser earth didst make,
And even with Paradise devise the snake—
For all the sin wherewith the face of man
Is blackened, man's forgiveness give—and take!

He signed to her to close the book.[64]

Chapter IV
Hardy's Early Writings

Despite the precocity recorded by Mrs Hardy, Hardy does not seem to have written anything during childhood and youth. If he did, no trace of it has remained, nor is there any record of such literary activity as that which for example, was a feature of Macaulay's childhood.[65] The earliest flowering of his genius was in poetry; and this must be discussed in a later chapter. About his first recorded production in prose there hangs a mystery. According to Mrs Hardy, this was a skit which appeared in a Dorchester paper, and was in the form of a plaintive letter from the ghost of the Alms House clock, removed from its bracket in South Street, Dorchester; Mrs Hardy has told the present writer that she has never seen this letter, having based her account of it on her husband's recollections.[66] A search has not discovered anyone who has seen it, nor can it be traced either in the *Dorset County Chronicle* or the *Dorset County Express*, the only two Dorset papers of the period preserved at the British Museum. The Editor of the *Chronicle* replied to an inquiry that he had never been able to trace anything from Hardy's pen to his paper during the 'sixties. The date of the letter must have been between 1856 and 1862. His biographer says that Hardy also wrote some prose articles, which were never printed, before leaving Dorchester in April 1862. No further information about these is available.

In one of the letters written to his sister Mary during his first year in London,[67] Hardy says that he used in the evenings to go and read in the

reading room of the Kensington Museum. This was in preparation for an
Essay for the competition organized yearly by the Royal Institute of British
Architects. The *Sessional Papers* of the Institute for 1862–3 (No. 2, Pt. 5),
record that at a special general meeting of members on March 16th, 1863,
the medal was adjudicated 'To Mr Thomas Hardy of 9 Clarence Place,
Kilburn, for his Essay *On the application of coloured bricks and terra cotta in modern
architecture*; Motto: "Tentavi quid in eo genere possem."' It has proved
impossible to find this Essay, either in print, or in manuscript; its disappearance from the Library of the Institute may be due to Hardy's having
borrowed it to make a copy and having failed to return it. We know all that
probably ever will be known about it from its title, and from the regulation
with which it presumably complied that 'The Essays are to be written very
legibly on alternate pages and are to be accompanied by suitable illustrations.' In A.P. Webb's *Bibliography of Thomas Hardy* there is reproduced
what is described as 'the text of the judges' criticism,' presumably preserved
by Hardy himself. This is as follows:

> The author of this essay has scarcely gone sufficiently into the subject
> proposed, and that portion referring to moulded and shaped bricks has scarcely
> been noticed. The essay, as far as it is written, is a very fair one, and deserves the
> medal; but, for the above reason, we cannot recommend that the supplemen-
> tary sum of £10 be given with it.

A suggestion made to Hardy at this time that he might combine literature
with architecture by becoming an art critic[68] does not seem to have been
followed up. But in *Chambers' Edinburgh Journal* for Saturday, March 18th,
1865, there appeared an unsigned article entitled 'How I built Myself a
House,' which Hardy wrote for his own amusement, and that of his fellow
assistants at Blomfield's. Mrs Hardy suggests that 'it may have been the
acceptance of this *jeu d'esprit* that turned his mind in the direction of prose.'[69]
The article is the earliest of Hardy's surviving compositions in prose. Apart
from its being quasi-autobiographical, the interest of 'How I built Myself a
House' is not great. There is a certain pawky humour; but the style is, on the
whole, remarkably undistinguished for the work of a great novelist in his
twenty-sixth year. Contrasted with the poems which he wrote at that age, it
shows how late was the development of his power of self-expression in prose.
There are, nevertheless, one or two touches which foreshadow the maturer
Hardy: for example:

> 'If it could only be in the Chinese style, with beautiful ornaments at the corners,
> like Mrs Smith's only better,' she continued, *turning to me with a glance in which a
> broken tenth commandment might have been seen.*

The Chinese conservatory is foolery; but the broken tenth commandment in
the woman's glance tells of a greater power to come.

Towards the end of July 1867, Hardy's health having for some time been
giving way in London, he returned to Dorchester, 'leaving most of his books

and other belongings behind him at Westbourne Park.'[70] Being determined to do something in literature, and having learnt by experience that no one would pay for poetry, he began to write a novel, searching his own experiences for material. The original title of this novel was:

THE POOR MAN AND THE LADY
    A Story with no Plot
Containing some original Verses.

This was later abridged to

THE POOR MAN AND THE LADY
    By the Poor Man.[71]

One point of interest about this title is that it seems to indicate that the narrative was written in the first person. This was a continuation of the method of 'How I Built Myself a House.' The writing of the novel was continued throughout the winter; when it was completed, Hardy made a fair copy of the MS., and this was finished on June 9th, 1868.[72] At this point it will be convenient to give a plain statement of the further events without reference to authorities. The evidence upon which the statement is based will then be given.

Hardy posted the MS. on July 25th to Alexander Macmillan. On August 12th he received a reply. The substance of this was that Macmillan thought it undesirable to publish the story as it stood, but was considering whether it might do with modifications. Meanwhile he had shown the story to a friend, who had written a criticism, which Macmillan enclosed. The friend was John Morley. Nothing further seems to have happened until December, when Hardy went to London and called on Macmillan. He there met Morley in person. Macmillan said he could not publish the novel, but that Chapman and Hall might do so. Hardy took the MS. to Chapman. Nothing happened until January 1869, when Hardy again went to London and called on Chapman. Chapman said he would publish it if Hardy would guarantee him twenty pounds. This Hardy did, and the book was put in hand. After some weeks, Chapman wrote to Hardy asking him to come and meet 'the gentleman who read your MS.'[73] Hardy went in March and met the gentleman, who was George Meredith. Meredith talked to Hardy about his novel, and advised him not to publish it. Hardy took away his MS.

This closes the first chapter in the history of Hardy's first novel. It has not hitherto been known what became of the manuscript. Mrs Hardy writes:

> What he did with the MS. is uncertain, and he could not precisely remember in after years, though he found a few unimportant leaves of it—now also gone. He fancied that he may have sent it to some other publisher just as it stood to get another opinion before finally deciding its fate.[74]

Edmund Gosse reported Hardy as having said, in a discussion of this lost novel in 1921, that

... some time afterwards he destroyed, as he thought, the whole MS., but lately he had come upon four or five pages of it, spared by some accident.[75]

Mr V.H. Collins, who in 1928 published a small book called *Talks With Thomas Hardy*, there reported that he had asked Hardy whether there was any chance of his first novel being published, to which Hardy replied:

> It no longer exists. When I was moving I got rid of it. It does not occur to authors when they are young that some day their early unsuccessful efforts may come to have value.[76]

It is clear that when he was over eighty, Hardy had actually forgotten what he had done with the MS. half a century before. All the above evidence, including that of Mrs Hardy, simply derives from Hardy himself. It is the more remarkable that the MS. should have vanished because Hardy seems generally to have taken care of his MSS., almost all of which are extant. But the most remarkable feature of the whole business is that SOME of the MS. survived, and was found by Hardy towards the end of his life, although it now no longer exists. Had he destroyed his early novel, as he told Collins, this would have been impossible, for all of it would then have perished together.

Sir Sydney Cockerell was kind enough to give me an account of what actually happened concerning the discovery of some of the MS. at Max Gate. He wrote:

> Hardy showed me in the latter half of 1916 a good portion of the MS. of *The Poor Man and the Lady* and I undertook to get it handsomely bound in blue morocco. This I did at a cost of two pounds and he seemed very pleased. But about ten years later he came to the conclusion that it ought not to be preserved and he burnt it himself in his study fire.

It may be noted that this MS. which came to light in 1916 did not consist only of a few leaves, as Hardy told his wife and Gosse; also that the date of Hardy's decision to burn it coincided with that when, possibly as a result of American publications, he burnt his private papers and diaries, and erased inscriptions in some of his books.

There is one explanation which covers all the facts, and one only. It is a perfectly simple one; and, although proof is wanting, circumstantial evidence that this is the true explanation is overwhelmingly strong. What happened was this: Hardy did not destroy the MS. of *The Poor Man and the Lady* in 1869. He saved it up. Some years later, when he was becoming an established novelist, he took his first novel (parts of which he had already used in *Desperate Remedies* and *Under the Greenwood Tree*), recast it, excised some portions, rewrote others, and published it under another title. For the purpose of recasting, he used the old MS., only taking out of it the sheets which contained cancelled matter. These were the sheets which he found in 1916, having probably preserved them as a memento, possibly with an idea that he might still make use of some of them. The rest of the MS., with all the alterations, went to the publisher.

In 1878 the July number of the *New Quarterly Magazine*, published by Chatto and Windus, contained a story, filling some sixty-five pages, entitled *An Indiscretion in the Life of an Heiress*, signed by Hardy. The pages which follow will show that this story was a version of Hardy's first, lost, novel, *The Poor Man and the Lady*. There is no doubt that if we could recover from Limbo the MS. which Hardy sent to Chatto and Windus for the *New Quarterly* in 1878, it would prove to be the revised and altered MS. of *The Poor Man and the Lady*.

An Indiscretion in the Life of an Heiress had not been reprinted until recently, when Mrs Hardy privately printed one hundred copies at the Curwen Press, Plaistow. Facing the title page of this reprint is the following:

> *An Indiscretion in the Life of an Heiress* is an adaptation by the author of his first novel, *The Poor Man and the Lady*, which was never published. The manuscript of the latter was destroyed by Thomas Hardy some years before his death and no copy remains. This version appeared in the *New Quarterly Magazine* for July 1878, but was not published in book form.

In the spring of 1935, the press of the Johns Hopkins University published the story as a volume in the United States, with an introduction and notes by Carl J. Weber, Professor of English Literature in Colby College, and the author of a number of articles on Hardy in American periodical publications. The source from which his text was taken is a copy of the *New Quarterly Magazine* for July 1878, in the possession of Mr Paul Lemperly, an American collector. Professor Weber's introduction consists of an hypothetical reconstruction of *The Poor Man and the Lady* in the form of one hundred numbered items: this is then compared with *An Indiscretion* in which Prof. Weber finds forty of the hundred. He concludes his introduction with these words:

> Hardy's first attempt at fiction was obviously intended to meet the usual Victorian three volume requirement. It seems reasonably clear that the contents of one volume were destroyed, the contents of a second found their way into other novels by Hardy, and the contents of the third may be read, in a slightly revised form, in the story which is here presented for the first time to American readers.

Professor Weber's convenient disposal into volumes is a little too good to be true. How much of *The Poor Man* Hardy used in later novels we shall never know. Prof. Weber does not mention the fact that *Desperate Remedies*, which was written in 1870, shortly after *The Poor Man*, but eight years before the publication of *An Indiscretion*, contains three sentences, and two quotations, which are to be found in *An Indiscretion*, of which more anon.

The remaining evidence concerning *the Poor Man and the Lady* consists of three main items: the account given by Mrs Hardy on pp. 75 to 83 of *Early Life*; an article by Sir Edmund Gosse which appeared in *The Sunday Times*[77] on January 22nd, 1928, just after Hardy's death; and the letter which Macmillan wrote to Hardy after reading his MS., which was published in *The Life and Letters of Alexander Macmillan*, by Charles L. Graves, in 1910. The second of these will be reproduced here, and the third in Appendix I.

Mrs Hardy's account is easily accessible. She tells the genesis and early history of *The Poor Man and the Lady*, as already related, up to the interview which Hardy had with Macmillan (and perhaps Morley also) in December 1868. It is curious, in view of the fact that Mrs Hardy's narrative must be wholly based upon her husband's recollections, that he told her nothing of the interview with Morley of which he gave an account to Gosse. Mrs Hardy, however, gives something more valuable than a recollection; and that is an extract from a written criticism of *The Poor Man* by Morley, which, she says, was enclosed in Macmillan's letter:

> He said that the book was 'A very curious and original performance; *the opening pictures of the Christmas Eve in the tranter's house* are really of good quality; much of the writing is strong and fresh.'

From the sentence italicized in the above, it becomes apparent that one of the best scenes in *Under the Greenwood Tree* originally appeared in *The Poor Man*. We know that Hardy used bits of his rejected novel of 1868 in *Desperate Remedies* in 1871 (possibly more than bits, but this can only be guessed); so that nothing is more likely than that he used others in *Under the Greenwood Tree* in 1872. The second and third, and parts of the seventh and eighth, chapters of that book may, if we only knew, be taken almost word for word from *The Poor Man and the Lady*. Mrs Hardy relates the interview in the offices of Chapman and Hall in March 1869 in some detail. The substance of Meredith's criticism was: that Hardy's story was a sweeping dramatic satire of the squirearchy and nobility, with a socialistic, not to say revolutionary tendency; the style was not argumentative, but affectedly simple, with a naïve realism which Hardy had imitated in part from Defoe; but this did not deceive Meredith, who said that if Hardy published so pronounced a piece of propaganda the press would be about his ears like hornets, and his future would be injured.[78].

> The upshot of this interview was that Hardy took away the MS. with him to decide on a course. *Meredith had added that Hardy could rewrite the story, softening it down considerably*; or what would be much better, put it away altogether for the present and attempt a novel with a purely artistic purpose, giving it a more complicated 'plot' than was attempted with *The Poor Man and the Lady*.

Hardy partly took both pieces of advice. The sentence here italicized is clearly the genesis of *An Indiscretion in the Life of an Heiress*. The complicated plot appears in *Desperate Remedies*.

> Extract from an article entitled 'Thomas Hardy's Lost Novel,' by Sir Edmund Gosse, which appeared in *The Sunday Times*, January 22, 1928.

(The first five paragraphs of the article in question are prefatory, or refer to other matters. In the following transcript of the remainder, those details of the plot of *The Poor Man and the Lady* which are to be found in *An Indiscretion in the Life of an Heiress* are italicized):

It was on an earlier occasion that he volunteered some precious reminiscences of his earliest effort at fiction, *The Poor Man and the Lady*. He said that he wrote it in 1867, soon after he left London and went to Weymouth. It took him a long time to finish, and now and then he could not get the story to move; it 'stuck,' but he persevered and ended it early the next year. He sent the MS. to Messrs Macmillan, and for some time he heard no more. Then came a letter declining the book, but asking him to call at the publishing office.[79] Hardy came up to town and paid his visit. He was shown in to a gentleman whom he believed to be old Mr Alexander Macmillan, who said that he would like to introduce him to their reader, Mr Morley. This he did, to Hardy's perturbation, since he had lately read with great admiration the *Edmund Burke*, and since this was the first time he had ever met an author of distinction. John Morley received him very kindly, but said they could not possibly publish the story, because it was crudely put together, but that it had interested him very much, and, oddly enough, he made the suggestion that he thought Hardy would do well to get practice by writing reviews of books. He offered the young architect a letter to John Douglas Cook, the editor of the *Saturday Review*. Hardy, however, thought to himself 'there is nothing in the world I could do less well,' and declined the introduction. As Cook was even then a dying man, it would in no case have been very serviceable. Hardy formed, however, a very lively enthusiasm for John Morley, who seemed to him the greatest man he had ever met. He took his own MS. away, and sent it to to Messrs Chapman & Hall, where it was read by George Meredith, and rejected in circumstances which are already known.

The moment seemed favourable for further information, so I pressed Hardy to tell me something of the plot of *The Poor Man and the Lady*, which he proceeded to do as follows:

'*The scene was laid in Dorsetshire, in the nineteenth century, and the hero was the son of peasants working on the estate of the great local squire.*[80] *The squire had a beautiful and spirited daughter who was his heiress.* The hero showed remarkable talent at the village school, and was patronized by the people of the great house, who had him educated as a draughtsman. When he was just grown up, *he was thrown by accident much into the company of the squire's daughter, who took a romantic interest in him.* Her parents, discovering this, *forbade her to communicate with him*[81]—for they had begun to write letters to each other—and the lad was sent up to London, where he was taken into the office of an eminent architect, and made striking progress.[82] *The lovers, however, were not able to resist the temptations of letter writing, and considered themselves betrothed.*[83] The squire discovered his daughter's disobedience, and intervened again. The young man became very hostile to the father, and took up radical politics in pique. *The great Wessex family now came up to their town house,* and, The Lady and the Poor Man contriving to meet, their engagement was secretly renewed. But he took to addressing public meetings, and once, while he was speaking passionately to a crowd in Trafalgar Square, the Lady drove by in her carriage, recognized him, and stopped to hear what he was saying. (Hardy paused here to remark that this was a rather remarkable prophecy, because at that time no such meetings had ever been held in Trafalgar Square, and John Morley actually pointed out this scene to him as absurd and impossible.)

The Lady's Conservative feelings were deeply wounded by this radical speech, and she broke off all relations with the young architect. A short time afterwards, however, *there was given a public concert at which the Lady happened to be seated alone in the last row of the expensive places, and the Poor Man immediately behind her in the front row of the cheap seats. Both were extremely moved by the emotion of the music, and, as she chanced to put her hand on the back of her seat, he took it in his and held it till the close of the performance.* They walked away together, and all their affection was renewed. She asked him to call upon her openly, at the great town house, and he did so.[84] Unluckily the Lady was out, and her mother received him with much anger and arrogance. He lost his temper, and they both became so excited that the mother fainted away. He found some water, and flung it over her face, with the result that the rouge ran down her cheeks. On coming to she discovered this, with redoubled rage, and the squire himself now coming in, ordered the footman to turn the architect out of the front door. *The family returned to Dorsetshire*, and no more letters passed between the lovers. In the course of time, however, the Poor Man learned from his relatives in Wessex that *the squire's daughter was just about to marry* the heir of a wealthy neighbouring landowner. On *the night before the wedding, hanging about the churchyard, the church still being open, the architect saw a muffled figure steal into the church, and, following it, found himself alone with the Lady. They had a very emotional interview*, she being at first very angry, and *then confessing that she had never loved any man but him*'.[85]

The story then ended, but Hardy could not recollect whether she married the proposed bridegroom or no. He racked his brain to remember, but in vain; he could not tell at all. Some time afterwards, he continued, he destroyed, as he thought, the whole manuscript, but lately he had come upon four or five pages of it, spared by some accident. I should read them next time I came to Max Gate, but we both forgot it. Hardy said that they were from the least interesting part of the book. I recall one other scrap of information about *The Poor Man and the Lady*. At some quite different, and much earlier time, he spoke to me of the lost novel, and admitted that it was very crude. 'The only interesting thing about it,' he added, 'was that it showed a wonderful insight into female character. I don't know how that came about!' He said this with the utmost detachment. When in 1921 he gave me the particulars which I have repeated as nearly as possible in his own words, I told him I should write down notes of what he had said. 'Oh, very well!' he replied; 'they may be amusing some day. But it is hunting very small deer!' The student of his mind in its early development will hardly, I think, agree with him.

The third piece of evidence as to the nature of *The Poor Man and the Lady* is the letter which Macmillan wrote to Hardy when he rejected it. This is published in *The Life and Letters of Alexander Macmillan* (p. 289 *et seq.*) Some of Macmillan's allusions require brief comment:

The description of country life among working men, which remained Hardy's own peculiar province, and of which he had a mastery probably unique in English literature, was the particular which struck the first experienced reader of his first novel. As will later be seen, even the author of the review which killed *Desperate Remedies* paid tribute to Hardy's power of describing country folk.

That the squire in *The Poor Man and the Lady* sent for the hero in a desperate attempt to save his daughter's life, and that this ran counter to his prejudices, corresponds exactly to the dying scene in *An Indiscretion*. There, it was only by the insistence of the Doctor that Geraldine's husband was told of what had happened; and to Geraldine's request that she might be left alone with Egbert, her father replies: 'Anything you wish, child ... and anything can hardly include more.'

It is only *supposition* that the award by 'The Palace of Hobbies Company' was an architectural one made to the hero in an architectural competition. The probability not only seems the only explanation which will cover all the requirements, but is also greatly strengthened by the fact of Hardy's own winning of the prize of the R.I.B.A. Having drawn on personal experience so far as to make his hero a budding architect, it was very natural that Hardy should go even further. Although this particular incident was removed from *An Indiscretion*, Hardy did not refrain from introducing there another one, drawn from his own architectural experience.

Although in the recasting of the early into the later narrative, most of the satire of a political nature, to which all the advisers objected so strongly in 1868–9, has disappeared, chap. IV of *An Indiscretion* retains traces of it. Some sentences may well be the original ones of *The Poor Man and the Lady*:

> To further complicate his feelings, there was the sight, on the one hand, of the young lady with her warm rich dress and glowing future, and on the other of the weak little boys and girls—some only five years old, and none more than twelve—going off in their different directions in the pelting rain, some for a walk of more than two miles, with the certainty of being drenched to the skin, and with no change of clothes when they reached their home. He watched the rain spots thickening upon the faded frocks, worn-out tippets, yellow straw hats and bonnets and coarse pinafores of his unprotected little flock.... Miss Allenville, too was looking at the children, and unfortunately she chanced to say, as they toddled off, 'Poor little wretches!' A sort of despairing irritation at her remoteness from his plane, as implied by her pitying the children so unmercifully impelled him to remark 'Say poor little *children*, madam.'

That Hardy's first story should contain extreme, not so say ridiculous, improbabilities is as characteristic as that it should contain masterly descriptions of country life and folk. These two characteristics seem like two strands of startlingly incompatible colour which are yet present all through the woof of his art. As has often been remarked, the former becomes particularly noticeable when Hardy tries to draw high society. The supreme examples of the two are probably the scenes in the malt house in *Far from the Madding Crowd*, and that truly amazing tale 'Barbara of the House of Grebe' in *A Group of Noble Dames*. They were evidently both present in embryo in *The Poor Man and the Lady*.

The scene in the churchyard at midnight which Macmillan criticized seems, to judge by Gosse's report, to have been substantially the same in *The Poor Man* as it is in *An Indiscretion*. The only differences are that the time is changed to evening; whereas in the first version the meeting began with anger on the lady's part, in the second it begins with feigned indifference on the man's (probably due to Hardy's increased knowledge of life); and whereas in the early version the lady confessed that she had always loved him, at the end of the interview, in the second she runs away from her father's house in the middle of the night on purpose to tell him. The difference may be due to different endings, for it is this which precipitated the ending, and what the ending of *The Poor Man* was is not quite clear. The second version makes it impossible for the hero not to take her if he has the least feeling for her, which he might otherwise hesitate to do. In both versions, the incident is characteristically melodramatic, and equally unlikely. That Hardy did not agree with Macmillan's criticism 'Could it happen?' is abundantly clear from all his novels.

That he so often outrages what Macmillan called 'the modesty of nature' is the burden of all his critics, from Lionel Johnson to Macdowall.

Macmillan asked if any gentleman would pursue and strike his wife at midnight. It is very much to be regretted that he was so allusive and not a little more explicit here. There is no really decisive answer to any of the questions: Who was it who pursued his wife at midnight and struck her? Was the wife the heroine? Was she unhappily married? Was this before or after the church scene? If before, what was the outcome of the church scene? If after (which seems less likely), did the second meeting correspond to Geraldine's nocturnal visit in *An Indiscretion*, the difference between the two versions being in that case that in *The Poor Man* she was running away from a husband, whereas in *An Indiscretion* it was only from a prospective bride-groom? The suggestion of Professor Weber, that the husband was the Squire, and that he struck his wife, not only does not fit in with what Gosse's report suggests concerning the relationship between the parents of the heiress, but seems also to lack applicability of any kind; nor does Prof. Weber explain how it 'brought about a meeting of the lovers.' Had the Squire been at variance with his dame, the story of *The Poor Man and the Lady* would have been quite a different one.

All the evidence hitherto given primarily concerns *The Poor Man and the Lady*, written in 1868, and incidentally shows its resemblances to *An Indiscretion in the Life of an Heiress* published in 1878. To show in full how far the latter is a version of the former, it would be necessary to give a summary of *An Indiscretion* in great detail. This would demand more space than is available, and the plot must be taken as known. A number of points in the story demand notice, nevertheless.

Tollamore Church is obviously Stinsford, the Mellstock of *Under the Greenwood Tree*. Here Hardy came to church as child and boy; here there is a memorial window to him; and here his heart is buried near the grave of his first wife. Egbert Mayne, gazing at Geraldine during evening service, sees her face 'modified in his fancy till it almost seemed to resemble the carved marble skull immediately above her head.' That monument with the carved marble skull, which may be seen on the wall of Stinsford Church to this day, had often terrified Hardy as a child. It may be noted that although *An Indiscretion* was not published until 1878, the place names in it are not normalized to conform to the toponomy which Hardy first adopted in 1871 in *Under the Greenwood Tree*, as they were normalized in all editions of *Desperate Remedies* subsequent to 1896. Although not proof positive, this strongly suggests that *An Indiscretion* existed in some form before 1871.

In chapter three, when Egbert waylays Geraldine, she is reading *Childe Harold's Pilgrimage*. We know that Hardy was reading that poem in July 1865.[86] In the recital of the first love passages between the two, the general situation and the girlishness of Geraldine's character bear a close resemblance to the situation in *A Pair of Blue Eyes* and to the character of Elfride. All this part looks like having been written nearer to 1870 than to 1880. In chapter five, however, there is a later touch. Egbert chooses a strategic spot for his critical encounter with Geraldine: 'having previously surveyed the sport and thought it suitable for the occasion, much as Wellington antecedently surveyed the field of Waterloo.' This passage seems the earliest reference in Hardy's writings to Napoleonic matters. With a view to the 'Drama of Kings' which was even then taking shape in his mind, he himself surveyed the field of Waterloo in 1876.[87]

Chapter seven contains an account of an incident which Hardy witnessed in 1865, that of the laying of the foundation stone:

> Geraldine laid down the sealed bottle with its enclosed memorandum ... and taking a trowel from her father's hand, dabbled confusedly in the mortar, accidentally smearing it over the handle of the trowel ... The dainty-handed young woman was looking as if she would give anything to be relieved of the dirty trowel; but Egbert, the only one who observed this, was guiding the stone with both hands into its place, and could not receive the tool of her. Every moment increased her perplexity. 'Take it, take it, will you?' she impatiently whispered to him, blushing with the consciousness that people began to perceive her awkward handling.

This incident almost certainly figured in *The Poor Man*, for Hardy had witnessed it in 1865. The account which he gave to Mrs Hardy half a century later, and which appears in *Early Life* (p. 63), even preserves the same phrase:

> Subsequent historic events brought back to his (Hardy's) mind that this year (1865) he went with Blomfield to New Windsor, to the laying of the memorial stone of a church there by the Crown Princess of Germany (the English Princess Royal). She was accompanied by her husband the Crown Prince, afterwards the Emperor Frederick. Blomfield handed her the trowel, and during the ceremony she got her glove daubed with the mortar. In her distress she handed the trowel back to him with an impatient whisper of 'Take, take it!'

In chapter eight, apropos of the social disparity between Egbert and his beloved we are told:

> That the habits of men should be so subversive of the law of nature as to indicate that he was not worthy to marry a woman whose own instincts said that he was worthy, was a great anomaly, he thought with some rebelliousness.

This is a very striking foretaste of Hardy's quarrel with social conventions that run counter to the apparent laws of nature, which forms so great a part of *Tess*. The rôle of the sexes is reversed, but the attitude of mind is the same. We have here, indeed, a link between Hardy's earliest effort in fiction, and his most famous work. As a young man, his quarrel with 'this sorry scheme of things entire,' and more particularly with the organization of human society, seems to have taken a political tinge. There is no trace of politics in *Tess*; but there is a passionate indictment of the warping, contorting and trammelling of existence 'by those creeds which futilely attempt to check what wisdom would be content to regulate.'[88]

The descriptions of Egbert's experiences as a man of letters in London clearly owe something to Hardy's own experiences between 1862 and 1868. The scene at the concert of the *Messiah* (in Chap. II, of Pt. 2), is probably hardly, if at all, altered from the concert scene which we know to have been in *The Poor Man*. The meeting of the long parted lovers in such an atmosphere is very well done: 'They were like frail and sorry wrecks upon that sea of symphony.' The modifications which the church scene underwent with its transference from *The Poor Man* to *An Indiscretion* have been noted. Despite Macmillan's strictures, Hardy evidently considered this melodramatic situation a valuable means of bringing about the *dénouement*, for a very similar device is used in *Desperate Remedies*. The scene in chapter thirteen of that novel, when Edward Springrove appears at the wedding of Cytherea, is at a further remove from the original scene in *The Poor Man*, but clearly derives from it.

The ending of *An Indiscretion* is a fine one, and recalls those of much more mature work, for example that in *The Trumpet-Major*. Of stately endings Hardy was especially fond. An account of the death of the heiress may well have figured in the early version; and the supposition is strengthened by the fact that the most memorable sentence occurs again in the description of the death of Miss Aldclyffe in the twenty-first chapter of *Desperate Remedies*; it may be noted that this sentence contains a suggestion which is repeatedly introduced, with very great effect, in *The Return of the Native*; that of the latent hostility of the external universe to human life. Its effectiveness lies largely in the artistry with which it is used, for it is never more than a suggestion.

We are now in a position to make a concise statement of the relationship between *The Poor Man and the Lady*, written in 1868 and only known to us by the evidence already quoted, and *An Indiscretion in the Life of an Heiress*, published in 1878.

(*a*) *An Indiscretion* is a version of *The Poor Man*, considerably shortened, partly simplified, but substantially the same novel.

(*b*) Some parts of *The Poor Man*, retained in *An Indiscretion*, have been partially rewritten; nevertheless, as will shortly appear even more conclusively, much of the later version remains verbatim as originally written.

(c) Three scenes, which we know to have been in the early novel, figure in the later one. The concert scene may be taken as being, with the alteration of two or three sentences, as it was first written. The church scene, while having undergone more modification, still bears many traces of its original state. The scene of the hero's call at the town house of the heiress has been rewritten, but retains its original purpose in the plot.

(d) The following features in the later novel were almost certainly not in the early one. They were introduced in the late 'seventies, and their interest is their connection of Hardy's later work with his early writings:

    (1) The stress laid upon the instinctive and uncalculating nature of love, and its fatal consequences.

    (2) The quarrel with conventions of society which run counter to the apparent laws of nature. This was a transformation of the critical faculty, which seems first to have tended to a political complexion, and is psychologically most interesting.

(e) The following features of the early novel still to be found in the later one show how very far from general was the revision, and how close *An Indiscretion* must in many ways to be to *The Poor Man*:

    (1) Two events of Hardy's own life which occurred in 1865 are to be definitely traced, the episode of the laying of the foundation stone, and the reading of *Childe Harold*. A number of reminiscences of his early years in London are probably also present, but cannot be definitely identified.

    (2) The place names in the story are not the place names of all the other Wessex Novels. This was also the case with the first edition of *Desperate Remedies* in 1871; but the familiar names first appeared in 1872 in *Under the Greenwood Tree*, and were thereafter Hardy's standard practice.

    (3) Several touches of a sort which in a modern author would be called 'class-conscious' are clearly perceptible. There is no parallel to these in any of Hardy's later writings.

    (4) There are certain analogies with *Desperate Remedies*, and possibly one or two with *A Pair of Blue Eyes*, in certain details of plot and treatment, which suggest a date of composition much nearer to 1870 than to 1880.

It has been suggested already that the manuscript of *An Indiscretion*, if it could now be found, would prove to be the MS. of *The Poor Man*, with excisions and alterations. How far the later version actually reproduces the wording of the early one, as this hypothesis would demand, cannot be known with certainty. That, for example, the concert scene dates almost entirely from 1868 is only very strong probability. It so happens, however, that there is even stronger circumstantial evidence to the probably verbal fidelity of *An Indiscretion* to *The Poor Man*. This is the fact that three rather striking phrases to be found in *An Indiscretion* are also to be found in *Desperate*

Remedies. It might be argued that Hardy, in 1878, took them out of the novel in which he first wrote them in 1871. This cannot be positively disproved. But the onus of proof rests with those who would advance a theory for which there seems no reason; for Hardy can have had no motive for doing in this instance what he never did again, that is, borrowing from his own earlier work. Besides, if he had wanted to borrow in 1878 it seems probably that he would have gone to more finished work than *Desperate Remedies.* But the opposite theory, that the appearance of these sentences in the novel of 1871, is due to his having borrowed them from the suppressed story of 1868, provides not merely a plausible, but the only reasonable, explanation. Assuming that he was fond of these sentences, nothing is more likely than that, having had to suppress the story in which they appeared, he afterwards used them again in his next novel.

The following are the passages in question:

(1) In chapter seven (Pt. 1) of *An Indiscretion*, at the end of the love scene between Egbert and Geraldine on the night after Broadfoot's death, she again asks him, as they leave, whether he forgives her:

> 'Do you forgive me entirely?'
> 'How shall I say "Yes" without assuming that there was something to forgive?'
> 'Say "Yes." It is sweeter to fancy I am forgiven than to think I have not sinned.'

Towards the end of the twelfth chapter of *Desperate Remedies*, when Manston is pressing Cytherea to fix a date for their wedding, she at first refuses, then relents and asks forgiveness:

> 'Will you forgive me?'
> 'How shall I say "Yes" without judging you? How shall I say "No" without losing the pleasure of saying "Yes"?' He was himself again.
> 'I don't know' she absently murmured.
> 'I'll say "Yes"' he answered daintily. 'It is sweeter to fancy we are forgiven, than to think we have not sinned; and you shall have the sweetness without the need.'

(2) In chapter eight (Pt. 1) of *An Indiscretion*, when Egbert is just about to leave Geraldine to catch his boat, at the end of their interview through the window on the morning on which he sets out to seek his fortune, her parting words to him are these:

> 'If you cannot in the least succeed, I shall never think the less of you. The truly great stand on no middle ledge; they are either famous or unknown.'

In the third chapter of *Desperate Remedies*, Springrove is telling Cytherea of his ambitions, and that he has got to the stage of being content to aim at reasonable wealth sufficient for his needs:

> 'And if you should fail—utterly fail to get that reasonable wealth,' she said

earnestly, 'don't be perturbed. The truly great stand upon no middle ledge; they are either famous or unknown.'

(3) The last paragraph of *An Indiscretion*, describing the death of Geraldine:

> Everything was so still that her weak act of trying to live seemed a silent wrestling with all the powers of the universe.

In chapter twenty-one of *Desperate Remedies* Cytherea comes to Knapwater House in answer to an urgent summons and finds Miss Aldclyffe dying:

> In the room everything was so still, and sensation was as it were so rarified by solicitude, that thinking seemed acting, and the lady's weak act of trying to live a silent wrestling with all the powers of the universe.

It will be noticed that in all three instances, the version of *An Indiscretion* is the simpler as well as the more effective, whereas the version of *Desperate Remedies* is padded out. This fits in with the theory that the versions of *An Indiscretion* are the earlier; which amounts to saying that, in part at least, *An Indiscretion* retains the actual wording of *The Poor Man*. It is, of course, quite possible, that other parts of *Desperate Remedies* were transferred thither out of *The Poor Man*, although their absence from *An Indiscretion* leaves us without clues. Prof. Weber's conjecture, that the description of Knapwater House in chapter five of *Desperate Remedies* originally figured in *The Poor Man*, would fit in with this.

Two other, much less important, points of contact between *An Indiscretion* and *Desperate Remedies* remain to be mentioned. The quotations at the chapter headings of the former have already been referred to. There are four from Shakespeare, three from Browning, two from Shelley, one each from Tennyson, Thackeray, Ecclesiastes and Waller, and one from Dryden's translation of the *Aeneid*. Three of these are also used in *Desperate Remedies*. This of course proves nothing as to date; one of the Shelley quotations appears again in *The Woodlanders*; but it is worthy of mention.

The most interesting of them, from the point of view of the student of Hardy, is that from Dryden's *Aeneid*, for this was one of the first books Hardy ever possessed, having been given it by his mother about 1850. The lines at the head of the first chapter in the second part of *An Indiscretion*, where they apply to Egbert's tactics towards Geraldine, appear also in the twelfth chapter of *Desperate Remedies*, where they apply to Manston's tactics towards Cytherea:

> *He, like a captain who beleaguers round*
> *Some strong-built castle on a rising ground,*
> *Views all the approaches with observing eyes,*
> *This and that other part in vain he tries,*
> *And more on industry than force relies.*

> (*Aeneid*, Bk. V)

Chapter eight of *An Indiscretion* is headed by four lines from Browning's 'The Statue and the Bust':

> *The world and its ways have a certain worth,*
> *And to press a point while these oppose*
> *Were a simple policy, best wait,*
> *And we lose no friends and gain no foes.*

The poem was a favourite with Hardy. Cytherea quotes three of these lines to Edward in the thirteenth chapter of *Desperate Remedies*. Three other lines from the same poem occur in the third chapter, where Hardy uses them of Edward and Cytherea. In the sixth chapter of *Desperate Remedies*, Miss Aldclyffe quotes to Cytherea a stanza from Shelley's 'When the lamp is shattered.'

> *Love's passion shall rock thee*
> *As the storm rocks the raven on high,*
> *Bright reason will mock thee*
> *Like the sun from a wintry sky.*

The last two lines stand at the head of the third chapter in the second part of *An Indiscretion*.

This last point of contact is a small, and by itself inconclusive, one. Taken with the other evidence it tends to confirm that, despite the later date of its publication, *An Indiscretion* is in the main the work of Hardy's late twenties rather than of his late thirties.

Considered purely as literature, *An Indiscretion* is disappointing; it is easy to understand why Hardy never reprinted it, and put off inquiries about his first novel from Gosse and Mr Collins with remarks that it 'was hunting very small deer',' or that he 'got rid of it when moving.' When we remember that by 1878, when it appeared, Hardy had written *Far from the Madding Crowd* and *The Return of the Native*, the conclusion that *An Indiscretion* had been written many years before is irresistible. This somewhat feeble composition belongs to the period of *Desperate Remedies*. That it happened to be first published in the same year as one of Hardy's masterpieces was a coincidence which does not confer upon it any distinction.

DESPERATE REMEDIES

The particular field of English letters in which Hardy, in the later 'sixties, set out to make himself a place, was already crowded almost to overflowing. There have been few decades in the whole history of English prose fiction when four novelists of the calibre of Thackeray, Dickens, Meredith and 'George Eliot' have all been in the field simultaneously, as they were then. And beside these four there were many other considerable novelists who are not forgotten to-day: Trollope, Charles and Henry Kingsley, Mrs Gaskell, Mrs Henry Wood, Mary Braddon, R.D. Blackmore; while Wilkie Collins hardly gets the credit for having virtually invented, in *The Woman in White*, what has become by far the largest branch of contemporary fiction. Hardy, in search of a popular method of treatment after the failure of *The Poor Man and the Lady* to achieve publication, chose as a model the work of Wilkie Collins; who was then, following the publication of *The Moonstone* in 1868, the most popular living novelist. The result was *Desperate Remedies*; but its debt to Collins does not seem to have been noticed by any of the critics except Madame Cazamian.[89] Detailed comparison of Hardy's book with certain aspects of *The Woman in White*, *No Name*, *Armadale* and *The Moonstone*, the most successful of Collins' novels in the 'sixties, will come more appropriately later. Only twice in his career did Hardy write a mystery novel. The second time was when circumstances compelled him, although desperately ill, to continue *A Laodicean*, upon which the success or failure of the periodical in which it was appearing depended. But traces of his early apprenticeship to Wilkie Collins appear now and then throughout his work. His taste for coincidence, and the occasional lapses into the sensational which occur even in his late novels, are partly due to this influence. Even if the bloodstain on the ceiling in *Tess* be not indecent, as it was accused of being, it is highly sensational.

In April 1869, Hardy was working in Dorchester for an architect called G. R. Crickmay, who had purchased the practice of Hicks, lately deceased, and taken on various schemes of church restoration which Hicks had had in hand. Crickmay's business was in Weymouth, and during the summer Hardy went to his office there and lived in Weymouth until the following February. It was during these nine months in Weymouth that *Desperate Remedies* was written, all but the last chapters. Having returned to his father's house, Hardy sent the MS. on March 5th, 1870, to Alexander Macmillan, together with a synopsis of the final chapters. He then went on a commission for Crickmay to St Juliot, near Boscastle in Cornwall, where he met Emma Lavinia Gifford, who later became his wife.[90]

There are a few clear traces of the Weymouth sojourn in the novel. Edward Springrove the younger was sketched, partly, from an assistant who came to Crickmay's office during the summer. But the history of the literary aspirations which he confesses to Cytherea in the course of the rowing expedition which concludes chapter three is Hardy's own:

> When I found all this out that I was speaking of, whatever do you think I did? From having already loved verse passionately, I went on to read it continually; then I went rhyming myself. If anything on earth ruins a man for useful occupation and for content with reasonable success in a profession, it is the habit of writing verses on emotional subjects, which had much better be left to die from want of nourishment.

Passages from the early parts of *Desperate Remedies*, the poem called 'The Dawn after the Dance,' dated 'Weymouth 1869,' in *Time's Laughingstocks*, and allusions by Mrs Hardy to a 'quadrille class,' suggest that the

Weymouth sojourn may not have been devoid of subjects for verses of the kind in question.

In April 1870 Hardy returned from Cornwall. On the 5th of that month he had received a letter from Macmillan declining to publish his MS. In May he went to London, and apparently got his MS. from Macmillan, and sent it to Tinsley Brothers.[91] This firm anticipated the publishers of the twentieth century in regarding MSS. submitted to it wholly from a commercial stand-point, and did not trouble itself with fine points of literary criticism. The policy had served it well; for the firm followed the guidance of its adviser in publishing *Lady Audley's Secret* in 1862, which had been such a success that it had made the fortunes, not only of its publishers, but even of its author. Tinsleys had also been fortunate enough to find another excellent investment in 'Ouida,' for whose first novel *Held in Bondage* they had paid £80 in 1863. Hardy, who was no fool, doubtless knew these things. What he wanted was to be published, not to receive sermons on his writings from Macmillan, Morley and Meredith. This seems to be the reason, which Mrs Hardy cannot find, why he went to Tinsleys rather than to Chapman, after having been a second time refused by Macmillan.

On May 6th Tinsley wrote stating the terms upon which he would publish *Desperate Remedies* if Hardy would send him the concluding chapters. Mrs Hardy, who gives this information,[92] does not say what those terms were. What happened during the next few months is not clear; except that during the autumn

> There were passing between him and Miss Gifford chapters of the story for her to make a fair copy of, the original MS having been interlined and altered, so that it may have suffered, he thought, in the eyes of a publisher's reader by being difficult to read. He meanwhile wrote the three or four remaining chapters and the novel—this time finished—was packed off to Tinsley in December.[93]

Hardy marked the date December 15th, 1870, in his *Hamlet* against the words:

> *'Thou would'st not think how ill all's here about my heart.'*

Tinsley again wrote his terms, which, says Mrs Hardy, 'for some unaccount-able reason were worse now than they had been in the first place.' What they were is evident from Hardy's reply[94]

> Bockhampton, Dorchester, December 20th 1870.
>
> Sir,
>
> I believe I am right in understanding your terms thus—that if the gross receipts reach the cost of publishing I shall receive the £75 back again, and if they are more than the costs I shall have £75 added to half the receipts beyond the costs (i.e., assuming the expenditure to be £100 the receipt £200 I should have returned to me £75 plus £50—125). Will you be good enough to say too if

the sum includes advertising to the customary extent, and about how long after my paying the money the book would appear?

Yours faithfully.

THOMAS HARDY.

These terms cannot be considered unfavourable by modern standards. Hardy accepted them, and the book appeared on March 25th, 1871. In reply to a request a year later, Tinsley sent Hardy an account according to which 500 copies of *Desperate Remedies* had been printed, of which 370 had been sold, and enclosed a cheque for £60. Mrs Hardy says that Hardy was 'much gratified thereby.'[95]

Desperate Remedies was published anonymously on March 25th, 1871. It was well reviewed in the *Athenæum* of April 1st, and as 'an eminent success' in the *Morning Post* of the 13th. On the 22nd, in Mrs Hardy's words:

> The *Spectator* brought down its heaviest-leaded pastoral staff on the prematurely happy volumes, the reason for this violence being mainly the author's daring to suppose it possible that an umarried lady owning an estate could have an illegitimate child.[96]

In the absence of more adequate explanation, this seems possible; even in 'Victoria's formal middle time,' however, such situations were not absolutely without precedent in fiction which was not of the lowest order. A novel which Wilkie Collins published in 1862, *No Name*, opens with the far more unlikely situation of a country squire with grown-up daughters, whose mother has never been legally married, and continues with a plot much more objectionable than Hardy's, occasionally sugared with moralizing. Whatever his reasons, the anonymous critic in the *Spectator* applied the rod with vigour:

> This absolutely anonymous story bears no assumption of a nom-de-plume which might, at some future time, disgrace the family name, and still more the Christian name, of a repentant and remorseful novelist—and very right too. By all means let him bury the secret in the profoundest depths of his own heart, out of reach, if possible, of his own conscience. The law is hardly just which prevents Tinsley Brothers from concealing their participation also.[97]

Were this review simply a piece of wrongheadedness, it would not be worth notice; but it contained rational criticism also. The substance of the critic's quarrel with Hardy was 'here are no fine characters, no original ones to extend one's knowledge of human nature, no display of passion except of the brute kind (which is not true), 'no pictures of Christian virtue.' In view of subsequent developments, the notion of going to Hardy for pictures of Christian virtue is not without piquancy. But this critic was not quite blind:

> But there is ... an unusual and very happy facility in catching and fixing phases of peasant life, in producing for us, not the manners and language only, but the tone of thought ... and the simple humour of consequential village worthies and gaping village rustics ... The scenes allotted to these humble actors are few and slight, but they indicate powers that might be and ought to be extended largely in this direction instead of being prostituted to the purposes

of idle prying into the ways of wickedness ... This nameless author, too, has one other talent of a remarkable kind—sensitiveness to scenic and atmospheric effects, and to their influence on the mind, and the power of rousing similar sensitiveness in his readers.

The review contained long quotations from the descriptions of the cider pressing (Chap. VIII), the bell ringing (sequel) and Cytherea's vision of her father's accident in chapter one, by way of illustration, and the critic said 'we wish we had space' for more quotation. He concluded: 'We have said enough to warn our readers against this book, and, we hope, to urge the author to write far better ones.'

It was by largely extending the powers which this critic recognized that Hardy produced the scenes depicting Joseph Poorgrass and his cronies, or the description of Egdon heath.

The review hurt Hardy badly when he read it. 'The bitterness of that moment,' says Mrs Hardy 'was never forgotten; at the time he wished that he were dead.'[98] Some time later, the critic seems privately to have written a sort of apology.[99] On returning in June from a visit to Cornwall, Hardy saw his novel in Smith's surplus catalogue at Exeter Station for half a crown the three volumes. It cannot be said that *Desperate Remedies* marked the beginning of Hardy's reputation as a novelist. It was one of those false starts which seem to be almost the rule in the case of really great authors.

Before the attack by the *Spectator*, *Desperate Remedies* had also been reviewed in the *Morning Post*, on April 13th; and by the *Athenæum* on April 1st. The writer of the latter article indulged in speculation as to the sex of the author, and, while returning an open verdict, inclined to the opinion that it must be a man, on the ground that some of the expressions in the book were too coarse to have been written by a lady! He acknowledged, however, that it was 'a powerful novel.' *The Saturday Review* in an article which appeared on September 30th, tried to bring Hardy's novel to life again. A review which ran to two and a half columns ended with the sentence: 'We sincerely hope to hear of him again, for his deserts are of no ordinary kind.' Although this cannot be verified, it is possible that this review was written by Hardy's friend, Horace Moule, who reviewed *Under the Greenwood Tree* in the same paper the next year.

The novel contains occasional touches traceable to Hardy's own experiences. In addition to the Weymouth scenes, and the subject of poetical aspirations, there is the architectural motif. Both the young men in the story, Graye and Springrove, are architects. There is also the visit of Miss Aldclyffe to the Institute of Architects in chapter seven; and some touches clearly taken from Hardy's life in London. But there is nothing in the story itself which can be considered remotely autobiographical; it is an elaborate fiction *à la* Wilkie Collins. The chief light which it throws upon its author is in the astonishing number of its allusions to English literature, and particularly English poetry. If, as Mrs Hardy says, Hardy read nothing except poetry for two years while in London, he made haste to unburden himself of some of his reading as soon as he got a pen into his hands. It is probable that *The Poor Man and the Lady* was, in its original state, rich in similar allusions, although they have all disappeared from *An Indiscretion*. Perhaps the poem to Eunice, which Springrove found among Manston's papers, was one of the 'original verses' alluded to in the discarded title of *The Poor Man*, although this is mere conjecture. However that may be, Hardy's reading is abundantly clear in *Desperate Remedies*. There are some forty allusions to, or quotations from, English literature; not including the Biblical ones already enumerated. Among them are four to Shakespeare, three to Shelley, two to Milton, two to Browning (both 'The Statue and the Bust'), two to Coleridge, one to Wordsworth, one to Keats ('Ode to a Nightingale'), one to Rossetti's 'Blessed Damosel,' one to Sterne's letters, one to de Quincey and one to Dryden's translation of the *Aeneid*. There are three quotations from Virgil in the original, one from Walt Whitman, and an allusion to a passage in Dante.

By way of example, a passage may be quoted from chapter three. In the previous chapter, Hardy has described Edward Springrove as: 'some years short of the age at which the clear spirit bids goodbye to the last infirmity of noble minds, and takes to house hunting and investments.' Just before his departure for London, Springrove asks Cytherea to go for a row round the bay at Budmouth (as Hardy so often went at Weymouth). The two are described in Browning's words:

> *He looked at her as a lover can;*
> *She looked at him as one who awakes—*
> *The past was a sleep, and her life began.*

When they are in the boat, Hardy returns to *Lycidas*, as witness their conversation:

> 'It doesn't matter to me now that I "meditate the thankless Muse" no longer—but ...' He paused, as if endeavouring to think what better thing he did.
>
> Cytherea's mind ran on the succeeding lines of the poem, and their startling harmony with the present situation suggested the fancy that he was *sporting* with her, and brought an awkward contemplativeness to her face.
>
> Springrove guessed her thoughts ... 'If I had known an Amaryllis was coming here, I should not have made arrangements for leaving.'

This one example out of many will show how in his first published work Hardy was already addicted to the habit of literary allusion which is such a feature of his late novels.

There are other features in the novel which also anticipate what was to come after. Chapter three contains two passages descriptive of feminine nature which belong to that much discussed subject, Hardy's view of women[100], and there is another in chapter twelve. There is a very characteristic remark about the short-lived bliss of love in the third chapter; and

chapter twenty-two contains some sentences on sudden death which ought not
to have been overlooked by those who have discussed Hardy's 'determinism':

> There's no such thing as a random snapping off of what was laid down to
> last longer. We only suddenly light upon an end—thoughtfully formed as any
> other—which has been existing at that very same point, though unseen by us to
> be so soon.

Desperate Remedies provides several instances of the delicate and minute use of
nature which Hardy was to carry to a fine art; notably the description, in
chapter seventeen, of the sound made by rain on various field surfaces.

Apart from such passages as these, the Hardy of the later Wessex Novels is
to be seen in the descriptions of country life and folk, and especially in their
conversation; in the scene of the cider pressing, and in that of the bell
ringers. The rest is a very artificial dish, confectioned to a popular recipe
perfected, if not invented, by Wilkie Collins.

What Hardy in *Desperate Remedies* owed to Wilkie Collins can best be seen
by comparing the novel with Hardy's subsequent work, and by a glance at
the novels which Collins published in the 'sixties. *Desperate Remedies* stands
apart from the Wessex novels, chiefly by virtue of its construction. Much of
Hardy's most characteristic work is constructed upon simple plots. Just as
the story of Clarissa Harlowe may, it is said, be told in two hundred words, so
may the stories of *Under the Greenwood Tree, A Pair of Blue Eyes, The Return of
the Native, Tess* and *Jude. Far from the Madding Crowd* is hardly more complicated in plot, though the wealth of incidents is greater. The most
complicated of Hardy's great novels is *The Mayor of Casterbridge*; which is,
nevertheless, most definitely a novel of character rather than of incident. And
even *The Mayor of Casterbridge* is simple beside the involutions of *Desperate
Remedies*. Hardy's first published novel is a 'mystery novel'; one in which the
movement of the story and the final solution are quite independent of
character and humour, but result from arbitrary combinations and devices
such as the discovery of a secret or the detection of a crime. *Desperate Remedies*
and *A Laodicean* are the only two such novels which Hardy wrote.

Hardy did not take the plot of *Desperate Remedies* from Wilkie Collins; he
constructed it himself. But he took from Collins all its essential elements,
merely grouping them into a different combination. The novels which
Collins published in the 'sixties were *The Woman in White* (1860), *No Name*
(1862), *Armadale* (1866) and *The Moonstone* (1868).[101] The last two concern the
student of Hardy least. Sergeant Cuff is a prototype of Sherlock Holmes,
even to some details; *The Moonstone*, indeed might be a modern detective tale
but for the prolixity of its telling; while the sensational and involved tale of
the two Allen Armadales is too preposterous to have originated any literary
genre. But *The Woman in White*, which is probably the first English detective
story, and to a slight extent *No Name*, contain all the elements of the plot of
Desperate Remedies. Apart from the matrimonial irregularity of the elder

Vanstone, which is the cause of the whole story of *No Name*, and that of Miss Aldclyffe, which is the cause of that of *Desperate Remedies*, there is no great contact between the two novels. The trials of Magdalen have no close resemblance to those of Cytherea, nor is Captain Wragge any counterpart to Manston. But *The Woman in White* contains close parallels. There is the underlying mystery: Manston is a rather pale version of Sir Perceval Glyde. There is the sacrifice of the beautiful heroine, Cytherea Graye or Laura Fairlie, who loves and is loved by the virtuous but impecunious young hero, to this mysterious villain whose mystery and villainy only become apparent after the marriage. There is the elucidation of the mystery, not by Sergeant Cuff or Sherlock Holmes, but by the person chiefly interested in it, whether he be called Edward Springrove or Walter Hartright. This person is assisted, not by an obtuse if admirable Watson, but by the nearest relative of the distressed heroine; in one case her brother, in the other her half sister. In both cases this relative had in the first instance been instrumental in thwarting the true love of hero and heroine, and in assisting the marriage of the villain to the heroine. All these parallels with *The Woman in White* are very close. There are many others. Manston is finally driven into a corner by Springrove very much as Glyde is driven by Hartright. The deliberate confusion of the identity of one woman with another for criminal purposes is essentially the same in both novels, whether the woman be Lady Glyde and Ann Catherick, or Eunice and Ann Seaway.

Different as are the actual developments, it is hard to resist the conclusion that Hardy took all these elements of the plot of *Desperate Remedies* from *The Woman in White*. Hardy's novel, it is true, is a pale and feeble affair beside that of Collins. There is no Fosco; and in general there is little technique in the handling of the mechanics of a mystery story, of which Collins is an acknowledged master. But Hardy was recognizably imitating the manner of that master—whose manuscripts drew from his publishers, not literary lectures but substantial cheques. It ought not to be forgotten that Hardy was writing for his living, as he reminded Gosse long afterwards.[102] Tinsley Brothers published *The Moonstone*; Tinsley, indeed, complained that Collins had driven a hard bargain with him;[103] and Hardy sent his MS. to Tinsley in the following year.

To a lesser degree than with the construction of the plot, *Desperate Remedies* may even owe a certain element of style to Collins. This is the manner of telling the story by building up an effect of verisimilitude through the device of accumulating minute realistic details. The first, and perhaps greatest, master of this method was Defoe, who carried it to such perfection that, while we know the narratives of Robinson Crusoe and Colonel Jack to be fictitious, the exact proportion of fiction to history in such a narrative as the *Journal of the Plague Year* can only be ascertained by external evidence. The passage in which Mrs Hardy compares a similar style of narrative, adopted by Hardy in *The Poor Man and the Lady*, to Defoe, was referred to in the last chapter. She accounts for it as deliberate imitation of Defoe. It is as certain that Hardy had read *Robinson Crusoe* as it is that most boys read it;[104] and he doubtless read more Defoe besides. But the circumstantial narrative of *Desperate Remedies* may well have been imitated from Collins, as was the construction of the plot. An editor of Collins has pointed out that Collins himself owed something to Defoe: 'The inevitable comparison (of Collins' style) is with Defoe, for it was Defoe who first discovered this mechanical art of story telling.'[105] In any case, the narrative style of much of *Desperate Remedies* is indistinguishable from that of Collins. The following paragraph taken at random (Chap. XIII) will illustrate:

> He hesitated as to the propriety of intruding upon her in Manston's absence. Besides, the women at the bottom of the stairs would see him—his intrusion would seem odd—and Manston might return at any moment. He certainly might call and wait for Manston with the accusation upon his tongue, as he had intended. But it was a doubtful course. That idea had been based upon the assumption that Cytherea was not married. If the first wife were really dead after all—and he felt sick at the thought—Cytherea as the steward's wife might in after years—perhaps at once—be subjected to indignity and cruelty on account of an old lover's interference now.

That is not Defoe, but it might be Collins. The 'propriety' and 'intrusion' and 'assumption' are as like Collins as they are unlike the style that was to give us Egdon Heath or the milking scene in Var Vale. It is true that even in *Desperate Remedies*, Hardy never descends to Collins' pseudo-grandiose; and that he can when he likes sketch a picture in a few words with a touch of which Collins was never capable. For example, that of the elder Springrove at the cider pressing:

> He wore gaiters and a leather apron, and worked with his shirt sleeves rolled up, disclosing solid and fleshy rather than muscular arms. They were stained by the cider, and two or three brown apple pips from the pomace he was handling were seen to be sticking on them here and there.

Although Hardy does not adopt the method which Collins claimed to have invented in *The Woman in White*, of telling the story throughout in the persons of its characters, the narrative left by Manston at his death, which finally clears up all remaining mysteries, is exactly in the manner of Collins, while the occasional insertion of letters or extracts from letters to help on the narrative, which is sparingly used in *Desperate Remedies*, was a great favourite with Collins.

The deduction, from internal evidence, that Hardy made a deliberate study of *The Woman in White* as a preliminary to writing a novel which he hoped would be commercially successful, is strongly confirmed by the presence of Collins' novel in his library. The library at Max Gate does not now contain any of the fiction which Hardy must have read in the 'sixties. He certainly obtained the popular books of the time from Mudie, Smith or the Library Company. Such little money as he had for buying books went for poets, or Bohn classics, or a copy of a Rhyming Dictionary, which is marked 'Westbourne Park Villas 1865.' The earliest contemporary fiction which he *bought* seems to have been in the 'seventies, when he invested in Trollope's *The Eustace Diamonds*, which he admired for its construction. It is all the more noteworthy that his library *does* contain the very book to which *Desperate Remedies* owes its chief debt. There can be little doubt that Hardy invested in the one volume edition of *The Woman in White* published in 1861 because it was cheaper than the three volume edition, which he had probably got from Mudie; and because he wished to possess it as a text-book for the aspiring novelist, writing for the relief of his necessities, and to study it more minutely than would be possible in borrowed volumes.

The acceptance of *Desperate Remedies* by William Tinsley, whom Hardy long afterwards described as 'shrewd' in his dealings with young writers,[106] proves sufficiently that it had the elements necessary to popular fiction. Tinsley's remarks upon it, written thirty years later, are coloured by Hardy's subsequent career; but are none the less interesting:

> I read a good many MSS. almost every year during the time I was a publisher. One I read, and took an especial interest in, was Thomas Hardy's first novel called *Desperate Remedies*. In fact, I read the work twice, and even though I never thoroughly made up my mind that it was the sort of work to be a great success, I certainly thought that it contained some capital characters and character drawing. But Mr Hardy had dragged into the midst of excellent humorous writing almost ultra sensational matter, in fact, incidents unworthy of his pen and the main portion of his work. Still, I quite thought that there was enough of the bright side of human nature in it to sell at least one fair edition. However, there was not, but for a first venture I do not think Mr Hardy had much to complain about.[107]

UNDER THE GREENWOOD TREE

Under the Greenwood Tree was written in the first half of 1871, and finished towards the end of the summer. The original title on the first page of the manuscript was 'The Mellstock Quire'; this was deleted because titles from poetry were in fashion at the moment; it was restored as a sub-title in later editions, but is not to be found in the two-volume first edition, nor the one-volume second edition of 1876. It appears that Hardy still had enough faith in the house of Macmillan to send them the MS. during the autumn of 1871. He received a letter in reply which he construed as refusing his work; wrote, asking for the return of the MS.; and 'threw it into a box with his old poems, being quite sick of all such.'[108] Macmillan had enclosed the opinion of his critic (whose identity remains unknown), which is quoted by Mrs Hardy: but the letter seems to have been ambiguous for she says: 'It was not till its acceptance and issue by another publishing house the year after that he discovered they had never declined it, and indeed would have been quite willing to print it a little later on.' *Under the Greenwood Tree* remained the

327

copyright of Tinsley Brothers until 1891, when it was published by Chatto and Windus, with whom, as the publishers of the *New Quarterly Magazine*, Hardy had connections. It was first published by Macmillan in 1903, when that firm had become the publisher of all Hardy's works.

The publication of the book seems to have been due to two chance meetings in London, to which Hardy returned in the spring of 1872. He first happened to meet in Trafalgar Square his friend Horace Moule, who advised him not to give up writing altogether in case his eyes should not be equal to the strain of architectural drawing. Some little while later, William Tinsley saw Hardy in the Strand, and persuaded him to produce the MS. of his new book. Hardy wrote home for it in the first week of April and:

> sent it on to Tinsley without looking at it, saying he would have nothing to do with any publishing accounts. This probably was the reason why Tinsley offered him £30 for the copyright, which Hardy accepted. It should be added that Tinsley afterwards sent him £10 extra, and quite voluntarily, being, he said, half the amount he had obtained from Tauchnitz for the continental copyright, of which transaction Hardy had known nothing.

Under the Greenwood Tree was published in two volumes in the last week in May 1872. The evidence as to its early fortunes is conflicting. The fact that Tauchnitz later published the book would seem to indicate considerable previous popularity in England. This would also appear from Tinsley's reluctance to part with the copyright only two years later. After the appearance of *Far from the Madding Crowd* in the *Cornhill Magazine* in 1874 had made Hardy's name, Smith, the *Cornhill* publisher, suggested that he should get back the copyright from Tinsley. Tinsley first said he would not part with it under any conditions; then he asked for £300. Hardy offered £150; Tinsley did not reply, and the negotiations ceased.

As might be expected, Tinsley's own account of the book he was so anxious to keep is rather less rosy:

> I purchased the copyright of Mr Hardy's second novel, called *Under the Greenwood Tree*. In that book I felt sure I had got hold of the best little prose idyll I had ever read. By 'little' I mean as regards the length of the book, in which there is not more than about four or five hours' reading; but to my mind it is excellent reading indeed. I almost raved about the book; and I gave it away wholesale to pressmen and anyone I knew interested in good fiction. But, strange to say, it would not sell. Finding it hung on hand in the original two-volume form, I printed it in a very pretty illustrated one-volume form. That edition was a failure. Then I published it in a two shilling form, with paper covers, and that edition had a very poor sale indeed; and yet it was one of the best press-noticed books I ever published. But even though it is as pure and sweet as new mown hay, it just lacks the touch of sentiment that lady novel readers most admire. In fact, to my thinking, if Mr Hardy could have imported stronger matter for love, laughter and tears in *Under the Greenwood Tree*, the book would have in no way been unworthy of the pen of George Eliot.[109]

In later years, *Under the Greenwood Tree* became one of the most popular of Hardy's novels.

The discriminating appreciation of the book by good critics in its earliest days is exemplified by the review of it in the *Athenæum* of June 15th, 1872.

> It is an old commonplace to say that there is just as much romance, together with just as keen interest, in the loves of two young persons of this humble station, as in any courtship which ends at St George's. But it is not everyone who can make as good a novel out of the one as out of the other, or produce out of such simple materials a story that shall induce us to give up valuable time in order to see the marriage fairly consummated.

Quotations were then given, particularly one from the description of the honey-taking at Geoffrey Day's; concerning whose apostrophe to the bees inside his shirt, the critic wrote 'We have seldom met anything much better.' The most serious criticism which the reviewer had to make was that the book displayed a mixture of styles, and that its rustics were not rustic enough to contrast with the other characters.

> A little more observation, or rather cultivation of the gift which the author possesses in abundance, would show him this; and he would then give us what this book, in spite of its second title, falls short of being—a Rural Painting of the Dutch school. His present work is rather a number of studies for such a painting. The ability to paint is there; but practice only can give the power of composition.

One other review may be quoted, from the equally influential *Saturday Review* on September 28th, 1872, because it came from the pen of Horace Moule, the friend who had urged Hardy not to give up writing.[110]

> This novel is the best prose idyll that we have seen for a long while past. Deserting the more conventional, and far less agreeable, field of imaginative fiction which he worked in his earlier book called *Desperate Remedies*, the author has produced a series of pictures of rural life and genuine colouring, and drawn with a distinct minuteness reminding one at times of some of the scenes in *Hermann und Dorothea* ... *Under the Greenwood Tree* is filled with touches showing the close sympathy with which the writer has watched the life, not only of his fellow-men in the country hamlets, but of woods and fields and all the outward forms of nature. But the staple of the book is made up of personal sketches ... Regarded as a whole, the book is one of unusual merit in its own special line, full of humour and keen observation, and with the genuine air of the country breathing through it.

Writing in 1912, for the issue of the book in the collected edition of his works, Hardy expressed regret that *Under the Greenwood Tree* was the work of his youth, still not sicklied o'er with the pale cast of thought, although he did not put it quite in those words:

> In rereading the narrative after a long interval there occurs the inevitable reflection that the realities out of which it was spun were material for another kind of study of this little group of church musicians than is found in the chapters here penned so lightly, even so farcically and flippantly at times. But circumstances would have rendered any aim at a deeper, more essential, more transcendent handling unadvisable at the date of writing.[111]

To most readers, the great charm of *Under the Greenwood Tree* is that it is almost the only one of Hardy's writings which does not contain a tragedy. The episode of Fancy and Mr Maybold lies on the edge of tragedy, and that is enough. Art should not always be tragic. It has been brought as a very sound criticism against the art of Hardy that, as a whole, it insists too much upon the 'lacrimae rerum.'[112] It is no small part of the pleasure with which *Under the Greenwood Tree* can be read, and read again, that it does not end in a grave.

Under the Greenwood Tree, considered as a work of art, has a freshness about it which Hardy never again achieved. *Far from the Madding Crowd* comes nearest, as a whole; and the first part of *A Pair of Blue Eyes* achieves a spontaneous poetry which is admirable; but upon both of them there lies a deeper shadow; and both of them are clearly works of fiction; whereas *Under the Greenwood Tree* owes much of its charm to the feeling that the subject of this 'rural painting of the Dutch school' is the real life of Dorset as Hardy knew it in his youth. Out of the characters who made up the 'Mellstock' choir, out of William Leaf and Parson Maybold, Hardy took the elements from which the Wessex characters of his later novels were constructed. But here he was drawing from the life. We come across traces of 'that vanished band' occasionally in other places in his writings. They appear briefly in *Two on a Tower*; and again in the short story called 'Absent-Mindedness in a Parish Choir.'[113] The bell ringers in *Desperate Remedies* are their near relatives; and rather more distant is the choir in the thirty-third chapter of *The Mayor of Casterbridge*. They appear sometimes in Hardy's poetry. 'Friends Beyond,' in *Wessex Poems*, and 'The Dead Quire' in *Time's Laughingstocks* recall their memory. The headstones of some of the men immortalized in *Under the Greenwood Tree* still stand in Stinsford Churchyard. Mrs Hardy gives an account of the death of the man from whom the 'Tranter' was drawn.[114]

Apart from a certain debt to William Barnes, already discussed, *Under the Greenwood Tree* owes practically nothing to other writers. There are Christmas scenes in Dickens; indeed, it has been said that Dickens invented the English Christmas; but in describing the activities of the Mellstock Quire, Hardy was not borrowing suggestions from literature; he was painting from life. The music of Stinsford church had been practically created by Hardy's grandfather, Thomas Hardy the first (1778–1837), who

> played in the gallery of Stinsford Church at two services every Sunday from 1801 or 1802 till his death in 1837, being joined later by his two sons (Thomas Hardy the Second, 1811–92, and James Hardy), who, with other reinforcement, continued playing till about 1842, the period of performance by the three Hardys thus covering inclusively a little under forty years.[115]

There is a full account of the quire and its doings in the first chapter of *Early Life*; and on p. 13 there is a plan of Stinsford church, showing the positions of its members in the West Gallery, about 1835, which was drawn up long afterwards by Hardy under the direction of his father. Thus, although the activities of the quire in Stinsford Church came to an end while Hardy was still an infant, he grew up in the atmosphere of these departed glories. Because he had never seen or heard them, Hardy was accustomed to say that he had rather burlesqued the quire, 'the story not adequately reflecting, as he could have wished in later years, the poetry and romance that coloured their time-honoured observances.'[116] There are actually some anachronisms in the book, for Hardy describes conditions which ceased in 1841 as co-existent with events which could hardly have occurred before 1860.[117] What happened was clearly that Hardy, when he wrote the novel, made use, both of what he knew only by report and of what he knew personally; the result, even if it does contain some anachronisms, certainly justifies the means. We have other records of church choirs;[118] but the Mellstock choir lives, with the life that only art can bestow.

The Preface to the novel clearly states that it is 'intended to be a fairly true picture, at first hand, of the personages, ways and customs which were common in the villages of fifty or sixty years ago.' Hardy also there describes the music of these instrumentalists:

> Their music in those days was all in their own manuscript, copied in the evenings after work, and their music books were home-bound. It was customary to inscribe a few jigs, reels, hornpipes and ballads in the same book, by beginning it at the other end, the insertions being continued from front and back till sacred and secular met together in the middle, often with bizarre effects, the words of some of the songs exhibiting that ancient and broad humour which our grandfathers, and possibly grandmothers, took delight in, and is in these days unquotable.

I owe it to the kindness of Mrs Hardy that I have been able to inspect three manuscript music books, in her possession, which were clearly those in Hardy's mind when he wrote these words.

The first and oldest of them is a home-made volume, composed of plain paper and bound in what appears to be vellum. Inside the cover, on a slip pasted in, is written 'Thomas Hardy. Puddletown 1799,' and across is written 'Thomas Hardy, Bockhampton.' Underneath is written in the hand of Thomas Hardy the author; 'The Carol Book of T.H. 1st (1778–1837). Bass. Used at Puddletown and afterwards at "Mellstock". (Violincello).' On the first page is a table of contents, written across and downwards, containing the first lines of twenty-five sacred items (mostly, but not all, carols). At the other end of the book is written: 'Thomas Hardy. His book. Puddletown. April 25 1800.' There follow sundry flourishes. On the second page from this end there begin the 'profane' songs, the music being ruled by hand (as throughout the book). The first six of these are:

'Gather ye rosebuds while ye may—'
'He comes, he comes, the hero comes—'
'The jolly bowl doth glad my soul—'
'What charms the heart and ear so sweet—

'The dusky night rides down the sky—'
'Jolly mortals, fill your glasses—'

Hardy the author seems to have studied this section with particular care; in 'The Maiden's Moan' he has written three suggested emendations. As a taste of the general quality of these 'profane' items, the last four stanzas may be quoted from the last song in the book (which has words, but no corresponding music). This is entitled 'Birds of a Feather,' which concludes as follows (the original spelling is retained):

> *If we meet with a female who has been gone astray*
> *By some artfull Villain Deluded away*
> *Lett us pitty her weakness & sooth of her Pain*
> *Prevent her from going the Same road again*

> *In all our misfortunes lett this be our plan*
> *To bear it with patients as well as we can*
> *In Justice love Mercy Walk humbly together*
> *And travel through life like Birds of a feather*

> *And when we arrive at the Inn at the Close of the Day*
> *And have a Refreshment leave nothing to pay*
> *And the Next Morning Journey sett all Matters Right*
> *So hear is wishing each other good Night.*

> *With Joyfull Assurance we will all go to Rest*
> *No Cares of the world can trouble our breast*
> *Awak'd by the Trumpett we will all go togeather*
> *And Climb up to heaven like birds of a Feather*

Surely a most unexceptionable ditty!

The second music book, belonging to Thomas Hardy the second, is a similar volume; it has written inside the paper binding: 'T. Hardy (Senr) from James Hook, to whose father it belonged (compiled probably about 1820).' On the opposite page, in Hardy the author's hand, is written a note describing the 'Figure of College Hornpipe as danced at Mellstock about 1840.' On an inserted page is a description of 'The Dorchester Hornpipe,' in the hand of Miss Katherine Hardy, and on the verso of this is a descriptive note, again by Hardy the author, of 'The Figure of Haste to the Wedding— as danced at Mellstock about 1840.' These call to mind the description of the dance at the Tranter's party in chapter seven of *Under the Greenwood Tree*, which opened with 'The Triumph, or Follow my Lover.' The original first page is missing, and has been replaced by Hardy the author, who gives an index in pencil of the contents. These contain a very few sacred items (such as 'Hymn 183' with the tune 'Linsted,' Psalm 117, and a Christmas Piece— 'Arise and hail the sacred day'). Most of the contents are such as these:

332

Alexandria
After many moving years
By the Fountain's Flowery Side
Banks of the Dee
Beggar Girl
Bewildered Maid, etc.

The third music book is a volume bound in brown paper, measuring eight and a half by six and a half inches, bearing on the cover, in the hand of Hardy the author, 'The "Mellstock Quire" Carol Book used on the rounds on Xmas Eve.' Inside is written, in the hand of Thomas Hardy the Second, 'Thomas Hardy. Bockhampton'; and, in the hand of Hardy the author: 'The Carol Book of T.H. II. (used on the rounds on Xmas Eve in the "Mellstock Quire" down to about 1842.') This volume contains only Christmas Carols and Hymns. The great interest of this volume is that it was clearly similar to the ones which are several times mentioned in *Under the Greenwood Tree*.

For example, in chapter three:

'Better try over number seventy-eight before we start, I suppose?' said William, pointing to a heap of old Christmas-carol books on a side table.

'Wi' all my heart,' said the choir generally.

'Number seventy-eight was always a teaser—always. I can mind him ever since I was growing up a hard boy-chap.'

'But he's a good tune, and worth a mint o' practice,' said Michael.

'He is; though I've been mad enough wi' that tune at times to seize en an tear en all to linnit. Ay, he's a splendid carrel—there's no denying that.'

'The first line is well enough,' said Mr. Spinks; 'but when you come to "O Thou man," you make a mess o't.'

In the following chapter, the choir sings this redoubtable carol:

'Number seventy-eight,' he softly gave out as they formed round in a semicircle, the boys opening the lanterns to get a clearer light, and directing their rays on the books. Then passed forth into the quiet night an ancient and time-worn hymn, embodying a quaint Christianity in words orally transmitted from father to son through several generations down to the present characters, who sang them out right earnestly:—

Remember Adam's fall,
  O thou Man;
Remember Adam's fall
  From Heaven to Hell.
Remember Adam's fall:
How he hath condemned all
In Hell perpetual
  There for to dwell.

Remember God's goodnesse,
  O thou Man;
Remember God's goodnesse,
  His promise made,
Remember God's goodnesse;

333

How He sent his Son sinlesse
Our ails for to redress;
 Be not afraid!

In Bethlehem He was born,
 O thou Man;
In Bethlehem He was born,
 For mankind's sake.
In Bethlehem He was born,
Christmas day i' the morn:
Our Saviour thought no scorn
 Our faults to take.

Give thanks to God alway,
 O thou Man;
Give thanks to God alway
 With heart-most joy.
Give thanks to God alway
On this our joyful day:
Let all men sing and say
 Holy, Holy!

Having concluded the last note, they listened for a minute or two, but found that no sound issued from the schoolhouse.

'Four breaths, and then "O, what unbounded goodness!" number fifty-nine,' said old William.

This was duly gone through, and no notice whatever seemed to be taken of the performance ... 'Four breaths, and then the last,' said the leader authoritatively. '"Rejoice, ye Tenants of the Earth," number sixty-four.'

In the Carol book which is still at Max Gate, number fifty-nine is 'O what unbounded goodness, Lord.' But 'Remember Adam's Fall' is not to be found in it. Number seventy-seven is 'Awake ye drowsy mortals all'; then there is a blank page' and number seventy-nine is 'Rejoice ye tenants of the Earth.' It is clear, however, that (with the slight difference of the numeration of 'Rejoice ye tenants of the Earth') this book was one of those used by the choir and described by Hardy in the novel.

If any other exemplars of the Mellstock carol book exist, they must be in private hands, and I have not been able to see any. Miss Katherine Hardy, Hardy's surviving sister, told me that Hardy got the words of 'Remember Adam's Fall' from their mother; this suggests that he did not have access to another copy of the carol book containing them, although many must have been extant when he was born.

The first occurrence of this very beautiful carol which I have been able to discover is in *Melismata: Musicall Phansies fitting the Court Citie & Countrie Humours*. To 3, 4, and 5 *Voices*, London. Printed by William Stansly & Thomas Adams, 1611; which was edited by T. Ravenscroft. 'Remember Adam's fall,' scored for four voices, is the last of the 'Countrie Pastimes' in this volume, where it is called 'A Christmas Carroll.' As printed by Ravenscroft, it consists of nine verses; of which the second, third, eighth and ninth correspond very closely to the version given by Hardy.

The following are the only noticeable variations:

Hardy:	Ravenscroft:
He hath condemned all—	We were condemned all
He sent His son sinlesse—	How He sent His Son, doubtless
Our ails—	Our sins—
Christmas day i' the morn—	For us that were forlorn
Our Saviour thought no scorn—	And therefore took no scorn
Our faults to take—	Our flesh to take
With heart-most joy—	With heart most joyfully
On this our joyful day—	For this our happy day

The carol is again to be found in *Cantus: Songs and Fancies*. To 3, 4 or 5 Parts apt for Voices and Viols, compiled in 1682 by John Forbes.[119] The tune which is given by Ravenscroft is also that given by Forbes. There is no evidence to show whether or not this was the tune found so troublesome by the Mellstock Quire.

The quire of Stinsford Church consisted, besides the singers, of two violins, a viola, and a violincello or 'bass viol' (the music book of Thomas Hardy the First being for the latter). Puddletown boasted of eight players, and Maiden Newton of nine, which included wood, wind and leather, that is to say clarinets and serpents.[120] These were the choirs alluded to in chapter four, who had been so ill advised as to admit clarinets:

> 'I can well bring back to my mind,' said Mr Penny, 'what I said to poor Joseph Ryme (who took the treble part in Chalk Newton church for two and forty year) when they thought of having clar'nets there, "Joseph," I says, said I, "depend upon't, if so be you have them tooting clar'nets you'll spoil the whole set-out. Clar'nets were not made for the service of the Lard; you can see it by looking at 'em," I said.'

But the serpent was no newcomer. When, in the same chapter, another member of the Mellstock Quire says that other choirs should have done away with serpents, Mr Penny replies: 'Yet there's worse things than serpents. Old things pass away, 'tis true; but a serpent was a good old note; a deep rich note was the serpent.' Although now a rare curiosity, the serpent was once a popular instrument. It was invented by a French Abbé at the end of the sixteenth century, and consisted of conical sections of wooden tube held together by a covering of leather, and having a cupped mouthpiece like that of the bass trombone. It somewhat resembled a serpent in shape. Its greatest vogue was in the eighteenth century, when it was introduced into the British Army by George III; and there is a part for the serpent in Handel's Water Music, now played upon the ophicleide.[121]

Besides the choir and its doings, there are other features of the country life of the very early nineteenth century in *Under the Greenwood Tree*. For example, the consultation of Mrs Endorfield by Fancy can be paralleled in the poems of Barnes,[122] and then there is the dialect. Hardy's principles on the use of dialect in his novels were set forth in two letters to the press, one of which, in answer to a review of *The Return of the Native*, appeared in the *Athenæum* on November 30th, 1878; and the other in the *Spectator* of October 15th, 1881. The substance of the former was that 'an author may be said fairly to convey the spirit of intelligent peasant talk if he retains the idiom, compass and characteristic expressions,' and implied that Hardy's own aim was to 'depict the men and their natures rather than their dialect forms.' In the second he wrote:

> The rule of scrupulously preserving the local idiom, together with the words which have no synonym among those in general use, while printing in the ordinary way most of those local expressions which are but a modified articulation of words in use elsewhere, is the rule I usually follow.

Concerning one expression, 'Good-now,'[123] Hardy was asked in July 1892 if he could explain the origin of it. The draft of his reply is among other papers at Max Gate, and runs as follows:

> The expression 'good now' is still much in use in the interior of this country, though it is dying away hereabout. Its tone is one of conjectural assurance, its precise meaning being 'You may be sure'; and such phrases as 'I'll warrant,' 'methinks,' 'sure enough' would be used as alternatives. The Americanism 'I guess' is near it.
>
> Though I should know exactly how and when to say it, I have never thought about its root meaning. As the people who use it are those who pronounce enough in the old way 'enow,' it is possible that 'good now' is 'true enow,' sure enough.
>
> The commentators are quite in error in taking 'good' to be vocative meaning 'goodman,' 'my good fellow,' as is proved by the frequency of such a sentence as this: 'You won't do it my lad, good now,' which would otherwise be redundant.

It may be added that Hardy was not, as has sometimes been wrongly stated, brought up to speak the Dorset dialect. Mr V.H. Collins reports Hardy as referring to this statement in a certain book, and adding: 'I did not speak it. I knew it, but it was not spoken at home. My mother only used it when speaking to the cottagers, and my father when speaking to his workmen.'[124]

Under the Greenwood Tree contains the seeds of most of the Wessex novels. The Wessex folk are here. The love story is here, not yet touched to tragic issues. The Hardy heroine is instinct in Fancy. The Hardy humour is here. There are touches of the Hardy pathos; for instance, the closing sentences. Above all, there is the power of conveying the moods of outer nature, and that deft poetic description of tiny details. There are foretastes of some of Hardy's favourite stylistic devices, as for example the biblical reference, so very apt, which passes between the grandfathers of bride and bridegroom after the wedding:

'Ah,' said grandfather James to grandfather William as they retired, 'I wonder which she thinks most about, Dick or her wedding raiment!'

'Well, 'tis their nature,' said Grandfather William. 'Remember the words of the prophet Jeremiah: "Can a maid forget her ornaments or a bride her attire?"'

Nevertheless, as a whole, *Under the Greenwood Tree* seems—to one reader of it, at least—to bear, not the stamp of fiction, but the stamp of life seen, remembered, and related by his elders to a child.

A PAIR OF BLUE EYES

A Pair of Blue Eyes was written during the latter half of 1872, in reply to a request from William Tinsley for a serial for *Tinsley's Magazine*.[125] The first instalment appeared in the September number, and the last in July 1873. It was published in three volumes by Tinsley Brothers towards the end of May 1873. Thereafter, every one of Hardy's novels made its first appearance in the pages of some periodical publication. The serial publication of fiction is a feature of literary history which is of much interest, and has not yet been adequately investigated. Nearly all the famous novels of the later nineteenth century first appeared as serial stories. In the years following 1850, there sprang up an enormous crop of new periodicals whose *raison d'être* was the publication of fiction. *Tinsley's Magazine* was one of these. Founded by Tinsley Brothers in 1867, it ran until 1886; and among its contributors was Mrs Henry Wood. Another was *Macmillan's Magazine*, in which *The Wood-landers* first appeared. Perhaps the most notable of these magazines, called into being by the demand for serial fiction, was the *Cornhill*, founded by Smith and Elder in 1860, of which Thackeray was the first editor. It was in the pages of the *Cornhill*, during the editorship of Leslie Stephen, that *Far from the Madding Crowd* was first published, and securely established Hardy as a novelist. The history of the *Cornhill* in its first fifty years is, as its editor wrote with pardonable pride at its Jubilee, almost the history of British fiction in that period. It was for the Jubilee Number that Hardy wrote a poem (reprinted in *Satires of Circumstance*):

Yes; your updated modern page—
All flower-fresh as it appears—
Can claim a time-tried heritage,
That reaches backward fifty years
Which, if but short for sleepy squires,
Is much in magazines' careers.

The account which Tinsley gives of the last book which he had the chance of publishing for Hardy shows very distinct traces of pique:

I tried Mr Hardy's third novel, called *A Pair of Blue Eyes*, as a serial in my magazine, and in book form, but it was by far the weakest of the three books I published of his. However, a good deal owing to my praise of him, and the merits of *Under the Greenwood Tree*, Mr Hardy was engaged to write his novel called *Far from the Madding Crowd* in the *Cornhill Magazine*, and for that he found more readers than for any book I published for him. Of course Mr Hardy was quite within his rights in not offering me his third (*sic*. i.e., fourth) book, although I had paid him rather a large sum of money for *A Pair of Blue Eyes*.[126] However, there is no doubt the Cornhill offer was a large one and started Mr Hardy afresh on his career as a novelist, for just about that time it was by no means certain he would not return to his profession as an architect, from which he could then have obtained a good income. At all events, he told me, soon after I did business with him, that unless writing fiction paid him well, he should not go on with it; but it did pay him, and very well indeed. Since Mr Hardy has become a noted writer of fiction, I have seen it stated that I refused more than one of his books. I never refused one of them, nor even had the chance of doing so.[127]

It is clear that we have there an authentic account of what really passed between Hardy and Tinsley, when the novelist began to feel his power, and was no longer 'much gratified' if he only lost fifteen pounds on every book he published!

The version of *A Pair of Blue Eyes* which appeared in *Tinsley's Magazine* is identical with that published in volume form, after the first half-dozen paragraphs. Hardy greatly improved his first draft; the first paragraph of the original is almost as horrible a specimen of 'journalese' as could be imagined. It is hard to realize how the same man could at the same sitting write such a paragraph, and then that describing Elfride's expression by illustrations from famous pictures; or that about her eyes—'blue as the blue we see between the retreating mouldings of hills and woody slopes on a sunny September morning.'

A Pair of Blue Eyes received more recognition in the Press than any of Hardy's previous works. It was reviewed simultaneously in the *Athenæum* and the *Spectator* on June 28th, 1873, in the *Graphic* on July 12th, in the *Saturday Review* on August 2nd, in the *Examiner* on October 10th, and in the *Pall Mall Gazette* on October 25th. The *Examiner* contrasted Hardy with George Eliot; and the *Saturday Review* wrote:

> Many readers of the fresher and truer sort of fiction will be glad to welcome another story from the author of *Under the Greenwood Tree*, who now for the first time assumes his real name ... It is one of the most artistically constructed among recent novels. And, from considerations affecting higher matters than mere construction, we should assign it a very high place among works of its class.

This review concluded:

> The author of *A Pair of Blue Eyes* has much to learn and many faults yet to avoid. But he is a writer who, to a singular purity of thought and intention, unites great power of imagination.

Shortly after the book appeared, Hardy received a letter from Coventry Patmore—a total stranger to him—expressing the view that the story of the novel was not a conception for prose, and regretting 'at almost every page that such unequalled beauty and power should not have assured themselves the immortality which would have been impressed upon them by the form of verse.'[128] It was penetrating on the part of Patmore to have seen that the new novelist was really a poet by nature. *A Pair of Blue Eyes* was Tennyson's favourite among Hardy's novels.[129]

The framework of the story was taken from Hardy's own experience; he himself visited Cornwall on a mission of church restoration; and on that mission, in the Vicarage itself, he met the girl who became his wife. There are one or two traces of Hardy's own experience. For example, the copying of the old seat ends in the church (in Chap. VII):

> He had a genuine artistic reason for coming, though no such reason seemed to be required. Six-and-thirty old seat ends, of exquisite fifteenth-century work-manship, were rapidly decaying in an aisle of the church, and it became politic to make drawings of their worm-eaten contours ere they were battered past recognition in the turmoil of the so-called restoration.

The drawings which Hardy made of the old seat ends are preserved to this day in the present church of St Juliot.[130] A number of incidents in the story had happened to people whom Hardy had known.[131] But further deductions on the value of the book as autobiography are not permissible. It should, in particular, be obvious that, if Hardy himself resembled any character in the novel, it was Henry Knight, and not, as has been unwisely stated, Stephen Smith. Hardy was in his thirtieth year when he went to Cornwall; he had written much poetry, and at least one novel; he had lived for years in London, and he had seen something of life.

A parallel between the relations of Stephen Smith and Knight, and those of Hardy and Horace Moule, was drawn by F.A. Hedgcock in his book *Thomas Hardy, Penseur et Artiste* (1911). In his first chapter, Dr Hedgcock wrote: 'On ne peut s'empêcher de voir dans le récit des luttes de Stephen Smith, de Clym Yeobright et de Jude Fawley une part de souvenir personel.' That sentence alone might have been upheld. To some extent, every man's life appears in his writings; and Hardy used his experiences in his work, although he only used them as the raw material out of which he constructed different situations. But Dr Hedgcock drew further deductions, the chief value of which was that they came to Hardy's knowledge and produced an interesting and valuable pronouncement upon this subject of autobiography in his novels. In *Talks with Thomas Hardy*, Mr V.H. Collins (on p. 73) reports a discussion with Hardy concerning the translation of Dr Hedgcock's book into English, in the course of which Hardy is reported to have repudiated his self-appointed biographer, saying 'I cannot understand how he could print such stuff.'

An interesting feature of *A Pair of Blue Eyes* is that Hardy returned in it to what seems to have been a very early practice, the heading of every chapter by a quotation. In his later books, the quotations were put in the text; not but that there is a fair sprinkling of quotations and allusions in the text of *A*

Pair of Blue Eyes, including ones to Adam Smith, Macaulay and Cicero; but there are far fewer than in *Desperate Remedies.* The epigraph of the book is taken from Hamlet. The scene between Smith and Knight in the Luxellian vault seems to have been suggested by the gravediggers' scene. The number of Shakespearian allusions in Hardy's early novels is interesting. There are five in *Desperate Remedies,* one or two in *Under the Greenwood Tree,* and three or four in *Far from the Madding Crowd.* Four of the chapter headings in *An Indiscretion* are from Shakespeare, and at least two of those in *A Pair of Blue Eyes.*

Hardy himself classed *A Pair of Blue Eyes* among his 'romances'; and, writing in 1912, he said: 'In its action it exhibits the romantic stage of an idea which was further developed in a later book.' The allusion is clearly to *Two on a Tower.* Although *A Pair of Blue Eyes* is a less satisfactory book than *Under the Greenwood Tree,* it contains passages of greater imaginative power than any which Hardy had hitherto written. The famous scene on the 'Cliff without a Name' in chapters twenty-one and twenty-two is almost too hackneyed for quotation. The early reviewers noted it, and the critic of the *Saturday Review* described it as 'worked out with extraordinary force.' The tragedy in the book is authentic Hardy; but it is not yet the searing tragedy of the later novels. The chief charm of *A Pair of Blue Eyes* is in the poetry which Patmore recognized; a poetical quality both in conception and execution which appears on nearly every page.

FAR FROM THE MADDING CROWD

The genesis of *Far from the Madding Crowd* is described in *The Life and Letters of Leslie Stephen,* by F.W. Maitland (1906), to which Hardy contributed some paragraphs, as well as his poem 'The Schreckhorn' (afterwards printed in *Satires of Circumstance).* On p. 270 of that volume Hardy writes:

> It was at the beginning of December 1872, on a wet and windy morning, when in a remote part of the country, that a letter stained with raindrops arrived for me in a handwriting so fine that it might have been traced with a pin's point.

The letter was from Stephen, and led to negotiations which ended in his accepting outright the novel which Hardy was in process of writing, without having even seen the whole manuscript. Hardy came to terms with Smith and Elder, the publishers, and proofs of the first number were sent to him. When returning from Cornwall on the last day of December 1873, he bought at Plymouth a copy of the *Cornhill,* and 'there, to his surprise, saw his story placed at the beginning of the magazine, with a striking illustration.'[132]

The appearance of the story raised a great deal of interest, and the *Spectator,* during the first week of 1874, hazarded a guess that it might be from the pen of George Eliot; a similar comparison was made later in other quarters when the book appeared in volume form. Leslie Stephen wrote to Hardy:

I am to congratulate you on the reception of your first number. Besides the gentle *Spectator*, which thinks that you must be George Eliot because you know the names of the stars, several good judges have spoken to me warmly of the *Madding Crowd*. Moreover the *Spectator*, though flighty in its head, has really a good deal of critical feeling. I always like to be praised by it—and indeed by other people! The story comes out very well, I think, and I have no criticism to make.[133]

Far from the Madding Crowd ran in the *Cornhill* from January until December 1874; it was published in two volumes by Smith and Elder in November, with the same illustrations by Helen Paterson that had accompanied it in the *Cornhill*; and it firmly established Hardy's career as a novelist. His next novel *The Hand of Ethelberta* was also to appear in the *Cornhill*; while Smith and Elder remained his publishers until 1880, and again published *The Mayor of Casterbridge* in 1886. We have seen how the friendship with Stephen deeply influenced Hardy's thought. Not the least of the results produced by *Far from the Madding Crowd* was that it enabled its author to marry Emma Lavinia Gifford in September.[134]

An incident occurred during the serial appearance of the story which was significant as a presage of what was to happen to Hardy in after years. He records it in *The Life and Letters of Leslie Stephen*. Stephen had written, warning him that the seduction of Fanny Robin must be treated in a gingerly fashion, and adding that this was necessary owing to 'an excessive prudery of which I am ashamed.' Hardy continues:

> I wondered what had so suddenly caused, in one who had seemed anything but a prude, the 'excessive prudery' alluded to. But I did not learn till I saw him in April. Then he told me that an unexpected Grundian cloud, though no bigger than a man's hand as yet, had appeared upon our serene horizon. Three respectable ladies and subscribers, representing he knew not how many more, had written to upbraid him for an improper passage in a page of the story which had already been published.
>
> I was struck mute, till I said 'Well, if you value the opinion of such people, why didn't you think of them beforehand and strike out the passage?'—'I ought to have, since it is their opinion, whether I value it or no,' he said with a half groan. 'But it didn't occur to me that there was anything to object to!'

The Grundian cloud apparently passed away without discharging its thunder further; and when the book was published in volume form, the very passage which had roused the reprobation of Stephen's lady subscribers was quoted in the review which appeared in *The Times* on January 25th, 1875. Whereupon Hardy triumphed over Stephen with: 'You cannot say that *The Times* is not respectable'; to which Stephen, being an editor and therefore infallible replied: 'You have no more consciousness of these things than a child!' Slight as it was, the incident foreshadowed the mutilation of *Tess* and the burning of *Jude*, which was to end Hardy's career as a novelist. The passage in question was in the eighth chapter, from the marvellous scene in the malthouse, where Master Coggan is describing Bathsheba's father:

'Well now, you'd hardly believe it, but that man—our Miss Everdene's father—was one of the ficklest husbands alive, after a while. Understand, a' didn't want to be fickle, but he couldn't help it. The poor feller were faithful and true enough to her in his wish, but his heart would rove, do what he would. He spoke to me in real tribulation about it once. "Coggan," he said, "I could never wish for a handsomer woman than I've got, but feeling she's ticketed as my lawful wife, I can't help my wicked heart wandering, do what I will." But at last I believe he cured it by making her take off her wedding ring and calling her by her maiden name as they sat together after the shop was shut, and so a' would fancy she was only his sweetheart, and not married to him at all. And as soon as he could thoroughly fancy he was doing wrong and committing the seventh, a' got to like her as well as ever, and they lived on a perfect picture of mutel love.'

Stephen's lady subscribers must indeed have found this very terrible; but they might have found comfort from the comment of Joseph Poorgrass:

'Well, 'twas a most ungodly remedy; but we ought to feel deep cheerfulness that a happy Providence kept it from being any worse.'

Far from the Madding Crowd was copiously reviewed in all the periodicals, and most of the reviews were very laudatory.[135] Several of the reviewers, including the critic of the *Times*, again made the comparison with George Eliot which the *Spectator* had first made on the strength of the opening chapter.[136] Mrs Hardy gives an interesting passage describing Hardy's own attitude to this comparison:

Why (it was made) he could never understand, since, so far as he had read that great thinker—one of the greatest living, he thought, though not a born story-teller, by any means—she had never touched the life of the fields: her country people having seemed to him, too, more like small townsfolk than rustics; and as evidencing a woman's wit cast in country dialogue rather than real country humour, which he regarded as rather of the Shakespeare and Fielding sort. However, he conjectured, as a possible reason for the flattering guess, that he had latterly been reading Comte's *Positive Philosophy*, and writings of that school, some of whose expressions had thus passed into his vocabulary, expressions which were also common to George Eliot.[137]

It seems much more likely that the critics in question made the comparison on the strength of a certain occasional similarity of phrasing which had nothing to do with positivism. *The Times* critic wrote:

Almost from the first page to the last the reader is never quite free from a suspicion that Mr Hardy is, consciously or unconsciously, imitating George Eliot's phraseology and style of dealing with the rough material of words. Having thus found almost the only fault that is worth finding, we will return to a brief description...

The charge is almost too indefinite either to confirm or refute. But it is true that occasionally there is a similarity of phrasing. For example:

The muddy lanes, green or clayey, that seemed to the unaccustomed eye to lead nowhere but into each other, did really lead, with patience, to a distant high road; but there were many feet in Basset which they led more frequently to a centre of dissipation, spoken of formally as the 'Markis o' Granby,' but among intimates as 'Dickison's.' A large, low room with a sanded floor, a cold scent of tobacco, modified by undetected beer dregs, Mr Dickison leaning against the door post with a melancholy pimpled face, looking as irrelevant to the daylight as a last night's guttered candle—all this may not seem a very seductive form of temptation; but the majority of men in Basset found it fatally alluring when encountered on their road towards four o'clock on a wintry afternoon.

That, especially the sentence describing the inn, might perfectly well be Hardy. Actually, it is from the eighth chapter of *The Mill on the Floss*. To try to carry further the resemblance between the two great novelists is unnecessary; for the critics of *Far from the Madding Crowd* carried it no further themselves; and not all of them acknowledged it. The critic in the *Athenæum*, for instance, wrote:

> How his present story could ever have been supposed to have been written by George Eliot we cannot conceive ... We should say, on the contrary, that some of the scenes, notably that where Sergeant Troy goes through the sword exercises before Bathsheba, are worthy in their extravagance of Mr Reade, and of him only; while the stronger parts are Mr Hardy's own. At least we know of no other living writer who could have so described the burning rick yard or the approaching thunderstorm, or given us the wonderful comicalities of the supper at the malt house.

The position which Hardy was making for himself can be gauged from the fact that a German translation of *Far from the Madding Crowd*, was asked for.[138] Hardy was never popular in Germany,[139] so that this was the more remarkable. But it was less surprising that the novel should meet with favour in France; for the French public has appreciated Hardy more thoroughly than any outside English-speaking countries; most of his works sell in good French translations, and when he died, the Académie, at a special meeting, voted an address of sympathy to the English nation, and the *Revue des Deux Mondes* wrote of the burial in Westminster Abbey: 'Il n'y a aucune doute que l'Angleterre vient de placer là un de ses immortels ... La Revue se devait de saluer sa grande ombre.'[140]

The first time that Hardy was brought to the notice of the French public was in a long review of *A Pair of Blue Eyes* and *Far from the Madding Crowd* which appeared in *La Revue des Deux Mondes* on December 15th, 1875. This article was headed 'Le Roman pastoral en Angleterre,' and was from the pen of Léon Boucher.

M. Boucher gave a brief sketch of the contemporary English novel, in which Wilkie Collins occupied the chief place. After a mention of *Desperate Remedies*, he briefly reviewed *Under the Greenwood Tree*, and at much greater length *A Pair of Blue Eyes*, which he praised very highly. Most of the article was devoted to *Far from the Madding Crowd*, from which long passages were translated.

> M. Hardy a voulu rajeunir le genre antique et souvent ennuyeux de la pastorale, et il y a mis une telle vérité d'observation, une passion si profonde, une poésie si fraiche, un style si puissant, tant d'idéal et de réalité à la fois, que cette transformation peut presque passer pour une création originale.

The criticism of the more highly-coloured parts of the book was essentially sound, and has been repeated by many later critics:

> Ici commence la partie pathétique du roman. Faut-il le dire? Quoique M. Hardy y ait déployé un singulier talent, c n'est peut-être pas celle qui lui fait le plus d'honneur. On y cotoie le bord du mélodrame, et, si l'on n'y tombe pas tout-a-fait, c'est que les situations, tout en étant violentes, ne deviennent jamais communes.

The conclusion of this article was:

> On ne saurait dire que M. Hardy appartient à une école, car par l'indépendance de son talent il ne relève que de lui-même. ... Ceux qui aiment à trouver dans le romancier un véritable écrivain sauront lui faire une place à part et le distinguer dans la foule.

Far from the Madding Crowd has been twice adapted to the stage. In March 1882 a dramatic version by Mr J. Comyns Carr was produced at the Prince of Wales Theatre, Liverpool, and afterwards at the Globe Theatre in London; apparently without financial success. It seems that Hardy himself, who went to Liverpool on purpose to see it,[141] considered it too far from the novel. A play based on *Far from the Madding Crowd* was produced in the Corn Exchange, Dorchester, in the autumn of 1909, and afterwards before the Society of Dorset Men in London. Mrs Hardy writes of this: 'Hardy had nothing to do with the adaptation, but thought it a neater achievement than the London version of 1882.'[142] Although many attempts have been made to dramatize various novels by Hardy, the most noteworthy being in the case of *Tess*, none of them have been really successful. However good in itself, the result is never Hardy; the transplantation into another form of literature cannot be effected without sacrificing almost all that makes the greatness of the novel. Had Hardy lived under Elizabeth or James I, he would probably have achieved great stage drama (which *The Dynasts* was never meant to be). As it was, he wrote fiction 'for the relief of his necessities'; and in due course produced *The Mayor of Casterbridge* and *Tess of the d'Urbervilles*. It seems best to be content with what he has given us; we already have *Othello* and *The Duchess of Malfi*.

In *Far from the Madding Crowd*, Hardy has come almost to his full stature. The sphere of experiment has been left behind; not only does he know what he wishes to do; he has the technique at command with which to do it. The humour of the Wessex rustic—and it was here that Hardy first used the word Wessex, immediately restoring it to the English language—is probably at its best in these pages. The descriptions; the opening chapter, the sheep-shearing, Gabriel Oak thatching the ricks before the storm; are worthy to

stand beside any that Hardy was to write. Bathsheba is that very characteristic compound called by critics 'the Hardy woman'; but Boldwood, who
has, strangely, no Christian name, is too much of a lay figure. The character
of Gabriel Oak, on the other hand, is an achievement. This strong, simple
and lovable shepherd is one of the most memorable figures in the Wessex
novels. The 'happy ending' is a concession; but even *The Return of the Native*
ends with such a concession; if a final sound of wedding bells can be called a
'happy ending' when it comes after such a breaking of hearts that the peace
of the grave is welcome. In *Far from the Madding Crowd*, tragedy stops short of
the intensity which the later novels achieve; indeed, there is more pathos
than real tragedy. The whole Boldwood episode is too artificial to grip the
heart; but the episode of Fanny Robin does. It was the development of the
manner in which the fortieth chapter is written that was to give us the Will of
Michael Henchard, and the baptism of Tess's Sorrow. But *Far from the
Madding Crowd* does not sear as *Tess* sears, or *The Mayor of Casterbridge*.
Moreover, it still lacks that power—so memorably put forth in *The Return of
the Native*—of enveloping the mere plot in an atmosphere more potent than
any single incident. It is, in short, a work which everywhere shows the
highest talent; but not yet, except perhaps occasionally in its comedy, genius.
Such a novel should be highly popular; and popular *Far from the Madding
Crowd* certainly was. It made Hardy's name as a novelist, and so paved the
way for the greater things to come.

Notes

1. 'It would, I suppose, be absurd to ask whether there is any philosophy in *The Dynasts*.'
2. *Thomas Hardy: An Illustration of the Philosophy of Schopenhauer*, Philadelphia. Winston, 1911.
3. G.R. Swann: *Philosophical Parallelisms in Six English Novelists*, Pennsylvania, 1931.
4. The preface to *Winter Words* concludes 'I also repeat what I have often stated, that no harmonious philosophy is attempted in these pages—or in any bygone pages of mine, for that matter.' Cf. the paragraph devoted to the Spirits in the Preface to *The Dynasts*.
5. A.P. Elliott: *Fatalism in the Works of Thomas Hardy*. Philadelphia, 1935.
6. Louise de Ridder Barzin: *Le Pessimisme de Thomas Hardy*. Brussels, 1932.
7. *Studies of a Biographer*, vol. 2, p. 129.
8. *Early Life*, p. 43.
9. *Early Life*, p. 66.
10. C.C.J. Webb: *A Study of Religious Thought in England since 1850*, p. 72.
11. *Jude the Obscure*, Pt. 3, Chap. IV.
12. The memorial is preserved in a collection of Oxford pamphlets in the Bodleian. Gough. Adds. Oxon 8°. 179.
13. *Dorset County Chronicle*, May 2, 1861.
14. *Early Life*, p. 198.
15. *Religious Thought in England since 1850*, p. 12.
16. *Early Life*, p. 269.
17. *Early Life*, p. 159.
18. *Life and Letters of T.H. Huxley*, by L. Huxley, Vol. 1, p. 176.
19. *Life and Letters of T.H. Huxley*, vol. I, p. 180 *et seq*. There was no official report of the

meeting issued, and the versions of the speeches given by eye-witnesses, in the *Life of Huxley* and in the *Life and Letters of Charles Darwin* by F. Darwin, vol. 2, p. 320 *et seq.*, have slight verbal differences. But the substance is common to all. The meeting had resounding publicity, in Press and from pulpit, all over the country.

The allusion to rock pigeons refers to Darwin's example that the four varieties of domestic pigeon all derive from the rock pigeon.

20. *Later Years*, p. 38.

21. Quoted in the article on Huxley by W.F.R. Weldon in the *Dictionary of National Biography*.

22. Preface to *Late Lyrics*. The poem is in *Poems of the Past and Present*.

23. Catalogue of the Ashley Library, vol. 10.

24. *On Liberty*, Chap. II.

25. Catalogue of the Ashley Library, Vol. 2, p. 169.

26. One of the epithets was 'an unclean fiery imp from the pit.' The famous article by Morley appeared in the *Saturday Review* of August 4th, 1866.

27. This sonnet was republished in *Poems and Ballads*, Second Series.

28. The 'Hymn to Prosperine' is also quoted in Chap. IV of Part 3 of *Jude*.

29. One of the choruses of *Atalanta* is quoted in *Tess*, Chap. XXXV.

30. In the essay 'Dreams and Realities,' reprinted in *An Agnostic's Apology*; like the other contents of that volume, it had first appeared in a periodical.

31. Charles Bradlaugh (1833–91), militant atheist and republican, author of *A Plea for Atheism*.

32. In 1888, Hardy noted in his diary 'When dogma has to be balanced on its feet by such hair-splitting arguments as the late M. Arnold's, it must be in a very bad way.' (*Early Life*, p. 281).

33. This is the account of the origin of the word given in the *New English Dictionary*.

34. In *Freethinking and Plain Speaking*.

35. To the Rev. Dr Grosart, whom Hardy advised to read Herbert Spencer, Stephen, who had also been asked, replied that it was the Doctor's business to explain to him, not his to the Doctor.

36. Hardy recounts the incident in *The Life of Leslie Stephen*.

37. *Later Years*, p. 121.

38. *Early Life*, p. 129.

39. *Early Life*, p. 189.

40. *La Philosophie positive* was translated by Harriet Martineau in 1853, and *Le Discours sur l'Ensemble* had been translated in 1852.

41. Dr de Ridder Barzin even suggests a comparison of Hardy with Renan, 'le philosophe du devenir,' *Le Pessimisme de Hardy*, p. 71.

42. For example, those on the relations between the sexes. Comte laid great stress on marriage and the importance of its being indissoluble.

43. Hardy meant by this that Aeschylus suspected the world to be an illusion. See p. 37.

44. *Later Years*, p. 91.

45. *Edinburgh Review*, Vol. 207, p. 421.

46. *Saturday Review*, Vol. 97, p. 136.

47. *Thomas Hardy*: A Critical Study.

48. A letter from Gosse to this effect is quoted at the end of Hedgcock's *Thomas Hardy: Penseur et Artiste*.

49. *Thomas Hardy: An Illustration of the Philosophy of Schopenhauer*, p. 40.

50. A Life of Schopenhauer appeared in 1875, and the *Westminster Review*, published an article upon him.

51. Schopenhauer has his own use of the word 'idea,' which he employs to mean 'phenomenon'; claiming this to be the Platonic, as opposed to the Kantian, sense.

52. In Hardy, who was not so subtle at metaphysics, space and time are part of the 'laws' of Immanent Will. But Schopenhauer simply means that the will is not subject to the *principium individuationis*.

53. See p. 275.

54. George R. Swann: *Philosophical Parallelisms in Six English Novelists*.

55. See *Westminster Review*, for 1876.

56. *Later Years*, p. 270.

57. According to the N.E.D., the word 'monism' first appears in the eighteen-sixties. There is one instance of 'monist' in the writings of Sir W. Hamilton, in the 'thirties.

58. 'As Gibbon blandly remarks on the evidence for and against Christian miracles, the duty of an historian does not call upon him to interpose his private judgment in this nice and important controversy.'

59. Part I, Chap. III, Section 28. (P. 139 in the edition of 1892.)

60. By Hedgcock, and also by Abercrombie.

61. Aulard renders: 'Voici maintenant que le monde est représenté dans une petite carte. Voici que tout est semblable et que les découvertes n'accroissent que notre néant.'

62. 'Rien, si ce n'est de savoir avec certitude que tout est vain, excepté la douleur, vous reste.'

63. Aulard renders thus: 'Maintenant tu te reposeras pour toujours, mon coeur fatigué. Elle a péri, l'erreur suprême que j'ai crue éternelle pour moi. Elle a péri. Je sens bien, qu'en nous des chères erreurs non seulement l'espoir, mais le désir est éteint. Repose-toi pour toujours. Tu as assez palpité. Aucune chose ne mérite tes battements, et de tes soupirs la terre n'est pas digne. Amertume et ennui, voila la vie; elle n'est rien d'autre, le monde n'est que fange. Repose-toi désormais. Désespère à jamais. A notre race le destin n'a donné que de mourir. Méprise désormais et toi-même, et la nature, et le pouvoir honteux, qui, caché, régne pour la ruine commune, et l'infinie vanité de ce tout.'

64. *Later Years*, p. 266.

65. *Life and Letters of Lord Macaulay*, by C.O. Trevelyan, vol. I, p. 30, *et seq*.

66. *Early Life*, p. 43.

67. *Early Life*, p. 50 *et seq*.

68. *Early Life*, p. 61.

69. *Early Years*, p. 62.

70. *Early Life*, p. 71.

71. *Early Life*, p. 75.

72. *Early Life*, p. 76.

73. All the foregoing paragraph is based on *Early Life*, p. 76, *et seq*.

74. *Early Life*, p. 83.

75. *Sunday Times*, January 22nd, 1928, 'Hardy's Lost Novel.'

76. P. 54.

77. Incorrectly described as 'the *London Times*,' by Prof. Weber.

78. That Meredith's advice, probably dictated by his own experience with *Modern Love* a year or two earlier, was correct, was proved by the fate which *Desperate Remedies* met with at the hands of the *Spectator* in 1871.

79. This is not in the letter of August 10th, 1868, as published in *The Life and Letters of Alexander Macmillan*. It may have been in a subsequent letter, as Hardy appears to have called on Macmillan in December (*Early Life*, p. 78); or possibly Hardy may have confused Macmillan with Chapman, at whose invitation he called in March 1869 to be given the opinion of Meredith, Chapman's reader. The parallelism between the interview with Morley, as related by Gosse, and that with Meredith as related by Mrs Hardy, is striking.

80. In *A Pair of Blue Eyes*, the fact that Stephen Smith is the son of local peasant parents is the cause of the whole calamity, without which there would have been no story.

81. In *An Indiscretion*, the forbidding comes at a later stage, but the situation is fundamentally the same.

82. Although the details are here different, the result achieved is the same; namely that the hero goes to London and begins to attain a success which places him upon a different footing. In *The Poor Man and the Lady*, he appears to have followed Hardy by becoming an architect, and in *An Indiscretion*, he follows Hardy by becoming an author, so that the very differences are interesting, as Hardy used the two experiences he had himself known as the two versions of his story.

83. In *An Indiscretion* the letter in which Geraldine tells Edward of her father's ban on their correspondence ends with a postscript 'Might we not write just one line at very rare intervals? It is too much never to write at all.'

84. In *An Indiscretion* the proposal to call is the man's. This, and Gosse's version of the episode, show how Hardy's increased knowledge of the world induced him to soften down the

wild impossibilities of *The Poor Man and the Lady* into the much more probable events of *An Indiscretion* without material alteration of the general situation.

85. In *An Indiscretion* the woman's avowal of her love comes a little later, when Geraldine comes to Egbert in the night.

86. *Early Life*, p. 64.

87. See p. 274. Prof. Weber remarks on this passage that 'it helps to date the action in the nineteenth century.' Being an author's remark, it no more dates the action than would a reference to the siege of Troy; moreover, the introduction of a steam threshing machine sufficiently indicates the nineteenth century.

88. *Tess.* Chap. XXV.

89. She calls it 'un sombre recit de terreur à la Wilkie Collins.' *Le Roman et les Idées en Angleterre*, p. 372.

90. *Early Life*, p. 84 *et seq.*

91. William and Edward Tinsley, whose offices were at 18 Catherine Street, Strand.

92. *Early Life*, p. 100.

93. *Early Life*, p. 109.

94. This letter was published in an article, 'Amenities of Book Collecting,' by A. Edward Newton, in *The Atlantic Monthly*, March 1915.

95. *Early Life*, p. 110.

96. *Early Life*, p. 110.

97. *Spectator*, April 22nd, 1871.

98. *Early Life*, p. 111.

99. *Idem*, p. 112.

100. At least two books have been entirely devoted to this subject: *La Femme dans le Roman de Thomas Hardy*, by A. Liron (Paris, 1919) and *Thomas Hardy's Frauen im Lichte seiner Weltanschauung*, by Gerda Salberg (Mulhouse, 1927).

101. All of them first appeared serially in *All the Year Round*, except *Armadale*, which was in the *Cornhill.*

102. In a letter dated February 18th, 1918, now in the Ashley Library, Hardy wrote to Gosse: 'For the relief of my necessities, as the Prayer Book puts it, I began writing novels and made a sort of trade of it.' Ashley Catalogue, Vol. X, p. 131.

103. *Random Recollections of an Old Publisher*, Vol. 1.

104. *A Pair of Blue Eyes*, Chap. XII: 'Elfride had known no more about the stings of evil report than the native wild fowl knew of the effects of Crusoe's first shot.'

105. The introduction to W.A. Brockington's edition of *After Dark* (1900).

106. V.H. Collins: *Talks with Thomas Hardy*, p. 55.

107. *Random Recollections*, Vol. 1, p. 127.

108. *Early Life*, p. 114. The details of this and following paragraphs are taken from Mrs Hardy's account of *Under the Greenwood Tree* on p. 113 *et seq.*, unless otherwise indicated.

109. *Random Recollections of an old Publisher*, Vol. 1, p. 127.

110. *Early Life*, pp. 115 and 120.

111. A parallel passage in the 1912 Preface to *A Pair of Blue Eyes* gives Hardy's own answer: 'To the ripe-minded critic ... an immaturity in its views of life and in its workmanship will of course be apparent. But to correct these by the judgment of later years, even had correction been possible, would have resulted, as with all such attempts, in the disappearance of whatever freshness and spontaneity the pages may have as they stand.'

112. A review of the collected edition of Hardy's works, which appeared in the *Spectator* on September 7th, 1912, rightly said: 'Great art is representative of life, not critical of it ... The art of Sophocles and Shakespeare does not leave our minds impressed by a pessimistic conception of existence. It represents the flux of all things, the cessation of pain and grief as well as of joy and pleasure. It has its compensating values ...'

113. This first appeared as one of nine 'Colloquial Sketches' in Harper's *New Monthly Magazine* March–June 1891, and is reprinted as 'A Few Crusted Characters' in *Life's Little Ironies*.

114. *Early Life*, p. 121. She also points out that Old Dewy was not, as has been supposed, a portrait of Hardy's grandfather. But the idea of the three generations probably came to Hardy from his own family.

115. *Early Life*, p. 11.

116. *Early Life*, p. 15.

117. I am indebted to Dr Percy Scholes for a note on this matter: he wrote to me: '*Under the Greenwood Tree* turns on the introduction of an American organ. That makes 1860 the earliest possible date, which is late for the conditions described. Even the Harmonium did not come into use much earlier or we might guess that Hardy had got a wrong name for the instrument. Note that Hardy mentions "Queen's Scholars," so the date must (I think) be subsequent to 1870.'

118. The prevalence and importance of village orchestras is illustrated in K.R. Macdermott's *Sussex Church Music in the Past* (2nd ed., 1923). Also in *Devon and Cornwall Notes and Queries*, 1916–17.

119. The version and tune given in Chappell's *Old English Popular Music* (2nd ed. by Wooldridge, 1893, Vol. 1, p. 144) are those of Ravenscroft.

120. *Early Life*, p. 12.

121. There is a full account, and a picture, of the serpent in *Old English Instruments of Music* (1910), by Francis W. Galpin, p. 195 *et seq.*

122. e.g., 'Haven Woone's fortune a-twold,' etc. There is a thorough study of Hardy's allusions to white and black witchcraft in *Folkways in Thomas Hardy*, by Ruth A. Firor (1931).

123. In Chap. IV, 'He's clever for a silly chap, good now, sir.' The same chapter contains the expression 'chips in porridge,' to which Hardy puts a footnote that it 'must be a corruption of something less questionable.'

124. *Talks with Thomas Hardy*, p. 73.

125. *Early Life*, p. 118.

126. According to Mrs Hardy, the sum for both the serial and three volume rights was double what Hardy could have earned by architecture in the same period (*Early Life*, p. 118), and was considered 'very reasonable.'

127. *Random Recollections*, Vol. 1, p. 127.

128. *Early Life*, p. 138.

129. *Ibid.*, p. 179.

130. *Ibid.*, p. 105.

131. *Ibid.*, p. 97.

132. *Early Life*, p. 128.

133. *Ibid.*, p. 129.

134. The serial form of *Far from the Madding Crowd* was identical with that published in two volumes, with the exception of a few words changed in chapter forty-eight. In the serial, this chapter was headed 'Doubts arise, doubts vanish.'

135. *Echo*, Nov. 28th 1874; *World*, Dec. 2nd, 1874; *Athenæum*, Dec. 5th 1874; *Examiner*, Dec. 5th, 1874; *Spectator*, Dec. 19th, 1874; *Saturday Review*, Jan. 9th, 1875; *Times*, Jan. 25th, 1875.

136. See also L. W. Berle's *George Eliot and Thomas Hardy: a Contrast* (1917).

137. *Early Life*, p. 129.

138. *Early Life*, p. 136.

139. In a letter which appeared in the *New Statesman* on January 21st, 1928, it was stated that 'quite recently a German bookman of repute told me that he had time and again tried to get the novels taken up by a German publisher, but that in every case the suggestion had been turned down.' Nevertheless, *Jude* had a successful career as a serial in Germany; and *Tess* has been translated into most European languages.

140. *Revue des Deux Mondes*, January 1928.

141. *Early Life*, p. 198.

142. *Later Years*, p. 140.

188
Thomas Hardy

---◆---

GEOFFREY GRIGSON

What is the common way of regarding Thomas Hardy, whose birth is commemorated this year, and whose life stretched across the nineteenth century to our own, through war and war? Other professionals—Henry James, for instance—have always patronized him a bit. Not quite an author, not quite a poet, not quite an artist; and also, no doubt, not quite a gentleman. Not at all Browning, not Mr T.S. Eliot. The man who wrote '*When I set out for Lyonesse*' and '*Only a man harrowing clods*'. Not quite a peasant, but nearly. And he said that the Odyssey or the Iliad was 'in the *Marmion* class'. I doubt if Mr Clive Bell would think of Hardy and Cézanne together. I doubt if many of those who read, or advise us to read, *The Dynasts* at the present time, go far deeper than the topicality of Napoleon's threat to invade England or the resemblance between Hitler and Napoleon as two products of the Unseen Forces and the interplay of the Eternal Abstractions.

Hardy was our prelude. He was not (nor was Cézanne) a lumpy, honest and simple peasant; but a complicated, cultured, resolute, narrow, sensitive man of the new professional classes of the nineteenth century; his profession, that is his preliminary profession, being architecture. He appeared simple, because his effects were reduced to the apparent simplicity of bone. He was a man without ambition, able to conceive ideas, roll them round, feed them, and mature them slowly through a very long time. He was penetrated by natural objects and phenomena, which he felt thoroughly as themselves, and, in one act, as images of the knot of human life. As he saw one thing, he saw another: the little old simpleton saw the affectation of his superior contemporaries (Walter Pater's manner 'is that of one carrying weighty ideas without spilling them'); but he did not wish to seem a depreciator and so he destroyed nearly all the notes he had made of this kind.

It seems to me facile to claim that the profession in which a man is bred—a passive act—must be related to the profession in which he discovers himself. The link may be there, but it can seldom be proved and it belongs

SOURCE *The Harp of Aeolus and Other Essays on Art, Literature & Nature* London, 1947, pp. 123–30.

usually to that order of unscientific and sentimental statements about descent which live in the first chapters of biography. An anthologist, for example, has just detected a strain of Celtic mysticism in the poet Robert Stephen Hawker, though he was English by descent and training, *because he lived in Cornwall.* So I am sure it is wrong to say that such and such happened in Hardy's writing, because he was an architect. Architecture was not vitally prominent in Hardy's work, certainly not in Hardy's imagination. How could it be? Architecture is a poor art—a poor professional art—for a strong sense of life. How can a young architect give form, except in drawings, to the urgencies of his feeling? I presume that architecture must be a profession of competent channels—competent hacks, if you like—through whom the already shaped ideas are put into stone, brick, or steel. The ideas change a little between entering and leaving the channel, but the architects who feel the time, and feel history and first shape the ideas, are very few. They are the rare, widely separated men of genius, fortunate in the coincidence of their own powers and a receptive time in which many buildings are demanded to fill some new social need. Since the means of architectural realization are costly, communal, and non-individual, so great an urgency as Thomas Hardy's in his youth must have broken out elsewhere unless there had been some fluke of favourable circumstance. And, as it was, Hardy showed little architectural talent, either as a draughtsman or a designer. He acquiesced in architecture, and was pushed into it by his father, who was a builder, and had worked for Mr John Hicks, the Dorchester architect and church restorer by whom Hardy was first instructed. 'Hardy was a born bookworm, that and that alone was unchanging in him; he had sometimes, too, wished to enter the Church, but he cheerfully agreed to go to Mr Hick's'.[1]

So much for that. And now it is established that Hardy and architecture came accidentally together (much as a lawyer's son may become a lawyer and then a landscape painter), it will be safe to say how his practice of architecture tinged, for example, his poetry; and to affirm that if Hardy's architectural talent was mediocre, he had that sense of human history in physical images which architecture needs and which so few architects ever possess.

Hardy worked chiefly on church restoration, vicarages and rectories, and schools for the London School Board. He stayed for some time with Mr Hicks, sketching and surveying churches in the West of England, and destroying (to his later sorrow) much medieval, Jacobean and Georgian detail. He came to London in 1862, and after getting politeness but no employment from Benjamin Ferrey, Pugin's pupil and biographer, he found a job with Arthur Blomfield. For ten years Hardy wavered between architecture and letters. Sir Arthur Blomfield—he became one of mediocrity's knights—was congenial to work with. They sang hymns together, when there was little to do. Hardy was continually writing poems—to Blomfield's knowledge—and even began to turn *Ecclesiastes* in Spenserian stanzas. He drew funny pictures on the Adam mantelpiece in the offices in the Adelphi. He did strange jobs—superintending the removal of the tombs and corpses and skeletons of Old St Pancras churchyard for the Midland Railway, for example. Behind a hoarding, by gas flares, the work went on all night, the loose skeletons being carried on boards. He won the R.I.B.A. silver medal in 1862 with an essay on Architectural Polychromy (the essay was presumably not good enough to be printed in the transactions of the Institute, and is now lost). He paid much attention to pictures, he began to write novels. He went back to Dorchester and helped Mr Hicks. He helped a Weymouth architect who took over Hicks's practice—and this brought him a wife when he went down to advise on the restoration of St Juliot Church in North Cornwall. His wife, Miss Emma Gifford opened the door to him in the rectory; and so one could say that architecture introduced him to some of his happiest and bitterest times and led to such poems as 'Lyonesse' (written—and how that knowledge revives it!—on the way back from Cornwall) and, forty years later, to the deeply pathetic emotional retrospect, 'After a Journey.' In 1872 he was designing schools with Professor Roger Smith, but *Under the Greenwood Tree* had now been written and his own impulse and the prescience of Miss Gifford were pushing him absolutely away into literature.

At Blomfield's his not being ambitious was observed; and he recorded in his old age how his mind was then beginning to fill with poetry:

> A sense of the truth of poetry, of its supreme place in literature, had awakened itself in me. At the risk, of ruining all my worldly prospects I dabbled in it ... was forced out of it ... It came back upon me ... All was of the nature of being led by a mood, without foresight or regard to whither it led.

'Churchy' was how Hardy described himself; but Hardy's churchiness was that of a man involved in humanity; who believed that everything should be done to ease 'mortals' progress through a world not worthy of them.' 'I have been looking for God for fifty years,' he wrote down in 1890, 'I think if He had existed I should have discovered Him.' Churches were to Hardy places sacred to tragedy rather than to God, where an answer had been pitifully looked for and never found. So it is ironic from one angle, and right from another, that he tidied up so many churches in the interests of a creed he believed to be no longer of use. If he had wished to build and set up in practice, it is not easy to see anything he could have built out of his full and peculiar churchy heart in the fifty years after 1870. *His* churches to *his* God, a Cause neither moral nor immoral, loveless and hateless, are something for which no one would have provided the stone and cement. Yet, I repeat, Hardy began where the rare and true architect should begin—with man, not first with those forms which sprout from man, or with his clothes, however expressive they may be. The accidentals of his union with architecture brought him not only into the happy and sad experience of his marriage ('the ultimate aim of the poet', he wrote down from Sir Leslie Stephen, 'should be to touch our hearts by showing his own'), gave him not only persons to write about (such as the church-restorer in *A Pair of Blue Eyes* or George Somerset in *A Laodicean*), but forced him into the company of vital images. They brought him into the yet intolerable London of 1862, the cruel capital of Baal which Dostoevsky saw in that year or the next,[2] the prediction from the Apocalypse, with the fish-flares of gas, the drunkenness, evident wealth, evident poverty, the Haymarket full of whores, and the City still drained into cesspits built after the Great Fire, a ten-foot bank of human droppings piling up where the river Lea emerged at Barking Creek, and a stink from the same substance in the river pervading the Houses of Parliament. And so Hardy observed year after year the false clean-up—the cleansing of the Lea and the accumulation of filth in the human heart, breaking into wars; the black comparison between material growth and moral repression on which he speculated so much in so many poems.

Herein, with his power of sight and vision, is rooted Thomas Hardy's human sensibility; by which the pilers-up of Maiden Castle or the Thames-side business blocks are hardly possessed. Whether he had that architectural sensibility in a more restricted way—that feeling for the historicity and humanity of form and ornament and the fitting of building into landscape, which is commoner among amateurs than architects, I doubt, although I could quote such remarks as 'the ashlar backyards of Bath have more dignity than any brick front in Europe'. Hardy digs rather for the general root of all buildings. He goes to St Marks, he is anti-Ruskin, he finds it squat, oriental, barbaric, built on 'weak, flexuous, constructional lines.' He records chiefly that the floor 'of every colour and rich device, is worn into undulations by the infinite multitudes of feet that have trodden it'. He goes to Salisbury into the Close, at night, 'walked to the West front and watched the moonlight creep round upon the statuary of the façade—stroking tentatively and then more firmly the prophets, the martyrs, the bishops, the kings and the queens'. He goes round Westminster Abbey by lantern at midnight, or into Wimborne Minster:

> *How smartly the quarters of the hour march by*
> *That the jack-o'-clock never forgets;*
> *Ding-dong; and before I have traced a cusp's eye,*
> *Or got the true twist of the ogee over,*
> *A double ding-dong ricochetts.*
>
> *Just so did he clang here before I came,*
> *And so will he clang when I'm gone*
> *Through the Minster's cavernous hollows—the same*
> *Tale of hours never more to be will he deliver*
> *To the speechless midnight and dawn.*

I grow to conceive it a call to ghosts,
  Whose mould lies below and around.
Yes; the next 'Come, come', draws them out from their posts,
And they gather, and one shade appears, and another,
  As the eve-damps creeps from the ground. . .

Always, you see, a church, always a meeting place of the dead, the living, and the unborn. On architecture as an art, and as an art of the age through which he was living, I do not know that Hardy pronounced anything peculiar or deep. He was much impressed by the Englishness of the Perpendicular (read 'The Abbey Mason' in *Satires of Circumstances*). He discerned that architecture and poetry resembled each other, 'both arts having to carry a rational content inside their artistic form'; and perhaps it is truly said that his poems have a precise Gothic intricacy, even on the page. But it is curious—curiously instructive—that he interprets his period more certainly when he thinks of painting, than when he thinks of his own profession. 'I am more interested,' he said, 'in the high ideas of a feeble executant than in the high execution of a feeble thinker.' He preferred Zurbarán to Velásquez. He put down in 1886 'my art is to intensify the expression of things, as is done by Crivelli, Bellini, etc., so that the heart and inner meaning is made vividly visible'. More to be remarked—one thinks of Balzac's *Chef d'oeuvre Inconnu* or justly again of Cézanne—is the statement he made to himself in January, 1887:

> After looking at the landscape ascribed to Bonington in our drawing-room I feel that Nature is played out as a Beauty, but not as a mystery. I don't want to see landscapes, i.e. scenic paintings of them, because I don't want to see the original realities—as optical effects, that is. I want to see the deeper reality underlying the scenic, the expression of what are sometimes called abstract imaginings.
>
> The 'simply natural' is interesting no longer. The much decried, mad, late-Turner rendering is now necessary to create my interest. The exact truth as to material fact ceases to be of importance in art—it is a student's style—the style of a period when the mind is serene and unawakened to the tragical mysteries of life; when it does not bring anything to the object that coalesces with and translates the qualities that are already there—half hidden it may be—and the two united are pictured as the All.

That is the best gloss on Hardy's own aims in his poetry, in which, and not in his novels, he has given us the most to feed upon.

> A skeleton—the one used in these lectures—is hung up inside the window. We face it as we sit. Outside the band is playing, and the children are dancing. I can see their little figures through the window past the skeleton dangling in front . . .

—there he is. I understand, I think, why Mr Eliot, setting Yeats beside Hardy, believes Hardy to be obviously a minor poet. Hardy and Eliot interpret life very differently. The churchiness of each is differently composed; and Yeats is a pagan, but a purer writer, less crinkle-crankle in his substance. Hardy works more by seeing, less by the imagination. The scope of his sensuality is limited, and he repeats himself with too little variation. But I also understand why it is that poetry in English cannot avoid Hardy, as, I believe it can well and does avoid Mr Eliot. It is not dealing in insolence with insularity, but pointing to a fact of inheritance, of transmission, if I remark that Mr Eliot is an American (who has spoken too much in ungenerative fragments and qualification), and Thomas Hardy an Englishman. What Mr Auden has admitted, that Hardy was his 'poetical father', that he provided him with a 'modern rhetoric which was more fertile and adaptable to different themes than any of Eliot's gas-works and rats' feet which one could steal but never make one's own',[3] many more poets of my generation could also admit, with gratitude. He recorded 'impressions, not convictions', was an artist, not a moralist or philosopher, and observed at once the language, the age, and the world. 'Style—consider the Wordsworthian dictum (the more perfectly the natural object is reproduced the more truly poetic the picture). This reproduction is achieved by seeing into the *heart of a thing* (as rain, wind, for instance) ...' He admired the realism of Crabbe, and narrow as he may have been, he brought back a selective appropriate realism, a truth, a congruence, an honesty. In 1909, in answer to an enquiry from Berlin:

> We call our age an age of Freedom. Yet Freedom under her incubus of armaments, territorial ambitions smugly disguised as patriotism, superstitions, conventions of every sort, is of such stunted proportions in this her so-called time, that the human race is likely to be extinct before Freedom arrives at maturity.

In 1920, when he was seventy-nine: 'January 19th Coming back from Talbothays by West Stafford Cross I saw Orion upside down in a pool of water under an oak.' Here, then, are two observations, and I reverence Hardy as an observer, one who discerned with terrible accuracy the intensification of evil and was glum and numb less, on the whole, over individuals than over the events which victimize them and kick them on through a world to which they are superior.

I recall the last lines of his poem on the Armistice of the earlier war (we are less charitable):

> *Calm fell. From Heaven distilled a clemency;*
> *There was peace on earth, and silence in the sky;*
> *Some could, some could not, shake off misery;*
> *The Sinister Spirit sneered: 'It had to be!'*
> *And again the Spirit of Pity whispered, 'Why?'*

I recall now a letter written by Rainer Maria Rilke in the intensity of the last war:

... no longer can the measure of the single heart be applied, yet at other times it was the union of earth and sky and of all distances and depths. What, at other times was the cry of a drowning man; and even if it *was* the village idiot who reached up from the water with a cry grown suddenly clearer, everything rushed towards him and was on his side and against the disaster, and the quickest man risked his life for him ... people cling to the war like misers with all the weight of their heavy consciences. It is a human bungling, just as every-thing in the last decades was human bungling, bad work, profiteering, except for a few painful voices and figures, except for a few warning prophets, except for a few zealots who held to their own hearts, which stood contrary to the stream. Rodin, how often, how everlastingly did he reiterate words of dis-approval and suspicion against the course of things. It was too much for me, I took it for exhaustion and yet it was judgement. And Cézanne, when they told him of outside affairs, in the quiet streets of Aix, he could burst out and shriek at his companion: '*Le monde, c'est terrible.*' One thinks of him like a prophet and one longs for another to cry and howl so,—but they have all gone, the old men who might have had the power to weep now before the peoples of the world.[4]

Thomas Hardy was one of them. How bitterly appropriate that the centenary of his birth should fall to be celebrated in the year of the no less terrifying and even more immense and complicated war in Europe.

Notes

1. This, and the quotations which follow, and the biographical details, are taken from Florence Hardy's *Life of Thomas Hardy*.
2. In 'Winter Notes on My Summer Impressions', translated in the *European Quarterly* No. 2, August 1934.
3. In *The Southern Review*, Summer 1940.
4. The translation is by R.F.C. Hull.

189

The Novels
of Hardy Today

———————◆———————

HERBERT J. MULLER

In this knowing age, centennials are apt to be rather trying for the spirits of the departed. Critics come not to praise or to bury the artist but to 'revalue' him; and in this performance they often treat his work primarily as a cultural symptom, a by-product of an age, an issue of deep unconscious forces—as an incidental illustration of something larger or more serious than the individualized imaginative creation that meant everything to him. The historical perspective is necessary, of course, for his sake as well as ours; it would be unfair even to Shakespeare to read his plays as if they were written by a timeless spirit, not by a popular playwright of Elizabethan England. But this approach may also be unfair to the artist. Critics are usually looking for particular historical tendencies, and their value judgments are loaded accordingly. 'To see a "century" in a cathedral or the revolt of the masses in a play,' remarks George Boas, 'is believed to be a more valuable experience than to see something else in them.' Hence literary reputations rise and fall with social or political theory—as William Dean Howells has gone up since Granville Hicks discovered that he had some perception of the class struggle. In general, critics tend to abstract a few generic traits and ignore the unique quality of the work as a whole, just as physicists ignore the color, feel, and particularity of things in order to measure and weigh them.

Now, Thomas Hardy is not, it seems to me, in crying need of revaluation—at least as a novelist. Upon rereading his novels I can discover no unsuspected depths or complexities, no reason for considering him more or less significant or pertinent; I discover chiefly the problem of how to avoid merely quoting myself. His virtues and his faults are plain, and for some time have ceased to stir controversy. He has been seen clearly enough against the transition from the Victorian to the modern age, aligned with enough tendencies, adequately labeled, sufficiently 'explained.' He is unusually poor

SOURCE *The Southern Review*, 1940–1, vol. 6, pp. 214–24.

material for Marxist or Freudian interpretation, or for subtle analysis in any mode. Although his pessimism might be regarded as a sign of the decay of capitalistic society, or a symptom of psychic maladjustment, such explanations would have to lean heavily on the unconscious in Hardy; at best they would be marginal notes, explaining little or nothing about his greatness as an artist. Yet they are pretty sure to be offered, and then to prejudice or confuse judgment of his art. Hardy is likely, indeed, to suffer considerably from prevailing critical attitudes. His greatness is of an elemental kind to which one cannot easily pay tribute in the precise language—or pseudo-precise jargon—now demanded of critics; his limitations appear more serious because of current preferences in beauty and truth; in general his interests and attitudes now seem so old-fashioned that contemporaries seldom give themselves up to him, seldom have had the sustained intimacy with his work that makes possible a justice beyond the letter of critical law. And so there is, after all, more reason for returning to Hardy than the sentiment of this occasion.

Even for pious purposes, however, it is well to have done at once with his serious faults. Most obvious is his mania for hounding his characters to the grave and for employing the most fantastic means to get them there. Only the disenchanted sophomore can be deeply impressed by Hardy's view of life. Although it was an outcome of the new scientific views, it now seems like a simple variant of supernaturalism. The President of the Immortals, the First Cause, the Great Foresightless, even the It he so proudly invented for *The Dynasts*—these are but different names for God, arbitrary inventions that find no place in any scientific scheme; his conception of evil as an absolute and ultimate reality, not merely a human judgement with reference to human purposes, is as naïvely anthropomorphic as any religious dogma. And although Hardy properly objected to treating his fiction as a 'scientific system of philosophy,' the trouble is that he often wrote as if it were. The scheme of his novels is typically all too rigid and diagrammatic, their argument all too formal and explicit. Hence one protests as much against his last novels, in which the governing ideas are more valid by contemporary standards. By now Hardy perceived that society as well as It was responsible for human misery and that an inexorable determinism lay behind blind chance; but the discovery of another villain and a more relentless machinery so exasperated his resentment at the conditions of life that his own machinery became more relentless. *Jude the Obscure* is at once the most and the least convincing of his novels. The serious objection, at any rate, is not to his philosophy *per se*, the dismal generalizations he illogically induces from the extraordinary actions he invents. It is to his artistry, the inventions themselves.

This objection is deepened, moreover, because of Hardy's simple conception of the duties of a story-teller, which was further simplified by the custom of serial publication that demanded a wallop in every instalment.

The 'real' purpose of fiction, he once said, is 'to give pleasure by gratifying the love of the uncommon in human experience.' Hence the grotesque accidents that seemed to him the natural workings of Providence would also give readers their money's worth. Hence his novels are over-stuffed with incident, especially with mistaken identities, untold secrets, miscarried letters, and all the forced misunderstandings without which there would be 'no story'—and which are not at all uncommon to readers of popular fiction. Few important novelists have worked their characters so hard, made them sweat through so many theatrical situations. And again, when Hardy came to introduce a more logical chain of events, he also introduced a new kind of artificial contrivance. In his last novels his characters have to sweat through formal disputation, get their arguments by heart. (Sue Bridehead 'exclaims' in a moment of passion: 'It is none of the natural tragedies of love that's love's usual tragedy in civilized life, but a tragedy artificially manufactured for people who in a natural state would find relief in parting!') Harassed as he was both by the demon Plot and the demon gods above, Hardy too seldom maintained entire responsibility to his characters.

These faults are obtrusive enough, and they are the more irritating because they are so externalized, detachable, in a way unnecessary. The primitivism of Lawrence, the super-refinement of James, the neurotic hyper-sensitiveness of Proust—such qualities may be objectionable in themselves, but they are nevertheless the source of the peculiar power of these novelists. What is most objectionable in Hardy is not so intrinsic and seems almost perverse. Yet it does point to defects in the quality of his mind: some blunt-ness of perception, coarseness of discrimination, crudeness of response to the possibilities of experience. These limitations also appear as a degree of provincialism. The strangers to his little land of Wessex, the more worldly types like Fitzpiers and Troy and Alec D'Urberville, are often stagey, never have the vitality of the natives. Furthermore they are usually his shabbiest or most vicious characters; he always tried to be fair to them, but like his rustics he distrusted them. And despite his gloominess he tended to exaggerate the humble virtues, romanticize the simple annals of the poor.

One may note other flaws in Hardy's fiction: some stiffness and awkward-ness of style, a deal of perfunctory and mechanical journeywork, the usual lapses into mediocrity or downright banality (as in 'The Romantic Adven-tures of a Milkmaid'). One may even say that he was not altogether at home in the novel; in an earlier age he probably would never have deserted poetry, his first and last love. Nevertheless contemporaries are apt to dwell too much on his limitations. The fault is partly an incomplete analysis, an overstress on certain aspects of Hardy's work and a neglect of the work as a whole. It is especially, however, a disposition to undervalue even the total or final effect of his art. And so I believe that we cannot do him justice merely by a conscientious tribute to his specific virtues, balancing accounts by listing his nature poetry, the rich humor of his Shakespearean rustics, the vivid recreation of Wessex, etc. We need to reconsider the assumptions that govern our whole response.

'Criticism,' Santayana writes, 'surprises the soul in the arms of convention.' Criticism is too often caught there itself. It is caught, more specifically, in the two-sided, sheep-or-goat concept of truth expressed in Aristotle's law of the excluded middle: a thing is either A or not A, a statement is either true or not true. Its proper logic is rather the principle of the *included* middle: the recognition that generalizations about literature are both true and not true, that qualities and values lie on a scale between A and not A and can be described accurately only in relative terms. In practice there is both a 'good' way and a 'bad' way of describing everything. Regionalism, for example, appears to be a relatively simple adaptation to life, a return to the familiar meanings of the family and the home. It may accordingly be stigmatized as an evasion of the problem of assimilating the complex material of modern life, a shirking of responsibility, an 'escape'; it may also be applauded as a return to the grass roots of art and life, a recovery of deep natural pieties, a means of stabilizing a confused, giddy generation. These descriptions of motives and values are the poles of a sliding scale. Ideally, then, the critic will command the whole scale as he tries to locate a given writer, remembering that motives are never pure and values never absolute. The natural tendency of critics, however, is to take a stand at one end, as if it were the absolute A of beauty and truth, and then to describe all writers in its terms.

In this way Hardy suffers today: our special interests and attitudes predispose us to the 'bad' description of many of his qualities. He confined himself to the little world of Wessex, a world at that already vanishing. Few critics, I imagine, would say that nostalgia was the matrix of his art, accuse him of seeking refuge from the pressing problems of his society. But many are prone to regard his novels as a temptation to nostalgia: to dwell on the quaintness and coziness of his rustic scene, to stress his failure to enter either the drawing room or the industrial arena of modern society, to consider his drama remote or even irrelevant to our problems. Nevertheless his main themes—the elemental passions against the elemental background of nature, the timeless problems of life and death—are still pertinent because they are elemental and timeless. If Wessex is a little world, it is still a *world*; and the final stress should be upon the vast dimensions he gave it—a kind of spaciousness not to be found, for example, in the whole continent of John Dos Passos. That American pilgrims to the Hardy country are apt to be disappointed by the patch of ground he called Egdon Heath is the clue to his achievement. He invested these few acres with grandeur, he erected on them one of the sublime conceptions of fiction. At his best, in short, he was *not* confined to Wessex. He realized his ideal conviction, that the tragedy of obscure men far from the stage of momentous events could be endowed with a majesty 'truly Sophoclean.'

Still more are we likely to condescend to Hardy's simplicity. We are very fond of subtlety, we are obsessed with complexity; when we return from James, Lawrence, or Virginia Woolf, not to mention Proust or Joyce, Hardy seems woefully obvious and uncomplicated. Although he did a respectable job of psychologizing in *Jude the Obscure*, his typical characters are compounded of relatively few elements and his issues are relatively naked. Above all, his methods are simple. Where more recent novelists weave back and forth in space and time, he marches in a straight line; where they evoke, intimate, render impressionistically, present character by indirection, carefully consider point of view, he is always the omniscient author, presenting directly and in so many words. He is indeed too omniscient and explicit. His simplicity is in one aspect, again, a lack of fineness of discrimination. Yet it is also the source of his dignity and strength. He did have a firm hold on the basic elements of character, render eloquently the primary passions, dramatize powerfully the major crises; and he did not oversimplify. Great passion may have mysterious sources and intricate ramifications, but it appears as a whole and remains primitive; all the fine consciences have to deal with the same elemental necessities and face the same final issues of mortality. Like the Greeks, at any rate, Hardy was concerned with the primal, the ultimate, the common destiny, and he as freely made large statements about life and death and the gods. To sophisticates and lovers of the three dots, this ancient tradition may seem naïve, crude, a little embarrassing. Nevertheless they have no reason to feel so superior to it—least of all at a time when bombs fall on subtle and simple alike.

Even our judgements of Hardy's plots may be too harsh. In our more advanced fiction, plot has been scrapped with the other simplicities. A well-regulated, unbroken, finished action appears to falsify our complex experience, with its waver and scatter and incessant flux; formal contrivance, the stock-in-trade of the most austere artists in the past, is suspect as mere trickery and trumpery. Hence the contrivance of Hardy, often mechanical or sensational as it is, will be especially offensive to cultivated tastes. But even the magnificent architectural structure of *The Return of the Native* may now seem too artificial, and his most powerful scenes melodramatic.

The chief source of suspicion, however, remains Hardy's general ideas; and it raises an issue that we need to consider at greater length. 'The truest philosophy,' T.S. Eliot declares, 'is the best material for the greatest poet.' It sounds like a reasonable principle—until he begins to specify the true philosophy. Doubt grows when from other quarters comes the same doctrine, but with different specifications. Thus Ralph Fox asserted that without Marxism 'there is no approach to that essential truth which is the chief concern of the writer'—in one sentence making a clean sweep of the world's acknowledged masterpieces. Everywhere critical discussion now centers about the writer's 'ideology,' everywhere he is judged according to its 'soundness'—just as professional moralists and simple readers judge him by the plainness and wholesomeness of his moral. This concern is no doubt a tribute to the effectiveness of literature as a social force; but when critics themselves fail to get together on the common garden variety of truths, much less the 'essential truth,' the responsible writer must be in a quandary.

Now, an obvious objection to Mr Eliot's attitude is what D'Avenant called 'such saucy familiarity with a true God'; when he laments that Shakespeare stuck fast in an 'inferior philosophy,' Santayana answers properly that what Shakespeare stuck fast in was the facts of life. Moreover, Mr Eliot would not commit himself to the theory implied by his concern for the true philosophy, that the expression of ideas is the primary purpose of art. But the record of fiction is alone sufficient answer to all these manuals of what every great writer must know. Hardy knew that man is the butt of wanton celestial jokers; Balzac knew that religion and monarchy are the eternal twin-principles of the good society; Dostoievsky knew that intellect is a false god and that Soul alone matters; Zola knew that there is no Soul and that an absolute determinism governs human behavior. From such testimony truth would seem to come out nowhere. Yet in our experience with these novelists something valuable comes out everywhere. Plainly, then, the enduring value of their work cannot lie in their soundness as philosophers or sociologists. It must lie in what they have in common; and this, in necessarily general terms, is the vividness and vitality of their concrete representations of life. It is the significance, not of their general ideas, but of their felt response to the immediate data of experience. Like the events in 'real life,' the characters and actions they create may be interpreted differently by different observers, but the creations have a life independent of these interpretations.

This is by no means to deny the novelist the luxury of a philosophy. Inevitably he has one and unquestionably he needs one: to order his immediate materials, to focus his creative energy, to enable him to be nourished instead of simply confused or dismayed by the activity of his age. The quality of his thought, furthermore, has much to do with the aesthetic value of his work: a shallow, confused, trivial, sentimental, or distorted view of life will obviously limit his felt response, weaken his command of immediate experience. But these adjectives are to be got by no rule of thumb, no consultation of the critic's own tastes in philosophy. The value of art lies not in the specific ideas and ideals expressed but in the power to suggest and nourish other ideas and ideals. The value of an artist's thought lies not in its essential truth but in the possibilities it permits him of so dealing with experience as to transcend any specific version of essential truth. And the serious objection to his thought arises in so far as it literally cramps his style.

Similarly the most serious objection to the excessive concern with a writer's general ideas is not that it warps the critic's judgment but that it narrows and impoverishes his actual experience in art. So naturally sensitive a critic as Paul Elmer More became simply unable to experience the values in most modern literature; Granville Hicks openly confessed what ideology has done to him: 'There is no bourgeois novel that, taken as a whole, satisfies me.' In this way, at any rate, not only Hardy but his contemporary readers are likely to suffer; and in this view one can make out more clearly the values that survive his obsessions.

Aside from his annoying habit of periodically translating the poetry of his imaginative creations into a crabbed, literal prose, dropping the reader into the world of the 'village atheist,' Hardy's philosophy was clearly a limitation. It tended to cramp his imagination, blunt his perceptions, mechanize his responses, harden his aesthetic arteries generally. It sapped his fictions of some vitality: his characters are at times slighted or manhandled for the sake of wildly improbable events, the relations between character and plot seem at times mechanical and arbitrary rather than organic and inevitable. Yet his obsessions were not fatal. Hardy survives because his poetry and drama are not confined within the angular frame of his plots and his syllogisms, his imaginative reach and emotional force are not measured by his intellectual convictions. Logically, his philosophy makes all self-assertion futile, leaves no room for self-realization; his characters should be the puppets that in *The Dynasts* he specifically tells us all men are. Actually, his characters at best have a vigorous life of their own; they have dignity and force, they aspire and assert themselves passionately, their full measure is taken. And his own vigorous creative activity makes nonsense of his philosophy. With all his limitations, Hardy was not one of our frustrate spirits. He was gnarled but whole, flawed but ripe on the bough, few contemporaries have more fully realized their potentialities.

It follows, too, that Hardy's tragedies are not finally so depressing as many readers still believe. Few of his heroes achieve the final reconciliation of Tess, who at the end can say simply, 'I am ready'; Michael Henchard and Jude Fawley die in an appalling bitterness of spirit, some episodes culminate in a sheer horror that numbs all pity and awe. The immediate impact of his tragedy is at times, indeed, terrific. But more important are the after-effects of the whole experience. What is explicitly stated in his novels is a gospel of despair: life is only a thing to be put up with, and mute resignation is the only wisdom. What is eloquently represented, however, is not only a deep compassion but a deep faith: a natural reverence for man, an illogical ideal belief that he is superior to the forces that destroy him, above all a conviction that at stricken moments (in the words of Robinson Jeffers) he 'can shine terribly against the dark magnificence of things.' Although Hardy's heroes do not have the stature or force of the ancient heroes, they do have this capacity for feeling greatly, and although he had a low opinion of the gods, the poet in him invested them with this dark magnificence. Hence the bitterness passes. There remains the qualities 'truly Sophoclean.'

And so, too, with the 'universality' of his stories. The past always changes with the present, is never seen or felt exactly as it was lived; and in this ceaseless process nothing is affected more surely than versions of universal, eternal truth. Few readers today will accept Hardy's specific ideas, any more than they will the gods that ordained the fate of Oedipus or the angels that sing Hamlet to his rest. In any event his novels could not have precisely the same meaning for us that they had in the last century or will have in the next. Yet process has its logic and its laws, and in human affairs its underlying uniformities: the primary desires and emotions, the basic patterns and rhythms of experience, the laws that give all behavior continuity and consequence, exact payment from all men in accordance with their capacity for feeling. Of these Hardy has given a vivid and compelling account. His theme of the rise and fall of Michael Henchard is significant for any culture. In art as in science, which alike represent a dynamic, unfinished world, the universal is to be sought not in particular truths but in modes of truth-making.

At the end it is well to return to the obvious. Hardy *exists*, when countless 'sounder' writers are dead. If we have no satisfactory explanation of genius, we have no substitute for it; as Schelling said, it is to art what the ego is to philosophy, 'the only supreme and absolute reality.' Hence Hardy survives the most damaging criticism—as he survives this labored apology. His greatest achievements in fiction have a poetic, elemental quality that calls for the lyrical appreciation of simpler days. One could argue, indeed, that we could now do with more of the old specialists in adjective and epithet, who expressed very vague ideas but who might communicate very live emotions. In this hyper-technical, hyper-practical, hyper-critical age one encounters too little whole-hearted enthusiasm and reverence for literature, too much worried introspection and nervous rationalization of its effects, too much suspicion of its 'emotive' function or semantic impurity, too much fear of letting oneself go. We have a laudable desire to be precise and never to be taken in. But the precious difference between great art and the good second-rate escapes precise verbal definition; and it is our loss if our admiration of the subtler, finer, more brilliant art of modern novelists should make us fearful of being taken in by the simple but majestic fictions of Thomas Hardy.

190
The Traditional Basis of Thomas Hardy's Fiction

———————— ◆ ————————

DONALD DAVIDSON

In the eighty-eight years of his life Thomas Hardy got used to a great many of the oddities of terrestrial experience, and was resigned to most of them, even to the seeming unapproachableness or indifference of the Deity. One thing, however, he never got used to, and was apparently not resigned to. I find a peculiar pertinence in the fact that Mrs Hardy, in *The Later Years*, has inserted a rather lengthy reminiscence of Hardy's visit to Oxford in 1920, written by Charles Morgan, who was then an undergraduate at the University and one of the leaders in arranging for the performance of *The Dynasts* at Oxford on this particular occasion. After an account of Hardy's visit, Morgan goes on to record a later conversation with Hardy at Max Gate, on the subject of literary criticism. Hardy spoke out against the critics with an animus that startled the younger man. Dramatic criticism, Hardy thought, had some merit because the dramatic critics had less time 'to rehearse their prejudices.' But Hardy was bitter about literary criticism.

> The origin of this bitterness [writes Morgan] was in the past where, I believe, there was good reason for it, but it was directed now against contemporary critics of his own work, and I could not understand what general reason he had to complain of them. He used no names; he spoke with studied reserve, sadly rather than querulously; but he was persuaded—and there is evidence of his persuasion in the preface to the posthumous volume of his verse—that critics approached his work with an ignorant prejudice against his 'pessimism' which they allowed to stand in the way of fair reading and fair judgment.
>
> This was a distortion of the facts as I knew them. It was hard to believe that Hardy honestly thought that his genius was not recognized; harder to believe that he thought his work was not read. Such a belief indicated the only failure of balance, the only refusal to seek the truth, which I perceived in Hardy ...

But Morgan was wrong, and Hardy was right, and the 'bitterness' of the aged poet toward literary criticism, as thus recorded, is something to give pause to the presumptuous critical interpreter. Hardy could not explain

SOURCE *The Southern Review*, 1940–1, vol. 6, pp. 162–78.

himself clearly to the younger man, and perhaps the reference to pessimism comes in only for want of a better verbal statement of the strange misunderstanding Hardy felt he had encountered. There was a real intellectual distance between Hardy and the critics—indeed, between Hardy and almost three generations of critics. The critics had not so much underrated—or overrated—Hardy as missed him, in somewhat the same way as, in our opinion, Dr Johnson missed John Donne. When we look over the impressive list of those who have made literary pronouncements in Hardy's time and ours, they do not seem to be the kind of people who would have affinity with Hardy. From George Meredith, his first literary adviser, up to T.S. Eliot, one can hardly think of a critic whose view of Hardy's work, however well-intentioned, would not be so external as to set up a gross incongruity like what we find in Marxian criticisms of Shakespeare.

Possibly the critics have been most in error in not realizing the comparative isolation of Hardy in modern literary history. Misled by the superficial resemblance between his work and the product current in their day, they have invariably attempted to treat him as a current author—or at least as a queer blend of tendencies receding and tendencies coming on. They have been further misled by Hardy's own attempt (not always happy) to shape his work into a marketable form or to bring it up to what he conceived to be a good current literary standard. For Hardy seems to have had little idea of being an innovator or an iconoclast. He sought to please and entertain, and perhaps to instruct, and he must have been amazed to find himself now acclaimed, now condemned, as heretic.

The appearance of Thomas Hardy among the temporal phenomena of the England of 1870 to 1928—that is the amazing, the confusing thing. I believe we ought to begin consideration by admitting that though Hardy was *in* that time, and was affected by its thought and art, he was not really *of* that time whenever he was his essential self. It is not enough to say that Hardy is 'old-fashioned' or 'quaint.' Certainly he did not try consciously to be old-fashioned. Although there are archaisms of language in his poetry and prose, and much general display of the antique in subject matter, there is nowhere in Hardy the affectation of archaism (found in such ironic romanticists as Cabell) or the deliberate exploitation of archaism (found in a great many of the literary specialities offered in America). The old-fashioned quality in Hardy is not in the obvious places, but lies deeper. It is in the habit of Hardy's mind rather than in 'folk-lore' or the phenomena of language and style.

Hardy wrote, or tried to write, more or less as a modern—modern, for him, being late nineteenth century. But he thought, or artistically conceived, like a man of another century—indeed, of a century that we should be hard put to name. It might be better to say that he wrote like a creator of tales and poems who is a little embarrassed at having to adapt the creation of tales and poems to the conditions of a written, or printed, literature, and yet tries to do his faithful best under the regrettable circumstances. He is not in any case a 'folk author,' and yet he does approach his tale-telling and poem-making as if three centuries of Renaissance effort had worked only upon the outward form of tale and poem without changing its essential character. He wrote as a ballad-maker would write if a ballad-maker were to have to write novels; or as a bardic or epic poet would write if faced with the necessity of performing in the quasi-lyrical but non-singable strains of the nineteenth century and later.

Hardy is the only specimen of his genus in modern English literature, and I do not know how to account for him. He has no immediate predecessors; and though he has some imitators, no real followers as yet. For his habit of mind has seemingly disappeared in England, and threatens to disappear in America; and without the habit of mind to begin with no real following can be done. I am almost ready to characterize Hardy (if he must be 'placed') as an American whose ancestors failed to migrate at the proper time and who accordingly found himself stranded, a couple of centuries later, in the wrong literary climate. In this connection it is amusing to remember that Hardy has been charged with borrowing a description from Augustus Baldwin Long-street's *Georgia Scenes* for use in *The Trumpet-Major*. The truth is that his general affiliation with the frontier humorists of the Old Southwest is a good deal more discernible than his affiliation with Victorian romantic-realists or with French Naturalists. It is an organic affiliation, not a literary attachment, because the Southwestern humorists drew their art, such as it was, from the same kind of source that Hardy used, and wrote (when they had to write) under the same embarrassment. If Hardy's distant seventeenth-century progenitor had migrated to America at the time of the Monmouth Rebellion— as some of his progenitor's relatives and many of his neighbors did, in all haste, migrate, then Thomas Hardy might easily have been a frontier humorist of the Longstreet school. And then he would never have been accused of pessimism, though he might, to be sure, have caused eyebrows to lift in Boston.

In the two volumes which are the second Mrs Hardy's Memoir of her husband (*The Early Life of Thomas Hardy* and *The Later Years of Thomas Hardy*) there is a good deal of scattering and fragmentary evidence to indicate the bent of Hardy's mind. It is enough to aid a speculation, though not enough, probably, to prove the case for a professional researchist. I refer to the recorded experiences of Hardy's childhood and youth which seem to suggest his inward preoccupation better than the interests generally emphasized by critics, such as his study of Greek, his knowledge of architecture, or his tussle with Darwinian theory and modern social problems. Another age than ours would have made something out of the fact that when Hardy was born he was at first cast aside for a stillbirth and was saved only by the shrewd perception of a nurse; or that when the infant Hardy was reposing in his cradle a snake crawled upon his breast and went to sleep there. These are

367

omens that I profess no ability to read. But the many little items that seem to make Hardy a 'crusted character,' like so many of the personages of his fiction, are not of minor or dubious importance.

Hardy was born early enough—and far enough away from looming Arnoldian or Marxian influences—to receive a conception of art as something homely, natural, functional, and in short traditional. He grew up in a Dorset where fiction was a tale told or sung; and where the art of music, always important to him, was primarily for worship or merriment. The Hardys, up through the time of Thomas Hardy's father, were 'church-players' of the type of the Mellstock Choir—performers on the violin, cello, and bass who adhered to a traditional psalmody and instrumental performance (of which echoes are preserved here today in the music of the 'shape note' singers of the South). Thomas Hardy, as a child, was "extraordinarily sensitive to music." He danced to 'the endless jigs, hornpipes, reels, waltzes, and country-dances' that his own father played and, without knowing why, was contradictorily moved to tears by some of the tunes. Later he himself could 'twiddle from notation some hundreds of jigs and country-dances that he found in his father's and grandfather's old books'—he was an 'oldtime fiddler.' Young Thomas played the fiddle at weddings and in farmer's parlors. On one occasion he bowed away for a solid three-quarters of an hour while twelve tireless couples danced to a single favorite tune. At one notable harvest-home he heard the maids sing ballads. Among these Hardy remembered particularly 'The Outlandish Knight'—a Dorset version of the ballad recorded by Child as 'Lady Isabel and the Elf Knight.'

And of course he must have heard, in time, many another ballad, if we may make a justifiable inference from the snatches of balladry in the novels and tales, and if Dorset was the kind of countryside we are led to think it to be. Mrs Hardy would have us believe that upon the extension of the railway to Dorset in the middle nineteenth century 'the orally transmitted ballads were slain at a stroke by the London comic songs,' but she underestimates the vitality of folk art. As late as 1922, one R. Thurston Hopkins published a book entitled *Thomas Hardy's Dorset*, in which he tells how he found a singing blacksmith at Lyme Regis, in Devon. Hopkins gives the blacksmith's song, but evidently does not know enough of balladry to recognize it. It is a perfectly good version of the ballad known as 'Mollie Vaughn' or 'Mollie Bond.'

For what it may be worth I note that Hardy first conceived *The Dynasts* as a ballad, or group of ballads. In May, 1875, he wrote in his journal: 'Mem: A Ballad of the Hundred Days. Then another of Moscow. Others of earlier campaigns—forming altogether an Iliad of Europe from 1789 to 1815.'

This, Mrs Hardy says, is the first mention in Hardy's memoranda of the conception later to take shape in the epic drama. Again, on March 27, 1881, Hardy referred to his scheme: 'A Homeric Ballad, in which Napoleon is a sort of Achilles, to be written.'

To evidence of this kind I should naturally add the following facts: that

Hardy wrote a number of ballads, like 'The Bride-Night Fire,' and ballad-like poems; that his poems like his novels are full of references to old singers, tunes, and dances, and that many of the poems proceed from the same sources as his novels; that he is fond of inserting in his journals, among philosophizings and other memoranda, summaries of anecdotes or stories he has heard. Of the latter sort is the following entry:

> Conjurer Mynterne when consulted by Patt P. (a strapping handsome young woman), told her that her husband would die on a certain day, and showed her the funeral in a glass of water ... She used to impress all this on her inoffensive husband, and assure him that he would go to hell if he made the conjurer a liar. He didn't, but died on the day foretold.

Such notations should not be unduly emphasized. Yet they appear in his journal with such frequency that we are justified in assuming Hardy's special interest in such material. On the other hand, in the record of Hardy's life thus far available to us, there is little evidence to indicate that, in devising the greater stories, he had some specific literary model before him, or was trying out some theory of fiction, or had, at the beginning of his conception, a particular philosophical or social thesis. Critics may show that such and such a literary influence reached him, or that a theory or philosophy ultimately engaged his mind; but I cannot believe that such elements controlled the original conception or determined the essential character of the greater novels and stories. The poetry offers a somewhat different field of critical speculation, which I do not propose to enter, but it seems worth while to argue that his characteristic habit of mind, early established and naturally developed, has much to do with certain peculiarities of his fiction.

My thesis is that the characteristic Hardy novel is conceived as a *told* (or *sung*) story, or at least not as a literary story; that it is an extension, in the form of a modern prose fiction, of a traditional ballad or an oral tale—a tale of the kind which Hardy reproduces with great skill in *A Few Crusted Characters* and less successfully in *A Group of Noble Dames*; but, furthermore, that this habit of mind is a rather unconscious element in Hardy's art. The conscious side of his art manifests itself in two ways: first, he 'works up' his core of traditional, or nonliterary narrative into a literary form; but, second, at the same time he labors to establish, in his 'Wessex,' the kind of artistic climate and environment which will enable him to handle his traditional story with conviction—a world in which typical ballad heroes and heroines can flourish with a thoroughly rationalized 'mythology' to sustain them. The novels that support this thesis are the great Hardy novels: *Under the Greenwood Tree, Far from the Madding Crowd, The Mayor of Casterbridge, The Return of the Native, The Woodlanders,* and *Tess of the d'Urbervilles*—in other words, the Wessex novels proper. *Jude the Obscure* and *The Trumpet-Major* can be included, with some reservations, in the same list. The novels that do not support this thesis are commonly held to be, by comparison with those named above, of inferior quality: *The Hand of Ethelberta* and *A Laodicean,* for example. These are Hardy's attempt to be a fully modern—and literary—novelist.

The fictions that result from Hardy's habit of mind resemble traditional, or nonliterary, types of narrative in many ways. They are always conceived of as stories primarily, with the narrative always of foremost interest. They have the rounded, often intricate plot and the balance and antithesis of characters associated with traditional fiction from ancient times. It is natural, of course, that they should in such respects resemble classic drama. But that does not mean that Hardy thought in terms of dramatic composition. His studies in Greek (like his experience in architecture) simply reinforced an original tendency. The interspersed descriptive elements—always important, but not overwhelmingly important, in a Hardy novel—do not encumber the narrative, as they invariably do in the works of novelists who conceive their task in wholly literary terms; but they blend rather quickly into the narrative. Action, not description, is always foremost; the event dominates, rather than motive, or psychology, or comment. There is no loose episodic structure. Hardy does not write the chronicle novel or the biographical novel. Nor does he build up circumstantial detail like a Zola or a Flaubert.

Hardy has an evident fondness for what we might call the 'country story'—the kind of story *told* by the passengers in the van in *A Few Crusted Characters*; or *sung* in ballads of the type attributed by scholars to the seventeenth and eighteenth century and sometimes called 'vulgar' ballads to distinguish them from the supposedly more genuine 'popular' ballads of an earlier day. In *Under the Greenwood Tree*, the coquettish behavior of Fancy Day is a delicate feminine parallel to the difficulties of Tony Kytes, the Arch-deceiver, related in *A Few Crusted Characters*. The coy maiden, after involvement with the solid farmer Shiner and the excellent Vicar, rejects them both at last for the brisk young country lad, Dick Dewy. Gabriel Oak, in *Far from the Madding Crowd*, is the 'faithful lover' of many a ballad, who has many of the elements of a masculine 'patient Griselda'; he endures a kind of 'testing' not irretrievably remote from the testings that ladies put upon their lovers in romances and ballads; and he is also obviously the excellent lover of 'low degree' who aims his affections high and is finally rewarded. Fanny Robin, of the same novel, is a typical deserted maiden, lacking nothing but a turtle-dove on her tombstone; or perhaps she is the more luridly forsaken girl found in 'Mary of the Wild Moor.' Her lover, Sergeant Troy, is the soldier (or sailor) of any number of later ballads. And it is worth remarking, in this connection, that Hardy's fondness for soldiers has everywhere in it the echo of many ballads about the military composed in the half-century or more preceding his birth and even in his own time. It flavors strongly, that is, of such pieces as 'Polly Oliver,' 'Bold Dighton,' 'High Germany,' and 'Bloody Waterloo.'

The Return of the Native gives us far more complexity, but many of its focal incidents are of the stuff in which tale-tellers and ballad-makers delight. Mrs

Yeobright is bitten by a snake; Eustacia and Wildeve are drowned in one pool, to make a simultaneous romantic death, and we almost expect to learn that they were buried in the old churchyard and presently sprouted—a rose from her breast, a briar from his. We should not forget that Eustacia disguises herself in man's clothing (as heroines of traditional stories have long done) for the mummer's play.

Henchard, in *The Mayor of Casterbridge*, undergoes the rise and fall traditional in English story from Chaucer to *The Mirror for Magistrates*. More clearly, as the man who sold his own wife, he is of ballad or folk tale quality. And the man to whom he sold her is none other than a sailor, of all persons, who returns from the salt, salt sea to claim his woman, as sailors do.

The Woodlanders, of the Wessex novels, seems furthest from the type; but again, the love of Marty South for Giles Winterborne is ballad love; and the women of *The Woodlanders*, like most of Hardy's women, have the frantic impulsion toward love, or the cruel and unreasoning capacity to reject faithful love, which we find in balladry. Then, too, Grace Melbury is caught, after the setting of the sun, in a murderous mantrap inadvertently placed in the path by her own lover. Happily she is released, and so escapes the fate of Molly Vaughn of the ballad; Mollie was *shot* by her own lover, who went hunting after the setting of the sun.

Tess of the D'Urbervilles, whatever else she may be, is once more the deserted maiden who finally murders her seducer with a knife in the effective ballad way. And she, with the love-stricken trio—Marian, Retty, and Izz—is a milkmaid; and milkmaids, in balladry, folk song, and folk tale, are somehow peculiarly subject to seduction.

The high degree of coincidence in the typical Hardy narrative has been noted by all observers, often unfavorably. Mr Samuel Chew explains it as partly a result of the influence of the 'sensation novelists,' and partly as a deliberate emphasis on 'the persistence of the unforeseen'—hence a grim, if exaggerated, evidence of the sardonic humor of the purblind Doomsters. Let us pay this view all respect, and still remember that such conscious and artful emphasis may be only a rationalization of unconscious habit. The logic of the traditional story is not the logic of modern literary fiction. The traditional story admits, and even cherishes, the improbable and unpredictable. The miraculous, or nearly miraculous, is what makes a story a story, in the old way. Unless a story has some strange and unusual features it will hardly be told and will not be remembered. Most of the anecdotes that Hardy records in his journal savor of the odd and unusual. And occasionally he speaks directly to the point, as in the following passages:

> The writer's problem is, how to strike the balance between the uncommon and the ordinary, so as on the one hand to give interest, on the other to give reality.
> In working out this problem, human nature must never be abnormal, which is introducing incredibility. The uncommonness must be in the events, not in the characters ... (July, 1881).

> A story must be exceptional enough to justify its telling. We tale-tellers are all
> Ancient Mariners, and none of us is warranted in stopping Wedding Guests (in
> other words, the hurrying public) unless he has something more unusual to
> relate than the ordinary experience of every average man and woman.

Thus coincidence in Hardy's narratives represents a conviction about the
nature of story as such. Hardy's world is of course not the world of the most
antique ballads and folk tales—where devils, demons, fairies, and mermaids
intervene in human affairs, and ghosts, witches, and revenants are commonplace. It is a world like that of later balladry and folk tale, from which old
beliefs have receded, leaving a residue of the merely strange. Improbability
and accident have replaced the miraculous. The process is illustrated in the
ballad 'Mollie Vaughn' (sometimes Van, Bond, or Baun), in which the
speaker, warning young men not to go shooting after sundown, tells how
Mollie was shot by her lover. I quote from an American version recorded by
Louise Pound:

> *Jim Random was out hunting, a-hunting in the dark;*
> *He shot at his true love and missed not his mark.*
> *With a white apron pinned around her he took her for a swan,*
> *He shot her and killed her, and it was Mollie Bond.*

In many versions, even the American ones, Mollie's ghost appears in
court and testifies, in her lover's behalf, that the shooting was indeed
accidental. But the ballad very likely preserves echoes, misunderstood by a
later generation, of an actual swan maiden and her lover. This particular
ballad is certainly unusual in admitting the presence of a ghost in a court of
law. But at least the apparition is a ghost, not a swan maiden, and so we get
the event rationalized in terms of an unlikely but not impossible accident: he
saw the apron and 'took her for a swan.'

Hardy's coincidences may be explained as a similar kind of substitution.
He felt that the unlikely (or quasi-miraculous) element belonged in any
proper story—especially a Wessex story; but he would go only so far as the
late ballads and country tales went, in substituting improbabilities for super-
naturalisms. Never does he concoct a pseudo-folk tale like Stephen V.
Benét's 'The Devil and Daniel Webster.' Superstitions are used in the background of his narrative; coincidence, in the actual mechanics. Tess hears the
legend of the D'Urberville phantom coach, but does not actually see it,
though the moment is appropriate for its appearance. In *The Return of the
Native* Susan Nonesuch pricks Eustacia Vye for a witch and later makes a
waxen image of her, just before her drowning; but coincidence, not superstition, dominates the action. Henchard visits the conjurer just before his
great speculation in grain, but only out of habit and in half-belief; and it is
coincidence that makes Farfrae a winner just at the moment when Henchard
is a loser. The supernatural, in Hardy, is allowed in the narrative, but in a
subordinate position; the quasi-miraculous takes its place in the main position.

If we use a similar approach to the problem of Hardy's pessimism, it is easy to see why he was irritated by insensitive and obtuse critics. Are the ballad stories of 'Edward,' 'Little Musgrave,' and 'Johnnie Armstrong' pessimistic? Were their unknown authors convinced of the fatal indifference of the Universe toward human beings? Should we, reading such stories, take the next step in the context of modern critical realism and advocate psycho-analysis for Edward's mother and social security for Johnnie Armstrong? In formal doctrine Hardy professed himself to be an 'evolutionary meliorist,' or almost a conventional modern. But that had nothing to do with the stories that started up in his head. The charge of pessimism has about the same relevance as the charge of indelicacy which Hardy encountered when he first began to publish. An age of polite literature, which had lost touch with the oral arts—except so far as they might survive in chit-chat, gossip, and risqué stories—could not believe that an author who embodied in his serious stories the typical seductions, rapes, murders, and lusty love makings of the old tradition intended anything but a breach of decorum. Even today, I suppose, a group gathered for tea might be a little astonished if a respectable old gentleman in spats suddenly began to warble the outrageous ballad of Little Musgrave. But Hardy did not know he was being rough, and had no more notion than a ballad-maker of turning out a story to be either pessimistic or optimistic.

To be sure, Hardy is a little to blame, since he does moralize at times. But the passage about the President of the Immortals in *Tess* and about the persistence of the unforeseen in *The Mayor of Casterbridge* probably came to him like such ballad tags as 'Better they'd never been born' or 'Young men, take warning from me.' He had a mistaken idea, too, that he could argue and philosophize with impunity in verse, whereas he might have to go carefully, say, in an essay or speech. 'Perhaps I can express more fully in verse,' he wrote in 1896, 'ideas and emotions which run counter to the inert crystal-lized opinion ... which the vast body of men have vested interests in supporting ... If Galileo had said in verse that the world moved, the Inquisition might have let him alone.' The good and innocent Hardy could somehow not easily learn that a bard was no longer a bard but a social critic.

The most striking feature of Hardy's habit of mind, as traditional narrator, is in his creation of characters. The characters of the Wessex novels, with certain important exceptions, are fixed or 'non-developing' characters. Their fortunes may change, but they do not change with their fortunes. Once fully established as characters, they move unchanged through the narrative and at the end are what they were at the beginning. They have the changelessness of the figures of traditional narrative from epic, saga, and romance to broadside balladry and its prose parallels. In this respect they differ fundamentally from the typical characters of modern literary fiction. Our story-writers have learned how to exploit the possibilities of the changing, or changeful, or 'developing' character. The theory of progress has seemed to influence them to apply an analogical generalization to the heroes of their stories: to wit, the only good hero in a serious novel is one that *changes* in some important respect during the course of the narrative; and the essence of the story is the change. This has become almost an aesthetic axiom. It is assumed that a story has no merit unless it is based on a changing character. If the modern author uses the changeless character, it is only in a minor rôle, or as a foil; or he may appear as a caricature.

But we have forgotten a truth that Hardy must have known from the time when, as a child, he heard at the harvest home the ballad of the outlandish knight. The changeless character has as much aesthetic richness as the changeful character. Traditional narrative of every sort is built upon the changeless character. It is a defect in modern fiction that the value of the changeless character is apparently not even suspected. But since the human desire for the changeless character is after all insatiable, we do have our changeless characters—in the comic strips, the movies, the detective story. Perhaps all is not well with a literary art that leaves the rôle of Achilles to be filled by Pop-Eye.

At any rate Hardy made extensive use of the changeless character. The habit of his mind probably forbade him to do otherwise; or at least he could not with complete success build his stories upon the changeful character. And so his novels of manners and genteel society are failures. At the same time, Hardy was no untutored child of the folk but a great author who learned by trial and error how to utilize self-consciously the rich material which by unself-conscious habit crowded his mind. He was thinking of his problem, I believe, when he wrote: 'The uncommonness must be in the events, not in the characters.' He did not make the mistake of exploiting his material for its mere picturesqueness—its *special* quality. He did not write dialect poems like William Barnes or romantic reconstructions like Black-more's *Lorna Doone*.

What Hardy did is, in its astonishing completeness and verity, a rebuke to superficial quasi-regionalists and to all who attempt to exploit 'folk material' with the shallow assumption that the 'folkishness' of the material is alone enough to dignify it. Hardy rationalizes the changeless characters by creating in highest circumstantiality not only the local environment in which they move, but the entire social order—the tradition itself, and the basis of the tradition—which will accommodate them. The basis of the tradition is a natural environment—a nature not very much despoiled or exploited, a town life neither wholly antique nor wholly modern, and the whole removed a little in time from the strictly contemporary, but not so far removed as to seem like a historical reconstruction. The antiquities, the local color, the folk customs are not decorative or merely picturesque; they are organic with the total scheme. They are no less essential and no more decorative than the occupations, ambitions and interrelationships of the changeless characters. He accepts the assumptions of the society that he depicts, and neither apologizes for it nor condescends to it. The stories are stories of human beings, not of peasants or moor-dwellers as such.

The scheme is somewhat more complex than it might appear to be. The changeless characters of the Wessex world are of both minor and major order; and they are generally set in juxtaposition with one or two characters of a more changeful or modern type. The interplay between the two kinds of characters is the focus of the struggle that makes the story. Hardy is almost the only modern novelist who makes serious use of this conflict and at the same time preserves full and equal respect for both sets of characters. His great art lies in not setting up too great or obvious a distance between his changeless and his changeful characters. The difference between Hardy and other novelists will be clear if I cite a typical example. Ellen Glasgow's *Barren Ground*, a novel which seems to copy Hardy at certain points, reduces all the thoroughly rustic characters to a condition either of amusing oddity or of gross ineptitude; and the excellent Dorinda, who makes such an obviously admirable change from rustic backwardness to rural progressivism, is at all times infinitely above all the rest.

Nature, itself unchangeable and inscrutable, is the norm, the basis of Wessex life. Those who accept nature as unchangeable and passively accommodate themselves to nature in the ordered ritual of their lives, not rebelling against it or attempting rash Promethean manipulations—these are the changeless characters.

Nearest to nature, and therefore most changeless, are the rustics (all crusted characters) who throng Hardy's pages. In the rural comedies, like *Under the Greenwood Tree* and *Far from the Madding Crowd*, they dominate the scene. Only the vicar, in *Under the Greenwood Tree*, with his newfangled church organ, and perhaps in a slight way Sergeant Troy, in the other novel, foreshadow the kind of disturbance set up by the changeful character. But these novels are essentially comedy, joyful and almost idyllic. In Hardy, tragedy does not arrive until changeless and changeful are engaged in bitter conflict.

Such a conflict is found in *The Return of the Native*. Here the rustics are Timothy Fairway, Grandfer Cantle, Christian Cantle, Susan Nonesuch and her son Johnny, and the mummers. It would be wrong to regard these persons as curiosities, or as interesting literary fossils planted in the environment for the verisimilitude that they give. They not only take part in the series of festivals that provide a symbolic chronological pattern for the novel; but they also participate in the critical action itself, as agents of destiny. Timothy carries the letter which was so fatally not delivered at last. Johnny Nonesuch is liaison agent between Eustacia and Wildeve. Christian Cantle carries the guineas, and gambles them away. Susan Nonesuch and her son intervene actively in the lives of both Eustacia and Clym. Their part is organic, not decorative; they are much more than the 'Greek chorus' that they have been called. They are, in fact, the basic pattern to which other characters conform or from which they differ. Diggory Venn and Thomasin,

375

at a slightly higher level, conform more or less; they are changeless characters who venture near the danger line of changefulness but do not pass over it. Eustacia and Clym have passed over the line, though not beyond the possibility of retraction. They are changeful characters, strongly touched by Promethean influences—as Wildeve, in a vulgar way, is also touched. Modernism has worked on Eustacia to lure her away from Egdon Heath; but Clym, who has already lived in Paris, has reached a second stage of revulsion against modernism. Yet when this native returns he brings with him a characteristically modern program of education and evangelism. Eustacia and Clym, as changeful characters, do not diverge extravagantly from the changeless pattern, but their rebellion is great enough to render their life-courses inconstant and tragic.

Hardy has taken some pains to mark the essential nature of Clym's character. The motto for the chapter that describes Clym is: 'My mind to me a kingdom is.' Clym is a Renaissance, or non-traditional, man. His face, already marked with disillusionment, foreshadows 'the typical countenance of the future.' Jude, another changeful character, is like Clym in some ways. He too is a rebel against nature, whose rebellion is also idealistic; but it leads him away from Wessex. His story might have been entitled: 'The Migration of the Native.' In Jude's life the changeless and the changeful are further represented in Arabella and Sue; Arabella, the changeless but too gross; Sue Bridehead, the changeful but too refined. In *Tess* there are two changeful and ruin-wreaking characters. In Alex Stoke-D'Urberville the changeful character takes on a vulgar form. He is an imposter, who has appropriated an old country name and bought his way into Wessex; and the Stoke-D'Urberville establishment, with its preposterous chicken culture, is a fake rural establishment. Angel Clare, on the other hand, is a rarefied form of alien. He is willing, condescendingly, to accept Wessex, and dairy farming, and Tess, provided he can possess all this in an abstractly 'pure,' or respectable form. The tragedy arrives when he cannot adjust (the sociological term is necessary) his delicate sensibility to a gross, but, in the natural order, an understandable biological fact. It is the changeful modern character in Angel that cannot abide Tess's delinquency. The changeless characters might have found fault, but would not have been shocked, would not have sulked, would not have been too slow to pardon. A similar opposition appears in *The Woodlanders*, where changefulness appears in Fitzpiers and Mrs Charmond; changelessness in Giles Winterborne and Marty South.

Perhaps these are dangerous simplifications. I do not offer them as definitive explanations of Hardy's fictions, but rather as possibilities not yet explored. Hardy's habit of mind, and his method of using his habit of mind in fiction, seem to me the least discussed of the aspects of his work. I have found no other approach that does not seem to improve a critical explanation from without, with an arbitrariness that often seems to do violence to the art work itself.

There is surely no other example in modern English fiction of an author who, while reaching the highest levels of sophisticated artistic performance, comes bringing his tradition with him, not only the mechanics of the tradition but the inner conception that is often lacking. The admonitions we hear so often nowadays about the relation of the artist and his tradition seem dry and academic when we look closely at Hardy's actual performance. He seems to illustrate what we might think the ideal way of realizing and activating a tradition, for he did, without admonition, what the admonishers are always claiming ought to be done; and yet for that particular achievement he got no thanks, or even a notice. The achievement is the more extraordinary when we consider that he worked (if I read his career rightly) against the dominant pattern of his day. He did what the modern critic (despite his concern about tradition) is always implying to be impossible. That is, Hardy accepted the assumptions of a society which in England was already being condemned to death, and he wrote in terms of those assumptions, almost as if Wessex, and perhaps Wessex only, would understand. From his work I get few of the meanings, pessimistic or otherwise, that are commonly ascribed to him. His purpose seems to have been to tell about human life in the terms that would present it as most recognizably, and validly, and completely human. That he succeeded best when he wrote of rural Wessex is significant. He probably had strong convictions on one point—convictions that had little to do with his official inquiries into Darwinism and the nature of Deity.

191

Hardy in Defense of His Art: The Aesthetic of Incongruity

◆

MORTON DAUWEN ZABEL

The first artists, in any line, are doubtless not those whose general ideas about their art are most often on their lips—those who most abound in precept, apology, and formula and can best tell us the reasons and the philosophy of things. We know the first usually by their energetic practice, the constancy with which they apply their principles, and the serenity with which they leave us to hunt for their secret in the illustration, the concrete example. None the less it often happens that a valid artist utters his mystery, flashes upon us for a moment the light by which he works, shows us the rule by which he holds it just that he should be measured. This accident is happiest, I think, when it is soonest over; the shortest explanations of the products of genius are the best, and there is many a creator of living figures whose friends, however full of faith in his inspiration, will do well to pray for him when he sallies forth into the dim wilderness of theory. The doctrine is apt to be so much less inspired than the work, the work is often so much more intelligent than the doctrine.

—[HENRY] JAMES on MAUPASSANT

I

That Hardy's was a native and persistent order of genius; that he expressed it in a style and drama which he made unmistakably his own; that his work carries the stamp of a theme and vision which have impressed a large area of art and experience in the last eighty years; that he exists as a force in modern literature in spite of some of the severest critical reservation any notable writer has been subjected to—these we may take as facts which have survived excesses both of distaste and of eulogy and become part of the record of modern English literature. In Hardy's middle years the scorn of Henry James and George Moore joined with the scandalized protests of press and pulpit to deny him aesthetic as much as public respect. In his old age and after, a reckless apotheosis has proved almost as damaging. Hardy survives

SOURCE *The Southern Review*, 1940–1, vol. 6, pp. 24–45.

them both. Virginia Woolf, when she visited him at Max Gate in 1926, was sincere in recognizing a fact of history.

> I wanted him to say one word about his writings before we left and could only ask which of his books he would have chosen if, like me, he had had to choose one to read in the train. I had taken *The Mayor of Casterbridge* ... 'And did it hold your interest?' he asked. I stammered that I could not stop reading it, which was true but sounded wrong.

Few readers have missed the spell, and few have missed feeling in some sense confused about it.

Yet the radical quality is less likely to be mistaken in Hardy's work than in most writers of his rank. It can easily be simplified to a convenient fault or virtue, according to the prejudice of the critic. It often remains crudely defined in memory. The conflicting elements that shape it may be minimized by admirers who are anxious to forget the difficulties they met in salvaging his genius from the uneven and erratic body of his work. But it is a quality as unmistakable in his prose and verse as in his personality and thought; as prominent in his style as in that reading of life which he insisted on disclaiming as a 'philosophy.'

It derives from the conjunction, in his temperament, of conformist and skeptical tendencies; in his humanism, of stoic acquiescence with moral protest; in his response to human character, of a kinship with gifted, rebellious, or destructive aberrations from the human norm as against his sympathy with the rudimentary types and stable humors of the folk. In his thought it appears in his leaning toward cosmic simplifications so large and unwieldy that their grandeur becomes inflexible, an impediment to critical thinking and an oppression to the imagination, and conversely in his humble loyalty to the claims of life in all its elusive and stubborn deviations—its vital struggles and appeals that protest and so make bearable the mindless negation of the universe. What this ambivalence of temper did to Hardy's style is apparent on almost every one of his pages. Their salt, tang, and sincerity are continuously accompanied by habits of rhetoric, pretension, and straining eloquence, even by astonishing repetitions and laborings of effect, that exceed those in most of the writers in a century abnormally conscious of crisis and the 'urge to rhetoric.'

To credit these divergences to Hardy with any special emphasis is to say that the large schemes into which he cast his problems, and the stormy dramas he made of them, make the central discordance in his work insistent, the basic clue to his talent. Obviously this discordance exists widely in modern art and thought. Hardy saw it as a primary rift or dichotomy in man which post-rationalist Europe had thrown into a new relief. His contemporaries were torn and distraught by it; it is the frame and condition of the modern man's typical agony. Nor does one distinguish Hardy particularly by saying that his style and form are inordinately marked by rough contrasts and antitheses. Such contrasts—of aesthetic logic and selection at odds with the rough justice and violence of experience, or plots shaped and contrived to the point of artifice against the disorder of life, of characters reduced to the basic patterns of human nature against the subtle divinations of modern psychologists—are apparent throughout modern fiction; they swarm through that chaotic and amorphous medium to which the courtesy title of novel is applied. The same heterogeneity exists in modern poetry, where serious purposes are offset by startling levities, where the grand manner is deflated by vulgar intrusions, where moral earnestness is scoffed by the scurrilities of cynicism, and where a sense of responsibility to the traditional dignities of the human spirit became so violently reproached by the squalor of modern society that satirists like Laforgue and Corbière wrought these jarring collisions into a critical medium that has descended to Pound, Eliot, Joyce, Auden, and the satirists and realists of contemporary poetry and fiction.

Hardy participated little in these developments and showed small interest in the artistic results of the modern man's skeptical consciousness. But he was too much a child of his time to remain unmarked by the traits of nineteenth century art. He inherited the aesthetic disorder of the age, its unresolved antipathies, its sprawling appetite for life, and the instability that reflected the surrounding distraction. That instability is deeply imbedded in his books, and if popular reverence now tends to slight its prominence there, two other factors insists on emphasizing it. For one thing, Hardy wrote and matured during a period in which aesthetic reformers in fiction and poetry were grappling with the problem of reducing the elements of the arts to a new unity and integrity, of bringing them into harmony that might enhance their value, force, and intelligence. He was the contemporary, in other words, of Baudelaire, Flaubert, and Turgenev, of James, Moore, Yeats, Proust, Pound, Valéry, and Eliot, but a colleague of none of them. He was, secondly, conscious throughout his life of the struggle in himself of a distressing opposition of faculties—of immediate personal sympathies and large intellectual ambitions—and in the face of the critical hostility that surrounded him through two-thirds of his literary career he struggled to formulate a defense of his talent and method. Thus he shaped a personal aesthetic for himself; and though it shows something of the amateur's pedantry that is evident in his early fiction and in his metaphysical excursions, it demands attention from anyone concerned with the artistic progress of the modern novel and with the interrelations of modern fiction and poetry.

He was no adept at critical or aesthetic reasoning; he felt a life-long suspicion of its practitioners; his literary notes and prefaces sound a note of peremptory impatience toward them. Yet his methodical habit of mind exercised itself over many years in notations on structure, form, style, and aesthetic ideas and in a continuous effort to generalize these into working principles. The craft of fiction had not come to him easily. Poetry was his first ambition, and until he was sixty he was in doubt whether his real vocation had been obstructed or merely painfully slow in maturing. 'I was quick to bloom; late to ripen.' 'I was a child till I was 16; a youth till I was 25; a young man till I was 40 or 50.'[1] The groping awkwardness he showed in mastering the business of fiction-writing is equaled by the step-by-step pains he took to come into some kind of conscious knowledge of his aesthetic purposes. One of the first things he discovered about himself was a natural lack of artistic sophistication. He knew he was unequipped for competition with the rising schools of Paris and London. He felt the pull of older traditions of romance and a brotherhood with the rough-and-ready masters of Victorian fiction, the dramatic and sensation novelists of the Sixties from whom he learned his trade. The homeliness of his tastes is evident in 'An Ancient to Ancients.' In music his favorites, when not the hymns of Tate and Brady, were *The Bohemian Girl* and *Il Trovatore*. In painting, though he carefully studied the Dutch and Italian schools, he warmed to the Academy pictures of Etty, Mulready, and Maclise. In fiction the 'throbbing romance' of Bulwer, Scott, Dumas, and Sand had made a golden age. His poetic loyalties, rooted in the romanticism of Keats, Shelley, and Tennyson, spent their last real enthusiasm on Browning and Swinburne. As early as 1873 we find him attempting to justify natural impulse and fancy as the basis of art:

> Read again Addison, Macaulay, Newman, Sterne, Defoe, Lamb, Gibbon, Burke, *Times* Leaders, in a study of style. Am more and more confirmed in an idea I have long held, as a matter of common sense, long before I thought of any old aphorism bearing on the subject: 'Ars est celare artem.' The whole secret of living style and the difference between it and a dead style, lies in not having too much style—being in fact, a little careless, or rather seeming to be, here and there. It brings wonderful life into the writing:
>
> > *A sweet disorder in the dress ...*
> > *A careless shoe-string, in whose tie*
> > *I see a wild civility.*
> > *Do more bewitch me than when art*
> > *Is too precise in every part.*
>
> Otherwise your style is like worn half-pence—all the fresh images rounded off by rubbing, and no crispness or movement at all.
> It is, of course, simply a carrying into prose the knowledge I have acquired in poetry—that inexact rhymes and rhythms now and then are far more pleasing than correct ones.

He began to turn to nature for his justification of such defect and awkwardness:

> So, then, if Nature's defects must be looked in the face and transcribed, whence arises the *art* in poetry and novel-writing? which must certainly show art, or it becomes merely mechanical reporting. I think the art lies in making these defects the basis of a hitherto unperceived beauty, by irradiating them with 'the light that never was' on their surface, but is seen to be latent in them by the spiritual eye.

'Faultlessness,' he once agreed with Browning, 'avails neither a man nor book anything unless it can be surmounted by care and sympathy,' and when he read Henry James's *Reverberator* on its appearance in 1888 he emphatically dissociated himself from the new motives in fiction:

> After this kind of work one feels inclined to be purposely careless in detail. The great novels of the future will certainly not concern themselves with the minutiae of manners ... James's subjects are those one could be interested in at moments when there is nothing larger to think of.

This defense of casual vitality now appears inseparable from Hardy's emphasis on the significance of chance and accident in life. In his aesthetic morality it results in a defense of instinctive and emotional qualities above the intellectual. The purpose of great fiction is not basically critical, intellectual, dialectic, or minutely discriminative; it is to seize and embody the values of the heart, of instinct and intuitive sympathy, of the passions which Hardy shared with the Victorian moralists and humanitarians and which he saw exhausted and vitiated among the critical efforts of the modern schools. The 'seemings' which he held, in the preface to *Jude* and elsewhere, to be the sum and substance of his work, as against the imputation of philosophical pessimism or negation (in 1917 he wrote: 'I find I wrote in 1888 that "Art is concerned with seemings only," which is true'), are for him exactly those responses which are authorized by the heart as against the cancelling judgments of the head. 'I hold,' he said late in life,

> that the mission of poetry is to record impressions, not convictions. Wordsworth in his later writings fell into the error of recording the latter. So also did Tennyson and so do many other poets when they grow old. Absit omen! ... I believe it would be said by people who knew me well that I have a faculty (possibly not uncommon) for burying an emotion in my heart or brain for forty years, and exhuming it at the end of that time as fresh as when interred.

Hardy, recognizing the undeviating identity of his feeling and style over a space of seventy years, took that fact as a means of justifying the permanence of 'impressions' above the instability of intellectual doctrines and convictions. 'Poetry must feel,' he maintained. 'The Poet takes note of nothing that he cannot feel emotively.' 'There is a latent music in the sincere utterance of deep emotion, however expressed, which fills the place of the actual word-music in rhythmic phraseology on thinner emotive subjects, or on subjects with next to none at all.' The translation of that emotion into style became his single assurance of success as a poet:

> Consider the Wordsworthian dictum (the more perfectly the natural object is reproduced, the more truly poetic the picture). This reproduction is achieved by seeing into the *heart of a thing* (as rain, wind, for instance), and is realism, in fact, though through being pursued by means of the imagination it is confounded with invention, which is pursued by the same means. It is, in short, reached by what M. Arnold calls 'the imaginative reason.'

Such a view of the matter made drudgery for Hardy of any intense technical discipline. When, in his earlier books, he was obliged to treat of modern artificial life, he particularly felt the strain. He had 'mostly aimed at keeping his narratives close to natural life and as near to poetry in their subject as the conditions would allow, and had often regretted that those conditions would not let him keep them nearer still.' When he reread Henry James in old age, he marveled and was perplexed that 'a writer who has no grain of poetry, or humor, or spontaneity, in his productions, can yet be a good novelist. Meredith has some poetry, and yet I can read James when I cannot look at Meredith.' He saw Meredith's failure in the fact 'that he would not, or could not—at any rate did not—when aiming to represent the "Comic Spirit," let himself discover the tragedy that always underlies Comedy if you only scratch deeply enough.' 'If all hearts were open and all desires known—as they would be if people showed their souls—how many gapings, sighings, clenched fists, knotted brows, broad grins, and red eyes should we see in the marketplace!'

The prejudice here is clear. Hardy saw the growth of sophistication and critical intellection in art as evils at its root. His scruples as a workman and his methodical seriousness as a student, even his systematic ambition for literary fame, were outbalanced by his sense of being an outsider to art's higher mysteries. It is no wonder that James and Stevenson, though compelled to admire, groaned over the flaws in *Tess*, or that George Moore spent his harshest invective on that book and its author, or that T.S. Eliot, in *After Strange Gods*, has set Hardy down as a 'symptom of decadence,' a victim of emotion run morbid, 'a minor poet' whose matter of communication is not 'particularly wholesome or edifying.' The approach to Hardy through his artistic medium ('he was indifferent even to the prescripts of good writing,' says Eliot, '... at times his style touches sublimity without ever having passed through the stage of being good') has often resulted in this inclusive contempt. This approach is inescapable; it is necessary; but in the case of Hardy's sharply qualified and unstable talent, the approach must be made in unusually wide and comprehensive terms. His own anti-aesthetic position committed him to a search for the timeless qualities of life and destiny, to a sense of history that shares little of the critical scrutiny of time and experience that was soon to become a major prepossession of the modern artist. Hardy stood, indeed, in an honored English line. He felt that poetry and fiction, if they bowed to the critical faculty, would ultimately meet an enervation of their strength, their native daemon and validity. He held in this with Bacon, Goldsmith, and Macaulay; he anticipated some of the fears that I.A. Richards has voiced in *Science and Poetry*. Caught between the intimacy of his physical sensations and the enveloping grandeur of his imaginative and scientific visions, he based his faith as a poet on a magical conception of man and nature. This sympathy suffuses his literal-mindedness, his prosaic tedium, his almost mawkish dissection of passionate fact. And he proposed to defend and exemplify it in his work as long as he lived.

Accordingly we find Hardy arguing that fiction must share with poetry the task of relieving the oppression of life's fact and commonplace. He opposed the naturalists, whom he saw joining forces with aesthetic rationalists in making an unbearable oppression of the actual.

> The real, if unavowed, purpose of fiction is to give pleasure by gratifying the love of the uncommon in human experience, mental or corporeal.
> This is done all the more perfectly in proportion as the reader is illuded to believe the personages true and real like himself.
> Solely to this latter end a work of fiction should be a precise transcript of ordinary life: but,
> The uncommon would be absent and the interest lost. Hence,
> The writer's problem is, how to strike the balance between the uncommon and the ordinary so as on the one hand to give interest, on the other to give reality.
> In working out this problem, human nature must never be made abnormal, which is introducing incredibility. The uncommonness must be in the events, not in the characters; and the writer's are lies in shaping that uncommonness while disguising its unlikelihood, if it be unlikely.

He subscribed to Coleridge's view that the aim must be 'at *illusion* in audience or readers—*i.e.*, the mental state when dreaming, intermediate between complete delusion (which the French mistakenly aim at) and a clear perception of falsity.' As late as 1919, long after he had abandoned fiction, he felt a weight on his conscience that he had led the novel too much toward positive realism, and had by that means aided in stultifying the suggestive and poetic force of modern novel-writing. He would, he said, write at the beginning of each new romance: 'Understand that however true this book may be in essence, in fact it is utterly untrue.' Two days after completing *The Mayor of Casterbridge* in 1885 he had written, 'The business of the poet and novelist is to show the sorriness underlying the grandest things, and the grandeur underlying the sorriest things.' Nature, if left unprejudiced and uninterpreted, becomes a curse and burden to man, and this can be alleviated only by the imaginative penetration of her meaning which it is the function of art to supply. 'Nature is an arch-dissembler. A child is deceived completely; the older members of society more or less according to their penetration; though even they seldom get to realize that *nothing* is as it appears.' And again:

> Nature is played out as a Beauty, but not as a Mystery ... I don't want to see the original realities—as optical effects, that is. I want to see the deeper reality underlying the scenic, the expression of what are sometimes called abstract imaginings.
> The 'simply natural' is interesting no longer. The much decried, mad, late-Turner rendering is now necessary to create my interest. The exact truth as to material fact ceases to be of importance in art—it is a student's style—the style of a period when the mind is serene and unawakened to the tragical mysteries of life; when it does not bring anything to the object that coalesces with and

translates the qualities that are already there,—half hidden, it may be—, and the two are depicted as the All.

Thus he came to suspect any rationalization that pretended to account for the totality of life or reality, and any literary theory that maintained it is the purpose of art to convey a sense of such totality. 'Since I discovered,' he said in 1882,

> that I was living in a world where nothing bears out in practice what it promises incipiently, I have troubled very little about theories ... Where development according to perfect reason is limited to the narrow region of pure mathematics, I am content with tentativeness from day to day.

So it comes about that Hardy, whatever his connection with post-Darwinian fashions in determinism, resisted the formulation of a logic of experience or history.

> Is not the present quasi-scientific system of writing history mere charlatanism? Events and tendencies are traced as if they were rivers of voluntary activity, and courses reasoned out from the circumstances in which natures, religions, or what-not, have found themselves. But are they not in the main the outcome of *passivity*—acted upon by unconscious propensity?

Just before the War, viewing the rise of a new generation of documentary realists, he said that 'they forget in their insistence on life, and nothing but life, in a plain slice, that a story *must be worth the telling*, that a good deal of life is not worth any such thing, and that they must not occupy a reader's time with what he can get at first hand anywhere around him.'

What is 'worth telling' is what recedes from the apparent, the external, the visible. It is the part of experience that withdraws into the private, the subjective, the subconscious, and hence into the mysterious energy of living matter.

> People who to one's-self are transient singularities are to themselves the permanent condition, the inevitable, the normal, the rest of mankind being to them the singularity. Think, that those (to us) strange phenomena, *their* personalities, are with them always, at their going to bed, at their uprising!
>
> Footsteps, cabs, etc., are continually passing our lodgings. And every echo, pit-pat, and rumble that makes up the general noise has behind it a motive, a prepossession, a hope, a fear, a fixed thought forward; perhaps more—a joy, a sorrow, a love, a revenge.
>
> London appears not to see *itself*. Each individual is conscious of *himself*, but nobody conscious of themselves collectively, except perhaps some poor gaper who stares round with a half-idiotic aspect.
>
> There is no consciousness of where anything comes from or goes to—only that it is present.
>
> In the City. The fiendish precision or mechanism of town-life is what makes it so intolerable to the sick and infirm. Like an acrobat performing on a succession of swinging trapezes, as long as you are at particular points at precise instants, everything glides as if afloat; but if you are not up to time—

When he transferred this sense of the endless dichotomy of life, its mysterious dualism of subject and object, to the problem of narrative, Hardy saw that the inherent animus of experience is something more than the double vision of which the blessed simple folk of the world are unconscious but by which the seeing intellects are eternally tormented. It is a matter of maintaining a precarious balance, in art as in intelligent life, between the necessities of personal, practical, and localized experience, and the knowledge of universals which transcend all individuality. 'I do not expect much notice will be taken of these poems,' he said when publishing *Moments of Vision* in 1917; 'they mortify the human sense of self-importance by showing, or suggesting, that human beings are of no matter or appreciable value in this nonchalant universe.' This was only an echo of what he had written during the stormy aftermath of *Tess* in 1893: 'The whole secret of fiction and the drama—in the constructional part—lies in the adjustment of things unusual to things eternal and universal. The writer who knows exactly how exceptional, and how nonexceptional, his events should be made, possesses the key to the art.' Upon that conviction he based his idea of tragedy. 'The best tragedy—highest tragedy in short—is that of the WORTHY encompassed by the INEVITABLE. The tragedies of immoral and worthless people are not of the best.' When *Jude* fell under the lash of the reviewers in 1895, he committed himself to his final patience and wrote in his notebook:

> Tragedy may be created by an opposing environment either of things inherent in the universe, or of human institutions. If the former be the means exhibited and deplored, the writer is regarded as impious if the latter, as subversive and dangerous; when all the while he may never have questioned the necessity or urged the nonnecessity of either.

Thus he made consoling generalizations on his creative plight. But he was able to localize the tragic sense in himself. That he had reasons for doing so, especially during his first marriage, we have come to understand only lately (Mr Carl Weber's biography makes them clear enough). Sometimes the twist of this pathos seized him with a pang almost as ludicrous as that which so frequently strikes his Clyms, Bathshebas, Judes, and Henchards. Once in middle life he found himself afflicted with toothache.

> I look in the glass. Am conscious of the humiliating sorriness of my earthly tabernacle, and of the sad fact that the best of parents could do no better for me ... Why should a man's mind have been thrown into such close, sad, sensational, inexplicable relations with such a precarious object as his own body!

II

Everybody has experienced certain tests of credulity and assent in reading Hardy. All lovers of his work, at one time or another, are caught up by the strain he places on belief and sympathy. Perhaps his own word best labels the pervading quality of his effects: they are 'tentative.' His appeal is cumulative, seldom concentrated; deliberate with a patient confidence in the latent meaning of life, not immediate and assumptive in its acceptance of cosmic justice. His reading of experience, whatever sense he conveys of implacable forces and blind principle, is groping, experimental, suspended, empirical. As is well known, he explicitly repudiated the imputation of pessimism in his thought, just as he implicitly broke with the monistic conception of life and matter. He practiced, 'by the exploration of reality and [a] frank recognition stage by stage along the survey,' the mode of thought which he called 'evolutionary meliorism.' At least three times he challenged directly the charge of his critics (Alfred Noyes on one notable occasion) that he argued from a position of dogmatic negation and that he reduced deity to nonentity and God to an 'imbecile jester.' The cosmic theater in which the warring nations of *The Dynasts* are mixed shows them obeying 'resistlessly the purposive, unmotivated dominant Thing,' but Hardy requested his reader not to make too close an inspection of his phantoms or arguments since they 'are but tentative, and are advanced with little eye to systematic philosophy.' *Jude* was offered to the public in 1895 as 'simply an endeavor to give shape and coherence to a series of seemings, or personal impressions, the question of their consistency or their discordance, of their permanence or their transitoriness, being regarded as not of the first moment.' And for the general preface of the Mellstock Edition in 1921 he wrote:

> Positive views on the Whence and the Wherefore of things have never been advanced by this pen as a consistent philosophy. Nor is it likely, indeed, that imaginative writings extending over more than forty years would exhibit a coherent scientific theory of the universe even if it had been attempted—of that universe concerning which Spencer owns to the 'paralyzing thought' that possibly there exists no comprehension of it anywhere ... That these impressions have been condemned as 'pessimistic'—as if that were a very wicked adjective—shows a curious muddle-mindedness. It must be obvious that there is a higher characteristic of philosophy than pessimism, or than meliorism, or even than the optimism of these critics—which is truth. Existence is either ordered in a certain way, or it is not so ordered, and conjectures which harmonize best with experience are removed above all comparison with other conjectures which do not so harmonize ... And there is another consideration. Differing natures find their tongue in the presence of differing spectacles. Some natures become vocal at tragedy, some are made vocal by comedy, and it seems to me that to whichever of these aspects of life a writer's instinct for expression the more readily responds, to that he should allow it to respond. That before a contrasting side of things he remains undemonstrative need not be assumed to mean that he remains unperceiving.

These statements of Hardy's reduce to several conclusions. He had no inclination to see science as absolute or final; its whole appeal to him lay in its dissolution of 'counters and fixities' in both experience and universal law. He inclined, with the natural leaning of his post-Romantic generation, toward the validity of individual perception. His respect for scientific thought was a respect for the goal it set for itself—a liberal, unprejudiced, and cumulative mode of truth. He was an empiric but not, as he insisted, a pragmatic. He sympathized less with the pessimistic arguments of Schopen-hauer than with the creative and evolutionary motives of English thinkers. Of *The Dynasts* he said, 'My pages show harmony of view with Darwin, Huxley, Spencer, Comte, Hume, Mill, and others, all of whom I used to read more than Schopenhauer.' The year 1859 was always remembered as a red-letter date in his career: he was one of the first readers of *The Origin of Species* and at once sensed its epoch-making importance. It was the evolutionary or progressive principle, with its creative implications, that won his sympathy for the historical patterns defined by Comte, Spencer, and Eduard von Hartmann's *Philosophy of the Unconscious*. The closing lines of *The Dynasts* are often overworked by embarrassed apologists, but they express what Hardy repeatedly insists on; their gleam of promise and aspiration in the universal order redeems, as with a flicker of faith, the darkness that drops on Tess, Jude, and Henchard.

Hardy was, in fact, more than is generally assumed a pioneer defender, with Butler and Shaw, of the creative principle in evolution. The will to live, as he dramatizes it, persists through every apparent confusion of local and individual purposes. It is never without its consolations. Momentarily it instructs man in accepting nature as the refuge of his tormented spirit. Prophetically it lends him the hope that his life will be harmonized with the unconscious or instinctive energy of nature. It even advances to a higher plane and glimpses a victory of intelligence, a release of the higher Will from its cosmic condition of 'immanence,' so that it may become assimilated to the conscious energy and vision of human beings.

'The discovery of the law of evolution, which revealed that all organic creatures are of one family,' he wrote to a New York correspondent in 1909, 'shifted the center of altruism from humanity to the whole conscious world collectively.' And he agreed with an Australian admirer that *The Dynasts* offered an idea harmonious with the principle of Christian revelation: the Immanent Will, far from showing fiendish malignance, may appear blind and irresponsible, but it implies a growth into self-consciousness. One recent critic, Mr Amiya Chakravarty, has extended this possibility in Hardy's thought by drawing the analogy of Freud's categories: the Spirit of the Years (of conscious or calculated experience) is analogous to the Freudian Ego; the Spirit of the Pities (of human purpose, identity, effort, frustration, tragedy) with the Super-ego; whereas the principle of unconscious and abiding energy, the Id, is represented by 'the continuum of blind forces which unites the instincts with Nature and whose actions are the main theme of the drama.'[2] These forces, basic and anterior to consciousness, may ultimately, with the arrival of a universal harmony, become lifted and approximated to the purposes of human will and aspiration. Another student, Pierre d'Exideuil, has echoed Hardy's distress that his version of Will should be regarded as an aimless one and that pessimism is the only adequate estimate of life, by going behind the Freudian analogy into the thinking of Hardy's middle years. He has proposed another affiliation: 'the fundamental difference between Schopenhauer's and Hardy's outlook perhaps lies in the fact that Schopenhauer is pre-Darwinian, whereas Hardy's thought was definitely moulded by the conception of evolution.' D'Exideuil sees that

> between Schopenhauer and Hardy, as between Schopenhauer and Nietzsche, stands Darwin, the channel whereby meliorism, the idea of the greatest possible enriching and perfecting of life, reaches the poet of *The Dynasts* and the hero of *Zarathustra*. Life, therefore, may become its own aim, whereas Schopenhauer stopped short with the denial of any final aim.[3]

This oversimplifies Schopenhauer's thought and minimizes its contribution to the Freudian principle of energy. But it points to an important fact. Hardy may have diverged from Schopenhauer but he saw with him the dualistic character of man, his division between compulsive force, supremely embodied in sexual urge, and his attraction toward the transcendence of idea—an aspiration of intellect rendered pathetic or tragic by the warfare of passion. Sex is for Hardy what it is for Schopenhauer—the focal point of Will, the final sublimation of sincerity. Yet Hardy never advanced as far as Schopenhauer did in 'his insight into the overweening power of instinct and the derogation of the one-time godlike reason, mind, and intellect to a mere tool with which to achieve security.'

Hardy, as both poet and novelist, was prevented by his response to man's character and courage from a dualism so extreme. Accordingly, the opposition of will and idea, instinct and intellect, is never absolute and rigorous with him. The two spheres interpenetrate. He conveys, by the dramatic reality of his characters and the poetic truth of his finest verse, a promise of ultimate unity among the forces that harry and destroy men which Schopenhauer, working within the frames of theory and ratiocination, stopped short of, Hardy's modest and confident temper never suffered the German's exacerbation. Yet what Thomas Mann has said of Schopenhauer is enlightening at this point: there is a fundamental connection between his pessimism and his humanism, 'this combined melancholy and pride in the human race which make up Schopenhauer's philosophy.'

> His pessimism—that is his humanity. His interpretation of the world by the concept of the will, his insight into the overweening power of instinct and the derogation of the one-time godlike reason, mind, and intellect to a mere tool with which to achieve security—all this is anticlassic and in its essence inhumane. But it is precisely in the pessimistic hue of his philosophy that his humanity and spirituality lie; in the fact that this great artist ... lifts man out of the biological sphere of nature, makes his own feeling and understanding soul the theater where the will meets its reverse, and sees in the human being the savior of all creation.[4]

What Schopenhauer arrived at by something resembling a counsel of desperation, Hardy arrived at by the humane insight and compassion of a great artist. Where Schopenhauer rests on the latent form of such 'artistry,'

Hardy succeeds by the imaginative immediacy of art. His Henchard, Tess, and Jude enter the sphere of 'saviors of all creation' where Hamlet, Macbeth, and Lear stand in the ranks of the triumphant.

The transition in Hardy from doubt and negation to humanistic hope was encumbered by an amateur's crudity in handling philosophical machinery, and the clumsiness is evident in all his dramas. He contrives his defeats and frustrations as a means of reducing to its final and minimal condition the saving heroism, dignity, and integrity of his characters. His use of every known portent, accident, and coincidence of chance destinies is notoriously excessive. The impression that survives such buffetings of the reader's patience corresponds, no doubt intentionally, to the indestructible essence of human worth and dignity with which his characters manage to survive, Greek-like, their havoc of ruin and defeat. The role of man in the universe is, for Hardy, comparable to the role of will and intelligence themselves: it is a role of emergent exoneration and supremacy. The word *emergent* is important. Man's exoneration is not to be taken for granted. It is not to be rashly assumed by means of defiance, ambition, or egotism. It materializes slowly, out of blight and despair. It materializes so slowly and painfully, indeed, that one is inclined to think that Hardy saw an analogy for this painful vindication in the equally painful and agonized degrees by which modern man had suffered the loss of his traditional dignity in the teachings of Bacon, Montaigne, Galileo, Newton, Locke, Lyell, and Darwin, and yet survived to declare a new faith and worth for himself through a sublimation of his egoistic individuality into the instinctive wisdom and slowly maturing intelligence of the natural universe itself. Some such allegory is conveyed by the stories of Clym Yeobright, Michael Henchard, and Jude Fawley; it is implicit in Hardy's children of nature—Gabriel Oak, Giles Winterborne, Marty South, Diggory Venn, and John Loveday.

Hardy's 'seemings' are rightly termed 'a tentative metaphysic.' His faith in nature and cosmic purpose is emergent. Correspondingly, the role of man—never demoted from his position of superiority to other parts of nature—must be emergent also. His dignity is arrived at by test, denial, humiliation, disillusion, and defeat—by every possible accident of fate, ironic mischance, and the apparently hostile action of nature. The vindication of man implies the vindication of purpose in the universe. It will appear by means of reserves that issue from the blind or instinctive life in order to become conscious and creative. This inspiration of personal will through violence and suffering corresponds to the gradualism whereby, in the closing chorus of *The Dynasts*,

> *the rages*
> *Of the ages*
> *Shall be cancelled, and deliverance offered from the darts that were,*
> *Consciousness the Will informing, till It fashion all things fair!*

III

Any reader of Hardy is continuously aware of difficulties exactly corresponding to Hardy's own slow, trial-and-error 'impressions' of the meaning of man's place in nature and to the deliberate, trial-and-error way by which he built them into his tales. His novels, teeming with contrivance, show the cumbersome plotting, the exaggerated mountings, the devious complexity, which the whole craft of modern fiction, from Flaubert and Turgenev to James, Conrad, and Proust, has insisted on rejecting, and which even such prodigal contrivers as Dickens, Trollope, and Hugo had managed to subdue to their more relaxed and spacious versions of modern life.

Almost any tale by Hardy, on first reading at least, nettles the sympathy, offers stumbling-blocks to attention, and is likely to make the suspension of disbelief a resentful ordeal. The selling of Mrs Henchard in the opening pages of *The Mayor of Casterbridge* is a violent instance of such assault on credulity, and others follow fast in the remainder of the book. It now takes persistence to move past these wrenchings of congruity, and one's faith in the novelist's seriousness must survive a good many tests before the gathering force of the local color, the Dorset speech, the richness of country customs, and the mounting grandeur of pathos slowly subsume the defects and crudities of Hardy's plots. The opening situation in *Tess* is relieved by the droll humor of its treatment, but minor tales like *Two on a Tower* are pitched at so violent an angle of improbability that they creak under the excesses of their romantic plots and the added burden of astronomical machinery that nearly crushes the lives out of the characters instead of rendering them tragically pitiable. Even the famous overture of *The Return of the Native* shows so exaggerated an air of portentous solemnity (and so much overwriting, dragging erudition, repetition of motives, and rhythmic orotundity) that it takes all the subsequent weight of the novel, all of its passions, rustic naïveté, and counter-balancing melodrama, to overcome the ponderous effect of the first chapters. Certainly *The Dynasts*, however it may impress many readers and however memorably it offers its flashes of historic synthesis and characterization, cannot survive as drama or history. The burden of its pretensions and the falseness they inflict on its style are too pervasive. Hardy admitted this to some degree; he told Henry Newbolt that 'instead of saying to themselves "Here is a performance hugely defective: is there anything in it notwithstanding the huge defects?" [the critics] have contented themselves with picking out bad lines, which any child could do, there are myriads of them, as I knew too well before they said so'; and he took consolation in Meredith's praise of the 'panoramic' validity of the work. But even as a panoramic achievement *The Dynasts* put our understanding of poetic integrity under a killing strain. The shorter poems are another matter; the finest are exquisite and superbly alive, and below the finest are three or four other levels of quality which one may richly enjoy; but even this leaves a considerable bulk that embarrasses Hardy's resources to a painful degree.

We are never permitted to forget the profound disparity in Hardy's taste and genius, a permanent division between his instinctive attraction toward life and his confusion by it, between his native feeling for words and character and his incurable tendency toward stiff erudition, toward ponderous generalizations on life and experience, toward grandiose symbolism and immensities of scale that wildly exceed the proportions necessary for maintaining his picture of man's atomic part in existence. There is an essential incongruity in Hardy's world. And he stretched the terms of the incongruity to such a degree that his tales often collapse under the test. It soon becomes apparent that the incongruity existed in his own temperament to a greater degree than most artists could ever hope to tolerate or justify. The imponderables of his thought and curiosity almost overwhelm the native and intimate resources of his personal character. 'The machinery contrived by the Gods for reducing human possibilities of amelioration to a minimum' which he mentioned in *The Mayor Casterbridge* often becomes a machinery contrived by Hardy for reducing the artistic possibilities of imaginative conviction to a vanishing point.

Yet in that incongruity, and in what he made of it, lies the secret of Hardy's success, and his success survives some of the severest criticism that has been made against an author of his rank. He was conscious of this hostility among critics; he never became thick-skinned enough, even in his final apotheosis, to disregard it. His prefaces, which are usually devoted to disclaiming charges made against his moral or philosophical ideas, are always mildly defensive and in the one prefixed to *Late Lyrics and Earlier* in 1922 he voiced a denunciation of contemporary reviewers as Isaiahan as anything one may find in the prose of Housman. (Charles Morgan, as an Oxford student in 1920, found in this querulous resentment the one 'failure of balance' in Hardy's personality.) But even when criticism is something more than the moral indignation of journalists or the snobbery of rising talents, its severity usually permits Hardy to emerge with the stature of a master. Mr Frank Chapman, in one of the best essays yet written on the novels, comes to the conclusion that 'his greatness [may be seen] as the greatness of the Victorian age, in its solidity and its sureness of what it really valued, yet Hardy is above the Victorian ethos and did not share the limitations that made tragedy impossible.' And Vernon Lee, in the severest analysis ever made of Hardy's style, concluded her merciless dissection by saying that superior stylists like 'Stevenson, Meredith, or Henry James would scarcely be what is wanted for such subject-matter ... the faults of Hardy are probably an expression of his solitary and matchless grandeur of attitude. He belongs to a universe transcending such trifles as Writers and Readers and their little logical ways.'[5] But here we return to Hardy's own analysis of his problem.

In 1888, in his essay on 'The Profitable Reading of Fiction,' he defended the novelist's right to be inconsistent and unequal.

> However numerous the writer's excellencies, he is what is called unequal; he has a speciality. This especial gift being discovered, he fixes his regard more particularly thereupon. It is frequently not that feature in an author's work which common repute has given him credit for; more often it is, while co-existent with his popular attribute, overshadowed by it, lurking like a violet in the shade of the more obvious, possibly more vulgar, talent, but for which it might have received high attention. Behind the broad humor of one popular pen he discerns startling touches of weirdness; amid the colossal fancies of another he sees strokes of the most exquisite tenderness; and the unobtrusive quality may grow to have more charm for him than the palpable one.

This is sufficiently astonishing as self-examination and prophecy. It is exactly in his touches of weirdness and strokes of exquisite tenderness that we now see the qualities that redeem the broad humor and colossal fancies that are the bane of Hardy's work. He said something equally cogent in 1891, in the essay on 'The Science of Fiction,' when he maintained that 'Art is science with an addition'; that while fiction must unquestionably show 'that comprehensive and accurate knowledge of realities which must be sought for, or intuitively possessed, to some extent, before anything deserving the name of an artistic performance in narrative can be produced,' it is in the addition that the vital and life-giving quality resides. Only when this 'constructive stage is entered upon, Art—high or low—begins to exist.' Accordingly Hardy takes issue with Zola's creed of the *roman expérimental* and repudiates the notion that fiction can ever be Truth, whole, consistent, and inclusive; that it can ever rely like science on the evidence of the outer senses; that it can ever rest on the logic and documentation of scientific naturalism; and that there is any possibility 'of reproducing in its entirety the phantas-magoria of experience with infinite and atomic truth, without shadow, relevancy, or subordination.'

> The fallacy appears to owe its origin to the just perception that with our widened knowledge of the universe and its forces, and man's position therein, narrative, to be artistically convincing, must adjust itself to the new alignment, as would also artistic works in form and color, if further spectacles in their sphere could be presented. Nothing but the illusion of truth can permanently please, and when the old illusions begin to be penetrated, a more natural magic has to be supplied.

Here Hardy is not only aware of his instinctive use of the poetic method in fiction and of his impulse toward metaphorical values; he is arguing again along the line of Richards: that 'the Neutralization of Nature, the trans-ference from the Magical View of the world to the scientific,' is robbing life of 'a shape, a sharpness, and a coherence that no other means could so easily secure,' and so deprives the artist of an 'ease and adequacy with which the universe ... could be emotionally handled, the scope offered for man's love and hatred, for his terror as well as for his hope and his despair.'[6] (The proem of *The Return of the Native* sounds this same danger when it raises the question 'if the exclusive reign of this orthodox beauty is not approaching its last quarter. The new Vale of Tempe may be a gaunt waste in Thule ... and ultimately, to the commonest tourist, spots like Iceland may become what the vineyards and myrtle-gardens of South Europe are to him now.') What he is further arguing is that the meanness and inconsequence to which scientific realism is reducing human life are despoiling both poetry and fiction of their traditional moral and heroic values; that these must be maintained or substituted for; that

> what cannot be discerned by eye and ear, what may be apprehended only by the mental tactility that comes from a sympathetic appreciativeness of life in all its manifestations, this is the gift which renders its possessor a more accurate delineator of human nature than many another with twice his powers and means of external observation, but without that sympathy.

Hardy was protesting here not only against realism—the confounding logic by which the naturalists were depriving art of meaning and power—but also against the aesthetic version of this discipline which Flaubert and Pater were advocating—the 'minutiae of manners' and of stylistic detail which spelled for him nothing but a revulsion to the 'purposely careless.' When he wrote on 'The Profitable Reading of Fiction' for *The Forum* in 1888, he told his readers:

> To distinguish truths which are temporary from truths which are eternal, the accidental from the essential, accuracies as to custom and ceremony from accuracies as to the perennial procedure of humanity, is of vital importance in our attempts to read for something more than amusement. There are certain novels, both among the works of living and the works of deceased writers, which give convincing proof of much exceptional fidelity, and yet they do not rank as great productions; for what they are faithful in is life garniture and not life ... A living French critic goes even further concerning the novelists of social minutiae. 'They are far removed,' says he, 'from the great imaginations which create and transform. They renounce free invention; they narrow themselves to scrupulous exactness; they paint clothes and places with endless detail.'

His own precepts were even simpler, in the end, than these. 'A story should be an organism.' 'Style ... can only be treatment, and treatment depends upon the mental attitude of the novelist.' 'Nothing but the illusion of truth can permanently please.'

Hardy becomes in his poetics something very different from the victim of scientific determinism that the literal reading of his novels and key-phrases makes him. He never resists the limitations of materialism so eloquently as when he resents the modern effort to yoke the artist with mechanisms of technique or with the utilitarian purposes of economic or physical theory. His force as a stylist, dramatist, and allegorist is clarified by his refusal to fall in with the restrictions of naturalism, or with an aesthetic based on the rigid and obvious congruities of physical fact. He defended the salient quality of his art, and any intelligent reader must be compelled by it in the end, whether it is represented by startling properties like Stonehenge and Edgon and Knight's vision as he hangs from the cliff's edge in *A Pair of Blue Eyes*, by extreme characters like Arabella, Sue, Eustacia Vye, Gabriel Oak, and Jude, by his use of obvious choral devices like the Shakespearean rustics and the Parcae of Casterbridge, or, best of all, by those brilliant strokes of dramatic incident which illuminate and suddenly justify the wildness of his plots—the door closed against Mrs Yeobright, the tree-planting by Marty and Winterborne, Tess's seeing the blood-stained paper as she stands ringing the bell of the empty house of Clare's parents. He now appears to us as a realist developing toward allegory—as an imaginative artist who brought the nineteenth century novel out of its slavery to fact and its dangerous reaction against popularity, and so prepared the way for some of the most original talents of a new time. He stands in a succession of novelists that includes Melville, Emily Brontë, and Hawthorne, that takes in James and Flaubert in the wider reach of their faculties, and that has arrived at the achievements of Joyce, Proust, Gide, and Kafka.

When his novels falter in that demonstration, his poetry takes it up. The shorter poems are, in fact, the spiritual center of his production. He was right in calling them 'the more individual part of my literary fruitage.' They reveal his rich and sympathetic humanity, alive with recognitions of spirit, alert in sensitive invention, and always correcting the arguments of human ignominy and defeat by their respect for man's capacity for passion, endurance, and sacrifice. They show at their best an originality that springs from deeply felt and tested experience in the ways of human ordeal. Their devices of stanza and rhythm, of verbal oddity and surprise, begin to lose the inhibiting effect of a personal convention and to take on the qualities of a genuine contribution to English diction and meter. In their finest development ('The Darkling Thrush,' 'He Abjures Love,' 'Voices from Things Growing,' 'The Schreckhorn,' 'To Meet or Otherwise,' 'The Something that Saved Him,' 'I Say I'll Seek Her,' the elegies of 'Veteris Vestigia Flammae') they arrive at an authentic poignance and wholeness of style. This is not only a matter of their delicacy of suggestion and tone or their candor in restoring personal appeal to poetry in the face of the impediments which modern sophistication and experiment have set against that appeal. It is a matter of Hardy's gradual mastery of effects: of subtle turns and balances of phrasing, of the fine shadings he is able to put on traditional emotions, of the sure hand with which he succeeds in justifying, by the time a poem ends, its apparently faltering progress from stanza to stanza. It is a matter also of Hardy's skill in restoring to poetry some usages which had fallen into neglect since the seventeenth century: for one, his exquisite use of the negative particle:

> *By briefest meeting something sure is won;*
> *It will have been:*
> *Nor God nor Demon can undo the done,*
> *Unsight the seen,*

395

> *Make muted music be as unbegun,*
>   *Though things terrene*
> *Groan in their bondage till oblivion supervene.*

This is 'our profound and powerful particle, in our "undone," "unloved," "unforgiven,"' which Mrs Meynell once named in describing the genius of English speech: 'the "un" that summons in order that it may banish, and keeps the living word present to hear sentence and denial, showing the word "unloved" to be not less than archangel ruined.' And in its homely archaism it reminds us of another description that suits Hardy's achievement in poetry almost exactly. 'It is his naturalness that strikes me most,' said Gerard Hopkins of Hardy's friend, the Dorset poet William Barnes,

> he is like an embodiment or incarnation or manmuse of the country, of Dorset, of rustic life and humanity. He comes, like Homer and all poets of native epic, provided with epithets and images and so on which seem to have been tested and digested for a long age in their native air and circumstances and to have a *keeping* which nothing else could give; but in fact they are rather all of his own finding and first throwing off.

Hardy never shared Barnes's privilege of writing poetry undistracted by the claims and disturbance of the outer world. He divided his life between Wessex and the tumult of his age. The two worlds gave him a dramatic stage on which to meet the conflicts of modern thought, to witness the tragic hostilities of life, to study the discord that marks the divided nature of man. But he mastered the 'keeping' of his art and brought it to the force of his long intellectual and moral struggle. How he harmonized these in the poetry of his last thirty years is one of the notable personal achievements of literary history. It crystallizes for us the conflicts of a great age of distress; it makes evident Hardy's success in forging, out of the baffling incongruities and discords of experience, not only an aesthetic but an art. It also emphasizes that he succeeded because he was a 'man of character,' and it makes unmistakable that character's central quality: its revolving sincerity.

Notes

1. The passages quoted from Hardy in this essay are from the prefaces as they appear in the Mellstock Edition (London, 1921–2), in *Late Lyrics and Earlier* (London, 1922), and in *Winter Words* (London, 1928); from Hardy's essays, notes, and letters as they appear in *Life and Art*, collected by Ernest Brennecke, Jr (New York, 1925); from his notebooks and letters as quoted by Mrs Hardy in *The Early Life of Thomas Hardy* (New York, 1928) and *The Later Years of Thomas Hardy* (New York, 1930); from several entries quoted by Carl J. Weber in *Hardy of Wessex* (New York, 1940) and in the studies of Lionel Johnson, H.C. Duffin, Arthur McDowell, and S.C. Chew; and from unpublished correspondence. The *Early Life* and *Later Years* published by Mrs Hardy after Hardy's death now take on an increased importance since Richard Little Purdy, in his *Thomas Hardy: A Bibliographical Study* (1954), pp. 262–7 and 268–73, has shown them to be 'in reality an autobiography,' prepared for posthumous publication by Hardy himself.
2. Amlya Chakravarty, *The Dynasts and the Post-War Age in Poetry* (Oxford, 1938), p. 22.

3. Pierre d'Exideuil, *The Human Pair in the Work of Thomas Hardy* (London, 1929), p. 209.

4. Thomas Mann, *The Living Thoughts of Schopenhauer* (New York, 1939), p. 29.

5. Frank Chapman, 'Hardy the Novelist,' in *Scrutiny* (Cambridge, England), Vol. III (June 1934), pp. 22–37. Vernon Lee, *The Handling of Words* (London, 1923), pp. 222–41.

6. I. A. Richards, *Science and Poetry* (New York, 1926), cf. pp. 53–63. The quotations in the last two paragraphs of the present essay are from Alice Meynell, *The Second Person Singular and Other Essays* (Oxford, 1922), p. 140; and from *Further Letters of Gerard Manley Hopkins*, edited by Claude Colleer Abbott (Oxford, 1938), pp. 222–3.

192
Hardy the Novelist, An Essay in Criticism

———◆———

DAVID CECIL

Chapter II
His Power

I

Hardy's imaginative range, then, covers the struggle of mankind with Destiny as exemplified by life in the humbler ranks of a rural society, now specifically the society of early nineteenth-century Wessex. Compared with that of some great novelists, this is a limited range. The theatre of Hardy's drama is built on the grandest scale, but it is sparsely furnished. His range does not allow him to present the vast, varied panorama of human life that we find in *War and Peace* or *L'Education Sentimentale*. His scene is too narrow. Many people in the world are not Wessex countrymen, and many of the most important types of people; statesmen, for example, or artists, or philosophers, or men of the world. You will not find these people in Hardy's books. Nor do you find any account of the sort of worlds in which they live. The subtleties of intellectual life, the complexities of public life, the sophistications of social life, these do not kindle Hardy's imagination to work. In fact, it is no good going to him for a picture of the finer shades of civilised life or of the diversity of the human scene as a whole. The life he portrays is life reduced to its basic elements. People in Hardy's books are born, work hard for their living, fall in love and die: they do not do anything else. Such a life limits in its turn the range of their emotions. There is comedy in Hardy's books, and poetry and tragedy; but his comedy is limited to the humours of rustic life, his poetry is the poetry of the folk-song, his tragedy is the stark and simple tragedy of the poor.

The limits imposed by his scene are increased by those of the perspective in which he sees them. After all, only a very few situations illustrate man's relation to the universal plan. There are many other facets of human nature

SOURCE London, 1943, ch. II, IV.

besides those which appear in the conflict of mankind with Fate. Let us imagine a typical figure of man, let us call him John Brown. In addition to Hardy's John Brown—a soul facing the universe—there is also John Brown the citizen, John Brown the Englishman, Jack the family man, John the friend, Brown the member of a profession and Mr Brown the snob.

Hardy's appreciation of the basic human character enables him to give some account of Jack the family man, his sense of the past reveals to him something of John Brown the Englishman; though even these aspects of John Brown's nature he portrays only in summary outline. But of the others—the citizen, the professional man, the snob—he gives us nothing at all. For, seen in the terrific perspective in which Hardy surveys the human being, man's struggles as a political and social character seem too insignificant to fire his creative spark. Compared with his relation to the nature of the universe, his relation to government and social systems dwindles to such infinitesimal proportions as to be invisible. And the working of the individual consciousness seems equally insignificant. How can we bother, when we are watching mankind's life-and-death struggle with Fate, to examine the process of the individual's private thought and feeling with the elaborate introspectiveness of Henry James or Proust?

Indeed, Hardy—and here he is very different from almost every other great novelist—does not put his chief stress on individual qualities. As I have said, he writes about man, not about men. Though his great characters are distinguished one from another clearly enough, their individual qualities are made subsidiary to their typical human qualities. And as their stories increase in tension, so do his characters tend to shed individual differences and to assume the impersonal majesty of a representative of all mankind. Giles stands for all faithful lovers, Tess for all betrayed women, Eustacia for all passionate imprisoned spirits.

Hardy's characters linger in our imagination as grand typical figures silhouetted against the huge horizon of the universe. Here they resemble characters of epic and tragedy. Indeed, alike in his themes and his treatment of them, Hardy has less in common with the typical novelist than with the typical author of tragedy and epic. And we must adjust our mental eye to envisage life in the tragic and epic focus if we are to see his vision in the right perspective.

II

We are assisted to do this by the convention he adopts. For our preparations for judging him are not complete when we have realised his range. We must also acquaint ourselves with the conventions within which he elected to compose his pictures. We should in criticising any writer. Every artist constructs his work within certain conventions, which we must accept before we are in a position to estimate his success. Some of the most famous ineptitudes of criticism are due to a failure to realise this obligation.

Macaulay read Racine without understanding the conventions of French classical tragedy; he expected all good tragedies to be like Shakespeare's. The consequence was that Racine's subtle and passionate presentation of the drama of the human heart struck him as intolerably stilted and artificial. Voltaire, on the other hand, read Shakespeare's plays expecting them to be like Racine's. He thought, therefore, that Shakespeare was a barbarian. That two persons of this eminence should talk such nonsense should be a warning to the ordinary reader to be careful to acquaint himself with an author's convention before starting to criticise him. He should be particularly careful with Hardy. For Hardy does not write in the convention that one might expect.

Hardy's convention was that of an earlier age, the convention invented by Fielding. The novel is a new form, as forms go, and it was some time before it discovered the convention most appropriate to its matter. It aimed at giving a realistic picture of actual life. How was this to be given a shapely form? Various writers experimented to solve the problem in various ways. Defoe put his tales in the form of autobiography, Richardson in the form of a correspondence. Fielding, who had begun his career as a dramatist, turned to the drama for help. The English novel, as created by Fielding, descends directly from the English drama. Now, that drama was unrealistic. In Shakespeare's day it did not even try to be realistic. It aimed at entertaining its audiences by showing them a world as little like their own as possible: a world in which heroic and dramatic personages took part in picturesque, sensational adventures. The writers of Restoration comedy modified this convention a little. They set their scene in contemporary England and made their characters talk in something approaching the language of real conversation. But essentially their plays remained unrealistic; their plots were highly artificial, their dialogue stiff with ornament and their characters stylised.

Bred to this tradition, Fielding and his followers took for granted that a mere accurate chronicle of ordinary life would be intolerably dull to the reader. So they evolved a working compromise. The setting and characters of their stories were carefully realistic, but they were fitted into a framework of non-realistic plot derived from the drama, consisting of an intrigue enlivened by all sorts of sensational events—conspiracies, children changed at birth, mistakes of identity—centring round a handsome ideal hero and heroine and a sinister villain, and solved neatly in the last chapter. As in the drama, the characters revealed themselves mainly through speech and action—there is not much analysis of them by the author—and the serious tension is relieved by a number of specifically comic characters drawn in a convention of slight caricature.

In one respect this type of novel was even more limited than the drama had been. It was intended as light reading. It might point a moral—it generally did—but it did not deal with those profounder and more impersonal aspects of life which were the subject of serious poetry. It was not supposed to be an intellectual strain, and themes that would set its reader's intellect seriously to work were, except in a few instances, avoided.

This convention was a loose makeshift affair. But it proved less clumsy and more effective than any other hitherto proposed. And, though it gradually discarded its more artificial devices, some elements at least of it were accepted by most English novelists until the time of George Eliot. She was a revolutionary in her sober way. In her books we are presented for the first time with a form of fiction freed from the last vestiges of the dramatic tradition—novels without romantic heroes and villains, with lengthy analysis of motive and character, and in which action is determined by no conventions of plot, but solely by the logical demands of character and situation. In addition, George Eliot, extremely intellectual and uncompromisingly serious, employed her books to expound her most considered reflections on human conduct.

The next generation of novelists carried this change still further. With Henry James, Meredith and George Moore, the novel showed itself as fully entered on a new phase.

Now, Hardy has been looked on usually as part of this new phase. It is natural. For one thing, he was the contemporary of the new novelists; and for another, his books do have some elements in common with theirs. Intellectually, Hardy was a man of the new age—a so-called advanced thinker, in open rebellion against traditional orthodox views about religion, sex and so on—and he used his novels to preach these heretical opinions. Drawing his inspiration largely, as we have seen, from his vision of man's relation to ultimate Fate, he welcomed the movement to deepen and elevate the subject-matter of the novel. Since he wanted to write about tragic and epic subjects, he was pleased that the novel should be regarded as a form capable of achieving tragic and epic dignity. Enthusiastically he discarded the happy ending and made his stories the mouthpieces of his most serious views.

But although intellectually Hardy was a man of the future, aesthetically he was a man of the past. His broad conception of the novel form was much more like that of Fielding than it was like that of Henry James. Circumstances were partly responsible for this. His taste in story-telling was that of the simple rural society in which he had been brought up. He liked a story to be a story. It should have a beginning and an end. It should be full of action. And, above all, it should be sufficiently unusual to arouse the interest of its hearers. It is significant that his first novel, *Desperate Remedies*, is prefaced by a quotation from Scott: 'Though an unconnected course of adventure is what most frequently occurs in nature, yet, the province of the romance writer being artificial, there is more required from him than a mere compliance with the simplicity of reality.' In some scattered notes Hardy expanded the same thesis:

The recent school of novel writers forget in their insistence on life, and nothing but life, in a plain slice, that a story must be worth the telling, that a good deal of life is not worth any such thing, and that they must not occupy a reader's time with what he can get at first hand anywhere around him.

A story must be exceptional enough to justify its telling. We tale-tellers are all Ancient Mariners, and none of us is warranted in stopping Wedding Guests (in other words, the hurrying public) unless he has something more unusual to relate than the ordinary experience of every average man and woman.

There was also a more serious motive in his adopting the old convention. It harmonised with the peculiar nature of his inspiration. The presentation of any special vision of reality must involve a process of elimination. The artist, in order to bring out the distinguishing characteristics of his vision of the world, must select and emphasise these features in the real world which illustrate his view. Hardy realised this, and in his private notes he refers to it again and again:

Art is a changing of the actual proportions and order of things, so as to bring out more forcibly than might otherwise be done that feature in them which appeals most strongly to the idiosyncrasy of the artist.

... As, in looking at a carpet, by following one colour a certain pattern is suggested, by following another colour, another: so in life the seer should watch that pattern among general things which his idiosyncrasy moves him to observe and describe that alone. This is, quite accurately, a going to Nature: yet the result is no mere photograph, but purely the product of the writer's own mind.

This is profoundly true and it is true for any artist. It is his capacity to select and isolate what are to him the significant features in the panorama of experience that differentiates the artist from the photographer. But the nature of their vision requires some artists to be much more careful than others to give an illusion of ordinary reality. Jane Austen, for instance, who is out to show us the comedy that lies in the everyday life of the average person, must not allow us to doubt for a moment that we are reading about such a life. We must be under the impression that we are getting a genuine glimpse of an ordinary drawing-room, and listening to the conversations there. Any obvious discrepancy between what she shows us and what we should expect to find in such a drawing-room will destroy this illusion, and with it our belief in her comic vision of life.

Hardy, concerned not with the everyday surface of things but with the deeper principles and forces that lie behind them, does not need to do this. On the contrary, too much preoccupation with the surface of things would distract our attention from the facts which he wishes to emphasise. If our eyes are always being directed to superficial details they will not penetrate below them to perceive fundamental causes: we shall not notice the pattern, to use his phrase, in the carpet of experience which his idiosyncrasy moves him to observe. In consequence, it would be mistaken for him to adopt a realistic convention. As he says, 'My Art is to intensify the expression of things so that the heart and inner meaning is made vividly visible,' and 'Art is a disproportioning—(i.e. distorting, throwing out of proportion)—of realities, to show more clearly the features that matter in those realities, which, if merely copied, might possibly be observed, but would more probably be overlooked. Hence "realism" is not Art.' He required a convention that would give full scope for the expression of the spiritual and imaginative aspects of experience, and would eliminate the necessity for describing the mere superficial features of its appearance. Naturally the greater realism, to which the go-ahead novelists of his time were turning, held no attraction for him.

So far from disliking the dramatic intensity and regularity which the first novelists had taken on from the playwrights, he found it necessary for the expression of his vision. He turned backwards, not forwards, in order to discover the most appropriate mode for his art. If he had masters, they are Shakespeare and that British novelist who learnt most from Shakespeare, Sir Walter Scott.

I do not know if you have remarked how often I have mentioned Scott when seeking for a parallel to Hardy. It was inevitable that I should; for Hardy has more in common with Scott than with any other British novelist. Intellectually, of course, they were poles apart. Their kinship is aesthetic. Scott, like Hardy, was inspired by rural life, country humours, traditional customs. His imagination was also fired by ancient stories, ballads and superstitions, and, even more strongly than Hardy, he saw the life of his own day in terms of its history, with every house, every landmark stamped all over by the associations of its past. Further, Scott also envisaged human beings simply and epically—as grand, tragic figures fired by elemental passions. Hardy, therefore, searching for an appropriate form through which to express his inspiration, turned away from his contemporaries—turned away even from George Eliot—to the Waverley novels.

Everything in Hardy's make-up, then—his temperament as well as his circumstances—directed him to adopt the older conventions of fiction. Even in his latest and most experimental book, *Jude the Obscure*, he does not escape from it. He may deck it up with realistic trappings, but the substance of Jude's story is old-fashioned tragic drama expressed with old-fashioned tragic eloquence. The rest of Hardy's successful works are conceived firmly within the limits of the older convention. We may sometimes regret this. As I hope to show later on in these lectures, it is responsible for some grave defects in his books. Still, if we are to appreciate him, we must school ourselves to accept these conventions for the time being. It is simply no good going to him expecting the eye-deceiving realism of Tolstoy or the psychological subtleties of Proust. We must read him in the spirit we read *The Antiquary*—or *King Lear*, for that matter: prepared to swallow naïve melodramatic plots, full of mystery and coincidence and sensational improbable events, and complete with hero and heroine, villain and comic relief.

III

If we do, we shall not be disappointed. Hardy's talent was equal to its very opportunity. Like his range, it is narrow. He rings the changes on a few situations, a few motives, and a few types of character. He is not a player with many strokes. But those he has are winners.

Within its range Hardy's imagination is unfailingly fresh, unforced, fertile in expression and of the highest power. And it is before all things a creative imagination. If a book is a work of art in so far as the imagination inspiring it has transfigured the author's experience, no novels are more aesthetic than Hardy's. He never presents us with a mere record of his observations; always it is observation coloured by the idiosyncrasy of the artist's personality, vitalised by the energy of the artist's temperament. Hardy's books are always pictures, and never photographs; and we like them as we like pictures—for aesthetic reasons: not only because they recall reality to us but because they stir our emotions directly by their own individual quality.

It is a unique quality too. Hardy may learn from other writers but he never imitates them. His individuality is so strong that it transforms anything he touches. Even when he is bad, it is in his own peculiar way. One paragraph of his sweeps us straight away into the unmistakable atmosphere of Hardy's world.

This imaginative power owes its strange individuality to a mixture of qualities seldom found together. In the first place, it is in the deeper sense in which Hardy uses the word, extremely true to nature. Hardy uses a convention, but it is not an idealising convention. The harsh reality of the world, in which he was brought up, combined with a natural sincerity of disposition to keep him vigilantly faithful to the truth about life as he saw it. Whether he is describing a landscape or a state of mind, he never shuts his eyes to what is ugly in it or what is drab. Indeed, if it were divested of any of its significant qualities, however ugly or drab, the subject would have no interest for him; it would not stimulate his creative powers. To convey the spirit of it as it is, is his sole aim.

On the other hand, the essence which Hardy divines in his subject is not one that would be apparent to an ordinary mind. For the second distinguishing quality about his imagination is that it is poetic. This is such an ambiguous word that you must forgive me if I pause for a moment to explain what I mean by it.

The word poetry is nowadays used habitually in two different senses; it can just mean verse form, as when we say, 'I hear Mr So-and-so writes poetry.' But it is also used to denote a certain type of imaginative inspiration, as when we say, 'Mr So-and-so is full of poetic feeling.' That is the sense in which I am employing it about Hardy. Now, since this inspiration very frequently expresses itself in verse form, the two have sometimes come to be considered as necessarily connected; and when people find them separate from one another they think there is something wrong. Matthew Arnold meant that there was something wrong in Pope's work when he said he was a classic of our prose. In the same way, people have criticised De Quincey on the ground that although he wrote in prose he was really a poet. Now, of course, this is all nonsense. No subject matter is bound to one form. The fact that most novelists write in prose, and that many lovers choose to express their raptures in verse, does not mean that it is impossible to write a good novel in verse or to make a moving declaration of love in prose. All that matters is that they should be successful.

When I say that Hardy's imagination is poetic, therefore, I mean that it is of a type that more often chooses verse as its mode of expression. In this he is very English. The English literary genius is, most characteristically, a poetic genius. For one good book in prose there are three good English lyrics. The poetic impulse of the English shows itself often in other forms. That drama which is the instrument of England's greatest literary glory is a poetic drama: Shakespeare conceives his picture of life in a mood which requires the lyrical rhythms and heightened imagery of verse for its expression. The novel, too, has been tinged with a poetic spirit. Some of our most famous novelists are poetic in a sense no Continental novelist is. Scott, Dickens, the Brontës, Meredith, D.H. Lawrence, Virginia Woolf present a picture of life intensified by the ardour and freaked by the fancy of a poetic vision. Three of these, moreover (this is noteworthy)—Scott, Emily Brontë and Meredith—are also distinguished poets in verse. Hardy was of the same family. His creative imagination had two strains in it. First, it was intensely poetic; so much so that he thought of himself as a poet rather than a novelist. But there was also in him that love of story-telling, that interest in the lives of human beings that is the characteristic mark of the novelist. And his genius only found complete fulfilment when both these strains in him had scope.

This duality is the central, most important fact about Hardy's work considered in its purely aesthetic aspect. He seems always to have been feeling about for some form which would satisfy both these impulses. He aimed consciously, so his wife tells us, at keeping his narratives at once as close to natural life and as close to poetry as conditions would allow. And he often regretted that conditions would not let him keep them closer still. In his most ambitious work, *The Dynasts*, he actually devises a new form to achieve this purpose, combining a realistic study of Napoleonic history, cast in the form of a Shakespearean historical play, with an allegorical drama about personified spiritual forces, modelled on the *Prometheus Unbound* of Shelley. But his novels and poems are also hybrids. Hardy's most characteristic type of poem is a narrative with a contemporary plot, a realistic detailed setting, and told in a colloquial and prosaic diction. This is half-way to a short story. Equally, his novels are half-way to poems. They have a great deal of the normal novel about them—so much so that they could not, most of them, be cast in a verse form. Hardy, like other novelists, wants to give a full-length picture of human life, and needs the space and flexibility of prose narrative to do this. He could not accumulate the detail necessary to illustrate his drama in the condensed mode of verse. But he did aspire to write a novel which should have the emotional and imaginative intensity of a poem; and those aspects of experience which inspired him to write, and which, in consequence, he wished to emphasise, were those which have more usually stirred writers to choose verse as their vehicle of expression.

'The poet,' he once remarked, 'takes note of nothing that he cannot feel emotively.' In this sense Hardy was a poet in all his work. He is stirred by what is momentous and moving and picturesque in life—by its phases of heightened passion or spiritual illumination; and the picture of the world he desires to present is one in which these hold the centre of the canvas. In consequence, he presents his theme in a higher emotional key than most novelists do, and conceives it in more imaginative terms. Madame Bovary's first meeting with Rodolphe is just as important an event in her life as Bathsheba's first meeting with Troy. It is important in the same way, too. Each woman is encountering the lover who is to bring her to disaster. But in Madame Bovary the encounter is, on the face of it, a perfectly commonplace incident. Rodolphe is calling on Emma's husband on business, and is brought in to be introduced to her as a matter of common politeness. How different is the scene in *Far from the Madding Crowd*, when Bathsheba, walking alone through a wood at night, knocks against an unknown man, and then, opening her dark lantern to see who he is, is dazzled by the figure, glittering in scarlet and gold, of the stranger Sergeant. Hetty Sorrell, in *Adam Bede*, is arrested for murder, just like Tess; but there is nothing spectacular about the scene of her arrest. In fact, it takes place off-stage. Tess is found by the police, in the first mysterious gleam of dawn, asleep amid the immemorial monoliths of Stonehenge. Hardy seizes every opportunity that his subjects afford for poetic treatment; gets every ounce of picturesque value from that country life which is its subject—from its natural beauty or its historic traditions and association. And, so far as his material has a romantic element in it, Hardy emphasises that romantic element. The life at the dairy where Tess meets Angel, as described by Hardy, is as much an essay in pastoral poetry as an idyll of Theocritus. The military life in *The Trumpet-Major* is military life as seen by the poet—steeped in gallant sentiment and brilliant colour, and lilting with martial music. The sordid district of Mixen Lane, in *The Mayor of Casterbridge*, where the underworld of the town gathers to plot and revel, is made imaginative by the lurid, macabre light with which Hardy's vision suffuses it. Even when he is out to make an effect of ugliness, he cannot help tinging it with a poetic colour:

> The brown surface of the field went right up towards the sky all round, where it was lost by degrees in the mist that shut out the actual verge and accentuated the solitude. The only marks on the uniformity of the scene were a rick of last year's produce standing in the midst of the arable, the rooks that rose at his approach, and the path athwart the fallow by which he had come,

trodden now by he hardly knew whom, though once by many of his own dead family.

'How ugly is it here!' he murmured.

The fresh harrow-lines seemed to stretch like the channellings in a piece of new corduroy, lending a meanly utilitarian air to the expanse, taking away its gradations, and depriving it of all history beyond that of the few recent months, though to every clod and stone there really attached associations enough and to spare—echoes of songs from ancient harvest-days, of spoken words and of sturdy deeds.

This passage illustrates another effect of Hardy's poetic approach to his subject. He presents the objects of his description subjectively. He is concerned not only to give us the facts but to discover their significance to the observer's imagination. He says somewhere:

Consider the Wordsworthian dictum (the more perfectly the natural object is reproduced, the more truly poetic the picture). This reproduction is achieved by seeing in the heart of a thing (as rain, wind, for instance), and is realism, in fact, though through being pursued by means of the imagination it is confounded with invention, which is pursued by the same means. It is, in short, reached by what M. Arnold calls 'the imaginative reason.'

Hardy's 'imaginative reason' is an intensely subjective affair. His description of anything is soaked in the atmosphere of the mood which it evokes in him, with all the attendant trains of thought it suggests. Let me give an example; here are the first paragraphs of *The Woodlanders*:

The rambler who, for old association's sake, should trace the forsaken coach-road running almost in a meridional line from Bristol to the south shore of England, would find himself during the latter half of his journey in the vicinity of some extensive woodlands, interspersed with apple-orchards. Here the trees, timber or fruit-bearing as the case may be, make the wayside hedges ragged by their drip and shade, their lower limbs stretching in level repose over the road, as though reclining on the insubstantial air. At one place, on the skirts of Blackmoor Vale, where the bold brow of High-Stoy Hill is seen two or three miles ahead, the leaves lie so thick in autumn as to completely bury the track. The spot is lonely, and when the days are darkening the many gay charioteers, now perished, who have rolled along the way, the blistered soles that have trodden it, and the tears that have wetted it, return upon the mind of the loiterer.

The physiognomy of a deserted highway expresses solitude to a degree that is not reached by mere dales or downs, and bespeaks a tomb-like stillness more emphatic than that of glades and pools. The contrast of what is with what might be, probably accounts for this. To step, for instance, at the place under notice, from the edge of the plantation into the adjoining thoroughfare, and pause amid its emptiness for a moment, was to exchange by the act of a single stride the simple absence of human companionship for an incubus of the forlorn.

You see how the forlorn loneliness of this autumnal scene is conveyed, partly by descriptive detail—the dripping hedges, the drifts of fallen leaves— but more powerfully by the exactness with which Hardy perceives the melancholy associations which the scene calls up: how he recalls the gay chariots driven by persons now dead that one thronged the solitary road; how he notices that a solitary road is bleaker because more unexpected than the solitary woods that surround it. Such a description is a poet's description. But it is not a novelist's description, according to the practice of most novelists. Turgenev is a writer with a sensibility to natural beauty at least as refined as Hardy's; and he, too, often begins a story with a picture of its natural setting. But his method is very different. Listen to one of his opening descriptions:

> Give me your hand, reader, and come along with me. It is glorious weather: there is a tender blue in the March sky: the smooth young leaves glisten as though they had been polished. The ground is all covered with that delicate grass with the little reddish stalks that the sheep are so fond of nibbling: to the right and left over the long sloping hillside the green rye is softly waving: the shadows of small clouds glide in thin long streaks over it. In the distance is the dark mass of forests, the glitter of ponds and yellow patches of village: larks are soaring, singing, falling headlong with outstretched necks, hopping about the clods. The crows, in the road, stand still, look at you, pick at the earth. On a hill beyond a ravine, a peasant is ploughing: a piebald colt with a cropped tail and ruffled mane is running with unsteady legs after its mother; its whinnying reaches us. We drive on to the birth wood, and drink in the strong sweet fresh fragrance.

It is not a contrast? There is nothing about the spectres who haunt the road, no whimsical meditation inspired by the emotion the scene evokes. Turgenev is painter, not poet. With taste and accuracy he selects the typical features of the scene and leaves them to rouse the appropriate emotions in the reader.

Nor is Hardy's poetic method of treatment confined to description. He tells the story in the same way. Let us look once again, and more closely, at Bathsheba's first meeting with Troy:

> 'Is that a dark lantern you have? I fancy so,' said the man.
> 'Yes.'
> 'If you'll allow me, I'll open it and set you free.'
> A hand seized the lantern, the door was opened, the rays burst out from their prison, and Bathsheba beheld her position with astonishment. The man to whom she was hooked was brilliant in brass and scarlet. He was a soldier. His sudden appearance was to darkness what the sound of a trumpet is to silence. Gloom, the *genius loci* at all times hitherto, was totally overthrown, less by the lantern-light than by what the lantern lighted. The contrast of this revelation with her anticipations of some sinister figure in sombre garb was so great that it had upon her the effect of a fairy transformation.

This scene is vividly presented to the eye, but still more vividly does Hardy penetrate beneath the material facts to reveal their imaginative significance. 'His sudden appearance was to darkness what the sound of a trumpet is to silence ... The contrast was so great that it had upon her the effect of a fairy transformation.' These sentences are the operative sentences in the passage, and they are operative because they drench it in a poetic light. They infuse into the bare facts of the chance encounter that mystery and magic which make it memorable. This mystery and magic spring not from the scene so much as from Hardy's reaction to it, the way in which it sets his fancy working. His creative power shows in his ability to communicate to us, not only the facts of the scene, but its significance to the imagination. It is an extremely good method of description, but not one usually found in a novel. It is the method, not of Flaubert or Tolstoy, but of Keats or Coleridge.

Keats and Coleridge, I need not remind you, were Romantic poets. So was Hardy. The poetic strain in his creative imagination is of the romantic type—sublime, irregular, quaint, mysterious and extravagant, showing itself most typically now in a wild grandeur of conception, now in some vivid particularity of detail. A particular circumstance had accentuated this innate disposition. Hardy started his career as an architect, and the architecture that pleased him best was Gothic church architecture. He thought it the peak of man's artistic achievement. To him, as to all very aesthetically minded spirits, the different arts were of a piece. Further, he noted a special connection between architecture and letters. Both, he said, 'were alike, and unlike the other arts in having to convey a rational context in an artistic form.' His standard of taste in architecture became his standard of taste in letters. There is nothing classical about it, nothing lucid or symmetrical. It is a Gothic cathedral, all soaring pinnacles and shadowy vistas, clustered over with spreading foliage, and grinning, sinister gargoyles. In addition to being steeped in a poetic mood, his descriptions are thickly embroidered with the freaks of a Gothic fancy:

> It was the first day of June, and the sheep-shearing season culminated, the landscape, even to the leanest pasture, being all health and colour. Every green was young, every pore was open, and every stalk was swollen with racing currents of juice. God was palpably present in the country, and the devil had gone with the world to town. Flossy catkins of the later kinds, fern-sprouts like bishops' croziers, the square-headed moschatel, the odd cuckoo-pint—like an apoplectic saint in a niche of malachite,—snow-white ladies' smocks, the tooth-wort, approximating to human flesh, the enchanter's nightshade, and the black-petaled doleful bells, were among the quainter objects of the vegetable world in and about Weatherbury at this teeming time ...

You can see how Gothic and fanciful this is. Nothing is described plainly and objectively, everything is ornamented in the Elizabethan manner with conceits and similes—the ferns are like bishops' croziers, the cuckoo-pint is like an apoplectic saint, the toothwort like human flesh. They are very odd similes, are they not? Indeed, strangeness is a salient element in Hardy's imagination. Instinctively his eye gravitated towards the queer. He always takes the opportunity to make use of any odd manifestation of Nature's power. Clym makes passionate love to Eustacia out on the heath during an eclipse of the moon, and Hardy emphasises the strangeness added to the scene by the lurid, joyless light in which it is drenched. Even when he is out to give an effect of loveliness and sweetness he likes to blend the strain of oddness with it. May I recall to you the scene when Giles meets Grace home from abroad? He has gone to the market to sell his apple trees, and she catches sight of him standing amid the stone and brick of the town with an apple tree blooming above his head as if it had grown miraculously out of the pavement. We get a pleasant little shock of surprise at the picture of him 'standing with his specimen apple tree, the boughs rising above the heads of the farmers and bringing the delightful suggestion of orchards into the heart of the town.'

His pictures of the historic past, too, are made vivid by some queer detail. It is instructive to contrast the vision of the retreat from Moscow in *The Dynasts* with Tolstoy's in *War and Peace*. Tolstoy makes his impression by a soberly recorded communication of probable facts; we are told exactly how cold it got, how the French army lost morale by the gradual increase of discomfort and danger; all is brought home to us by a thousand details, none particularly striking in itself, but combining to build up an absolutely solid and convincing picture of despair and disaster.

Hardy gets his effect in one short scene; and that scene depends for its force on a single extraordinary, macabre fact. The pursuing Russians find some French soldiers with their backs to them, huddling round a fire. These soldiers do not turn at their approach, and when they get close, they discover they are stiff; frozen to death in the very act of trying to get a little warmth into their bodies.

The grotesque is an essential of Hardy's imaginative make-up. It is a marked characteristic of the plots of his stories. Here, of course, it can be explained partly in terms of his philosophy of life. He wants to stress the strange irony of Fate. Also, as we have seen, he thought that fiction ought to be odder than life. Did he not model himself on the Ancient Mariner? But grotesqueness is also a feature of his taste. Like the Gothic sculptors, he liked gargoyles. He could convince us that Fate was ironical without making it play such extraordinary pranks on poor bewildered mortals. He called one of his collections of short stories *Life's Little Ironies*, and there are moments when he seems to take a sinister pleasure in presenting Destiny as a sort of superhuman perpetrator of jokes in poor taste. This is particularly noticeable in his briefer narratives, *Wessex Tales, A Changed Man*.[1] What could be more fantastic than the history of the Duchess of Hamptonshire, whose clergyman lover comes back, after years spent in America, to claim his true love, now a widow, only to find that she had travelled, disguised, on the same boat with him, had died during the voyage, and had been consigned to the deep at a funeral conducted by himself!; or that of the Fiddler of the Reels, which recounts how a woman's life is ruined by the fact that when a certain fiddler plays a certain dance-tune, she is constrained to dance and to go on dancing till he stops?

Yet in his greatest work this streak of the grotesque does not dominate his

410

imagination. The other strain in it, the sincere, truthful strain, keeps it in check. For the fantastic is not a necessary stimulant to his creative power. It can work equally vigorously on the normal, given that his subject-matter has sufficient poetic sentiment inherent in it to fire his interest at all. He can extract all the appropriate poetry from the homely gaieties of *Under the Greenwood Tree*—the carol-singers' supper, the wedding breakfast—or from the sober everyday toil of the rural labourer's year, thatching and hedging, reaping and sowing.

Nor does the imaginative atmosphere in which he writes these things diminish their substantial reality. Hardy's world is never dreamlike or phantasmal even when his feet are on the earth. Giles tending the apple trees in the market is a solid flesh-and-blood English working-man, not an idealised Corydon of pastoral poetry. The spring wood in *Far from the Madding Crowd* is a real wood with its ferns and cuckoo-pints and catkins.

Hardy said that the highest art was that which, though changing the appearance of what it describes, only does so in order the better to bring out its essential reality., He himself had this kind of art. In his union of bold fantasy and fundamental truth he is unique amongst English novelists. To find a parallel we must go back to the anonymous authors of the Border ballads, 'Clerk Sanders' and 'The Twa Corbies.' Like theirs, Hardy's most extravagant flowers of fantasy are firmly rooted in the common soil of human life.

Chapter IV
His Weakness

The Athenians, it is said, grew weary of hearing Aristides called 'The Just.' And you may, I fear, have grown weary of hearing me call Hardy a creative genius. If so, the following pages may bring you relief; in them I propose to examine Hardy's faults. For he was a faulty writer—so faulty that, in spite of all his gifts, his most successful works are stained by noticeable blemishes, and his least successful are among the worst books that ever came from the pen of a great writer. His genius works in flashes. When the flash comes it is dazzling, but out it goes, and then the reader is left in the dark, groping about, bothered and bewildered. Like Dickens or Scott, Hardy is liable at any moment to let us down. The reason for this is that his equipment for the task was as defective on one side as it was rich on another. The creative gift, the power to apprehend his material aesthetically, he possessed in the highest degree; but, for complete success, a writer cannot rely on the aesthetic qualities alone. He must know how to present his imaginative conceptions to best advantage. For this he needs the critical qualities—the qualities of craft. Hardy was a great artist, but not a great craftsman.

This appears, first of all, in the design of his books. A craftsman's gift shows primarily in his ability to construct a fitting form in which to incarnate his inspiration. Hardy took trouble to do this: and indeed there are many worse designers. His plots are clear; and he sticks to them. All the same, his hold on design is slack and clumsy. In *Two on a Tower*, for instance, form and content have no organic connection. The story describes the romance of Lady Constantine and the young astronomer, St Cleeve, and the germ of the conception, the idea that inspires Hardy to write it, is the contrast between the cold inhuman stellar universe, which is the theatre of the hero's professional activities, and the hot human passions agitating the two chief characters. It is an imaginative idea, most effectively symbolic of that conflict between man and the nature of things which is a root inspiration of Hardy's creative process. But, in order to make a full-length novel about it, Hardy incorporates it in an intricate and improbable tale of intrigue in high life, featuring a jealous peer and an unscrupulous bishop, and interspersed with reflections on the difficulty of woman's lot in conventional society. This plot is feeble in itself, and it has nothing to do with the imaginative stimulus which prompted him to write the book. The two pull against each other. The more we are moved by the spectacle of the love scenes under the stars, the more are we annoyed when we are forced to divert our eyes from it in order to follow the working of the plot. Indeed, even if he had thought of a better story, Hardy would not have got over his difficulty, for his germ idea, imaginative though it be, is not suitable to a novel. It is not capable of sufficiently varied development. The poetic strain in Hardy's creative process here led him astray. This limited his choice of themes in a way that more prosaic talents are not limited. The theme had to be of a kind susceptible to poetic treatment, and yet it must be full enough to fill a novel. Such themes exist. The emotions stirred by *The Woodlanders* or *The Return of the Native* are of lyrical force; yet they demand a story long and complex enough to make a novel. In fact, you could not have explored all their imaginative possibilities in a short poem. This is not so with *Two on a Tower*. The contrast between the stellar universe and human passion is too simple a theme. For the stellar universe is uninhabited and cannot be made to produce the variety of subject and character needed to develop the drama to novel length. Once the author has realised the feelings of Swithin and Lady Constantine, and related them to their background, he has exhausted the artistic potentialities of his subject. Lack of critical sense has led Hardy to choose fiction as the vehicle for an inspiration which is appropriate only to a lyric.[2] He falls into the same error in *The Well-beloved*. This tells how a man fell in love with a mother, a daughter and a granddaughter, for instinctively he is drawn to the mysterious quality constant in one family. This theme could, of course, have been developed to novel length if Hardy had approached it in a spirit of pyschological interest. But he was not a pyschologist. It is just the idea of a family face, with its own mysterious, unique fascination, appearing generation after generation, which fires his fancy. Looked at in this way, the theme affords enough material for a ballad, not for a novel; and, in fact, *The Well-beloved* has to be eked out with an irrelevant and conventional plot. Perhaps he could have made a short novel in verse out of it—something like Patmore's *Angel in the House*. It is interesting that Patmore—a very acute critic—did urge him on one occasion to put his novels into verse form. And in this instance he would have been right. Hardy's lack of critical sense leads him to misunderstand the nature of his inspiration, and therefore to choose the wrong mode for its expression.

These books, though, are among Hardy's failures. At his best, he does choose themes for which fiction is the right form. Even them, however, he often executes his design loosely and carelessly. Consider the last part of *The Woodlanders*. Clearly, after Giles's death, the trend of the story makes it inevitable that Grace should be reconciled with Fitzpiers. In fact, it is so obviously the logical conclusion of the story that it should be got done with as quickly as is decently possible: Hardy takes forty pages over it! The reader grows impatient to reach a goal so long in sight, and his impatience brings with it a most undesirable slackening of emotional tension. A similar disproportion also mars *The Trumpet-Major*. Here Hardy's primary intention is to give us a series of pictures of Wessex life during the Napoleonic period, and he threads these pictures together on the string of a love story—the love story of Anne and the two Loveday brothers. It is a sufficiently adequate string for the purpose, but Hardy does not stretch it taut enough. In order to make room for all his pictures, he ekes out the plot by repeating the same incidents in slightly varied form several times; first, Anne is shown as preferring Bob, then John, then Bob, then John, then Bob again. No development of character is revealed by these fluctuations in her feelings. They are the consequence of outside events, arbitrarily introduced by Hardy to make the story long enough. The result is that the book, delightful though its separate episodes may be, is a little monotonous as a whole.

The novel is peculiarly liable to expose an author's weakness in the art of design. For it sets him some peculiarly difficult problems. The novel proposes to give a convincing picture of real life; but, like other works of art, it is only successful if it composes its material in an orderly pattern. Life, however, fecund, heterogeneous life, is anything but orderly. How then is he to satisfy both his obligations? How is he to devise a picture which satisfies us equally as a pattern and as an illusion of life? How is he to reconcile form with fact? It can be done, even by authors working within as strict a convention of plot as Hardy did. Jane Austen, to name no others, did it. Her stories are exquisitely shapely, and yet create a convincing illusion of reality. Not so Hardy. His vision of life is effective enough. Even though it is not a realistic one, it has the profusion and energy of reality. But, in order to force it into a pattern, he tends to impose a plot on it which is not convincing at all. There is an instance of this at the crisis of *The Woodlanders*. In order to achieve the reconciliation between Grace and Fitzpiers, Hardy has to get rid

413

of Mrs Charmond, who has been seducing Fitzpiers's truant heart away from Grace. It should not have been beyond the mind of man to invent some probable way of doing this. Fickle, and capricious as she is, she might have tired of Fitzpiers; she might even have contracted an illness and died, without putting too great a strain on our credulity. Hardy, however, scorns such unsensational devices; and instead invents a desperate foreign lover for her, who arrives at the hotel where she is staying abroad and shoots her. Hardy does not even describe the lover in detail. He has made a brief appearance once or twice in the story before—not enough for us to get to know his personality. The actual murder is hurriedly reported, second-hand. The lover is revealed as what he is—a piece of machinery, introduced in order to give form to the plot. In *A Laodicean*, again, Abner Power has to be got out of England in order that his niece shall marry the hero. It seems that there is no special reason why he should go; so Hardy suddenly tells us that, in his earlier days, he had been an international spy, and that someone had found this out and has now taken to blackmailing him, so that he has to flee the country. The incident is unlikely in itself, it jars violently with the prevailing tone of the story—a social comedy—and there is nothing in Power's character, as described up till then, to make one expect it of him. But the most disastrous example of Hardy's failure in this kind is in *Tess of the d'Urbervilles*. It is essential to the development of his plot that Alec should get Tess into his clutches again after she has been deserted by Angel. But how is this going to be managed? For Tess had never liked Alec and now hated him as the author of all her woes. Indeed, he has been presented to us—in so far as he has any individuality at all—as a cigar-smoking, rich young vulgarian, living only for his own animal pleasure. Hardy, however, suddenly reintroduces him into the book in the unexpected character of a Revivalist preacher. Alec, he tells us, has been converted. Far be it from me to deny that pleasure-loving vulgarians can undergo religious conversions. But the event is too odd for the reader to be expected to accept it without explanation. Alec should have been described to us as possessing some emotional streak in his disposition which might make such an occurrence probable. Hardy never attempts to do this: indeed, when, once more for the purposes of the plot, Alec has to behave like a villain again, Hardy simply says airily that his conversion lost its power and that he has reverted to what he was before. All through his books, the reader is liable to knock up against these crude pieces of machinery, tearing the delicate fabric of imaginative illusion in tatters.

The novelist has not finished his task when he has reconciled form with fact. His second problem is to reconcile fact with imagination. He has to give a convincing impression of the real world, but he has also to express his personal vision. And he only achieves complete success in his art if he satisfies both these conditions equally. This is an even harder problem. Many distinguished novelists have never achieved it. *Women in Love* blazes with the fire of Lawrence's temperament. But as a picture of country society in twentieth-century England it is—to say the least of it—far-fetched. Gissing, on the other hand, gives us a most reliable record of the life of the serious-minded poor in Victorian London. But it is only intermittently tinged with an individual colour. Hardy is no more successful than these eminent authors. He errs, as we might expect, with Lawrence rather than with Gissing. His creative power is so much stronger than his critical sense that he always disregards probability if it stands in the way of the emotional impression he wishes to make. As a matter of fact, he was not a good judge of probability. The plot of *The Return of the Native* in the form we possess it concludes with the marriage of Venn and Thomasin. But Hardy did not originally intend to end it like this. He had conceived Venn as a sort of benevolent, mysterious spirit, who appears, from no one knows where, to save Thomasin at the crises of her fortunes, and then, once more, vanishes into obscurity. This, however, would have meant that the book ended sadly for everyone concerned in it. Not only Clym and Eustacia, but the virtuous Venn and Thomasin would fail to attain happiness. His publishers told Hardy that the public would not stand for this; and in deference to his publishers Hardy modified his plan. He regretted doing so, because a happy end conflicted with the aesthetic image he had formed of Venn. But the publisher was right, if the claims of probability were to be respected. Venn did want to marry Thomasin. Once she was free, he would certainly have asked her, and Thomasin—a clinging, timid woman, left alone when still young—would almost certainly have accepted a lover so attractive and who had treated her so nobly. Hardy does not seem to have considered this. If an idea pleased his imagination, that was good enough for him.

Alas! Hardy did not always have the luck to be saved from himself in this way. We see this in two of his most famous books— *Tess* and *Jude.* Here his lawless imagination, unchecked by a publisher's wise hand, bolted with him. Both books describe how an innocent and amiable person, after a life of unrelieved misfortune, comes to complete catastrophe. Such a theme is exceptionally tragic, even for Hardy. Indeed, it is so exceptional that the author who chooses it must be particularly careful to make it seem inevitable. Otherwise he will not carry the reader along with him. We shall simply refuse to believe such dreadful things could happen. Hardy starts off in both books convincingly enough, but in both, two-thirds of the way through, his imagination gets out of hand; and to give his catastrophe the required intensity of blackness he breaks with probability altogether. Tess is, first of all, seduced by Alec. Later on she becomes engaged to Angel, who knows of her lapse. After her wedding she tells him. Angel is a doctrinaire idealist, who loves her because to him she has been the incarnation of innocent virtue. Horrified at her confession, he deserts her. So far, so good. It is a painful story and it is a possible story. But now Hardy begins to lose grip. First of all, as we have seen, he brings Alec back into her life, unconvincingly disguised as a Revivalist preacher. Then he would have us believe that Tess goes back to him in order to get money to support her poverty-stricken family—though she could more easily have got money from Angel's relations. Finally, Angel comes back, penitent for his heartlessness and willing to forgive her. She flees with him, but makes use of the few moments before she starts to murder Alec with a breakfast knife: with the result that she is shortly afterwards arrested and hanged at Winchester. This last section of the book is imagined with such intensity that, on first reading, it sweeps us off our feet. But a cooler perusal begins to shake our faith. Why on earth should Tess murder Alec if, in the first place, Angel is penitent, and, in the second, she is willing to go back to him? The only explanation can be that Hardy has imagined the work aesthetically as a gradually darkening tragedy, the appropriate climax of which must be a catastrophe as black and brutal as an official hanging. If he can get this emotional effect, he does not care if the factual structure on which it is built is convincing or not.

The end of Jude violates probability, if possible, more flagrantly. The theme of *Jude* is the conflict between a sensitive, passionate temperament, with a cruel, conventional world. Once more, Hardy begins well enough. Jude, a poor country boy, longs for satisfaction, both of mind and heart. After difficulties, he succeeds in going to Oxford, where he hopes to get some education to fulfil his mental wants; but before he has got there his passionate temperament has already betrayed him into a short-lived marriage with the coarse Arabella. Now the blow begins to fall upon him. First, Oxford rejects him, and secondly, he falls in love with his true affinity, his cousin Sue. She, in order to drive him from her heart—for there seems no legal way to get free of Arabella—marries Philotson, a schoolmaster. It is all in vain; desperately in love, they defy convention and elope. Up to this point the plot is credible; and if Hardy wanted a sad ending, it should have been possible for him to devise a convincing one which would illustrate how happiness—pursued in defiance of convention—is unattainable, and that all the efforts of Sue and Jude must end in misery. However, this was not enough—his wild, Gothic imagination wanted something more appalling and terrific. In his efforts to attain this, once more he flings probability to the winds. First of all, though they both obtain a divorce, they neither marry nor leave the district they live in. In consequence, they are ostracised. Jude gets no work, and they sink lower and lower. This is unlikely enough. People as poor as they are and with children simply would not have yielded to such fancies. They would most likely have married, and certainly have left the district. But, in order to bring them to full disaster, Hardy now embarks on his most extraordinary flight of fancy. Jude has had a child by Arabella, who is introduced to us as a symbol of the tragedy of modern life. Already, at ten years old, his mind has been so impressed by the incredible misery of human life that he does not know how to smile and longs only for death. This unprepossessing infant—'Little Father Time' is his nickname—arrives to make his home with Sue and Jude, and, after listening for a time to their lamentations, takes it upon him to hang both himself and his step-brothers and sisters in a cupboard. Understandably shattered by this preposterous misfortune, Sue and Jude break down completely. She feels that she is being punished for her infidelity to her husband, and goes back to live with him, although his every caress is a horror to her. Jude falls into the clutches of Arabella again, and shortly afterwards dies from a combination of drink and bronchitis. Long before the end is reached, the reader's outraged credulity has made him unresponsive to the emotion Hardy wishes to evoke. How can we believe such a story at all, let alone blame Providence for allowing it, as Hardy would have us do? Once more, Hardy has broken one of the primary laws of the novel. To satisfy the demands of his imagination, he neglected the claims of probability.

We may note, incidentally, that the most obvious lapse in the book—the character of the child—is made worse by a misuse of Hardy's most conspicuous talent—his poetic talent. As in *Two on a Tower*, the poetic strain in Hardy's imagination has failed to reconcile itself with the laws governing the medium he has chosen. The novel may present a poetic vision of life, but it must also give a sufficiently convincing illusion of objective reality. Now the figure of Little Father Time as presented to us on his first appearance in the railway carriage is a very poetic conception:

> In the down train that was timed to reach Aldbrickham station about ten o'clock the next evening, a small, pale child's face could be seen in the gloom of a third-class carriage. He had large, frightened eyes, and wore a white woollen cravat, over which a key was suspended round his neck by a piece of common string: the key attracting attention by its occasional shine in the lamplight. In the band of his hat his half-ticket was stuck. His eyes remained mostly fixed on the back of the seat opposite, and never turned to the window even when a station was reached and called. On the other seat were two or three passengers, one of them a working woman who held a basket on her lap, in which was a tabby kitten. The woman opened the cover now and then, whereupon the kitten would put out its head and indulge in playful antics. At these the fellow-passengers laughed, except the solitary boy bearing the key and ticket, who, regarding the kitten with his saucer eyes, seemed mutely to say: 'All laughing comes from misapprehension. Rightly looked at, there is no laughable thing under the sun.' He was Age masquerading as Juvenility, and doing it so badly that his real self showed through crevices. A ground swell from ancient years of night seemed now and then to lift the child in this his morning-life, when his face took a back view over some great Atlantic of time, and appeared not to care about what it saw.

This is an imaginative picture; more than that, it is true to its author's interpretation of human life. The pale, sad child in the train is an effective, arresting symbol of the predicament of latter-day mankind, as conceived by Hardy. But he is only a symbol—I had almost said only a metaphor—not a human creature with an independent life of his own. Static and labelled, as much an allegorical figure as the Giant Despair in *Pilgrim's Progress*, Little

Father Time exists on the plane of allegory and can no more be transferred to the plane of objective reality, on which any novel, however imaginative, must move, than Giant Despair could. And, in fact, when he does meet Sue and Jude and has to talk and act and take part in their life, his unreality becomes painfully obvious. Here, in his effort to give a poetic intensity to the novel, Hardy has overreached himself and upset the delicate balance between fact and imagination which, for success in his medium, it should be one of his primary objects to preserve.

But over and above these sins against the specific laws governing the novel, Hardy's lack of critical sense makes him at times offend against the first rule of all imaginative compositions. He writes outside his range. If a certain area only of his experience inspires the writers' creative imagination, his first obligation is to remain within it. The great craftsmen, like Defoe or Turgenev, always did, so that their work is continuously alive. Hardy does not, so that a large portion of his work is wasted. It is not genuinely creative. He spent a great deal of time, for instance, writing about people whom he could not bring to life—people in the higher ranks of society, for instance. The chief characters in *A Laodicean*, in *Two on a Tower*, and in *The Hand of Ethelberta*, belong to this category. We can see why Hardy chose to write about them. Such people were the inhabitants of the great houses of the Wessex countryside; and these houses made a real appeal to his imagination, susceptible, as it was, to the imaginative charm of the antique and the picturesque. He wanted to embody his response to them in some story, so he wrote stories about their inhabitants. One collection of short stories is given up to such tales—*A Group of Noble Dames*. But there are noble dames in his other books too—Lady Constantine, Mrs Charmond, Paula in *A Laodicean*. The result is what might be expected. The setting of the tales is vivid and beautiful. The feeling awoken by the houses was part of his imaginative experience. But the noble dames were not: he never came across them until he was too old to be receptive. In order to draw them, therefore, he follows conventional models of the 'grande dame' to be found in novels of the day. These have no life at all: and Hardy's too are just stuffed dummies of high life—Madame Tussaud wax figures of Countesses and Baronesses. The circle they live among is as unreal as themselves. These are the terms in which Hardy imagined that Lady Constantine's brother would urge her to make a prudent second marriage:

> You are still young, and, as I imagine (unless you have vastly altered since I beheld you), good-looking: therefore make up your mind to retrieve your position by a match with one of the local celebrities; and you would do well to begin drawing neighbouring covers at once. A genial squire, with more weight than wit, more realty than weight, and more personality than realty (considering the circumstances), would be best for you.

Or, in a lighter vein, listen to his notion of the conversation of a society debutante at a fashionable London party:

> A young friend of Pierson's, the Lady Mabella Buttermead, appeared in a cloud of muslin. A warm-hearted emotional girl was Lady Mabella, who laughed at the humorousness of being alive. She asked him whither he was bent, and he told her that he was looking for Mrs Pine-Avon. 'Oh yes, I know her very well,' said Lady Mabella. 'Poor thing—so sad—she lost her husband. Well, it was a long time ago certainly. Women ought not to marry and lay themselves open to such catastrophes. I never shall. I am determined never to run such a risk. Now do you think I shall?' 'Oh no, never,' said Pierson drily. 'That's very satisfying.' But Mabella was scarcely comfortable under his answer, even though jestingly returned: and she added, 'Sometimes I think I shall, just for the fun of it!'

This is fashionable life as imagined by Miss Daisy Ashford. Lady Mabella is a Young Visitor.

Hardy's excursions among complex intellectual types of human being are nearly as disastrous. Here he was led astray by a different motive. The nineteenth century was an age of growing self-consciousness. People were investigating psychology and analysing motive as never before. The novelists, led by George Eliot, were doing it too. Hardy was aware of this tendency. He even said that it was not to be resisted: novels must be more analytical. Luckily for him, his practice was usually different from his precept. But now and again he does attempt something in the new style. He chooses what he considers some typical figure of the new age—Knight, a modern thinker; Fitzpiers, a modern sceptic; Sue, an advanced woman—and he does his conscientious best to make them true to life. Their opinions and doubts are painstakingly detailed to us. Unfortunately the result is no more convincing than Lady Mabella. Once again, he was describing people he had only learned to know after he ceased to be receptive imaginatively. Moreover, such characters cannot be fully described through word and action, and it is only through word and action that Hardy is able to give his creatures vitality. Sue is a regular Hardy woman, incongruously decked out with advanced opinions. Fitzpiers and Knight are collections of views, imperfectly clothed in flesh and blood. Hardy's descriptions of their thoughts are just essays on the subjects they are thinking about; their conversations are like debates in college societies. This is how Sue, spending her first night alone in her lover's room, converses with him:

> 'I have no respect for Christminster whatever, except, in a qualified degree, on its intellectual side,' said Sue Bridehead earnestly. 'My friend I spoke of took that out of me. He was the most irreligious man I ever knew, and the most moral. And intellect at Christminster is new wine in old bottles. The Mediaevalism of Christminster must go, be sloughed off, or Christminster itself will have to go.'

Alas, she was mistaken. Christminster remains; and it is Sue herself—just because her creator persisted in making her talk in this fashion—who is gone from the world of living characters.

Indeed, *Jude*, remarkable book though it be, does suffer from the fact that

419

its subject-matter trespasses often into territory outside its author's range. It sets out, as no other of his novels do, to give not only a real but a realistic picture of life. Hardy's tender heart, stirred by the sufferings of working-men with intellectual aspirations and uncomfortably warm sexual temperaments, wished to write a book bringing home these sufferings to others. And he is therefore at pains to give an accurate presentation of such a life. But his imagination is not a realistic one. The result is that the book is discordant. Hardy's intention and Hardy's natural bias quarrelled with one another all the way through it. He takes trouble to check his instinctive bias towards the fanciful. The plot is less formalised than in his other books, the conversation more naturalistic; there are fewer flights of poetic fancy; there is no chorus of humorous rustics. Yet the effect is never realistic in the way Hardy wanted it to be. It is as if some actor of the old heroic school were to attempt to play a part in a modern drama of ordinary life. Painstakingly he dresses himself in the appropriate costume and mutes down his voice to the inflections of everyday conversation; but the moment he warms to his work he betrays himself. Back come the flashing glance, the thrilling tones, the grandiose gesture, shattering the illusion he has taken such trouble to create. Sue shows herself to be the old-fashioned Hardy heroine; Jude's little boy is a figure of wild poetic symbolism; Oxford and Shaftesbury are the old, picturesque Hardy setting, steeped in historical and romantic associations. And, as we have seen, when the story begins to work up to its climax, Hardy throws realism to the winds and plunges, head foremost, into a whirlpool of macabre fantasy.

No doubt it is very hard for the novelist to remain undeviatingly within his range. For most plots involve dealing with some aspects of experience that have not stirred the author's imagination. But a competent craftsman, with a good critical sense, will generally avoid the worst consequences of leaving his range. Trollope is an example. If his story requires him to write about some aspect of life which does not inspire him, he takes trouble to study it sufficiently for his picture to be, at any rate, not inaccurate. Even though it is not vividly alive, it is not so flagrantly unreal as to weaken the aesthetic vitality of the inspired passages. It may not delight, but it does not jar. Hardy had not the skill to skate over thin ice in this way. He did his best to acquire it. Before describing the fashionable parties in *The Hand of Ethelberta* he actually went up to London—poor, simple, conscientious Hardy!—in order to attend some society dinner-parties. But the spontaneous nature of his talent, combined with his simple rustic upbringing, made him incapable of learning in this way; and his picture of society is a mixture of the conventional novel of the day and the rural person's simple dreams of rank and fashion—filled with courtly Earls and gorgeous Duchesses and haughty Dowagers and sprightly Lady Mabellas. When Hardy gets on to thin ice—crack! splash! he is in head first and drowned.

It must be admitted that he is not certainly safe even on firm ice. Hardy can come to grief right within his range. He lacked another essential quality of the critical sense—restraint. He lets his imagination have its head too often. He repeats himself, he overdoes his effects; so that his very virtues at times become defects. The grotesque element in his imagination, for instance, needed to be disciplined with a firmer hand than Hardy's. At moments he seems to seek the preposterous for its own sake. Perversely enough, too, Hardy is most fantastic when fantasy is most out of place, as in his two unfortunate excursions into the realm of social life, *The Hand of Ethelberta* and *A Laodicean*. In the first of these we are asked to believe that Ethelberta, though possessed of no special literary skill or aptitude, should suddenly take to writing poems, and that these poems—*Metres by E* is their curious title—should take the reading public of London by storm. Further, she follows up this achievement by hiring a hall, where, without any previous experience as a public speaker, she holds huge audiences spellbound by telling them long stories sitting in a chair. The plot of *A Laodicean* is diversified by yet odder flights of imagination. The villain, Dare, wishes to blacken the hero, Somerset, in the eyes of the heroine, Paula. He therefore takes a photograph of Somerset, and then, by means of some new and subtle photographic process known only to himself and Hardy, alters it in such a way as to make him appear dead drunk. He then presents it to Paula, who, properly shocked, breaks with Somerset. Dare's mind was fertile of such unusual expedients. Earlier in the story, he wishes to make Captain de Stancy fall in love with Paula. So he takes him to a remote wood, in which, surprisingly enough, is concealed a gymnasium, and persuades him to look through a hole in its wall. Here de Stancy is transfixed to see Paula, dressed in a gymnasium costume of pink flannel, disporting herself on the parallel bars. The spectacle, Hardy tells us, was so bewitching that de Stancy, forgetting all other obligations, immediately became Paula's slave. This scene certainly illustrates Hardy's originality. No other writer, as far as I know, has ever represented a romance as inspired by the sight of physical jerks performed in pink flannel. But such originality is not a merit.

There is no doubt that, if we approach them in an irreverent spirit, we can get a deal more fun out of Hardy's books than he ever intended. He could not resist an effect, provided it was queer enough. Nor, even when an idea was not in itself grotesque, was he safe from overdoing it. His comic characters are meant to be a little caricatured—that is the convention in which they are conceived. But sometimes they are caricatured too much. Festus in *The Trumpet-Major* is an amusing study of the cowardly braggart who has been a stock figure of English comedy since Parolles. But he is overdone: always he brags, always he runs away, chapter after chapter. Tragic irony, too, sometimes gets out of Hardy's control. It is a fine stroke in *A Pair of Blue Eyes* that Elfride's two inconstant lovers should arrive to make reparation to her on the very day of her funeral. But they should not discover they have been travelling down in the same train as her coffin. Such tragic irony appears as a practical joke on the part of the author: it is not consistent with the atmosphere of tense emotion which should colour the scene.

Again, Hardy is liable to over-emphasize the part played by chance in producing catastrophe. That it should play such a part is, of course, an essential element in his view of life. Chance is the incarnation of the blind forces controlling human destiny. The smallest incident may help to determine a great event. But no author should make chance condition action too often, or he will strain the reader's credulity. For, even if man is not a free agent, the powers that direct his fortunes—his general circumstances, his inherited disposition—are too constant to be diverted at every turn from achieving their ends by some trivial accident. If we are really in love with someone, we shall not be stopped from declaring it just by missing a train. Blind chance must only be introduced in fiction as a determining element at some crucial moment when time is everything, as when Mrs Yeobright's visit of reconciliation coincides with Eustacia's visit from her lover. In such an instance, Hardy's use of chance is legitimate. But his lack of critical restraint causes him sometimes to employ it illegitimately. Tess's fear of Angel's disapproval, for example, should have been enough to stop her telling him about her seduction before marriage. Why must we be expected to believe that she wrote him a letter of confession and put it under his door, but that, owing to the fact that it slipped under the carpet, he did not see it?

Further, we ought not to be required to believe that so many unfortunate accidents happened in a short space of time. Once again, let me ask you to consider the catastrophe in *The Return of the Native*. We can believe that Mrs Yeobright called on Eustacia and Clym at the wrong moment. We can also just believe that she was bitten by a poisonous snake on the way home. This double calamity does answer Hardy's purpose by giving the effect of a hostile Fate, driving the characters to destruction, despite all their efforts to save themselves. But when, two chapters later, Eustacia's letter of appeal to Clym goes astray because her messenger forgets to post it, scepticism begins to creep in. Hardy seems to be twisting his plot to suit his purpose. The characters seem puppets all right; but puppets not in the hands of Fate but of the author.

There is another reason for this failure than a mere indiscretion of taste. Hardy insists on this aggregation of evil chances the better to illustrate his doctrine that man is the sport of an indifferent Destiny. The most fatal error into which he was led by his lack of critical sense was preaching. At moments, obsessed by his views about the universe, he turns from an imaginative creator into a propagandist.

The relations of art to propaganda are much discussed today by writers. On the one hand, we find young writers, worried by the painful state of the world and anxious to prove that they are justified in using their talents to set it right, maintaining that all literature is propaganda, in so far as it expresses the author's view of life. There is no difference in kind between *Pride and*

Prejudice, they say, and Mr Wells's last blue-print, in the form of fiction, for the reformation of mankind. Jane Austen is just more cunning at concealing the powder of her views in the jam of her art. On the other side stand a group—they are mostly disgruntled and elderly survivors from the age of the aesthetes—who protest irritably that art has nothing to do with morals, nay, that, in so far as it points any moral at all, a novel is a failure. Both views have some truth in them; but both are wrong. It is nonsense to say that art should not point a moral. Every artist, like every human being, has moral beliefs; and since his work is the expression of himself, it must also express his moral beliefs. It is the point of view from which Jane Austen regards Darcy and Elizabeth which determines the form of the story in which she exhibits them, and her picture is all the more impressive for the fineness of the moral sensibility which illuminates it. But of course—and this is where the aesthetes are on the right track—though moral quality may enrich a work of art, it is not a condition of its existence. Without her moral sensibility, Jane Austen would still be an artist. And we read *Pride and Prejudice* not because we agree with its author's view of life, but because it presents us with a lively, entertaining and beautifully expressed vision of the world.

It follows, then, that the artist's first obligation is to his vision rather than to his moral point of view. This does not mean that he should never write with a moral purpose. If his creative inspiration happens to coincide with his moral purpose, well and good. The *Germinal* of Zola is none the worse for the fact that, in addition to being a novel, it is a pamphlet on behalf of the oppressed miners of France. For the spectacle of the life of the mine happened to stimulate Zola's imagination, so that he is able to produce a successful work of art and a successful pamphlet at the same time. However, no amount of virtuous indignation would have availed him if the mine had not appealed to his imagination. Mrs Gaskell felt just as strongly about the cotton-spinners of Lancashire as Zola did about the miners, yet *Mary Barton* is a failure. The artist must stick to his range, whatever is fidgeting his conscience. And even when writing within his range, he must be careful not to point his moral so ostentatiously that it diverts our attention from the imaginary world he has created. Still less must he let his propagandist purpose modify his conception against the judgement of his imagination. Indeed, his moral views are best left to reveal themselves involuntarily. The artist's only conscious duty should be to the truth of his creative vision. Every other consideration must be sacrificed to it. Hardy realised this. 'I hold,' he said, 'that the mission of poetry is to record impressions, not convictions. Wordsworth, in his later writings, fell into the error of recording the latter.' But so did Hardy; his practice was not always true to his precept. Like other Victorians, he was a stern moralist, absorbedly interested in working out his philosophy of life. Now and again, undisciplined as he was by a strong critical sense, his moral intention dominates his artistic inspiration. Just when we are spellbound by Hardy the novelist, Hardy the preacher bobs up, and instantly the spell is broken. Tess, a country girl of eighteen, is riding with her little brother on the waggon under the stars:

> 'Did you say the stars were worlds, Tess?' asks the child.
> 'Yes.'
> 'All like ours?'
> 'I do not know, but I think so.'

This is all right, but she goes on:

> 'Most of them seem splendid and sound— a few blighted.'
> 'Which do we live on? The splendid one or the blighted one?'
> 'A blighted one.'

Here is no unsophisticated country girl speaking. Through her lips comes the voice of a middle-aged novelist, brooding in gloomy mood on the riddle of the painful earth. For *Tess* is a late book. The preaching tendency grew on Hardy. Alas, as people grow older their imaginative faculties tend to grow weaker, and their interest in morals stronger. Not that Hardy's ideas changed—he would have called the earth a blighted star when he was twenty-four. But in his early works— *Under the Greenwood Tree* or *Far from the Madding Crowd*, for example—he feels no impulse to proclaim it so openly. They are the expressions of the same philosophy, but it is implicit. The impulse grew gradually stronger. There is a little more preaching in *The Return of the Native* and *Two on a Tower*, and yet more in *The Mayor of Caster-bridge* and *The Woodlanders*. Indeed, *The Woodlanders* was only saved from moralistic excess by the convention of the age. At the time he was writing it, Hardy, possibly for personal reasons, was concerned about the marriage question, and wished to show what a cruel tie an incompatible marriage entailed. He therefore wished at the end of the book to point out that, though officially reconciled, Grace and Fitzpiers were likely to be unhappy. But he softened this in deference to the popular desire for a happy ending. Aestheti-cally, it is an improvement, like the happy ending of *The Return of the Native*. The tragedy of *The Woodlanders* is the tragedy of Giles and Marty; and though we cannot expect Grace and Fitzpiers to be very happy, it is better that their departure from the stage should take place in an atmosphere of comparative tranquillity; otherwise we shall be diverted from yielding ourselves exclusively to the poignant emotion evoked by the figure of Marty in her lonely, faithful despair, which should dominate the last scene of the book. But Hardy, for the sake of expounding his views, was himself prepared to run the risk of ruining his final effect.

Still, these are small blemishes in a successful work. *The Woodlanders* was not designed in the first place in order to provide a vehicle for Hardy's opinions on life. This is less true of *Tess* and not true at all of *Jude*. In these two books Hardy the preacher takes far too much hand in the matter, and interferes in the design of the ground plan of the story. *Tess* is an indictment of Providence—a parable whose moral is that it is not possible to justify the ways of God to men. One cannot call it a failure: the heroine is the most pathetic of all Hardy's creations, and the book is full of magnificent passages. But there is a flaw in the design. Not only, as we have seen, is the catastrophe highly improbable, but we feel that Hardy has devised it too obviously in order to prove his point. He twists reality, partly to get the requisite tragic effect, but still more to draw a moral. *Jude* fails more disastrously for the same reasons. He says somewhere that he thought someone ought to write a book exposing the hardships to which intellectually minded working-men were liable, and, moreover, that that someone ought to be himself. This was an inauspicious beginning. No artist should ever choose a subject because he thinks he ought to, but only because he wants to.[3] And, as we have seen, it took Hardy right off his own territory. Then, the catastrophe is even more improbable than that in *Tess*. For again—partly to make the close black enough, but still more to satisfy his itch to give the universe a piece of his mind—Hardy indulges in the wildest fantasy. It is not, it may be remarked incidentally, even successful in achieving its moral purpose. In matters of art, those who load the dice seldom win the game. In order to prove his point, Hardy overstates his case grossly. No doubt, working-men of intellectual aspirations and strong sexual impulses did tend to have a poor time in Victorian England; but there is no reason to suppose that their children were particularly liable to hang each other. Like a charitable institution appealing for funds, Hardy piles on the agony in order to win pity for a deserving object. And he is punished for it. The muse of the novel writing is not to be flouted in this way. Not only is Hardy's story an artistic failure, but his indictment of Providence fails by reason of its overstatement.

Compare *Jude* with *The Mayor of Casterbridge*. Here Hardy's moral judgements are under the control of his artistic sense. The tragic hero, Henchard, is not a perfect character. He sins, and his misfortunes are partly the consequence of his sins. His story could have been told by an author who believed in the righteous governance of the universe and wished to show that Henchard got his deserts. Hardy does not twist the facts. But, seen from his angle of vision, Henchard's tragedy appears as the result not of his fault but of his circumstances. He was born with a faulty disposition which he did all he could to mend. Fate, however, was too much for him. He comes to disaster, and his sufferings are more than he deserved. Here Hardy's indictment of Providence is fairly stated: and it is the more convincing for its fairness.

Further, the fact that Henchard's tragedy is presented against a more cheerful background adds to its impressiveness. We are shown a world which is not all sorrow and evil—which contains virtuous people, leading reasonably happy lives. The world Jude lives in is a world without joy. It is Hardy's only book without any humour, any picture of pleasure. Jude starts life as a normal man, with normal instincts, but not for one instant does he enjoy himself. He does not even come across any likeable people, except Sue and

Philotson, and they are neurotics. We may note that here the general gloom in which Hardy was wallowing when he wrote *Tess* and *Jude* did betray him into philosophic inconsistency. In them he does not only attack the universal plan, he also goes for human institutions and human beings. *Tess* contains outbursts against the current view on sexual morality, and more especially the clergy who uphold them. In *Jude* Hardy makes an onslaught on the marriage laws and on snobbish dons. These double indictments are inconsistent one with another. If all human beings are equally the puppets of circumstance, circumstance is also responsible for their views and institutions. The unfortunate clergy and dons are as much the creatures of cruel destiny as Tess and Jude; and as such are no more to be judged as responsible for their errors. In his earlier books, Hardy makes this point clear. The characters who play the part of the villain of the piece—Eustacia, Wildeve, Troy, Fitzpiers—are depicted more with pity than anger. Are they not, equally with the heroes, victims? But in the mood in which he wrote *Tess* and *Jude*, Hardy is so indignant about everything that he attacks human beings—Angel and Alec, Arabella and the dons—as bitterly as though they were the President of the Immortals himself. And even when he has finished with them, he has some anger left to splash over on to lesser objects of his disapprobation—on the supporters of blood sports, or the promoters of the enclosure of common land. This shows an indefensibly muddled mind. But when Hardy's preaching mood is on him, preach he must, whatever muddles it gets him into.

Notes

1. This love of sensational plots makes him succeed better in a novel than in a short story. There is no time in a short story to create the atmosphere that might persuade us into believing it. We are confronted with its bones in all their stark improbability.

2. He did write two lyrics inspired by this theme: 'At a lunar eclipse' and 'In vision I roamed'; and has no difficulty in concentrating the whole fertilising content of *Two on a Tower* into their brief span.

3. Other causes may have contributed to produce the unbridled didacticism of *Jude*. The influence of Ibsen had lately started the notion that serious literature should comment on problems of the day. Hardy saw *Rosmersholm* shortly before writing *Jude*; and, whether intentionally or not, there is a noticeable similarity between Sue's story and that of Rebecca West. Both are 'emancipated' women who are forced by the tragic consequences of putting their revolutionary views into action, to admit the compelling power of the beliefs against which their reason rebelled.

Further, we know that Hardy was at odds with his wife at this time. And, though it is always dangerous to interpret an imaginative work in terms of its author's biography, this may be why he felt it his duty to expose the dreadful consequences of indissoluble marriage. The unbalanced and uncharacteristic bitterness with which he speaks of the subject suggests this; so too does the unreal impersonality of much of the talk about it, like a tract put into dialogue form. Personal experience must be digested, personal emotion must cool, before they are susceptible material for the action of the creative imagination.

193
Thomas Hardy

———————— ◆ ————————

FRANK O'CONNOR

By 1882, when Trollope died, the novel as the nineteenth century knew it was already done for. In Russia, Chekhov had begun to be known; in France, Maupassant. Both were short-story writers rather than novelists, and both had affiliations with naturalism, the literary theory that evolved about *Madame Bovary*. In England, naturalism was still almost unknown, and was finally introduced by an Irishman, George Moore. In fact, the social groundwork for naturalism had never been laid, and writers and public were still wedded to the idea of the novel as entertainment. But the tendency to symbolism had already shown itself in the form of a revived romanticism, and novels and tales were being largely written by poets who managed to sustain their dual identity. Hardy and Meredith are good early examples, as Stevenson and Kipling are good later ones. Both Hardy and Meredith were fine poets, and Hardy, at least, was a great one.

At the same time, poets do not make great novelists. Theirs is an interior world, to begin with. The novelist's is an exterior world that he tries to assimilate to an interior world. Their characters are nearly always more than life-size; they act with extraordinary boldness in landscapes of surpassing beauty, and the accidents that befall them, while picturesque, are rarely of human significance. They are also more easily influenced by general ideas than the novelist, whose thoughts have to be passed through human channels not remarkable for their powers of retention. I have already quoted the anonymous critic who suggests that the teaching of philosophy in German universities may have something to do with the fact that Germany has never produced a great novelist.

Thomas Hardy and George Meredith were both influenced by the Darwinian theory. Hardy was very deeply influenced by it. Already, before Darwin, there had been among the educated classes in England a decline in religious belief. Among the working classes both Arnold and Florence Nightingale noticed that the decline took the form of atheism. Atheism is the

SOURCE *The Mirror in the Roadway*, London, 1957, pp. 237–50.

poor man's agnosticism, and the Darwinian theory hastened the process.

Up to this point it might have been said that in the novel science and art were working together toward a more rational picture of human existence, but Darwin left the poor artist's part in this far behind. In his field, tradition seemed useless, for this was something unknown to the thinkers of Greece and Rome. It opened up a vast and frightening panorama of cosmic history, put a new edge on the conflict that people like Dostoevsky were portraying between science and religion, and even divided the rationalists themselves.

In fact, there were two ways in which they could accept Darwin's world-picture. One was the way of the optimists, who merely regarded it as fresh and incontrovertible evidence of a supernatural force operating through all life, whether they called it God, the First Cause, the World Spirit, the *élan vital*, or the Life Force. It was something they shared and could help to direct. This was largely how Shaw and Wells regarded it, and for them there was no essential difference between it and the ordinary nineteenth-century creed of progress. Things were obviously getting better, and now it turned out that they had been doing so from the beginning. One could rely on Nature. As Meredith put it,

> *Into the breast that gives the rose*
> *Shall I with shuddering fall?*

To which Hardy would have replied: 'Emphatically.' For there was a darker interpretation possible: that these changes in the forms of life followed no laws but their own, and that human consciousness, instead of being part of the process, was merely an accident. One might have to postulate the existence of a First Cause, but not of any concern on its part for the develop-ment of its handiwork. 'We have reached a degree of intelligence which Nature never contemplated when framing her laws,' he wrote, 'and for which she consequently has provided no adequate satisfactions.' 'Thought,' he wrote in *The Return of the Native*, 'is a disease of the flesh.' In other words, God created a world containing an accidental element of intelligence which he was not intelligent enough to anticipate or provide for. It is a view that differs only slightly from Shakespeare's after his study of Montaigne, and which I once defined as putting the Almighty on trial for murder and then faking the evidence. It seems to me a peculiarly British view. The insular temperament has reserves of idealism unknown to the cynical Latin, and the shock experienced by an Englishman when he discovers that God does not play cricket is often an overwhelming one.

It was among the working classes that Arnold and Florence Nightingale discovered atheism, and Hardy belonged to these. Nor, English society being what it was, was it ever possible for him to leave them. He died a wealthy man, but long after his death, when I asked a Dorchester man if he had known the great writer, I realized that I had failed to insult him only because I was a foreigner and knew no better. He explained with great patience and gentleness that '*Mister* Hardy was what is known in this country as a self-made man,' but admitted that his wife knew Hardy's wife 'socially.' There is an embarrassing passage in Mrs Hardy's reminiscences which describes Hardy's mother being wheeled down to the roadside by her daughter to see the guests departing from her son's garden party, and the vain attempts of the younger woman to prevent the old lady from cheering.

Darwinism affected Hardy more deeply than it affected other novelists because he was essentially simpler than any of them. He was driven to atheism because he was unaccustomed to the agnosticism of the educated classes, and remained till the day of his death, at least with a considerable portion of his mind, religious and even superstitious. 'Half my time,' he says, '(particularly when I write verse) I believe—in the modern use of the word—not only in the things that Bergson does but in spectres, mysterious voices, intuitions, omens, dreams, haunted places, etc., etc.' The qualification is particularly revealing. Superficially his mind is critical and pessimistic, but in that part of him which writes poetry, it is still the mind of the folk at any age in any part of the world.

He is a fascinating example of historic schizophrenia, standing on the frontier of two cultures, watching traditions older than the Celts, whose barrows topped the neighboring hills, disappear as the extending railway line brings in the latest music-hall song, the latest melodrama, the latest scientific theory. When two cultures clash in this way, what happens at the time is not that the more sophisticated one triumphs, but that the less sophisticated takes refuge in the depths of the heart. This is what he means when he says that half his time he believes in 'spectres, mysterious voices, intuitions, dreams, haunted places, etc., etc.' At the same time he is slightly ashamed of his own weakness. What takes place in the conscious part of a mind like that is the spread not of sophistication, but of naïveté. Hardy as a thinker is naïve because he thinks with only half his mind. His feelings, on the other hand, are profound.

The problem for the critic is to distinguish between the two Hardys. If one considers him as a novelist in the way in which one considers Tolstoy or Trollope, it soon becomes plain that he is not a novelist at all. More than any other novelist who ever lived he is socially limited and naïve. Naturally, he is a genius, but his genius is akin to that of the *douanier* Rousseau or an American primitive. Not only has he no notion of how men and women other than the working classes of Dorset live and think, but also when he tries to apply to these people the romantic conventions of the novel he has no idea of how they would behave. 'Can a man fooled to utter heart-burning find a reason for being merry?' asks one lovelorn farmer. 'If I have lost, how can I be as if I had won? Heavens, you must be heartless quite! Had I known what a fearfully bitter sweet your love would be, how I would have avoided you and never seen you and been deaf to you.' This has the genuine quality of the American primitive, delighting us not because it resembles anything in the created world, but because it so plainly does not resemble anything while passionately attempting to do so.

The only characters in Hardy who can be described as satisfactory (apart from the character of Henchard in *The Mayor of Casterbridge*, which has a certain rough consistency) are the choruses of rustics, and this is not because he understood rustics any better than he understood other classes, but because he did not attempt to treat them as characters. The idea that humble and inarticulate people could be treated as characters probably occurred to him as little as the idea that his mother could be invited to a garden party. The rustics in Hardy are considered not from the point of view of the novelist, but from that of the poet, as part of an anonymous, idyllic rural background. Accordingly, he was able to give them a richness and quaintness of vocabulary which he would have felt it improper to give his more articulate characters.

All Hardy's faults are faults of simplemindedness. His invention is largely meaningless and frequently highly embarrassing. The plot of *Far from the Madding Crowd* is as stagy as anything in Dickens, but it is unsatisfying because, unlike Dickens and, indeed, unlike most Victorian novelists, Hardy is not in the least a stagy man. He writes in this way only because he has read and seen too many melodramas and is lacking in the critical insight that would enable him to see how far removed they are from those things which came natural to himself.

The Mayor of Casterbridge is easily his best-planned novel, but even in this the plotting is unnecessarily complicated. Consider it for a moment. Henchard sells his wife to a sailor at the fair while he is drunk. When he comes to his senses and realizes that his simpleminded wife believes in the legality of the sale and has gone off with the sailor, the shock is so great that he vows to give up drink for twenty-one years, and as a result makes his fortune as a grain-dealer. His wife returns with their daughter, Elizabeth-Jane, and to avoid scandal he marries her a second time. At the same time he takes as partner a young Scotchman, Farfrae, who falls in love with Elizabeth-Jane. But in the meantime he has had a love affair with a comparatively wealthy woman, Lucetta (the name alone is ominous), who comes to live near him, in Casterbridge. Gradually, Farfrae, a younger and more brilliant man, pushes Henchard from his high place in the business life of the town. Mrs Henchard dies, and he then discovers that Elizabeth-Jane is not really his daughter, but that of the sailor, Newson. He forces her to leave his house, and she takes up residence with Lucetta, as her companion. By this time Lucetta has fallen in love with Farfrae, and she eventually marries him. By a coincidence, the gossips of the town get hold of Lucetta's correspondence with Henchard and she is held up to ignominy at a time when she is pregnant. Farfrae is away and Henchard follows him to give him warning, but Farfrae does not trust his rival's message, and, as a result of this, his wife dies. Farfrae then marries Elizabeth-Jane, but not before her real father, the sailor, has returned from the dead and revealed the imposture of Henchard, who by this time is clinging frantically to Elizabeth-Jane as the only creature life has left him to love.

The plot is intended to strip the proud, emotional Henchard of everything and send him to die in the wilderness, but it overshoots the mark. It is needlessly complicated, and it is not complicated for the purpose of demonstrating Hardy's thesis that we are mere flies to the gods who 'kill us for their sport,' but for the modest purpose of providing serial entertainment for Hardy's readers, who liked surprises at proper intervals. It gives us an embarrassing picture of a simpleminded, meditative man doing his best to say things he does not really wish to say in an involved manner that does not come naturally to him when what he does wish to say is something as simple, clear, and poignant as an old song.

2

On the other hand, it must be said in Hardy's favor that much of this melodrama revolves about old beliefs, old customs, old buildings, and old crafts. At the worst, this diminishes the commonness of the contrivance; at its best, it gives the contrivance a new life by withdrawing its conventionality and replacing it by the description of things timeless and beautiful in their very nature. Any Victorian writer who had heard of it would have used the sale of the wife for the sake of its dramatic quality. Only Hardy was interested in it as the survival of a whole world of belief regarding the marriage bond.

It may even be said to justify itself because, in fact, the second and greater Hardy had little or nothing of the true novelist in him. In *Under the Greenwood Tree* he wrote the only novel of his which does not depend on meretricious coincidence and melodrama; which is absolutely authentic; and, enchanting as it is, it is clearly not a novel at all. It is an idyll that will be remembered as long as fiction is read, not for the sake of its characters or their emotions, but for its picture of life in rural England before it was swamped by railway culture.

This was the real inspiration of the second Hardy, Hardy the poet. Whenever he looked forward, he saw only chaos and gloom; whenever he looked back, his memory filled with enchantment. He was not only one of the great folklorists and historians; he was also the greatest master of local color that the nineteenth century had seen, greater even than Dickens.

Here, whether or not he knew it—and probably he did not—Hardy was affected by the naturalists, and we can trace in him the development of a purely pictorial kind of writing which must ultimately derive from Flaubert. Unlike Flaubert, he never allows it to settle into neat little miniatures, and long before the cinema he had invented a technique that anticipates it, as in the wonderful chapter of *The Mayor of Casterbridge* where the two women see the town for the first time. Hardy begins in the air high above the town as it lies in evening light; fades to a horizon view of it, far away and flat upon the plain; and then tracks slowly toward the tree-lined rampart that surrounds it and down the Main Street, pausing now and again to give a close-up view of bow windows, shutters, or inn signs.

> The lamplights now glimmered through the engirdling trees, conveying a sense of great snugness and comfort inside, and rendering at the same time the unlighted country without strangely solitary and vacant in aspect, considering its nearness to life. The difference between burgh and champaign was increased too by sounds which now reached them above others—the notes of a brass band. The travellers returned to the High Street, where there were timber houses with overhanging stories whose small-paned lattices were screened by dimity curtains on a drawing string, and under whose barge-boards old cobwebs waved in the breeze. There were houses of brick nogging which derived their chief support from those adjoining. There were slate roofs patched with tiles, and tile roofs patched with slate, with occasionally a roof of thatch.

Consider the difference between the tempo of such a passage and the tempo of the plot of *The Mayor of Casterbridge*, and you will almost feel the difference between the two Hardys; the one whose mind slides through character and event like a knife through butter, and the other whose mind crawls blindly and lovingly over the surface of things like an old spider weaving his web of enchantment about them. To read him is like looking at a Cotman drawing in which one can identify the very quality of materials, wood, stone, and tile, from the draughtsmanship. The second Hardy is a matchless describer of all natural phenomena, and of all objects and characters to which time has given the patina of natural phenomena; old inn signs, roofs, walls, church pews, old tools, old customs, old people chattering in the twilight as they chattered in the time of the Celts. He dismisses Lucetta's house with a phrase because it was Georgian, either not old enough in his day to have acquired the historic patina or because in its conscious symmetry it sought to impose itself upon the landscape.

Because he does not read himself into what he describes, Hardy is not a realist, but though, like Flaubert, he may be said to read himself out of it, he is not a naturalist either. Flaubert reads himself out because he believes that an artist must not become involved with his subject matter, but Hardy does so for a different reason. One can see it in the way he frequently intrudes an observer on the scene, and the observer is present even when not mentioned. He is present in the use of the passive voice: 'were heard,' 'were found,' 'were to be seen,' 'were to be discovered,' 'was apparent,' and in phrases like 'a close examination revealed,' 'the inside of the hut as it now presented itself,' 'that stillness which struck casual observers,' 'we turn our attention to the left-hand characteristics,' 'his face now began to be painted over.' Curiously, Leon Edel points out that exactly the same device occurs in Henry James.

Partly this is due to a pictorial imagination of almost unnatural sensitiveness which is not always easy to distinguish from naturalism, a style of writing deeply influenced by painting. But naturalism cannot explain why the observer—the watcher and listener—is so often obtruded where no such obtrusion is necessary or even desirable. *Far from the Madding Crowd* opens with Gabriel Oak watching from cover while Bathsheba Everdene looks approvingly at herself in the mirror. In the second chapter he sees her again, through a crevice in the wall of the cowshed where she and her aunt are working by night, and in the third he observes her once more, as she practices tricks on a horse, unaware of being watched. So too, in *The Return of the Native*, we have the great opening in which the reddleman watches from a hollow while Eustacia Vye climbs on the barrow to look for signs of her lover's return.

> There the form stood, motionless as the hill beneath. Above the plain rose the hill, above the hill rose the barrow, and above the barrow rose the figure. Above the figure was nothing that could be mapped elsewhere than on a celestial globe.

It is not as though Hardy were excluding himself from the scene. Rather, it is as though he were being excluded and returning as a sort of dis-embodied presence, *a revenant*, someone of different substance who cannot mix with the human materials he observes, and happy only in the contemplation of their physical surroundings or in the presence of rustics to whom he is invisible; who are, as it were, only portions of the landscape made visible and audible; men and women who are eternal only because, like the animals, they remain dumb and patient and uncomprehending.

> 'Joseph Poorgrass, are you there?'
> 'Yes, sir—ma'am, I mane ... I be the personal name of Poorgrass.'
> 'And what are you?'
> 'Nothing in my own eye. In the eye of other people—well, I don't say it; though public thought will out.'
> 'What do you do on the farm?'
> 'I do do carting things all the year, and in seed time I shoots the rooks and sparrows and helps at pig-killing, sir.'
> 'How much to you?'
> 'Please nine and ninepence, and a good ha'penny where 'twas a bad one, sir—ma'am, I mane.'

There is a curious passage in Hardy's journals which seems to me to throw a great light on this attitude.

> For my part, if there is any way of getting a melancholy satisfaction out of life it lies in dying, so to speak before one is out of the flesh; by which I mean putting on the manners of ghosts, wandering in their haunts, and taking their views of surrounding things. To think of life as passing away is a sadness; to think of it as past is at least tolerable. Hence, even when I enter into a room to pay a simple morning call I have unconsciously the habit of regarding the scene as if I were a spectre not solid enough to influence my environment; only fit to behold and say, as another spectre, said: 'Peace be unto you.'

This was no mere chronic pessimism or passing mood, for again and again in his poetry he speaks as for the dead, for 'the Squire and Lady Susan' as well as 'poor Fanny Hurd.' If Hardy is not a realist like Dickens, it is that he is 'not solid enough to influence his environment,' but neither is he a Flaubert or Joyce, 'like God, paring his nails.' He is a ghost; a ghost that finds the spectacle of passing life intolerable, and can contemplate it only as if it were already gone by, its sufferings ended. All his characters are treated as though they were already dead, and even among the shadows he evokes he will turn from any face too fair or venturesome to contemplate some Celtic fort or fifteenth-century cottage that has already outlasted generations of such eager souls. It is almost impossible for the artist to evade the spirit of an age, and even in the west of England, far from the bustle of James's society world, the novel was closing in on itself and the novelist being pushed to the extreme periphery of experience. Hardy was as incapable as James of placing himself again where Trollope and Tolstoy stood, in its burning center.

194

Hardy's Major Fiction

———————◆———————

JOHN HOLLOWAY

The deepening and harshening pessimism of Hardy's later novels has been stressed often enough in the past. All that need be done here is to remind readers of how it is usually located in two particular aspects of his work: first, his 'philosophical' asides ('the President of the Immortals, in Aeschylean phrase, had ended his sport with Tess' will be enough in illustration of this familiar story; the phrase itself will need re-examination later); and second, his apparently growing preoccupation with problems of marriage. One should perhaps add that to see this second issue as the product of difficulties in Hardy's own married life is very uninformative. Much more to the point are the divorce cases (the Parnell case being the best known) which became national sensations in the later 1880s and early 1890s; and besides this, the important influence of Ibsen, at least in the case of *Jude the Obscure*.

Recent criticism of Hardy has also emphasized something else: a special part of his connection with the southwest of England. An earlier generation of writers on Hardy underestimated this. Amiably if innocently equipped with haversack and large-scale map, they cycled over Wessex and noted Hardy's faithful geography, or his intimate and affectionate knowledge of rural occupations and customs. More recently, the stress has fallen on Hardy as one who registered the impact upon rural England of a great historical change, which went to the very roots of life. One cause of this was the swift and decisive decline in British agriculture which followed almost instantaneously on the completion of the railroad links to the American Middle West in about 1870. The other, less spectacular but in the long run much more far reaching, was the industrial revolution in agriculture. This was progressing steadily in the later years of the century, and has even now far from completed its radical transforming work. As symbol of this second force, one might take a pair of incidents from Hardy's own work. In *The Mayor of Casterbridge* (1886) the new mechanical seed-drill which is to replace the methods in use since the time of the Anglo–Saxons is for sale in the market place. Someone has still to buy and use it. In *Tess of the d'Urbervilles*,

SOURCE *Jane Austen to Joseph Conrad*, Minneapolis, 1959.

only five years later the mechanical harvester dominates and controls the whole scene of the cornstacking (Chapter 48) and reduces the tired, dazed human beings who serve it to mere automatons. The contrast is no proof of how rural life was changing; but as an illustration it is vivid.

Modern criticism of fiction often seems at its weakest in trying (or failing) to consider the forces in a book which unify it from beginning to end. This weakness is perhaps the result of a certain uneasiness which (for reasons obvious enough) often shows itself when the critic turns his attention to the plot. Yet such attention is necessary if the pervasive unifying drives of the work are to be located; and certainly the full seriousness and import of Hardy's major novels will be concealed from the reader who fails to apprehend their plots: plots, that is, not as mere summarizable sequences of events, but as the central unifying and significating forces of the books. These I hope now to approach.

The first step in that approach is not difficult, for it is taken simply by combining the two more or less familiar points from which this discussion started; by seeing Hardy's deepening and harshening gloom as not a mere self-ingraining philosophical bias, but rather as something in most intimate relation to his vision of the passing of the old rhythmic order of rural England. Once the novels are seen from this point of view, they suggest a surprising development in Hardy's thought. They suggest not just a growing preoccupation with the rural problem, not even a growing sense that an earlier way of life was inevitably vanishing. They suggest something more disquieting: a gathering realization that that earlier way did not possess the inner resources upon which to make a real fight for its existence. The old order was not just a less powerful mode of life than the new, but ultimately helpless before it through inner defect.

When one is arguing that a thought or an attitude comes increasingly into focus in a writer's work, it is always easy to claim too much and hide too much; yet in the present case the change looks convincingly steady. *The Return of the Native* (1878) has a half-tragic ending in its present form; and Hardy's original intention seems to have been to have made it more tragic rather than less so. Yet throughout the book, the stress falls on the revitalizing power of rural life, and on how its vitality is intrinsically greater than that of modernity. Eustacia and Wildeve, and at first Clym too, are alienated from it: indeed, this very alienation lies behind their ostensible successes (the marriages, for example). But because of the alienation, the successes are ill-placed and precarious, they are the successes of those who have lost the soundness, the inner strength, the power to choose and to achieve wisely which belongs to men whose life is in harmony with their world. By contrast, Venn the reddleman suffers reverses, but they do not impair his integrity; his vitality runs submerged, but it runs with the tide of life. The gambling scene on the heath is fantastic enough, but it tellingly conveys this. Moreover, the whole rural ambience can ultimately assert a greater vitality than the city life from which Clym has come. As he gives himself to it, he is regenerated from a basic source. By the end, Egdon has triumphed, even if on its own stern terms. The renegades have been destroyed or won over: even if Venn had never married Thomasin, the faithful would have been in possession. The novel resolves in an assertion of the old order, its regenerative austerity, its rewarding unrewardingness.

The next novel is very different. Henchard is the only major figure in *The Mayor of Casterbridge* (1886) who stands integrally for the traditional qualities. Farfrae is an agriculturalist, but of the new kind: he prospers by chemistry, machinery, and bookkeeping and elementary economics. His traditional songs are partly a social accomplishment, neither sincere nor insincere; his kindliness and even his amorousness are conventional. Henchard's daughter Elizabeth-Jane is turning into a cultivated young lady (I would sooner over-rate than underrate Hardy's own educatedness, but I cannot help seeing something of importance in his seeming assurance here that education could without loss be self-education). Lucetta is entirely *déraciné*. On these premises, contrast with *The Return of the Native* is vivid. From beginning to end Henchard's course is downward. Whenever his older way of life meets the new, it is defeated. Step by step, he comes to work for the man whom he once employed, and in the end he feels himself driven away to his death; while those who were once his laborers work the new, harder (and easier) way, for a shilling a week less than they had had from him.

Yet, although this relentless decline of Henchard's is (as we take its meaning) what unifies the book, Henchard still stands above the others in what might be called psychic virtue. In the conventional sense, he is both less moral than they, and more so. He is violent and a liar and in one sense intensely selfish, but his generosity is true magnanimity, and he has reserves of affection and humility that they quite lack. The essential is something else, though: that his whole nature, good or bad, is centered upon a deep source of vital energy. The rich stream of life still issues from life's traditional order. It does not bring success, but it brings greatness and in a sense goodness. Farfrae prospers through *skill* which the new mode of life has impersonally taught him: Henchard is able to struggle on, though defeated, not because of what he has learned but because of what he *is*. He blocks out something like the full contour of the human being.

That Henchard should stand out as a human rather than a man was surely part of Hardy's intention. His lack of interest in 'womankind' is stressed more than once, and we are reminded of how Marty South is also in a sense made sexless at the end of *The Woodlanders* (1887). But to turn to *The Woodlanders* is to find that Hardy has now moved further still. Marty South and Giles Winterborne do not display, like Henchard, a defeated strength. On the contrary, they leave the impression of debility. So far as goodness itself goes, they are, to be sure, alone in having contact with it: 'you was a good man, and did good things.' But the springs of goodness are now no longer the springs of strength. Rather the opposite. Such vitality as there is lies on the other side, in the self-assurance and plausible fluency of Fitzpiers, or the passionate sensuousness of Felice. Grace Melbury has a thwarted contact, anyhow, with the traditional order: but what it does is chiefly to make her impassive and acceptant.

In *Tess of the d'Urbervilles* (1891), Hardy moves further. Tess is 'a pure woman,' admittedly; but this is not the feminine counterpart to Henchard's 'A Man of Character.' It is not Tess's sexual misadventures which impugn her as a woman of character, and Hardy is indeed at pains to show, in the later part of the book when she resists the now twice-reprobate Alec, that she is comparatively faithful and steadfast. But she has a weakness nearer her center: an alienation, a dreaminess which Hardy depicts unsuccessfully in the ride at night when she tells her young brother that we live on a 'blighted' planet (and becomes so engrossed that she causes a fatal injury to the horse), and which he depicts again, this time with brilliant success, at Talbothay's dairy when she tells Dairyman Crick how 'our souls can be made to go outside our bodies when we are alive' (Chapters 4 and 18). Again, this incident is nodal in the book, and I must return to it. For the present it is enough to say that its nodality is stressed by Hardy, in that he makes this the moment when Angel Clare first gives Tess any special notice.

This dreamy unreality in Tess is no personal quirk. It results from her heredity, and is reflected in both her parents. Moreover, Hardy is at pains to stress that among country folk, degeneration of an old stock is common enough. The stock is in decline. It seems a positive disparagement of the old order. The contrast with Henchard is revealing. Quietly but clearly, Hardy indicates that in Tess there is something self-destroying. So there was, in a sense, in Henchard. Yet how differently does the stress fall, provided that the reader follows only the contours created by the author!

Tess of the d'Urbervilles also dwells, quite for the first time, upon another unattractive side of rural life. This is what appears in the barrenness and crippling toil of life on the upland farm of Flintcomb-Ash. Hardy links his picture to contemporary agricultural realities—the farm belongs to an absentee landlord—but the essential things which make life hard on it are those which have made the rural life hard since the beginning: stony soil, cold wind, rain, snow, callous masters—things that can be found in the Wakefield *Second Shepherds' Play* as easily as in *Tess*. Should this be in doubt, it may be confirmed from *Jude the Obscure* (1895). In fact, there is something like a parallel here to the double indictment of *Tess*. Jude Fawley is 'crazy for books ... It runs in our family ... Later, when the now adult Jude sees a stone-mason's yard and glimpses for a moment that happiness for him lay only in a life like that, Hardy passes decisive judgment upon bookish tastes in laborers' families. A still clearer parallel with *Tess*, however, is Hardy's insistence in this novel upon the essential harshness of rural life. 'How ugly it

438

is here,' thinks Jude, as he drives off the rooks from the brown, featureless arable of the upland. This is in part an ironical judgment upon Jude. Hardy is at pains to stress the rich human associations of the scene. Yet some of these associations are themselves associations of human unhappiness; and the whole chapter goes far to endorse Jude's revulsion from the drab landscape and the inevitable greed and callousness of the farmer. Nor are this revulsion, and the inescapable grounds tending to justify it, incidentals. They initiate the whole train of events. Jude's quest for learning is to escape from a life of grinding toil that he could not but wish to escape. And what are the compensations of rurality, as they now appear? Only Arabella, whose work is to wash the innards of the newly slaughtered pig, and whose attractions take their force from brutal humor, coarse sensuality, and a rooted tradition of deceit.

This discussion of the later novels is not by itself, of course, anything like the whole truth about them. It virtually ignores Hardy's rich and intimate contact with the rural tradition in every book before *Jude*, and his profound dependence upon, and loyalty to, its characteristic virtues. It ignores these matters because they have often been discussed elsewhere, and its concentration upon Hardy's growing sense of weakness in the country world must be taken in the context of Hardy criticism as it now stands. Yet it remains true that in these later works the essence of plot, the distinctive trajectory of the narrative, is the steadily developed decline of a protagonist who incarnates the older order, and whose decline is linked, more and more clearly, with an inner misdirection, an inner weakness.

Two of the novels stand out as inviting a closer scrutiny, if we wish to see how this kind of movement lies at the heart of unity and meaning. These are *The Mayor of Casterbridge*, and *Tess of the d'Urbervilles*. *Jude the Obscure* clearly has another kind of concern; and *The Woodlanders*, surprisingly enough, proves largely to have it as well. Indeed, there is a sense in which this novel has a much looser organization than the other late ones. Deep and powerful as its awareness of rural life undoubtedly is (one cannot keep from mind the pictures of Giles spattered all over with his apples and their juice), yet much at the center of this work pursues another concern. Grace's response to Fitzpiers' infidelity, and the gradual rebirth of her affection for him, are not Wessex products. The novel resolves itself by amiably decanting these two characters into the middle-class urban life of the Midlands. The psychological change that we see in Grace is barely connected with Hardy's rural interest; and that, I think, is why the whole episode of their reconciliation is treated with a lightness and even something of a gentle half-ironical detachment that distinguishes the book clearly from *Tess*. At one point Hardy brings the difference out starkly through a metaphor. This occurs when Grace, running swiftly through the wood to meet Fitzpiers, just misses the mantrap (which is in itself, by the way, another scrap of evidence for the view

439

that Hardy was beginning to dwell on the harsher side of country life). Her destiny is to evade, though barely, the issues of life in their brutal sharpness. All the man-trap does is whisk her skirt off: in Hardy's making this the occasion of her being reconciled to Fitzpiers we are to see, I think, that the whole sequence has about it something of the essentially trivial. Tess turns back to Angel over her rush-drawing labor in the snow-laden barn, as she comes to grasp her case, and Angel's, in terms of the plainest, the essential relations between women and men as human animals. We are in a much different world, a world that has not skipped over the waiting man-trap. For these reasons, among others, it is *The Mayor of Casterbridge* and *Tess* that best warrant further questioning. They are the novels which have a single-minded organization along our present line of thought.

The world 'theme,' now the most hackneyed of clichés in criticism, is also one of its bugbears. An essay, a philosophical discourse, even a collection of different pieces, all these may equally well have a theme, or several themes. The word has no necessary connection even with imaginative literature, let alone with the narrative forms of it, and is therefore a standing temptation to the critic to overlook the whole narrative dimension. But almost always, the narrative trajectory is what makes a novel a novel and what makes any particular novel the novel it is. Only within the framework of this central drive can the real significance of the detail (incident, imagery, metaphor, local contrast) be grasped at all. Examples may be needed here; let us revert to *The Woodlanders*. To connect, say, Giles Winterborne's meeting with Grace while he holds up his apple tree in the market-place with 'the theme of rural fertility,' or Marty South's selling her hair with 'the commercial theme,' would be grotesquely uninformative. The significance of both these incidents, prominently placed at the outset of the narrative, is that the two characters are made to carry out, at the start, ritual gestures by which they formally (though unwittingly) surrender their essential strength. From this point out, we know what kind of character we are to watch, we are put on the track of the path their lives must take.

A tree also embodies the essential strength of Marty's father. In an aberration from his proper rural life, he wants it cut down. When this is done, he dies. As for Marty's hair, Hardy invests this with almost talismanic virtue. While Felice wears it as her own, her luck prospers. Toward the end of the book, her secret comes out. At once she loses her power over Fitzpiers, and almost immediately after she meets her death. Similarly with the contrast between how Grace meets Winterborne (under the flowering apple tree in his hand) and how she first meets Fitzpiers (he has bought the right to dissect her old nurse's body after she is dead, and Grace goes to buy it back). These meetings are no mere specimens of a theme, but exact pointers to a narrative movement; and they come at the start of the relation and show what its significance is, and what (if pursued) it will bring. For Grace to progress with one is to pursue the forces of life, with the other to pursue those of death. Similarly with the incident where Marty helps Giles to plant the young trees (Chapter 8). This does not merely take up the theme of rural order; it exactly indicates how Marty is Giles's proper strength and counterpart. His trees will flourish if he chooses her to help. When he turns elsewhere, we know what he has done. But all these details have significance within the frame of the basic narrative movement of the book, a movement which, as it takes its shape out of them, reciprocally determines what meaning they shall have.

'From beginning to end,' it was suggested above. 'Henchard's course is downward. Whenever his older way of life meets the new, it is defeated.' It is this narrative movement in the book which embodies Hardy's deepest interest and the essence of his moral insight. But there is more to be said about the exact nature of the struggle and the downward movement, as he envisages it; and it is at this point that such matters as incident and imagery can take their proper and proportionate place in our awareness of the whole work. For it seems that Hardy has employed a single basic metaphor through which to embody the war between Farfrae and Henchard; local incidents and metaphors have their allotted place within it; and in spite of the recurrent suggestions that Henchard (like Old Hamlet) is 'a man, take him for all in all,' the basic metaphor through which Hardy sees the struggle between Farfrae and him, is that of a struggle between a man and an animal. This begins with the animal in possession of its territory. Henchard arrived on the scene during, as it were, the prehistory of the narrative. Now he is in occupation at Casterbridge. Farfrae is passing through on his way to emigrate. As the novel pursues its course, Farfrae takes possession. It is his rival who thinks to emigrate. But instead he is persuaded to live in his own old home, now occupied by Farfrae; and like an animal, he becomes domesticated. 'Henchard had become in a measure broken in, he came to work daily on the home premises like the rest.' Later he is likened to a 'netted lion,' or to a lion whose fangs have been drawn. When he describes how Farfrae, now mayor, as he himself once was, forced him away on the occasion of the royal visit, he says. '. . . how angry he looked. He drove me back as if I were a bull breaking fence . . .'

Several of the incidents of the book enter into this sustained metaphor. Henchard and Farfrae fighting in the cornstore is, in a sense animal against man: it is very like the earlier fight in the barn between Henchard and the bull. The parallel extends even to Farfrae's 'wrenching Henchard's arm . . . causing him sharp pain, as could be seen from the twitching of his face,' and Henchard when he 'wrenched the animal's head as if he would snap it off . . . The premeditated human contrivance of the nose-ring was too cunning for impulsive brute force, and the creature flinched.' Finally, at the end of the novel, Henchard crawls away, like a wounded beast, to die in an empty hovel that is more like an animal's hole than a place for men. His final instructions for how he is to be buried are not appropriate for *felo-de-se*: they are appropriate for the burial of an animal.

Henchard's character, moreover, is that of a beast; in the true, not the townee, sense of that word. His immense natural energy, his simplicity, his having no skill of any kind save that of hay-cutting, and his liability to enslavement above all through a disabling, yearning, dog-like need for human affection, all these features of his nature make their contribution. There is no need to remind readers that Henchard is not *simply* an animal. Far from it. At no point does metaphor become literal truth. But it is through this metaphor that we must see the struggle which constitutes the narrative and the unity of the book, and which predominantly defines its significance. Indeed, nothing but awareness of this metaphor will fully bring out the issues between old and new that are involved, or the length to which Hardy pursues them. 'My furniture too! Surely he'll buy my body and soul likewise!' Henchard says at one point. (One cannot but—though it is an unhappy touch—see the caged singing-bird which Henchard brings Elizabeth-Jane at the end as a wedding present, and which he leaves behind when he goes away to die, as linking with this idea of his giving up 'body and soul' together.) Yet even this is insufficient to bring out the lengths to which Hardy pursues his central conflict. Henchard is more than enslaved, he is *tamed*. That is something far more thoroughgoing. It is the measure of what Hardy sees as at issue.

Tess of the d'Urbervilles also has unity through a total movement; and the nature of this may also largely be grasped through a single metaphor. It is not the taming of an animal. Rather (at least for a start) it is the hunting of one. Several remarks and incidents in the book make this explicit, notably Tess's letter to her absent husband when he has deserted her: 'I must cry out to you in my trouble—I have no one else ... if I break down by falling into some dreadful snare, my last state will be worse than my first.' So does the night she spends in the wood with the wounded pheasants: strongly reminiscent, of course, of her earlier night in a wood, when she fell into the snare set for her by Alec. Throughout, Tess is harried from place to place at what seems like gradually increasing speed. Even the very start of her relation with Alec is relevant: 'the handsome, horsey young buck' drove up early in the morning in his gig to fetch her. At the end, it is especially clear. When the hunt is over, Tess is captured on the sacrificial stone at Stonehenge, the stone where once, like the hart at bay, the victim's throat was slit with the knife. With these things in mind, Hardy's much-abused quotation from Aeschylus ('the President of the Immortals, in Aeschylean phrase, had ended his sport with Tess') takes on a new meaning and aptness.

Yet Tess's career represents more than a hunt. What this is, can again be summed up in a metaphor, one to which we are almost inadvertently led, if we attempt to summarize. That Hardy should have divided his book into 'phases' is itself, perhaps, an indication of the field in which his mind was partly working: the word was good nineteenth century currency in history and natural history, and Carlyle was fond of it. 'Phase Three' is entitled 'The Rally.' In it, Tess strikes out for new country. She leaves the snug and familiar environment of the 'Vale of the Little Dairies,' surmounts the challenge of barren Egdon Heath which lies across her path, and enters a new territory, the 'Vale of the Great Dairies,' where life runs upon a basically different pattern. To this she almost completely adapts herself: so much so, that she finds a mate in Angel Clare, and almost succeeds in—there is only one word to use—in germinating. This word is less odd than it seems at first. Hardy lays great stress on the rich, blossoming fertility of Tess's whole environment during this period, and also stresses, discreetly but with great force, her own richly sensuous nubility, her genuine bond, in the truest sense, with the milch cows and the lush blossoms where the fruit is setting.

The rally fails. Tess has to abandon her favorable environment, and is forced on to a harsh upland soil where existence is more difficult. She struggles not at the level of reproduction, but for mere survival. She is resistant, though, and for a long time she does survive. But her strength is shaken when her family is finally driven off the soil; and in the end, what Darwin called sexual selection begins to work contrariwise to natural selection. Tess gives up the struggle. She is driven out of her natural habitat altogether, and goes to live, kept like a pet, with Alec in Sandbourne.

Here, I think, is the second, bigger metaphor, embracing the first, through which Hardy embodies his central fictional movement. The central train of events demands description in Darwinian terms: organism, environment, struggle, adaptation, fertility, survival, resistant—and one more: Hardy has envisaged an individual life at the depth of, and to the length of, the ultimates for a species—establishment at one end, and at the other, extinction.

Many of the incidents in the book bring this total movement into focus. For example, Hardy provides the reader with an index to it by two scenes, one at the beginning and one at the end. In the first, Angel looks back down the road and sees the village girls in white, dancing in spring time on the green: Tess, still integrated with them, stands by the hedge. In the other, he looks back after what he thinks is their final parting, over bare, open countryside and an empty road: 'and as he gazed a moving spot intruded on the white vacuity of its perspective. It was a human figure running.' It is Tess, now alienated and isolated. Tess and her family take refuge in the family vault (Chapter 52). In terms of the hunt metaphor, they have been run to earth; and this parallels the sleepwalking scene (Chapter 37) when Angel lays Tess in the open tomb: within the larger movement there is a recurrent smaller pattern. Tess at the dairy says that 'our souls can be made to go outside our bodies' if we 'lie on the grass at night and look straight up at some big bright star.' (This is exactly what she does at the end of the book,

443

on her fatal last night on Salisbury Plain.) Meanwhile, Dairyman Crick was balancing his knife and fork together 'like the beginning of a gallows.' Most striking of all, Hardy reinvites us to register the total movement of Tess's career, in all its integration, by an ingenious and vivid résumé of it, toward the close of the book. He does this through the final days that Tess and Angel spend together—partly a psychological fugue, partly a kind of total recall, partly both. Leaving her sin with Alec behind her, she rejoins Angel, and the rich woodland of the first two days together corresponds to the rich vale of the dairies. The empty manor house they sleep in corresponds to the ancient house where their marriage was so nearly consummated before. Barren Salisbury Plain corresponds to the uplands of Flintcomb-Ash. The scene at Stonehenge corresponds both to Tess in the vault, and to the moment when she hung on the wayside cross to rest and looked like a sacrificial victim. Her whole tragic life is mirrored in little at its close.

To notice things of this order is to realize, in effect, that Hardy's novels (like many others) need a special mode of reading. The incidents in them which strike us as improbable or strained or grotesque invite (this is not to say that they always deserve) the kind of response that we are accustomed to give, say, to the Dover Cliff scene in *Lear*. Admittedly, Hardy has local failures; but incidents like these are intrinsically at one remove from the probable and the realistic. Almost, it is necessary for them to be unrealistic in order that their other dimension of meaning, their relevance to the larger rhythms of the work, shall transpire. Again and again, it is those larger rhythms which finally expand into the total movement of the novel, transmitting the author's sense of life, the forces that operate through it, the values that chart it out and make it what it is.

From what has so far been said, a new reason may perhaps be advanced as to why Hardy gave up fiction. It is both the strength (because of the integrity that it brought) and the limit of his achievement, to have seen the source of life-creating strength for human beings as connected always with a certain limited context, the traditional rural order. As time passed, he lost confidence in the strength of this order to resist and survive, and in part, even seems more and more to have regarded the element of drabness and harshness in rural life as not a product of change and modernity, but intrinsic. This being so, he had no position to which to retreat. He does not seem ever to have viewed human nature as itself ineradicably vital, as possessing an innate power to transform, from its own resources, its waste land into a fertile one. To say this is not necessarily to make a point against him. He may very well have been right in thinking that the human species, like others, wilts out of its natural habitat and communal order. It is merely to recognize that by the middle 1890s, Hardy's course in fiction had become one that he could neither retrace, nor pursue.

195

Hardy's 'Gurgoyles'

———————◆———————

RICHARD C. CARPENTER

On a typical summer evening in June, when the atmosphere is 'in such a delicate equilibrium ... that inanimate objects seem endowed with two or three senses, if not five,' Tess of the D'Urbervilles, walking in the garden alone hears the 'thin notes' of a 'second-hand harp' in the hands of Angel Clare. Often she has heard this strumming before in the attic above the dairymaids' sleeping room, but it never appealed to her then as it does now, wandering 'in the still air with a stark quality like that of nudity.' As she listens, Tess, 'like a fascinated bird' draws near the harper in the unweeded garden, the fringe of which 'uncultivated for some years ... was now damp and rank with juicy grass which sent up mists of pollen at a touch; and with tall blooming weeds emitting offensive smells.' Through these Tess goes 'stealthily as a cat'; as she walks, 'gathering cuckoo-spittle on her skirts, cracking snails that [are] underfoot, staining her hands with thistle-milk and slug-slime, and rubbing off upon her naked arms sticky blights which, though snow-white on the apple-tree trunks, [make] madder stains on her skin.' (pp. 157–8).[1]

As Tess listens, the floating pollen seems to her 'his notes made visible' and 'the dampness of the garden the weeping of the garden's sensibility' (p. 158). All is idyllic, ecstatic on Tess's part, and even the rather dull philosophical conversation that follows does not destroy the illusion—at least for her. She and Angel part, feeling the first burgeonings of love. But to the reader's illusions much damage has been done. No longer can he believe in the Talbothay's idyll; he carries with him in his imagination stains as indelible as those left by the 'sticky blights' on Tess's naked arms, images of slug-slime and cuckoo-spittle; he has been forewarned that a nasty catastrophe is in the offing.

Certainly we have here one of Hardy's most effective scenes: the clustered images reinforcing one another to create a complex picture of purity stained and corrupted, and the picture in turn carrying with it symbolic nuances of sexuality, other gardens and other temptations by a sanctimonious sceptic.

SOURCE *Modern Fiction Studies*, vol. VI, no. 3, Autumn, 1960, pp. 223–32.

We have here a vital objective correlative which communicates more power-fully and accurately to the reader's thoughts and feelings than could any amount of discursive philosophizing. We are seeing Hardy at the peak of his creative powers.

But is this passage unique? Is Hardy managing here to do something he did not do elsewhere? In some respects the answer must of course be yes—*Tess of the d'Urbervilles* is unique. But twenty years earlier Hardy had written similar passages in his first novel, different in intensity and poetic force but bearing the mark of the same imagination.

Manston, the villain of *Desperate Remedies*, is trying to press Cytherea into a marriage for which she has no great desire, by a kind of blackmail. They are standing by the 'ruinous foundations of an old mill in the midst of a meadow':

> Between grey and half-overgrown stonework—the only signs of masonry remaining—the water gurgled down from the old millpond to a lower level, under the cloak of rank broad leaves—the sensuous natures of the vegetable world. On the right hand the sun, resting on the horizon-line, streamed across the ground from below copper-coloured and lilac clouds, stretched out in flats beneath a sky of pale soft green ... Thinking and hesitating, she looked as far as the autumnal haze ... would allow her to see distinctly. There was the fragment of a hedge—all that remained of a 'wet old garden'—standing in the middle of the mead, without a definite beginning or ending, purposeless and valueless. It was overgrown, and choked with mandrakes, and she could almost fancy she heard their shrieks. (pp. 254–5)

In comparison to the scene from *Tess* this is crude, too obvious and dis-cursive. Nevertheless, here are many of the same elements that made the greater scene: the interconnection of man and nature; the hint of corruption in the rank, broad leaves and the colors of the sky; the bizarre concept of the mandrakes. Although *Desperate Remedies* is known as a complicated detective story in the fashion of Wilkie Collins, such scenes as this strike a different note, present us with a grimmer dissonance than characterizes the usual nineteenth-century melodrama.

Consider, for example, an earlier scene where Manston is pondering how he may achieve his object of marrying Cytherea. For a while he walks up and down in his yard, then pauses and leans upon the edge of the rainwater-butt, where 'the reflection from the smooth stagnant surface tinged his face with the greenish shades of Correggio's nudes.' He watches the staves of sunlight slanting down through the water, and can see 'with wonderful distinctness' multitudes of 'minute living creatures' as they sport and tumble about in the depths 'with every contortion that gaiety could suggest' (p. 245). This is not the stuff of most action stories but rather one of those moments where we look into the depths, not of a still pool only, but also of reality. Here also is the parallelism or reflection between human affairs and those of the animal world, made ironic and faintly gruesome by the implied comparison of man's life with mindless and minuscule water-snakes.

Five novels later, Hardy uses the same scene—or what amounts to the same scene—in a great novel and with a concomitant increase in force and meaning. Mrs Yeobright, in *The Return of the Native*, sets out across the heath on a scorching August day on a peace mission toward Clym. As she labors across the ancient and alien heath under a 'metallic violet' sky, she comes to a place where 'independent worlds of ephemerons were passing their time in mad carousal, some in the air, some on the hot ground and vegetation, some in the tepid and stringy water of a nearly dried pool.' Mrs Yeobright, like Manston in this respect if different in most others, is inclined to philosophize; and she sits down to watch where 'all the shallower ponds had decreased to a vaporous mud amid which the maggoty shapes of innumerable obscene creatures could be indistinctly seen, heaving and wallowing with enjoyment' (p. 327). Oddly enough, Mrs Yeobright, who hopes for some joy herself as the outcome of her visit to Clym, derives a sort of empathetic happiness from watching these creatures, who seem to be enjoying themselves in their own way.

As with *Tess*, however, the images Hardy presents are in ironic tension with the happiness he talks about. There is something nightmarish in these pictures of decay, as there is in the slimy water of the rainwater-butt and the sticky blights of the unweeded garden. No matter how casually they are slipped into a current which seems to tend in an opposite direction, they carry with them other overtones that guide our sensibilities to the real meaning beneath the surface.

I believe that this type of imagery, which usually is compounded from unit-images of corruption, and of animation or personification, is one of Hardy's more powerful iconic devices.[2] It does not always function just as I have indicated in the above examples, nor can we always find such motifs as rank gardens and obscene ephemerons running through several novels. But it does appear again and again in various guises throughout Hardy's work. In general, I believe we can term it imagery of the *grotesque*. In the first place it is usually so incongruous to the tone of the incidents we are encountering and so intense in its evocation of physical sensations that it merits this designation. In the second place, the word carries with it connotations of perversion, of violent connections between the real and unreal, the mundane and the surrealistic. And finally, as Webster says, the grotesque 'originally, and still technically ... is applied to a type of [art] which employs natural details (animals, men, flowers, foliage, etc.) and conventional designs and figures (scrolls, garlands, satyrs, etc.) in unnatural combinations.' In verbal arts I take it this would mean the kind of situation, scene, or image which yokes man and his environment together in strange relationships.

Obviously, not all images of the grotesque will display all these qualities simultaneously. Occasionally an image may strike our attention forcibly as incongruous and yet not relate man and nature in an unnatural way. Or, on the other hand, some extremely effective instances of the grotesque may seem at first perfectly congruous with reality—demonstrating 'existential particularity' to use the fashionable phrase—yet warrant being termed grotesque because of the unnatural combination of man and nature. Furthermore, some instances of the grotesque may be due to a failure of the artistic sense. Hardy was not Henry James, and we cannot be sure that an image is going to be aesthetically effective simply because it is supremely out of place. It may just be bad writing.

Nonetheless, a careful perusal of objects, figures of speech, scenes, and incidents throughout the novels turns up a great number of examples of the grotesque, many of which serve an aesthetic purpose. Perhaps the most obvious of them all is an object which I believe appears only once in Hardy's work but which is emphasized and used in a bizarrely effective way: the gargoyle—or as Hardy calls it, the 'gurgoyle'—in *Far from the Madding Crowd*. Hardy's attitude toward this object is clearly indicated in his preliminary description where he tells us, 'It has been sometimes argued that there is no truer criterion of the vitality of any given art-period than the power of the master-spirits of that time in the grotesque' (p. 360). He goes on to tell us about it: 'too human to be called like a dragon ... too animal to be like a fiend, and not enough like a bird to be called a griffin.' It is a

> horrible stone entity ... covered with a wrinkled hide ... [with] short, erect ears, eyes starting from their sockets,and its fingers and hands ... seizing the corners of its mouth, which they thus seemed to pull open to give free passage to the water it vomited. ... Here and thus, jutting a couple of feet from the wall against which its feet rested as a support, the creature had for four hundred years laughed at the surrounding landscape, voicelessly in dry weather, and in wet with a gurgling and snorting sound (p. 361).

This epitome of the grotesque serves Hardy well both imagistically and symbolically—or iconically we might say—in that it is the proximate cause of ruining Troy's romantic attempt to make amends, or at least make a gesture in that direction. The flowers he has planted on the grave of the girl he has wronged, Fanny Robin, are washed away by a stream from the gargoyle's mouth.

> The persistent torrent from the gurgoyle's jaws directed all its vengeance into the grave. The rich tawny mould was stirred into motion, and boiled like chocolate. ... The flowers so carefully planted by Fanny's repentant lover began to move and writhe in their bed. The winter-violets turned slowly upside down, and became a mere mat of mud. Soon the snowdrop and other bulbs danced in the boiling mass like ingredients in a cauldron (p. 362)

No clearer communication of the futility of belated good intentions when opposed by the ineluctable forces of nature could we have. And the quasi-human aspect of the personified gargoyle makes the point with more force than could pages of narrative or exposition. Undoubtedly the entire incident is strained and manipulated to give us this effect, and if the ultimately grotesque distortion of the gargoyle were not there we would probably object to the lack of realism. But the gargoyle sets the tone, lets us know that this is symbolic event, an instance of the disproportion that is art. As Hardy said in one of his journals:

> Art is a disproportioning—(*i.e.*, distorting, throwing out of proportion)—of realities, to show more clearly the features that matter in those realities, which, if merely copied or reported inventorially, might possibly be observed, but would more probably be overlooked. Hence 'realism' is not Art.[3]

Isolated objects of this sort, grotesque in themselves, do not appear frequently; but there is at least one other which is made grotesque by the imagery associated with it and which illustrates Hardy's typical method in employing this imagery. Edward Springrove, the hero of *Desperate Remedies*, goes to a London slum where he encounters a 'depressing picture' of domesticity in a large city. The major part of the description is conveyed by such naturalistic details as 'pap-clogged' spoons and such, but the most striking aspect of the scene is a Dutch clock. Although one would think this an innocuous enough object, it is made to serve an iconic purpose. Fixed out of level, it ticks 'wildly in longs and shorts, its entrails hanging down beneath its white face and wiry hands, like the faeces of a Harpy' (p. 350).

In conjunction with the faintly nauseating implications of the atmosphere in the Higgins home, its whining babies and unnamed but easily imaginable odors, the clock serves a remarkably concise grotesque function. Its wild ticking can be specifically related to the general slatternliness and disorder of the household (thus showing Hardy's prejudice against the city poor as contrasted with his beloved peasantry); and without being quite so symbolic, the white face and wiry hands remind us of the pallid, undernourished children of a London slum. The final detail speaks for itself.

Beyond this, the image of the clock illustrates some of the typical characteristics of Hardy's use of the grotesque. In particular we see the combination of personification and corruption which he habitually employs in similes of this sort, probably his most common grotesque device. In the same novel he speaks of the shuttered windows in London looking like 'the white and sightless orbs of blind men' (p. 122); the line of stable roofs of the Three Tranters Inn now 'sunk into vast hollows till they seemed like the cheeks of toothless age' (p. 138); trees which stretch their boughs 'like hairy arms into the dull sky' (pp. 164–5); and a shadow from Cytherea's head dancing 'like a demon, blue and grim' (p. 236).

Such similes are more startling in a novel like *The Woodlanders*, that drama of 'a grandeur and unity truly Sophoclean' which takes place in a 'sequestered spot outside the gates of the world' (p. 4), where amid the living wood we hardly expect harping on the string of morbidity. As Albert Guerard has pointed out, the incursion of decadence into the novel is symbolized at the outset by Mrs Charmond's purchase of Marty South's hair—'an extreme violation of natural right and property ... by the sophisticated ennui of the overcivilized world.'[4] At least two similes convey the emotive significance of this incursion by reflecting Marty's attitude toward her self-spoliation. As she works late into the night cutting spar-gads, the two sovereigns with which the barber has tempted her 'confronted ... her from the looking-glass in such a manner as to suggest a pair of jaundiced eyes on the watch for an opportunity' (p. 14). And six pages later, after the deed has been done, the long locks of hair lie on the 'scrubbed deal of the coffin-stool table ... like waiving and ropy weeds over the washed white bed of a stream' (p. 20). While these comparisons are pretty obvious, they still convey a strong implication of morbidity, of disease, guilt, and even of death. Though Marty is not drowned in ropy weeds like some of Hardy's other heroines, selling her hair is the first step on the road to spiritual demise, which images of drowning effectively symbolize.

Similarly, the morning after the hair-cutting emerges as a 'bleared white visage' like that of a 'dead-born child' (p. 24); and later come references to glossy plants coming out 'like weak lidless eyes' (p. 295), and puddles that have a 'cold, corpse-eyed luminousness' (p. 313). Brief as such figures are, they form a startling, grotesque contrast to the general tone of the novel.

These similes illustrate one typical method by which Hardy makes his figures grotesque, in that they relate nature (or sometimes an inanimate object) to unpleasant human attributes. Tess, subjected to hearing Dairyman Crick's tale of the wronged maid, sees the evening sun as 'ugly to her, like a great inflamed wound in the sky' (p. 173). Angel arises on the morning after the confession scene 'in the light of a dawn ... ugly and furtive, as though associated with a crime' (p. 302). The stack of straw beside the threshing machine appears 'as the *faeces* of the same buzzing red glutton' (p. 424).

The other common method by which he constructs a grotesque simile is just the opposite: humanity is compared to the less pleasant manifestations of nature. Tess is twice compared to a fly crawling across the landscape (pp. 136, 364), an iconic indication of her—and humanity's—insignificance against the vast and indifferent bosom of Nature. The calm of that Nature, symbolized by Egdon Heath, is disturbed by activities which beside those of a town would appear only 'a creeping of the flesh of somnolence' (p. 123). Charley, approaching Eustacia, also looks 'like a fly on a negro' against the blackness of the heath; and after Eustacia has become intrigued by Clym, Wildeve has to her only the 'rayless outline of the sun [seen] through smoked glass' (p. 172).

Perhaps these similes are not unduly grotesque, but two others of the same sort certainly seem to be, as well as seeming to be profoundly iconic. Twice Hardy describes the inside of his most fascinating heroines' mouths: Eustacia laughs at Venn, unclosing her lips 'so that the sun shone into her mouth as into a tulip, and lent it a similar scarlet fire' (p. 104). The clustered associations of beauty and passion, combined with the clinical comparison are as bizarre, almost, as one could wish. But when Hardy describes Tess's mouth when she is yawning we are even more disturbed: 'he saw the red interior of her mouth as if it had been a snake's' (p. 217). Freudian implications to one side, here is clearly a startling and compressed indication of perception. In a flash Angel's character is revealed to us, for it is he who sees his beloved this way. In the midst of the Talbothays idyll, of Eden, as it were, we catch hints of evil and betrayal. Angel is not only a sanctimonious sceptic but also the type of man— like Clym Yeobright in this respect—who sees in the fundamental innocence and beauty of natural things a still more fundamental depravity. And because he thus sees we are informed as to the state of his soul—the bottomless crack that lies within it. The rest of the description of Tess—'her face ... flushed with sleep ... the brim-fulness of her nature' breathing from her, and 'the most spiritual beauty bespeak[ing] itself flesh'— emphasizes this theme. Angel's relation to her is perverted by the corruption of cold heart, as Alec's is the corruption of a burning wilfulness; between them they destroy her because her direct and natural sexuality fascinates beyond their capacity for love. We might say that Angel's seeing her mouth like a serpent's symbolizes that she is going to bring about his destruction, too. There is a perverted kind of truth in Alec's saying that she has ruined him; similarly she is to wreck the upside-down Eden of Angel's cold intellectual existence.

Not the least extraordinary thing about this simile is its place, appearing as it does as a sudden fissure or crevasse in the smooth surface of the Talbothays world. Momentarily we glimpse a cold and frightening depth beneath our feet which we may half forget as we go on but which still lingers in the back of our memory, haunting us. In many places Hardy uses this technique of the sudden fissure, more usually in brief scenes and descriptions rather than in isolated similes:

> They went noiselessly over mats of starry moss, rustled through interspersed tracts of leaves, skirted trunks with spreading roots whose mossed rinds made them like hands, wearing green gloves; elbowed old elms and ashes with great forks, in which stood pools of water that overflowed on rainy days and ran down their stems in green cascades. On older trees still than these, huge lobes of fungi grew like lungs (*Woodlanders*, pp. 58–9).

Here is the corruption of Tess's garden again, while toward the end of the novel Hardy shows us a beech tree with 'vast arm-pits' and a black slug climbing it, more fungi, rotting stumps 'rising from their mossy setting like black teeth from green gums' (p. 376). Repellent enough, certainly, and sufficiently grotesque, this description serves an iconic function as well because it reflects Grace Melbury's despair, her projection into nature of her state of mind. Hardy's genius for the macabre was seldom more aptly combined with his metaphysical intent. Despite its 'unreality'—or perhaps because of it—the scene is one of his best.

Especially is this marriage of meaning and feeling true of the splendid

Stonehenge scene in *Tess of the d'Urbervilles*, assuredly one of Hardy's greatest imaginative moments. Usually this is viewed as painfully pat symbolism: that Tess should be immolated to chaos and old night in this temple dedicated to human sacrifice and ancient superstition is only too appropriate, clear evidence of Hardy's scheming. But the result of the daring incongruity and the brilliant evocation of sensory effects far outweighs the manipulated obviousness of the scene. We are right there, with Angel and Tess, stumbling among the monoliths, hearing the wind strumming against them 'like the notes of some gigantic one-stringed harp.' And it is like a dream, as real as touch, yet as eerie and fantastic as the nightmare from which we cannot wake. Like the gurgoyle, an incident which in itself has existential particularity undergoes a sea-change because of its situation and emphasis, and becomes monstrous, unearthly.

There are many other similar scenes about which it would be interesting to speculate as to their function and the reasons why Hardy used them in just the way he did. Perhaps he merely wished to add some dramatic color, in a kind of expressionistic way; or perhaps he regarded the scenes and figures primarily as a means of portraying character or as symbolism. Or perhaps there are less rational reasons for the constant evocation of morbidity, reasons which an amateur Freudian would enjoy probing into. That Hardy wrote primarily 'realistic' novels in which staring dead eyes, decaying teeth, and loathsome fungi obtrude suddenly like a piece of bad meat at a country picnic might be very revealing.

But such speculations are bad psychology and not very illuminating criticism. A more useful inquiry would be into the aesthetic results of Hardy's grotesque imagery. Here we can say that it is important, first, in contributing to what Geurard terms Hardy's 'anti-realism.' Hardy himself felt that Art requires disproportion, distortion from reportorial reality. Thus we find the intentional coincidence, formal counterpointings, the characters warped out of resemblance to ordinary people. The grotesque increases this wrenching and twisting of the frame of the real to provide a more penetrating vision, a more significant aesthetic experience. Imagery, as we now realize, is as much a part of the meaning in a novel as are character and plot; the peculiarly trenchant imagery of the grotesque is especially meaningful in its emotive meaning, its presentational effect.

The obtrusiveness of the grotesque is also aesthetically effective. In its sudden incongruity it provides an enrichment and thickening of the aesthetic texture, comparable to the effect of dissonance in music or an eccentric distortion of perspective in painting. While Hardy's novels would still have much to say without the grotesque, they would often lack that essential touch of strangeness which lifts them above the ruck of Victorian melo-dramatic or realistic fiction. When the beautiful Tess shows the red interior of her mouth, we are presented with a dissonance that raises this part of the novel to another plane of artistic interest. The casual nature of the detail does not detract from its impact, but may in fact intensify it. A glimpse of hell is a glimpse of hell, and no lengthy perusal is necessary.

Dissonance not only enriches the aesthetic effect but also bears with it a metaphysical implication. The nightmare quality of the imagery is symptomatic of a basic corruption in Hardy's world, a green and pleasant land where the herbage is occasionally brushed aside to reveal the morass which lies beneath. The imagery is thus iconic—it *means* rather than just is. The gurgoyle calls up old horrors usually hidden by the light of reason, and to picture a wood as decayed and lacerated is not only to set up an equation between the world of men and Nature, but also to suggest that decay and laceration are fundamental.

Thus it seems safe to say that the grotesque plays an important role in Hardy's fiction. Though there is not a great deal of it, it is startlingly effective and evocative. To portray the quaint 'volk' or a universe in which the President of the Immortals holds sway is hardly enough to make Hardy the fascinating and powerful novelist that he is. It is his poetic insight, his sensitivity to the image, which makes his thesis live. Gurgoyles and Dutch clocks, dead eyes and fungi, ephemerons and cuckoo-spittle—these are essential ingredients in presenting to us the unique quality of Hardy's vision.

Notes

1. Page references to Hardy's novels are from Harper's Modern Classics Edition (New York, 1918–22) except *Desperate Remedies* (Harper, 1912).

2. I use *iconic* in the same sense as W.K. Wimsatt: an image 'which is not merely a bright picture ... but also an interpretation of reality in its metaphoric and symbolic dimensions' (*The Verbal Icon* [University of Kentucky Press, 1954], 'Note on the Title,' facing p. i).

3. Florence E. Hardy, *The Early Life of Thomas Hardy* (New York: Macmillan, 1928), p. 299.

4. *Thomas Hardy: The Novels and Stories* (Harvard University Press, 1949), p. 22.

196
Hardy the Novelist: A Reconsideration

———————— ◆ ————————

ARNOLD KETTLE

A recent number of *The Critical Quarterly* contained a review-article by Philip Larkin under the title: 'Wanted: Good Hardy Critic'. [see ch. 156, vol. III—ed.] I refer to this not because I wish to put myself forward as an applicant for the vacant post but because I think Mr Larkin's title illuminates a situation. There is a fairly widespread doubt about Hardy among current practitioners of Eng. Lit., and I think the doubt (which tells us as much perhaps about twentieth-century literary criticism as about Hardy) is associated with a sense that he has not yet been adequately 'dealt with' by the profession.

The situation is not unlike that surrounding the reputation of Dickens until fairly recently. Everyone was sure that Dickens was a great writer except the highbrows and the academics. Now Dickens has been instated and you can find as many symbols, themes, archetypal myths and Freudian neuroses (as well as PhD subjects) in his work as anywhere outside Shakespeare. But for a long time there was a rather ridiculous discrepancy between Dickens's reputation as one of the handful of writers whom almost everyone thought one of the very great and the general unwillingness of serious literary criticism to come to terms with him. I think there is something of the same problem with Hardy. And although Hardy as a novelist is not at all like Dickens I suspect that some of the underlying difficulties we have had with both of them are not unrelated.

For myself, I have no doubt that Hardy is one of the great novelists and feel very suspicious of any attempt to present a 'tradition' of the English novel which leaves him out or plays him down. I do not think he is adequately 'placed', as Dr Leavis does, by a patronizing reference to 'the good little Thomas Hardy'. Nor can I feel much happier about the urbane treatment meted out by Mr J.I.M. Stewart in the last volume of the *Oxford History of English Literature*. Of relatively recent books on Hardy much the best seems to me to be Douglas Brown's, but that is a small book and rather

SOURCE The W.D. Thomas Memorial Lecture, University College of Swansea, 1966.

disappointingly jibs when it reaches the two main hurdles—*Jude* and *The Dynasts*. So I understand what Philip Larkin means when he complains about the state of Hardy criticism.

What links Hardy with Dickens—and makes them both a problem to many twentieth-century critics—is that they were both, in a rather basic sense, unsophisticated writers. I do not mean by this that they were not interested in the moral and formal aspects of their art, but rather that they both looked at life, as artists, from below rather than above. This is really the essence of my theme: the need to see Hardy in a more 'popular', 'democratic' tradition than has sometimes been done. Hardy was, for an artist, an exceptionally well-read man who kept abreast of current philosophical and even scientific developments with remarkable conscientiousness; but his sensibility was not at all that of the typical modern intellectual. His almost pathological inability (in marked contrast to Dickens) to live in London or any large town reflects far more than a preference for the peace and quiet of country life: it was the *values* of urban life that oppressed him.

Perhaps I am over-simplifying. For the cozy picture of Hardy the simple countryman perpetually surrounded by rustic pleasures and no less rural calamities is a false one too. Perhaps it is more to the point to emphasize, deep in Hardy's life and art, a contradiction, and a strangely fruitful one, between two tendencies. On the one hand there is the rather conservative and conventional literary man, prepared to be guided by his snobbish wife through the London season and finding himself, with surprise but pleasure, accepted by the very best people; a figure who achieved a certain niche in the Establishment and an inevitable place in Poet's Corner (with Prime Minister, Leader of the Opposition, and the major literary lions of the day carrying his coffin): and on the other hand the curiously lonely and uncompromising figure who terrified the publishers and shocked the bishops and maintained throughout his life attitudes so radical and unpopular that even nearly forty years after his death we cannot always easily persuade ourselves that he really believed what he wrote.

This contradiction—between the conservative and the radical—informs Hardy's art just as persistently as it divided his life. Already in one of the first and least disturbing of his fictions—*Under the Greenwood Tree*—you can see it operating. Fancy Day, the lively little school-teacher, has to choose between the simple country virtues of honest Dick Dewy and the more glamorous sophistication of the young parson—the contrast symbolized at one point by the possession, or not, of an umbrella. The issues involved have already been dramatized by the competition for priority in the musical aspects of the church services between the old-fashioned quire to which the Dewy family are attached and the new organ which Fancy herself, dressed to the nines for the occasion, plays.

> So they (the Quire) stood and watched the curls of hair trailing down the back of the successful rival, and the waving of her feather as she swayed her head. After a few tuned notes and uncertain touches her playing became markedly correct, and towards the end full and free, but, whether from prejudice or unbiassed judgement, the venerable body of musicians could not help thinking that the simpler notes they had been wont to bring forth were more in keeping with the simplicity of their old church than the crowded chords and interludes it was her pleasure to produce.

A little scene like this does more than dramatize the conflict between older and newer ways; it illustrates one of Hardy's recurring dilemmas. Fancy's playing becomes 'markedly correct' and finally 'full and free'. Fancy, you see, has had the advantages of education, and these help her, through learning 'correctness', to flower. But whose side is Hardy on? The whole tendency of *Under the Greenwood Tree* is to celebrate the virtues of the older, rural culture of the Dewys at the expense of the newer liveliness and instability which Fancy touches off, (and Fancy herself is a predecessor of the more dangerously corrupted girls like Bathsheba and Eustacia and Grace Melbury). Yet Hardy knows very well that the issue isn't so simple. He cannot reject education for his heroines any more than he can reject the realities of Darwin and T.H. Huxley for himself. The somewhat naïve phrase 'markedly correct' (presumably she didn't strike too many wrong notes) to describe Fancy's accomplishment tells us a good deal not merely about Hardy's dilemma but about his style too. He is deeply suspicious of sophisticated attitudes but recognizes the need for a more 'advanced' culture and in some respects accepts rather innocently its values and vocabulary. Already the desperate fate that was to destroy Jude—his need for Christminster and his contempt for Christminster—is at work.

Hardy's style certainly has its problems. The self-conscious philosophical asides, the conscientious toning up of key passages by classical allusions and poetic quotations (only too often from Swinburne), the not infrequent use of absurd long words: none of these characteristics is calculated to win over the twentieth-century reader. At the very climax of *Tess* when Angel's feelings are tested and extended to the utmost he exclaims—in all the intimacy of mutual self-revelation—'My God—how can forgiveness meet such a grotesque—prestidigitation as that!' Fitzpiers replies to Giles Winterborne, who has asked if he is not rightly in love with Grace Melbury, in these terms (and, although implying a different way of life, they are not meant to be ridiculous):

> 'People living insulated, as I do by the solitude of this place get charged with emotive fluid like a Leyden jar with electric, for want of some conductor at hand to disperse it. Human love is a subjective thing—the essence itself of man, as that great thinker Spinoza says—*ipsa hominis essentia*—it is a joy accompanied by an idea which we project against any suitable object on the line of our vision; just as the rainbow iris is projected against an oak, ash or elm tree indifferently. So that if any other young lady should have appeared instead of the one who did appear I should have quoted the same lines from Shelley about her as about the one I saw. Such miserable creatures of circumstances are we all.'

This seems to have been how Hardy really thought an educated man talks.

One could without difficulty find more examples. But do they really, when all's said, matter much? Or, rather, does not Hardy's 'provincial gaucheness' which Dr Leavis finds so inferior to George Eliot's poise, make its own important contribution to the effect he is after? Hardy's style has, very often, some of the qualities that one associates with self-education in general and the particular climate of the rationalist movement of his day—one thinks of Winwood Reade, the South Place Ethical Society and the beginnings of the WEA; this seems to me an authentic and essential part of the Hardy world. He was not unaware of the challenge it offered to Establishment critics like Matthew Arnold and frankly met the charge of provincialism. 'Arnold is wrong about provincialism' he wrote in his note-book, 'if he means anything more than a provincialism of style and manner in exposition. A certain provincialism of feeling is invaluable.'

I think it is important to face the problem of Hardy's naïveté squarely and not feel the need either to ignore or excuse it. It is a bit like Dickens's vulgarity, a trial to refined persons but inseparable from his strength. One of the merits of some recent emphases that link Hardy with the ballad tradition is that they recognize this. But when Mr Donald Davidson says 'He wrote as a ballad-maker would write if a ballad-maker were to have to write novels' one feels impelled—while applauding the insight—to add a ballad-maker with very nineteenth-century preoccupations and an unusual number of 'advanced' opinions. Mr Davidson, in the essay I have just quoted from—'The Traditional Basis of Thomas Hardy's Fiction'—is bothered about Hardy's uniqueness as ballad-maker among modern writers. 'I do not know how to account for him' he says. And the very sophisticated Harvard critic, Albert J. Guerard, states the same problem in another form: 'Why Hardy grew more and more pessimistic—as his own fortunes waxed, as he moved towards success both literary and financial—appears to be beyond the biographers' reach.'

I do not think, myself, that the problem is really quite so intractable. Of course, in one sense a great writer can never be 'explained': no-one could have foreseen his existence or created the conditions for an inevitable flowering. But that a writer born and bred in rural Dorset in the middle of the nineteenth century should have felt deeply—upon his pulses—the tragic situation of the South-of-England peasantry at this time does not strike me as so very extraordinary. It is all very well for Professor Guerard to complain that Hardy's pessimism does not accord with the facts, because the standard of living of the agricultural population actually improved during this period; but Hardy wasn't chiefly concerned with standard of living: it was the destruction of the old rural *culture* that worried him and the replacement of the older relationships, grounded in centuries of custom and shared neces-sities, by new relationships based on nothing kinder than the negotiation of a wage contract. The way in the novels (and especially in *Tess*) we see the age-old festivals of the countryside—Lady Day, Candlemas, Michaelmas—originally based on the movement of the seasons and later overlaid with a Christian significance, becoming merely dates for the commencement and expiry of wage agreements illustrates very potently Hardy's awareness of this process. A few years back I described *Tess* as being 'about' the destruction of the peasantry rather than about a pure woman. I would not put it quite that way any longer—what I wrote now seems to me a bit one-sided and insufficiently close to Hardy's deepset intention and impact—but I still feel quite sure that Tess's tragedy, like Marty South's, is indissolubly bound up with a social process of which Hardy was, on every level, deeply, hauntedly aware.

The danger of putting too much emphasis on the rural basis of Hardy's novels is that of making them seem quaint and folksy. Everyone notices the recurring themes that wend through the books—in particular the conflict between the values of the town and those of the rural community. Almost all the figures who cause the trouble in the books—from the perverse Miss Aldclyffe in *Desperate Remedies* to Sergeant Troy, Eustacia, Fitzpiers, Mrs Charmond and Angel Clare (to say nothing of Alec D'Urberville)—share in some way the corrupting and cosmopolitan sophistication of the town—and are not infrequently linked—if only by marriage—with the North of England, an area for Hardy of unknown but sinister qualities all connected with industrialism. It is therefore tempting to stress a contrasting 'idyllic' flavour in the country communities which are being undermined. But this is not in fact Hardy's note. Life in the Hintocks in the wonderful novel *The Woodlanders* is not idyllic. Giles and Marty are not 'pastoral' figures. Nor is there anything mystic about their close relationship with nature and its processes. It is based on observation, experience and work. It is true that at certain points they take upon themselves qualities and implications of a wider significance than their personal parts in the story. When Grace, about to be married to Fitzpiers, looks out of the in-window in Sherton Abbas, the scene she watches evokes a whole culture and Giles takes on a more than personal role.

> In the yard between Grace and the orchards there progressed a scene natural to the locality at this time of the year. An apple-mill and press had been erected on the spot, to which some men were bringing fruit from divers points in mawn baskets, while others were grinding them, and others wringing down the pomace, whose sweet juice gushed forth into tubs and pails. The superintendent of the proceedings, to whom the others spoke as master, was a young yeoman of prepossessing manner and aspect, whose form she recognized in a moment. He had hung his coat to a nail in the outhouse wall, and wore his shirt sleeves rolled up beyond his elbows, to keep them unstained while he rammed the pomace into the bags of horsehair. Fragments of apple-rind had alighted upon the brim of his hat—probably from the bursting of a bag—while brown pips from the same fruit were sticking among the down upon his fine round arms, and his beard.

The contemporary critic, well up on Dionysiac revels and fertility ritual, will not fail to appreciate such a passage. A comparison with the fourth act of *The Winter's Tale* is perhaps irresistible. Yet Hardy is of course working in a convention far more basically realistic than Renaissance Pastoral. Nature, one might say, is presented in contrast to the artificiality of the sophisticated life into which Grace's education has introduced her. But even that gives a somewhat false, because over-simplified, impression. *The Woodlanders* is as permeated with the social problem of the perils of 'rising' in the world as is *Our Mutual Friend.* Nature, in the novels, is not simply the world of fruit and trees, sticks and stones—splendid as he is with them—it is always linked with man and his history and his work and almost always used as a contrast with ideas.

Sometimes the ideas are contemporary trends and fashions from a more cosmopolitan world. A figure like Eustacia Vye in *The Return of the Native* with her restless boredom and frustrated romanticism has her affinities with Madame Bovary and Hedda Gabler and it is not, I think, irrelevant to link the 'regional' Hardy occasionally with some of the major issues of European contemporary culture. He was not, after all, unaware of them. But the chief point one would wish to emphasize is the negative rôle, in novel after novel, of any way of thinking that gives abstract ideas or principles a priority over the actual needs of specific situations. This is particularly striking in *Tess of the d'Urbervilles*. It is interesting that at the climax of the novel, when Angel cruelly rejects Tess, part of the background of the scene is a ruined abbey behind the mill where the newly-married couple are staying. The mill had been 'in centuries past attached to the monastic establishment. The mill still worked on, food being a perennial necessity; the abbey had perished, creeds being transient.' Hardy's authorial comment on Angel's tragic mistake is that he has allowed himself to be influenced by general principles to the disregard of the particular instances'. In opposition to the limitation and inadequacies of the conventional social attitudes of his time Hardy consistently evokes a world of actions and values more truly 'natural' and therefore more fully human. Against the false, unnecessary sorrow Tess is forced to bear because of her social sin is posed the genuine, natural sorrow involved in the death of her child: against the unsatisfactoriness of creeds and dogmas is posed: ' "the appetite for joy" which pervades all creation, that tremendous force which sways humanity to it purpose ...'. The positive value to which Hardy appeals in *Tess of the d'Urbervilles* is life, 'the great passionate pulse of existence, unwarped, uncorrected, untrammelled by those creeds which futilely attempt to check what wisdom would be content to regulate'. The purity of Tess, warm and natural, is contrasted with that of Mercy Chant, cold and class-bound. Tess is pure because in the central quality of her life and feelings she is, in this sense, natural.

But nature is not, in Hardy's novels, contrasted with society as such. On the contrary, the natural and the social are never fully separable. Man is a part of nature which he touches and transforms through his work, thereby transforming himself. Hardy may suspect ideas and hate idealism but he never questions the social nature of man and the profundity of his sense of this emerges in his all-pervasive sense of history. Take the description of the village of Marygreen at the beginning of *Jude*:

> It was as old-fashioned as it was small, and it rested in the lap of an undulating upland adjoining the North Wessex downs. Old as it was, however, the well-shaft was probably the only relic of the local history that remained absolutely unchanged. Many of the thatched and dormered dwelling-houses had been pulled down of late years, and many trees felled on the green. Above all, the original church, hump-backed, wood-turreted, and quaintly hipped, had been taken down, and either cracked up into heaps of road-metal in the lane, or utilized as pig-sty walls, garden seats, guard-stones to fences, and rockeries in the flower-beds of the neighbourhood. In place of it a tall new building of modern Gothic design, unfamiliar to English eyes, had been erected on a new piece of ground by a certain obliterator of historic records who had run down from London and back in a day. The site whereon so long had stood the ancient temple to the Christian divinities was not even recorded on the green and level grass-plot that had immemorially been the churchyard, the obliterated graves being commemorated by eighteenpenny cast-iron crosses warranted to last five years.

Visually this is excellent; but the principal effect is less visual than historical. That the architect of the new church should have come down from London and returned the same day tells its own tale. Nor is it an easy nostalgia that Hardy is playing on. He is not against metal-based roads, it is the actual process of historical change in their complex ramifications upon the countryside and its people that he is most concerned to capture.

All of Hardy's novels are, in the broad sense, historical novels and not least the final, most problematical and most contemporary book from which I have just quoted. *Jude* may not be Hardy's masterpiece—it lacks the extraordinary artistic unity and radiance of *Tess* and *The Woodlanders*—but it is certainly his most ambitious, most courageous book. The remarkable thing, of course, is that, in some ways an old-fashioned and even clumsy Victorian novel, it presses so insistently into the twentieth century. Jude's decision to turn his back on Marygreen and seek not only his education but his living in Oxford represents Hardy's own recognition that the rural society to which he was so deeply committed was in fact, for better or worse, irrevocably gone. If Tess is the last peasant-heroine Jude is the first working-class hero. He moves into, and feels an instinctive solidarity with, the world of the twentieth-century urban proletariat. The most surprising thing about the Christminster section of *Jude the Obscure* is not so much the bitter disillusionment with the university set-up (impressive as this is when one recalls Hardy's naturally respectful attitude towards established learning and the layers of romantic glamour surrounding Oxford) but Jude's discovery, in the university town itself, of quite another kind of life.

> He began to see that the town life was a book of humanity infinitely more palpitating, varied and compendious than the gown life. These struggling men and women before him were the reality of Christminster, though they knew little of Christ or Minster. That was one of the humours of things. The floating population of students and teachers, who did know both in a way, were not Christminster in a local sense at all.
>
> He looked at his watch, and, in pursuit of this idea, he went on till he came to a public hall, where a promenade concert was in progress. Jude entered, and found the room full of shop youths and girls, soldiers, apprentices, boys of eleven smoking cigarettes, and light women of the more respectable and amateur class. He had tapped the real Christminster life.

Jude is not, of course, a typical working-man in the sense of being an average one; but he is typical in a far more fruitful way, artistically; for he embodies in his thoughts and feelings so many of the deepest aspirations of his class and generation—for education, for an enlarged professional skill, for a more scientific philosophy, and above all for personal and sexual relationships based on a new level of candour and equality. And Jude, for all his misfortunes and mistakes, his inadequacies and sillinesses, is a true hero of our time. His own analysis of his predicament, as he lies dying, is true and, for that reason, very moving.

> As for Sue and me when we were at our best, long ago—when our minds were clear, and our love of truth fearless—the time was not ripe for us! Our ideas were fifty years too soon to be any good to us. And so the resistance they met with brought reaction in her, and recklessness and ruin on me!

It is not fortuitous that D. H. Lawrence should have found so much in Hardy to touch and stimulate him. His analysis of the relationship of Jude and Sue is on one level absurd but on a deeper one highly relevant. Lawrence is, of course, bitterly unsympathetic to Sue whom he regards—not without some justification—as an intellectual version of the strip-tease girl. What is good about his 'Study of Thomas Hardy' is his instinctive recognition that Hardy had got on to so many central contemporary issues in his analysis of personal relationships.

What bothers many readers about *Jude*—and, for that matter, about Hardy's novels as a whole—is the determinist implication which lies so deep in it. It is this that is generally referred to when people complain of Hardy's pessimism—a sense that he gives his books too rigid a pattern and takes a certain perverse pleasure in turning the screws of coincidence or fatality to do down the aspirations of his characters. Isn't it a bit much that when Jude finally persuades Sue to live with him (though as yet platonically) they should land up at the very hotel in Aldbrickham where he has previously taken Arabella? Near the beginning of the book poor Jude can't even take the fatal Arabella out to tea without finding a picture of Samson and Delilah on the wall of the cottage. One can understand a reader's exasperation at these coincidences, especially since Hardy writes in a convention deceptively near to a naturalistic realism. But I think the complaints betray a rather

461

fundamental failure to respond to Hardy's basic methods. These are not naturalistic novels. Dr Leavis's category 'the novel as a dramatic poem' really describes them best, and it is almost as irrelevant to object to the use of the Martyrs' Memorial as Jude and Sue's first meeting place as it would be to complain about the coincidences in *Romeo and Juliet*. Star-crossed lovers have to be star-crossed. If the underlying emotional truth and historical plausibility of a situation are established the author has the right (even the necessity) to find what expression for it he can. Of course there are moments in the novels when Hardy does fail to meet a challenge—I am inclined to think the actual seduction scene in *Tess* is one—but by and large the plots of the novels, including *Jude*, do reinforce the underlying patterns of their conception.

Are these patterns deterministic to a point which robs them of the impulse and resilience of actual life and replaces that by a limiting and abstract dogmatism? I don't think so. There are moments in all the books, it is true, when it is hard to acquit Hardy of a certain morbid self-indulgence, the sort of thing one associates with A. E. Housman in his more parodiable moments. In some of the novels—in *Two on a Tower* for instance and even in the much better *Mayor of Casterbridge*—there is a rather deep tendency for Hardy's pattern to impose itself on the life he touches in a restrictive way. But on the whole the charge of mechanism seems to me quite untrue—and even in some of the apparently more vulnerable passages like the Father Time episodes of *Jude* or the final phase of *Tess*. The extraordinary thing about the achievement here is the sense Hardy succeeds in conveying—in those few pathetic and, in one sense, unreal days Tess and Angel spend together after the murder—of a triumph as well as of a defeat, so that the title of this section of the book, 'Fulfilment', is by no means wholly ironical.

Hardy was always indignant and hurt when he was accused of pessimism, and I think he was right. He recognizes, of course, a very strong element of determinism in human existence; his people are not wholly free: but they are free enough—free enough to recognize and make real choices, free enough to be defeated like Grace and Sue or to go on battling, like Marty and Jude, to the end of their lives; free enough to make irreparable mistakes or to struggle to make their lives whole and unified, at one with the external world; free enough, in short, to be human beings.

197

Thomas Hardy and Turner—The Painter's Eye

——————◆——————

EVELYN HARDY

It is strange that among all of the many painters referred to in his novels and notebooks Thomas Hardy never once mentions Constable. One would have suspected that this painter of the Suffolk Stour, with his pre-impressionist visions of mill streams and cottages, rotting posts and locks under cloud-burdened skies, would have appealed more than any other painter to a writer who knew and loved the Dorset Frome and Stour landscapes as intensely as Constable loved his own. Unexpectedly, Hardy's favourite painter proves to be none other than Turner, who died when he was eleven years old, an artist who came to have a profound influence on his work at a time when Turner was not generally acknowledged to be 'one of the major painters of the world'.

In all that has been written on Hardy by the scholars of many countries no one has commented on his possession of the painter's eye. Even Lord David Cecil, a discerning critic, dismissed Hardy's love of painting as merely that of the self-made man in search of culture. But it was more than this, for Hardy was born with the painter's love of the miracle of light and colour and—later—in variations in the quality of both. We have his own account of how he used to sit on the stairs of the Bockhampton home as a small child, waiting for the afterglow of the setting sun to 'intensify' the Venetian red of the staircase walls. This awareness, this observation of, and attempt to depict in words the effects of light and colour—or the *lack* of both—became a life-long preoccupation. One finds endless examples of this in his prose—less in his poetry, although we might quote 'O the opal and the sapphire of that wandering western sea' as one example of Turner-like, contrasted colours in his poetry.

In his first published novel—*Desperate Remedies*—we find Hardy's description of the cook moving serenely about in the great house kitchen among the reflections of firelight on the polished surfaces of copper and brass sauce-

SOURCE *London Magazine*, June, July, 1975, pp. 17–27.

pans, kettles, knobs, jacks and handles. The sub-title of his second novel, *Under the Greenwood Tree*, was 'A Rural Painting of the Dutch School', revealing those twenty-minute periods stolen from his lunch hour when he was working for Blomfield, in which he studied paintings in the National Gallery—studies that he continued in the South Kensington Museum Exhibition of 1862, the Grosvenor Gallery, and later in the long galleries of manor houses to which he had *entrée* when he had become famous. The number of painters alluded to by him comes to more than sixty, ranging through the Italian, French, Dutch, Spanish and English schools. Hardy himself was no mean artist in pen-and-ink sketches, like that of the fiddles in his Max Gate study, or the one showing the view from his London lodgings where he sat up late at night writing his early poetry. But the proof of his discerning eye for light and colour lies in his novels, in the countless descriptions of landscape—the dun tones of Egdon Heath or Thorncombe Wood at twilight, the yawning darkness of a churchyard vault lit by candlelight; or in the vivid colours of country clothing and vehicles picked out with the accuracy of David Cox—a farmer's yellow gaiters, a dairyman's 'snowy smock', the field-women's 'rusty wroppers', a man's primrose-coloured waistcoat or 'a neckerchief as bright as a marigold'. An old woman wears a shawl with 'a steeped aspect' which comes from age—'neither tawny, russet, hazel nor ash'. The wheels of gigs and farm-carts are painted with the brush strokes of Stubbs—a 'gorgeous yellow' gig streaked with blue ... has 'red wheels outlined with a darker shade', while old farm wagons look like nothing so much as 'ships of the line at Trafalgar'.

Degrees of, and variations in, darkness fascinate this writer, and thorn patterns attract him. In the demonic storm of *Far from the Madding Crowd* Gabriel's smock is covered with 'a dancing pattern of thorn twigs, the light reaching him through a leafless intervening hedge'; and the light from an early morning candle throws 'a moving pattern of shade on Marty's face' in *The Woodlanders*. Profiles also attract him—Tess's against the flank of a cow she is milking, or of an old woman's against a cottage wall, likened by Hardy to a charcoal drawing; a third is described as having the 'shadowlessness' of a Holbein drawing. One of the most memorable of these profiles is that of John Stuart Mill, who influenced Hardy strongly in his youth, to be found in the pages of *The Times* in 1906. Here Hardy describes Mill as an old man standing in front of St Paul's, Covent Garden—'his vast, pale brow, so thin-skinned as to show the blue veins', exposed in relief against the blue shadow of the church 'with cameo clearness'. His marvellous description of the painter Watts in old age combines a visual impression with an intuitive one: 'that old small man with a grey coat and black velvet skull-cap who, when he saw one of his picture-frames pressing against a figure on canvas, moved it away gently, *as if the figure could feel.*'

But what of Turner's influence on this young man with the impressionable eye and retentive memory? Where do we find *proof* of Hardy's love for this painter in his writing, or of Turner's influence on it? The answer is in his novels, and also in the notebook entries included in his autobiography. Out of the scores of artists mentioned by Hardy in his prose Turner is the only one to be mentioned twice by name in his novels, and four times in his notes. In *A Pair of Blue Eyes* his third novel written when he was thirty-two, Hardy names Tuner for the first time, in a short description with colours as vivid as some of the painter's own. Stephen and Knight are looking down from the upper rooms of a London house onto a crowd below—'surging, bustling and packing up and down. Gaslight flared from the butchers' stalls, illuminating the lumps of flesh to splotches of vermilion, *like the wild colouring of Turner's later pictures.*'

In the next year, 1874, *Far from the Madding Crowd*, the greatest of the novels of his first period, was published. Again we have a direct reference to Turner closing a description, this time of Gabriel's sheep-dog who:

> exhibited an ebony-tipped nose, surrounded by a narrow margin of pink flesh and a coat marked in random splotches approximating in colour to white and slaty grey: but the grey after years of sun and rain had been scorched and washed out of the more prominent locks, leaving them of a reddish brown, as if the blue component of the grey had faded, *like the indigo from the same kind of colour in Turner's pictures.*'

The other proofs are in the notebook entries. The first of these occurs in January, 1887, when Hardy was forty-six. He had been studying an alleged Bonnington in his drawing-room at Max Gate and had come to the conclusion that he was no longer interested in the depiction of the

> ... 'simply natural'. The much decried, mad, *late-Turner* rendering is now necessary to create my interest. The exact truth ... ceases to be of importance in art—it is a student's style ... of a period when the mind is serene and un-awakened to the tragical mysteries of life ...

Two months after making this important note he and Emma set out for Italy, nearly seventy years after Turner's first brief visit in the autumn of 1819. The effect on the two men was explosive. Both were natives of a northern island, familiar with the misty vagaries of light on the Thames. Venice heightened their perceptions, intoxicating them with its heat and glitter and the marked contrasts in cavernous shadows. Turner responded with a flood of paintings over the years, Hardy in recording what intoxicated him when the weather was not 'wet and windy'. He is fascinated by the 'shining *ferri* of the gondolas curtseying down and up against the wharf wall'. (Who but Hardy would have noted the deeper downward motion first?) For him the faces of the Doges in the frieze of the Hall of the Great Council 'float out' into the air of the room in front of him—living wraiths of their former selves; and with his mind sweeping over the intervening centuries he notes, in a phrase similar to the brush strokes and light of Turner, 'the wonderful *diaphanous*, alabaster pillars that were once in Solomon's temple', when a man stooping in a dark corner to strike a match reveals their colour. At night the lanterns above the heads of the singing gondoliers throw 'a diffused light on their faces and forms—a sky as of black velvet stretching above with its star points.' He sums up these impressions with 'Venice requires *heat* to contemplate the picture of her'.

With his architectural eye he studied buildings and their materials, noting that even a doorway in the Genoese slums was made of marble: in Florence the overpainting of the Giottos troubled him, while in Rome the sheer weight of pile upon pile of ancient ruins, stripped of their Piranesi-like draperies of ivy, depressed him. But light, always the variations in, and the quality of light is what he notes again and again. The soft, 'amber light' of Florence, he admits, is a relief after the fiercer one of Rome. In the Piazza della Signoria, in the 'stagnant' hour of three in the afternoon, he notes the 'intense white' of Neptune 'against the brown-grey houses behind', and the 'bronze forms round the [fountain's] basin ... starred with rays on their noses, elbows, knees, bosoms and shoulders'—Neptune throwing '*a secondary light*' into the nearby café.

Having made that most significant note about the 'mad, late-Turners' little more than two months before, we may assume that the writer was looking at Venetian buildings, waters, skies, dawns, sunsets and especially light, with a half-Turner eye.

Hardy's study of contrasting lights and shadows made on this visit to Italy is reflected almost immediately in one of the greatest of his novels, *Tess of the d'Urbervilles*, which he set about writing after he had crossed back to Dorset.

The second notebook entry was made two years later, again in *January*, 1889, at a Royal Academy Old Master Exhibition. It reads,

> Turner's watercolours: each is a landscape *plus* a man's soul ... What he paints chiefly is *light modified by objects*. He first recognizes the impossibility of really reproducing on canvas all that is in a landscape; then gives for that which cannot be reproduced as something else which shall have on the spectator an approximate effect to that of the real. He said, in his maddest and greatest days: 'What pictorial drug can I dose man with, which shall affect his eyes somewhat in the manner of this reality which I cannot carry to him?'—and set to make such strange mixtures as he was tending towards in 'Rain, Steam and Speed', 'The Burial of Wilkie', 'Agrippina landing with the Ashes of Germanicus', 'Approach to Venice', 'Snowstorm and a Steamboat', etc. Hence one may say, Art is the secret of how to produce by a false thing the effect of a true.

(I shall revert to the *double* importance of this note later.)

The last two references to Turner in the notebook entries were made in 1906, when Hardy was in his sixties, and in 1922, in his eighties. The 1906 entry is significant because Hardy refers to two artists working in different but closely related *media*—painting and music. He prefers, he writes,

> late Wagner as I prefer late Turner ... the idiosyncrasies of each master being more strongly shown in these strains. When a man not contented with the

grounds of his success goes on and on, and tries to achieve the impossible, then he gets profoundly interesting to me.

I do not think that Sir Kenneth Clark—as he then was—knew of this sentence in Hardy's autobiography, but fifty years after it was written Sir Kenneth remarks that, in late-Turners 'we may note a similarity to Wagner, occasionally in our minds when looking at Turner's pictures'.

The final entry, in 1922, six years before Hardy's death, is in a letter to General Morgan who had questioned just how Hardy knew that Napoleon had entered Berlin by the Potsdam-strasse. Hardy replied that he did not think he would have done so 'without authority', adding:

> You have to remember that the events generally in *The Dynasts* had to be pulled together into dramatic scenes, to show themselves to the mental eye of the reader as a picture viewed from one point; and hence it was sometimes necessary to see round corners, down crooked streets, and to shift buildings nearer each other than in reality, *as Turner did in his landscapes.*

I have called that note of 1889 'doubly important' because not only does it name Turner again, but it gives the titles of five of his paintings. These have been difficult to identify because the names have been changed since Turner's day, and without the assistance of the Librarian of the Royal Academy I should not have been able to do so. The note reveals something we had no proof of before, that Hardy had been studying Turner from the age of twenty-nine onwards. How do we know this? Because not one of the five paintings named in this entry was at the Royal Academy Exhibition of this year. Hardy was retaining in his memory what some of Turner's paintings looked like twenty years earlier—carrying Turner's vision with him for two decades. When he spoke of visiting South Kensington to study paintings in 1869, when he was twenty-nine, he was looking at the Turners which had been removed there from Marlborough House in 1859, a decade earlier—unless he had seen them on some unrecorded occasion at the National Gallery in 1876 or thereafter, when the Turners were removed to the Gallery upon its enlargement, so Martin Butlin tells me.

There were in all seventy-three Turners in the Royal Academy Exhibition of 1889. Fifty-one were *Rhine Sketches* from Ayscough Fawkes's collection at Farnley Hall. Of the remaining twenty-two, fourteen were painted after Turner's first visit to Venice in 1819, sixty-eight years before Hardy went there. Among the remaining eight were *The Field of Waterloo* (1815) and *Nelson's Monument, Great Yarmouth* (1828). Turner visited the battlefield on his second visit to the continent in August-September 1817; Hardy on his honeymoon in September 1874, a visit not recorded by him, but by his wife in her pocket *Wedding Diary*, as I have called it. Both subjects would have interested Hardy intensely, with his mind brooding since boyhood on what was to become *The Dynasts*. Like Turner's painting some of the scenes in this are in muted colours. For this Turner was criticized adversely, the Waterloo painting being called 'a night-piece against heroics', showing the suffering, or dying soldiers in half-light, the field darkened by heavy clouds that sweep across a sky dramatically lit by lightning.

As for the paintings named by Hardy the now-called *Burial of Wilkie*—Turner's name was *Peace: Burial at Sea*—was immensely popular in Hardy's day. One wonders whether he knew of Turner's *riposte* to a critic who remarked that the sails of the ship were too dark. Turner replied that if he had had a black more black in his paintbox he would have used it. Today, two of the other paintings named by Hardy have far outdistanced *The Burial* in popularity—*Rain, Steam and Speed* and *The Snowstorm* called *Snowstorm and a Steamboat* by Hardy. (Turner's title was four times as long.) What Hardy calls *The Approach to Venice* has been identified for me as *St Benedetto, looking down towards Fusina*, out of the confusing welter of Turner's Venetian paintings—a favourite of Ruskin, whom Hardy had been reading from the age of twenty-two onwards. (Three out of the four paintings given were in the recent exhibition at the Royal Academy.)

The Snowstorm is a revealing choice for Hardy. In this painting there are no visible human figures, but it was the painter's problem to indicate their supposed presence emotionally and imaginatively. Heroic endurance and human effort are suggested by the two points of lemon light from the *Ariel's* stoke-hole and the tiny speck of red light from the porthole reflected on the tumultuous waters. The colours may have been brighter when Hardy studied them since the colours today are obscured by 'dirt and discolouration under the varnish applied forty or fifty years ago', according to the Tate Gallery's Keeper of Conservation. The dark, revolving paddle-wheel—a human invention—about which the snow, smoke and salt sea-spray whirl in confusion, centres the eye on what would otherwise depict only dizzy chaos. Here was an artist who depicted, who echoed one of Hardy's deepest convictions, frequently stated in his work—that nature in her most destructive, heartless moods reveals, in man's struggle against her, his puniness but also his nobility. The *effort* to outwit her and to survive is what counts, not his death. Put more simply, in a lower key, 'The mark of man on a scene' is worth 'more than any such formed by unconscious nature.'

In *Tess of the d'Urbervilles*, which he 'settled down to write daily' seven months after returning from Venice, we find deeply poetic, deeply observed depictions of tenuous light and half-revealed substances, bearing witness to his study of light abroad and in Turner's paintings. His contrasted settings for these are north and south Dorset. In the Frome water-meadows he is concerned with dawns and sunsets, with mist, snow and fog, with 'phosphorescence' and '*evanescence*', a word also used by Turner's contemporary critics. Getting up at three in the summer mornings to call the other dairy-maids Tess meets Angel Clare in 'spectral, half-compounded, aqueous light which pervaded the open mead' impressing them 'with a feeling of isolation'. They walk in 'a mixed luminous gloom ... whilst all the landscape was in a neutral shade', in which Tess's face looks 'ghostly'. In another passage describing the valley-light on a foggy summer morning the meadows lay

> like a white sea, out of which the scattered trees rose like dangerous rocks. Birds would soar through it into the upper radiance, hang on the wing sunning themselves, or alight on the wet rails ... which now shone like glass rods. Minute diamonds of moisture from the mist hung ... upon Tess's eyelashes, and drops upon her hair, like seed pearls.

Her beauty was 'ethereal'.

But it is in the passage describing the Arctic winter in the uplands of north Dorset that Hardy achieves in words what Turner had done in paint. The arrival of 'the polar birds' shows what I mean—

> gaunt spectral creatures with tragical eyes—which had witnessed scenes of cataclysmal horror in inaccessible polar regions of a magnitude such as no human being had ever conceived, in curdling temperatures that no man could endure; which had beheld the crash of ice-bergs and the slide of snowhills by the shooting light of the Aurora; been half blinded *by the whirl of colossal storms and terraqueous distortions...*

The presage of the snow's approach is a 'blast that smelt of icebergs, arctic seas, whales and white bears, carrying the snow so that it licked the land but did not deepen on it'. Finally, in a sentence more like Turner's work than anything else that he ever wrote (having said that individual snowflakes could not be distinguished) he adds: 'The air, afflicted to pallor with the hoary multitudes that infested it, twisted and spun them eccentrically, suggesting an *achromatic chaos of things.*' Here, surely, is Turner's 'Snowstorm' remembered, and transmuted into words. Here violence, disorder and heartlessness, to which both men were attracted, is depicted.

'Eccentrically spun': what does this mean except that the snowflakes lack a placed axis and are not concentric with a fellow circle, lacking a regular orbit? And 'achromatic chaos'—what is this except chaos without colour? The wintry elements in their 'furious rages' mirror a disorder of nature provoking the same 'sense of giddiness' that Sir Kenneth Clark felt when looking at Turner's *Snowstorm*, in which the sloping horizon causes the viewer to participate in the storm. Hardy has, consciously or unconsciously, transmuted into words what Turner had done in paint. There is the same preoccupation with the whirling gyrations and vortices of nature's forces that had fascinated Turner from youth onwards, as his first painting exhibited at the Royal Academy when he was only twenty-one shows.

But it is in his descriptions of sunrises and sunsets that Hardy comes closest to Turner. (I will confine myself to the sunsets only.) These begin to appear in his first novel—*Desperate Remedies*—and continue on into a late one—*The Woodlanders*. They are the counterpart of Turner's 'sunset-cloud architecture'—Sir Kenneth's phrase. Here is a sunset in *A Laodicean*:

the sun ... streamed across the ground from below copper-coloured and lilac clouds, stretched out ... beneath a sky of pale soft green. All dark objects on the earth that lay towards the [setting sun] were overspread by a purple haze, against which a swarm of wailing gnats shone forth luminously, rising upward and floating away like sparks of fire.

Not content with describing light at eye-level he describes it reflected upward, or downward. Here it is thrown downward: 'fading away, yellow and mild as candle-light ... upper windows, facing north-west, reflected to persons in the street dissolving views of tawny cloud with brazen edges ...' (*The Hand of Ethelberta*).

In *The Mayor of Casterbridge* there is an exquisite description of 'a yellow flood of reflected light' from a passing haywain in the street below, thrown upwards into an inn room. In yet another novel a seascape sunset is painted, the northwest wind provoking frightening phenomena in the waves (stained as if with blood), and cloud colours—just such a scene as Turner, with his intimate knowledge of storms at sea, actually experienced by being lashed to the mast of the *Ariel* of the *Snowstorm* rejoiced to paint. In *Tess* the sun settles down upon the level meadows 'with the aspect of a great forge in the heavens' as 'a monstrous pumpkin moon' rises 'on the other hand'. In the lesser-known *Well-beloved*, city-dwellers on the tops of omnibuses stare at curiously-shaped, grey cloud-patterns against a sunset sky of 'topaz hues darkened here and there into richest russet'.

Lastly, in *The Woodlanders*, the most magnificent of all these sunset descriptions appears:

...the whole western sky was revealed. Between the broken clouds they could see far into the recesses of heaven, the eye journeying on under a species of golden arcades past fiery obstructions, fancied cairns, logan-stones, stalactites and stalagmites of topaz. Deeper than this their gaze passed thin flakes of incandescence till it plunged into a bottomless medium of soft green fire.

Topaz and russet; incandescence and soft-green fire; copper and lilac with soft pale green; gold and fiery red; great forges in the heavens, and waters stained with blood beneath skies of unnatural pallor; the 'opal and the sapphire' of the wandering Cornish sea—it is in descriptions of colour like these that Hardy attempted in words what Turner had achieved in his unpatterned cloud-and-sky water-colour sketches, that often appeal to us today more than the luminous sunsets of his great finished oil paintings. Turner's words on his death bed are said to have been 'The sun is God'; and for that other agnostic, Thomas Hardy, who from early childhood until old age had worshipped the sun, this belief may also have been true.

198

Thomas Hardy

———————◆———————

RAYMOND WILLIAMS

It is now conventional in critical accounts of the English novel to go on from George Eliot to Henry James. There is of course a real relation there, especially from parts of George Eliot's later novels—from the Transomes in *Felix Holt*, from Dorothea's relationships in *Middlemarch*, from Gwendolen and Grandcourt in *Daniel Deronda*. We shall need to follow that through.

But first I am interested in emphasizing a more central English tradition: from George Eliot to Hardy and then on to Lawrence, which is a very clear and in my view decisive sequence. Some years ago a British Council critic described George Eliot, Hardy and Lawrence as 'our three great auto-didacts', and as it happens his prejudice serves to indicate a very crucial fact. Why, we must ask, 'autodidact'? For all three of these writers were actively interested in learning and while they read a good deal for themselves had also a significant formal education. Their fathers were a bailiff, a builder and a miner. George Eliot was at school till sixteen and left only because her mother died and she had to go home to look after her father, though she still took regular lessons there. Hardy was at Dorchester High School till the same age and then completed his professional training as an architect. Lawrence went into the sixth form at Nottingham Hill School and after a gap went on to Nottingham University College. It is not only that by their contemporary standards these levels of formal education are high. It is also that they are higher, absolutely, than those of four out of five people in mid-twentieth-century Britain. The flat patronage of 'autodidact' can then be related to only one fact: that none of the three was in the pattern of boarding-school and Oxbridge which in the late nineteenth century came to be regarded not simply as a kind of education but as education itself. To have missed that circuit was to have missed being 'educated' at all. In other words a 'standard' education was that received by one or two per cent of the population.

All the rest were seen as 'uneducated' or else as 'autodidacts' (the later phrase was grammar-school boy and will soon, no doubt, be comprehen-

SOURCE *The English Novel from Dickens to Lawrence*, London, 1970, ch. 4, pp. 78–96.

sive). They were seen also, of course, as either comically ignorant or when they pretended to learning as awkward, over-earnest, fanatical.

The effects of this on the English imagination have been deep. To many of us, now, George Eliot, Hardy and Lawrence are important because they connect directly with our own kind of unbringing and education. They belong to a cultural tradition much older and more central in this country than the comparatively modern and deliberately exclusive circuit of what are called the public schools. And the point is that they continue to connect in this way, into a later period in which some of us have gone to Oxford or Cambridge; to myself, for instance, who came from that kind of family to Cambridge and now teach here. For it is not the education, the developed intelligence, that is really in question. How many people, if it came to it, on the British Council or anywhere else, could survive a strictly intellectual comparison with George Eliot? It is a question of the relation between education—not the marks or degrees but the substance of a developed intelligence—and the actual lives of a continuing majority of our people: people who are not, by any formula, objects of record or study or concern, but who are specifically, literally, our own families. George Eliot is the first major novelist in whom this question is active. That is why we speak of her now with a connecting respect and with a hardness—a sort of family plainness—that we have learned from our own and common experience.

It is also why we come to Hardy with interest and respect. The more I read Hardy the surer I am that he is a major novelist, but also that the problem of describing his work is central to the problem of understanding the whole development of the English novel. It is good that so many people still read him, and also that English students are reading him increasingly and with increasing respect. Yet some influential critical accounts have tried to push him aside, and even some of those who have praised him have done so in ways that reduce him. Thus he can very easily be praised as what we now call a regional novelist: the incomparable chronicler of his Wessex. Or he can be taken as the last voice of an old rural civilization. The acknowledgement, even the warm tribute, comes with the sense that the substance of his work is getting further and further away from us: that he is not a man of our world but the last representative of old rural England or of the peasantry.

Actually, the very complicated feelings and ideas in Hardy's novels, including the complicated feelings and ideas about country life and people, belong very much, I think, in a continuing world. He writes more consistently and more deeply than any of our novelists about something that is still very close to us wherever we may be living: something that can be put, in abstraction, as the problem of the relation between customary and educated life; between customary and educated feeling and thought. This is the problem we already saw in George Eliot and that we shall see again in Lawrence. It is the ground of their significant connection.

Most of us, before we get any kind of literary education, get to know and to value—also to feel the tensions of—a customary life. We see and learn from the ways our families live and get their living; a world of work and of place, and of beliefs so deeply dissolved into everyday actions that we don't at first even know they are beliefs, subject to change and challenge. Our education, quite often, gives us a way of looking at that life which can see other values beyond it: as Jude saw them when he looked across the land to the towers of Christminster. Often we know in ourselves, very deeply, how much those educated values, those intellectual pursuits, are needed urgently where custom is stagnation or where old illusions are still repeated as timeless truths. We know especially how much they are needed to understand *change*—change in the heart of the places where we have lived and worked and grown up.

The ideas, the values, the educated methods are of course made available to us if we get to a place like Christminster: if we are let in as Jude was not. But with the offer, again and again, comes another idea: that the world of everyday work and of ordinary families is inferior, distant; that now we know this world of the mind we can have no respect—and of course no affection—for that other and still familiar world. If we retain an affection Christminster has a name for it: nostalgia. If we retain respect Christminster has another name: politics or the even more dreaded sociology.

But it is more than a matter of picking up terms and tones. It is what happens to us, really happens to us, as we try to mediate those contrasted worlds: as we stand with Jude but a Jude who has been let in; or as we go back to our own places, our own families, and know what is meant, in idea and in feeling, by the return of the native.

The Hardy country is of course Wessex: that is to say mainly Dorset and its neighbouring counties. But the real Hardy country, I feel more and more, is that border country so many of us have been living in: between custom and education, between work and ideas, between love of place and an experience of change. This has a special importance to a particular generation, who have gone to the university from ordinary families and have to discover, through a life, what that experience means. But it has also a much more general importance; for in Britain generally this is what has been happening: a moving out from old ways and places and ideas and feelings; a discovery in the new of certain unlooked-for problems, unexpected and very sharp crises, conflicts of desire and possibility.

In this characteristic world, rooted and mobile, familiar yet newly conscious and self-conscious, the figure of Hardy stands like a landmark. It is not from an old rural world or from a remote region that Hardy now speaks to us; but from the heart of a still active experience, of the familiar and the changing, which we can know as an idea but which is important finally in what seem the personal pressures—the making and failing of relationships, the crises of physical and mental personality—which Hardy as a novelist at once describes and enacts.

473

But of course we miss all this, or finding it we do not know how to speak of it and value it, if we have picked up, here and there, the tone of belittling Hardy.

I want to bring this into the open. Imagine if you will the appearance and the character of the man who wrote this:

> When the ladies retired to the drawing-room I found myself sitting next to Thomas Hardy. I remember a little man with an earthy face. In his evening clothes, with his boiled shirt and high collar, he had still a strange look of the soil.

Not the appearance and the character of Thomas Hardy; but of the man who could write that about him, that confidently, that sure of his readers, in just those words.

It is of course Somerset Maugham, with one of his characteristic tales after dinner. It is a world, one may think, Hardy should never have got near; never have let himself be exposed to. But it is characteristic and important, all the way from that dinner-table and that drawing-room to the 'look of the soil', in that rural distance. All the way to the land, the work, that comes up in silver as vegetables, or to the labour that enters that company—that customary civilized company—with what is seen as an earthy face.

In fact I remember Maugham, remember his tone, when I read Henry James on 'the good little Thomas Hardy;' or F.R. Leavis saying that *Jude the Obscure* is impressive 'in its clumsy way'. For in several ways, some of them unexpected, we have arrived at that place where custom and education, one way of life and another, are in the most direct and interesting and I'd say necessary conflict.

The tone of social patronage, that is to say, supported by crude and direct suppositions about origin, connects interestingly with a tone of literary patronage and in ways meant to be damaging with a strong and directing supposition about the substance of Hardy's fiction. If he was a countryman, a peasant, a man with the look of the soil, then this is the point of view, the essential literary standpoint, of the novels. That is to say the fiction is not only about Wessex peasants, it is by one of them, who of course had managed to get a little (though hardly enough) education. Some discriminations of tone and fact have then to be made.

First, we had better drop 'peasant' altogether. Where Hardy lived and worked, as in most other parts of England, there were virtually no peasants, although 'peasantry' as a generic word for country people was still used by writers. The actual country people were landowners, tenant farmers, dealers, craftsmen and labourers, and that social structure—the actual material, in a social sense, of the novels—is radically different, in its variety, its shading, and many of its basic human attitudes from the structure of a peasantry. Secondly, Hardy is none of these people. Outside his writing he was one of the many professional men who worked within this structure, often with uncertainty about where they really belonged in it. A slow gradation of classes is characteristic of capitalism anywhere, and of rural capitalism very clearly. Hardy's father was a builder who employed six or seven workmen. Hardy did not like to hear their house referred to as a cottage, because he was aware of this employing situation. The house is indeed quite small but there is a little window at the back through which the men were paid, and the cottages down the lane are certainly smaller. At the same time, on his walk to school, he would see the mansion of Kingston Maurward (now happily an agricultural college) on which his father did some of the estate work, and this showed a sudden difference of degree which made the other distinction comparatively small though still not unimportant. In becoming an architect and a friend of the family of a vicar (the kind of family, also, from which his wife came) Hardy moved to a different point in the social structure, with connections to the educated but not the owning class, and yet also with connections through his family to that shifting body of small employers, dealers, craftsmen and cottagers who were themselves never wholly distinct, in family, from the labourers. Within his writing his position is similar. He is neither owner nor tenant, dealer nor labourer, but an observer and chronicler, often again with uncertainty about his actual relation. Moreover he was not writing for them, but about them, to a mainly metropolitan and unconnected literary public. The effect of these two points is to return attention to where it properly belongs, which is Hardy's attempt to describe and value a way of life with which he was closely yet uncertainly connected, and the literary methods which follow from the nature of this attempt. As so often when the current social stereotypes are removed the critical problem becomes clear in a new way.

It is the critical problem of so much of English fiction, since the actual yet incomplete and ambiguous social mobility of the nineteenth century. And it is a question of substance as much as of method. It is common to reduce Hardy's fiction to the impact of an urban alien on the 'timeless pattern' of English rural life. Yet though this is sometimes there the more common pattern is the relation between the changing nature of country living, determined as much by its own pressures as by pressures from 'outside', and one or more characters who have become in some degree separated from it yet who remain by some tie of family inescapably involved. It is here that the social values are dramatized in a very complex way and it is here that most of the problems of Hardy's actual writing seem to arise.

One small and one larger point may illustrate this argument, in a preliminary way. Nearly everyone seems to treat Tess as simply the passionate peasant girl seduced from outside, and it is then surprising to read quite early in the novel one of the clearest statements of what has become a classical experience of mobility:

> Mrs Durbeyfield habitually spoke the dialect; her daughter, who had passed
> the Sixth Standard in the National School under a London-trained mistress,
> spoke two languages: the dialect at home, more or less; ordinary English
> abroad and to persons of quality.

Grace in *The Woodlanders*, Clym in *The Return of the Native* represent this
experience more completely, but it is in any case a continuing theme, at a
level much more important than the trivialities of accent. And when we see
this we need not be tempted, as so often and so significantly in recent
criticism, to detach *Jude the Obscure* as a quite separate kind of novel.

A more remarkable example of what this kind of separation means and
involves is a description of Clym in *The Return of the Native* which belongs in a
quite central way to the argument I traced in *Culture and Society*:

> Yeobright loved his kind. He had a conviction that the want of most men
> was knowledge of a sort which brings wisdom rather than affluence. He wished to
> raise the class at the expense of individuals rather than individuals at the expense of
> the class. What was more, he was ready at once to be the first unit sacrificed.

The idea of sacrifice relates in the whole action to the familiar theme of a
vocation thwarted or damaged by a mistaken marriage, and we shall have to
look again at this characteristic Hardy deadlock. But it relates also to the
general action of change which is a persistent social theme. As in all major
realist fiction the quality and destiny of persons and the quality and destiny
of a whole way of life are seen in the same dimension and not as separable
issues. It is Hardy the observer who sets this context for personal failure:

> In passing from the bucolic to the intellectual life the intermediate stages are
> usually two at least, frequently many more; and one of these stages is sure to be
> worldly advance. We can hardly imagine bucolic placidity quickening to intel-
> lectual aims without imagining social aims as the transitional phase.
> Yeobright's local peculiarity was that in striving at high thinking he still cleaved
> to plain living—nay, wild and meagre living in many respects, and brotherliness
> with clowns. He was a John the Baptist who took ennoblement rather than
> repentance for his text. Mentally he was in a provincial future, that is, he was in
> many points abreast with the central town thinkers of his date ... In con-
> sequence of this relatively advanced position, Yeobright might have been called
> unfortunate. The rural world was not ripe for him. A man should be only
> partially before his time; to be completely to the vanward in aspirations is fatal
> to fame ... A man who advocates aesthetic effort and deprecates social effort is
> only likely to be understood by a class to which social effort has become a stale
> matter. To argue upon the possibility of culture before luxury to the bucolic
> world may be to argue truly but it is an attempt to disturb a sequence to which
> humanity has been long accustomed.

The subtlety and intelligence of this argument from the late 1870s come from
a mind accustomed to relative and historical thinking, not merely in the
abstract but in the process of observing a personal experience of mobility.
This is not country against town, or even in any simple way custom against
conscious intelligence. It is the more complicated and more urgent historical

476

process in which education is tied to social advancement within a class society, so that it is difficult, except by a bizarre personal demonstration, to hold both to education and to social solidarity ('he wished to raise the class'). It is the process also in which culture and affluence come to be recognized as alternative aims, at whatever cost to both, and the wry recognition that the latter will always be the first choice, in any real history (as Morris also observed and indeed welcomed).

The relation between the migrant and his former group is then exceptionally complicated. His loyalty drives him to actions which the group can see no sense in, its overt values supporting the association of education with personal advancement which his new group has already made but which for that very reason he cannot accept.

> 'I am astonished, Clym. How can you want to do better than you've been doing?'
>
> 'But I hate that business of mine ... I want to do some worthy things before I die.'
>
> 'After all the trouble that has been taken to give you a start, and when there is nothing to do but keep straight on towards affluence, you say you ... it disturbs me, Clym, to find you have come home with such thoughts ... I hadn't the least idea you meant to go backward in the world by your own free choice ...'
>
> 'I cannot help it,' said Clym, in a trouble tone.
>
> 'Why can't you do ... as well as others?'
>
> 'I don't know, except that there are many things other people care for which I don't ...'
>
> 'And yet you might have been a wealthy man if you had only persevered ... I suppose you will be like your father. Like him, you are getting weary of doing well.'
>
> 'Mother, what is doing well?'

The question is familiar but still after all these years no question is more relevant or more radical. Within these complex pressures the return of the native has a certain inevitable nullity, and his only possible overt actions can come to seem merely perverse. Thus the need for social identification with the labourers produces Clym's characteristic negative identification with them; becoming a labourer himself and making his original enterprise that much more difficult: 'the monotony of his occupation soothed him, and was in itself a pleasure'.

All this is understood and controlled by Hardy but the pressure has further and less conscious effects. Levin's choice of physical labour, in *Anna Karenina*, includes some of the same motives but in the end is a choosing of people rather than a choosing of an abstract Nature—a choice of men to work with rather than a natural force in which to get lost. This crucial point is obscured by the ordinary discussion of Hardy's attachment to country life, which would run together the 'timeless' heaths or woods and the men working on them. The original humanist impulse—'he loved his kind'—can indeed become anti-human: men can be seen as creatures crawling on this timeless expanse, as the imagery of the heath and Clym's work on it so powerfully suggests. It is a very common transition in the literature of that period but Hardy is never very comfortable with it, and the original impulse, as in *Jude the Obscure*, keeps coming back and making more precise identifications.

At the same time the separation of the returned native is not only a separation from the standards of the educated and affluent world 'outside'. It is also to some degree inevitably from the people who have not made his journey; or more often a separation which can mask itself as a romantic attachment to a way of life in which the people are merely instrumental: figures in a landscape or when the literary tone fails in a ballad. It is then easy, in an apparently warm-hearted way, to observe for the benefit of others the crudity and limitations but also the picturesqueness, the rough humour, the smocked innocence of 'the bucolic'. The complexity of Hardy's fiction shows in nothing more than this: that he runs the whole gamut from an external observation of customs and quaintnesses, modulated by a distinctly patronizing affection (as in *Under the Greenwood Tree*), through a very positive identification of intuitions of nature and the values of shared work with human depth and fidelity (as in *The Woodlanders*), to the much more impressive but also much more difficult humane perception of limitations, which cannot be resolved by nostalgia or charm or an approach to mysticism, but which are lived through by all the characters, in the real life to which all belong, the limitations of the educated and the affluent bearing an organic relation to the limitations of the ignorant and the poor (as in parts of *Return of the Native* and in *Tess* and *Jude*). But to make these distinctions and to see the variations of response with the necessary clarity we have to get beyond the stereotypes of the autodidact and the countryman and see Hardy in his real identity: both the educated observer and the passionate participant, in a period of general and radical change.

Hardy's writing, or what in abstraction can be called his style, is obviously affected by the crisis—the return of the native—which I have been describing. We know that he was worried about his prose and was reduced by the ordinary educated assumptions of his period to studying Defoe, Fielding, Addison, Scott and *The Times*, as if they could have helped him. His complex position as an author, writing about country living to people who almost inevitably saw the country as empty nature or as the working-place of their inferiors, was in any case critical in this matter of language. What have been seen as his strengths—the ballad form of narrative, the prolonged literary imitation of traditional forms of speech—seem to me mainly weaknesses. This sort of thing is what his readers were ready for: a 'tradition' rather than human beings. The devices could not in any case serve his major fiction where it was precisely disturbance rather than continuity which had to be communicated. It would be easy to relate Hardy's problem of style to the two languages of Tess: the consciously educated and the unconsciously customary. But this comparison, though suggestive, is inadequate, for the truth is that to communicate Hardy's experience neither language would serve, since neither in the end was sufficiently articulate: the educated dumb in intensity and limited in humanity; the customary thwarted by ignorance and complacent in habit. The marks of a surrender to each mode are certainly present in Hardy but the main body of his mature writing is a more difficult and complicated experiment. For example:

> The season developed and matured. Another year's instalment of flowers, leaves, nightingales, thrushes, finches, and such ephemeral creatures, took up their positions where only a year ago others had stood in their place when these were nothing more than germs and inorganic particles. Rays from the sunrise drew forth the buds and stretched them into long stalks, lifted up sap in noiseless streams, opened petals, and sucked out scents in invisible jets and breathings.
>
> Dairyman Crick's household of maids and men lived on comfortably, placidly, even merrily. Their position was perhaps the happiest of all positions in the social scale, being above the line at which neediness ends, and below the line at which the *convenances* begin to cramp natural feeling, and the stress of threadbare modishness makes too little of enough.
>
> Thus passed the leafy time when arborescence seems to be the one thing aimed at out of doors. Tess and Clare unconsciously studied each other, ever balanced on the edge of a passion, yet apparently keeping out of it. All the while they were converging, under an irresistible law, as surely as two streams in one vale.

This passage is neither the best nor the worst of Hardy. Rather it shows the many complicated pressures working within what had to seem a single intention. 'The leafy time when arborescence' is an example of mere inflation to an 'educated' style, but the use of *'convenances'*, which might appear merely fashionable, carries a precise feeling. 'Instalment' and 'ephemeral' are also uses of a precise kind, within a sentence which shows mainly the strength of what must be called an educated point of view. The consciousness of the natural process, in 'germs and inorganic particles' (he had of course learned it from Darwin who with Mill was his main intellectual influence) is a necessary accompaniment, for Hardy's purpose, of the more direct and more enjoyed sights and scents of spring. It is loss not gain when Hardy reverts to the simpler and cruder abstraction of 'Dairyman Crick's household of maids and men', which might be superficially supposed to be the countryman speaking but is actually the voice of the detached observer at a low level of interest. The more fully Hardy uses the resources of the whole language, as a precise observer, the more adequate the writing is. There is more strength in 'unconsciously studied each other', which is at once educated and engaged, than in the 'two streams in one vale', which shares with the gesture of 'irresistible law' a synthetic quality, here as of a man playing the countryman novelist.

Hardy's mature style is threatened in one direction by a willed 'Latinism' of diction or construction, of which very many particular instances can be collected (and we have all done it, having taken our education hard), but in the other direction by this much less noticed element of artifice which is too easily accepted, within the patronage we have discussed, as the countryman speaking (sometimes indeed it is literally the countryman speaking, in a contrived picturesqueness which is now the novelist's patronage of his rural characters). The mature style itself is unambiguously an educated style, in which the extension of vocabulary and the complication of construction are necessary to the intensity and precision of the observation which is Hardy's essential position and attribute.

> The gray tones of daybreak are not the gray half-tones of the day's close, though the degree of their shade may be the same. In the twilight of the morning, light seems active, darkness passive; in the twilight of evening, it is the darkness which is active and crescent, and the light which is the drowsy reverse.

This is the educated observer, still deeply involved with the world he is watching, and the local quality of this writing is the decisive tone of the major fiction.

The complication is that this is a very difficult and exposed position for Hardy to maintain. Without the insights of consciously learned history and of the educated understanding of nature and behaviour he cannot really observe at all, at a level of extended human respect. Even the sense of what is now called the 'timeless'—in fact the sense of history, of the barrows, the Roman remains, the rise and fall of families, the tablets and monuments in the churches—is a function of education. That real perception of tradition is available only to the man who has read about it, though what he then sees through it is his native country, to which he is already deeply bound by memory and experience of another kind: a family and a childhood; an intense association of people and places, which has been his own history. To see tradition in both ways is indeed Hardy's special gift: the native place and experience but also the education, the conscious inquiry. Yet then to see living people, within this complicated sense of past and present, is another problem again. He sees as a participant who is also an observer; this is the source of the strain. For the process which allows him to observe is very clearly in Hardy's time one which includes, in its attachment to class feelings and class separations, a decisive alienation.

> If these two noticed Angel's growing social ineptness, he noticed their growing mental limitations. Felix seemed to him all Church; Cuthbert all College. His Diocesan Synod and Visitations were the mainsprings of the world to the one; Cambridge to the other. Each brother candidly recognized that there were a few unimportant scores of millions of outsiders in civilized society, persons who were neither University men nor Churchmen; buy they were to be tolerated rather than reckoned with and respected.

This is what is sometimes called Hardy's bitterness, but in fact it is only sober and just observation. What Hardy sees and feels about the educated world of his day, locked in its deep social prejudices and in its consequent human alienation, is so clearly true that the only surprise is why critics now should still feel sufficiently identified with that world—the world which coarsely and coldly dismissed Jude and millions of other men—to be willing to perform the literary equivalent of that stalest of political tactics: the transfer of bitterness, of a merely class way of thinking, from those who exclude to those who protest. We did not after all have to wait for Lawrence to be shown the human nullity of that apparently articulate world. Hardy shows it convincingly again and again. But the isolation which then follows, while the observer holds to educated procedures but is unable to feel with the existing educated class, is severe. It is not the countryman awkward in his town clothes but the more significant tension—of course with its awkwardness and its spurts of bitterness and nostalgia—of the man caught by his personal history in the general structure and crisis of the relations between education and class, relations which in practice are between intelligence and fellow-feeling. Hardy could not take the James way out, telling his story in a 'spirit of intellectual superiority' to the 'elementary passions'. As he observes again of the Clare brothers: 'Perhaps, as with many men, their opportunities of observation were not so good as their opportunities of expression.' That after all is the nullity, in a time in which education is used to train members of a class and to divide them from other men as surely as from their own passions (for the two processes are deeply connected). And yet there could be no simple going back.

> They had planted together, and together they had felled; together they had, with the run of the years, mentally collected those remoter signs and symbols which seen in few are of runic obscurity, but all together made an alphabet. From the light lashing of the twigs upon their faces when brushing through them in the dark, they could pronounce upon the species of tree whence they stretched; from the quality of the wind's murmur through a bough, they could in like manner name its sort afar off.

This is the language of the immediate apprehension of 'nature', for in that form, always, Hardy could retain a directness of communication. But it is also more specifically the language of shared work, in 'the run of the years', and while it is available as a memory, the world which made it possible is, for Hardy, at a distance which is already enough to detach him: a closeness, paradoxically, that he is still involved with but must also observe and 'pronounce upon'. It is in this sense finally that we must consider Hardy's fundamental attitudes to the country world he was writing about. The tension is not between rural and urban, in the ordinary senses, nor between an abstracted intuition and an abstracted intelligence. The tension, rather, is in his own position, his own lived history, within a general process of change which could come clear and alive in him because it was not only general but in every detail of his feeling observation and writing immediate and particular.

Every attempt has of course been made to reduce the social crisis in which Hardy lived to the more negotiable and detachable forms of the disturbance of a 'timeless order'. But there was nothing timeless about nineteenth-century rural England. It was changing constantly in Hardy's lifetime and before it. It is not only that the next village to Puddletown is Tolpuddle, where you can look from the Martyrs' Tree back to what we know through Hardy as Egdon Heath. It is also that in the 1860s and 1870s, when Hardy was starting to write, it was what he himself described as 'a modern Wessex of railways, the penny post, mowing and reaping machines, union work-houses, lucifer matches, labourers who could read and write, and National school children'. Virtually every feature of this modernity preceded Hardy's own life (the railway came to Dorchester when he was a child of seven). The effects of the changes of course continued. The country was not timeless but it was not static either; indeed, it is because the change was long (and Hardy knew it was long) that the crisis took its particular forms.

We then miss most of what Hardy has to show us if we impose on the actual relationships he describes a pastoral convention of the countryman as an age-old figure, or a vision of a prospering countryside being disintegrated by Corn Law repeal or the railways or agricultural machinery. It is not only that Corn Law repeal and the cheap imports of grain made less difference to Dorset: a county mainly of grazing and mixed farming in which the coming of the railway gave a direct commercial advantage in the supply of milk to London: the economic process described with Hardy's characteristic accuracy in *Tess*:

> They reached the feeble light, which came from the smoky lamp of a little railway station; a poor enough terrestrial star, yet in one sense of more importance to Talbothays Dairy and mankind than the celestial ones to which it stood in such humiliating contrast. The cans of new milk were unladen in the rain, Tess getting a little shelter from a neighbouring holly tree ...
> ... 'Londoners will drink it at their breakfasts tomorrow, won't they?', she asked. 'Strange people that we have never seen? ... who don't know anything of us, and where it comes from, or think how we two drove miles across the moor tonight in the rain that it might reach 'em in time?'

It is also that the social forces within his fiction are deeply based in the rural economy itself: in a system of rent and trade; in the hazards of ownership and tenancy; in the differing conditions of labour on good and bad land and in socially different villages (as in the contrast between Talbothays and Flintcomb Ash); in what happens to people and to families in the interaction between general forces and personal histories—that complex area of ruin or survival, exposure or continuity. This is his actual society, and we cannot suppress it in favour of an external view of a seamless abstracted country 'way of life'.

It is true that there are continuities beyond a dominant social situation in the lives of a particular community (though two or three generations, in a still partly oral culture, can often sustain an illusion of timelessness). It is also obvious that in most rural landscapes there are very old and often unaltered physical features, which sustain a quite different time-scale. Hardy gives great importance to these, and this is not really surprising when we consider his whole structure of feeling. But all these elements are overriden, as for a novelist they must be, by the immediate and actual relationships between people, which occur within existing contemporary pressures and are at most modulated and interpreted by the available continuities.

The pressures to which Hardy's characters are subjected are then pressures from within the system of living, not from outside it. It is not urbanism but the hazard of small-capital farming that changes Gabriel Oak from an independent farmer to a hired labourer and then a bailiff. Henchard is not destroyed by a new and alien kind of dealing but by a development of his own trade which he has himself invited. It is Henchard in Casterbridge who speculates in grain as he had speculated in people; who is in every sense, within an observed way of life, a dealer and a destructive one; his strength compromised by that. Grace Melbury is not a country girl 'lured' by the fashionable world but the daughter of a successful timber merchant whose own social expectations, at this point of his success, include a fashion-able education for his daughter. Tess is not a peasant girl seduced by the squire; she is the daughter of a lifeholder and small dealer who is seduced by the son of a retired manufacturer. The latter buys his way into a country house and an old name. Tess's father and, under pressure, Tess herself, are damaged by a similar process, in which an old name and pride are one side of the coin and the exposure of those subject to them the other. That one family fell and one rose is the common and damaging history of what had been happening, for centuries, to ownership and to its consequences in those subject to it. The Lady Day migrations, the hiring fairs, the intellectually arrogant parson, the casual gentleman farmer, the landowner spending her substance elsewhere: all these are as much parts of the country 'way of life' as the dedicated craftsman, the group of labourers and the dances on the green. It is not only that Hardy sees the realities of labouring work, as in Marty South's hands on the spars and Tess in the swede field. It is also that he sees the harshness of economic processes, in inheritance, capital, rent and trade, within the continuity of the natural processes and persistently cutting across them. The social process created in this interaction is one of class and separation, as well as of chronic insecurity, as this capitalist farming and dealing takes its course. The profound disturbances that Hardy records cannot then be seen in the sentimental terms of a pastoral: the contrast between country and town. The exposed and separated individuals, whom Hardy puts at the centre of his fiction, are only the most developed cases of a general exposure and separation. Yet they are never merely illustrations of this change in a way of life. Each has a dominant personal history, which in psychological terms bears a direct relation to the social character of the change.

One of the most immediate effects of mobility, within a structure itself changing, is the difficult nature of the marriage choice. This situation keeps recurring in terms which are at once personal and social: Bathsheba choosing between Boldwood and Oak; Grace between Giles and Fitzpiers; Jude between Arabella and Sue. The specific class element, and the effects upon this of an insecure economy, are parts of the personal choice which is after all a choice primarily of a way to live, of an identity *in* the identification with this or that other person. And here significantly the false marriage (with which Hardy is so regularly and deeply concerned) can take place either way: to the educated coldness of Fitzpiers or the coarseness of Arabella. Here most dramatically the condition of the internal migrant is profoundly known. The social alienation enters the personality and destroys its capacity for any loving fulfilment. The marriage of Oak and Bathsheba is a case of eventual stability, after so much disturbance, but even that has an air of inevitable resignation and lateness. It is true that Hardy sometimes, under pressure, came to generalize and project these very specific failures into a fatalism for which in the decadent thought of his time the phrases were all too ready. In the same way, seeing the closeness of man and the land being broken by the problems of working the land, he sometimes projected his insistence on closeness and continuity into the finally negative images of an empty nature and the tribal past of Stonehenge and the barrows, where the single observer, at least, could feel a direct flow of knowledge. Even these, however, in their deliberate hardness—the uncultivable heath, the bare stone relics—confirm the human negatives, in what looks like a deliberate reversal of pastoral. In them the general alienation has its characteristic monuments, though very distant in time and space from the controlling immediate disturbance.

But the most significant thing about Hardy, in and through these diffi-culties, is that more than any other major novelist since this difficult mobility began he succeeded, against every pressure, in centring his major novels in the ordinary process of life and work. For all his position as an educated observer, he still took his actions from where the majority of his fellow-countrymen were living. Works enters his novels more decisively than in any English novelist of comparable importance. And it is not merely illustrative; it is seen as it is, as a central kind of learning. Feeling very acutely the long crisis of separation, and in the end coming to more tragically isolated catastrophes than any others within this tradition, he yet created continually the strength and the warmth of people living together: in work and in love; in the physical reality of a place.

> To stand working slowly in a field, and feel the creep of rainwater, first in legs and shoulders, then on hips and head, then at back, front, and sides, and yet to work on till the leaden light diminishes and marks that the sun is down, demand a distinct modicum of stoicism, even of valour. Yet they did not feel the wetness so much as might be supposed. They were both young, and they were

talking of the time when they lived and loved together at Talbothays Dairy, that happy green tract of land where summer had been liberal in her gifts: in substance to all, emotionally to these.

The general structure of feeling in Hardy would be much less convincing if there were only the alienation, the frustration, the separation and isolation, the final catastrophes. What is defeated but not destroyed at the end of *The Woodlanders* or the end of *Tess* or the end of *Jude* is a warmth, a seriousness, an endurance in love and work that are the necessary definition of what Hardy knows and mourns as loss. Vitally—and it is his difference from Lawrence, as we shall see; a difference of generation and of history but also of character—Hardy does not celebrate isolation and separation. He mourns them, and yet always with the courage to look them steadily in the face. The losses are real and heartbreaking because the desires were real, the shared work was real, the unsatisfied impulses were real. Work and desire are very deeply connected in his whole imagination. That the critical emotional decisions by Tess are taken while she is working—as in the ache and dust of the threshing-machine where she sees Alec again—is no accident of plot; it is how this kind of living connects. The passion of Marty or of Tess or of Jude is a positive force coming out of a working and relating world; seeking in different ways its living fulfilment. That all are frustrated in the essential action: frustrated by very complicated processes of division, separation and rejection. People choose wrongly but under terrible pressures: under the confusions of class, under its misunderstandings, under the calculated rejections of a divided separating world.

It is important enough that Hardy keeps to an ordinary world, as the basis of his major fiction. The pressures to move away from it, to enter a more negotiable because less struggling and less divided life, were of course very strong. And it is even more important, as an act of pure affirmation, that he stays, centrally, with his central figures; indeed moves closer to them in his actual development, so that the affirmation of Tess and of Jude—an affirmation in and through the defeats he traces and mourns—is the strongest in all his work.

Beginning with a work in which he declared his hand— *The Poor Man and the Lady, by the Poor Man*; finding that rejected as mischievous, and getting advice, from Meredith, to retreat into conventional plots; letting the impulse run underground where it was continually disturbing but also always active; gaining a growing certainty which was a strengthening as well as a darkening of vision: Hardy ran his course to an exceptional fidelity.

'Slighted and enduring': not the story of man as he was, distant, limited, picturesque; but slighted in a struggle to grow—to love, to work with meaning, to learn and to teach; enduring in the community of this impulse, which pushes through and beyond particular separations and defeats. It is not only the continuity of a country but of a history that makes me now affirm, with his own certainty and irony: Hardy is our flesh and our grass.

199

Hardy's Secret Love

◆

LOIS DEACON

One of the most important contributions to Hardy studies in recent years was made by Lois Deacon, who writes here of her accidental discovery of Hardy's first love, for his cousin Tryphena Sparks. Her revelations caused a storm of controversy, and not all her hypotheses are accepted, but nevertheless Tryphena has been established as a highly influential, though long-concealed factor in Hardy's life and work. There is no doubt about the fact that Hardy loved her, courted her, and broke off his relationship to her. In this essay, Lois Deacon describes her belief that Hardy broke off the relationship because he discovered that Tryphena was in reality not his cousin, as he had supposed, but his niece, being the illegitimate daughter of Hardy's own sister. His love for Tryphena may also have been further complicated by her emotional involvement with Hardy's older friend and mentor, Horace Moule: such an involvement is strongly supported by literary evidence, though there is no factual evidence for it as yet. But, as Lois Deacon points out, there is much still to be discovered about Tryphena's role in Hardy's life.

Moule, Hardy and Tryphena all went their separate ways, breaking up the complex triangle which seems to appear in *A Pair of Blue Eyes*, one of Hardy's earliest novels, and *Jude the Obscure*, his last. Moule committed suicide in 1873, Hardy married his first wife Emma in 1874, and Tryphena married Charlie Gale in 1877, after working for some years as a schoolmistress. After his marriage, Hardy never saw Tryphena again. But Lois Deacon believes, and produces much literary evidence to support her view, that his early and tragic love inspired and coloured most of his poetry and prose, though he felt obliged to conceal his sources. Certainly, as we know from his own words, he did not forget her. And it remains a striking fact that a woman who played so large a part in Hardy's emotional life should have remained unrecognized and undiscussed for so long. Here, Lois Deacon tells the story of her discoveries, and suggests reasons for Hardy's long concealment of Tryphena.

MARGARET DRABBLE

In the summer of 1959 I was living alone in a Dartmoor border village, writing my Dartmoor novels. An isolated Quaker, I was shut off from meeting other Quaker Friends because I had no car. About eight miles away there lived in a remote twelfth-century Dartmoor mill-farm one Eleanor, who was also a Quaker, but she was unknown to me.

SOURCE *The Genius of Thomas Hardy*, ed. Margaret Drabble, London, 1976, pp. 19–31.

Earlier, I had lived for two years at Dartmeet, the heart of the Moor, and a friend who stayed in a nearby caravan, discovering my interest in Hardy as we walked together, began to lend me, one by one, her pocket edition of Hardy's novels. On her death a few years later she unexpectedly bequeathed all her books to me, including the complete Wessex edition of Hardy's works. So I began to read the lesser-known books in my thatched cottage at North Bovey, and it happened that soon after reading the puzzling—but later, quite explicable—*The Well-beloved*, I decided to join a party of twelve Devon Quakers who were planning to visit the Quakers of the Rhineland.

We twelve Friends were present at a Quarterly Meeting of German Quakers in Darmstadt, and after the Meeting for Worship a Frau from Weisbaden whom I had never met or heard of before seated herself beside me at a tea-table, turned to me without any preliminary, and not even knowing my identity, asked 'Are you an admirer of Thomas Hardy?'

I said I was a student of Hardy, and had *The Trumpet-Major* in my hotel bedroom at that moment. She said, 'There is never a time when I am not reading Hardy,' and added that she did so because he wrote about the Moors; that she herself loved the Moors, having been brought up on the Moors near Bremen.

'I love the Moors also!' I said, 'I love them so much that I live alone on Dartmoor!' She said, 'Then perhaps you know some of these places?' and she produced the *Country Life Book of English West Country Pictures.* I opened the book at random and beheld my village green. I tapped the page excitedly, and said 'This is where I live! My cottage is just above this Green.' I then turned the page, saw Dartmeet and the roof of my former residence, and exclaimed 'This is where I lived before I came to the village of North Bovey!'

That night I related these coincidences to my room-mate, Eleanor, and she said to me:

'My mother is a cousin of Thomas Hardy, and her mother was engaged to be married to him.'

The effect of this was to silence me for that night. In the morning I said, 'You told me that your grandmother was engaged to be married to Thomas Hardy. What was her name?'

'Tryphena.'

'Well, if they were engaged to be married, and they loved each other, why were they not married?'

'She sent back the ring because they were cousins,' said Eleanor.

I came home and started fifteen years of the hard labour of research. But it was not merely a fifteen-year stretch, but a happy life sentence. Incredible coincidences piled up around me, wherever I went, resulting among other things in an avalanche of Tryphena's personal possessions being deposited from a lorry into Eleanor's farmyard—the family Bible of Tryphena's mother

Rebecca Sparks, Tryphena's photograph albums, her sampler, worked as a schoolgirl at Athelhampton, near Puddletown, her autograph album, with a handwritten poem—only doggerel, but breathtaking in what it revealed—by her bridegroom, Charlie Gale; a certificate that she won at the training college for drawings of an architectural nature, and many other mementoes. Her album contained the photograph of himself, aged twenty-two which Hardy had given Tryphena five years later. It also contained several photographs of herself, and one of a small boy.[1]

Tryphena's daughter, Nellie Bromell (the mother of my friend Eleanor), identified the photographs for me, and gave them into my safe keeping, at my bank, until such time as my book about Hardy and Tryphena could be written and published. She eagerly poured out to me, over and over again, everything she could remember about her mother, who had died when Nellie was still a child. She told me how Tryphena was clever at old English lettering—a skill also possessed by Sue Bridehead in *Jude the Obscure*. Nellie showed me pieces of the dresses her mother had worn, and told me how Tryphena had talked constantly to her about 'Tom, Tom, it was always Tom,' and how Tom came to Topsham with his brother Henry after Tryphena's death, and was entertained to lunch by herself, because her father, Charles Gale, did not wish to meet Tom Hardy.

I never questioned Nellie Bromell in my many talks with her, but simply listened to all she told me so eagerly. She insisted on writing out her 'Recollections' and giving them to me, and members of her family told me of their gratitude for my interest. 'Mother is always talking about these things, and we are busy farm folk and haven't time to listen to her!'

In the past fifteen years I think I have studied and restudied every work of poetry and prose that Hardy published, some things that he did not publish, but wrote in his own hand, and a great mountain of books that have been written about him, his literature and his countryside. I have walked in the places where he walked, and where he and Tryphena had their being.

One of the first puzzles to clear up before writing an account of Hardy's secret love was *why* a pair of cousins who had been engaged to each other for five years should then decide that they could not marry because it was 'against the laws of the Church'. At the outset I consulted my own Rector and the Rural Dean on that point, and of course found that it was never against the laws of the Church for cousins to marry, although the Church had sometimes 'frowned upon it'. So there must have been another reason, or reasons, why Tryphena 'sent back the ring', which she undoubtedly did, and we have supporting evidence of this from more than one quarter. There is still new evidence to be found: there is much about this story that is not yet known, as is implied by a letter of Tryphena's that came to light recently, and has been published.

On the original letter Tryphena's nephew, Nat Sparks, Junior (a Royal Academician), had made a covering note dated 7 November 1955, which included the words 'Thomas Hardy first wanted to meet Martha [Tryphena's sister], but Grandmother [Maria Hand Sparks of Puddletown] put a spoke in his wheel on the grounds of its being against the laws of the church. This information was given to me by my Father, Nathaniel Sparks, Snr' (violin maker of Puddletown, and later of Bristol).

Photographs of the lovely Martha, closely resembling Tryphena, were long ago found by me in both Tryphena's album and that of the young Tom Hardy, which was for a while in my keeping—I having been asked by the owner to identify the old photographs in the album. I also have a facsimile of a letter written by Tom Hardy, at the age of twenty-two, from Kilburn, London, to his sister Mary at Salisbury. This letter was published in his autobiography, *Early Life*, omitting one telling passage from the original letter—'I have found Martha Sparks, and went one evening to the exhibition with her. She is now gone home for a short time.'

Home was the thatched cottage, only a mile from where Hardy's parents lived, at Sparks' Corner, beside the Mill at Puddletown, where Tryphena lived. When Hardy wrote this letter Martha was aged twenty-seven (five years older than Hardy) and Tryphena was eleven (eleven years younger than Hardy).

PROBABLE TRUTH OF TRYPHENA'S PARENTAGE

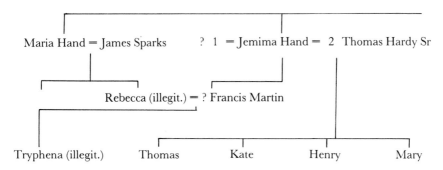

ACCEPTED VERSION OF TRYPHENA'S PARENTAGE

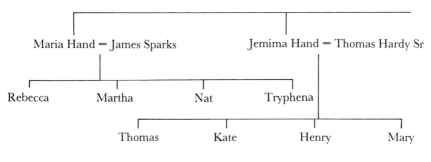

Gradually, the full explanations of the mysterious relationships between the Sparks family and Thomas Hardy came to me. After many wanderings, hundreds of interviews and exchanges of letters, and endless study, fraught with coincidences, the revelations began to fit together like a gigantic, intricate jigsaw. Many of the pieces so fitted came straight from the pen of Hardy.

The reason why Hardy did not marry Tryphena was as follows. Although Tryphena was ostensibly Hardy's first cousin, living near him on the other side of Puddletown ('Egdon') Heath, she was actually—though we shall never be able to prove it in a court of law—the niece of Thomas Hardy, being the illegitimate child of the illegitimate daughter of Hardy's mother, Jemima Hand. There is evidence that Jemima bore children before her marriage to Hardy's father, Thomas Hardy the second, of Higher Bockhampton, Stinsford, near Dorchester, Dorset. The writer Hardy was Thomas Hardy the third of that place.

It was not too uncommon for countryfolk of that region in those days to bear children before marriage. On the Isle of Portland, for instance, it was known and honoured as 'the island custom'. We need to read Hardy's novel, *The Well-beloved*, to realize the truth of this.

A close study of Hardy reveals that he necessarily veiled the truth by many a clever but simple device, so that no outsider during his lifetime or that of his family was likely to penetrate his secrets. But at the same time he signposted the truth for the enlightenment of future generations. It is a long time ago that Jemima Hand gave birth to a child who was entered in family Bibles as being that of her respectably married sister.

'Too late!—Too late!' cried the anguished Tess to her remorseful Angel Clare. Hardy, at the age of twenty-seven, found too late that he had unwittingly planned to marry his sister's daughter, which is forbidden in the Church prayerbook.

If, in the mid-nineteenth century, an obscure young Dorset countryman fell deeply in love with a sixteen-year-old cousin, eleven years his junior, and met her secretly in defiance of his and her parents' estrangement and prohibitions, and if, in accordance with the known custom in West Country villages, the girl became pregnant, what would the young man do? He immediately planned to marry her, but if the alarmed parents of the pair tell them that the banns are forbidden 'because of the laws of the Church', what is left to do but to plight their troth privately, and go through their own form of marriage alone in a church? This is what Hardy and Tryphena evidently did, and he tells us about it in more than one poem, novel and short tale; notably and directly in his poem 'A Poor Man and a Lady':

> *We knew it was not a valid thing,*
> *And only sanct in the sight of God.*

The plight of the lovers on making the first tragic discovery of their true blood relationship is heartbreakingly presented in Hardy's poem, 'Neutral Tones':

> *We stood by a pond that winter day,*
> *And the sun was white, as though chidden of God,*
> *And a few leaves lay on the starving sod;*
> *— They had fallen from an ash, and were gray.*
>
> *Your eyes on me were as eyes that rove*
> *Over tedious riddles of years ago;*
> *And some words played between us to and fro*
> *On which lost the more by our love*
>
> *The smile on your mouth was the deadest thing*
> *Alive enough to have strength to die;*
> *And a grin of bitterness swept thereby*
> *Like an ominous bird-a-wing . . .*
>
> *Since then, keen lessons that love deceives,*
> *And wrings with wrong, have shaped to me*
> *Your face, and the God-curst sun, and a tree,*
> *And a pond edged with grayish leaves.*

There is strong literary evidence that Tryphena was the illegitimate daughter of Francis, the Lord of the Manor, who lived at Kingston Maurward, close beside Hardy's home; the squire's wife, Julia Augusta, who passionately loved the little Tommy Hardy, was herself childless. Kingston Maurward was made the setting for at least three of Hardy's earliest novels: he wrote his first novel, *The Poor Man and the Lady*, during the four months in 1867 when he was ardently and secretly wooing Tryphena on Egdon Heath, and the book's heroine is, of course, a 'lady', the daughter of the squire.

The history of that book is now well known. It was suppressed, resurrected and suppressed again; torn to pieces and privately burned. But careful and—let us confess it—very crafty genius preserved a great deal of its beautiful and valuable contents in *Desperate Remedies, Under the Greenwood Tree* and in the extremely telling and rarely read remnant of the original novel, *An Indiscretion in the Life of an Heiress*, the history of which could fill a whole book. To read this *Indiscretion* is to become completely enlightened about the young author and his love: it is a glorious and rhapsodic piece of writing, though a point that emerges strongly from this idyll is the inevitable opprobrium the illicit lovers encountered in their own locality during their youthful romance. There are echoes of these events in startling personal poems, as well as in other tales and novels. Students of Hardy have noticed other echoes in his fondness for using the same phrases to describe the heroines of different novels: often these cherished phrases can be tracked back to *The Poor Man and the Lady*. Of his abundant primary materials Hardy wasted nothing—ever.

491

By the time that *Desperate Remedies* was written and published, anonymously—March 1871—the love relationship between Hardy and Tryphena
had developed on Egdon Heath and had been drastically thwarted by
denizens of the Heath—Hardy's close relations. The desperate remedies of
the book were for an impossible situation.

Also, by 1869, Tryphena had met Horace Moule. This unlikely bachelor
scholar and leader-writer, son of the vicar of Fordington St George,
Dorchester, brother of several men who were destined to become eminent
clerics and scholars, met Tryphena, who was twenty years his junior, in
London, where she was training to be a teacher. He fell hopelessly in love
with her.[2] Hardy tells the story very clearly in *A Pair of Blue Eyes*, and other
novels, but most particularly in his personal confession, *Jude the Obscure*,
blaming himself endlessly because he had been personally responsible for
placing his young cousin under the tutelary care and guidance of his trusted
mentor and friend—Moule knowing nothing of the true relationships and
ties between Tom and his supposed young cousin from Puddletown, who
could now enter college because she was eighteen.

Tom Hardy, meanwhile, was trying to earn a little money by part-time
architectural work in Weymouth, and was also writing self-revelatory poems
and his first published novel, *Desperate Remedies*. Poems and novel alike
demonstrate his desperation, but he was to be far more deeply desperate in a
few years' time.

Moving between Weymouth and Stockwell, London, where Tryffie was at
training college, Hardy became aware of the position between Moule and
Tryphena—and himself went what I can only describe as stark, staring mad.
(Read all the novels.) I have shown elsewhere[3] that there was a natural two-
year estrangement between Hardy, Tryphena and Moule, for which we have
abundant literary evidence. But Moule had not yet committed suicide in his
chambers in Cambridge when *Desperate Remedies* and *A Pair of Blue Eyes* were
written, though he appears prominently in both books, and is immediately
recognizable in *A Pair of Blue Eyes*. This novel, written by Hardy when he was
very angry with both Tryphena and Moule, was in accordance with the
ruthless Irony of Circumstance throughout Hardy's life, published under his
own name shortly before Moule's suicide. Hardy's original title for the book
was *A Winning Tongue Had He*, and the winning tongue was Horace Moule's.

There is abundant indication that the chastened but flattered Tryffie, with
a second brilliant Abelard at her feet, had seen no harm in promising to
marry him, there being insuperable impediments to her marrying her
dearest Tom. *That* is one key to a better understanding of Hardy's novels.

Tryphena had already been described as she really appeared and
behaved, as Fancy Day in *Under the Greenwood Tree*, and as Cytherea in
Desperate Remedies, also as the heroine, Geraldine, of the hidden first novel,
but by the time that *A Pair of Blue Eyes* appeared she had wisely been
disguised with the eyes, hair, riding-habit and Cornish setting of Hardy's

future wife Emma, whom he met when they were both thirty, and married a few years later. Emma's marriage with Hardy was a matter of expedience to them both.

From the moment of the tragic culmination of Moule's inadvertent intervention in Hardy and Tryphena's joint story, it became vitally important to conceal real identities in everything that Hardy wrote in the future. So, in *Far from the Madding Crowd, The Return of the Native* and most of the other novels, Hardy adopted the ingenious expedient of telling variations of the true story of his life by means of cutting real life characters into two parts and depicting them and their circumstances in two fictional characters in every book. Sometimes the heroine had three heroes, reminiscent of Thomas Hardy, Horace Moule and Charlie Gale, whom Tryphena married in 1877.

It can be seen that sometimes Hardy moulded together his own characteristics and those of Moule in one fictional character, and occasionally he moulded Emma with Tryffie. Thus we find Tryphena in both Eustacia and Thomasin in *The Return of the Native*, while the two warring sides of young Tom Hardy—passionate reckless fellow and scholarly, austere worthy—are presented in the guise of Damon Wildeve and Clym Yeobright. In the early days of my research I found myself writing the names of these two fictional men side by side and seeing that the real names 'Tom Hardy, Horace Moule and Charlie Gale' were all to be found in the available letters. This would be the sort of way Hardy spoke to Tryphena of matters very weighty to them— without transgressing his self-imposed rule never to see or write to her again, once she was the wife of Charlie Gale.

In *Tess* the 'angelic' side of the writer (the aspect which injures the beloved woman even more than the rascality of the wanton fellow) is portrayed in Angel Clare, and the wild aspect in Alec d'Urberville. Moule is also always to be found in one of the main male characters.

Once we hold the key of Tryphena and the concatenation of affections between herself, Hardy, the spouses they eventually thought fit to marry, and Moule, who by his death turned drama into tragedy, we can faithfully unravel and interpret every tangled tale Hardy ever wrote. None of these stories would have been written but for the part Tryphena played in the author's life, and many of the thousand poems are even more obviously and confessedly personal than the prose. In published monographs, lectures and articles, as well as in unpublished books, I have demonstrated these truths, but only Time can firmly establish them.

Hardy was a stricken, contrite man, deeply immersed in spiritual values and timelessness; a Seer always, possessed of insight, hindsight and foresight. He endeavoured to work out his expiation—that of the 'obscure Judas Iscariot', as he saw himself while writing his last book. There are close factual links between the names 'Thomas' and 'Judas', as readers will find on studying 'Thomas' in the *Oxford Dictionary of Christian Names*. Our Thomas ('Jude') saw himself as the triple betrayer of his Lost Love, the woman he married without love, and his closest man friend, who is largely 'Phillotson' in the novel *Jude the Obscure*. The strange, un-named children in the book, who were killed by an 'actual' child, 'Little Father Time', are, of course allegorical; that is, children of what might-have-been, but for what-was. Little Father Time himself, the 'Ancient of Ancients', has a compelling resemblance to the boy in Hardy's poem 'Midnight on the Great Western (the Journeying Boy)' and to a small boy with an ancient face in Tryphena's photograph album.[4]

Working out his 'sad science of renunciation', Hardy bore himself tenderly and with long-suffering during forty years of increasing incompatibility with his wife Emma, and after her death he expressed his regret in beautiful poems of remorse which cannot possibly be mistaken for the passionate poems of a young lover.

I am convinced that Hardy never would have married Emma, nor would Tryphena have married Charlie Gale of Devon after he had persistently wooed her for six years, if Horace Moule had not committed suicide, throwing up the necessity for suppression of facts during the lifetime of all participants in the tragedy. They had become involuntarily involved, like puppets on a stage.

There is much literary evidence in Hardy that before the lovers were forced to go their separate ways with other partners, there was a strong plea from the man to the woman to flee to a far corner of the earth. We are told this in the poem 'The Recalcitrants', which was also a title chosen originally by Hardy for *Jude the Obscure*:

> *Let us off and search, and find a place,*
> *Where yours and mine can be natural lives . . .*
> *We have found us already shunned, disdained . . .*

Holding the key in our hands we open secret door after secret door, so that even when Hardy writes allegorically it is easy to perceive the inner significance. The truth is signposted for our generation, now that the immediate victims of 'Heredity' and 'the blood's tendence' of the 'Family Portraits' in the poems have been laid to rest—these 'dear people' as Hardy described them when he was eighty-three. That is when the arresting, ingenious *Tragedy of the Queen of Cornwall* was shaped. In this work Tryphena was the dark-haired Queen Iseult; Emma was the unloved fair-haired Iseult (wife of Tristram), and Hardy was Tristram himself. The fact that he wrote this version of the old Cornish love story, after long postponements, shows two things—first, that he still adored his dead Tryphena when he was approaching the end of his life, and secondly that he still thought it necessary to present his romance so that contemporary readers would at once assume that it enshrined memories of his courtship of his wife in Cornwall. Having adopted the same ruse more than fifty years earlier, in the novel, *A Pair of Blue Eyes*, Hardy had specially requested his publisher to take pains to keep

494

this novel, with its Cornish associations, well before the public eye.

The method adopted by Hardy in his old age was to write his auto-biography in the third person and to arrange for it to be published posthum-ously as a biography written by his second wife, Florence, who acted as his secretary, both before and after she married him. She was not born until well after the drama of her husband's early life had been played out to a bitter conclusion. The effects of autobiography masquerading as well-informed but secretive biography are profoundly interesting. Confusion, puzzledom and exasperation are just a few of the inevitable results. In his *Life* Hardy omitted to mention his Sparks relations, only once referring to Tryphena and then as 'a cousin', and, in his published *Pedigree*, Hardy significantly ignored the Sparks family altogether, although Maria Hand Sparks was his aunt, an elder sister of his mother, Jemima, and lived only two or three miles away from Hardy's birthplace.

It has been shown, in print, that the young Jemima Hand's illegitimate daughter Rebecca was almost certainly baptized as being the daughter of James and Maria (Hand) Sparks of Puddletown, and that Rebecca later became the mother of Tryphena—illegitimately.

What Hardy does not tell us in his autobiography he reveals clearly in such poems as 'The Christening', 'A Wife and Another', 'On a Heath', 'At Rushy Pond', 'The Place on the Map', 'The End of the Episode', 'Beyond the Last Lamp', 'Her Love Bird', 'Midnight on the Great Western', 'The Revisitation', 'To a Motherless Child', 'Thoughts of Phena', 'In a Eweleaze near Weatherbury', 'Her Immortality' and dozens of other poems.

Occasionally Hardy omitted from published collections important stanzas which he left in the manuscripts, and sometimes poems were ante-dated or post-dated in collections, for obvious reasons of secrecy. None of the collected poems appeared until eight years after Tryphena's death, which was in 1890.

Some of the most revealing poetry was not published until after Hardy's death, in *Winter Words* (1928). This volume includes the supremely important 'Standing By The Mantelpiece', with Horace M. Moule's initials, indicating the facts behind Moule's suicide.[5] 'Family Portraits' in the same collection, is also exceptionally important, with its references to veiled secrets in the Hardy family.

What was Tryphena like? We have plenty of indications. A winsome introduction to her can be found, we may assume, in *Under the Greenwood Tree*, a sweet, fresh and happy novel, published anonymously in 1872, before Horace Moule died. The heroine, Fancy Day, shows the 'colossal incon-sistency' that characterizes all Hardy's heroines, who almost always had two, sometimes three strings to their bow. Here is Fancy:

> Flexibility was her first characteristic, by which she appeared to enjoy the most easeful rest when she was in gliding motion. Her dark eyes—arched by brows of so keen, slender and soft a curve that they resembled nothing so much

as two slurs in music—showed primarily a bright sparkle each. This was softened by a frequent thoughtfulness, yet not so frequent as to do away, for more than a few minutes, at a time, with a certain coquettishness, which in its turn was never so decided as to banish honesty. Her lips imitated her brows in their clearly-cut outline and softness of bend; and her nose was well-shaped— which is saying a great deal, when it is remembered that there are a hundred pretty mouths and eyes for one pretty nose. Add to this, plentiful knots of dark-brown hair ... and the slightest idea may be gained of the young maiden who showed, amidst the rest of the dancing-ladies, like a flower among vegetables.

This is the Hardyan girl we meet again and again. The phrase about arched brows 'like two slurs in music' is used by Hardy to describe the heroine of more than one of his novels, and her identity with Tryphena, 'the lost prize', is supported by the photograph of Tryphena, aged eighteen, which her daughter, old Nellie Bromell, brought to me from Tryphena's own album.

Of Geraldine in *An Indiscretion in the Life of an Heiress*, Hardy wrote:

The clear, deep eyes, full of all tender expressions; the fresh, subtly-curved cheek, changing its tones of red with the fluctuation of each thought; the ripe tint of her delicate mouth, and the indefinable line where lip met lip, the noble bend of her neck, the waving lengths of her dark brown hair, the soft motions of her bosom when she breathed, the light fall of her little feet, the elegant contrivances of her attire, all struck him as something he had dreamed of and was not actually seeing.

Another notable thing about Hardy's fictional young women is their rich contralto speaking voices, deepening in moments of great emotion, 'in the stopt-diapason note which her voice acquired when her heart was in her speech.' The quotation is from *Tess of the d'Urbervilles* and Hardy so far forgot that he was writing of a *fictional* character that he added to the sentence—'and which will never be forgotten by those who knew her.' He was quite carried away when he wrote these words, and perceptive readers saw what he saw, and heard what he heard. Indeed—ah, indeed—he who runs may read!

Of Eustacia, in *The Return of the Native*, Hardy recorded, 'She had Pagan eyes, full of nocturnal mysteries', and 'In heaven she will probably sit between the Heloises and the Cleopatras.' Hardy's Heloises always sat at the feet of *two* Abelards, and so, I think, did Tryphena.

'Tess' was 'a fine and handsome girl ... her mobile peony mouth and large innocent eyes adding eloquence to colour and shape ... Her lower lip had a way of thrusting the middle of her top one upward, when they closed together after a word.' She spoke 'two languages, the dialect at home, more or less; ordinary English abroad and to persons of quality'.

In making Tess say, of a youthful aspect of her appearance, that 'it was a fault which time would cure,' Hardy was actually quoting Tryphena. When she was interviewed for the post of head mistress at a girls' school in Plymouth, she was told that she was very young, at twenty, for the appointment, and she replied, 'That is a fault which time will cure.' She secured the post, and kept it, satisfactorily, until she yielded to Charlie Gale's reiterated proposals at the end of 1877.

Between *Greenwood Tree* and *Tess* we can meet the wayward, loveable girl many times in Hardy's other tales, and very notably as Eustacia in *The Return of the Native*, and as Bathsheba in *Far from the Madding Crowd*.

Hardy had finally parted from his Lost Love before he married Emma, and well before Tryphena married Charlie, and there are many indications that these two marriages may have been largely matters of expediency, to provide an alibi and a refuge to the pair, who were animated by a spirit of atonement and of personal sacrifice.

Hardy indicated that his last novel, *Jude*, was an amplification of the theme already presented in *A Pair of Blue Eyes*, which can clearly be seen from a comparison of the two books. He also explained in the preface to *Jude* that the circumstances of the novel were 'suggested by the death of a woman in 1890' (the year Tryphena died). In a postscript which he added in 1912 to this preface Hardy expressed his earlier hope, which had been disappointed, that 'certain cathartic qualities' might have been found in the book when it was published in 1895. Actually *Jude* had met with a storm of misunderstanding and downright abuse.

In *A Pair of Blue Eyes* and *Jude* the author stressed the 'curious epicene tenderness' and 'unconsciousness of gender' of the young woman at the centre of the complicated plots. She would give her photograph or warm sympathy and attention to any man as naturally as to a friend of her own sex.

After Hardy had written *Jude* he said, 'All my stories are written', and refused to write another novel. But when *The Return of the Native* was being written Hardy was in the early years of his marriage to Emma (the calmest years), and Tryphena was about to be married to Charles. The ill-starred lovers were irrevocably parted, and Hardy was in honour bound never to approach Tryphena again in person, or by letter. So what did he do? He sat in the bay window of his sitting-room, turned his back on Emma (and told us so in a reminiscent poem), and reconstructed the true love story in *The Return of the Native*, with the two real young lovers presented in four different fictional characters. The book is full of tender, loyal, secret yet obvious messages to Tryffie.

The Return of the Native was first printed serially in *Belgravia* from January to December, 1878—the first instalments appearing in January, the month after Tryphena had married Charles Gale in Plymouth and gone with him to live at Topsham, near Exeter, where she died.

Tryphena read that book. She read all Hardy's books as they appeared, and even gave them to her very young daughter, Nellie Tryphena, to read, telling her 'All the people in Tom's stories are *real* people.' In her old age Nellie Tryphena repeated that information to myself.

Tryphena herself recognized the truth that Hardy was telling, though secrecy, which held that articulate man in her firm grip until his death, demanded often that he should disguise places as well as people; hence, for instance, the setting of *Jude the Obscure* in remoter parts of Wessex—places where Tryphena had never been, and Sue Bridehead is without doubt a portrait of the very Tryphena. Yet, as always, from time to time he whisked off the coverlets by writing such frank poems as 'In a Cathedral City' (Salisbury), telling us that his beloved had never been there, so that he who bore her 'imprint through and through' might sojourn there to gain forgetfulness.

Scores of poems owe their origin in this way to Hardy's secret love for Tryphena: they cover the entire period, from 1867 when he was twenty-seven, to when he was in his eighties, just before his death in 1928.

More than a hundred years have now passed since Hardy and his beloved met 'in a secret year' beside Rushy-Pond on Egdon Heath. The truth about their relationship, so long concealed and so accidentally discovered, can now be told, without harm or distress to any living person, provided we refrain from probing the privacy of living descendants of the protagonists. Hardy himself certainly yearned for the revelation, and employed the power of his pen to bring it about: and Tryphena's grand-daughter Eleanor wrote to me at the outset of my researches; 'All things that are hidden shall be made known,' and 'Truth cannot be hidden at the bottom of a well.' The letter is treasured by me now that Eleanor too has departed.

Hardy's love for Tryphena has rendered her immortal. To those who mistakenly imagine that the truth will damage the reputation of Hardy or Tryphena, one can only point out, with complete sincerity, that she was the lifelong inspiration of his incomparable works.

Notes

1. Lois Deacon and Terry Coleman have suggested in *Providence and Mr Hardy* that this photograph was of a supposed illegitimate son of Hardy and Tryphena, a boy called Randy. A monograph by F.R. Southerington, published by J. Stevens Cox, argues the case in favour of this hypothesis more fully. *Hardy's Child. Fact or Fiction?* Monographs No. 42, 1968.

2. It must be pointed out that although literary evidence for a relationship between Moule and Tryphena is strong, there is no factual evidence of their having known each other (Margaret Drabble's Note).

3. In *Providence and Mr Hardy.*

4. See note 1 above.

5. Lois Deacon and Coleman believe that Moule, who died in 1873, having severed his own wind pipe with a razor, had been involved with Tryphena. The report of the inquest spoke of depression caused by difficulties in his academic career, not unlike Jude the Obscure's, and Moule's brother Charles spoke of 'circumstances to lead to such depression', which may hint at troubles with Tryphena, and his friend Hardy (Margaret Drabble's Note).

200

Thomas Hardy as
a Cinematic Novelist

───────◆───────

DAVID LODGE

This essay is a revised and extended version of an article, 'Thomas Hardy
and Cinematographic Form', published in *Novel*, VII (1974) pp. 246–54.

Thomas Hardy's last novel, *Jude the Obscure* (1895), was published well before
film had properly evolved as a narrative medium. By calling him a 'cinematic' novelist, therefore, I mean that he anticipated film, not that he was
influenced by it. In a general sense this is true of all the great nineteenth-
century realistic novelists. As Leon Edel has observed:

> Novelists have sought almost from the first to become a camera. And not a
> static instrument but one possessing the movement through space and time
> which the motion-picture camera has achieved in our century. We follow
> Balzac, moving into his subject, from the city into the street, from the street into
> the house, and we tread hard on his heels as he takes us from room to room.
> We feel as if that massive 'realist' had a prevision of the cinema ... Wherever we
> turn in the nineteenth century we can see novelists cultivating the camera-eye
> and the camera movement ...[1]

One way of explaining this affinity between film and classic realistic fiction is
to say that both are 'metonymic' forms, in Roman Jakobson's sense of that
term. According to Jakobson, a discourse connects one topic with another
either because they are *similar* to each other or because they are in some
sense *contiguous* with each other in space-time. Most discourse uses both
types of connection, but usually one or other predominates. Jakobson calls
them metaphoric and metonymic, respectively, because these tropes are
models or epitomes of the processes involved: metaphor being a figure of
substitution based on similarity, while metonymy (and the closely related
figure of synecdoche) deletes from or rearranges naturally contiguous
entities, substituting cause for effect or part for whole, or vice versa.

In Jakobson's scheme, drama and lyric poetry are typically metaphoric
forms, while film and realistic prose fiction are typically metonymic.

SOURCE *Thomas Hardy after Fifty Years*, ed. Lance St John Butler, London, 1977, pp. 78–89.

'Following the path of contiguous relationships, the realistic author meto-nymically digresses from the plot to the atmosphere and from the characters to the setting in space and time', says Jakobson (this matches Edel's des-cription of Balzac's technique exactly). 'He is fond of synecdochic detail. In the scene of Anna Karenina's suicide Tolstoy's attention is focused on the heroine's handbag ...'[2] The handbag is a synecdoche for Anna. It will be remembered that she throws it aside as she jumps beneath the train, and that her first attempt is checked when the bag becomes entangled in her clothing. One could easily imagine a cinematic treatment of the scene in which the camera cuts away from the fatal leap to a close-up shot of the poignantly abandoned handbag on the platform. Close-up is the filmic equivalent of synecdoche (part standing for whole). Film has its metaphors too, of course (e.g. waves pounding on the shore signifying sexual intercourse in the pre-permissive cinema), but this kind of montage must be used sparingly in narrative film, or disguised as contextual detail, if intelligibility is to be preserved. For the same reasons modernist or symbolist novels in which the metaphorical principle of similarity largely determines the devel-opment of the discourse (e.g. Joyce's *Ulysses*) are much more difficult to translate into film than realistic novels.

'Realism' as an aesthetic effect depends upon the suppression of overt reference to the conventions employed, so that the discourse seems to be a transparent window on reality, rather than a code. Avant-garde and experi-mental movies may draw attention to their own optics, but most narrative films do not. As experienced viewers of films we tend to take the camera eye for granted and to accept the truthfulness of what it shows us. Though its perspective is never that of ordinary human vision, it is close enough to the latter to seem a transparent medium for the rendering of reality rather than an artificial system of signs. Similarly the narrative style of realistic fiction, derived from non-fictional types of discourse such as biography, confession, letters and historiography, bestows upon the fictitious narrative a pseudo-historical authenticity. Both novel and film are able to shift their point of view between an 'omniscient' or impersonal perspective and the perspective of a particular character without sacrificing realistic illusion. Roland Barthes has observed that 'the discourse of the traditional novel alternates the personal and the impersonal very rapidly, often in the same sentence, so as to produce, if we can speak thus, a proprietary consciousness which retains the mastery of what it states without participating in it',[3] and the same may be said of film.

If there is so close an affinity between the classic realist novel and film, what is the justification for distinguishing Hardy as a 'cinematic novelist'? To answer that question we must emphasise the *differences* between novel and film. Apart from dialogue and monologue (which are available to both) and the use of music for emotive suggestion, film is obliged to tell its story purely in terms of the visible—behaviour, physical appearance, setting—whereas the verbal medium of the novel can describe anything, visible or invisible (notably the thoughts passing through a character's head), and can do so as abstractly as it pleases, A cinematic novelist, then, is one who, as it were, deliberately renounces some of the freedom of representation and report afforded by the verbal medium, who imagines and presents his materials in primarily visual terms, and whose visualisations correspond in some significant respect to the visual effects characteristic of film.

That description, especially description of the natural settings of his stories, plays a crucially important part in Thomas Hardy's fiction is, of course, a commonplace. But I don't think it has been observed how remarkably 'cinematic' he is, both in the way he describes landscape and in the way he deploys his human figures against it. Hardy uses verbal description as a film director uses the lens of his camera—to select, highlight, distort and enhance, creating a visualised world that is both recognisably 'real' and yet more vivid, intense and dramatically charged than our ordinary perception of the real world. The methods he uses can be readily analysed in cinematic terms: long shot, close-up, wide-angle, telephoto, zoom, etc. Indeed, some of Hardy's most original visual effects have since become cinematic clichés. One thinks of his use of mirrors to dramatise encounters in which there is an element of guilt, suspense or deception (e.g. Eustacia realising that Clym had discovered the truth about her treatment of his mother when she sees his grim face reflected in the mirror of her dressing-table, or Grace in *The Woodlanders* startled to discover in the mirror of Fitzpiers' sitting-room that he is regarding her from his couch, though when she turns round he is apparently asleep);[4] and his use of 'aerial shots' (of Tess on the floor of the valley of the Great Dairies, for instance, or of Wildeve and Eustacia on Egdon Heath at night in *The Return of the Native*).[5]

Hardy, like a film-maker, seemed to conceive his fictions, from the beginning, as human actions in a particular setting: the dense woods of *The Woodlanders*, the wild heathland of *The Return of the Native*, the contrasting valleys and heights of *Tess*, are integral to the imaginative unity of those novels. He called them 'novels of character and environment', and it is his ability to make concrete the relationship between character and environment in a way that is both sensuously particular and symbolically suggestive that makes him such a powerful and original novelist, in my opinion, rather than his skill in story-telling, his insight into human motivation or his philosophic wisdom. This emphasis on the visual presentation of experience makes him no less of a *writer*—quite the contrary, since he must do through language what the film-maker can do by moving his camera and adjusting his lens; correspondingly, it is difficult for film adaptation to do justice to Hardy's novels precisely because effects that are unusual in written description are commonplace in film.[6]

To illustrate my argument I will comment in some detail on the opening chapters of *The Return of the Native* (1878). This novel begins, like so many films, with an emotionally loaded, panoramic establishing shot of the *mis-en-scène*, Egdon Heath:

> A Saturday afternoon in November was approaching the time of twilight, and the vast tract of unenclosed wild known as Egdon Heath embrowned itself moment by moment. Overhead the hollow stretch of whitish cloud shutting out the sky was as a tent which had the whole heath for its floor.

The emphasis in the first chapter is on the heath's symbolic properties, especially its consonance with the mood of late nineteenth-century cosmic pessimism in which this novel is, a little self-indulgently, steeped. For this purpose the heath is empty (Chapter 2 is headed, 'Humanity appears upon the Scene, Hand in Hand with Trouble') but it is noteworthy that at several points Hardy postulates an observer as a kind of descriptive formula: 'Looking upwards, a furze-cutter would have been inclined to continue work; looking down, he would have decided to finish his faggot and go home' ... 'To recline on a stump of thorn in the central valley of Egdon, between afternoon and night, as now, where the eye could reach nothing of the world outside the summits and shoulders of heathland which filled the whole circumference of its glance' ... 'On the evening under consideration it would have been noted that, though the gloom had increased sufficiently to confuse the minor features of the heath, the white surface of the road remained almost as clear as ever.'

The invocation of a hypothetical or unspecified observer in description is one of the signatures of Hardy's narrative style. His novels are full of phrases like, 'An observer would have remarked', 'a loiterer in this place might have speculated', or verbs of perception, often in the passive voice ('it was seen', 'it was felt', etc.) that are not attached to any specified subject. Why should a novelist who did not shrink from exercising the authorial privilege of intrusive philosphical comment feel compelled to invent surrogates for himself when it came to description? The habit is linked with Hardy's heavy reliance on *specified* observers in his fiction: there are an extraordinary number of scenes in which one character observes, spies on or eavesdrops on others. J. Hillis Miller has plausibly traced this feature of Hardy's novels to the writer's own unconscious wish 'to escape from the dangers of direct involvement in life and to imagine himself in a position where he could safely see life as it is without being seen and could report on that seeing'.[7] But we may also interpret Hardy's reliance on specified and unspecified observers as evidence of the importance he attached to visual perspective—it is as though he is trying to naturalise devices of presentation that would require no such explanation or justification in film. These observing eyes act like camera lenses—and if there is often something voyeuristic about their observations, this only reminds us that film is a deeply voyeuristic medium.

To return to the *Native*: the opening paragraph of Chapter 2 introduces an old man, walking along the road whose whiteness was remarked at the close of Chapter I. The physical appearance of the old man is described, followed by these words: 'One would have said that he had been, in his day, a naval officer of some sort or other.' Again, the unspecified observer: 'One would have said ...' There is nothing to prevent Hardy from telling us that this is Captain Vye, retired, but he prefers to enact the process by which we interpret purely visual information, thus restricting himself voluntarily to a limitation that is binding on the film-maker. The old man now becomes the 'lens' through which we see. The road stretches before him, 'dry, empty and white. It was quite open to the heath on each side, and bisected that vast dark surface like a parting line on a head of black hair, diminishing and bending away on the furthest horizon.' Then, 'at length he discerned, a long distance in front of him, a moving spot which appeared to be a vehicle ... It was the single atom of life that the scene contained.' This is a very character-istic, and very cinematic, effect in Hardy's fiction: the little speck of human life in a vast expanse of nature, expressing (though one doesn't wish to interpret too allegorically) the vulnerability of the individual human life, its relative insignificance in the temporal and spatial scale of the earth and the universe at large.

Gradually Captain Vye overtakes the van, which turns out to be 'ordinary in shape, but singular in colour, this being a lurid red. The driver walked beside it; and like his van, he was completely red. In a Technicolor film, this would surely be a stunning moment. Indeed, Diggory Venn the reddleman is one of Hardy's most cinematically-conceived characters. There is little to him psychologically: he is honest, chivalrous, loyal, a rather dull 'goodie'. The interest and appeal of his character is all in his picturesque appearance and behaviour: his weird pigmentation, his lonely nomadic existence, his dramatic interventions into the action—notably the scene in Chapter 8 of Part III where, like the strong silent hero of a Western, he strides into the circle of lamplight on the heath where Christian has just lost to Wildeve all the money entrusted to him by Mrs Yeobright:

> Wildeve stared. Venn looked coolly towards Wildeve, and without a word being spoken, he deliberately sat himself down where Christian had been seated, thrust his hand into his pocket, drew out a sovereign, and laid it on the stone.
> 'You have been watching us from behind that bush?' said Wildeve.
> The reddleman nodded. 'Down with your stake,' he said. 'Or haven't you pluck enough to go on?'

In Chapter 2 of Part I, Diggory, having been presented to us first through the eyes of Captain Vye, himself provides the eyes through which we first glimpse the heroine of the story, Eustacia Vye: a carefully composed visual sequence that begins with a wide-angle shot of the heath and then zooms in on the distant barrow where a figure is outlined against the sky.

> There the form stood, motionless as the hill beneath. Above the plain rose the
> hill, above the hill rose the barrow, and above the barrow rose the figure. Above
> the figure was nothing that could be mapped elsewhere than on a celestial
> globe ... The figure perceptibly gave up its fixity, shifted a step or two, and
> turned round. As if alarmed, it descended on the right side of the barrow, with
> the glide of a water drop down a bud, and then vanished. The movement had
> been sufficient to show more clearly the characteristics of the figure, and that it
> was a woman's.
>
> The reason of her sudden displacement now appeared. With her dropping
> out of sight on the right side, a newcomer, bearing a burden, protruded into the
> sky on the left side, ascended the tumulus, and deposited the burden on the
> top. A second followed, then a third, a fourth, a fifth, and ultimately the whole
> barrow was peopled with burdened figures.
>
> The only intelligible meaning in this sky-backed pantomime of silhouettes
> was that the woman had no relation to the forms who had taken her place, was
> sedulously avoiding these, and had come thither for another object than theirs.

Once again information is conveyed to the reader through visualised action,
made striking and vivid by an unusual perspective, interpreted by a narrator
who could have used his authorial privilege to simply *tell* us the facts.

The third chapter begins characteristically: 'Had a looker-on been posted
in the immediate vicinity of the barrow, he would have learned that these
persons were boys and men of the neighbouring hamlets.' The transition
from Diggory's distant view-point to the hypothetical 'looker-on' is equivalent to a cinematic 'cut' from a long-distance shot to a close-up of a given
subject. It situates us on the barrow, able to observe the local rustics as they
build their bonfire, and to overhear their conversation. And now *they* become
the observing eyes of the narrative, surveying the dark expanse of Egdon on
which 'Red suns and tufts of fire one by one began to arise, flecking the
whole country round. They were the bonfires of other parishes ...'

To work through the entire novel in this way would be tedious, and I
hope I have indicated clearly enough my grounds for regarding *The Return of
the Native* as a 'cinematic novel' *avant la lettre*. That it is the product of an
intensely visual imagination is surely undeniable. The plot, *qua* plot—
considered as a sequence of human actions connected by cause and effect—
has little to recommend it, heavily dependent as it is on melodramatic
stereotypes in character and action. Yet we scarcely register these things as
flaws because they are overlaid by, or are actually the occasion of, stunning
visual effects. The reasons, the circumstances, that cause Eustacia not to
open the cottage door to her mother-in-law, thus bringing about the latter's
death and eventually her own, matter less than the visual image, perceived
by Mrs Yeobright and frequently recalled later, of Eustacia's cold, hostile
face at the window. The business of the gold guineas which are won by
Wildeve from Christian, and then by Diggory from Wildeve, is not particularly interesting as plot, is indeed, entirely dispensable on this level, but one
would be sorry to lose that memorable and intensely visual scene where the
two men gamble on desperately into the night, surrounded by insects and

cattle attracted by the light, and then, their candle extinguished by a moth, continue their game by the light of glow-worms. The same is true of the characters. For instance, all Hardy's efforts to dignify Eustacia with classical allusion cannot make her into a complex or morally interesting character. She is essentially a rather shallow-minded, self-dramatising young woman, primarily interesting (like many heroines of the screen) because of her physical beauty, which Hardy evokes very powerfully by close-ups of her lips, throat, eyes and hair ('rich romantic lips' and 'beautiful stormy eyes' are representative phrases), and by posing her picturesquely against the background of the heath.

Subtract the description of the heath from the novel, and you would be left with a rather contrived melodrama of unhappy love, relieved by some amusing comic dialogue from the rustics. The novel as we have it, with the descriptions of Egdon, is powerful and memorable. A line in Chapter 7 of Book Four, 'moving figures began to animate the line between heath and sky', epitomises the characteristic visual motif of the novel, established in its opening chapters: the two masses of heath and sky, one dark and the other lighter, both inscrutable and indifferent to the pathetically small, vulnerable human figures occasionally visible against these backgrounds. Usually the perspective is horizontal, but on at least one occasion Hardy switches to the vertical, when Wildeve and Eustacia are walking back from the country dance:

> The moon had now waxed bright and silvery, but the heath was proof against such illumination, and there was to be observed the striking scene of a dark, rayless tract of country under an atmosphere charged from its zenith to its extremities with whitest light. To an eye above them their two faces would have appeared amid the expanse like two pearls on a table of ebony. (IV, 3)

This emphasis throughout the novel on the smallness and vulnerability of the human being is conveyed primarily through panoramic views with deep perspective, combined with effects of 'zooming in' on distant figures. But it is worth noting that Hardy's visual imagination is just as active in close-up treatment of small-scale subjects. As blindness encroaches on Clym, for example,

> His daily life was of a curious microscopic sort, his whole world being limited to a circuit of a few feet from his person. His familiars were creeping and winged things ... Bees hummed around his ears with an intimate air, and tugged at the heath and furze-flowers at his side in such numbers as to weigh them down to the sod. The strange amber-coloured butterflies which Egdon produced, and which were never seen elsewhere, quivered in the breath of his lips, alighted upon his bowed back, and sported with the glittering point of his hook as he flourished it up and down. Tribes of emerald-green grasshoppers leaped over his feet, falling awkwardly on their backs, heads or hips, like unskilful acrobats ... Litters of young rabbits came out from their forms to sun themselves upon hillocks, the hot beams blazing through the delicate tissue of each thin-fleshed ear, and firing it to a blood-red transparency in which the veins could be seen. (IV; 2)

This passage has the eye-opening beauty of a good natural history film, and in the treatment of the grasshoppers anticipates the witty anthropomorphism of Disney at his best.

Hardy's most powerful and characteristic descriptive passages are generally 'exteriors'; but it is worth noting that his treatment of interiors is equally cinematic, both in the way he lights them and in his choice of viewpoints from which to observe them. *The Woodlanders* is especially rich in instances of this kind, perhaps because the dense, all-enclosing woods in which the action is mainly set made impossible the broad, panoramic descriptions of scenery at which Hardy excelled. (The notable exception is that remarkable scene in Chapter 28, so like a film Western in effect, when Grace watches Fitzpiers cross White Hart Vale on her horse Darling, the setting sun catching the white coat of the horse and making it visible until it is a mere speck on the opposite ridge.) In Chapter 2, Barber Percomb regards the unsuspecting Marty South through the open door of her cottage as she sits making spars by the light of her fire, which is also dimly and ominously reflected in the scissors protruding from the barber's waistcoat pocket. Here, as so often, Hardy invokes the art of painting to convey the particular visual effect he had in mind, but it is one that the cinema has since made very familiar:

> In her present beholder's mind the scene formed by the girlish spar-maker composed itself into an impression-picture of extremest type, wherein the girl's hair alone, as the focus of observation, was depicted with intensity and distinctness, while her face, shoulders, hands, and figure in general were a blurred mass of unimportant detail lost in haze and obscurity.

The situation in which a figure in an illuminated interior is observed from outside, through a door or window, is a recurrent motif in the novel. After bringing Grace back to her home in Chapter 6, Giles, outside the house, wistfully watches through a door the family gathered round the parlour fire, and observes an effect of light on Grace's hair similar to that described in the earlier scene. Immediately afterwards Grace is alerted to the presence of Fitzpiers in the woodland by the coloured lights in his window. Later, Giles sees Grace looking at herself in her bedroom mirror by candlelight as she anticipates the next day's visit to Mrs Charmond (Chapter 7). When Giles agrees to keep Fitzpiers company on his nocturnal drive in Chapter 16, the latter identifies Grace when they both catch sight of her drawing the curtains of her bedroom. After summoning Fitzpiers to attend Mrs Charmond following her accident, Giles 'stepped back into the darkness ... and ... stood for a few minutes looking at the window which, by its light, revealed the room where Grace was sitting' (Chapter 26). When Fitzpiers is asked to leave the Melbury house, he does so without meeting her, but 'while passing through the gate he turned his head. The firelight of the room she sat in threw her figure into dark relief against the window as she looked through the panes, and he must have seen her distinctly' (Chapter 44). The most bizarre variation on this theme, with the point of observation reversed, comes in Chapter 36 when Mrs Charmond pulls back the shutter of her drawing-room window to reveal on the other side of the plane, 'the face of Fitzpiers ... surrounded with the darkness of the night without, corpse-like in its pallor, and covered with blood'—a moment worthy of Hitchcock.

Hardy's most stunning visual effects are however never introduced just 'for effect' (as they are sometimes in Hitchcock); they are invariably part of some larger aesthetic and thematic pattern. The recurrent motif in *The Woodlanders* of the illuminated figure inside, observed by an unobserved observer outside, symbolises the imperfect understanding and defective communication that obtains between the main characters in the novel; just as the diminutive figures on the rim of a huge horizontal landscape in *The Return of the Native* symbolise the vulnerability of human creatures and the indifference of Nature to their agonies and ecstasies. The same kind of patterning of visual effect is observable in the most substantial relic we have of Hardy's first work of fiction, *The Poor Man and the Lady*. Before Hardy destroyed the manuscript of this work, he carved out of it a short serial story, called 'An Indiscretion in the Life of an Heiress', which was published in the *New Quarterly Magazine* in 1878, and recently reprinted in book form.[8] The plot is simple and melodramatic: Egbert Mayne, a gifted but poor young man, falls imprudently in love with Geraldine, the beautiful daughter of the local squire, and she with him. He goes to London to make his fortune, and after a number of years have passed she almost gives herself in loveless marriage to an aristocratic suitor. After a dramatic meeting on the eve of the wedding the lovers elope and marry. The strain of attempting a reconcili-ation with her stern father, however, proves fatal to Geraldine. The story is certainly among Hardy's less impressive achievements, as he acknowledged by excluding it from his collected works, but it demonstrates his ability to give power and poignancy to commonplace and even stereotyped emotions by artful effects of lighting and perspective. The opening chapter, set in a parish church closely modelled on Hardy's own at Stinsford, is represen-tative in this respect. Afternoon service in winter is in progress. From the gallery Egbert looks down intently at Geraldine in her pew below, as the natural light fades from the windows:

> The lady was the single person besides the preacher whose face was turned westwards, the pew that she occupied being the only one in the church in which the seat ran all around. She reclined in her corner, her bonnet and dress growing by degrees invisible, and at last only her upturned face could be discerned, a solitary white spot against the black surface of the wainscot. Over her head rose a vast marble monument, erected to the memory of her ancestors, male and female; for she was of high standing in that parish. The design consisted of a winged skull and two cherubim, supporting a pair of tall Corinthian columns, between which spread a broad slab, containing the roll of ancient names, lineages, and deeds, and surmounted by a pediment, with the crest of the family at its apex.

> As the youthful schoolmaster gazed, and all these details became dimmer, her face was modified in his fancy, till it seemed almost to resemble the carved marble skull immediately above her head.[9]

This intensely visualised scene symbolises the social gap between the lovers, expresses the effort of will required of Egbert to maintain their relationship, and hints at its tragic conclusion. All the most important encounters between the lovers take place in darkness, or the melancholy half-darkness that follows dusk or precedes dawn, fitfully illuminated by candlelight or firelight: their first embrace, their parting when Egbert leaves for London, their meeting on the eve of the wedding. The final fatal meeting of Geraldine with her father also takes place at night, and its melodramatic character is somewhat muted by the fact that it is not presented directly. Instead, as Geraldine goes into the house, the narrative stays outside in the dark grounds with the anxious Egbert. The passage subtly echoes the opening scene in the church:

> he watched her crossing the grass and advancing, a mere dot, towards the mansion. In a short time the appearance of an oblong of light in the shadowy expanse of wall denoted to him that the door was open: her outline appeared on it; then the door shut her in, and all was shadow as before. (Chapter 7)

Nothing could be more 'cinematic'—the best word, it seems to me, to describe what Hardy himself called his 'idiosyncratic mode of regard'.[10]

Notes

1. Leon Edel, 'Novel and Camera', *The Theory of the Novel*, ed. John Halperin (New York, 1974) p. 177.

2. Roman Jakobson, 'Two Aspects of Language and Two Types of Linguistic Disturbances' in R. Jackobson and M. Halle, *Fundamentals of Language* (The Hague, 1956) p. 78. For a full discussion of the theory see my *The Modes of Modern Writing: Metaphor, Metonymy and the Typology of Modern Literature* (1977).

3. Roland Barthes, 'To Write: An Intransitive Verb?', *The Structuralist Controversy*, ed. R. Macksey and E. Donato (Baltimore, 1972) p. 140.

4. *The Return of the Native* V, 3; *The Woodlanders*, Chapter 18.

5. *Tess of the d'Urbervilles*, Chapter 16; *The Return of the Native*, IV, 3.

6. John Schlesinger's *Far from the Madding Crowd* (1967) made a good attempt in the early part of the film—particularly with a striking shot in which the camera moves rapidly and vertically away from Gabriel's flock until the sheep and the contours of the countryside become two-dimensional shapes in an abstract design—but gradually the melodrama of the story came to predominate.

7. J. Hillis Miller, *Thomas Hardy: Distance and Desire* (1970) p. 43.

8. Thomas Hardy, *An Indiscretion in the Life of an Heiress*, ed. with an introduction by Terry Coleman (1976).

9. This passage adapts a similar moment of speechless courtship in Stinsford church between Hardy's own parents, which he made the subject of a poem, 'A Church Romance: (Mellstock *circa* 1835)'.

10. In *The Life of Thomas Hardy* (London, 1962) p. 225.

201

Lawrence on Hardy

———— ◆ ————

MARK KINKEAD-WEEKES

Perhaps the most brilliant and certainly the most individual essay on Hardy
has been sadly neglected. Although D.H. Lawrence's *Study of Thomas Hardy*
was written in 1914, it was only published in 1936, among the large
miscellany of essays and sketches gathered in *Phoenix*.[1] Too long and
complex to be included in collections of essays on Hardy, too short to be
published alone, the *Study* has led a fugitive existence in Hardy criticism,
more referred to than read, and certainly more read in anthologised extracts
torn from context than as a coherent whole. Recently, it is true, the *Study* has
become a recognised stopping-place for critics of Lawrence en route for *The
Rainbow* and seeking some help with the 'ideas' which inform that novel. Yet
extrapolation of 'ideas' has done little justice either to the imaginative quality
of the work, or to the impact of Hardy at this crucial moment of Lawrence's
development. As a book, supporting the claims of its title, it remains virtually
ignored. There are however reasons for this. The bulk of the *Study* appears to
be concerned with Lawrence, seemingly at his most arcane. It is also a study
of art and the artist in painting as well as literature; a book about sex and
marriage and not having enough to live on in 1914; a response to the
outbreak of war. In a 'miserable world' it is a confession of faith[2] about
creativity in nature, human relationship and art; a 'philosophy' or even
'theology' by a 'passionately religious man'[3] trying to adapt the language of
Christianity to express his growing insight into the relation of man and
woman. It is an attempt to clarify what he had been struggling towards in a
novel he had thought was complete, but which had to be taken up again and
restructured, with a newly sharp sense of form and purpose, as soon as the
Study was finished. In all this, it is not too surprising that the sections actually
on Hardy should seem isolated and disjunct. Yet the sense in which the book
is any of these things is also the sense in which it is all, and Hardy is the
centre. What I would like to indicate, within the limits of a short essay, is a
way of reading which could make the *Study* more available not simply to the
student of Lawrence's development, but to the student of the Wessex novels.

SOURCE *Thomas Hardy after Fifty years*, ed. Lance St John Butler, London, 1977, pp. 90–103.

Inescapably, the account will seem to be more 'of Lawrence' than 'of Hardy'; but this is to overlook the mode of the book, which has more in common with creative than with critical writing. It is an imaginative exploration, beginning in one position, moving out into another, and concluding in a third; and in that exploration, though Lawrence is the traveller, it is Hardy who defines the journey. Though Hardy appears, so to speak, only on three separate occasions, each appearance is a dramatic intervention marking a phase of exploration, and summoning Lawrence to a more radical self-scrutiny. Seen like this, Hardy is not there for Lawrence as merely a text for a literary critic, but as a profoundly creative influence, shaping his own imagination in an unfolding drama whose resolution—in one's response—ought to be a final recognition of the nature of both protagonists.

Lawrence begins, however, not with Hardy, but with a poppy—and it is important to see why. We might start by distinguishing his kind of thinking from Eliot's, in opening *Notes towards the Definition of Culture.* ('The term *culture* has different associations according to whether we have in mind the development of an *individual,* of a *group* or *class,* or of a *whole society* ...'[4]) Lawrence is to be no less concerned with culture (the tending of natural growth), the individual, and society; but he is not concerned with the kind of thinking that puts reason to work on terms, definitions, concepts. Human growth, in life or art, is an aspect of life itself, so Lawrence seeks to capture at the start a sense of something alive. This involves a consonant liveliness: a tone which refuses to take Lawrence or 'Man' too solemnly; a teasing humour which loosens up attitudes; an energy and fun which allow writer and reader to be on holiday with once-upon-time stories of cavemen, and phoenixes, and pastry-knobs on pies, and Dido. (One still comes across people who solemnly aver that Lawrence lacks humour.) But behind this is a grasp of parable as a way of getting down to basics, of teasing the intellectual scribe or pharisee out of conceptual thought into the extraordinary challenge of simplicity. Lawrence is, after all, obeying the charge to consider the lilies of the field, how they grow; and enforcing the same challenge as Christ's, to take no thought of self-preservation. To consider a poppy, growing, alive, is to see deeper and more simply than its 'careful architecture, all the chemistry, the weaving and the casting of energy' (399); it is to treat with contempt the concept of the red flower as the excess which always accompanies reproduction, or as a mere device to bring bees and help propagation. It is its flowering that makes a poppy a poppy: the thing itself at its maximum being.

As against, then, the urge to self-preservation from which society, government and industry have evolved, Lawrence contends that the final aim of every living thing is the full achievement of itself—after which it will bear the fruit of its nature. In the second chapter he reads this back into a radical criticism of society. If society is sick in its political, sexual and economic relationships, if there is war, the cause lies within individual men and women and there is no remedy in seeking to reform social systems. The suffragettes (whom he respects), and movements for parliamentary, legal and economic reform, are all misdirected towards the symptoms rather than the disease. That lies in the urge to self-preservation itself, the obsession with material needs, and the fear of risking security in the only final human right: to be oneself to the maximum of one's individual nature. For this very little is materially necessary (as Christ thought too); but men fear it as they fear the unknown. Yet for Lawrence, as for Blake, to repress the inner drive to be oneself, is inevitably to produce rottenness and destruction. Even the pity which seeks to redress poverty, 'loving one's neighbour as oneself', is false and destructive if it means reducing one's sense of one's neighbour or oneself to a matter of material needs; or if it leads to the false egalitarianism of holding back the self-development of any so that none should grow further than his neighbour.

> Every step I move forward into being brings a newer, juster proportion into the world, gives me less need of storehouse and barn, allows me to leave all, and to take what I want by the way, sure that it will always be there; allows me in the end to fly the flag of myself, at the extreme tip of life (409)

—like a poppy, or a phoenix, or a kindled bonfire on the edge of space. (The outbreak of war, on the other hand, is a sign of the loss of all sense of the value of life, a mass-movement of self-hate, a reaction of nausea against self-preservation, a death-wish.)

It is defiantly, even outrageously said, with a Blakean kind of truth, though it will hardly do as it stands. At least, however, Lawrence was practising what he preached. It is useful to realise that this chapter was primarily addressed to himself and his own cry 'What is going to become of us?'[5] when Methuen's return of his novel meant that there was not going to be enough to live on. Only now does he turn to Hardy, and only now can one see why the first of the three essays on the Wessex novels should take the line it does—and why it should be *The Return of the Native* that occupies the centre. Humour returns in a cheerfully cavalier précis of the first six novels as variations on a single theme—vastly oversimplified, of course. Yet the X-ray picture of the walled city, the poppy-characters, and the wilderness does have disconcerting insight, especially in the remarkable diagnosis of *The Return of the Native* which is Lawrence's real concern. There are three main contentions. The typical Hardy tragedy comes from the attempt to fulfil the self by breaking the confines of established forms of life in the community and its social morality; but the poppy-characters perish in the wilderness or come back reduced, while the prize of happiness and stability goes to those who stay within the walls. So the tragedy in *The Return* is the waste of Eustacia, through the 'subtle cowardice' and ultimate conventionality of Clym, who has original force of life but chooses 'to improve mankind rather than to struggle at the quick of himself into being' (414), and is consequently reduced to half-blindness and half-life, while Thomasin and Venn get the prize within the walls. But the second contention, which Lawrence urges more cogently than any other critic, is that Egdon Heath is the great power in the book.

> This is a constant revelation in Hardy's novels: that there exists a great back-ground, vital and vivid, which matters more than the people who move upon it ... The vast, unexplored morality of life itself, what we call the immorality of nature, surrounds us in its eternal incomprehensibility, and in its midst goes on the little human morality play' (419).

Hardy shares this quality with the great writers, Shakespeare, Sophocles, Tolstoy. But, finally, Hardy and Tolstoy are smaller because their tragedy lies not in trangression of nature, but merely of society, which for Lawrence is not necessarily tragic at all.

Of course this is Lawrence's *Return of the Native* rather than Hardy's. This first criticism is too skeletal: the bone structure without the play of expression across the face. It ignores the many-sidedness of Hardy's vision and the curiously shifting relation between the author and the fiction. It produces an Eustacia too tragically heightened and released from ironies, a reddleman too reduced from enigmatic suggestiveness, an Egdon too much a Lawrentian life-force to be faithful to Hardy's multiple view of the heath and its inhabitants. Yet the deep structure Lawrence sees is there, significantly so; and the analysis of Clym is in many respects sharper than Hardy's own Victorian uncertainty about his hero. What is most significant, however, and seldom grasped, is that this first essay on Hardy is only an initial move. Lawrence is about to change his mind, and the direction of his exploration.

His fourth chapter, 'An Attack on Work, and the Money Appetite, and the State', is apparently an extension of the earlier argument. Potentially man is a constantly brimming fountain of life, but he mostly has to spend it in work. It is true that he must work to eat, but he must not merely eat to work again; he needs the means of self-preservation not just to exist, but to live more fully. There is a satisfaction in work, in executing efficiently an habitual movement or a known process; the happiness and security of staying 'safe within the proven, deposited experience' of humanity, as it were within 'the trunk of the tree, in the channels long since built' (424). But this is always, in the end, an imprisonment; for man's deepest urge is to project himself as a leading-shoot into further realms of being, and so he will always long to be free from work, 'for the unresolved, quivering, infinitely complex and indefinite movement of new living' (425). He must claim this freedom. The machine is a labour-saver which can help us produce all we really need, and can be honoured thus far; but it is time for man to renounce his greed for more than he needs, to renounce the money appetite which governs industrialist and worker alike, to affirm that the individual is more important than the state, to move outside the walled city of the existing system.

Yet something new is happening, suggested perhaps by the metaphor of the tree, for in the next chapter Lawrence has changed his mind about work. It is not, after all, mere self-preservation but something more creative: a kind of knowledge, as man learned to plough and sow by becoming conscious of the significance of the fall of seeds and the covering of earth. So man is dual, Janus-faced: in both being ('the living stuff of life itself, unrevealed'); and 'knowing, with unwearying labour and unceasing success, the manner of that which has been, which is revealed' (430). Knowledge is also a force of life: 'It seems as if the great aim and purpose in human life were to bring all life into the human consciousness' (430–1); and as if conscious knowledge, involving increasing self-distinction of the individual from that which is not-him, were part of a universal process of progressive differentiation, from mass, to orders, to species, to distinct individual, to perfected individual, hero, or angel. Still the movement into being is primary, for knowledge can only be of that which already is; but the new sense of the value of distinct individuality forces Lawrence, in the middle of his chapter, to go back to Hardy again, from a different point of view.

The 'great background' is in abeyance, and the focus is now on the characters. Lawrence still urges his previous argument, but sees more clearly now that Hardy, too, has a *prédilection d'artiste* for the 'aristocrat'—by which he means someone who believes he or she has a right 'to be himself, to create himself' (436), to 'fulfil his own individual nature' (439)—as against the 'bourgeois', meaning someone whose existence and loyalty are tied to the community. But this makes it all the more striking that all the aristocrats are doomed to failure or death, and that it is the bourgeois who prosper. The physical aristocrats fall before the community; the physical and spiritual aristocrats fall because of their own isolation; the physical aristocrats who are spiritually bourgeois fail physically and are reabsorbed into the community; the bourgeois with civic virtues usually succeeds in the end. But there are three new kinds of perception. If Hardy, having a predilection for the aristocrats, is so driven to show them destroyed by the community or create them fatally flawed, it must be because of some deep division in himself. Moreover, to follow the 'little morality play' from the beginning to the end of the Hardy novels is to detect a *volte-face* of feeling. The sympathy at the beginning is all for the white knight and heroine against the dark villain and the red-and-black villainess; but in *The Mayor* the black villain 'is already almost the hero'; in *Tess* the condemnation 'gradually shifts' from the dark villain to the blond bourgeois hero; in *Jude* the white virgin 'is the arch-sinner against life at last' (437). Thirdly, in comparing Hardy with Shakespeare again, Lawrence now puts the Shakespearian stress not on transgression against nature, but on a fatal division within the self of the hero. He still thinks Hardy's tragedies fall short of this in being caused by something outside; the aristocrats still have to die even though the direction of sympathy has been reversed. But something is stirring in the *Study*; the beginning of a new sense of duality about being and knowing, and about Hardy. The second critique is still unsatisfactory. One cannot rip characters from their context and attempt to force them into categories, and Lawrence doesn't seem to know quite what to do with his new ideas. But if there were a way to bring the 'great background' back in, and somehow to fuse *that* with the division in Hardy and a more internalised sense of character . . .?

There is a way, and Lawrence finds it by going right back to the beginning, to consider the poppy again. Only this time he opens the flower, to look inside. Chapter 6, the shortest of all, is the centre on which the whole book turns: the completion of one movement of argument; the impulsion to another. The poppy 'lives' in two ways, not one. A movement of life has sprung from seed, grown a green pillar, and then both burst into flower and held back in seed. It is both the bonfire on the edge of space, the thing at its maximum being, and (*also* in its nature) poppy-preservation, security against the future. But deeper than that, looking inside, the poppy reveals a dynamism of two 'sexual' forces in the stamens and the pistil. Both flower and seeds are the product of the clash of 'female' and 'male'—a dualism, but also a two-in-one, a creative dialectic, and this becomes a central truth for Lawrence about all life and creativity.

It is at this point in the *Study* that Lawrence's deepest concerns come together: his marriage, his struggle to write *The Wedding Ring*, his 'passionately religious' sense of the world, his thoughts about the nature of art. In Chapters 7 and 8 he tries to formulate a way of looking at all personality, relationship, religion and art as the outcome of creative conflict between two opposed forces, impersonal and universal. I shall have to summarise brutally, but some caveats may be helpful first. This burst of creative imagination is essentially *exploratory*. One must not look for the philosopher's logic or careful consistency; but one will find an extraordinary movement, and expansion, of consciousness. The thought is dialectic rather than dualistic: both forces are vital to creative growth, and the deepest concern is with the marriage and consummation, in life and art, that springs from their conflict. Though they are separable for the sake of understanding, they are ultimately one, as the movement at the rim of a wheel and the stillness at its centre are one. Lawrence is well aware that all his terminologies, female and male, the axle and the wheel, God the Father and God the Son, Law and Love, are 'arbitrary, for the purpose of thought' (448).[6] We must not translate 'male' and 'female' into 'man' and 'woman', for though the exploration begins that way, it soon becomes clear that both 'male' and 'female' forces exist and conflict within every man and woman as well as between them. 'Sex' is a fully religious mystery. On the one hand 'the sexual act . . . is for leaping off into the unknown, as from a cliff's edge' (441); on the other, sexual acts as such are not essential for laying hold of the 'beyond', and consummation may take place in the spirit as well as the body. With these cautions we may speak of the 'Female', the force of Law, of God the Father; and of the 'Male', the force of Love, of God the Son.

God the Father is immutable, stable, all-embracing, one. Life according to this Law is pure being, in complete unity with the universe of created things. Man exists in the flesh, in nature, in sensation, linked with all creation in one whole. But equally there operates throughout creation the opposite force of Love, of God the Son. This is the impulse to movement and change, from being to knowing, from undifferentiated oneness to perception of what is not-self, defining the self against the other. It is differentiation into the many, into separation, into distinct self-awareness, thought and utterance. The ideal of the Son is ever more complete individuation. The two forces are always in conflict, but the conflict is the ground of all growth. From every successive clash, in an endless process, is born a new dimension of personal life, or religion, or art. Beyond God the Father and the Son is the Holy Spirit; beyond sexual conflict is consummation, giving man and woman more completely to themselves and opening up the beyond; out of the dualism in the artist is created the work of art.

Religions express what the race or the collective consciousness aspires to, in order to complete its partiality. Men create art to utter what they know in themselves. So, both developing and testing the formulation of his dialectic, Lawrence looks at a series of particular paintings and statues. If one tries to look at them too, what may appear to be pretentious generalisations about the history of art or the psychic states of artists turn out to be remarkably precise and illuminating perceptions. The central quality of the 'Madonna with the Iris'.[7] 'in the style of' Dürer, is how completely she occupies the picture in 'stable, incontrovertible being' (456). Plants and butterflies in her rustic bower (hardly distinguished from nature), and the suckling child which is an extension of her, all unite in togetherness with her tranquil centrality. But Botticelli's 'Mystic Nativity'[8] is a marvellous fusion of stability with ecstatic movement, centrifugal with centripetal force. At the still centre is the child. But, as one looks again, the child is in motion. The curious pose of the father, 'folded up' like a boulder (455), pulls the eye round to the right; the statuesque mother pushes it round to the left, suggesting a circular movement around Him. The angels clapsing humans at the foot of the picture are both frozen in a moment of communion, and seem about to turn in dance. The four planes of the picture from bottom to top initiate movement, spiring and counterspiring, which culminates in the joyous whirl of angels at the top, but the painting is *composed* about a still centre, tranquil. In 'Dürer's' picture God the Father predominates; in Botticelli's the Father is 'married' to the Son. Raphael and Michelangelo intensify in opposite directions. In Raphael's 'Ansidei Madonna'[9] the Virgin and Child are oddly abstracted-looking; but he 'rings her round with pure geometry, till she becomes herself almost of the geometric figure, an abstraction. The picture becomes a great ellipse crossed by a dark column' (460). It is still a marriage of 'male' and 'female', the column and the ellipse, but though there is unity and stability, almost static, it is produced by an act of abstract mind. But if Raphael is 'the

515

male reaction upon itself' (458) creating abstraction, Michelangelo 'sought the female in himself, aggrandized it, and so reached a wonderful momentary stability of flesh exaggerated till it became tenuous, but filled and balanced by the outward-pressing force'. So, the Moses looms 'announcing, like the Jewish God, the magnificence and eternality of the physical law'; the David is 'young, but with too much body for a young figure, the physique exaggerated, the clear, outward-leaping, essential spirit of the young man smothered over'; the slaves heave in body 'fastened in bondage that refuses them movement', the Adam on the Sistine ceiling 'can scarcely stir into life. That large body of almost transparent, tenuous texture is not established enough for motion', yet it is not motion he requires, but body. 'Give him but a firm, concentrated physique. That is the cry of all Michelangelo's pictures' (462). Yet other constations of the forces are to be found in Correggio, Rembrandt, and Turner. In the 'Madonna of the Basket'[10] the Virgin has become secular, a natural young girl with her baby and her workbasket, while her husband carpenters in the background. Correggio is concerned not with 'her great female mystery, but her individual character' (456). She is almost a woman he knows, though there is still a hint of mystery, a strange light and expressiveness in her face and in the stretch of the child to something beyond. In Rembrandt the light of knowledge is turned on to the flesh in increasing individuality. The human being is a separate self, distinct, 'and he must study himself ... So Rembrandt paints his own portrait again and again, sees it again and again within the light.' But though this is a great act of progressive individuation it is also more. 'It is the declaration that light is our medium of existence, that where the light falls upon our darkness there we *are*: that I am but the point where light and darkness meet and break upon one another' (471). So the light is also the light of the spirit which in 'The Jewish Bride'[11] or even in the 'Portrait of Himself and Saskia',[12] the man looks towards, past the embrace with the woman. And in the late portraits the light both enables individuality to materialise in every wrinkle, and is itself made manifest. But Turner 'did not seek to mate body with spirit ... what he sought was the mating of the Spirit ... Ever, he sought the Light, to make the light transfuse the body, till the body was carried away.' Turner's final picture might have been a pure white incandescent surface, but 'such a picture as his *Norham Castle, Sunrise*,[13] where only the faintest shadow of life stains the light, is the last word that can be uttered, before the blazing and timeless silence' (474). But, Lawrence adds, 'I cannot look at a later Turner picture without abstracting myself, without denying that I have limbs ... If I look at the Norham Castle and remember my own knees and my own breast, then the picture is a nothing to me' (475). What he looks for is an art in which all the contraries are married, not affirmed at one another's expense.

Critics of both Lawrence and Hardy have tended to shy away from the art-criticism in the *Study*, yet it is crucially important in enabling Lawrence to return to Hardy in an altogether deeper dimension, and to judge by the highest standards. In the art-criticism the 'ideas' have been authenticated, the contraries shown to be actually there in works of art. But in the process the multiplicities of creative tension have been revealed as far more complex than the dialectic theory itself could have suggested. So, in getting down to Hardy for the third time, the earlier positions have to be subsumed, complicated, deepened. The 'great background' can no longer be merely a background or a single life-force, for it has been *internalised* in the conflict of opposed forces of nature *within the self* and *in relationship*. It cannot be 'more important' (or less) than the people who move 'upon it', for universal forces have been so fused with character and into relationship that the classifications of the 'aristocrats' and the dichotomy of individual and community have become far too simple. The author's division is the ground of creativity; and it is the tension of opposed forces within characters—the Shakespearian mode from which Hardy had previously been excluded – and between them, that now holds all the attention. The stress must fall on *Tess* and *Jude*.

But what kind of criticism emerges? Lawrence formulates expectations for Tess that Hardy doesn't voice; and the way she is seen as destroyed by the opposite imbalances of Alec and Angel leaves aside the contingencies of the narrative. Yet the X-ray diagnosis is essentially true, both to one's sense of the stature of Tess, and to the basic impression the novel leaves on the memory long after the details have gone. This is because of the new sureness with which Lawrence cuts right through the dimensions of behaviour, and even feeling and self-consciousness—both the older morality of conduct and the newer morality of sensibility—to the fundamental nature of Hardy's people; and because Hardy's art was moving in the same direction. So the characteristics and the actions of Alec and Angel become symptoms of intrinsic imbalance in their natures, indeed of radical insufficiency of self through the atrophy of one or other of the essential natural drives. Alec will inevitably seek Tess for self-gratification, since (though masculine enough) he lacks the 'male' drive to discover a further dimension of selfhood through what is beyond himself. He is bound to see Tess 'as the embodied fulfilment of his own desire: something, that is, belonging to him. She cannot, in his conception, exist apart from him nor have any being apart from his being' (483). It is inevitable that Angel will deeply despise the woman in her, substitute ideas for her, desert her to go wandering, because of the atrophy in himself of all that Law, the 'female', has come to mean. Whereas Tess, intrinsic 'female', also has the 'male' respect for the Other, never seeing others as extensions of herself or herself as the centre of the universe, but accepting herself, and others, as they are. This is a big quality, more than passivity or fatalism. It helps to explain a reader's respect for Tess, and his feeling that she deserves a full 'consummation' of her complex human potentialities. To appreciate the depth of Alec's betrayal of her *being* is to see the murder as deeply credible, however clumsily managed; but also to see why no full life is possible with Angel, even apart from policemen and the law. As Lawrence moves from *Tess* to *Jude*, however, he does more than extend his previous analysis. He begins by noting the parallel between Alec and Arabella; though he also argues very acutely that they are intrinsically bigger than the materialisation Hardy allows in the *nouveau-riche* cad, or in the false hair and the practised dimple. (This is clear from the great scenes, on the harvester, or the pig-killing, where they demonstrably have a stature and a pressure they are often denied elsewhere.) He goes on to show Jude, both 'male' and 'female', pulled apart between Arabella and Sue as Tess had been between Alec and Angel. What is new, however, is the way Lawrence grows to see Jude as contributing to his own tragedy. Having realised half of himself through Arabella he is only too willing to deny it, wanting 'to arrest all his activity in his mind' (495) and being drawn inevitably to Sue. Yet the tragedy with Sue is very different. The previous logic suggests that, having 'produced an individual flower of his own' (499) through his 'male' relationship with Sue, it was natural that he should also want to sleep with, and have children by her. Yet Lawrence's critical imagination, responding with increasing compassion and understanding, sees more deeply into the radical incapacity in Hardy's Sue which rendered the sexual relationship fatal, and the death of the children artistically inevitable. He cuts through the 'bisexuality' of Sue (in ordinary terms) to a deeper and more accurate perception of a highly specialised being-in-one-kind, who is as surely destroyed by Jude's blind dragging 'his body after his consciousness' as he is by her. Jude and Sue 'are damned, partly by their very being, but chiefly by their incapacity to accept the conditions of their own and each other's being' (505). The change from the 'aristocrat' section, where she is the arch-sinner against life, is very marked. 'Sue had a being, special and beautiful. Why must not Jude recognize it in all its speciality? ... She was not "a woman". She was Sue Bridehead, something very particular. Why was there no place for her?' (510).

It is because, Lawrence concludes, Hardy came at the end of an epoch of the supremacy of God the Son. Deeply drawn to the opposite world of the older Law, Hardy feared it and tended always to write it down—hence Alec, Arabella and their predecessors. His art had moved, ever more surely, to assert the impulse to individuation in mind and spirit, denying the body which unites man with the natural universe. But Hardy could only pit one force *against* the other, tragically; he could see no possible reconciliation. What remained to strive for was a 'supreme fiction' in which both sides of the dialectic would have full expression, neither overbalancing the other; but in which there would also be 'the final reconciliation, where both are equal, two in one, complete' (516). As Lawrence began, at once, to rewrite *The Wedding Ring* into *The Rainbow*, that was his aim.

His dialogue with Hardy finally brought about the revolutionary change in his own fiction he had struggled so hard to achieve. By exploring Hardy's people he had found a language in which to articulate his vision; and also, as

I have argued elsewhere,[14] the outlines of a new structure for the first of the two novels (not one) that would be needed. The *Study* showed him how to begin, how to divide *The Rainbow* into its three 'testaments', and where to end in near-tragedy, but with a vision of reconciliation to be achieved in the second novel. It also awakened images which his novelist's imagination could explore in terms of human relationship, with marvellous sensitivity and insight.[15] But above all, his experience of Hardy must have been the greatest possible authentication and encouragement of his own vision. Here, of all English novelists, was one who saw human life against a vast impersonal landscape, and whose characters already existed in terms of being and consciousness rather than the conduct and sensibility of 'the old stable ego'.[16] As he pondered more deeply he had come to see how, as Hardy's fiction developed, the great background had become internalised in the conflict of universal forces within the characters themselves, at such a depth that they already clarified, in credibly human complexity, the interplay of contraries which he had been trying to understand in his own life and art. Yet he must have felt—the most liberating perception of affinity—that Hardy had neither seen clearly where he was going nor gone far enough, that there was room to move beyond him and, above all, to move beyond his pessimism. What *Tess* and *Jude* began, *The Rainbow* could complete.

Yet the very depth and clarity of his insight shows up the limitations of its focus. He took one dimension of Hardy criticism as far as it would go; but in so doing he poses, all the more sharply because of his affinity with the most 'Lawrentian' of the Wessex novels, the challenge to pin down the other dimensions he seems blind to, but which make Hardy himself, and not an incomplete D.H. Lawrence. Significantly, *The Mayor of Casterbridge* is hardly there in the *Study* and everything implied by 'of Casterbridge' is underplayed: Hardy's stubborn sense of how unavoidably 'character' is conditioned and action limited by place and time, by being-in-society and being-in-history. The way a Hardy character is himself must also be the way in which he locates an interplay of economic conditions, social mores, a past which is a living presence, and the history-within-the-blood. Lawrence can show the inevitability of the death of Sue's children in one sense, because of what their parents are in themselves; but he largely ignores the multiple pressures of place and history which brought them where they are, and the tragically foreshortened sense of Time that names the executioner. One must be careful here: the complex ways in which *The Rainbow* is a social history will show that Lawrence was not as single-minded as he seems in the *Study*. Yet always his drive is to free his characters from society and history, determining themselves. For Lawrence, Hardy's sense of limitation is an imaginative failure; for Hardy, Lawrence's sense of freedom would be delusion. This is an opposition so radical that it must give rise to fundamentally different kinds of art. If I have used the X-ray metaphor for Lawrence's criticism, it was to suggest his search 'beneath the surface' for some basic structure in art and life. But Hardy's whole way of seeing is different: if a Hardy novel is a 'series of seemings' or a 'great web', it is because no single way of seeing will do. Vision, to be inclusive enough, must be from this angle, *and* that, *and* this; and the multiple perspectives do not fuse so much as sustain one another by a sense of interweaving. Hardy is more tentative, more aware of how one way of looking is different from as well as linked to another, more sceptical. He is also more aware of multiplicity, and of the sheer difficulty of seeing enough and of holding what one sees together. (It was probably the erosion by the late 1890s of the possibility of using 'Wessex' as an *externally* coherent world any longer that made Hardy abandon fiction.) The 'series of seemings' has to be articulated by a Narrative which both allows for accident and holds design; and which, in moving narrator and reader from one location and mode of observation to another, never allows point-of-view to settle. Where Lawrence tends to be immersed in and committed to everything he writes, Hardy moves in and out of his fiction, now sympathetically involved, now wryly distanced, shifting stance from sentence to sentence or even within a sentence. No two novelists, in being so like each other, are in fact so different.

'Where *Jude* ends, *The Rainbow* begins.'[17] This is true both in the sense in which, together, they mark the change from nineteenth-century to modern, from the novel of behaviour to the novel of being, from character to consciousness; and also in the sense in which Hardy helped Lawrence to find himself, and carry to completion what he saw in the Wessex novels. Yet it is no less important to see how, and why, Hardy 'ends' with *Jude*. Indeed Lawrence's own dialectic gives one the final clue to the significance of his study of Hardy, in emphasising how both the 'self' and the 'other' are 'singled out' in themselves, through the discovery of true relationship.

Notes

1. Phoenix—*The Posthumous Papers of D. H. Lawrence*, ed. E.D. McDonald (London, 1936) pp. 398–516. Page references in the text are to this edition. The Study is now also available in *Lawrence on Hardy and Painting*, ed. J.V. Davies (London, 1973).

2. To Pinker, 5 September 1914: 'What a miserable world. What colossal idiocy, this war. Out of sheer rage I've begun my book about Thomas Hardy.' *The Collected Letters of D.H. Lawrence*, ed. Harry T. Moore (London, 1962) I, p. 290; hereafter referred to as 'C.L.'. Lawrence told Amy Lowell on 18 November that he was almost finished—S. Foster Damon, *Amy Lowell. A Chronicle* (Boston, 1935) p. 279—and, later, that it had 'turned out as a sort of Story of My Heart, or a *Confessio Fidei*'—C.L. 298. For a fuller account of the circumstances of composition of the *Study* and its relation to the making of *The Rainbow* and *Women in Love*, see Mark Kinkead-Weekes, 'The Marble and the Statue' in *Imagined Worlds*, ed. Maynard Mack and Ian Gregor (London, 1968) pp. 371–418.

3. C.L. 273. In a 'Foreword to Sons and Lovers', written in January 1913 and never meant for publication, he had first attempted to rewrite Christian theology in terms of the relation of man and woman. See *The Letters of D.H. Lawrence*, ed. Aldous Huxley (London, 1932) pp. 95–102.

4. T.S. Eliot, *Notes towards the Definition of Culture* (London, 1948) p. 21.

5. C.L. 289. Methuen claimed later to have returned the manuscript because 'it could not

be published in its then condition'—see the report of proceedings at the trial of *The Rainbow*, *Sunday Times*, 14 November 1915, p. 13. There is evidence however that many publishing ventures were being retrenched because of the war. In a moment, the financial security of Methuen's lucrative offer had turned into serious embarrassment for the Lawrences.

6. As if to mark the point, Lawrence *reversed* 'male' and 'female' in the opening pages of *The Rainbow*. I prefer the terminology of God the Father and the Son as less liable to misunderstanding.

7. In the National Gallery, London (the lower gallery).

8. In the National Gallery, London.

9. In the National Gallery, London.

10. In the National Gallery, London.

11. In the Rijksmuseum, Amsterdam.

12. In the Pinakotek, Dresden.

13. In the Tate Gallery, London.

14. 'The Marble and the Statue', op. cit., pp. 380–6.

15. For example, the use of the axle and the wheel in the chapter on the honeymoon of Anna and Will; the expansion of the *Study's* remarks on medieval cathedrals and on the column and ellipse in the Cathedral chapter; the pervasive exploration of Rembrandtesque light and dark; the Turneresque incandescence in the scene with Skrebensky on the beach.

16. C.L. 282. The *Study* helps us, as it helped Lawrence, to grasp what he had been struggling to say in this letter. In *The Rainbow*, Ursula does pass through 'allotropic states' in which, while still recognisably Ursula, she seems radically different; as she is patterned in different ways by differing interactions of the 'male' and 'female' forces within and upon her, in the successive phases of her story.

17. The final sentence in Ian Gregor, *The Great Web* (London, 1974).

202

Either Side of Wessex

———————◆———————

MICHAEL IRWIN and IAN GREGOR

I

'The following novel, the first published by the author, was written nineteen years ago, at a time when he was feeling his way to a method.'

Hardy is writing a preface for *Desperate Remedies*, and looking back, in the manner of an author secure in his achievement, at problems now happily resolved. For Hardy, writing in 1889, such an attitude was appropriate and understandable. For us, the longer perspective makes the position appear differently.

This is particularly true now that the New Wessex Edition has restored the 'minor' novels to general currency. Looking at the line of fiction that extends a quarter of a century from *Desperate Remedies* (1871) to *The Well-beloved* (1897) we can see that there never was a time when Hardy ceased 'feeling his way to a method'. Critical concentration on the six famous 'Wessex' novels has made his art appear simpler and more homogeneous than it was. To study the minor works is to be reminded that Hardy's creative talents involved tensions and contrarieties not easily or always reconciled in fictional terms.

By examining the beginning and the end of Hardy's career as a novelist we hope to show why he might have found it peculiarly difficult to evolve a 'method', why his method should have led him to the idea of Wessex, and why that idea should finally have been abandoned in the interests of an apparently new development. It is not our present purpose to attempt a revaluation of the minor novels, but at least, and unquestionably, *Desperate Remedies* can tell us a great deal about Hardy's early aims and problems, and *The Well-beloved* can enlarge our understanding of *Jude*. Our central concern, however, is not with this or that particular novel, but with Hardy's own imaginative journey—a voyage of exploration that neither began nor ended in Wessex.

SOURCE *Thomas Hardy after Fifty Years*, ed. Lance St John Butler, London, 1977, pp. 104–15.

II

Hardy himself was to say of *Desperate Remedies* that 'the powerfully, not to say wildly, melodramatic situations had been concocted in a style which was quite against his natural grain ...' But the modern reader who comes to this first novel from the later ones finds not merely an excellent tale of mystery and suspense but a work which is in its very texture Hardyesque. There is a singularity in the descriptive writing that reveals a distinctive imagination, a distinctive vision. The author is already following his own later prescript: '... the seer should watch that pattern among general things which his idiosyncrasy moves him to observe, and describe that alone.'

His own 'idiosyncrasy' is perhaps best illustrated from the *Life*, where he is free to write for himself. In the course of a long illness he makes this note:

> *January 13.* Incidents of lying in bed for months. Skin gets fair: corns take their leave: feet and toes grow shapely as those of a Greek statue. Keys get rusty; watch dim, boots mildewed; hat and clothes old-fashioned; umbrella eaten out with rust; children seen through the window are grown taller.

The entry is striking in several ways. Hardy has found in particularities a very effective notation for an abstract experience. The sights he records are individually pleasing in their unexpectedness, but gain force from juxtaposition. A variety of aspects of living are brought into implied connection; decay and regeneration are curiously linked. Somehow the bare factual memorandum comes to suggest a view of life. As an account of a serious illness the passage is at the same time intensely personal and intensely impersonal.

In *Desperate Remedies*, too, Hardy frequently chooses to isolate—to focus attention on, say, a single hair from Mrs Manston's head or a single raindrop, or 'a warm foot in a polished boot'. The same habit leads him to define scenes by means of salient detail: '... their clothing touched, and remained in contact'; 'The shovel shone like silver from the action of the juice ...' At a further stage of reduction many an incident is sketched solely in sounds: '... the click of the smoke-jack, the flap of the flames, and the light touches of the women's slippers upon the stone floor.' Repeatedly Hardy looks at an ordinary place or landscape from an unusual angle, or sees it under an unusual aspect. The palings in Lincoln's Inn Fields are 'rusted away at their base to the thinness of wires'. Conversely, in a dramatic frost Cytherea sees that 'A shoot of the diameter of a pin's head was iced as thick as her finger ...' Scene after scene is brilliantly coloured, or is distinctively lit by sun, moon, candle, lantern, firelight or match.

As in the extract quoted from the *Life* the descriptive habit implies a habit of thought, a stance towards experience. There is a constant attempt to present the familiar in a new guise—to make the reader look with fresh eyes and see unsuspected relationships. On the merely stylistic level the same instinct is seen in the surprising similes: 'countless stars fluttering like bright birds'; 'high-hipped, rich-coloured cows with backs horizontal and straight as the ridge of a house'; 'her small taper fingers extended like the leaves of a lupine.' At the narrative level the oddity of vision can be dramatised within the episode. For conveniently hyperbolic examples we must look beyond *Desperate Remedies*. In *A Pair of Blue Eyes* Elfride undressing on the cliff-top, Knight hanging from the cliff-face, Smith sailing home from Egypt and a fossil some millions of years old are brought into a pattern of mutual regard. In *The Well-beloved* Pierston takes in at one view Avice's moving coffin 'with its twelve legs', a church, a lighthouse, the sea and even the twinkle of a school of mackerel.

It is not, perhaps, immediately apparent that these various practices involve a tension, or even a contradiction. They express not a single tendency but two opposed tendencies. One is towards vividness, immediacy. There is a sense of being brought into direct contact with a certain sight or sound. Yet at the same time the peculiarity of the perspective, or the almost 'metaphysical' quality of the simile, can seem deliberately obtrusive—designed, not to present the thing itself, but an attitude to, or an idea about, that thing. Again, the extravagance of Hardy's visual effects is no more characteristic than a countervailing precision: 'she acquired perceptions of the newcomer in the following order: unknown trousers; unknown waistcoat; unknown face.' Altogether Hardy's 'idiosyncrasy of regard' involves a series of opposites: immediacy against detachment, spontaneity against reflection, flamboyance against formality. Such antinomies are ingeniously reconciled in Hardy's incidental perceptions—are indeed the very thing that makes them intriguing; but it might be suspected that in a developed story antagonistic intentions might lead the author into difficulty.

That is a question to which we will return. When he was writing *Desperate Remedies* Hardy was necessarily concerned with the more basic problem of whether his descriptive skills were appropriate to fiction at all. Would he be able to do more than work into his narrative arresting visual material taken, as it might be, from a commonplace book? From our vantage-point we might pose the question differently: Hardy's art is often called cinematographic— might not *Desperate Remedies* be compared to the work of a director prolix in stark images and novel camera-angles, but with nothing much to say? Are style and subject-matter brought into relationship? Is the novel more than a mystery-story with descriptive decorations?

A defence of its unity of purpose might begin from the fact that the scenes Hardy describes often alter the mood or motive of those who witness them. After Cytherea has rejected Manston's advances he is walking in his back-yard and turns to look into a water-butt:

> Hundreds of thousands of minute living creatures sported and tumbled in its depths with every contortion that gaiety could suggest; perfectly happy, though consisting only of a head, or a tail, or at most a head and a tail, and all doomed to die within the twenty-four hours.

524

This is pure Hardy: it isn't easy to think of another novelist who would describe the contents of a water-butt. But the passage is no mere interlude. Manston is affected by what he sees: 'Damn my position! Why shouldn't I be happy through my little day too? Let the parish sneer at my repulses, let it. I'll get her, If I move heaven and earth to do it!'

Shortly afterwards, when he is renewing his advances to Cytherea, her tendency to submit to them is partly traceable to the effects of her surroundings, a meadow at sunset:

> The stillness oppressed and reduced her to mere passivity. The only wish the humidity of the place left in her was to stand motionless. The helpless flatness of the landscape gave her, as it gives all such temperaments, a sense of bare equality with, and no superiority to, a single entity under the sun.

It must be admitted that these effects are local ones. The characters of Manston and Cytherea are insufficiently developed to permit any real latitude of motive. In any case the plot requires that they must behave as they do were the landscape hilly and Manston's water-butt empty. But Hardy is surely not just demonstrating his 'idiosyncrasy of regard' but already 'feeling his way' towards the creation of a context that will give it narrative relevance. When he uses again, in *The Return of the Native*, the passage about the effect of a flat landscape, it takes on far greater significance, but significance of a similar kind.

There is an interesting congruity between the unlikely relation of character and background suggested by such episodes and the unlikely relationships implied by Hardy's strange images and tricks of perspective. Both story and description deal in curious links, resemblances, affinities, influences. The freaks of nature—sudden storms or frosts, for instance— parallel the freakishness of human conduct. The fire which destroys the Three Tranters is necessary to Hardy's plot; but as he describes it, circumstantially, from its minutest beginnings it could be a metaphor for the accidentally initiated destructiveness of Manston. Both in substructure and in superstructure *Desperate Remedies* demonstrates the strangeness and the interconnectedness of the world.

Such a summary might suggest that Hardy the novelist would find matter and manner in easy harmony. But in fact it embodies the very contradiction mentioned earlier. 'Strangeness' pulls one way, 'interconnectedness' the other. Again extravagance and pattern are in conflict. The problem becomes clearer if one goes beyond detail and incident to look at a complete episode. A useful example to analyse might be that of Mr Graye's death; partly because it is the first directly-narrated episode in the novel, partly because it is gratuitous. Mr Graye could be disposed of as summarily as his unfortunate wife: a heart-attack would seem the obvious and humane way of eliminating him. Instead Hardy has him fall off a church-tower in full view of his daughter. The manner of his death has no consequences in the story: it seems solely designed to provide a lurid start.

Yet in the telling the episode is *not* lurid. Neither Cytherea nor the reader sees Mr Graye hit the ground: he merely disappears downwards. His death, like the others in *Desperate Remedies*—like the great majority of deaths in Hardy—takes place *just* off-stage. But a more important factor is stylisation. Hardy is at pains to formalise the picture Cytherea sees from the Town Hall: 'It was an illuminated miniature, framed in by the dark margin of the window, the keen-edged shadiness of which emphasised by contrast the softness of the objects enclosed.' Naturally the men on top of the steeple are physically diminished. They 'appeared little larger than pigeons, and made their tiny movements with a soft, spirit-like stillness.' Another kind of distancing effect is achieved by Hardy's comment on Cytherea, who is idly looking on: 'as listless and careless as one of the ancient Tarentines, who, on such an afternoon as this, watched from the Theatre the entry into their Harbour of a power that overturned the State'.

Having devised a needlessly sensational episode, then, Hardy makes it carefully, almost pedantically, unsensational. The 'framing' device he uses here he later, of course, resorts to again and again. It neatly figures the author's instinctive subjection of narrative or descriptive extravagance to control.

Already in *Desperate Remedies* there are signs of a spasmodic attempt by Hardy to discipline his plot, too, by patterning. Miss Aldclyffe is made to see herself and Cytherea as counterparts: each of them falling in love with a man who is already engaged. But she herself is a counterpart to Edward Springrove, in that for each the course of true love is obstructed by premature entanglement with a cousin. From this point of view Cytherea's plight corresponds to her father's and is only a mirror-image of Miss Aldclyffe's. There is further parallelism between Cytherea and Edward, as they are simultaneously drawn towards undesired marriages through unselfish willingness to help a relative.

If Hardy had gone further in this direction he might have groped his way towards a very modern kind of novel: the kind in which structural symmetries signal to the reader that extravagances of plot are meant to have a figurative, not a literal force. The kind of novel, in fact, that Iris Murdoch writes. Already in *A Pair of Blue Eyes* Hardy produces at least a near-success in just such a mode. Yet this is not the line that he chooses to follow; and it is intriguing to speculate why.

One obvious reason is that over a large area of his interests Hardy was predominantly a realist. Authenticity is natural to his descriptive mode. He does not lightly invoke fire or storm: he knows how a blaze starts and what noises wind and rain make. He knows about landscape, local history, geology, dialect, work. The *Life* shows that the kind of anecdote he liked to record combined the unusual or even the melodramatic with just such authenticity. The characteristic narrative impulse is not: 'There was once a man who sold his wife—', but rather: 'There was once a hay-trusser named

Henchard who sold his wife in a drunken fit at Weydon Fair.' Such a story is, of course, highly recalcitrant to patterning. The unusualness might be retained, but the authenticity will be lost.

But, as often in discussion of Hardy's art, the general statement needs immediate qualification. This authenticity is itself limited. Hardy sees vividly, but sees as a detached observer—through a window, through a keyhole, from the summit of a hill. The vision tends to be static—less a film than a sequence of slides. Some things he fails to see at all. The on-stage doings of Hardy's major characters may be sharply specific; by contrast their off-stage and antecedent lives can be so shadowy as to be almost unimaginable. Almost every novel has some markedly theoretical aspect. Manston is the first of a long line of characters who try to regulate their conduct in terms of a private system of belief or disbelief. In a substantial, working, rural world these theoreticians are alien figures in more senses than Hardy intended. Throughout his career he was to hesitate between the predominant realism and a formalism that might accommodate such visitors. There is often a sense, even in his greatest novels, of ideas extrinsic to the story that is being told, or of vivid episodes that have yet drifted away from significance or control.

III

The context that brought 'the ideas' and 'the story' into a relationship to be sustained through most of Hardy's career as a novelist came into being with *Far From the Madding Crowd*. It was, of course, Wessex. In a preface written twenty years after the novel Hardy says that he envisaged 'a series of novels ... requiring a territorial definition of some sort to lend unity to the scene.' The kind of unity involved however, is not so simply described. 'Wessex' enabled Hardy to shift his narrative stance slightly, but crucially, so that he was freed from a manner of narration which suggested the inventor of tales, to a manner which suggested he was their chronicler. He was able to convey a sense of time which was suggestive both of the historian and 'The Shepheardes Calender'. Fact and fiction could be brought into a new relationship. If there was melodrama in Wessex it was because there was a melodrama in nature, in the sudden violence of storm and fire, or because it invaded our workaday lives when a prosperous shepherd could be rendered destitute by the sudden self-destruction of his sheep, or our emotional lives because the gargoyles of some churches in Wessex are sadly in need of repair. This glaze of circumstantiality laid upon a fiction is present in the first thing we encounter in every Wessex novel—the map. We see a region immediately recognisable in outline and contour, but wholly fictive in name; a region with a history but peopled by romance. Hardy had created an imagined world in which contraries could coexist. If 'detail' could be endlessly accommodated in the texture of that world, in woods and heath and trackways, in methods of work, in the business of the market-place, in the pleasures of the ale house, 'pattern' could find expression in its structure, in the rhythm of the seasons, in simple plots about three men and a girl, about fickle soldiery and abandoned serving girls. It allows, too, a place for the ubiquitous observer, labelled variously 'a wayfarer' or 'a bystander', to overhear voices in the dark or behind a wall, to glimpse people moving in the shadows or framed suddenly in a window or a doorway, and by an accumulation of such impressions to be able to convey a sense of a whole community being looked at and appraised by a vigilant eye.

As originally conceived, however, this 'world' had a crucial limitation which Hardy soon recognized: it could make his work narrow and stereotyped.

> He was aware of the pecuniary value of a reputation for a speciality ... yet he had not the slightest intention of writing for ever about sheepfarming, as the reading public was apparently expecting him to do, and as, in fact, they presently resented his not doing.'[1]

It was in the process of writing *The Return of the Native*, with the introduction of Clym, that Hardy realised that Wessex need no longer be thought of as 'writing about sheepfarming', but in Matthew Arnold's phrase, could be made to include 'the dialogue of the mind with itself'. Into Wessex Hardy was able to introduce not simply the structure provided by indigenous customs and plots, but more inclusively, the structure of a contemporary consciousness, ambivalent in its sympathies and sceptical in outlook. The development of Wessex could, in other words, be made commensurate with the development of the author.

As Hardy's novels developed in the 1880s we see him continuing 'to extend his method', but comfortably within the frontiers set by Wessex. Emphases change, but the basic pattern remains. In form, a contemplative narrator broods over a community evoked in loving detail; in substance, the narrative is structured in major conflicts, Henchard against Farfrae, Grace against Melbury and Giles, Angel against Tess. But that very sequence of names indicates the change overcoming Wessex, which was to be more than a change of emphasis. The region is becoming as much an interior landscape as an external one. If we compare the presentation of Weatherbury Farm with Talbothays we see the nature of the shift. Perhaps no landscape in Hardy is presented with more scrupulous care and loving attention to detail than the farm which Tess enjoys as a milkmaid, but if we compare it with Weatherbury, we recognise that the feeling it evokes is inseparable from the love of Angel and Tess; and behind that lie the feelings of an author who knows that his idyll is really an elegy. Wessex, as it goes through successive presentations, becomes gradually more and more stylised, the region shaped increasingly by the feelings of the author and by the invading of a world elsewhere. When Tess dies—the last and richest embodiment of the region—Wessex dies too.

But Hardy, like Angel Clare, has to 'go on', to write a fiction that will express those feelings about isolation, about love, about the modern world, which were released by Wessex and came finally to overwhelm it. The challenge was to find a method to express the contraries which had haunted his imagination but without the support which the rural background had given him for so long.

IV

Fitzpiers and Angel Clare are obliged to adjust their different brands of romantic idealism to the demands of the real world. In *The Well-beloved* modern, self-conscious man, the theoretician, is examined on his own terms. The result is by definition a formal, patterned novel. Hardy stylises into new significance what seems at first to be a familiar situation. The concentration is on Jocelyn Pierston and on 'the lonely rock of his birthplace' where he seeks his beloved. It is the return of the native again—with a difference. Clym comes 'home' to find 'some rational occupation among the people I know best'; Jocelyn's only 'home' is in peace of mind, his occupation, so far from being 'among people', is the product of his own imagination, carved out of the rock of his birthplace and shaped into art by the frustrations of his solitary life. The novel is the tale of a self-enclosure which lasts a lifetime; this native is not estranged from his birthplace, but from himself.

To convey the intensity and the duration of this self-dislocation, Hardy puts into practice a prescription he wrote in his notebook at the beginning of 1893. 'The whole secret of fiction and the drama—in the constructional part—lies in the adjustment of things unusual to things eternal and universal.' In *The Well-beloved* 'things unusual' are juxtaposed to 'things external' with stark severity. The story of the Sculptor, with a metropolitan reputation, in love with three generations of girls from the same family is seen against a background of Hardy's profoundly held beliefs about the nature of love and the inexorable passing of time. To facilitate 'the constructional part' Hardy availed himself of the Platonic belief in the transmigration of the beloved. This was the machinery which enabled him, as he puts it, 'to introduce the subjective theory of love into modern fiction'. Without interrogating that phrase too closely, its direction can be felt if we compare the difference in emphasis of Arnold's phrase 'the dialogue of the mind with itself' when applied to *The Return of the Native* and then to *The Well-beloved*.

By laying the emphasis so firmly on the interiorisation of *The Well-beloved*, it might seem that we are overlooking 'the island' as presenting a substantial reality which is indifferent to Jocelyn's dilemma. In a sense, the 'treeless rock' does have a function similar to Egdon, it too is 'a face upon which time makes little impression' and provides therefore an ironic counterpoint to the characters. But where 'the vast tract of unenclosed land' has a reality quite independent of the drama acted out upon it, the Isle of Slingers, vivid and detailed as it is, has about it an hallucinatory clarity reminiscent of expressionist films:

> The towering rock, the houses above houses, one man's doorstep rising behind his neighbour's chimney, the gardens hung up by one edge to the sky, the vegetables growing on apparently almost vertical planes, the unity of the whole island as a solid and single block of limestone four miles long, were no longer familiar and commonplace ideas. All now stood dazzlingly unique and white against the tinted sea, and the sun flashed on infinitely stratified walls of oolite … with a distinctiveness that called the eyes to it as strongly as any spectacle he had beheld afar.

For all the visual sharpness of that scene, it is the observer we are finally reminded of, and when later, Jocelyn sees the huge cubes of white oolite on the wharves of the Thames, we feel the landscape has moved and begun to acquire the 'insubstantiality of the well-beloved'.

If the construction of *The Well-beloved* enables Hardy to present in fiction the idea of love with the directness we associate with his poetry and to dramatise in the character of Jocelyn, a subjective awareness of that idea, it also allows him to convey something further: the sense of the passage of time.

The fantasy of the plot shows the lapse of time to operate in two ways which seem at first almost antithetical. The repetition of the drama over three generations and Jocelyn and Avice Caro gives the sense of a universal predicament, a dilemma intrinsic in man's emotional aspirations, where the reach and the grasp are always at odds. In that perspective the successive generations give the sense of duration, of endless sequence; in another perspective the very similarity of the drama within each generation telescopes them, so that they become aspects of a single conflict. But whichever way we look, these two perspectives are united in a third which sees the process of time as endlessly destructive. We have the tension and pathos expressed in the titles of each part of the novel, 'A Young Man of Twenty', 'A Young Man of Forty', 'A Young Man of Sixty', and succinctly, in a poem of the same period.

> *But Time, to make me grieve,*
> *Part steals, lets part abide;*
> *And shakes this fragile frame at eve*
> *With throbbings of noontide.*

Time is destructive but it is sadly teasing too; it is only when Jocelyn looks at himself in the mirror or looks at Marcia that the full force of Time's passage is seen:

> She stood the image and superscription of Age—an old woman, pale and shrivelled, her forehead ploughed, her cheek hollow, her hair white as snow. To this the face he once kissed had been brought by the raspings, chisellings, scourgings, bakings, freezings of forty invidious years—by the thinkings of more than half a life-time.

It would be false to the spirit of *The Well-beloved* to leave an account of it, however brief, on that bleak and uncompromising note. It would be false because when Hardy was 'feeling for a method' he needed the distance which fantasy would bring not only to reveal the tragedy in Jocelyn's situation, but also to release the comic spirit which, for Hardy, kept it close company. It is a spirit which 'surprises Jocelyn into stillness', when Avice the second, the least attractive and intelligent of the girls, says by way of explaining her resistance to his advances, 'I have loved *fifteen* a 'ready! Yes, fifteen I am almost ashamed to say', she repeated laughing. 'I can't help it, sir, I assure you. Of course, it is really to me, the same one all through, only I can't catch him ...' That Avice should be allowed to state the theme so bluntly suggests that Hardy was nicely aware that *The Well-beloved*, for all its seriousness, should keep a modest sense of its scope.

The modesty consists, in its abstract construction, in the sense that this is *merely* a novel of pattern, that Love, Art and Time seek to be spelt with capital letters and exist virtually outside a context of historical circumstance. To restore that context became Hardy's aim as he turned Jocelyn into Jude, the well-beloved into Sue, and 'the lonely island' into Chrisminster and elsewhere. Through the obliquities of *The Well-beloved* Hardy had prepared himself for a more direct treatment of the idea of love, so that he now felt ready to write, as he says in his preface,

> a novel addressed by a man to men and women of full age; which attempts to deal unaffectedly with the fret and fear, derision and disaster, that may press in the wake of the strongest passion known to humanity; to tell, without a mincing of words, of a deadly war waged between flesh and spirit ...

Hardy had never been more passionate, more direct, more candid in introducing a novel, and it is a sign of the remarkable confidence that he now felt in his abilities that he was able to use a rhetoric so plain.

The feeling that *Jude* conveys is so direct and so powerful, that 'without a mincing of words' seems not an inappropriate description, but the structure which conveys that feeling is more carefully calculated than ever. Hardy, profiting from the experience of writing *The Well-beloved* where he had made the symmetry of plot carry its own meaning, extends this in *Jude* so that the structure itself derives from that clash of contraries so basic to his imagination.

> Of course the book is all contrasts—or was meant to be in its original conception. Alas, what a miserable accomplishment it is, when I compare it with what I meant to make it!—e.g. Sue and her heathen gods set against Jude's reading the Greek testament; Christminster academical, Christminster in the slums; Jude the saint, Jude the sinner; Sue the Pagan, Sue the saint; marriage, no marriage; etc. etc.[2]

Jude is the case of a novel not merely embodying a man's imagination, but miming the way it works. It is an index of how completely Hardy has come to know himself as an artist. This is not to say that *Jude* is an unequivocal success, but that by the time of *Jude* Hardy has assimilated his past as completely as a writer can and knows precisely what he can do. Or he almost does.

Father Time is the last, but in some ways the most dramatic, instance of Hardy continuing 'to feel for a method' in a novel where that whole notion had been ostentatiously put to one side. As a character Father Time marks the place where two kinds of fiction cross, in one he is 'Arabella's boy', in the other he is 'Age masquerading as Juvenility'. The crossing is an awkward one. But for our purpose, it is not the character, but the function of Father Time that matters. In Father Time Hardy was seeking to fill the gap created by the absence of Wessex, he needed the long perspective which reveals that while men may make their own plots, a plot may be made for them, the scenario of which can only be guessed at. Father Time was an actor in that script, forever old where Pierston was forever young. But Father Time has to carry more than his years, he is 'the expression in a single term' of the situation between Jude and Sue, and it is a function too great for him to bear. We sense the immensity of feeling behind his creation, but as an expression of those feelings, he is baffled, mute. Nevertheless, if we try to think of *Jude* without Father Time, it becomes a lesser novel, a tragedy not about the universe, but more about unfulfilled ambitions, domestic strife. Father Time marks the outermost reach of Hardy's art: the extravagance is too great—the stylisation fails; the formal and the realistic modes collide. But there is a sense in which the very violence of that collision is a measure of the author's creative energy, of his undiminished eagerness to encompass something new.

Notes

1. F.E. Hardy, *The Life of Thomas Hardy*, Macmillan, 1962, p. 102.
2. *Ibid.*, pp. 272–3.

203

Hardy and the 'Cell of Time'

◆

PATRICIA INGRAM

In chapter twenty-two of *A Pair of Blue Eyes*, Henry Knight finds himself by a ludicrous accident clinging for life to the edge of a cliff. Hardy then describes how—'By one of those familiar conjunctions of things wherewith the inanimate world baits the mind of man when he pauses in moments of suspense'—he sees opposite his eyes in the cliff face an imbedded fossil:

> It was a creature with eyes. The eyes, dead and turned to stone, were even now regarding him. It was one of the early crustaceans called Triolobites. Separated by millions of years in their lives, Knight and this underling seemed to have met in their place of death.[1]

Hardy draws out from this confrontation a contrast: he relates the fossil to other low types of animal existence but adds that

> The immense lapses of time each formation represented had known nothing of the dignity of man. They were grand times, but they were mean times too, and mean were their relics. He was to be with the small in his death.

This sense of the immensity of time which had pre-dated man was obviously one of the most striking revelations of nineteenth-century geology. Hardy spells it out by making Knight think back through all the stages of evolution and all the ungraspable centuries. 'Time closed up like a fan before him. He saw himself at one extremity of the years, face to face with the beginning and all the intermediate centuries simultaneously.'[2]

This new grasp of time's almost unthinkable extent is used as a forceful counterpoint elsewhere in the novels, notably in *Tess of the d'Urbervilles*. What I wish to argue is, that for all the obsession with time in Hardy's poems, the geological time scheme is strangely lacking. Only rarely as in 'The Clasped Skeletons' (858) is it used in the poetry. In place of the sense of geological time and an accompanying impression of movement, another is obsessively present in the poems: of limited and characteristically human time, un-

SOURCE *The Poetry of Thomas Hardy*, eds Patrician Clements and Juliet Grindle, London, 1980, pp. 119–36.

related to anything outside itself. Such a view of time creates, when certain recurring elements which accompany it are somehow fused and focused, some of Hardy's best and most moving poems. Crudely these might be described as claustrophobic. They are the antithesis of a number of the poems in the 1912–13 sequence.

This is not an impression gleaned from the many direct references to time in the poems. These are, on the whole, heavy-handed attempts to emphasize, even by a capitalizing of the initial letter. But emphasis fails. The concept does not unfold. Many of these references are personifications and banal at that: 'Time the tyrant', 'dicing Time', 'the toils of Time', 'never-napping Time', 'marching Time', 'Time's transforming chisel', 'dull defacing Time'. And the personifications act predictably: 'Time the tyrant' merely 'ruled Amabel', the once beautiful. 'Dicing Time' casts 'a moan' and not 'a gladness', the 'toils of Time' carry off the 'lauded beauties' of the woman who speaks, 'never-napping Time' uses a chisel to deface the body of the speaker, 'marching Time' marks the passing of hours which reveals a broken tryst, and 'Time's transforming chisel' turns curve to crease.

It is not direct reference that reveals the grip of time on Hardy's imagination, but certain recurrent features in his treatment of it. Hynes long ago pinned Yeats' word 'antinomial' on Hardy's poetry:

> thesis ... marriage, youth, young love, the reunion of husband and wife ... is set against antithesis ... infidelity, age, death, separation ... to form an ironic complex, which is left unresolved.[3]

Hynes is concerned with the irony, the relation (ambiguous here) between appearance and reality. But when one considers the sequence in which the contrasting elements are shown, a striking aspect of Hardy's treatment of time (as opposed to his references to it) is revealed: its retrospective nature. The passing of time is seen when it has already taken place.

This is the reverse of, say, Shakespeare's sonnets on time, where youth and beauty are present but will fade. In Hardy, conversely, the withering has already happened:

> Shadows of the October pine
> Reach into this room of mine:
> On the pine there swings a bird;
> He is shadowed with the tree.
> Mutely perched he bills no word;
> Blank as I am even is he.
> For those happy suns are past,
> Fore-discerned in winter last.
> When went by their pleasure, then?
> I, alas, perceived not when.   (273)

Priority is here given to the defacement and diminution, increased by the repetition of the chinese-box reference to another spring-winter cycle.

In this retrospective treatment, the unblemished state of things is less immediate to the imagination than the blemished. He sees 'The Faded Face' (377) and regrets that he did not 'know you young'; he presents to us the 'naked sheaf of wires' that was once 'The Sunshade' (434) and only behind it the picture of it 'silked in its white or pink' and the 'Little thumb standing against its stem'.

The justification for describing the pattern of retrospection as obsessive lies in its occurrence in poems ranging from the unsuccessful to the profound. In poems of situation, typical of *Satires of Circumstance*, events have already passed from better to worse at the moment when the speaker describes them. 'The Newcomer's Wife' (304) is already married when he discovers that his wife is 'the Hack of the Parade' and drowns himself. The girl pregnant by a married man is already married to a man she does not love when she learns on her honeymoon of the death of the lover's wife (305). The wife has already accepted her husband's ingenious present of a workbox for all her 'sewing years' before she realizes that it is made from the coffin of her lover (330).

And it is, characteristically, in retrospect and from an icy, colourless, present that the complexities of 'In Tenebris I' (136) spring:

> *Wintertime nighs;*
> *But my bereavement-pain*
> *It cannot bring again:*
> *Twice no one dies.*

> *Flower-petals flee;*
> *But, since it once hath been,*
> *No more that severing scene*
> *Can harrow me.*

> *Birds faint in dread:*
> *I shall not lose old strength*
> *In the lone frost's black length:*
> *Strength long since fled!*

> *Leaves freeze to dun;*
> *But friends can not turn cold*
> *This season as of old*
> *For him with none.*

> *Tempests may scath;*
> *But love can not make smart*
> *Again this year his heart*
> *Who no heart hath.*

> *Black is night's cope;*
> *But death will not appal*
> *One who, past doubtings all,*
> *Waits in unhope.*

Even when Hardy's viewpoint is not retrospective but forward into the future, he is inclined to a characteristic perspective. He will look forward in order to look back: to '1967' when there will be

> *... nothing left of me and you*
> *In that live century's vivid view*
> *Beyond a pinch of dust or two;*   (167)

to 2000 A.D. when Max Gate will have become 'The Strange House' (537) and himself a ghost to the new inhabitants; or even 'The Minute before Meeting' (191) he looks forward to a point beyond the expected meeting when the present anticipation will be turned into looking back despondently. The future is merely a way of turning the present into the past. The ultimate in retrospective treatment comes in 'The Clock of the Years' (481), when in a sensational and ballad-like story, 'The Spirit' moves time backward to bring the lost woman back to life but ironically does not stop there: finally she is unborn.

Here in the clock poem, another recurrent feature of Hardy's view of time is associated with his retrospective view of it. Time, as elsewhere, is seen not as a corrupter but as an almost chemically negating force. It does not so much destroy as denature things, removing the natural qualities of life, warmth, colour. In 'The Dead Man Walking' (166) he describes himself:

> *I am but a shape that stands here,*
> *A pulseless mould,*
> *A pale past picture, screening*
> *Ashes gone cold.*   (166)

Shape has gone, pulsing life has gone, colour has gone, warmth has gone. The picture is one of that privation which reaches it ultimate in 'In Tenebris I'. And it is pictorially typical too in its reduction of everything to mono-chrome in a world of neutral tones, that other obsession of Hardy's.[4]

This negating, undoing force of time can produce, in his best treatment, a superb lament which is not evoked by the remains of anything once living, beautiful, young or happy:

> *Regret—though nothing dear*
> *That I wot of, was toward in the wide world at his prime,*
> *Or bloomed elsewhere than here,*
> *To die with his decease, and leave a memory sweet, sublime,*
> *Or mark him out in Time ...*   (78)

Not even the skeleton of a sunshade starts this regret, and yet it has a power reminiscent of Shelley's *Ode to the West Wind* as, 'turning ghost', 'A Commonplace Day'

> *... scuttles from the kalendar in fits and furtively,*
> *To join the anonymous host*
> *Of those that throng oblivion ...*

The day had a 'pale, corpse-like birth', his 'colourless thoughts' of it slide like rain. Here we have a sense of pure loss because the poem has no central focus. There is no reason that Hardy can find for the feeling of privation except the negative one that (perhaps) a potential something has been crushed:

> *... maybe, in some soul,*
> *In some spot undiscerned on sea or land, some impulse rose,*
> *Or some intent upstole*
> *Of that enkindling ardency from whose maturer glows.*
> *The world's amendment flows;*
>
> *But which, benumbed at birth*
> *By momentary chance or wife, has missed its hope to be*
> *Embodied on the earth;*
> *And undervoicings of this loss to man's futurity*
> *May wake regret in me.*

There is ambivalence here: the postulated might-have-been seems less the centre of Hardy's concern than

> *... this diurnal unit, bearing blanks in all its rays—*
> *Dullest of dull-hued Days!*

Similarly he writes more effectively when he (typically) considers 'The Unborn' better off *not* born (235), or movingly urges the unborn pauper child (91):

> *Breathe not, hid Heart: cease silently,*
> *And though thy birth-hour beckons thee,*
> *Sleep the long sleep ...*

It seems a natural result of this idea of a benumbing, icing, denaturing force that while geological time essentially moves in order to create, this human time has little sense of movement. Such movement as Hardy gives it is often as repetitive and pointless as that of 'On One Who Lived and Died where He Was Born' (621);

> *Wise child of November!*
> *From birth to blanched hairs*
> *Descending, ascending,*
> *Wealth-wantless, those stairs;*

> *Who saw quick in time*
> *As a vain pantomime*
> *Life's tending, its ending,*
> *The worth of its fame.*
> *Wise child of November,*
> *Descending, ascending*
> *Those stairs!*

The internal rhymes, the rapidity of the brief lines with their almost dizzying effect, mime the futility of that ascending and descending, however the weak expostulation ambivalently asserts its wisdom. Something physically giddying can hardly affect us as wise.

So Hardy's retrospective, negating, almost unmoving time leaves him usually on the wrong side of a limited stretch of existence. He is in a position not of looking forward to transience in the sense of time moving on, but almost of its opposite: stasis. Time has done its denaturing, and he is its prisoner, trapped already in the irretrievable. Once, in 'The Caged Goldfinch' (436), he merely embodies in a commonplace metaphor this strong sense of being a prisoner:

> *Within a churchyard, on a recent grave,*
> *I saw a little cage*
> *That jailed a goldfinch. All was silence save*
> *Its hops from stage to stage*
>
> *There was inquiry in its wistful eye,*
> *And once it tried to sing;*
> *Of him or her who placed it there, and why,*
> *No one knew anything.*

Significantly the stress on the cage was here increased by Hardy when he cut out from this poem the third stanza (found in the manuscript):

> *But a woman was found drowned the day ensuing,*
> *And some at times averred*
> *The grave to be her false one's, who when wooing*
> *Gave her the bird.*[5]

More usual, however, than the unexplicated metaphor of the final version of 'The Caged Goldfinch' are the recurrent poems which deal specifically with being trapped in a small place. A characteristic example is 'Not Only I' (751). Here death has already come and so of course the retrospective, static, trapped state is supposed to be literally accurate:

> *Not only I*
> *Am doomed awhile to lie*
> *In this close bin with earthen sides ...*

As in the poems on time's transience, mentioned earlier, we here again see the joys of life at one remove, like the sunshade and its owner:

> *But the things I thought, and the songs I sang,*
> *And the hopes I had, and the passioned pang*
> > *For people I knew*
> > *Who passed before me,*
> *Whose memory barely abides;*
> > *And the visions I drew*
> > *That daily upbore me!*

Then a central stanza recalls these 'joyous springs and summers' and 'far-off views' only to be shut in by the third and final stanza closing trap-like, round them:

> *Compressed here in six feet by two,*
> > *In secrecy*
> > *To lie with me*
> > *Till the Call shall be,*
> *Are all these things I knew . . .*

This sense of physical imprisonment is, like the retrospective view of time, one that recurs in poems of all types. It may be found in the would-be philosophical 'Fragment' (464):

> *At last I entered a long dark gallery,*
> > *Catacomb-lined; and ranged at the side*
> > *Were the bodies of men from far and wide*
> *Who, motion past, were nevertheless not dead.*
>
> > *'The sense of waiting here strikes strong;*
> *Everyone's waiting, waiting, it seems to me;*
> *What are you waiting for so long?—*
> > *What is to happen?' I said.*

Or it may occur in the unspectacular picture of 'Molly Gone' (444) where the speaker sees himself, though out of doors, in a 'prison close-barred'. Or, in what sounds like an occasional piece, written 'In a Former Resort after Many Years' (666) he asks:

> *Do they know me, whose former mind*
> *Was like an open plain where no foot falls,*
> *But now is as a gallery portrait-lined,*
> > *And scored with necrologic scrawls,*
> *Where feeble voices rise, once full-defined,*
> > *From underground in curious calls?*

Time's denaturing has here already affected mind, and voices, and turned plain into prison. Or in the ballad-like story, 'Jubilate' (461), where the dead rise and dance to invisible instruments, they sing with joy—'We are out of it all!—yea, in Little-Ease cramped no more!' And in the narrative piece on 'The Clock-Winder' (471) we find the trap in fuller and characteristic form:

> *It is dark as a cave,*
> *Or a vault in the nave*
> *When the iron door*
> *Is closed, and the floor*
> *Of the church relaid*
> *With trowel and spade.*

In this setting the parish clerk ascends to wind 'the rheumatic clock' and his movement is reminiscent of the pointless 'Descending, ascending' of the stairs in 'On One Who Lived and Died Where He Was Born' (621):

> *Up, up from the ground*
> *Around and around*
> *In the turret stair*
> *He clambers, to where*
> *The wheelwork is,*
> *With its tick, click, whizz,*
> *Reposefully measuring*
> *Each day to its end*
> *That mortal men spend*
> *In sorrowing and pleasuring.*
> *Nightly thus does he climb*
> *To the trackway of Time.*

The short lines, the internal and end rhymes with their metronome-like regularity, give the lie to 'reposefully', and the thoughts of the clock-winder yearning for a dead woman are far from peaceful resignation. In fact, the earliest version of the poem had no reference to a lost lover.[6]

The trap is here found in a form that I have suggested is more characteristic of Hardy because it is an interior. His *Huis Clos* is, essentially, the house, the room. His finest claustrophobic poems, in which the obsessive sense of being trapped by unmoving time is embodied in an interior, make us grasp almost painfully what he meant in *A Pair of Blue Eyes* by 'those familiar conjunctions of things wherewith the inanimate world baits the mind of man'. Shut in, he confronts 'Old Furniture' (428) which surrounds him:

> *I know not how it may be with others*
>   *Who sit amid relics of householdry*
> *That date from the days of their mother's mothers,*
>   *But well I know how it is with me*
>   *Continually.*

I see the hands of the generations
   That owned each shiny familiar thing
In play on its knobs and indentations,
   And with its ancient fashioning
     Still dallying . . .

The furniture serves to mock the human beings whose memory it recalls as

Hands behind hands, growing paler and paler,
   As in a mirror a candle-flame
Shows images of itself, each frailer
   As it recedes, though the eye may frame
     Its shape the same.

The undoing effect of time is captured along with the sense of being trapped within this permanently furnished room.

Similarly there is all the domestic intensity of Emily Dickinson in his picture of the man shut up in the house with a figure left colourless and formless by time.

We two kept house, the Past and I,
   The Past and I;
Through all my tasks it hovered nigh,
   Leaving me never alone.
It was a spectral housekeeping
   Where fell no jarring tone,
As strange, as still a housekeeping
   As ever has been known.   (249)

There is the familiar ambivalence of the statement that there was 'no jarring tone' contrasting with the pointlessly repetitive movement which follows:

As daily I went up the stair
   And down the stair . . .

As elsewhere, the past is dimly seen through the ravages of the present now that

   gaunt griefs had torn old troths
And dulled old rapturings.

The personified figure of the Past itself, of course, 'dwindles' into a 'far-off skeleton'.

But the poem which, above all, expresses through a stifling domestic interior claustrophobic trap into which time has shut the speaker and from which all except pointless, giddying movement is excluded is 'The Masked Face' (473):

541

I found me in a great surging space,
  At either end a door,
And I said: 'What is this giddying place,
  With no firm-fixéd floor,
  That I knew not of before?'
  'It is Life,' said a mask-clad face.

I asked: 'But how do I come here,
  Who never wished to come;
Can the light and air be made more clear,
  The floor more quietsome,
  And the doors set wide? They numb
  Fast-locked, and fill with fear.'

This question is mockingly answered in the third and final stanza by an opaque statement:

The mask put on a bleak smile then,
  And said, 'O vassal-wight,
There once complained a goosequill pen
  To the scribe of the Infinite
  Of the words it had to write
  Because they were past its ken.'

This trite assertion, that he cannot understand because he is an uncomprehending instrument, seems to shut him in more securely.

The isolation that a prisoner feels is suggested ironically by the very presence of the masked face. And so too it is in 'Who's in the Next Room?' (450), said by Purdy[7] to have been identified as taking place at Max Gate:

'Who's in the next room?—who?
  I seemed to see
Somebody in the dawning passing through,
  Unknown to me.

That this is not another prisoner attempting to communicate is made clear by the following chilling stanzas:

'Who's in the next room?—who?
  I seem to hear
Somebody muttering firm in a language new
  That chills the ear.'
'No: you catch not his tongue who has entered there.'

Who's in the next room?—who?
  I seem to feel
His breath like a clammy draught, as if it drew
  From the Polar Wheel.'
'No: none who breathes at all does the door conceal.'

It is also made clear that the next room contains the figure of death and horrors worse than this one:

> *'Who's in the next room?—who?*
>   *A figure wan*
> *With a message to one in there of something due?*
>   *Shall I know him anon?'*
> *'Yea, he; and he brought such; and you'll know him anon.'*

The ballad form reminiscent in its development of 'Edward' (or 'Lord Randal'), captures the sinister note superbly. The door to the next room hardly tempts the prisoner to open it.

The dramatizing of an attempt to break out of the stifling, enclosed space is found in 'A Wasted Illness' (122) where physical distemper and the building become fused:

> *Through vaults of pain,*
> *Enribbed and wrought with groins of ghastliness,*
> *I passed, and garish spectres moved my brain*
>   *To dire distress.*
>
> *And hammerings,*
> *And quakes, and shoots, and stifling hotness, blent*
> *With webby waxing things and waning things*
>   *As on I went.*

He sees an apparent end to 'this foul way' in a door ahead, 'The door to Death', but it slips from him—

> *And back slid I*
> *Along the galleries by which I came,*
> *And tediously the day returned, and sky,*
>   *And life—the same.*

Yet he still knows that the same movement must be made—

> *And those grim chambers, must be ranged again*
>   *To reach that door.*

In contrast to 'Who's in the Next Room?' there is the muffled suggestion here that death might be a way out. But the relief appears uncertain and ambiguous.

Only in the poem on his mother's death is he able to convey a sense that death is a relief, a breaking out from the trap into which his static view of time seems to lock humanity: again gazing round a domestic interior he sees the persistently surviving inanimate things; the creased sheets, pillows, and

> *The lettered vessels of medicaments*
> *Seem asking wherefore we have set them here;*   (223)

543

but this time they are conquered by the pervading sense of relief:

> *Each palliative its silly face presents*
>   *As useless gear.*
>
> *And yet we feel that something savours well;*
> *We note a numb relief withheld before;*
> *Our well-beloved is prisoner in the cell*
>   *Of Time no more.*

The mere escape is enough, 'the deft achievement', and the poem dwells on the sense of ease at the fact that

> *There's no more to be done, or feared, or hoped . . .*

It does not focus on what lies beyond 'the cell of Time'.

Only here does the escape asserted seem to be conveyed as real. This is not so in those poems which try to assert that there is an escape from time possible by other means. They make use of the idea used, for instance, in Shakespeare's sonnets that one lives on through descendants and so transcends time's limits. This idea is plainly stated in 'Heredity' (363):

> *I am the family face;*
> *Flesh perishes, I live on,*
> *Projecting trait and trace*
> *Through time to times anon,*
> *And leaping from place to place*
> *Over oblivion.*
>
> *The years-heired feature that can*
> *In curve and voice and eye*
> *Despise the human span*
> *Of durance—that is I;*
> *The eternal thing in man,*
> *That heeds no call to die.*

But this, despite its assertiveness, is oddly self-contradictory, since the life that heredity perpetuates is still seen as 'the human span/Of durance'.

More convincing is the negative implication of the idea drawn out in 'Sine Prole' (690), that because he is without offspring the potential transcending of time will fail:

> *Forth from ages thick in mystery,*
> *Through the morn and noon of history,*
>   *To the moment where I stand*
> *Has my line wound: I the last one—*
> *Outcome of each spectral past one*
>   *Of that file, so many-manned!*

But no poem accepting that by heredity of flesh or spirit man transcends his 'span of durance' carries the force of those poems in which such an idea visibly crumbles as the speaker attempts to expand it.

In 'His Immortality' (109) this is precisely what happens:

I

I saw a dead man's finer part
Shining within each faithful heart
Of those bereft. Then said I: 'This must be
His immortality.'

II

I looked there as the seasons wore,
And still his soul continuously bore
A life in theirs. But less its shine excelled
Than when I first beheld.

III

His fellow-yearsmen passed, and then
In later hearts I looked for him again;
And found him—shrunk, alas! into a thin
And spectral mannikin.

IV

Lastly I ask—now old and chill—
If aught of him remain unperished still;
And find, in me alone, a feeble spark,
Dying amid the dark.

The characteristic denaturing and 'dwindling' of the man represents a crumbling before our eyes of the thesis that he can live on through his descendants, and so transcend the cell of time. Such a development carries all the conviction that the poems asserting transcendence through heredity lack.

The negative idea is as compelling here as in the situation poem 'The Pedigree' (390). There the written pedigree itself mocks the speaker physically:

The branches seemed to twist into a seared and cynic face
Which winked and tokened towards the window like a Mage
Enchanting me to gaze again thereat.

What he sees in the window is the powerful image of the mirror showing, as usual, man dwindling:

III

It was a mirror now,
And in it a long perspective I could trace
Of my begetters, dwindling backward each past each

> *All with the kindred look,*
> *Whose names had since been inked down in their place*
> *On the recorder's book,*
> *Generation and generation of my mien, and build, and brow.*

The mirror then suddenly seems to become one more inanimate object which 'baits the mind of man':

IV

> *And then did I divine*
> *That every heave and coil and move I made*
> *Within my brain, and in my mood and speech,*
> *Was in the glass portrayed*
> *As long forestalled by their so making it . . .*

There is a sense here of action being so predetermined that it enwraps him like a snake, in whose grip he heaves and coils like a snake himself. He is trapped, not released, by the written pedigree: time's stasis is inescapable. So, at least, the poem convinces us as it reasserts the familiar claustrophobia. The only movement, as before, is a backward, dwindling one.

And in this poem, as in several others, the metre and diction underline the effect of the trap. In some, as has been pointed out, the jingling metre enacts the repetitive, pointless movement. In others including 'The Pedigree', 'The Masked Face' and 'A Wasted Illness' there is a characteristic effect of impeded movement. This is created either by qualifications and inversions like

> *Through vaults of pain,*
> *Enribbed and wrought with groins of ghastliness,*
> *I passed . . .*

or by consonant groups which are difficult to enunciate as in a 'mask-clad face'. The metre is slow and cumbersome often in Hardy's poems, but here to a purpose.

Similarly, adding to the effect in these poems, is the scattering of archaism. When the masked face answers the speaker's question as to why he has been brought to the 'giddying place' it says obliquely:

> *O vassal-wight,*
> *There once complained a goosequill pen*
> *To the scribe of the Infinite*
> *Of the words it had to write*
> *Because they were past its ken.*

The phrases 'O vassal-wight' and 'past its ken' are archaic-poetic. An archaism is a dead word revived. It carries with it to any native speaker an element of artificiality. It is felt as a sterile form, not part of a usable language; it is essentially static by contrast with other words. Such sterility fits perfectly where man is seen in an artificial and virtually inescapable trap. And what is true of 'vassal-wight' and 'past its ken' is true also of the trivial archaic forms *ere, yea, nay, troths, whilom, blent* which sprinkle the other poems under discussion. Consider for instance:

> *And hammerings,*
> *And quakes, and shoots, and stifling hotness, blent*
> *With webby waxing things and waning things . . .*

where *blent* is used for the more normal *mixed*. The increase in artificiality is self-evident. It refutes the idea sometimes expressed that in Hardy archaic words 'serve to shift the tone upward and out of time'.[8] A word which cannot be used freely, which is in effect a verbal fossil, is locked in time. Only when it recalls an earlier, specific and powerful context, as does Keats' ironic use of *trammel up* in *Lamia*, can it open up associations. The very triviality of Hardy's archaisms works against this.

In summary, I have described the recurring features of Hardy's treatment of time which occur, sometimes separately, sometimes fused together, as that it is retrospective, denaturing, static, claustrophobic and largely inescapable. There is no development to be traced in these obsessive qualities: they may occur as early as the 1880s in 'A Wasted Illness', or as late as 'The Pedigree' (which was not published, at least, till 1917). The 'cell of time' seems to have been a constant in Hardy's poems including many not cited.

It accounts perhaps for the added sense of release found in some of Hardy's best poems in the 1912–1913 sequence, written after Emma's death and recalling the past in a way which in almost every respect differs from that outlined above; it is more vivid than the present and more alive, full of a sense of movement and freedom and usually in an outdoor setting. There is, indeed, one poem (740), which clearly belongs with the 1912–13 group[9] and which marks the transition:

> *She opened the door of the West to me,*
> *   With its loud sea-lashings,*
> *   And cliff-side clashings*
> *Of waters rife with revelry.*

> *She opened the door of Romance to me,*
> *   The door from a cell*
> *   I had known too well,*
> *Too long, till then, and was fain to flee.*

> *She opened the door of a Love to me,*
> *   That passed the wry*
> *   World-welters by*
> *As far as the arching blue the lea.*

She opens the door of the Past to me,
Its magic lights,
Its heavenly heights,
When forward little is to see!

For once the way out of the present was the past which here expanded instead of dwindling. So, the 1912–13 poems seem to constitute stepping out of the cell.

Notes

1. Wessex Edition, p. 241.
2. *Ibid.*, p. 242.
3. S. Hynes, *The Pattern of Hardy's Poetry* (Chapel Hill, 1961), p. 44.
4. See No. 79 in *The Complete Poems*: 'At a Lunar Eclipse'.
5. *Ibid.*, p. 963.
6. *Ibid.*, p. 963.
7. R.L. Purdy, *Thomas Hardy: A Bibliographical Study* (Oxford, 1968), p. 202.
8. Hynes, pp. 104–5.
9. It was published in *Human Shows* in 1925.

204
Short Stories

———— ◆ ————

NORMAN PAGE

Hardy wrote nearly fifty short stories—a substantial body of work, equivalent in length to four or five of the novels; but it has not received a proportionate amount of attention from his critics. It is true that the wide variation in quality characteristic of Hardy's writings is at least as prominent in the short stories as in the novels and poems; but the judgment of a recent critic that 'Most of them ... are not worth salvaging' seems to overstate the case, and the comment in another study of Hardy that 'The short stories *are* pot boilers' seems to miss the point. All Hardy's fiction, like Shakespeare's plays, was prompted by motives that were, in part at least, opportunist and commercial; but this is, *per se*, hardly a damaging consideration in estimating their literary worth. The best of the stories are no more and no less pot-boilers than *The Return of the Native*—or, for that matter, *King Lear*.

Their author at least appears to have deemed most of them 'worth salvaging', since he collected thirty-seven stories in four volumes over a period of a quarter of a century. *Wessex Tales* (1888) contains six stories written between 1879 and 1888; *A Group of Noble Dames* (1891), ten stories mainly dating from 1889–90, though two had appeared considerably earlier; *Life's Little Ironies* (1894), nine stories written between 1882 and 1893, the majority of them belonging to the years 1890 and 1891; and *A Changed Man* (1913), twelve stories written during the period 1881–1900. (Firm evidence of the date of composition is often lacking, but it seems reasonable to assume that it did not normally precede that of magazine publication by more than a short interval.) All these stories had appeared before the public in a variety of British and American periodicals before being collected. Some of the un-collected stories date from a little earlier in the 1870s than any of those collected, the earliest of all ('Destiny and a Blue Cloak') having been first published in 1874. Hardy's career as a writer of short stories therefore extends over more than twenty-five years, beginning soon after he made his début as a novelist with *Desperate Remedies*, and continuing for a few years

SOURCE *Thomas Hardy*, London, 1977, pp. 121–30.

after the publication of his last novels. (Indeed, the two parallel careers, as novelist and short-story writer, are of exactly equal length.)

As to how many or which of these fifty items, varying considerably in length, are of permanent interest there seems to be little agreement. Hardy told his American admirer Miss Rebekah Owen that he considered 'The Son's Veto' his finest short story; her vote went to 'The Three Strangers'; Florence Emily Hardy on another occasion nominated 'On the Western Circuit'. John Wain's recent selection is limited to seven stories and includes neither the first nor the third of these titles; among critics who have taken the stories into account in their assessment of Hardy's achievement, Douglas Brown mentions ten by title, George Wing about fifteen. Most, however, are passed over in a silence that, given Hardy's recognized status as a novelist, is somewhat puzzling.

Nor need we feel obliged to take at face value Hardy's own occasionally disparaging allusions to this branch of his art: he made similar and oft-quoted references to his novels, but the attitude of contempt towards both stories and novels is belied by the careful attention both received in the processes of composition and revision. When we have the kind of manuscript evidence assembled for Hardy that exists for Dickens (notably in the work of John Butt and Kathleen Tillotson), the famous remark that limited his ambition as a novelist to being 'a good hand at a serial' will be conclusively seen for what it is—excessive modesty or assumed indifference.

As far as the short stories are concerned, there are, apart from the issue already raised of their intrinsic literary quality, at least three ways in which they merit the attention of the serious Hardy student: they show very strikingly the range of his art and his exceptional capacity for mingling disparate types of fictional convention; they stand in a significant relationship to the major novels written during precisely the same period; and they exhibit in miniature some of the complex problems of composition and revision that make Hardy's text a territory full of interest and by no means yet exhaustively charted.

In answer to those who dismiss the stories as mainly negligible pot-boilers, one can point not only to the successive rewritings that Hardy patiently bestowed upon many of them, but also to the care he took in collecting them in volumes intended to possess a reasonable degree of internal unity. As late as 1912, for example, he took pains to reverse the positions of two stories—'A Tradition of 1804' in *Life's Little Ironies* exchanging places with 'An Imaginative Woman' in *Wessex Tales*—for this reason. Such continuing concern hardly looks like indifference. But the homogeneity of these collections must not be exaggerated, for all except *A Group of Noble Dames* contain a considerable range of types. Of the first three stories in the earliest volume, *Wessex Tales*, for instance, one is a realistic story of middle-class urban life with a bitterly ironic conclusion, one a stylized and ballad-like romantic tale set in the 1820s, and the third a macabre excursion into the supernatural; what unites them, perhaps super-ficially, is the Wessex setting.

More generally, four types of stories may be distinguished: (1) those revealing a humorous and affectionate observation of rustic life (e.g., 'A Few Crusted Characters' (1891, *LLI*: the date given is that of first publication, the initials those of the volume in which the story was collected) and 'The Distracted Preacher' (1879, *WT*)); (2) tales on romantic or supernatural themes, often reminiscent of balladry and folk-tales (e.g., 'The Withered Arm' (1888, *WT*) and 'The Fiddler of the Reels' (1893, *LLI*)); (3) realistic and often ironic or tragic stories of modern life, usually later in date of composition than most of those in the previous two categories (e.g., 'On the Western Circuit' (1891, *LLI*) and 'An Imaginative Woman' (1894, *LLI*)); (4) historical tales, set in the Napoleonic period ('A Tradition of 1804 (1882), WT), 'The Melancholy Hussar of the German Legion' (1890, *LLI*)) or earlier (*A Group of Noble Dames*). Though there is inevitably some overlapping between these groups, each of them may be related to a distinctive element in Hardy's work as a whole. (I) has obvious affinities with the rustic portions of the Wessex novels, (2) with the many poems of ballad type in the *Collected Poems*, (3) with the late novels, especially *Tess of the d'Urbervilles* and *Jude the Obscure*, and (4) with *The Trumpet-Major* and *The Dynasts*. The last of these groups is probably the least interesting: stories like 'A Tradition of 1804' seem to resemble a discarded episode from one of the longer works cited, and with the exception of the powerful story 'Barbara of the House of Grebe', *A Group of Noble Dames* shows neither Hardy's characteristic preoccupations nor his imagination as fully engaged. As always, he conveys a sense of the past most successfully when he is not explicitly working with historical or pseudo-historical material.

The examples in the first of the four groups are not without interest, but add little to the knowledge of Hardy that is derived from the major fiction. Such stories as 'The Distracted Preacher', in which observation and recollec-tion are shaped into rustic romance, with a stimulating touch of astringency, belong to the world of *Under the Greenwood Tree* and to comparable passages in some of the other novels. But the second and third groups contain stories that are not only successful in their own right but constitute an extension of Hardy's art, taking up (it is true) elements that exist elsewhere but develop-ing them with the clarity and concentration demanded by the genre. It is here that we find the by no means negligible best of Hardy's work in the short-story medium, though it has so far been accorded little recognition.

Since demonstration must be specific to be useful, it will be necessary to concentrate on a handful of examples. It is true that the impression conveyed by any selection of material is inevitably misleading, and only a reading of the collected stories in their entirety can convey a full sense of the variety and inventiveness of Hardy's handling of the genre. (The uncollected stories are mostly of inferior quality, and Hardy's judgment on them was sound, though 'Our Exploits at West Poley' (1892, but rediscovered and republished only in 1952) is an interesting example of the way in which his persistent moral preoccupations emerge even in the context of a boys' adventure story; and 'Old Mrs. Chundle', probably written in the 1880s, but unpublished during Hardy's lifetime, shows an impressive modulation from grotesque comedy, through irony, to genuinely touching sentiment.) What can be more directly demonstrated, however, is the relationship of the minor to the major writings, as well as the textual vicissitudes of some items, which throw a revealing light on Hardy's working methods and on his attitude towards editors and reading public. I shall discuss more fully, therefore, two examples from each of the second and third categories enumerated above.

The earliest of the four, 'The Romantic Adventures of a Milkmaid', was published in England and America in 1883 but waited thirty years before being collected in *A Changed Man*. Its quality has been a source of dis-agreement even among Hardy's admirers: Douglas Brown praises it as 'ballad-like' and showing 'inventive energy and delight,' but C.J. Weber, with unaccustomed tartness, dismisses it as a 'worthless trifle'. Whatever its weaknesses, it has a flavour that is sufficiently individual to raise it above the mass of late-Victorian magazine fiction. It opens in a familiar vein of careful realism that recalls Hardy's debt to George Eliot: it is 'half-past four o'clock on a May morning in the eighteen forties', and the symphony of rural noises as life begins to stir in the dairy farm—'the bark of a dog', 'the slamming of a gate', 'women's voices', and soon 'the milk ... buzzing into the pails'—is muted by a 'dense white fog'. The musical metaphors of the opening passage are of more than local interest, since the climax of the story is to involve music and dancing. When Hardy introduces the heroine, it is with a meticulous precision of visual detail (she wears 'a small woollen shawl of shepherd's plaid', a white handkerchief tied over her straw bonnet, and carries 'a withy basket, in which lay several butter-rolls in a nest of wet cabbage-leaves'); but her name, Margery Tucker, suggests not merely a rustic stereotype but the world of nursery-rhymes and folk-tales (Margery Daw, Tommy Tucker). The suggestion proves well-founded, for this realistic prologue precedes a story that strays to the frontiers of the supernatural and contains hints of Byronism and diabolism, as well as a recognizable debt to the Cinderella story. It exhibits, that is to say, the typically Hardyan mingling of disparate elements, realistic and fanciful or fantastic, implicit here in the title with its unfamiliar collocation of *romantic* and *milkmaid*. Such merging of apparently incompatible genres can also be found in the novels (*The Mayor of Casterbridge* is a case in point), and has proved a fertile source of puzzlement and disapproval among Hardy's critics.

The same story also incorporates some of the commonest ingredients of Hardy's fiction: the theme of class-distinctions (the milkmaid and the baron reversing the more familiar roles of the poor man and the lady); the conflict of old and new ways (Margery's 'Reels, and jigs, and country-dances' are scorned by the fashionable world in which she makes a brief appearance and which has 'gone crazy' over the newly arrived polka);the intrusion of the discontented and *déraciné* outsider into a happy and stable community (the Baron von Xanten is a spiritual brother to Fitzpiers in *The Woodlanders*); and the sometimes bizarre use of symbolism. Indeed, we have almost an anthology of his thematic and other preoccupations, full of echoes of what he had written and anticipations of what was still to come: Margery Tucker might, for instance, be seen as a very tentative first sketch for Tess Durbeyfield. There is, perhaps, *too* much, even for what is a short novel rather than a short story (its American serialization was in seven weekly instalments): although the tale is in essence a fairly simple one, it is padded out with description and dialogue and would have gained from a more disciplined structure and from more stylistic self-denial. It might have been even better as a ballad-poem; and it can fairly stand as an example of Hardy's failure to accommodate the kind of imaginative response prompted by his theme to the genre in which he was working. Yet it remains more readable and even memorable than Weber's curt dismissal allows for: as often, even Hardy's inferior work has, at moments at least, a curiously vivid and compelling quality. In one other respect it exemplifies a feature familiar in Hardy's fiction as a whole; the ending originally intended was abandoned in favour of one more likely 'to suit the requirements of the summer number of a periodical, *The Graphic*, in which the story was first printed' (the words are Hardy's, from a note written in his copy of *A Changed Man*, dated 1927 and now in the Dorset County Museum).

Ten years later, diabolism and dancing recur in a story that has often been regarded as Hardy's finest, 'The Fiddler of the Reels', and which serves to show how, working with somewhat similar materials to those in the earlier story, he was capable of a more controlled kind of art. Again, the story is set in a previous generation (it opens in the 1840s and moves on to the time of the Great Exhibition); and, like the Baron, 'Mop' Ollamoor, with his 'un-English' appearance, 'rich olive' complexion, and long dark hair, is an exotic, an orchid in the Wessex hedgerows. He represents paganism (he 'had never, in all likelihood, entered a church at all'), and effects conversion to his own creed of sensuality through his violin-playing ('All were devil's tunes in his repertory'). It is not too much to claim that, in 'Mop', described at the outset as 'a woman's man', Hardy achieved the near-impossible for a late-Victorian popular novelist in his account of the irresistible power of the sexual impulse stirred by a practised seducer. He does it by poetic rather than realistic means, and by metaphor rather than statement or analysis (compare the poem 'The Dance at the Phoenix', in which an elderly woman married to a steady husband leaves her bed to dance wildly under the spell produced by the music of the King's Own Cavalry). Mop's fiddling produces a semi-hypnotic effect, an involuntary impulse to abandon normal decorum and to dance until the point of exhaustion is reached: these 'compelled capers' (in Hardy's phrase) lead to the girl's seduction; and, years later, when she has made a respectable marriage, a second bout of dancing ends in the disappearance of 'Mop' with the child: a rape, that is, in another sense. The nearest parallel in the novels is probably Sergeant Troy of *Far from the Madding Crowd*, but there the handling of the theme of sexual power seems relatively crude. The simple patterning of 'The Fiddler of the Reels' is entirely satisfying, and the power of Mop's music-making is a perfect symbol for his personal magnetism; at the same time, fantasy is kept under control, and for all the hints as to the protagonist's true nature the background is reassuringly realistic—both in the rural settings and in the London scenes, with the excursion-train and the visit to the Exhibition.

The two stories discussed so far are poetic and romantic, with obvious affiliations to the early and middle-period Wessex novels. The remaining two show a different aspect of Hardy's art, one that recalls Gissing and George Moore, and which is exemplified in the major novels only by *Jude the Obscure*. 'On the Western Circuit' appeared alongside 'The Fiddler of the Reels' in *Life's Little Ironies*, but offers a striking contrast in mode. Set 'in the city of Melchester', its milieu is urban and bourgeois: the two protagonists are a young barrister and the wife of a prosperous wine-merchant; and, rather than looking back to a past generation, its period is apparently that of its composition. The situation is developed, and the central irony made plain, with admirable economy, and the story seems a sufficient response to critics who believe Hardy to have been incapable of a plot that was not mechanical and over-elaborate. It has, too, another kind of interest that is worth expounding, in the development of its text from manuscript to the various printed versions. Four distinct stages in its textual history may be observed: (1) Hardy's holograph, given to the Manchester Central Library in 1911, and described by Purdy (p. 84) as 'the original, unbowdlerized version'; (2) its first appearance in print in England, in *The English Illustrated Magazine* for December 1891 (and in America in *Harper's Weekly* for 28 November of the same year); (3) the galley-proofs of *Life's Little Ironies*, showing, according to Purdy, 'a number of interesting alterations', dated December 1893, and now in the Dorset County Museum; (4) the version in that collection, as published on 22 February 1894 by Osgood, McIlvaine & Co.

Purdy's description of the manuscript as 'the original ... version' implies that, as on other occasions, Hardy first wrote the story he wanted to write, subsequently modified it to satisfy his editor and Mrs Grundy, and finally restored the original text when the story appeared in volume form. An examination of the manuscript, however, suggests that this is not quite what happened. The original version was indeed bowdlerized, as I shall illustrate more fully in a moment; but the final version represents not simply a restoration of the original but to some extent a revision of it in which the frankness in the handling of the sexual situation is markedly increased. There were, that is to say, changes introduced both in the transition from manuscript to serial and, later, from serial to volume. Hardy's own dating of the final version of the story in *Life's Little Ironies* as 'Autumn 1891' is therefore misleading. After briefly considering the nature of the story, some specific examples of the changes introduced will make the trend of his revisions clearer.

The theme, like that of *Jude the Obscure*, relates to 'the marriage question': a young woman, sexually and emotionally unfulfilled by a marriage of convenience to an elderly and disagreeable husband, enters into a correspondence with a young barrister who has seduced one of her servants. Since the girl is illiterate, her mistress agrees to compose and write her love-letters, unknown to the recipient, and soon she finds herself pouring her deepest feelings into the letters and forming a close if one-sided attachment to the young man whom she has seen only once and briefly. It is not until he has married the girl, whom he has made pregnant, that the truth emerges, and he finds himself, like his true correspondent, 'chained' for the rest of his days to an incompatible spouse. Hardy, whose own marriage had by this time proved disastrous, had a more than detached interest in such a situation; but, in any case, from the point of view of a periodical intended for a family audience, the situation was hardly less explosive than that of *Tess*, which was actually in the process of serial publication when the story under discussion was written. Hardy's revisions ranged from the alteration of a single epithet to the omission of whole paragraphs, but it will be enough to note two major adjustments comparable to the mangling of *Tess* which he had found himself obliged to perform a little earlier. The wife of the original becomes a widow, her husband's role being taken over more or less intact by an uncle: at a stroke, that is, any hint of infidelity, even of the spiritual kind, is avoided. The numerous minor revisions consequent upon this change need not be noted, but two of them are of interest. When the servant-girl suggests, naively but with unconscious irony, that writing love-letters for her can have no effect on her mistress's feelings, Hardy wrote as her comment, '"Because you are married already!"' For the same reason, the wife's despairing cry towards the end of the story, '"Ah—my husband!—I forgot I had a husband!"' is sacrificed. Both reappear in the final version.

Second, all references to the fact that the marriage is necessitated by the girl's pregnancy are scrupulously excised. It is worth noting, however, that two of the most striking sentences in the story as we read it today did not appear in the manuscript: one is the comment that the wife's marriage 'had left her still a woman whose deeper nature had never been stirred', the other the even more unconventional remark 'That he had been able to seduce another woman in two days was his crowning though unrecognized fascination for her as the she-animal'. Editorial hands were never held up in horror at such a frank diagnosis of the power of sexual needs and impulse, since the sentences were afterthoughts inserted after the appearance of the story in magazine form.

In summary, Hardy revised his original version of this story twice, at different times and for different reasons. On the first occasion the pressures were external—those of the editor and readers of a popular magazine; and the example shows on a small scale what *Tess* and *Jude* display more extensively in their textual history: that he was prepared to undertake major alterations of content in order to produce an inoffensive, and therefore commercially viable, literary commodity. The second revision seems to have been undertaken, on the other hand, to please himself: it is partly concerned with sharpening some of the stylistic effects, but also stresses even more fully than the earliest version the sexual element, by way of belated compensation, as it were, for what had been omitted and distorted in the interim. Not only is 'On the Western Circuit' one of the most powerful of Hardy's short stories, but it provides additional evidence of his preoccupation with the theme of marital disharmony during the years that saw the publication of *Tess* and the writing of *Jude*.

My final example, 'An Imaginative Woman', which was eventually to stand first in *Wessex Tales*, having been included in the new edition of 1896, belongs to the same period—it was written (according to Hardy's note) in 1893 and first published in April 1894—and shares a similar setting and tone. The scene is 'a well-known watering-place in Upper Wessex', the social background is middle class (the heroine's husband is 'a gunmaker in a thriving city northwards'), and again the theme is a woman's attempt to find relief from an unsatisfactory marriage in fantasy—this time in an idealized relationship with a poet who has previously occupied their lodgings. Hardy seems to have been engaged on the planning of *Jude the Obscure* at the same time that this story was written, and *The Well-beloved* had been completed and published for the first time in the previous year. 'An Imaginative Woman' seems to derive its theme from both novels—the yoking together in matrimony of dissimilar temperaments from the former, and the pursuit of an ideal lover from the latter (with a female protagonist in place of the sculptor Pierston). The poignant conclusion of the story, with the widowed husband's unfounded rejection of his child (who resembles the dead poet) as a bastard, prompted a defence of the plausibility of this device in Hardy's Preface to *Wessex Tales* (dated April 1896): he wrote that there the story 'turns upon a physical possibility that may attach to women of imaginative temperament, and that is well supported by the experiences of medical men and other observers of such manifestations'. It is interesting that Hardy, who had elsewhere published stories far more fantastic without explanation, should have felt it necessary to speak in his own defence: nothing, perhaps, could better underline the essential difference of kind between stories such as this one and the unashamedly romantic type referred to earlier.

The manuscript of 'An Imaginative Woman', like that of 'On the Western Circuit', is heavily corrected, especially in the opening pages: the second leaf alone, for example, contains nearly forty alterations, insertions and deletions, made (it appears from the handwriting) at different times and including the addition of a substantial passage on the verso evidently inserted as an after-thought. This is not the place to discuss the nature of Hardy's revisions in detail, but their very existence gives the lie not only to the view of him as a careless stylist but to the notion that these unjustly neglected tales were dashed off in the intervals of more serious literary labours to satisfy a commercial need. Hardy took pains over these and other stories; and, apart from those mentioned, there are a dozen or more that deserve to be read by virtue of their intrinsic qualities as well as on account of the reflected interest which belongs to the minor work of a major writer. I have said nothing, for instance, of such tales as 'The Three Strangers' (*WT*), 'The Son's Veto' (*LLI*), 'A Tragedy of Two Ambitions' (*LLI*) or 'The Waiting Supper' (*CM*). Hardy's supposed indifference to his short stories is belied by the consider-able care he took in writing, revising and collecting them; he was in any case the most modest of great novelists where his own fictional achievements were concerned, and we would be wise not to insist upon taking the stories at his own valuation.

205

The Short Story: A Critical Introduction

—————— ◆ ——————

VALERIE SHAW

Literature abounds with stories which disclose a secret, offering the one 'true' version to replace conjectural accounts of events. In *The Turn of the Screw* (1898), for example, James plays with this device; he uses a narrative frame to vary the Dickensian Christmas fireside setting with which the story opens, delaying the story proper until the house has been cleared of inquisitive women and only a tiny circle of choice listeners remains. The implication is that only the few are sensitive enough to be made party to the governess's strange memoir. Hardy uses a somewhat similar technique in 'The Melancholy Hussar of the German Legion', another story which deals with hidden passion. The fact that the memory of Phyllis's unhappy love affair is passed from one generation of villagers to another, gives a folklore quality to her story and at the same time it sets the narrator his task of correcting false interpretations, 'since such fragments of her story as got abroad at the time, and have been kept alive ever since, are precisely those which are most unfavourable to her character'. Privileged as a boy of fifteen to hear the full story from Phyllis's own lips, and enjoined to keep silence until she is 'dead, buried and forgotten', the narrator has waited thirty years before sharing her secrets with the reader, who is correspondingly privileged. It is an aspect of Phyllis's fine sense honour—the sense which actually produces the tragedy of her story—that she hides her suffering, and the final reward for her reticence comes long after her death when the narrator substitutes the whole inner truth for the fragments pieced together into a distorted picture by narrow-minded village gossips.

In his aptly titled collection *Life's Little Ironies* (1894), Hardy repeatedly uses a decisive irony to reduce all sense of life opening out. Phyllis's misinterpretation of Gould's overhead words just as she is about to elope with 'The Melancholy Hussar' locks that moment on in a desolate situation; the single ironic occurrence is crucial and irrevocable. And in 'The Son's Veto'

SOURCE London 1983, pp. 94–5, 210–11, 218–19.

Sophy's marriage of convenience is a denial of nature that recoils on her, closing forever her prospects of happiness with the true man of nature, Sam Hobson. Misery taking the place of wished-for happiness provides an economical plot which can be unfolded rapidly, using the central ironic reversal as a pivot, the frontier within the story between comedy and tragedy.

In these stories the loss of hope as loneliness replaces anticipated joy has a melancholy effect in keeping with Hardy's belief that human beings are essentially powerless. But the short story is equally receptive to more robust moods, particular when 'justice' is not dispensed by fate but by the characters themselves. There is a large class of story in which an ironic structure is used to deal with the intrinsically lawless subject of revenge. Vengeance thrives as a short-story subject because it carries with it elements of clearly delineated conflict, vivid emotion and urgency. Revenge is a notion that collapses if its outlines are blurred, and for the storyteller the positive side of this is that a vendetta successfully accomplished can be described in a taut story which ends with a satisfying turnabout of the characters' positions. In Maupassant's bloodthirsty tale 'Vendetta' (1885), a frail old widow triumphs over the ostensibly stronger man who murdered her son; the story merely records the strategy by which the widow gains her revenge, strength and weakness changing places. Fascination with crafty stratagem is also apparent in a much later story, Borges's Kiplingesque 'The Bribe' (1975), though here the revenge theme is given an extra twist, since it is 'the vanity of not seeking revenge' which makes one scholar play into the hands of his cunning academic rival.

... Hardy's short stories, usually disqualified from inclusion in the genre because of their lack of form, are somewhat neglected instances of short fiction's power to examine social conventions and to provide endings which express a sense of wasted, rather than exhausted potentially. And for this purpose it was appropriate to choose as subject-matter unorthodox 'tri-angular' situations which could be resolved by reducing the number three to one, proposing solitariness as the inevitable outcome of rivalries and three-cornered relationships within a society where marriage was deemed the only acceptable context for sexuality.

Many of Hardy's shorter pieces take the basic ingredients of a romantic love plot and then dispose them in such a way as to undermine conventional views about 'right choices' and the equation of 'moral' behaviour with happiness. In 'the Melancholy Hussar', for instance, Phyllis is the familiar figure of a girl with two suitors, Tina and Gould, but by the end of the story fine-spirited Tina is dead and Gould has married for shallow prudential reasons, leaving Phyllis facing lifelong loneliness. The triangular plot-situation favours rapidly established contrasts between the two men, and introduces conflict into the story by placing the heroine in a dilemma. But where a conventional, romantic approach would insist that the moral soundness of the heroine's choice be rewarded by happiness, here she loses both the man she chooses for emotional reasons, and the man to whom she feels morally bound. Three-cornered relationships are particularly conducive to Hardy's brand of irony: in 'The Son's Veto', for example, the inflexible hostility of Sophy's son perpetuates the consequences of her first choice of husband, reflecting at plot level a larger irony which fates Sophy and Sam, the story's 'couple' by nature and disposition, to remain permanently apart. 'To please his Wife', another story collected in *Life's Little Ironies*, varies the pattern by attributing rivalry to two women, gentle Emily Hanning and envious Joanna Phippard, the third corner of the triangle being Captain Joliffe. Here the unhappy love-story is amalgamated with a retribution theme: Joanna, who marries Joliffe out of spite, is left desolate while the woman she deprived of happiness prospers financially, though not emotionally.

A Postscript

206

A Letter from
Alexander Macmillan on
The Poor Man and The Lady

———— ◆ ————

To Thomas Hardy, Dorchester.   August 10th, 1868.

I have read through the novel you were so good as to send me with care
and with much interest and admiration, but feeling at the same time that it
has what seem to me fatal drawbacks to its success, and what, I think,
judging the writer from the book itself, you would feel even more strongly—
its truthfulness and justice.

Your description of country life among working men is admirable, and,
though I can only judge of it from the corresponding life of Scotland, which I
knew well when young, palpably truthful. Your pictures of character among
Londoners, and especially the upper classes, are sharp, clear, incisive and in
many respects true, but they are wholly dark—not a ray of light visible to
relieve the darkness, and therefore exaggerated and untrue in their result.
Their frivolity, heartlessness, selfishness are great and terrible, but there are
other sides, and I can hardly conceive that they would do otherwise than
what they (i.e. you?) seek to avoid, 'throw down the book in disgust.' Even
the worst of them would hardly, I think, do the things that you describe
them as doing. For instance, is it conceivable that any man, however base
and soul-corrupted, would do as you make the Hon. Fay Allamont do at the
close, accept an estimate for his daughter's tomb—*because it cost him nothing?*
He had already so far broken through the prejudices of his class as to send
for Strong in the hope of saving his daughter's life. Then is it at all possible
that a public body would *in public* retract their award on the grounds you
make them avow in the case of the Palace of Hobbies Company?

The utter heedlessness of *all* the conversation you give in drawing-rooms
and ballrooms about the working classes, has some ground of truth, I fear,
and might justly be scourged, as you aim at doing, but your chastisement

SOURCE See Florence Emily Hardy, *The Life of Thomas Hardy*, London, 1962 edition, pp. 58–9.

would fall harmless from its very excess. Will's speech to the working men is full of wisdom (though, by the way, would he have told his own story in public, being, as you describe him, a man of substantially good taste?)—and you there yourself give good grounds for condemning very much that is in other parts of the book. Indeed, nothing could justify such a wholesale blackening of a class but large and intimate knowledge of it. Thackeray makes them not greatly better in many respects, but he gave many redeeming traits.

(Here follows a comparison, the substance of which is: 'He meant fair, you mean mischief,' but nothing is added about Hardy's novel.)

I like your tone infinitely better. But it seems to me that your black wash will not be recognized as anything more than ignorant misrepresentation. Of course I don't know what opportunities you have had of seeing the class you deal with ... But it is inconceivable to me that any considerable number of human beings—God's creatures—should be so bad without going to utter wreck in a week.

Of the story itself I hardly know what to say. I should fear it is very improbable, and would be looked on as a sort of Reynold's Miscellany affair, though your really admirable handling often gives a certain dignity and power that greatly redeems it. Much of the detail struck me as strained and unnatural. The scene in the church at midnight has poetical qualities—but could it happen? Then is it within the range of likelihood that *any* gentleman would pursue his wife at midnight and *strike* her? Though you give a good deal about the family life afterwards, there is nothing to justify that very exceptional scene. It is too palpably done to bring about a meeting of the lovers.

Much of the writing seems to me admirable. The scene in Rotten Row— seen as it is and described by an outsider—is full of real power and insight. And the characters, on the whole, seem to me finely conceived and presented. The fault of the book, as it seems to me, is that it lacks the *modesty of nature* of fact. *Romeo and Juliet* and *Hamlet* have many unnatural scenes, but Shakespeare puts them in foreign countries, and took the scenes from old books. When he was nearer home and in his own time you don't find such things in his writing. King Cophetua and the beggar maid made a pretty tale in an old ballad; but will a story in which the Duke of Edinburgh takes in lawful wedlock even a private gentleman's daughter? One sees in the papers accounts of gentlemen's daughters running away with their fathers' grooms, but you are not in that region. Given your characters, could it happen in the present day? The 'modesty of nature' takes into account all conditions.

You see I am writing to you as a writer who seems to me, at least potentially, of considerable mark, of power and purpose. If this is your first book I think you ought to go on. May I ask if it is, and—you are not a lady, so perhaps you will forgive the question—are you young?

I have shown your MS. to one friend, whose judgment coincides with my own—I wish to show it to another man of a different stamp of mind, who knows more of the upper class then either, and is yet a very noble fellow, that I may get his view as to whether it would do with modifications. Would you be willing to consider any suggestions?

P.S. I have just got my friend to write his opinion in his own words, and I enclose it. I mean the one who has already had the MS.